The Politics of Exile in Latin America

The Politics of Exile in Latin America addresses exile as a major mechanism of institutional exclusion used by all types of governments in the region against their own citizens, while at the same time these governments often provided asylum to aliens fleeing persecution.

The work is the first systematic analysis of Latin American exile on a continental and transnational basis and on a long-term perspective. It traces variations in the saliency of exile among different expelling and receiving countries; across different periods; with different paths of exile, both elite and massive; and under authoritarian and democratic contexts.

The project integrates theoretical hindsight and empirical findings, analyzing the importance of exile as a recent and contemporary phenomenon, while reaching back to its origins and phases of development. It also addresses presidential exile, the formation of Latin American communities of exiles worldwide, and the role of exiles in shaping the collective identities of these countries.

Mario Sznajder holds the Leon Blum Chair in Political Science at the Hebrew University of Jerusalem. He is also Research Fellow at the Truman Research Institute for the Advancement of Peace. Among his works are the books *The Birth of Fascist Ideology* (with Zeev Sternhell and Maia Asheri), *Constructing Collective Identities and Shaping Public Spheres: Latin American Paths* (coedited with Luis Roniger), and *The Legacy of Human Rights Violations in the Southern Cone: Argentina, Chile and Uruguay* (with Luis Roniger). He has also published numerous articles on Fascism, democracy, and human rights.

Luis Roniger is Reynolds Professor of Latin American Studies at Wake Forest University. A comparative political sociologist, Roniger's publications include books such as *Patrons, Clients and Friends* (with Shmuel N. Eisenstadt), *Hierarchy and Trust in Modern Mexico and Brazil, The Legacy of Human Rights Violations in the Southern Cone* (with Mario Sznajder), *The Collective and the Public in Latin America* (coedited with Tamar Herzog), and *Globality and Multiple Modernities* (coedited with Carlos Waisman). He is currently completing a book on *Transnational Politics in Central America*.

The Politics of Exile in Latin America

MARIO SZNAJDER
Hebrew University of Jerusalem

LUIS RONIGER
Wake Forest University

CAMBRIDGE
UNIVERSITY PRESS

CAMBRIDGE
UNIVERSITY PRESS

32 Avenue of the Americas, New York NY 10013-2473, USA

Cambridge University Press is part of the University of Cambridge.

It furthers the University's mission by disseminating knowledge in the pursuit of education, learning and research at the highest international levels of excellence.

www.cambridge.org
Information on this title: www.cambridge.org/9781316501122

© Mario Sznajder and Luis Roniger 2009

First published 2009
First paperback edition 2015

A catalogue record for this publication is available from the British Library

Library of Congress Cataloguing in Publication data

Sznajder, Mario.
The politics of exile in Latin America / Mario Sznajder, Luis Roniger.
   p.   cm.
Includes bibliographical references and index.
ISBN   978-0-521-51735-5 (hardback)
1. Exile (Punishment) – Latin America.   2. Exiles – Psychology.   3. Exiles – Social
conditions.   4. Statelessness – Latin America.   5. Latin America – Politics and
government.   I. Roniger, Luis, 1949–   II. Title.   III. Series.
HV9310.5.S96   2009
325'.21 – dc22   2009000952

ISBN 978-0-521-51735-5 Hardback
ISBN 978-1-316-50112-2 Paperback

To Shmuel N. Eisenstadt and Zeev Sternhell, in deep appreciation of their scholarship, intellectual wisdom, and public commitment

Contents

Acknowledgments

We owe a debt of gratitude to many individuals and institutions that contributed in various ways to the completion of this work. We are indebted to the Truman Research Institute for the Advancement of Peace, the Consejo de Investigaciones Científicas of Spain in Madrid, the Davis Center for International Relations, the Aims Byudks Research Fund and the Shain Center for Research in the Social Sciences of the Hebrew University of Jerusalem, the Social and Behavioral Sciences Fund of Wake Forest University, and the U.S.-Israel Bi-National Science Foundation for their support at different stages of the work. Special thanks are due to those who shared their experiences and hindsight with us, particularly the late Daniel Recanati, Elda González, Pablo Yankelevich, Clara Obligado, Mempo Giardinelli, Mauricio Frajman, Laurence Whitehead, Pinchas Avivi, Claudia García, Alan Angell, former Israeli ambassador Benjamin Oron, Yehuda Dominitz, Ran Curiel, Blas Matamoros, Abrasha Rotemberg, Adriana Muñoz, Arnoldo Liberman, Maria Luiza Tucci Carneiro, Tulio Halperin Donghi, Nora Bendersky, Ingrid Hecker, Orit Gazit, Ifat Bachrach, Avital Appel, Yuval Ben-Dov, Esther Lifshitz, Gustavo Silva, Fanny Muldman, Carlos Fuentes, Batia Siebzehner, Samuel Ouman, Nahum Solan, Leonardo Senkman, Florinda Goldberg, the late Dr. Mario Cohen, the late Daniel Moore, and librarians Brenda Golan, Regina Gruzman, and Amnon Ben-Arieh. Interviews with former president of Brazil Professor Fernando Henrique Cardoso and former president of Chile Professor Ricardo Lagos were particularly instructive. We are grateful to the directors and staff of the following institutions and libraries: the International Institute of Social History in Amsterdam, the Library of the Iberoamerican Institute of the Prussian Heritage Foundation in Berlin, the CIEMI-Centre d'Information et d'Etudes sur les Migrations Internationales in Paris, the Library of Congress in Washington, the National Library of Argentina, the National Library of Santiago de Chile, the Bodleian Library of the University of Oxford, the National Library in San José de Costa Rica, Cuba's National Library in Havana, the National Archives of Israel in Jerusalem, the library of the Ministry of Interior of Spain in Madrid, the FASIC and the Biblioteca del Congreso in Chile, the Library of the Center for Latin American Studies at the University of Cambridge, and the Fondazione Lelio and Lili Basso in Rome, Italy. We are indebted to Tamar Soffer of the Department of Geography of the Hebrew University of Jerusalem for her elaboration of the maps included in this book, and to Ronit Nirel and Bella Vakolenko-Lagun, of the Applied Statistics Laboratory of Jerusalem, for their advice and work on the statistical elaborations of the book. We would also like to thank Irina Babchenko of the Faculty of Social Sciences and Ronit Sasson of the Department of Political Science of the Hebrew University. The research assistance of Haim Portnoy, Nathan Brener, Leandro Kierszenbaum, Yaara Angres, Deby Babis, Caroline Kaplan, Andrés Lindner, Hillen Meirovich, Peter Morris, Melissa Velarde, and Orly Haimovich, at various stages of this project, is kindly acknowledged. We are also grateful to Eric Crahan, Editor of History and Politics at Cambridge University Press, who invested his talent and energy in bringing this project to completion. Parts of this work were presented in several forums and later appeared as articles in *Journal of Latin American Studies*, 37 (2005), *Soziologia Israelit*, 6 (2005), *Revista de Ciencia Política*, 27 (2007), *Latin American Perspectives*, 34 (2007), and *Estudios Interdisciplinarios de América Latina y el Caribe*, 18 (2007), we gratefully acknowledge these journals for granting us permission to reproduce parts of them here.[1] We are indebted as well to all those who commented on this work in seminars at the Department of Sociology and Anthropology of the Hebrew University of Jerusalem in 2003, the Department of Political Science of Wake Forest University in 2004, and the University of São Paulo in 2005; at the conference of the Centro de Documentación e Investigación de la Cultura de Izquierdas in Buenos Aires, Argentina, in August 2005; at the International Political Science World Congress in Fukuoka, Japan, in July 2006; at the Universidad Nacional Autónoma de México in Mexico in August–September 2006; at the annual meetings of the Chilean Association of Political Science at the Catholic University of Santiago in November 2006; at the MACLAS annual meetings in Reading in March 2007; at the Social Sciences Seminar of WFU in September 2007; at the Latin American Studies Association Conference in Montreal in September 2007; and at the Second International Congress on the Analysis of Genocidal Social Practices, held at the Universidad Tres de Febrero in Buenos Aires in November 2007.

[1] Thanks are due to the following: Cambridge University Press, for using materials from "From Argentina to Israel: Escape, Evacuation and Exile." *Journal of Latin American Studies*, 37, 2 (2005): 351–377; the Israeli Sociological Association, for using "Israel and the Escape of the Victims of Military Repression in Argentina (1976–1983)." *Israeli Sociology*, 6, 2 (2005): 233–263; Sage Publications, for "Political Exile in Latin America." *Latin American Perspectives*, 34, 4 (2007): 7–30; the Instituto de Historia y Cultura de América Latina of the School of History of Tel Aviv University, for "Los antecedentes coloniales del exilio político y su proyección en el siglo 19." *Estudios Interdisciplinarios de América Latina y el Caribe*, 18, 2 (2007): 31–51; and the Catholic University of Chile, for "Exile Communities and Their Differential Institutional Dynamics: A Comparative Analysis of the Chilean and Uruguayan Political Diasporas." *Revista de Ciencia Política* (Chile), 27, 1 (2007): 43–66.

List of Acronyms

AAA	Alianza Anticomunista Argentina/Argentine Anti-Communist Alliance
ACHA	Acción Chilena Anticomunista/Chilean Anti-Communist Action
ACNUR	Alto Comisionado de las Naciones Unidas para los Refugiados; Spanish acronym for UNHCR: Office of the United Nations High Commissioner for Refugees
AD	Acción Democrática/Democratic Action (Social Democratic Party of Venezuela)
AGELA	Asociación General de Estudiantes Latinoamericanos/General Association of Latin American Students
AHSDREM	Archives of the Foreign Affairs Ministry of Mexico
ALN	Ação Libertadora Nacional/National Liberation Organization (Brazil)
APE	Acuerdo Paraguayo en el Exilio/Paraguayan Accord in Exile
APEC	Asia-Pacific Economic Cooperation
APRA	Alianza Popular Revolucionaria Americana/American Popular Revolutionary Alliance (Peru)
ARDI	Alianza Revolucionaria de Izquierda/Revolutionary Alliance of the Left (Colombia and Venezuela)
CADHU	Centro de Abogados por los Derechos Humanos/Lawyers' Center for Human Rights (Argentina)
CAFRA	Comité Anti-Fascista contra la Represión en Argentina/Anti-Fascist Committee against Repression in Argentina (Italy)
CAIS	Centre Argentine d'Information et Solidarité/Argentinean Center of Information and Solidarity (France)
CAS	Comisión Argentina de Solidaridad/Argentinian Solidarity Commission (Mexico)
CBA	Comitê Brasil pela Anistia/Brazilian Committee for Amnesty (Brazil)

CCHR	Chile Committee for Human Rights (United Kindgdom)
CDPPU	Comité de Défense de Prisonniers Politiques en Uruguay/Committee for the Defense of Political Prisoners in Uruguay (France)
CELS	Centro de Estudios Legales y Sociales/Center of Legal and Social Studies (Argentina)
CEP	Conferencia Episcopal Paraguaya/Assembly of Paraguayan Bishops (Paraguay)
CEPAL	Comisión Económica para América Latina/Economic Commission for Latin America (ECLA)
CEPAR	Center for Psykosocialt Arbejde med Flygtninge og Indvandrere/Centre for Psychosocial Assistance to Refugees and Immigrants (Denmark)
CIDE	Centro de Investigación y Docencia Económica/Center of Economic Research and Teaching (Mexico)
CIMADE	Comité inter-mouvements auprès des evacués/Comité Inter-Movimientos por los Evacuados/Inter-Movements Committee for Refugees (France)
CIPAE	Comité de Iglesias para Ayudas de Emergencias/Council of Churches for Emergency Help
CNR	Comisión Nacional de Repatriación/National Commission of Repatriation (Uruguay)
CNRAE	Comisión Nacional de Retorno de Argentinos en el Exterior/National Commission for the Return of Argentines Abroad (Argentina)
CODEPU	Corporación de Promoción y Defensa de los Derechos del Pueblo/Corporation for the Promotion and Defense of People's Rights (Chile)
COLAT	Colectivo Latinoamericano de Trabajo Psicosocial/Latin American Collective of Psychosocial Work (Belgium)
COMAR	Comisión Mexicana de Ayuda a Refugiados/Mexican Commission of Aid to Refugees (Mexico)
CONADEP	Comisión Nacional Sobre la Desaparición de Personas/National Commission of Inquiry on the Disappeared (Argentina)
CONAR	Comisión National de Ayuda a Refugiados/National Commission of Aid to Refugees (Chile)
COPEI	Comité de Organización Política Electoral Independiente/Committee of Independent Electoral Political Organization (Venezuela)
CORFO	Corporación de Fomento/Development Corporation (Chile)
CO.SO.FAM	Comision de Solidaridad con Familiares de Presos y Desaparecidos en la Argentina/Commission of Solidarity with Family Members of Prisoners and Disappeared Persons in Argentina

COSPA	Comité Argentino de Solidaridad con el Pueblo Argentino/Argentinean Committee of Solidarity with the Argentinean People (Mexico)
CUT	Central Única de Trabajadores/Workers' Union Organization (Chile)
DAS	Departamento Administrativo de Seguridad/Administrative Department of Security (Colombia)
DC	Democracia Cristiana/Christian Democracy (Chile, Italy)
DIEX	Dirección Nacional de Identificación y Extranjería/National Directorate of Foreigners and Identification (Venezuela)
DINA	Dirección Nacional de Inteligencia/National Intelligence Directorate (Chile)
DOPS	Delegacia de Ordem Política e Social/Department of Political and Social Order (Brazil)
ERP	Ejército Revolucionario del Pueblo/People's Revolutionary Army (Argentina)
ESMA	Escuela de Mecánica de la Armada/Navy Mechanics School (Argentina)
FASIC	Fundación de Ayuda Social de las Iglesias Cristianas/Social Aid Foundation of the Christian Churches (Chile)
FLACSO	Facultad Latinoamericana de Ciencias Sociales/Latin American Faculty of Social Sciences
GAAEF	Groupe d'avocats argentines exiles en France/Group of Argentinean Lawyers Exiled in France
GDR	German Democratic Republic (also known popularly as East Germany, 1949–1990)
ICJ	Institute of Contemporary Jewry of Jerusalem (Israel)
IGO	international governmental organization
IISG	International Institute of Social History (Netherlands)
ILO	UN International Labor Organization
ILPES	Instituto Latinoamericano de Planificación Económica y Social/Latin American Institute of Social and Economic Plannning attached to CEPAL-ECLA
INE	Instituto Nacional de Estadística/National Institute of Statistics (Spain and other countries)
INSEE	Institut national de la statistique et des études économiques/National Institute for Statistics and Economics (France)
JA	Jewish Agency
MAPAM	Mifleguet Poalim Meuhedet/United Workers Party (Israel)
MAPU	Movimiento de Acción Popular Unitaria/Movement of United Popular Action (Chile)
MAPU-OC	Movimiento de Acción Popular Unitaria Obrero Campesino/Workers-Farmers MAPU (Chile)
MDP	Movimiento Democrático Popular/Popular Democratic Movement

MFA	Ministry of Foreign Affairs
MIDA	Movimiento de Izquierda Democrático Allendista/Pro-Allende Leftist Democratic Movement (Chile)
MIR	Movimiento de Izquierda Revolucionario/Revolutionary Leftist Movement (Chile)
MNRI	Movimiento Nacionalista Revolucionario de Izquierda/National Revolutionary Leftist Movement (Bolivia)
MOPOCO	Movimiento Popular Colorado/Red Popular Movement (Paraguay)
MPL	Movimiento Patria Libre/Free Fatherland Movement (Paraguay)
MR-8	Movimiento Revolucionário 8 de Outubro/Revolutionary Movement 8th October (Brazil)
NGO	non-govermental organization
NKVD	Narodniy komissariat vnutrennikh del/People's Commissariat of Internal Affairs (USSR)
OAS	Organization of American States
OBAN	Operação Bandeirantes/Operation Bandeirantes (Brazil)
OEA	Organización de Estados Americanos (Spanish-Portuguese acronym for OAS)
OFPRA	Office Français de protection des réfugiées et des apatrides/French Office of Protection of Refugees and Stateless Persons (France)
OIM	Organización Internacional de Migración/International Organization of Migration, or IOM
ONR	Oficina Nacional de Retorno/National Office of Return (Chile)
ORVEX	Organización de Venezolanos en el Exilio/Organization of Venezuelans in Exile
OSEA	Oficina de Solidaridad para Exiliados Argentinos/Office of Solidarity with Argentine Exiles (Argentina)
PADR	personal archive of Dany Recanati (Israel)
PASOK	Panhellenic Socialist Movement (Greece)
PCC	Partido Comunista de Chile/Communist Party of Chile
PCU	Partido Comunista de Uruguay/Communist Party of Uruguay
PDC	Partido Demócrata Cristiano/Christian Democratic Party (Chile)
PIT-CNT	Plenario Intersindical de Trabajadores–Convención Nacional de Trabajadores/Inter-syndical Plenary of Workers–National Convention of Workers (General Trade Union) (Uruguay)
PLRA	Partido Liberal Radical Auténtico/Authentic Liberal Radical Party (Paraguay)
PMDB	Partido Movimento Democrático Brasileiro/Brazilian Democratic Movement Party (Brazil)
PPC	Partido del Pueblo Cubano/Cuban Popular Party (Cuba)

PPD	Partido por la Democracia/Party for Democracy (Chile)
PRD	Partido Revolucionario Dominicano/Dominican Revolutionary Party (Dominican Republic)
PRD	Partido Revolucionario Democrático/Democratic Revolutionary Party (Mexico, Panama)
PREALC	Programa Regional de Empleo para América Latina y el Caribe/Employment Regional Program for Latin America and the Caribbean
PRI	Partido Revolucionario Institucional/Revolutionary Institutional Party (Mexico)
PRIN	Partido Revolucionario de Izquierda Nacionalista/National Leftist Revolutionary Party (Bolivia)
PRN	Proceso de Reorganización Nacional/National Reorganization Process (Argentina)
PRT	Partido Revolucionario de los Trabajadores/Workers Revolutionary Party (Argentina)
PRV	Partido Revolucionario Venezolano/Venezuelan Revolutionary Party (Venezuela)
PSDP	Panamanian Social Democratic Party (Panama)
PSI	Partito Socialista Italiano/Italian Socialist Party (Italy)
PSIUP	Partito Socialista Italiano di Unità Proletaria/Italian Socialist Party of Proletarian Unity (Italy)
PTB	Partido Trabalhista Brasileiro/Brazilian Workers' Party (Brazil)
RCTV	Radio Caracas Televisión/TV-Radio Caracas (Venezuela)
REDHER	Red de Hermandad y Solidaridad/Network of Brotherhood and Solidarity (Colombia)
ROE	Resistencia Obrero-Estudiantil/Workers' and Students' Resistance (Uruguay)
SCB	Central Bureau of Statistics (Sweden)
SD	Social Democracy organizations
SER	Servicio Ecuménico de Reintegración/Ecumenical Reintegration Service (Uruguay)
SERPAJ	Servicio de Paz y Justicia/Peace and Justice Service (Uruguay, Chile)
SIJAU	Secretariado Internacional de Juristas por la Amnistía en Uruguay/International Secretary of Jurists for Amnesty in Uruguay (France)
SIN	Servicio de Inteligencia Nacional/National Intelligence Service (Peru)
TYSAE	Travailleurs et syndicalistes Argentines en Exil/Trabajadores y sindicalistas argentinos en el exilio/Argentinean Workers and Syndicalists in Exile (France)
UAL	Unión Artiguista de Liberación/Artigas Liberation Union (Uruguay)

UN   United Nations
UNAM   Universidad Nacional Autónoma de México/National
            Autonomous University of Mexico
UNCHR   United Nations Commission for Human Rights
UNESCO   United Nations Educational Scientific and Cultural
            Organization
UNHCR   Office of the United Nations High Commissioner for Refugees
UP   Unidad Popular/Popular Unity coalition (Chile)
UPARF   Unión de Periodistas Argentinos Residentes en
            Francia/Association of Argentinean Journalists Living in
            France
UT   Unidad Técnica para la Reinserción Laboral/Technical Agency
            for Labor Reinsertion (Uruguzy)
WHO   World Health Organization

Introduction: The Politics of Exile

In this book, we analyze the resilience and transformation of political exile from colonial times to the present in Latin America. The premise of this study is that exile has been a regulatory mechanism for political systems unable to create pluralistic and inclusive models of participation; and although exile developed as an elite phenomenon in the 19th century when political participation was restricted, it became a massive trend in the 20th century as mobilizations and more inclusive participation led to authoritarian rule.

Exile is a perennial subject that signals the logic of political exclusion and displacement from internal public spheres. Western democracies have increasingly developed pluralistic and tolerant public spheres that enabled them to contain countervailing, opposition forces without expelling them from their midst, as long as all sides abided by the democratic game. Former ruling elites, whose misdeeds during tenure have been exposed publicly, as well as dissident intellectuals and vocal opponents of incumbent administrations, have been able to act and express themselves in the public domains without being forced to abandon their home countries. After impeachment procedures were recommended, Richard Nixon resigned the presidency in 1974 but did not leave the United States. Charles De Gaulle abandoned office in 1946 for the solace of Colombey les Deux-Eglises, to return to power in 1958 and establish the Fifth Republic. When Giulio Andreotti, prime minister of Italy for many terms, was accused of corruption and complicity with organized crime, he still could stay in his home country and trust justice. Under established democracies and within the rule of law, both leading and rank-and-file politicians have been able to remain in their country and be involved in the public domain. This has not been the case in Latin America.

Institutional exclusion has been a major constitutive feature of Latin American politics. Clearly enough, the area has witnessed many rebellions, movements of protest, and pressures for widening political participation and access to political power and resources. Yet, in parallel, the political domain has often been controlled by narrow circles of elites, ostracizing others, while the masses have been forced to work through mediating networks, clientelism, and favoritism. These trends have been present both in authoritarian, dictatorial environments and in situations in which those in power have professed to revolutionize their countries, and even in democratic situations. In other words and focusing on political actors, although exclusion of the opposition has been a natural correlate of authoritarianism, exclusion has not been absent from democratic openings. Under both authoritarianism and democracy, those fallen from power or directly in the opposition often have been forced to take the road of exile. Many opposition figures and rank-and-file citizens have moved abroad following Chávez's increasing control of the public sphere in Venezuela. In addition, former presidents such as Alberto Fujimori, Carlos Salinas de Gortari, Jamil Mahuad, and Alejandro Toledo have decided to leave their home countries instead of facing the difficulties of postpresidential life. Democracies have professed to respect the basic rights of every citizen, and yet, similar to the authoritarian polities that have used expulsion and exile as normative political tools, democracies too have been characterized by persecution, exclusion, and ostracism of citizens expressing voices dissenting with those in power. The recurrent use of exile reflects an ongoing challenge of the incomplete and exclusionary nature of the nation-states in the region.

Political exile has been a major political practice in all Latin American countries throughout most of the 19th and 20th centuries. It is our claim that exile has played a vital part in shaping the form and styles of Latin American politics.

Despite its ubiquity in these countries, political exile is still an underresearched topic. Although fascinating, until recently it has been conceived of as somewhat marginal for the development of these societies and has been studied in the framework of traditional concepts and concerns in history and the social sciences. It is not unusual to find numerous biographical monographs that mention exile as a formative political experience, from well-known cases such as those of Bolívar or Perón to less-renowned individuals, whose aggregate testimonies build up a collective story of communities of exiles and expatriates. Similarly, and not surprisingly, a testimonial literature accompanied the last wave of political exiles, first documenting the experiences of Brazilians who were forced to leave their country in the aftermath of the 1964 *coup d'état*,[1] and marking a trend that was to repeat itself continuously over the next three decades. A number of such biographies and testimonies has burgeoned in the past generation and include some outstanding and insightful works.[2]

---

[1] Pedro Celso Uchôa Cavalcanti and Jovelino Ramos, *Memórias do exilio: Brasil 1964/19??*. São Paulo: Editora Livraria Livramento, 1978; Abelardo Jurema, *Exilio*. Paraiba: Acauá, 1978.

[2] Among them: Albertina de Oliveira Costa, et al., *Memórias das mulheres do exílio: obra coletiva*. Rio de Janeiro: Paz e Terra, 1980; Albino Gómez, *Exilios (Por qué volvieron)*. Rosario: Homo Sapiens Ediciones, 1999; Flavio Tavares, *Memorias do esquecimento*. São Paulo: Globo, 1999; Carlos Ulanovsky, *Seamos felices mientras estamos aquí*. Buenos Aires: Editorial Sudamericana, 2001; Diana Guelar, Vera Jarach, and Beatriz Ruiz, *Los chicos del exilio. Argentina (1975–1984)*. Buenos Aires: Ediciones el País de Nomeolvides, 2002; David Cox, *En honor a la verdad*.

These biographical accounts and testimonies of exiles and expatriates contribute important building blocks toward a reconstruction of the collective experiences of exile. They also point out the ubiquity and profound impact of the phenomenon, which resulted from political exclusion and persecution by the military dictatorship of the 1960s to 1980s. And yet, most of these testimonies do not provide a systematic analysis of the role of exile in Latin American politics and societies and also do little to explain the recurrence of exile or its transformations over time, from the early 19th century to the late 20th century. Only recently have collective works moved in the direction of constructing building blocks for a comprehensive approach to specific communities of co-nationals exiled during the last wave of military dictatorships.[3]

In parallel, recent years have witnessed the proliferation of literary analysis and criticism focusing on the universal meaning of the experience of exile, from forced to self-imposed exile. This literature is mainly anchored in 20th-century writings, reflecting the pronounced impact of political repression and military dictatorships of the 1970s and 1980s on exile.[4] Often, these works provide in-depth theoretical hindsight of the existential experience of marginalization and the tensions it creates, especially for writers rooted in the language of communities that were silenced by repression and underwent processes of cultural transformation in which the exiles took only a tangential part while abroad. And yet, most works in this line are strongly permeated by postmodern emphases and have been less prone to contribute to the systematic social and political study of the impact and roles of exile in Latin American politics.

Memorias desde el exilio de Robert Cox. Buenos Aires: Colihue, 2002; Abril Trigo, *Memorias migrantes. Testimonios y ensayos sobre la diáspora Uruguaya.* Buenos Aires and Montevideo: Beatriz Viterbo Editora and Ediciones Trilce, 2003; Jorge Luis Bernetti and Mempo Giardinelli, *México: El exilio que hemos vivido.* Buenos Aires: Editorial de la Universidad Nacional de Quilmes, 2003; and Pilar Roca, *Ismael Viñas. Ideografía de un mestizo.* Buenos Aires: Dunken, 2005.

3 José del Pozo Artigas, Ed., *Exiliados, emigrados y retornados chilenos en America y Europa, 1973–2004.* Santiago: RIL Editores, 2006; Silvia Dutrénit-Bielous, Ed., *El Uruguay del exilio. Gente, circunstancias, escenarios.* Montevideo: Trilce, 2006; Pablo Yankelevich and Silvina Jensen, Eds., *Exilios. Destinos y experiencias bajo la dictadura militar.* Buenos Aires: Libros del Zorzal, 2007.

4 Gloria Da Cunha-Giabbai. *El exilio: Realidad y ficción.* Montevideo: Arca, 1992; Ana Vásquez, and Angela Xavier de Brito, "La situation de l'exilée: essai de génèralisation fondé sur l'exemple de réfugiés Latino-américains." *Intercultures,* 21 (1993): 51–66; William Rowe and Teresa Whitfield, "Thresholds of Identity: Literature and Exile in Latin America." *Third World Quarterly,* 9, 1 (1997): 232–255; Maria José de Queiroz, *Os males da ausência ou a literatura do exílio.* Rio de Janeiro: Topbooks, 1998; María-Inés Lagos-Pope, "Testimonies from Exile: Works by Hernán Valdés, Eduardo Galeano and David Viñas," in idem., Ed., *Exile in Literature.* Lewisburg, PA: Bucknell University Press, 1999; Hamid Naficy, Ed., *Home, Exile, Homeland.* New York and London: Routledge, 1999; Amy K. Kaminsky, *After Exile. Writing the Latin American Diaspora.* Minneapolis: University of Minnesota Press, 1999; Mike González, "Exile," in Daniel Balderston, Mike González, and Ana M. López, Eds., *Encyclopedia of Contemporary Latin American and Caribbean Cultures.* London and New York: Routledge, 2000, Vol. 2, pp. 539–540.

Another major corpus of work is that developed by psychologists, social psychologists, social workers, and psychiatrists on the difficulties that many exiles faced as they were displaced from their homeland. These works have elaborated, often in penetrating ways, the problems of adjustment, personal disarticulation, mental stress, distrust and isolation, cases of suicide, as well as high rates of family disruption and divorce. Outstanding is the pioneering work of Ana Vásquez and Ana María Araujo, *Exils Latino-americains. La malediction d'Ulysse,* which, on the basis of their professional experience with South American exiles in France, has elaborated a theoretical stage-by-stage analysis of exile. According to their analysis, also reminiscent of the Grinbergs' work, exiles live through an initial phase of pain and remorse, followed by a phase of transculturation, and a possible third phase of shattering illusions and deep questioning. Although we rely on the insights of this work and similar contributions, we refrain from reviewing in a systematic way their contribution to the understanding of the exilic condition.[5]

Our work follows a sociopolitical perspective, analyzing political exile, its background, patterns, and wider social and cultural impacts. Recent developments in political science and history, sociology, anthropology, and international relations have highlighted the centrality of diasporas and transnational studies, of transience and relocation, of cultural hybridity and multiple modernities. Following these analytical developments, we suggest that the study of Latin American exile can become a topic of central concern, closely related to basic theoretical problems and controversies in these disciplines. In parallel, we suggest that the systematic study of exile also promises to lead to new readings of Latin American development, away from the traditional readings of national histories and toward other more regional, transnational, or even continental dimensions.

On the theoretical level, the study of exile highlights an ongoing tension between the principle of national membership and the principle of citizenship. Once a person is pushed into exile, she or he may lose the entitlements attached to citizenship but, at the same time, he or she may become even more attached than before to what is perceived as the 'national soul.' There is a latent but distinct dimension of collective identity submerged in citizenship, necessarily recognized while in exile. Accordingly, it has been abroad that many of the displaced nationals discovered, rediscovered, or rather invented the 'collective soul' of their countries in primordial or spiritual terms. Whereas some migrants and sojourners became transnational and deterritorialized, many others sought to reconstruct their bonds of solidarity in terms of the home collective identity, thus opening a fascinating area of political and cultural debate as these societies returned to democracy and opened their public spheres.

---

[5] See, for instance, Jorge Barudy et al., *Así buscamos rehacernos. Represión, exilio y trabajo psico-social.* Santiago: COLAT-CELADEC, 1980; León and Rebeca Grinberg, *Psicoanálisis de la migración y del exilio.* Madrid: Alianza Editorial, 1984; Ana Vásquez and Ana María Araujo, *Exils Latino-americains. La malediction d'Ulysse.* Paris: CIEMI and L'Harmattan, 1988.

After periods of crisis, which produce a significant number of exiles, fascinating debates have been generated between those who stayed in the home country and those who moved abroad over the definition of the components of national collective identity. Concurrently, new bonds have been forged with exiles from 'sister-nations,' reinforcing a dynamic of mutual recognition and identification of shared problems and transnational interests in the inter-American system. Exiles, hoping to return someday to their home country, often attempt to define in novel ways the terms of collective identity. In many instances, exile seems to have played an important role in Latin America, in defining or redefining both the national and the pan-Latin American identity.

At the same time, though the exiles often claim they are the true representatives of 'the people' while abroad, they interact in new environments, are exposed to fellow exiles from other countries, and confront new models of organization that transform them, willingly or not. This poses a major dilemma for every exile at the personal, psychological, familial, and collective levels: how to relate to the host society and whether to become part of it, beyond the instrumental level of everyday life, and even develop hybrid identities and commitments. Moreover, if they settle in what they perceive as a more developed, organized, or cultured environment, they face this dilemma more poignantly. The longer the exile, the more likely this leads to fragmented identities, to visions of heterogeneity, migrancy, and heteroglossia, which some may celebrate and others mourn.

The experience in exile challenges the displaced persons to reconsider the ideals they came with and their notions of both the host country and the homeland that they left behind. A profound process of redefinition of cultural, social, and political assumptions thus takes place, which is crucial to trace as one analyzes later transformations in these countries.

This approach leads us to suggest that political exile is important in multiple ways. It is both the result of political processes and a constitutive factor of political systems. In causal terms, because it results from political persecution but stops short of annihilation of the opposition, exile speaks – in Gramscian terms – of an authoritarian hegemony in politics, whatever the formal definition of the political system may be. Such patterns of politics are built on exclusion and a situation set between a winner-takes-all competition for power and the perils of a zero-sum game broadened into civil wars.

Although resulting from such forms of political competition, the recurrent use of exile has ensconced it in the political culture of these countries, reinforcing the exclusionary rules of the political game in Latin America. In early stages of political development, the widespread practice of exile has limited democratic institutionalization, even if it projected pressures on a wider domain of political action. It affected democracy by limiting representation and contestation within the polity, hindering the scope of free debate and the possibility of contesting established power by the open channels of democratic action.

The study of exile requires a nuanced reading of context and history because it evolved and changed its character throughout the 19th and 20th centuries.

Political exile is dynamic, hinging on political action and evolving in a parallel fashion to processes of political institutionalization and deinstitutionalization and to the reformulation of political ground rules. In parallel, the dynamics of recurrent exile have been main components of limited or exclusionary democracies in Latin America.

It should be stated that the experience of exile is multiple, and yet there are trends and patterns in exile, which can be studied from various disciplinary vantage points. We follow a sociopolitical and macrohistorical approach that combines institutional and network perspectives. Our thesis is that political exile has been instrumental in defining key aspects of Latin American states, with consequences for the ways in which politics has been played and public life structured in these countries since independence. Although recognizing the early use of translocation in colonial times, we have identified in postindependence times the transformation of exile into a major mechanism for regulating authoritarian polities, with central consequences for the public spheres of these countries.

We also claim that exile has changed its structure with the passing of time. In the context of elitist politics, exile developed a three-tiered structure, shaped around the interplay among the expelling state, the exiles, and the host countries. By the late 19th century, and moreover in the 20th century, this tiered structure started developing a fourth tier in the form of an international public sphere with increasing impact in modulating the ways in which the other tiers interact.

In the early pattern, the combination of political factionalism and the lack of effective mechanisms of political turnover and representation created waves of individuals expelled into neighboring territories. Oppositions often found themselves ostracized from their home political scenarios. As the frontiers of the new states were still in the process of being defined, exile became a major mechanism of regional politics. In situations of defeat, exiles moved to neighboring areas to prepare themselves to regain control of the home political scene. Motivated by their own agenda, the host rulers exercised their regional influence by giving shelter to those fleeing detrimental constellations of power, turning them into sympathetic political allies. Therefore, it is not surprising that when a faction that a ruler sided with was defeated in a neighboring country, the ruler often welcomed the vanquished into his territory, hosting them, and even supporting their plans of return to the polity of origin. When the defeated faction was inimical to the host's political design, he could still host the expelled individuals and control their freedom of action, thereby curtailing the possibilities of plotting against an ally, the ruling government in the neighboring expelling country. In all cases, the translocated individuals and the communities of exiles played an important role in this three-tiered structure, within both the plans of regional hegemony of the host countries and their home country's strategies and pressures on the states hosting the translocated.

This dynamic was maintained throughout the first two centuries of independent political life. Still, major changes were effected in its workings as the result of social, economic, and political transformations, particularly the degree of institutionalization or deinstitutionalization of the different polities. Political factionalism reflected the format of elitist and mass politics. Political openings and mobilizations – both through civil wars and enlarged franchise – generated increasing complexity. This was reflected both in the diversification of the social and economic background of the exiles and in the extent to which the route of exile was followed by increasing numbers of individuals of varied background. In a certain way, exile mirrored the pace of modernization, evinced in pressures for political inclusion by incorporation of new social strata into politics and, at the same time, exclusion through banning, persecution, and translocation. Accordingly, exile progressively reflected the limited character of the political arena facing the mass activities of individuals in political associations, parties, professional associations, trade unions, and student organizations.

Exiles were not necessarily champions of political democracy. Many of the 'revolutionaries' going into exile were no less authoritarian and violent than the rulers who sent them into exile or from which they were fleeing. By tracing the characteristics of the exiles, research may reveal the changing tug-of-war between authoritarian politics and the pressures to democratize Latin American politics. The violence generated by this political process has been a major ingredient pushing people to flee their home country, even when their connection to politics was tangential. By the 20th century, massive migration resulting from political conflict, civil war, and violence was manifest throughout the continent. The refugee problem became evident both in civil war situations and in protracted and low-intensity conflicts.

The triangular structure of exile underwent a core transformation once a fourth and increasingly important element entered the exile equation: a global arena preoccupied with humanitarian international law and human rights. In Latin America, the ground for this fourth tier was laid in the 19th century. The proliferation of exiles, and later on of refugees, triggered Latin American efforts to internationally regulate the issue and move toward the creation of an inter-American set of international regimes of asylum. As early as the 1860s and 1870s, delegates of these countries discussed the right of asylum and progressively elaborated a corpus of norms of international private law and international penal law. The issue of exiles and refugees has increasingly resonated in the global arena, creating a more complex political environment in which the actions taken by expelling governments were increasingly questioned and placed under criticism. Exiles were incorporated into widening transnational and global networks with a voice not to be silenced by distance, time, or internal censorship. Networks of solidarity, non-governmental organizations (NGOs), international governmental organizations (IGOs), and global media created a new and more complex organizational environment to be taken into account. Toward the late 20th century, exile had already clearly evinced this four-tiered structure.

This study traces the origins of political exile in colonial translocation. We reconstruct the emergence of exile out of colonial forms of translocation, when it was used for juridical, administrative, and social purposes, into the modern form of political exile, and its subsequent transformations in the 19th and 20th centuries. After independence, colonial precedents were ingrained in the formation of exile as the mechanism to serve the hold of small elites over the masses by avoiding a zero-sum game and mutually destructive situation inherent in factionalism. One of the unintended consequences was that exiles became a factor in defining the boundaries and borders of nations and states in a region.

The emerging situation of being translocated helped shape the ways in which borders, identity, and alterity were defined in Latin America. Thus, it gave substance to the formal definitions that were taking place among both the mass and the elites in the process of defining new states in the Americas. In such a manner, exile was unwittingly instrumental for these states, based on formal administrative divisions inherited from colonial times, as their elites struggled to shape singular identities and construct their own ethos and nations. As the ostracized political actors took the road of exile within the American continent, they ascertained their status as 'nationals' of a 'polity' left behind as soon as they were out of the reach of the rulers of their place of origin but realized they were not accepted as full members in their place of destination. This phenomenon in itself has shaped in novel ways what turned out to be fragmented spheres of power emerging from former colonial boundaries. Hence, political exile helped in defining the new polities and forms of sovereignty characteristic of the emergence of modern nation-states out of disintegrating empires. We thus attribute to political exile not only a derivative function of former traditions but also a formative role in the transformation of politics and states in the Americas.

The Janus-face nature of political exile was evident as it continued to reinforce the authoritarian characteristics of the political game in these states. In the political culture of the various Latin Americas, to follow the expression coined by Renato Ortiz, exile turned into a major regulatory mechanism of political action. Exile and return allowed the new polities to stabilize by projecting political pressures outward and by ruling momentarily without being challenged by internally well-organized and effective oppositions. These phenomena also enabled their organization, on the basis of the formal political models of the time, to be coupled with the lack of political debate within their countries.

The very exclusion of exiles from the domestic public arena shaped, however, a transnational public sphere and multistate politics in the Americas and beyond, in which some of the exiles learned how to play their national politics from afar and the states were drawn into play politics on an international and, later, global scope.

Another important implication of this is the emergence of political cultures characterized by a lack of congruence between the boundaries of statehood and the definitions of national identity. Many nationals, including members of the elite, found themselves fleeing abroad. Whereas only by the late 19th century are there true diasporas, translocated individuals moved across territories as they debated and redefined their identity and their country's identity and boundaries. This also implies that there was a spillover of politics beyond the formal borders of any single Ibero-American state and that the very definition of a country's identity and borders turns into a function of exiles' personal and collective experience in the 19th century, as it will become a vector of political and cultural renovation in the 20th century.

That is, by excluding members of the political and cultural elites, the problems deemed internal to a polity are projected to an arena that only then becomes identified as 'abroad.' Accordingly, the interplay of exiles in the evolving realms helped in shaping the transnational and the national domains in ways that both linked the new states to the older administrative boundaries and projected them into new visions and definitions, while perhaps reducing the internal pressures for change.

The structure of this book follows the preceding claims and suggestions along an analytical line. Chapter 1 analyzes the exilic condition and focuses on the key issues, meaning, and scope of exile as an exclusionary social and political phenomenon. The chapter examines prevailing approaches on translocation and displacement and suggests analytical dimensions for the study of political exile.

In Chapter 2, the Latin American tradition of displacement and the historical antecedents of exile are analyzed. The chapter reviews Portuguese and Spanish practices of banishment; the early construction of differentiated Latin American collective identities in exile; and the formative role of exiles in the process of constitution of the new nation-states and their collective identities.

Chapter 3 is about the three-tiered format of early exile and the emergence of communities of exiles, addressing their role in the transnational dynamics of Latin American politics. Special attention is devoted to collective imaginaries and the formation of the new state identities through a politics of exit.

Chapter 4 elaborates on the role played by major sites of exile by reviewing the cases of Chile in the 19th century, Paris as the cultural Mecca attracting exiles and émigrés since independence, and Mexico in the 20th century. It examines receptivity of host countries and the limits set by them on the political activity of the exiles.

Chapter 5 treats the relationships between widening political and social participation and the massification of exile as the counterface of political inclusion. It elaborates on issues of international agreements of asylum and the transformation of the format of exile into a four-tiered structure, in which transnational networks played an increasingly important role.

In Chapter 6, the varied dynamics of communities of exiles in the late 20th century, their relationship to the diasporas of co-nationals, and the political role they played as part of the globalizing fourth tier of exile are examined through the cases of exiles from Brazil, Argentina, Chile, and Uruguay. Special attention is given to the way in which proactive communities of exiles have an impact on their home-country politics through the international arena. For reasons of space and research design, the focus is on the communities of exiles escaping repression in the Southern Cone, leaving aside other important exile communities such as those of Cuba, Haiti, and Central America.

Chapter 7 combines quantitative and qualitative data on the extent of Latin American presidential exile since independence and into the present, singling out the displacement of heads of states because of their centrality in the political process, both practically and symbolically. An original database of nearly 1,500 presidential terms in Latin America is analyzed in terms of the extent and forms of exile.

Finally, Chapter 8 explores the question of whether return and democracy mean the end of exile. It also touches on some of the transformations experienced during exile and those involved in the process of returning to the home countries. Living abroad and interacting with organizations and networks in the host countries and in the transnational arena, exiles experienced significant personal and ideological changes in how they understood political activism, gender, race, and national unity. On return of many of them, these new perspectives had an impact on the political and social processes in their home countries. The chapter concludes by indicating the broader implications of this study and future lines of research.

The combination of themes around political exile and its Latin American variants constitutes an attempt to see the theoretical implications of this phenomenon on the basis of its development in a region that has used and abused political exile as a regulatory mechanism of exclusion. The multifocal approach we follow escapes simple historical–developmental analysis. By encompassing different aspects and angles of political exile, we hope to raise awareness of the main problems of research ahead, as we suggest lines of analysis that are both theoretical and empirical, based on hundreds of past and contemporary cases of displacement in the Americas.

I

Defining the Exilic Condition

The purpose of this chapter is to place the study of political exile within the broader domain of studies of the exilic condition. We define political exile as a mechanism of institutional exclusion – not the only one – by which a person involved in politics and public life, or perceived by power holders as such, is forced or pressed to leave his or her home country or place of residence, unable to return until a change in political circumstances takes place. This definition covers both those directly persecuted by the authorities or by other violent political actors, such as paramilitary groups and guerrilla organizations, as well as those who choose displacement and expatriation as they sense an existential threat or problem originating in political quarters; and those who, once abroad as voluntary sojourners, discover that the changed political circumstances prevent their return. Ostracism, forced displacement, and exile are, in our view, the result of political settings prone to exclude a myriad of actors, whose political voice the power-holders cannot digest and contain within the polity. We thus consider exile to be a major form of institutional exclusion, a tool profusely used by states to ban political dissidents.[1]

Octavio Armand, a Cuban poet in exile, once said that for a displaced person, "to be is not to be [I am from where I am not present]. . . . "[2] In recent decades, political exile has been bracketed out to a large extent by focusing on the existential life challenges generated by displacement throughout history, seemingly irrespective of the political context in which it operated. Indeed, throughout history, individuals have been forced to abandon the place that

---

[1] Political dissent is to be interpreted here in the broadest possible sense, to include also social and cultural counter-elites and activists, defiant to established power and norms.

[2] Octavio Armand's "*ser es no estar*" playfully moves between the dual meaning of the verb to be in Spanish, which alludes both to the sense of identity [*ser*] and to being in a place [*estar*], so to stress the multiple dislocation of exile. Sophia McClennen translates Armand's dictum as "to be (someone) is not to be (somewhere)," and concludes: "In the case of the Spanish-speaking exile, to be is not to be, and that is the problem." (*The Dialectics of Exile: Nation, Time, Language and Space in Hispanic Literatures*. West Lafayette, IN: Purdue University Press, 2004, p. 119.)

they considered home and relocate to a 'foreign' land, triggering a series of psychological and social constraints as well as creativity and change. Such individuals have lived in the span between home and homeland, roots and movement, a lost past and an uncertain future, and between individual faith and collective endeavor, all these themes of central concern in phenomenological and narrative terms.

Since time immemorial, the exilic condition has become a practice and a core image reflected in the cultural tenets, stories, and myths of all societies. In Western imagery, for instance, it was encoded in the archetypical images of Adam and Eve's displacement from the Garden of Eden; Lot and his wife departing their city with the latter frozen as she did not detach herself from what she left behind; Jacob and his sons leaving the land of Canaan for Egypt, and, centuries later, the exodus of the Hebrew people from that land; Aeneas fleeing from defeat in Troy and reaching Italy; Ulysses being deterred for years from returning to Ithaca; ostracism as introduced by Cleisthenes in Athens; Jesus' family fleeing Bethlehem.

The exilic condition has also been encoded as part of the work of acclaimed authors who were forced to leave their home societies. From Ovid and Seneca to Dante Alighieri and Camões; from Madame de Staël and Victor Hugo to Joseph Korzeniowski-Conrad; from Witold Gombrowicz and Vladimir Nabokov to Rafael Alberti, Joseph Brodsky, and Thomas Mann; among many others. It is not by chance that the exilic condition has turned into a key paradigm for the human condition, especially under conditions of estrangement, alienation, and marginalization as well as displacement, relocation, and migration.[3]

It has been suggested that exile is a most recurrent and particularly pervasive motive in Latin American literature.[4] A very incomplete list of writers, poets, and essayists, intended only to provide a glimpse of this immensely vast phenomenon, could start in the early 19th century with Juana Manuela Gorriti, an early feminist voice in exile, and would include such figures as Pablo Neruda and José Donoso; Miguel Angel Asturias and Jorge Icaza; Augusto Roa Bastos, Herib Campos Cervera, and Gabriel Cassaccia; Mario Benedetti and Carlos Onetti; Jose Martí and Alejo Carpentier; Jorge Amado and Marcia Theophilo; Guillermo Cabrera Infante, César Vallejo, and Reinaldo Arenas; Tomás Eloy Martínez and Mempo Giardinelli; Antonio Skármeta and Ariel Dorfman; Clara Obligado, Tununa Mercado, and Manuel Puig; Eduardo Galeano and Jorge Edwards; Roque Dalton and Claribel Alegría; Rómulo Gallegos and Juan

[3] See, for instance, María José de Queiroz, *Os males da Ausencia*. Rio de Janeiro: Topbooks, 1998; Paul Tabori, *The Anatomy of Exile: A Semantic and Historical Study*. London: Harrap, 1972; Claudio Guillén, *Múltiples moradas*. Barcelona: Tusquets, 1998; Hamid Naficy, Ed., *Home, Exile, Homeland: Film, Media and the Politics of Place*. New York: Routledge, 1999; and Sophia A. McClennen, *The Dialectics of Exile*, West Lafayette, IN: Purdue University Press, 2004.

[4] Gloria da Cunha-Gabbai, *El exilio: realidad y ficción*. Montevideo: ARCA, 1992, pp. 27–52. See also Teresa Mendez-Faith, *Paraguay, novela y exilio*. Sommerville, NJ: SLUSA, 1992; and María Inés Lagos-Pope, Ed., *Exile in Literature*. Lewisburg, PA: Bucknell University Press, 1998.

Gelman; Noé Jitrik and Edgardo Cozarinsky; Antonio di Benedetto and Héctor Tizón; Fanny Buitrago and Fernando Vallejo; Cristina Peri Rossi and Alicia Kozameh; Edmundo Paz Soldán and Héctor Borda Leaño; Pedro Shimose and Víctor Montoya; Salomón de la Selva and Daisy Zamora; among many others.

In a fascinating analysis of Latin American exile and migrant writers, Florinda Goldberg follows Argentinean writer Julio Cortázar's remark that "the unavoidable consequence of the problem posed by exile in literature is the literature of exile," adding that such literature necessarily led also to the proliferation of "exilographers and exilophiles," central to literary analysis in our time.[5] It is not by chance that the current stage of increased movement of individuals, organizations, and networks across the globe seems to reinforce the typicality of the exilic condition as a metaphor of the human condition.

Correlating this emphasis on the exilic condition, attention has often been placed on the wide scope of denotations implied: displacement, translocation, *destierro*, forced migration, asylum, refugees, *relegación* [judicial internal banishment], insile, banishment, expatriation, *alejamiento* [estrangement], expulsion, deportation, proscription, and ostracism. At times, this great variety of terms has been brought to emphasize the ubiquity of the phenomenon across space and time. More often, the focus has been on the delineation of terminological nuances, as in many legal and literary studies.

Prevailing Approaches

Although we will focus on the political roles and significance of exile, let us start then with a short overview of some of the prevalent approaches to exile and the exilic condition, which address the widest possible framework of analysis, especially from the perspective of those individuals forced to take the road of exile. Our first observation is that even by confining our view to the paramount term, *exile*, the definitions are many. Some stem from the Latin root of *exilium*, which stands for a state of banishment. The *Oxford English Dictionary* defines exile as the "enforced removal from one's native land according to an edict or sentence, penal expatriation or banishment; the state or condition of being banished; enforced residence in some foreign land" but also as "expatriation, prolonged absence from one's native land, endured by compulsion of circumstances or voluntarily undergone for any purpose."[6] It thus encompasses both the condition of expulsion and a voluntary act grounded in a radical change of circumstances.

A definition with historical depth is provided by a major Italian dictionary, describing exile as a sanction that, since antiquity, was a substitute for the death penalty and, as such, a penalty of supreme gravity: "In a general sense, [exile is]

[5] See Florinda Goldberg, "Latin American Migrant Writers: 'Nomadic, Decentered, Contrapuntal'" in Luis Roniger and Carlos H. Waisman, Eds., *Globality and Multiple Modernities.* Brighton, UK: Sussex Academic Press, 2002, pp. 285–312, specifically p. 286.

[6] "Exile," in *The Oxford English Dictionary.* Oxford: Clarendon Press, 1989, p. 540.

a mandatory measure which sends an individual away from his homeland [*patria*], legally or arbitrarily, decided by the authorities in power, mostly because of political reasons."[7] In another dictionary, the fact that exile limits personal freedom is salient. Also, the possibility of voluntarily leaving the fatherland to escape persecution or civil and political violence is contemplated.[8] These definitions bring to awareness that exile can result from more or less legal proceedings or from authoritarian, arbitrary decisions, but qualifies both cases as an act of coercion. It also highlights that exile can result from situations in which authoritarian rulers are in command but also in situations in which legality is maintained and prevails.

In French, the term *exil* resonates of "expulsion of someone from his or her homeland with the prohibition of return; situation of the expulsed person" but also as "banishment deportation, expatriation, expulsion, proscription, relegation, transportation, ostracism and *lettre de cachet*."[9] In another French definition, we are dealing with "affective or moral estrangement; a separation which causes a [human] being a loss of his or her locus of attachment," referring in this case to a feeling of alienation. Relying on a passage from Madame Bovary by Flaubert, exile is depicted as "any change of residence, voluntary or not, which provokes a feeling or sense of *dépaysment* [loss of homeland]."[10] The French definitions thus bring into account not only the physical act of banishment but also a spiritual component, thus broadening the domains to be analyzed as impacted by political exile. Portuguese dictionaries include this element too because they mention the meaning of expulsion from home [*expeler da casa*], the cutting off of social relationships [*afastar da convivencia social*], and the relocation into an "unpleasant place to live" [*lugal desagradavel de habitar*].[11]

In Spanish, the term *exile* is linked with and preceded by the term of *destierro*, meaning the separation of a person from the land in which he or she lives; expatriation, for political reasons. It thus centralizes the territorial dimension as the core of the phenomenon of exile. The verb *desterrar* [to coercively make somebody to leave a land] implies a juridical action that obligates those considered to be 'damaging' socially, morally, or politically to leave a certain territory or place.[12] The conviction of *destierro* may imply a translocation that

7   "Esilio," in Salvatore Battaglia, Ed., *Grande dizionario della lingua Italiana*. Torino: Unione tipográfica editrice Torinese, 1968, p. 349.

8   "Esilio," in *Vocabolario della lingua Italiana*. Rome: Istituto della Enciclopedia Italiana, 1987, vol. II, 317.

9   "Exil," in *Le Grand Robert de la langue Francaise*. Paris: Le Robert, 1989, p. 289.

10 "Exil," in *Trésor de la langue Francaise*. Paris, 1980, vol. 8, pp. 445–446.

11 *Dicionario da Lingua Portuguesa de Candido Figueroa*. Lisbon: Livraria Bertrand, 13th ed., vol. 1, p. 1148; *Pequeno diccionario Brasileiro da lengua Portuguesa*. Rio de Janeiro: Editora Civilização Brasileira, 1964, 11th ed., p. 524. The Portuguese institution of expulsion [*degredo* or banishment], which has existed in Portugal since the Middle Ages, is subsequently analyzed.

12 "Desterrar," in Martín Alonso Pedraz, Ed., *Enciclopedia del idioma*. Madrid: Aguilar, 1958, vol. 2, p. 1521; *Enciclopedia Universal Ilustrada Europeo-Americana Espasa-Calpe*. Bilbao, Spain: Espasa-Calpe, vol. 8, part I, pp. 643–644.

may be temporary or for life.[13] Since Roman imperial times, in the Iberian realm, *destierro* has acquired the meaning of banning of an individual for a certain period – short, long, or perpetual – to a certain distance from his or her place of residence. Variants involved 'deportation' (i.e., expulsion taking place through a port to a place across the sea) or 'relegation' (i.e., a translocation to another specified place).[14]

Although it is a clearly recognized juridical figure, present in penal codes and regulations, in modern times *destierro* also came to signify a voluntary decision, in which the individual leaves the land, "never to return."[15] However, it often involved a strong sense of coercion, which projected a feeling of alienation and could be used even metaphorically. Thus, the 1809 rebellion led by Pedro Domingo Murillo in La Paz found justification in terms of redressing injustice, declaring in its manifesto that "until now we have tolerated a sort of *destierro* in the bosom of our own fatherland."[16] Sophia McClennen quotes the Cuban exile writer Guillermo Cabrera Infante, who pointed out that until 1956, the word exile was not included in the *Diccionario de la Real Academia de la Lengua Española*.[17] When it was finally included, it referred to the exilic condition and not to an exiled individual. Even though the roots of this semantic bias go far back in time to the linguistic uses of Spanish since the Middle Ages, perhaps Cabrera Infante's explanation that General Franco's dictatorship ignored the condition of those excluded from Spain for political reasons[18] has a kernel of truth. Authoritarian rulers tend to disregard exiles as legitimate political interlocutors.

Moving fully to the interface between linguistic definitions and social and political processes, Amy K. Kaminsky points out the close connection of exile to space and movement in space, which is mediated by language, while singling out exile as especially coercive: "Exile as I am using it here is, like nomadism, errance. Or [. . .] border-crossing, a process of movement and change, not solely a displacement beyond a border (although it is also that)."[19] She considers voluntary exile an oxymoron.[20] Susanna Bachmamn stresses the dialectic of exile in terms of a dual position, of belonging and being an outsider at the

---

[13] "Destierro," in Real Academia Española, *Diccionario de la lengua Española*. Madrid: Espasa Calpe, 1984.

[14] *Enciclopedia Espasa-Calpe*, p. 643.

[15] "Desterrarse," in Sebastián Covarrubias Orozco, Ed., *Tesoro de la lengua castellana*. Barcelona: S. A. Horta, 1943.

[16] Teresa Gisbert, "Situación jurídica de la Audiencia de Charcas y primeros levantamientos," in José de Mesa, Teresa Gisbert, and Carlos D. Mesa Gisbert, Eds., *Historia de Bolivia*. La Paz: Editorial Gisbert, 1999, p. 309.

[17] Sophia A. McClennen, *The Dialectics of Exile: Nation, Time, Language and Space in Hispanic Literatures*. West Lafayette, IN: Purdue University Press, 2004.

[18] Guillermo Cabrera Infante, "The Invisible Exile," in John Glad, Ed., *Literature in Exile*. Durham, NC: Duke University Press, 1990, pp. 36–37.

[19] Amy K. Kaminsky, *After Exile. Writing the Latin American Diaspora*. Minneapolis: University of Minnesota Press, 1999, p. xvi.

[20] Kaminsky, *After Exile*, p. 9.

same time, of being in a place (the site of exile) and yet being outside what is really important to the displaced individual, excluded from the social life she or he had before.[21]

Exile implies a break not only with the home territory and landscape but also with a social and cultural milieu, background, and imagery, a certain vision of collective history. In *The Oxford Book of Exile*, John Simpson defines the concept as "[t]o be wrenched from home, family, everything pleasant and familiar, and forced into a world that is cold and hostile, whether the expelling agent is the Angel of God or Stalin's NKVD: this is the defining experience of exile. The word itself carries powerful connotations of sorrow and alienation, of the surrender of the individual to overwhelming strength, of years of fruitless waiting. It was Victor Hugo who called exile 'a long dream of home'"[22] because, as Edwards indicates, exile implies "an uprooting from native soil and translation from the center to the periphery, from organized space invested with meaning to a boundary where the conditions of experience are problematic."[23] Hamid Naficy claims that "[e]xile is inexorably tied to homeland and to the possibility of return," although today exile is possible even at home, shaped by a sense of alienation and longing for other places and ideals.[24]

Translocation, Displacement

The phenomenon of exile exists within a wider spectrum of phenomena of individuals and groups moving across space, time, and culture. The dynamics of such translocation bring exiles close to a series of related phenomena, such as migrants, refugees, beneficiaries of asylum, cosmopolitan vagrants, nomads, and the networks that form diasporas. Although it is often difficult to separate exile from these related phenomena, the former has a distinctive political connotation, genesis, and implications, to be subsequently discussed.

Even if all the preceding concepts of mobility are linked, observers have tried to pinpoint their different connotations and partially shared characteristics. Argentinean writer Luisa Valenzuela distinguishes between exile and expatriation. She could have chosen to live quietly in Argentina under the military, but she would have then turned into an expatriate (i.e., a person who had her country taken from her).[25] Edward Said distinguishes among exiles, refugees, expatriates, and emigrants. A refugee

[21] Susanna Bachmann, *Topografías del doble lugar: El exilio literario visto por nueve autoras del Cono Sur*. Lausanne-Zaragoza: Hispanica Helvetica, No. 13, p. 16.

[22] John Simpson, "Driven Forth," in *The Oxford Book of Exile*. Oxford: Oxford University Press, 1995, p. 1.

[23] Edwards in Lagos, 1988: 16–17, quoted from Susanna Bachmann, *Topografías del doble lugar*. Hispanica Helvetica, No. 13.

[24] Hamid Naficy, "Framing Exile: From Homeland to Homepage," in *Home, Exile, Homeland*. New York: Routledge, 1999, p. 3.

[25] Kaminsky, *After Exile*, pp. 9–10.

...has become a political one, suggesting large herds of innocent bewildered people requiring urgent international assistance. Expatriates are people who live voluntarily in alien countries, usually because of personal or social reasons. Emigrants... enjoy an ambiguous status. Technically, an emigrant is anyone who migrates to a new country, choice in the matter is certainly a possibility. Although an emigrant was not banished, and can always return, he may still live with a sense of exile. Exiles... are people who were forced to leave their home, land, roots and are cut off from their past.[26]

Luis Miguel Díaz and Guadalupe Rodríguez de Ita distinguish between beneficiaries of asylum and political refugees. The former are politically persecuted persons who ask for protection in a diplomatic legation and, as such, are not subject to extradition, whereas the latter are persons expelled or deported or who fled their country of origin or residence, as victims of war, natural catastrophes, political turmoil, or persecution for various reasons, including ethnic or religious factors.[27]

Similarly, the Uruguayan intellectual, Angel Rama, distinguished between *exile*, a term dominated by precariousness and intentions to return, and *migration*, which encompasses a more definitive assimilation to a host society and culture.[28] Exiles differ from migrants in that exiles are forced to leave their country, whereas migrants choose to leave in order to solve a difficult economic situation. Exiles suffer from a prohibition to go back, whereas migrants have virtually at any time the possibility of returning. Many migrants do not have the means to go back, but they are not formally denied the right to do so. The possibility of return conditions the perception of self and of the homeland, placing the personal projects on different axes.[29] In the same line and following a cultural approach, Sharon Ouditt constructs the same distinction among displaced persons:

The conditions of the exile and the immigrant are differentiated by the fact that the exile experiences an unhappy or unwilled rupture with his or her original culture, while the immigrant leaves voluntarily, with the desire to become accepted as a member of the new society.[30]

John Durham Peters attempts to define and compare related concepts of mobility, primarily exile and diaspora. Peters considers that both concepts include

[26] Edward Said, "The Mind of Winter: Reflection on Life in Exile." *Harper's Magazine*, September 1984, pp. 49–56, cited in Yossi Shain, *In Search of Loyalty and Recognition: The Political Activity of Exiles*. Yale University, Ph.D. dissertation, 1988, p. 9.

[27] Luis Miguel Díaz and Guadalupe Rodríguez de Ita, "Bases histórico-jurídicas de la política mexicana de asilo diplomático," in Silvia Dutrénit Bielas and Guadalupe Rodríguez de Ita, Eds., *Asilo diplomático Mexicano en el Cono Sur*. Mexico: Instituto Mora and SER, 1999, pp. 63–85.

[28] Mentioned by Carlos Ulanovsky, *Seamos felices mientras estamos aquí. Crónicas del exilio*. Buenos Aires: Sudamericana, 2001, p. 25.

[29] Ana Vásquez and Angela Xavier de Brito, "La situation de l'exilé: essai de généralisation fondé sur l'exemple de réfugiés Latino-Américains." *Intercultures*, 21 (1993): 51–66.

[30] Sharon Ouditt, "Introduction: Dispossession or Repositioning?," in S. Ouditt, Ed., *Displaced Persons: Conditions of Exile in European Culture*. Aldershot, UK: Ashgate, 2002, pp. xiii–xiv.

a strong element of displacement and can imply variable measures of coercion and choice. However, diaspora alludes to networks among compatriots abroad, whereas exile suggests longing for home, with a strong element of pathos that does not appear as often in the diaspora. The author also claims that exile is always solitary, whereas diaspora implies a collective dimension by definition.[31] This binary contrast is too schematic, in our understanding. Exile may be constructed through networks and the construction of community, aimed both at strengthening individuals and fighting for return. Diaspora may include strong levels of individual alienation, both from the home country and the host settings, shaping strong feelings of solitude.

A more balanced characterization of diaspora has been elaborated by Thomas Tweed in his book on the religion of Cubans in Miami. According to Tweed, the defining event encoded in the collective identity and memory is the dispersion from a grounded center. From this perspective, *diaspora* can be defined as:

A group with some shared culture which lives outside the territory that it considers its native place, and whose continuing bonds with that land are crucial for its collective identity.... Those migrants symbolically construct a common past and future, and their shared symbols bridge the homeland and the new land.[32]

Gabriel Sheffer further elaborates the definition of a *diaspora* in ethnonational terms:

[as] a social-political formation created as a result of either voluntary or forced migration, whose members regard themselves as of the same ethno-national origin and who permanently reside as minorities in one or several host countries. Members of such entities maintain regular or occasional contacts with what they regard as their homelands and with individuals and groups of the same background residing in host countries. Based on aggregate decisions to settle permanently in host countries, but to maintain a common identity, diasporas identify as such, showing solidarity with their group and their entire nation, and they organize and are active in the cultural, social, economic, and political spheres. Among their various activities, members of such diasporas establish trans-state networks that reflect complex relationships among the diasporas, their host countries, their homelands, and international actors.[33]

These encompassing definitions bring the concept of diasporas closer to the experience of exiles. In many cases, the latter presupposes forced displacement but may also become blurred in cases of expatriates getting out of a home country because of tightening institutional exclusion. In general, as Sheffer points out, exiles also maintain regular or occasional contacts with what they regard as their homelands and with individuals and groups of the same background

---

[31] J. D. Peters, "Exile, Nomadism and Diaspora: The Stakes of Mobility in the Western Canon," in Naficy, *Home, Exile, Homeland*, pp. 19–21.

[32] Thomas A. Tweed, *Our Lady of the Exile: Diasporic Religion at a Cuban Cathlolic Shrine in Miami*. New York: Oxford University Press, 1997, p. 84.

[33] Gabriel Sheffer, *Diaspora Politics: At Home and Abroad*. Cambridge: Cambridge University Press, 2003, pp. 9–10.

residing in host countries. For exiles, the maintenance of a common identity is a *sine qua non* of their existence as they vacillate between their past back home and their present abroad. Exiles tend to establish trans-state networks with other exiles and co-nationals, with various degrees of social and political involvement, to use the terminology of Michael Hechter and Michael Banton.[34]

Despite these similarities, we should be aware that migratory processes in the 20th century have complicated the possibility of defining political exile and diasporas in ethnonational terms. This is especially true in the Americas, in the framework of mass migration coinciding with the establishment of states. Consequently, in many cases – such as those created by the political dynamics of institutional exclusion in Latin America – exile turns out to be focused on the relationships between citizenship and nationality. Second, exile may be the harbinger of the creation of new diasporas, as in the cases of Paraguay and Cuba, in which even economically motivated migration is colored and permeated with images, accounts, and strategies of exile. As long as authoritarian rule creates long-term situations of institutionalized exclusion, it is likely that large numbers of migrants could use reflexively an ethos of exile and shape strategies of survival and advancement of their interests in these terms. Third, the social and political involvement of the proactive exiles is geared mostly toward the home country, whereas the activities in the public spheres of the host country and transnational domains serve to promote changes in the home country.

There are many gradations of exile. In her book, *Exiled Governments*, Alicja Iwańska identifies three major groups within a national diaspora's social movement, according to their active or potential role in the actions of exile groups. First are the "core members," the active members of exile organizations. In the second circle are the "rear guard members," "those proven but temporarily passive exiles, who for lack of time, energy or access to an ideological milieu are not involved. . . . " The third, external layer consists of all others who share a cultural background, some solidarity derived from a common heritage, "and at least some latent patriotism which core members assume may be aroused and mobilized."[35] These networks may include, of course, not only forcibly displaced individuals but also migrants and their descendants, sojourners, and overseas students. From our perspective, it is crucial to assess the interaction among these groups, which shape in different ways the dynamics of communities of exiles and their relative capacity to impinge the state and transnational spaces in which they are active.

The decision to flee a place considered home can be shown to be closely related to a coercive or menacing institutional situation that left the exile without much choice, even in those cases in which she or he fled home as a result of a personal choice. For the exile, leaving home is related to coercion and fear of

34 Michael Hechter, *Principles of Group Solidarity*. Berkeley: University of California Press, 1987; Michael Banton, "Modeling Ethnic and National Relations." *Ethnic and Racial Studies*, 17, 1 (1994): 1–19.

35 Alicja Iwańska, *Exiled Governments*. Cambridge, MA. Schenkman, 1981, p. 44.

imminent danger. The element of personal choice is severely limited, although not totally eliminated, because exiles can decide when to leave and sometimes about where to go to. Contrastingly, the worker-migrant is perceived, justly or unjustly, as solely responsible for his or her departure. While far from home, the exile feels constrained to remain there as long as the conditions that brought him or her to leave did not disappear. Worker-migrants feel they can return at will, whereas exiles wait for the home government or regime to change. This means that, analytically, residence abroad is experienced differentially in each of these situations.[36] Martin A. Miller distinguishes among refugees, expatriates, exiles, and émigrés. Refugees are willing to resettle; expatriates have moved abroad by choice; exiles have been forced to move, most will not resettle but cannot return, meanwhile, to their homeland; and, finally, émigrés are exiles who engage in politics.[37] Related to this, sociologist Lewis A. Coser distinguished between refugees who intend to settle permanently in their new country and exiles who regard their exile as temporary and live abroad for the day they may return.[38]

Political scientist Yossi Shain has conceptualized this distinction in the following terms: "I define expatriates as political exiles if they engage in political activity, directed against the policies of a home regime, against the home regime itself or against the political system as a whole, so as to create circumstances favorable to their return."[39] But Shain also provides a psychologically oriented characterization: "what distinguishes the exile from an ordinary refugee, is above all a state of mind . . . the exile does not seek a new life and a new home in a foreign land. He considers his residence abroad strictly temporary and will not and cannot assimilate to a new society."[40] Exile is conceived by those who experience it as a transitory phase, a "life between parentheses," as outside the "real life" that remained in the homeland.[41]

Analytical Dimensions

Our inquiry has started by asking about the broadest common denominator and the distinctiveness of political exile. Such a combined strategy leads to uncover what the exiles have in common with the wider arena of translocating individuals and displaced groups and what singles them out. In other words, which are the basic themes that exile shares with other similar situations and

---

[36] Ana Vásquez and Ana María Araujo, *Exils Latino-americains: La malediction d'Ullyse.* Paris: CIEMI-L'Harmattan, 1988.

[37] Martin A. Miller, *The Russian Revolutionary Emigrés, 1825–1870.* Baltimore, MD: Johns Hopkins University Press, 1986, pp. 6–8.

[38] Lewis A. Coser, *Refugee Scholars in America.* New Haven, CT: Yale University Press, 1984, p. 1.

[39] Yossi Shain, *The Frontier of Loyalty: Political Exiles in the Age of the Nation-States.* Middletown: Wesleyan University Press, 1989, p. 15.

[40] Shain, *In Search of Loyalty and Recognition.* Yale University, Ph.D. dissertation, 1988, p. 8.

[41] Vásquez and Araujo, *Exils Latino-Américains.*

which are those that converge into the concept of political exile as distinguished from the encompassing exilic condition.

Although the exilic condition can be predicated both on situations of marginalization and inner alienation from society, as intrinsic to situations characterized by socioeconomic exclusion and a discriminatory politics of identity,[42] the meanings of political exile are more specific.

Political exile is structured around the institutional exclusion of individuals and groups of individuals from the national territory and the body-politic of a home country. As Alan Angell and Susan Carstairs concluded in a comprehensive article on Chilean exile,

Exile is not a capricious excess of authoritarian rulers in Chile: it is an intrinsic and indispensable part of the authoritarian system of rule.[43]

The central core of exile in its sociopolitical sense revolves around the closure of normative channels of political participation, negotiation, and dialogue in the body-politic. Institutional exclusion implies arbitrary use of power and violence in the service of political goals by those in power as well as the possible generalization of counterviolence, perceived by oppositions as the only feasible means of contestation. Whenever such a situation develops, public spheres slip into polarization. While limiting normative contestation, those in power exercise exclusion and proceed to use violence in arbitrary ways. They are likely to meet a radicalized opposition, which they persecute, imprison, kill, or banish from the body-politic. In such contexts, exile may increasingly affect a wider range of individuals only partially connected to the political domain, such as intellectuals, professionals, publicists, academics, union leaders, and student activists. Loss of place logically results then from the questioning of membership in a political community and of the banning of free participation in the public spheres of a certain society. Whether only a few prominent individuals or even entire social groups are banished will depend on the shifting definitions and boundaries of *the political* in various settings and historical circumstances.

Displacement from the national territory and exclusion from a community and the body-politic of a home state trigger a series of issues of crucial personal and collective transcendence. As Hannah Arendt perceptively stated,

The fundamental deprivation of human rights is manifested first and above all in the deprivation of a place in the world which makes opinions significant and actions effective. Something much more fundamental than freedom and justice, which are rights of citizens, is at stake when belonging to the community into which one is born is no longer a matter of course and not belonging no longer a matter of choice.[44]

---

[42] Iris Marion Young, *Inclusion and Democracy*. New York: Oxford University Press, 2000; and cf. Nancy Fraser, Ed., *Redistribution or Recognition? A Political-Philosophical Exchange*. London and New York: Verso, 2003.

[43] Alan Angell and Susan Carstairs, "The Exile Question in Chilean Politics." *Third World Quarterly*, 9, 1 (1987): 166.

[44] Hannah Arendt, *The Origins of Totalitarianism*. Cleveland, OH: Meridian, 1968, 12th printing (originally published 1951), p. 296.

Foremost, exile triggers questions of identity, leading to rethinking the tension between the political and the primordial components embedded in the nation-state. Doubts are cast on the collective and personal identity of the displaced person, who finds herself or himself detached from the environment in which routines were meaningful and daily practices and meanings could be taken for granted. The exilic experience demolishes well-established beliefs. The loss of such "markers of certainty," to use a term suggested by Claude Lefort and Shmuel N. Eisenstadt,[45] is deepened as displacement often follows the defeat of political projects envisioned in the country of origin. Furthermore, exile prompts the search for the reconstitution of life paradigms and political projects, albeit far away from the home polity and society.

Although, in this sense, being an exile is constraining in the short term, it also entails new openings in the transnational and international arena, rooted in the daily confrontation and exposure to new environments, institutions, and ideas. Existential plight forces a process of change, both individual and collective. Being abroad and attempting to retain an impact on the home society's fate and direction of development forces exiles to act in wider arenas, be they transnational, international, or global. As they struggle to regain public visibility in the host country and the global arena, exiles thus resist a mere acculturation and adaptation, typical of migrants.

Rooted in displacement and translocation, political exile has a clear geo-graphical dimension. The most generic trait shared by exiles with, for instance, *gastarbeiters* [guest-workers], expatriates, cosmopolitan vagrants, nomads, and tourists is that all these individuals or groups are defined by their mobility, free or forced, as they shift from one place to another, across borders and cultures. They also all move across temporal frameworks from past to present and backward in remembrance and imagination, while preserving hopes and plans for the future.

The time dimension is no less crucial in defining exile, and it tends to be conflated with it. Indeed, institutionalized exclusion breaks the normal flow of life. It disconnects the displaced individuals from the life of the home society. As soon as they arrive in a host society, the exiles begin to live in two time frames. One is the frame in which they physically move from the moment of their displacement. The other is the one that takes place in tandem with the inaccessible homeland left behind. Exiles are caught between the present and the past, and they try to reinterpret and reframe the past events and frameworks in terms of the new experience. This dynamic prompts a constant redefinition of their previous political and cultural premises and of their connection to the collective images and visions that, until recently, they took for granted. In this sense, exile is a harbinger of reflexivity and change, at both the personal and the collective level.

45 Claude Lefort, *Democracy and Political Theory.* Minneapolis: University of Minnesota Press, 1988; S. N. Eisenstadt, "The Reconstitution of the Realm of the Political in Modern Societies," unpublished manuscript, 2006.

Similar to other foreigners crossing borders, exiles are exposed to what Victor Turner and other anthropologists have defined as situations and experiences of liminality and that, from another perspective, Julia Kristeva characterizes as a condition of strangers moving back to places out of reach.[46] Thus, they may become, under certain circumstances, agents of social and cultural transformation both in the host countries in which they reside and in their home country, which they had to leave and to which they dream of returning. However, we should be wary of generalizations. For some individuals, exile is a trigger of deep depressive states. For others, it prompts an orientation to activism in the public sphere and a commitment to continue fighting for the 'cause' and return to the homeland. It is the proactive type of exile who often becomes an agent of transformation and serves as a bridge among societies, ideas, and institutional paradigms.

The broadest analytical elements denoting exiles are, first, their forceful institutional exclusion and displacement and their strong will to retain control of life decisions, all under constraining conditions and persecution. The second is their move to a foreign environment and the re-creation of life strategies and images of homeland from afar. The third is their impaired yet persistent will to return to the home country.

Together, these themes provide a characterization of exiles as they converge because each of them separately is not enough to define this phenomenon. For instance, there is a huge dimension of coercion in the displacement of groups of individuals and groups evolving into diasporas, such as the African slaves taken to the New World or the Irish people forced by the policy of enclosures and famine to cross the Atlantic Ocean. Similarly, the construction or reconstruction of a collective project of return connected to the reconstruction of the collective identity is not peculiar to exiles, as many other migrants form diasporas that engage in processes of cultural creation as they interact within their new environments.[47] Finally, the longing for the homeland left behind and the temporary impossibility to return are typical of long-term migrant groups as well as temporary residents such as *gastarbeiters* or diplomats.

It is the joint convergence of all these dimensions that forms a cluster that singles out political exile in phenomenological terms.

Forceful Exclusion and the Will to Retain Control of Life Decisions

The first and almost universal element is the institutional exclusion, with exiles being forced to leave their country of residence in order to escape repression, as they suffer the loss of civil and political rights, or as they fear persecution or even the loss of life.

[46] Victor Turner, *The Ritual Process: Structure and Anti-Structure*. New York: Cornell University Press, 1974; Julia Kristeva, *Strangers to Ourselves*. New York: Columbia University Press, 1991.

[47] Gabriel Sheffer, *Diaspora Politics*. Cambridge: Cambridge University Press, 2003.

Exile stems from public activities and positions, or suspicion of such activities and positions that are in opposition to the interests and policies taken by those in power, independent of whether or not the individuals were actually involved in politics. That is, their exile may be a result of proactive positions in the political sphere as well as in the professional, academic, intellectual, student, or labor-union domain, all having implications in the public sphere.

Those who become exiles feel forced to leave their place of residence by their evaluation of the home situation or are literally expelled by the authorities. Throughout Latin America, the options opened before those contesting power, or perceived as such by those in power, were very limited. Historian Félix Luna described in plastic terms the choices of those opposed to Juan Manuel de Rosas in the early 19th century as involving *encierro, destierro o entierro* (i.e., prison, exile, or death).[48] It is perhaps no coincidence that in her testimony, a victim of Tiburcio Carías Andino's rule used these same words to reflect on the fate of dissidents in the 1930s and 1940s in Honduras:

The Hondurean who did not agree with the dictatorship had the options of prison, exile or death (*podía escoger entre el encierro, el destierro o el entierro*); those were the alternatives. Unable to resist, protest or even criticize, the mental dumbness was such that people could not distinguish between good and evil. Human rights were not respected; private homes were profaned at any hour; people were put in prison without reason; those not siding with the government could not find a job; their children were subject to harassment and humiliation in public schools. In sum, those who did not submit to the despotic corruption were treated in an inhuman manner.[49]

Under normal conditions, those who move into exile would have liked to stay in their country of origin or residence and to continue their normal life and activity but find their normal life interrupted because of political developments, subjective premonitions, or a combination of both.

In addition to nationals being forced to move abroad as exiles, there is the phenomenon of *double* or *serial exile*. That is, individuals who had fled their country of origin and found refuge in a country willing to receive them as exiles or refugees find themselves in a situation in which, because of political change and still unable to return to the country of origin, they are forced to leave their new country of residence for a second exile.

From the moment the exiles leave their country of residence, borders acquire a special significance for them. "Borders are real concern for the exile, even in the post-modern age of hyper-capitalism [and globalization]. The exile does not float free, but must worry about such practical things as visas and prohibited re-entry into his or her nation."[50]

---

[48] Félix Luna, *Historia general de la Argentina*. Buenos Aires: Planeta, 1995, vol. 5, p. 202.

[49] Emma Bomilla, *Continuismo y dictadura*. Tegucigalpa: Litográfica Comyagüela, 1989, pp. 1–2, in Marvin Barahona, *Honduras en el siglo XX: Una síntesis histórica*. Tegucigalpa: Guaymuras, 2005, p. 101.

[50] Sophia McClennen, *The Dialectics of Exile*, p. 191.

Beyond the degree of institutional exclusion forcing individuals to leave, there is usually a 'deep structure' grounded in a closure of the political domain and the attempted authoritarian control of public spheres.[51] The impact of such authoritarian closure is felt far beyond the strict political arena. For instance, Bruce Gilman describes the oppressive atmosphere after the military took power in Brazil in 1964, which prompted many artists to flee the country. At the start of their careers, Chico Buarque de Hollanda, after being arrested in 1968, and singer–songwriter Geraldo Vandré resented the authoritarian controls imposed, as well as the use of self-censure and techniques to deceive the censors, and left the country. Buarque looked for refuge in Italy, while Geraldo Vandré escaped to Chile and later relocated to Algeria and Europe. Music critic Tárik de Sousa, who started to work for the press in 1968, described the atmosphere at that time: "We could not mention names like Chico Buarque, not even to report news that had nothing to do with music." Caetano Velhoso and Gilberto Gil were arrested in December 1968 in São Paulo, taken to Rio, and imprisoned. "A few months later they were moved to Salvador and 'invited' to leave the country. The *tropicalistas* found a cold refuge in London, where they remained in exile until 1972. Gal Costa, a singer whose lifestyle symbolized the openness and freedom of Tropicália, recorded their songs and served as a medium for Caetano and Gil while they were in exile."[52]

Accordingly, it is often difficult to discriminate among the political, cultural, and socioeconomic background elements prompting and motivating exile. We can state with confidence that in most situations of exile, one can find some combination of such elements conforming with what we define as *institutionalized exclusion*, a situation of marginalization of those who oppose – or are affected by – the policies taken by the rulers and, as a result, find themselves fleeing their country of origin or residence. In the case of Paraguay, there are hundreds of thousands of workers who became *gastarbeiters* [*peones golondrinas*] in Argentina and Brazil and planned a return to their families. In parallel fashion, thousands of individuals with political, professional, and intellectual aspirations were forced to take the road of exile, their ranks engrossed by hundreds of spies sent by General Stroessner's administration to infiltrate the communities of Paraguayans in the Southern Cone, as any visitor to the Archives of Terror in Asunción will see when checking the thousands of files there. Many of these background elements have a strong political core, as they are melted in the lack of options to debate policy freely in an authoritarian institutional environment without finding oneself at risk.

Unsurprisingly, as the military began to dominate Paraguay after 1936, especially after the coup of 1940, and, finally, as General Alfredo Stroessner took power in 1954, installing a decades-long military rule, a massive migratory

---

[51] Shmuel N. Eisenstadt, Wolfgang Schluchter, and Bjorn Wittrock, Eds., *Public Spheres and Collective Identities*. New Brunswick, Canada: Transaction, 2001.

[52] Bruce Gilman "Times of Gal," available at http://www.brazzil.com/cvrdec97.htm, accessed 4 May 2008.

movement of Paraguayan politicians, intellectuals, liberal professionals, union and student leaders, as well as workers left the country. In such an environment, as occurred in Paraguay increasingly after 1936,

being a friend, acquaintance, relative or somebody even unrelated but sympathetic to somebody persecuted politically is sufficient to be thrown out of the country [*desterrado*], imprisoned or tortured.... Even if the economic and the political factors are the two principal motives triggering the reality of exile, the fact that the great majority of the migrants did not opt to return as the result of the critical economic situation in Argentina and Uruguay in the last years, demonstrates or at least stresses the prominent character of the political factor.[53]

Toward the 1970s, estimates placed the number of Paraguayans residing abroad, especially in Argentina, Uruguay, and Brazil, as a third of the Paraguayan population:

An "island surrounded by land," Paraguay's post-independence history has been one of cyclical exoduses, each of which has only served to highlight the isolation and exile of Paraguay itself.... Paraguay's tiny population of two million people is today complemented by the estimated one million more who have chosen or have been forced to live outside their country.[54]

The massive process of exclusion leading to the crystallization of a Paraguayan diaspora in the Southern Cone consists of a complex continuum of individuals moving out of the country for a variety of reasons, from strictly economic motivations to those who were pushed out because of political persecution. The class origins are varied as well, including individuals of the lowest strata together with prominent members of the elites. Beyond the different motivations and life projects of the Paraguayans abroad, the presence of exiles in their midst became a factor of worries for those in power, who sent a huge number of spies to obtain information about possible anti-Stroessner activities abroad.

Authoritarian governments such as Stroessner's have been fully aware of the possible danger stemming from the political articulation of economic migrants by proactive exiles on the basis of common exclusion by the authoritarian system. Because authoritarianism is predicated on exclusion, political exiles may become central to all sorts of activities, leading eventually to its demise. The possible merger of political exiles and economic migrants becomes even more problematic from the perspective of authoritarian rulers as the international and global arena becomes increasingly committed to discussing both issues in terms of human rights.

The case of Paraguayan exile is illuminating in terms of the draining of the intellectual core out of a country sunk into political anarchy and subsequent authoritarian repression and closure of the public spheres. Teresa Méndez-Faith, who researched Paraguayan literary creation, indicates that nearly half

[53] Teresa Méndez-Faith, *Paraguay, novela y exilio*. Sommerville, NJ: SLUSA, 1992, p. 30.
[54] William Rowe and Teresa Whitfield, "Thresholds of Identity: Literature and Exile in Latin America." *Third World Quarterly*, 9, 1 (1987), 231.

of the greatest works written between 1949 and 1967 were completed and
published in exile, a trend that continued thereafter. Herib Campos Cervera,
the most renowned poet of the post-Chaco War period, wrote his most emo-
tive poems in exile and died in exile. Méndez-Faith mentions a large list of
exiled writers and intellectuals, such as Elvio Romero, Rubén Bareiro Saguier,
Justo Pastor Benítez, Lincoln Silva, Augusto Roa Bastos, and Gabriel Casaccia,
who have written in exile about the dramatic experience of their co-nationals,
reflecting nostalgically and critically on the home country and relating the
collective and personal drama of the exiles. Novels such as *Yo el Supremo*
(1974) by Augusto Roa Bastos and *Los herederos* (1976) by Gabriel Casaccia
were published in Argentina. The rich production abroad since the 1940s has
contrasted with the relative poverty of the creation in Paraguay itself.[55]

Without disclaiming the element of force and repression that pushes individuals into exile, it is important to stress that the decision to leave contains
an element of choice, albeit of a severely constrained kind. The politically persecuted person faces danger and is aware that she or he can adopt alternative
moves, such as taking the risk of going underground to continue being politically involved, keeping a high political profile regardless of the risks implied,
leaving the political arena, or even changing sides to avoid persecution.

To choose among these and additional courses of action implies a constrained choice, with high personal and collective prices that put pressure on
the prospective exile. Opting for exile, which poses a serious dilemma for the
prospective exile, is a choice open to criticism by those who opt to remain
behind in the home country. Often, after years, as the displaced individuals return, their exile may be severely criticized and defined as defection and
escape. In addition to the personal costs of being forced to leave, this element
of choice may be brought back in future debates as an easy way out of a situation of repression, as an individualistic move that, in most cases, did not
take into account the plight of those who remained behind. In short, exiles
may be defined by those attacking them as those who chose to escape frontal
confrontation.[56]

Exile – especially for those who are actively engaged in political activities
against their repressive home government – may be seen as changing the terms
of confrontation, from the internal public sphere to a foreign environment and
to the international and transnational realms.

One of the central issues distinguishing exiles from other forms of forced
displacement, such as refugees, is the will to retain control of their constrained
decisions, choices, and self-image. In her discussion of "Citizens of the World,"

55 Méndez-Faith, *Paraguay, novela y exilio*, ibid. On Gabriel Casaccia, see also Gloria da Cunha-
   Giabbai, *El exilio, realidad y ficción*. Montevideo: Arca, 1992. On Augusto Roa Bastos's views,
   see Kart Kohut, *Escribir en París*. Frankfurt am Main: Verlag Klaus Dieter Vervuert, 1983.
56 Saúl Sosnowski, Ed., *Represión y reconstrucción de una cultura: El caso argentino*. Buenos
   Aires: Universidad de Buenos Aires, 1984; Roniger and Sznajder, *The Legacy of Human Rights
   Violations in the Southern Cone*, Oxford: Oxford University Press, 1999, pp. 190–193.

Martha Nussbaum analyzes the classic case of Diogenes (404–323 B.C.E.), who coined the term *exile* and chose leaving his home city to be able to pursue a life of freedom, especially the freedom of speech that he defined as "the finest thing in human life":

This freedom from subservience, he held, was essential to philosophical life. "When someone reproached him for being an exile, he said, that it was on that account that he came to be a philosopher."[57]

In the context of Latin America, the testimony of Ariel Dorfman is equally paradigmatic. In *Heading South, Looking North*, as he found asylum in the Argentine Embassy in Santiago de Chile in 1973, Dorfman was interviewed by a UN High Commission for Refugees (UNHCR) representative, who explained to him the conditions and benefits of the refugee status he was offered according to the 1951 UN statute: "What I need to know – she said – is if you intend to avail yourself of refugee status." The advantages were clear: training and job placement, language courses in the country of asylum, preferred housing, free medical attention, social security, no need to renew visa approval each year from the local immigration authorities. Dorfman recollects clearly the reasons for declining that status: "I was now being offered a future in history as a victim." Contrastingly, he defined himself as an exile:

I chose it automatically because I wanted to see my emigration as part of another tradition.... There was something Byronic, defiant and challenging, about being an exile, something vastly more romantic and Promethean than the fate embodied in that recently coined word *refugee* that the twentieth century had been forced to officialize as a result of so much mass murder and wandering.... [B]y rejecting the passive term and opting for the more active, sophisticated, elegant one, I was projecting my odyssey as something that originated in myself and not in the historical forces seething outside my grasp. Instead of formulating my future in terms of what I was seeking, refuge, I conceived myself as ex-cluded, ex-pelled, ex-iled, as if I had absolute freedom to choose which of the many countries of the world my free person would wander.... I was going off into the wilderness like a rebellious, solitary, persecuted angel.[58]

Retaining autonomy over one's life is the crux of the exile's decision.[59] A similar hindsight into the attitudinal element of retaining choice and free will in the midst of taking forced, constrained steps can be found in the testimony of

[57] Martha Nussbaum, *Cultivating Humanity*. Cambridge, MA, and London: Harvard University Press, 1997, p. 56.
[58] Ariel Dorfman, *Heading South, Looking North: A Bilingual Journey*. New York: Farrar, Straus, and Giroux, 1998, pp. 236–239.
[59] The decision about exile affects family members unrelated to the political circumstances that produced exile, including life partners, parents, children, brothers, and sisters. Children are particularly vulnerable because they generally are not part of the decision to leave the home environment, yet suffer its consequences. A recent film by Cao Hamburger portrays the impact of exile on children, through the disorientation and grief of the son of a couple fleeing the Brazilian dictatorship in 1970 (*O ano em que meus pais saéram de férias* [The year my parents went on vacation], Brazil, 2006).

Uruguayan psychiatrists Julio C. Lamónaca and Marcelo N. Viñar. For them, looking for asylum was especially troublesome because the Spanish word *asilo* [asylum] had heavily loaded meanings for them as professionals. As psychiatrists, they were used to thinking of asylum in connection with the total institution for the mentally ill. Indeed, in Spanish, *asilo* or *manicomio* were words that stood for madhouses. Accordingly, their first impression of being granted asylum carried heavy negative meanings:

In our profession and since immemorial times, the word *asilo* . . . is lack of capacity and desolation, marginalized institution, often sordid, linking protection, solidarity and philanthropy with misery and contempt.[60]

As in the previous case, the fleeing individuals resented losing control of their fate and destinies. By defining themselves as exiles and assuming the élan of being exiles, they could possibly seclude themselves from losing a sense of control over their future, as their lives took a turn for the unknown. However, the legal and material benefits associated with their identification and categorization as refugees could be a very important aspect of making ends meet and therefore could not be easily sidelined and surrendered. This contradictory situation remained inimical throughout long processes of living abroad as exiles.[61]

Moving into Exile

Until they were forced to leave, the relationship of the future exiles with their home society was taken for granted. Once abroad, many exiles remain attached to the place they left and make this loss into a conscious and often central component of their personal identity. For many of them, it is only as they find themselves in alien environments and meet different social and cultural surroundings that they discover their lost home society as 'homeland,' realizing that what was left behind is central to their lives and plans. The experience of exile involves many tensions embedded in shifts in the linguistic, physical, and emotional landscapes that individuals grew to know and took for granted as long as routine life went on. Forced relocation carries with it drastic shifts and poses challenges to the manner in which individuals have perceived their

---

[60] Julio C. Lamónaca and Marcelo N. Viñar, "Asilo político: perspectivas desde la subjetividad," in Silvia Dútrenit Bielas and Guadalupe Rodríguez de Ita, Eds., *Asilo diplomático mexicano en el Cono Sur.* Mexico: Instituto Mora and SRE, 1999, p. 84.

[61] Among those escaping state repression was Andrew Graham-Yooll, a leading journalist persecuted for reporting on the Argentinean situation in the pages of *The Buenos Aires Herald.* Born to a Scottish immigrant and registered at birth at the British Consulate in Argentina, thereby receiving the privileges of dual nationality, he wrote a book of memoirs from his voluntary exile in Great Britain, in which he was highly critical of those "professional failures who assumed the role of the persecuted to win access to special allocations of funds, jobs and scholarships" (*A Matter of Fear: Portrait of an Argentinian Exile*, Westport, CT: Hill, 1982, p. 5).

life projects, involving a clear dimension of connecting personal and collective dimensions:

> It is necessary to establish a difference between mourning and the situation of exile. In a certain moment of life every human being knows this kind of loss. Mourning is felt as a private loss in which communication, in its deep nuances, is difficult. Contrastingly exile is not felt as an individual loss. The exiles do not mourn only their "dead" or their "prisoners." Their mourning is also social, in the sense that they are forced to accept the end of a *modus vivendi*, of a political and social context that cannot be reproduced as it was. Loss of their systems of reference, of their objects of love, of their poles of affection and aggression. Loss also of their megalomaniac projection acquired as revolutionaries and builders of a New World. The mourning of the exiles is collective and shared. However, the loss is always there and the process of mourning cannot but remain uncompleted, unfinished.[62]

Common assumptions and meanings are put to the test, and complex processes of personal and collective transformation are triggered by the traumatic experience of loss. Exile carries with it the sense of rupture and often of being projected into a precarious situation, potentially losing or at least redrafting one's positions, status, connections, and referents.

It is therefore not uncommon that the identity of the exile is often shaped or re-created far away from home. Whereas many immigrants are expected and may expect to become part of the host society, most exiles consciously remain attached to what they left behind. A particular salient case in this regard is that of the Irish trans-Atlantic emigration to North America. From the early 17th century to the early 20th century, as many as 7 million people emigrated from Ireland to North America. From the summer of 1845 to the early 1850s alone, in the period that came to be known as the Great Famine, the failure of the potato crop in Ireland precipitated the exodus of nearly 1,800,000 inhabitants, who "embraced emigration as their only escape from destitution and death."[63] Despite being a case of massive emigration because of economic and social changes taking place on both sides of the Atlantic, the Irish perceived the context of poverty and despair as prompting their sojourn as a result of British political oppression. Accordingly, a great majority of Irish portrayed themselves as involuntary exiles, using this account and symbols to explain and justify leaving the homeland. As analyzed by Kerby Miller,

> ... all but the most "cold" and "senseless" emigrants carried away burning memories and burdensome emotional obligations – that despite their physical departure, they would not break with the values and behaviour demanded by tradition and by parents, priests, and nationalist politicians.... Perhaps revealing were the promises which many emigrants, under the stress of these moments, gave to return someday to Ireland.... Of course, such promises were unrealistic and rarely fulfilled. However, the fact that they were made, remembered and cherished and that their failure was regretted on both sides

---

[62] Vásquez and Araujo, *Exils Latino-Americains*, pp. 45–46.
[63] Kerby A. Miller, *Emigrants and Exiles: Ireland and the Irish Exodus to North America*. Oxford: Oxford University Press, 1985, p. 280.

of the Atlantic served to keep Irish-Americans emotionally oriented to their childhood homes. Furthermore, even if they enjoyed material prosperity in the New World, their guilt about promises unfulfilled reinforced internalized obligations to ensure that most emigrants would send remittances and that at least occasionally they would still regard or portray themselves as involuntary "exiles".... Tradition and expediency merged, and emigration remained forced banishment – demanding political redress and the emigrants' continued fealty to sorrowing Mother Ireland.[64]

In all cases of exile or of migration conceived in terms of exile, a process of definition or recasting of identity takes place, being operated with some elaboration of the civil and political trends as well as some of the more primordial elements of the homeland.

These elements are processed anew by the exiles in forms that are not necessarily those sustained by the co-nationals at home. Political and cultural activism may become an essential part of this process of reconstruction of identity but may also be sidelined as a reaction to their ostracism. Nostalgia and the search to escape homelessness, the rupture of earlier confidence and sense of security produced by displacement, all these are interwoven in the re-creation of identity and, among some, the will to engage in political activities.

A further tension arises between the experience of exile and its various forms of representation. Intellectuals and artists in particular confront what seems to be the almost impossible task of narrating exile. This difficulty is rooted in distance and censorship, which they face as they try to confront a history that is being silenced by dictatorial regimes. Distance, in turn, projects the tension between a need to represent the precise background of their plight and the feasibility of translating it into a comprehensible and somehow objective report that the co-nationals back home can share. Students of literature have correctly observed that, in many cases, this tension leads to an intense literary creation, aimed at maintaining the identity and memory of the displaced individuals as well as at creating alternative imaginaries as a basis of future projects and hope. We claim that this problematique of exile is characteristic not only of writers and creators but also bears on exiles in general. Although it is true that not every exile is able to express himself or herself publicly in the preceding terms, for many this problematique triggers an intense review of conscience and redefinition of memories, identities, and political projects.[65]

The Impaired Yet Persistent Will to Return

These twin themes manifest themselves in a longing for the lost homeland, which combines with various forms and degrees of cultural, social, and political

---

[64] Miller, *Emigrants and Exiles*, pp. 567–568 and 557.

[65] These themes are profusely discussed by those who analyze the role of writers in exile. See, for instance, J. Gerald Kennedy, *Imagining Paris, Exile, Writing and American Identity*. New Haven, CT: Yale University Press, 1993, pp. 28–35; Méndez-Faith, *Paraguay, novela y exilio*, pp. 14–15; and McClennen, *The Dialectics of Exile*, pp. 29–34.

activism, while the exile is abroad. This life situation shapes a separate identity in the spaces that the exiles occupy in the host society and in the transnational social and political spaces in which they engage.

Many of the exiles try to remain updated with the developments of the home society, and some make a profession of being exiles. 'Activist' or 'proactive' exiles would like to contribute to a change in the conditions that had forced them into exile. For years, many of them tend to defy settled power in the home country, to create the conditions for political change, to press for their return, to replace power-holders, and eventually to attain power there.

In the nature of political activism in exile, we may find also exacerbated versions of regular political activism. For some exiles, their activism is contextualized within a subtext suggesting images of a 'golden age' and a 'lost paradise' back home. For others, 'home' becomes a political hell that requires serious analysis and political action geared to both personal and collective change. Some exiles idealize time and space images and exaggerate them into almost mythical proportions. Others engage in soul-searching processes, seeking a better understanding of past mistakes and failures leading into exile.

Even those exiles who remain politically active undergo a process of mourning. It is a process often perceived as following the social death of the displaced individual. Julio Cortázar, an expatriate turned exile, phrased it in the following terms:

Exile is the abrupt end of contact with the leaves and of the intimate touch with the air and land that was taken for granted. It is the sudden end of love, the unimaginably awful death, a death that a person continues to experience in full conscience.[66]

In less literary terms, the problems faced by the exiles are portrayed by Thomas Wright and Rody Oñate for the Chileans forced to move abroad, in a characterization that fits many other forced diasporas:

Regardless of their destinations and material circumstances, exiles carried heavy psychological baggage: the bitterness of defeat, feelings of guilt for having left dead, jailed, or disappeared comrades behind, memories of prison and torture they had endured – these and myriad other legacies of a sudden, violent, forced uprooting profoundly affected the exiles, compounding the challenges of adaptation. They arrived with dreams smashed, families torn apart, careers destroyed. Personal space contracted: Many of the men and some of the women, losing the public roles that their political involvement had given them in Chile, were forced by exile into the private realm. Parents became dependent on their children, who learned the host country's language quickly and became the link between household and outside world. In the developed countries, where most professionals were unable to work in their fields, many found menial jobs that provided a living but no satisfaction. These traumas had to be borne without the support and solidarity provided by the typical Chilean extended family.... The magnitude of the

[66] Julio Cortázar, "América Latina: exilio y literatura." *Araucanía de Chile*, No. 10 (1980): 60.

adjustment problem was such that, particularly beyond Latin America, exiles suffered high rates of depression, divorce, alcoholism, and suicide.[67]

Whereas the preceding extract reflects the individual sense of loss felt by many, exile also opens windows of opportunity for the individuals leaving their country of origin. It is while peregrinating abroad that many exiles grow to become leading and mature intellectuals, academics, researchers, or politicians. José Martí is one outstanding example of an intellectual who used his literary and oratory capacity for a political cause, the independence of his native Cuba. His proactive and tireless organizational and mobilization skills turned him into one of the most influential figures in the Cuban and Puerto Rican independence movements, reaching a continental projection in Latin America.

Very early in his life, Martí's sentence of prison was commuted by the colonial Spanish authorities' deportation from Cuba to Spain. It was during his first exile in Spain in the early 1870s that he received his formal education, earning degrees in philosophy and law in Zaragoza and Madrid. As he left Spain for Mexico in 1874, he was able to participate actively in the Mexican cultural life, organizing, debating, and writing widely, until the rise to power of Porfirio Díaz constrained his moves. After a short visit to Cuba, he settled in Guatemala, where he was appointed to the faculty of the Escuela Central to teach European literature and history of philosophy and contributed to the cultural life there. Again, a shift in the political ruling factions prompted him to leave Guatemala. He returned to Havana, where he made a living working in a law firm as he continued his revolutionary activities against the colonial status of the island. This resulted in 1879 in a second deportation to Spain, although he continued almost immediately to France, and then to the United States. In the United States, he once again engaged in journalism. In 1881, he attempted settling in Caracas but returned to New York, where he remained until May 1895, when he landed in Cuba and was killed as he tried to launch a war of liberation.[68]

In the United States, Martí became one of the leading figures of the Cuban and Puerto Rican revolutionary movements and an intellectual widely recognized for his many contributions. He wrote notes for periodicals in the Spanish-speaking countries, among them Argentina, Uruguay, Honduras, and Mexico; he worked as a translator and a clerk; he became a consul for Uruguay in 1887, for Argentina in 1890, and for the Dominican Republic in 1892. Foremost, Martí organized patriotic clubs in the New York area and in Florida, where there were concentrations of Cuban tobacco workers, whom he energized with his passion and rhythmic prose and speeches. He soon turned,

---

[67] Wright and Onate, "Chilean Political Exile." *Latin American Perspectives*, 34, 4 (2007): 38. The authors rely in this paragraph on interviews and on the works of Diana Kay, *Chileans in Exile: Private Struggles, Public Lives.* Wolfeboro, NH: Longwood Academic, 1987; and on Ana Vásquez and Ana María Araujo, *La maldición de Ulises.* Santiago: Sudamericana, 1990.

[68] Deborah Shnookal and Marta Muñiz, Eds., *José Martí Reader: Writings on the Americas.* Melbourne and New York: Ocean Press, 1999, pp. 10–13.

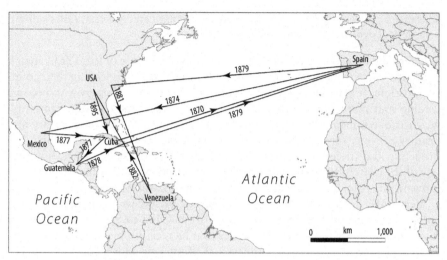

MAP 1. The serial exile of José Martí.

along with Generals Máximo Gómez and Antonio Maceo – with whom he maintained a tension-ridden relationship – into the living spirit and voice of those fighting for the cause of Cuban independence, organizing and galvanizing the communities of migrants, sojourners, and workers into a series of émigré groups committed to the cause of liberation.[69] Martí also befriended Ramón Emeterio Betances, considered to be the founding father of the Puerto Rican nationalism, and together they organized patriotic clubs, aimed at attaining the independence of both Cuba and Puerto Rico. They even collaborated on a project about a future Confederation of the Antilles, partially thought of as a preemptive stage to preclude the United States political hegemony after the envisioned independence.[70]

Exile involves a process of personal and collective transformation that begins only as the exiles leave their home country. One of the descriptions of this transformative process can be found in Mario Benedetti's book, *Andamios*. For him, exile involves a series of piecemeal and tense transformations encoded in the semantic structure of communication. In his eyes, those of a writer, exile involves a struggle between resistance and accommodation, sliding into a complex process of transformation. This process is no less troublesome when the newcomer moves to a country, such as Spain, which is the cradle of the

[69] On Maceo in exile in Costa Rica and his relationships with the other leaders of the Cuban Independence Movement, see Armando Vargas Araya, *Idearium Maceista: Junto con hazañas del General Antonio Maceo y sus mambises en Costa Rica, 1891–1895*. San José: Editorial Juricentro, 2001.

[70] Alfonso Rumazo González, *8 grandes biografías*. Caracas: Ediciones de la Presidencia de la República, 1993, vol. II, pp. 463–465.

language he grew to recognize as his mother tongue and the official language of his home country:

There are several stages. In the first, you refuse to undo your suitcases, because you still have the illusion that return will be tomorrow. Everything looks strange, indifferent, alien. When you listen to the news, you just pay attention to the international events, waiting (in a senseless way, of course) that something, even small, will be said about your country and your people. The second stage occurs when you begin paying attention to what happens around you, [taking interest] in the promises of politicians, in what they don't fulfill. At this stage you already feel at home, as you read the graffiti on the wall or listen to people's songs. Since nobody tells you how do [the Uruguayan soccer teams] Peñarol or Nacional or Wanderers or Rambla Juniors perform, you slowly become a fan of Zaragoza or of Albacete or Tenerife or any other team in which there is a Uruguayan player, or at least an Argentinean or Mexican or Chilean or Brazilian. In spite of the slow adaptation, in spite of the use of local idioms, . . . when you have already elbowed your way into the semantic jungle, you still suffer anguish in the most ridiculous corner of your little soul. You still feel the pleasure and pain of remembering what you left behind. . . . As time goes by (as Humphrey Bogart said) you are allowed to return. Only then, you enter the third and final stage [of exile]. Then you feel the sensuous and almost absurd itching, the fear of losing the blessed identity, the pressure on your heart and a ringing bell in your mind. And even though you are conscious that the move will neither be an act of bravery nor a cause for celebration, the return home becomes a must.[71]

The stages depicted by Benedetti resemble those described by other migrants and sojourners. Still, in exile, the political factor constitutes an axis around which the experiences of the displaced individuals are organized. The process of accommodation takes place as in the other cases. However, the prospects of relocation are seriously compounded by the redefinition of political projects and strategies to effect changes in the home country while one is abroad.

Because exile in general, and political exile in particular, is a universal phenomenon across societies and times, one needs to address the question of its generic traits and its transformations throughout Latin American political development. Some of its roots can be traced to colonial times, when traditions of displacement formed both in the Portuguese realm and in Spanish America. Whereas in this period displacement was *apolitical* and motivated mostly by social and economic considerations, in postcolonial times it acquired its distinctive political character, becoming a major mechanism for regulation of political conflict and access to power.

From the beginning of statehood, a significant number of founding fathers of the states found themselves in circumstances that led them to leave their countries and settle either in neighboring Latin American countries or elsewhere, mostly in Western Europe or the United States. Exile did not diminish the prestige and stature of these individuals, even though some died in exile and others were unable or unwilling to participate in the current events of their

---

[71] Mario, Benedetti, *Andamios*. Madrid: Alfaguara, 1997, pp. 19–21.

countries of origin for long periods of time. In some cases, the exiles, unpolluted by the home country's politics, reached larger-than-life stature as the result of the distance that separated them from their fellow country-people. Oblivion was the fate of many others, however. Future generations will wrangle with the image of the absent founding fathers and write history motivated by contemporary political concerns, while they played politics, searching for legitimacy in the historical mirror. In this mutual impact of power relations, discursive strategies, and citizenship practices, the great absentees or 'victims' of national politics – the exiles – played a central role.[72] With independence, exile becomes a landmark trait in Latin American states and politics.

Research Lines

The preceding analysis sharpens the need to address a series of research questions that have been sidelined until recently by most writings on exile and that we can partially address in this book. For instance, we do not know enough about the comparative geographical and historical salience of political exile. Similarly, it has yet to be determined whether we can refer to exile as a phenomenon that affected a whole region, across different societies. Additionally, the question of whether it has remained the same with the passing of time or whether it has been transformed along with other changes in the sociopolitical and cultural transformation of the different societies of Latin America stands. The place of exile in the political culture of the region and of the different countries remains a significant question yet to be manifestly pursued.

We should ask what the factors are that impel the phenomenon of exile as a recurrent feature in Latin America, why exile was the choice of rulers who might have instead chosen the death penalty for their opponents, and, in societies pervaded by violence and disregard of civil rights, why exile was another major option for the incumbents to power.

Other equally relevant questions include determining to what extent there are elements of choice in exile and how pressed the exiles have been to leave. This raises the question of the expatriate who, under changing circumstances, becomes a self-imposed exile. For instance, rich Latin Americans of the 19th century used to move to Paris because they perceived it as a cultural Mecca. Or the case of individuals such as the Argentine writer Julio Cortázar, who moved to Paris and decided to stay there while remaining intimately tied to Argentine culture, even though his home society seemed increasingly oppressive, which brought his experience of expatriation closer to that of an exile.[73]

---

[72] Diana Quattrocchi-Woisson, *Los males de la memoria: Historia y política en la Argentina.* Buenos Aires: Emecé, 1995; and Ana María Alonso, "The Effects of Truth: Representations of the Past and the Imagining of Community." *Journal of Historical Sociology*, 1, 1 (1988): 35–57.

[73] Living abroad, Cortázar stressed in his writings a perspective dividing the victims from within as censored and paralyzed from those living abroad, the exiles, who were detached from the

It also remains to be seen what alternatives there have been to exile and how effective these alternatives were for rulers and persecuted individuals at various critical periods. Moreover, to what extent can the exile decide to put an end to his or her situation and return to the country, or absorb himself or herself by moving toward fuller integration in the host country, and how did authoritarian rulers use the possibility of letting exiles return?

Research should also inquire into the factors operating in the selection of host countries during different periods. How did/do the countries of destination compare with one another as perceived by the exiles? Language and cultural affinity have certainly been important. Distance has also been key: moving to a European country made the possibilities of return harder than relocating to a neighboring country. On the other hand, the attractiveness of settling in 19th-century Paris was very high for individuals who perceived it as a cultural and political model. In the 1980s, being in Washington, London, or Rome could be beneficial for exiled Chileans, who could feel that they were impacting Chilean politics in greater fashion than if they remained in Santiago, a locale in which they could not protest or organize themselves against the Pinochet government. Also, one must explore what role has been played in such choices relative to the ideological background of the exiles, such as in the case of communist activists fleeing to communist countries and then, in turn, fleeing from those societies.

Furthermore, how is it possible to explain the fact that countries with relatively feeble democratic traditions have received large numbers of exiles from other countries in Latin America, and even from Europe? The paradigmatic case has been Chile and Montevideo in the 1830s and 1840s, as well as post-revolutionary Mexico – and, to some extent, other countries such as Argentina, Venezuela, Cuba, and the Dominican Republic – hosting exiles following the Spanish Civil War and the rise to power of Fascism and Nazism, as well as the coming of Nazis and fascists to the Southern Cone in the postwar period. Correspondingly, it has often been incorrectly assumed that only dictatorships and military governments produce exile. Nonetheless, it is important to remember, however, that under democratic rule, there are cases of political actors and intellectuals feeling harassed and claiming to be forced to leave their home country. Even if from a strict semantic perspective they might be defined as expatriates, because they leave their countries out of free will, these individuals often define their move as a forced displacement, and many of their sympathizers and supporters consider them exiles. As a consequence, these somehow 'atypical' cases of exile cast a shadow onto the commonly assumed interpretations

home sources and condemned to estrangement (e.g., in an article named "América Latina, exilio y literatura," published in the Colombian journal *Eco*, No. 205, November 1978). This perspective raised a series of debates and elaborations by Argentine intellectuals. See Liliana Hecker, "Polémica con Julio Cortázar." *Cuadernos hispanoamericanos*, 519–520 (1993): 591–595; and Kart Kohut, *Escribir en París*. Frankfurt am Main: Verlag Klaus Dieter Vervuert, 1983.

about exile occurring exclusively under dictatorships, and about the necessary correlation between the reception of exiles and the democratic character of the host countries.

Another central issue to be addressed concerns the tensions encoded in exile between the principle of national membership and the principle of citizenship. Once a person is pushed into exile, he or she may lose the entitlements attached to citizenship but, concurrently, he or she may become even more attached to the national soul. If this is true, the 'national soul' is a covert but potent dimension of collective identity in these societies and is often revealed in exile. Significantly, it is abroad that many of these nationals discover, rediscover or, rather, invent the 'national soul' of their countries in primordial or spiritual terms. Under a certain set of circumstances, exile may become a basic factor in the definition or redefinition of national and transnational identities in Latin America.

After periods of crisis producing significant numbers of exiles, debates were generated between those who stayed in the home country and those who moved abroad, over the definition of what are the 'essential' components of national collective identities. Exiles, hoping to return someday to their home country, may attempt to define in novel ways the terms of collective identity. The extraterritoriality of exile plays an important role in the redefinition and imagery of collective identity, and not only because of the exiles' contact with new institutions and identities in the host society, as well as with other groups of exiles. Rather, the loss of daily contact with the home society, coupled with the loss of civil and political rights, often prompts a review of consciousness that leads to a reconsideration of the mundane and transcendental assumptions they initially took for granted as the original basis of their previous political action. Consequently, exile is very shocking for many, because it casts doubts on some of the basic parameters along which previous life was organized and that moved almost on a natural path.

The view held by exiles may be less linked to a time-bound, immediate perception of politics in terms of contingency, and they may try to define 'real' identities on the basis of the enduring values of the nation. Many claim that the driving motive of exiles was their unwillingness to renounce the core principles and values of their nation. In other words, exiles may tend to present their cases, beyond the immediate causes of their plight, also in idealistic or principled terms. They give to their situation a future-oriented perspective, increasingly related in the 20th century to global themes and values, primarily the defense of human rights. Their holding of 'true' values places them on a privileged position in relation to the reestablishment of normal political life and freedoms in their home country or, at least, their own reinsertion into the public sphere of the countries of origin.

While abroad, and despite the fact that the exiles may claim they are the true carriers of the original collective soul (or real representatives of the people), they are interacting in a new environment and are exposed to new models of social organization that intervene in the process of creating or changing their identities, as well as their perception of the home country. This situation a dilemma for every exile at the personal, psychological, familial, and co...~~ive levels: how to relate to the host society, and how to willingly become part of it, beyond the instrumental level of everyday life. Moreover, if they settled in what they perceived as a more developed, organized, or cultured environment, they face this dilemma more poignantly. Many of the dreamt-of images of the host country are met every day in ways that make them reconsider both the ideals they came with and the imagined view of their country of origin.

Research could contribute understanding on the forms of communal, social, and political organization of exiles in different host societies, including what determined these forms. Was it mainly the models of organization that exiles brought with them from their home countries, or were these forms affected by the organizational culture of the host country, or by other transnational circumstances?

Research should also assess what impact exiles did have on their home country. How did they impinge the international arena? What were the ways in which their residence abroad modified their cultural and human capital and their views of society, politics, and culture? People often attribute a *constraining* effect to exile. Relocation is difficult; working conditions can lead to downward socioeconomic mobility; there is financial insecurity; psychological imbalances and alienation are generated; previous bonds of partnership disarticulate under the pressures of exile. For many, it may be hard to find a new purpose in life. Nonetheless, exile has also led to what we may call *expanding effects*, often triggered by new experiences, thus leading to unforeseen opportunities to change one's status, upgrade skills, and discover one's strength and develop new relationships. Particularly salient in the late 20th century was the emergence, especially in Europe, of an empowered feminine voice and a self-reliance among women, many of whom had arrived as spouses of exiles and, once abroad, adopted new visions of gender, partnership, and motherhood that would change them forever. Research should aim to assess how these experiences and new approaches crystallized in exile influenced their home societies on return and following democratization. In sum, what has been the impact and legacy of exile in different countries and various political circumstances?

Last, but not least, the question of whether democratization or redemocratization in Latin America necessarily entails the end of political exile also becomes central.

Forceful Displacement, the Construction of Collective Identities, and State Formation

> I beg you to order the implementation of my departure outside Colombia, since once far away from the country, I will no longer belong to factions and only live in peace and my name will not serve as a pretext to hamper public order.
>
> Francisco de Paula Santander to Simón Bolívar, 1828

Expulsion from the realm was a major instrument of imperial policy-making in Iberia, as elsewhere. The forceful and massive expulsion of the Jews in the 1490s and of the Iberian Moslems in the early 16th century, as well as the slave trade among Africa, Europe, and America as a perverse way of massive relocation of populations for economic profit, are salient cases. They were supplemented on a piecemeal level by the threat and use of displacement as a mechanism of regulation and control of subjects. In this chapter, we elaborate on the early forms of forceful displacement and discuss their intended and unintended consequences on the construction of collective identities and state formation, showing lines of continuity and change once the region underwent a major political transformation in the early 19th century.

Banishment as a Portuguese Colonial Practice

A tradition of *degredo* [exile or territorial banishment], implying institutional exclusion, had existed in Portugal since the Middle Ages. It was used by power-holders to get rid of criminals and undesirables by sending them to the borders of the kingdom while Portugal was involved in regional wars. The establishment of border landholdings [*coutos*] under the legal and administrative jurisdiction of noblemen in charge of defense created both places of absorption of individuals unwanted at the core of that society, as well as a tradition of displacement, later used in America. For certain crimes, such as homicide, displacement was the only option to escape the death penalty. The king also used displacement out of Portugal sometimes, as an alternative punishment to death and other heavy penalties, for serious crimes, including charges of treason.[1]

The development and history of Brazil as a Portuguese colony seems marked by the use of displacement [*degredo* and *desterro*] by the Portuguese since their first arrival on the coasts of America. When Pedro Alvares de Cabral accidentally reached Brazil in 1500, his fleet included two men condemned to *desterro*, whom he left behind on the continent, charged with the task of learning the languages of the indigenous peoples. This event marked the starting point of banishment in Brazil, reinforced during the rule of João III, the Colonizer King, who increasingly deported unwanted individuals to that land, instead of earlier destinations such as the island of São Tomé, and other territories in Africa and India.[2]

During the 16th century, a series of royal decrees institutionalized the deportation of criminals and undesirables from Portugal to Brazil instead of other parts of the Maritime Empire. Most probably, the reasons for this policy were rooted in the size of Brazil, as well as with a dearth of self-motivated colonizers for such unattractive territories as those of Brazil in the early colonial period (when the lands in the East constituted the center of Portuguese administrative and economic colonial endeavor). Local authorities and clergymen in Brazil complained from the start about this policy of banishment that brought people of criminal and undesirable backgrounds, who were suspected of continuing their activities in the colony.[3]

The General Council of the Inquisition also used banishment from the 16th to the 18th centuries, with nearly four-fifths of all *desterrados* exiled during the 17th century, 49 percent of all being sent from Portugal to Brazil (with Angola in second place, receiving 26 percent of those banished during these centuries). The number of Brazilian Marranos was enlarged by exiles transported from Portugal between 1682 and 1707 for the crime of judaizing. These exiles were closely watched, and, in the case of relapse, they were returned to Lisbon to be punished at *autos da fé*, conducted in the metropolis until the Marquis de Pombal ended the transportation of Marranos from Brazil to Lisbon.[4]

Spanish Americas: Practices of Expulsion

Since the inception of the Spanish Empire in the Americas, the legal figure of displacement, translocation, and banishment [*destierro*] was established by the

---

[1] Geraldo Pieroni, *Os excluídos do Reino*. Brasilia: Editora da Universidade Nacional de Brasilia, 2000, pp. 25–27; Marcelo Caetano, *Historia do Direito Portugues*. Lisbon: Verbo, 1981, pp. 251–252.

[2] Geraldo Pieroni, *Vadios e ciganos, heréticos e bruxas – os degradados no Brasil colonia*. Rio de Janeiro: Bertrand, 2000, p. 32.

[3] Pieroni, *Vadios e ciganos*, pp. 31–33.

[4] Cyrus Adler, Joseph Jacobs, and Elkan Adler, "South and Central America," available at JewishEncyclopedia.com, accessed 13 April 2008.

Consejo Real de Indias to deal with offenders. Mainly, it was conceived as a means against those who were identified as a cause of social disturbances and were seen as a menace to the social or political order:

From a very early time Spanish codes had recognized *destierro*, which frequently implied banishment to another locality in the same province, *relegación*, by which the culprit was banished to a colony beyond the seas, and *extrañamiento*, which involved banishment from the national soil with prohibition to return. These terms were used rather loosely, and it is not always that *destierro* was milder than the other two.[5]

Destierro was one of the possible punishments for crimes committed in the Americas. Researchers of Spanish America indicate that the use of punishments was far from systematic. Displacement, for instance, was variably applied to different misdemeanors and crimes, and its use varied according to the circumstances, social position of the indicted, potential consequences of the verdict, and feasibility of application of the punishment.[6]

Attempting to identify patterns in this varied and shifting field of jurisprudence and law enforcement, we tentatively find that such expulsions were initially enforced to prevent unemployment and vagrancy in the Americas. These were cases of individuals accused of misdemeanors, who were not able to find a place in a community by practicing a trade and working. Similarly, clergymen or soldiers who left their mission were prone to be sentenced to *destierro*, and sometimes to the galleys, after being flogged. Any Spaniard or foreigner trading in the Indian villages without license was also prone to be expelled. If a nobleman transgressed the law in these counts, the possibility of confiscation of half of his possessions and sentencing him to up to 10 years of *destierro* was contemplated. All of these possible ways of punishment were detailed, among others, in the *Ordenanzas de la Casa de Contratación* of 1552.[7]

The highest crime, according to Spanish jurisprudence, was treason against the king, to be punished with permanent expulsion from the Americas and loss of honor.[8] Nonetheless, Spanish legislation also contemplated death and slavery as possible punishments for those who revolted against the king and broke the loyalty oath that bound them to the monarch.[9]

The measure of displacement was to be used in a selective way, provided that the reason for punishment was serious enough, and that both the banished person [*desterrado*] and the authorities in Spain were informed about the precise reasons for this procedure. Reflecting a situation of unrest in Peru, the king issued in 1568 a *cédula*, in which he granted Francisco de Toledo, viceroy

[5] Robert G. Caldwell, "Exile as an Institution." *Political Science Quarterly*, 58, 2 (1943): 242.
[6] Héctor José Tanzi, "El derecho penal indiano y el delito de lesa majestad." *Revista de Historia de América*, 84 (1977): 51–62.
[7] Ernesto Schäfer, "La Casa de la contratación de las Indias de Sevilla durante los siglos XVI y XVII." *Archivo Hispalense*, 13–14 (1945): 149–162.
[8] Ismael Sánchez Bella, Alberto de la Heray, and Carlos Díaz Rementeria, *Historia del Derecho Indiano*. Madrid: Mapfere, 1992, pp. 390–394.
[9] Tanzi, "El derecho penal indiano," pp. 54–55.

of Peru in the "city of kings," Lima, power both to pardon or to displace to Spain "all those who committed any crime" and as the local authorities may see fit to "pacify the land."[10] Yet, the High Court of Mexico was instructed in 1530 to expel from the Indies to Spain those found liable to cause unrest, but only on the basis of sufficient and very serious evidence [*"no sea sin muy gran causa"*].[11]

With the consolidation of Spanish rule and the establishment of new administrative jurisdictions, *destierro* was increasingly used to displace individuals within and across American lands, sending people who were perceived as endangering social peace into marginal or far-away lands. In 16th-century Quito, the figure of *destierro* was used on a temporary – month-long – basis against those who perpetrated minor offences.[12] In 17th- and early 18th-century Quito, sentences of *destierro* were given for longer periods, from 2 to 20 years, in cases of violent crimes or cases of stealing by Indians and slaves.[13] In the mid-17th century, people were expelled from Quito and Peru to Chile, and by the end of the century, they were kept in the prison of Valdivia.[14] Others were sent intermittently to Guayaquil and, until 1750, many were placed on the Isla de Piedra, where they were subjected to forced labor.

Under conditions of lack of manpower, translocation served both the function of sending the offender far away from his or her community and providing remote and unattractive areas with costless labor sources. Borderlands such as Chile, where war was waged against the Indians, benefited from the forced displacement of individuals who reinforced the military defense of the Spanish settlers.[15]

From Mexico, individuals were mainly sentenced to forced labor in the Philippines and various regions of Spanish America, particularly Puerto Rico and Havana, where they were enrolled in the construction of fortresses and other public services. In the late 18th century, *desterrados* were also forcefully enrolled in the colonial army, which suffered from an acute lack of manpower.[16]

Michael Scardaville has conducted a statistical analysis of crime and the urban poor in Mexico City in the late colonial period, finding that the sentence of *destierro* was mainly used against those found guilty of *incontinencia* (i.e.,

[10] Diego de Encina, Ed., *Cedulario Indiano*. Madrid: Ediciones Cultura Hispánica, 1945, p. 267.

[11] Ibid., p. 266.

[12] Ricardo Descalzi, *La Real Audiencia de Quito: Claustro en los Andes*. Barcelona: Seix Barral, 1978, p. 87.

[13] Tamar Herzog, *La administración como un fenómeno social: La justicia penal de la ciudad de Quito, 1650–1750*. Madrid: Centro de Estudios Constitucionales, 1995, p. 18, on the basis of the Archivo Histórico Nacional of Quito.

[14] Personal communication, Professor Fred Bronner, 14 January 2001.

[15] The usual sentence was six years of service in the war of Chile. José María Mariluz Urquijo, *Ensayo sobre los juicios de residencia indianos*. Seville: Escuela de Estudios Hispanoamericanos, 1952, pp. 208–209.

[16] Gabriel Haslip, "Crime and the Administration of Justice in Colonial Mexico City 1696–1810." London: University Microfilm International, pp. 203, 208, 227.

lack of sexual restraint) and of violation of the night curfew. There was a positive correlation between young and bachelor offenders and the use of *destierro*. In addition, displacement was used particularly against people originally from beyond the city boundaries (i.e., migrants from the provinces) Furthermore, many more Indians and *mestizos* were punished than whites, thus indicating once more that the *destierro* was reluctantly applied to people well connected and firmly established in the community.[17]

In relation to the Indian populations, since the 16th century, many sentences of displacement originated from within the Catholic Church, being issued especially by those clergymen charged with the extirpation of idolatry in the Andean region. In the early 17th century, as the Church established a routine practice and mechanism of *visitas de idolatrías* [control of idolatry], the sentence was applied for long periods to punish those involved in the maintenance of former Andean religious beliefs and practices. Many *kurakas* and religious experts of both genders were sent either to work under the custody of city families or as prisoners and forced laborers in convents (e.g., the convent of Descalzos de San Francisco de Huara and the prison of Santa Cruz in Lima).[18]

There are indications that in cases of severe gravity, such as rebellions, people expected displacement rather than the death penalty if those involved were not Indians. The failed movement of Túpac Amaru in 1780 provides a good indication of the different punishments reserved for individuals of 'ethnic' backgrounds. As the prosecution opened the case in January 1781, it charged the leaders with the crime of "treason to the king" and asked for the death penalty, on the basis of Castilian laws. The defense argued for lenient penalties on the basis of the preferential treatment that Spanish laws granted Indians, invoking Indian [Spanish-American] laws, according to which natives were considered minors and ignorants. Such distinction had precedents in a 1550 law, included in the *Recopilación* of laws of 1680 (II, XV, 138). In the mid-17th century, Bishop of Quito, Alonso de la Peña Montenegro explained that the "rustic and simple nature of the Indians force the judges to use all possible mercy in punishing their crimes."[19]

On the basis of materials from the Audiencia of Quito between 1650 and 1750, Tamar Herzog reflected on the significance of *destierro*, indicating that the sentence was used to "translocate the problem (the prisoner) to another jurisdiction with the idea that far away from home and from the land of origin, he could be better controlled, as the community of destination would be less scrupulous in punishing him as a stranger, and therefore could freely use the whole spectrum of punishment measures." Displacement reinforced an image

---

[17] Michael C. Scardaville, *Crime and the Urban Poor: Mexico City in the Late Colonial Period*. London: University Microfilms International, 1977, pp. 327–350.

[18] Pierre Duviols, *Cultura andina y represión: Procesos y visitas de idolatrías y hechicerías. Cajatambo, siglo XVII*. Cuzco: Centro de Estudios Rurales y Andinos Bartolomé de las Casas, 1986, pp. 387–390; idem, *La destrucción de las religiones andinas*. Mexico: UNAM, 1977, p. 244.

[19] Tanzi, "El derecho penal indiano," pp. 59–60.

of swift and efficient administration, achieved with little investment and at low costs.[20] In parallel, the use of displacement as a tool also shows that justice was conditioned by the nature of small and closely knit communities, which were unable to punish their transgressors *in situ* and found it easier to transfer the 'problem' to another area. Far away, social networks would not stand in the way of justice. This tradition has its roots in Europe and has been prominent in situations of fragmentation of political authority developing within a common framework of shared language and culture, as was the case of Italy at least since the 12th century and particularly in the 15th century, as studied by Christine Shaw. It is worthwhile to quote Shaw at length:

The tradition that those who held power in a commune had the right to exclude and expel their rivals was widespread and firmly rooted (even if it might be contested, in the case of subject towns, by their superiors). If political differences appeared irreconcilable, not amenable to compromise, the exile of those worsted in the contest was the usual way of removing them from the scene. Long-term imprisonment was rare in Renaissance Italy. Locking up large numbers of political opponents for lengthy periods was not an option, though small groups might be incarcerated by a confident regime with secure prisons at its disposal. Political executions of those found guilty of political crimes were infrequent too and regarded as shocking, unless it was for an act such as an assassination attempt. Political executions for which there was less obvious justification were regarded as vindictive, and harmed the reputation of a regime at home and abroad. Exiling political opponents might be regarded as injudicious, or even in some cases unjust, but would not attract anything like the same adverse comment.[21]

Displacement [*destierro*] was a mechanism devised as a trade-off between the will to punish and the limited capacity of the social and administrative system to do so rigorously and in harsh terms. From the start, it left wide space for personal decisions, and it created a tradition in which local authorities enjoyed discretion to send individuals away who endangered local stability.

The use of displacement was widespread and permeated local culture, establishing a strong precedent for political exile. In many cases, *destierro* left no cultural imprint. Despite the problematique of individual incorporation into a new social and cultural environment, most of the displaced individuals dealt with these issues in a pragmatic, ad hoc, private manner.

Constructing Collective Identities from Afar

Displacement had wider significance on collective identity when the combination of distance and high intellectual capacity brought these personal concerns into the public sphere. Perhaps one of the earliest examples of this dynamic is that of Gómez Suárez de Figueroa, the son of Garcilaso de la Vega, a leading

---

[20] Tamar Herzog, *La administración como un fenómeno social. La justicia penal de la ciudad de Quito (1650–1750)*, p. 252.

[21] Christine Shaw, *The Politics of Exile in Renaissance Italy*. Cambridge: Cambridge University Press, 2000, p. 6.

conqueror and *corregidor* of Cuzco and of the Incan Princess Isabel Chimpu Ocllo, a granddaughter of Emperor Túpac Inca Yupanqui. Gómez Suárez de Figueroa arrived in Spain in 1560, at the age of 21, and failed to be accepted socially either by his distant relatives or the court because of his mixed Indian origins. He went as a soldier to Granada but again failed to win any social recognition. As he retired in Andalusia, he adopted the respected name of his father and wrote, among other works, the *Comentarios reales de los Incas* (Lisbon, 1609) and the *Historia General del Perú* (Córdoba, 1617).

Feeling himself a victim of spiritual exile, far away from his land of origin and his people, he elaborated what David Brading considers "the primordial image of Peru, the starting point of all inquiry into the history and reality of his country."[22] Garcilaso the son portrayed the Spanish wrongdoing in Peru, centering on the persecution of the Incan royal family and on the subsequent *destierro* from Cuzco of many of the *mestitzo* offspring, such as himself, of the conquerors and Incan noblewomen. In Garcilaso's view, neither miscegenation nor Spanish destructive policies contributed to yield the promise of a hybrid and united society: "The creation of a Holy Inca empire, based on the marriage of conquerors and Inca noblewomen, governed by a *mestitzo encomendero* class, Christian in religion, ruling a native peasantry in accordance with the principles of Inca legislation, had failed to emerge."[23] As he died in 1615 a recognized literary figure in Córdoba, his individual drama was projected into texts that suggested a collective identity, the full implications of which would be worked out during the failed rebellion of Túpac Amaru II in 1780.[24]

In 1759, Portuguese Chief Minister Marquis of Pombal and the Portuguese crown decided to expel the Jesuits from their domains. Eight years later, on 20 August 1767, Carlos III replicated the order of expulsion for the Jesuits in the Spanish Empire. This was not the first massive expulsion in the Iberian political tradition. The mass evictions of Jews and Moors figured prominently in the collective consciousness of these societies, in the Iberian Peninsula, and throughout the Portuguese and Spanish Empires.

The Spanish authorities used large army forces to implement the decision in the Americas. For instance, Francisco Bucareli y Ursúa organized a force of 1,500 soldiers in Buenos Aires to overcome any possible resistance in the area of Misiones. Such resistance in Guanajuato and San Luis de la Paz in New Spain was met by forceful repression.[25]

---

[22] David Brading, *The First America, The Spanish Monarchy, Creole Patriots and the Liberal State, 1492–1867*. Cambridge: Cambridge University Press, 1991, p. 272.

[23] Brading, *The First America*, p. 271 and see pp. 255–272.

[24] David Cahill, "After the Fall: Constructing Incan Identity in Late Colonial Cuzco," in Luis Roniger and Mario Sznajder, Eds., *Constructing Collective Identities and Shaping Public Spheres: Latin American Paths*. Brighton, UK: Sussex Academic Press, 1998, pp. 65–99.

[25] The background, character, and consequences of the expulsion are beyond the focus of this study. The reader can consult, among others, Christopher Hollis, *The Jesuits: A History*. New York: Macmillan, 1968; Magnus Moerner, *The Expulsion of the Jesuits from Latin America*.

More than 5,000 Jesuits found themselves expelled from the American lands, banished to Italy, where most lived, pursuing scholarly work and writing. Fourteen percent of them left the order until 1773, as a first step to be able to return to their homeland.[26] Homesick, other individuals in this cultured elite – with scholarly training and access to important libraries and to the Indian codices brought from the Americas – were enmeshed in intellectual debates, prompted by scholars who denigrated the image of the Americas. Such writers as Corneille de Pauw, William Robertson, and Guillaume-Thomas Raynal portrayed the Americas as a feeble replica of Europe.[27]

Facing such an intellectual climate and perceiving the partiality of these ideas, Jesuit scholars exiled in Europe wrote works in which they attempted to unravel the richness of their home traditions, history, antiquities, fauna, flora, climate, and geography.[28] Some of the most well-known works are those by Juan de Velasco, an Ecuadorian Jesuit who, during his exile in 1788, wrote *La Historia del Reino de Quito*; Juan Ignacio Molina, a Jesuit from Chile, who wrote the *Historia Geográfica, Natural y Civil del Reino de Chile* (1782–1787); and Francisco Javier Clavijero, author of the *Historia Antigua de México* (1780–1781).

Although these works were ordered by the Jesuit superiors, they led to the expression of distinct feelings of patriotism. Clavijero dedicated his work to the University of Studies of Mexico, lamenting the distanced separation from his homeland [*patria*] and claiming it was "a history of Mexico written by a Mexican."[29] Velasco launched a fierce attack on "the modern sect of anti-American philosophers" and their "chimerical systems."[30] These Jesuits, who professed love of the *patria* they left behind, were deeply influenced by the revolution in science, history, and philosophy from the Enlightenment and had access to the archival sources and libraries in Bologna, Ferrara, Modena, Rome, Florence, Genoa, Milan, Naples, and Venice. Although they were not the first Jesuits to write about the Americas (*vide* Alonso de Ovalle in the mid-17th century), their exile in Europe contributed to a shift from purely scholarly endeavors with locality in the Spanish Empire to particularistic patriotism, reflecting the early crystallization of the territorial collective identities.

A few of the members of the order went a step further. In the late 18th century, they attempted to convince the British to lend their support for the

New York: Knopf, 1965; and Enrique Giménez López, Ed., *Expulsión y exilio de los Jesuitas Españoles*. Alicante: Universidad de Alicante, 1997.

[26] See Enrique Giménez López, Ed., *Expulsión y exilio de los jesuitas españoles*. Alicante: Universidad de Alicante, 1997.

[27] Antonello Gerbi, *O novo mundo. Historia de uma polemica (1750–1900)*. São Paulo: Companhia das Letras, 1996.

[28] Eva Maria St. Clair Segurado, *Expulsión y exilio de la provincial Jesuítica Mexicana 1767–1820*. Alicante: Universidad de Alicante, 2006, pp. 408–423.

[29] Francisco Javier Clavijero, 13 July 1780, in Bologna. *Capítulos de historia y disertaciones*. Mexico: Imprenta Universitaria, 1943, p. 3.

[30] Juan de Velasco, *Historia del reino de Quito en la América Meridional*. Caracas: Biblioteca de Ayacucho, 1981; Brading, *The First America*, pp. 447–464, especially p. 447.

cause of Spanish-American independence. The best-known cases were those of Juan Godoy, a Jesuit born in Mendoza, then part of Chile and later on of Argentina, and Juan Pablo Vizcardo, a native from Peru.

According to Guillermo Furlong, Godoy stayed in England from February 1781 until August 1785, where he tried – together with other Jesuits – to convince high officials of the feasibility of their plan to create an independent state that would include Chile, Peru, Tucumán, and the Patagonia.[31] Godoy planned a revolution in Chile, Paraguay, and Peru. Harassed by the Spaniards in London, he moved to North America in 1785. Once there, he was lured to move to Jamaica, where he was promised a position as a clergyman. Instead, the ship carrying him arrived in Cartagena, and Godoy was delivered to the Inquisition and later was sent to Spain via Havana, where he was imprisoned.[32]

Both in Leghorn, Italy, in the 1780s, and in London, where he moved in 1789, Juan Pablo Viscardo y Guzmán tried to convince British officials that Spanish America was ripe for revolt, on the basis of Túpac Amaru's uprising in 1780. English support was needed. He elaborated a plan according to which the British would send an army to the Pacific coast of South America to precipitate the revolt against Spain and thus secure American independence, to be proclaimed in Arequipa, his home town. Despite early expectations, the plan failed. Nonetheless, the English continued their contacts with Viscardo and even paid him a pension while he lived in London. In 1791, Viscardo authored a "Carta dirigida a los espanioles americanos por uno de sus compatriotas."[33] In 1799, the letter, translated into French, was published with the support of Francisco de Miranda, one of the early leaders of the struggle for independence in Venezuela and Spanish America. The letter became widely known among Spanish-Americans because it was published in Spanish in London shortly threafter. Its incendiary rhetoric lit the imagination of many youngsters in the Americas a generation later.

These cases were exceptional among the thousands of Jesuits expelled from the Americas, in that they translated patriotism into conspiracy, as typical of later political exiles. In the other cases previously discussed, patriotism remained the work of those focusing on the realm of culture, contributing to the construction of collective identity.

We would like to stress that we do not support the 20th-century interpretation that seeks a linear connection among the political philosophies of Saint Thomas Aquinas and Francisco Suárez, the writings of the Jesuits, and Latin American modern national identities.[34] The patriotism of the expelled Jesuits preceded nationalism and was geared to achieving recognition of the richness

---

[31] Guillermo Furlong, *Los Jesuitas y la escisión del Reino de Indias*. Buenos Aires: Amorrortu, 1960, p. 88.

[32] Furlong, pp. 89–91.

[33] Literally, a letter written to Spanish-Americans by a person of their fatherland.

[34] We refer here mainly to Furlong, *Los Jesuitas y la escisión del Reino de Indias*. In his history of the Jesuits, David Mitchell refers to them, in a more modest way, as "literary nationalists."

of the cultural identity and the nature of Mexico, Quito, Chile, and the other "kingdoms" of the Americas. With the exception of the few individuals who followed a conspiracy strategy, most of the Jesuits were far from any national program. They did not articulate modern national ideas toward the development of sovereign statehood and the homogenization of different sectors under the aegis of the states. There is a wide difference between the articulation of particular collective identities and the adoption of clear emancipation principles leading to political rebellions and independence from Spain in the form of modern Latin American political states. Nonetheless, it is true that 20th-century Latin Americans, particularly – but not only – those of a Catholic background, have often referred to these Jesuits as national heroes. Illustrative is the case of Rafael Landívar, former rector of a seminary in the city of Guatemala, who once in exile became a parish priest in Bologna and wrote an epic poem in Latin, *Rusticatio Mexicana* [Mexican Country Scenes]. In 1950, his remains were moved from Bologna to an imposing tomb in Antigua, the Guatemalan ancient capital. In Guatemala, Landívar is considered a national poet and hero.[35]

Expatriation and the New States

Reading backward from the experience of political nationalism and the config-
uration of a world system of nation-states, late 19th-century and early 20th-century researchers tended to accept the vision of national constructivism about the early 19th-century emergence of national statehood and identity. When most Ibero-American states reached a certain measure of stability and managed to curtail civil wars, their political and intellectual elites elaborated national histories and education programs that projected the idea of national existence back to the early independence period. In this sense, these intellectuals created imaginary communities, to use Benedict Anderson's term, and projected them backwards, as if they had existed in their current format from at least the inception of the independent states. Driven by later processes and challenges such as modernization, the need to integrate immigration, and the drive to incorporate local and indigenous populations into more-or-less homogeneous political frameworks, they essentialized collective identities around the revolutionary myth of independence.

This interaction between politics and the manipulation of history is not peculiar to Latin America but has been particularly salient there because the rewriting of history according to modern political constructions served to accelerate the processes of nation-building in these societies.

(*The Jesuits: A History*. New York: Watts, 1981, p. 204). For an excellent analytical discussion of patriotism as distinct from modern nationalism, see David Brading, "Patriotism and the Nation in Colonial Spanish America," in Luis Roniger and Mario Sznajder, Eds., *Constructing Collective Identities and Shaping Public Spheres: Latin American Paths*. Brighton, UK: Sussex Academic Press, 1998, pp. 13–45.

[35] Mitchell, *The Jesuits*, p. 204.

   Departing from the analysis of political exile, a different scenario emerges –
that is, one consistent with developments in Latin American political historiography. According to the works of François-Xavier Guerra, Antonio Anino,
Brian Loveman, and José Carlos Chiaramonte, among others, it is recognized
that the establishment of new states in the former Spanish-American areas was
neither the result of protonational movements nor the consequence of the diffusion of new social and cultural carriers.[36] The process of independence of Spanish America was the long and unintended consequence of the implosion of the
Spanish Empire from within its center in the Iberian Peninsula. The processes of
disintegration that led to the wars of independence were followed by civil wars
and protracted political violence, with no clear national definitions emerging
with independence. On the contrary, the main terms of reference toward the
establishment of the new states remained plural, ranging from early Spanish
administrative jurisdictions, emerging royalist and patriotic strongholds, and
especially regional spaces with strong local identities and an aspiration for political autonomy.[37] In Portuguese America, the dynamic of territorial expansion
and control generated a long series of rebellions, many of them of a regional
character against the central government and its bureaucratic–absolutist policies. Among them stood out the rebellions of the Inconfidência Mineira in
1789, the Conjuração Baiana of 1798, and a long series of minor revolts in
the 1810s and 1820s. Often, after an initial wave of brutal punishment that
may have included a combination of hanging, beheading, and dismemberment
of leaders, especially if they came from lower-class and artisan backgrounds,
royal decrees of pardon and amnesties were declared, aimed at projecting the
image of benevolence of the rulers and creating a sense of reconciliation.[38] In
punishing the rebels, banishment [*banimento*] was often used, mainly to remote
areas in Africa or in Amazônia and Mato Grosso, the latter indirectly helping

---

[36] Antonio Anino, "Soberanías en lucha," in Antonio Anino, Luis Castro Leiva, and François-
   Xavier Guerra, Eds., *De los imperios a las naciones – Iberoamérica.* Zaragoza: Ibercaja, 1994,
   pp. 229–253; José Carlos Chiaramonte, *El mito de los orígenes en la historiografía latinoamericana.* Universidad de Buenos Aires: Cuadernos del Instituto Ravignani, 1991; idem, "Modificaciones del pacto imperial," in Anino, Castro Leiva, and Guerra, Eds., *De los imperios a
   las naciones,* pp. 107–128; François-Xavier Guerra, "The Implosion of the Spanish Empire:
   Emerging Statehood and Collective Identities," in Luis Roniger and Tamar Herzog, Eds.,
   The Collective and the Public in Latin America. Brighton, UK: Sussex Academic Press, 2000,
   pp. 71–94. Although patriotism and local patriotism existed, they differed in terms of discourse
   and symbolic representation from the ideology of nationalism that would be fostered toward
   the second half of the 19th and the early 20th centuries. See David Brading, "Nationalism and
   State-Building in Latin American History," *Ibero-Amerikanisches Archiv,* 20 (1994): 83–108;
   and idem, "Patriotism and the Nation in Colonial Spanish America," in Roniger and Sznajder,
   Eds., *Constructing Collective Identities and Shaping Public Spheres,* pp. 14–45.
[37] Federica Morelli, "Territorial Hierarchies and Collective Identities in Late Colonial and Early
   Independent Quito," in Roniger and Herzog, Eds., *The Collective and the Public in Latin
   America,* pp. 37–56.
[38] Roberto Ribeiro Martins, *Liberdade para os brasileiros: Anistia ontem e hoje.* Rio de Janeiro:
   Civilizacao Brasileira, 1978, 2nd ed.

expand the presence of the Portuguese-speaking peoples in the vast territory of Brazil.

In parallel, the displacement of the ruling House of Bragança and its entourage to Brazil – under the protection of the British and escaping the Napoleonic invasion – contributed to the growing importance of Brazil and the subsequent crystallization of a consciousness of collective identity. The translocation of the Bragança imperial rulers to the New World made possible the preservation of monarchical rule through independence in 1822 and up to the imperial demise in 1889.

We focus hereafter mainly on Hispanic America, emphasizing how translocation, itself a product of the weakness of national definitions and blurred state boundaries, played a formative role in shaping these definitions and identities, as the leaders of the independence movements moved across regions as if all those regions were part of the fatherland they were trying to re-create in the Americas.

Forceful Translocation as Tactical Movement

Relying on the colonial tradition of displacement, used against those who, through their action, disturbed public peace or were perceived as a menace to their community, many of the patriots could leave their countries through expulsion or were allowed to escape after defeat.

This possibility was open to those rebels who were part of the upper strata and denied to those who belonged to the popular classes and lower ethnic groups. Thus, for example, neither José Gabriel Condorcanqui (Túpac Amaru) nor José Antonio Galán was granted the privilege or 'doubt' of exile, as was granted to Bolívar and Sucre. Both Galán and Túpac Amaru were executed after their rebellions failed in the early 1780s in New Granada and Peru, respectively. Similarly, in Brazil, after the failure of the 1789 rebellion known as the Inconfidência Mineira, six leaders were sentenced to death by "hanging, decapitation and dismemberment." The sentence was commuted in 1792 to banishment by Queen Maria in five of the cases, being enforced only in the case of Tiradentes, the most humble and steadfast of the rebellious leaders. Interestingly enough, Tiradentes' martyrdom turned him, more than a century later, into a figure of protonational projection under the First 'Old' Republic (1889–1930). In the imagery and representations fostered in this period,

the image of Tiradentes was stripped of his anti-systemic potential and made into the martyr-like figure of a hero who prematurely invoked the Republic, and died, sacrificing himself for an idea that would fructify in due time. Tiradentes' reconstructed image was appealing where other images failed to connect with the prevailing cultural representations. Tiradentes was portrayed with a Christ-like look, his fall was due to treason by his co-plotters (again resembling Jesus), he seemingly refrained from recurring to violence (in fact, the movement he participated in aborted before reaching such a stage) and he forgave his executioners. All this served to ease the paradoxical promotion of his plebeian figure as the most prominent hero in the bloodlessly installed Brazilian conservative ("Old") Republic.[39]

Probably the same grounds may explain why the Portuguese authorities showed no clemency toward the rebels of the 1792 Bahia rebellion. Many of them were of lower-class background, in sharp contrast with the mostly upper-class and middle-class background of the Minas rebels:

The attorneys, magistrates and priests of Minas Gerais, the rich merchants and their dependents, the majority of whom were masters of slaves and members of rather exclusivist trade unions, were in marked contrast with the mulatto artisans, the soldiers, landless sharecroppers and salaried professors involved in the Bahian plot. Resentful and anticlerical, the mulattos in Bahia had in mind both the Portuguese rule and the Brazilian rich as targets [of their rebellion].[40]

In Hispanic America, in the early years of the 19th century, moving away from the native homeland was perceived as a tactical move within the antiroyalist struggle. The cases of Simón Bolívar, Antonio José de Sucre, and many others in the northern part of South America are paradigmatic.

In 1812, following his participation in the rebellion led by Francisco Miranda, the royalist authorities initiated a *causa de infidencia* [trial for rebellion] against Simón Bolívar, with the penalty of loss of properties in favor of the public treasury. After going underground between 2 August and 26 August 1812, Bolívar managed to meet Captain Domingo Monteverde, the royal authority, through the mediation of Francisco Iturbe, an individual highly respected in loyalist circles and an acquaintance of the fugitive rebel. Monteverde was willing to agree to let Bolívar leave the country for Curaçao, a Dutch island held by the British since 1807. Monteverde was grateful to Bolívar for his help in capturing Miranda and handing him over to the royalists, after Miranda was suspected by the patriots of planning to escape and defect the cause of independence. Bolívar managed to leave for Curaçao, and there he continued to play a central role in the struggle that eventually led to independence. His fate in Curaçao was that of many other exiles. In his case, he suffered from the seizure of his belongings by the British authorities.[41]

---

[39] Luis Roniger, "Citizenship in Latin America. New Works and Debates." *Citizenship Studies*, 10, 4 (2006). In this excerpt, Roniger analyzes José Murilo de Carvalho's *La formación de las almas: El imaginario de la República en el Brasil*. Buenos Aires: Universidad Nacional de Quilmes, 1997, pp. 81–112.

[40] Kenneth R. Maxwell, *A Devassa da Devassa: a Inconfidência Mineira: Brasil-Portugal – 1750– 1808*. São Paulo: Paz e Terra, 1985, p. 245, quoted from Ribeiro Martins, *Liberdade para os Brasileiros*, p. 29.

[41] As result of the Napoleonic wars, this Dutch colony was occupied by the British between 1801 and 1815. When Bolívar reached the island, penniless, he was helped by Mordechay Ricardo, a local Sephardic Jew, scion of families expelled from the Iberian Peninsula in the late 15th century and cousin of the renowned British economist David Ricardo. Mordechay Ricardo was probably motivated by his recognition of the ills of exile and helped both Bolívar, in 1812, and his two sisters and children, whom Bolívar sent to Curaçao in 1814, so that they would escape the wave of repression by Spanish commander José Tomás Boves. See Roberto J. Lovera

Escaping persecution, imprisonment, or harsher punishment was sometimes a path adopted by entire groups. Another independence leader, Antonio José de Sucre, escaped the royalist siege of Margarita Island in early 1815, together with other officers and troops, such as José Francisco Bermúdez, Justo Briceño, and Pedro María Freites. Their ship brought them to Grenada; from there, they moved to French Martinique, and then to the British island of St. Thomas. After three months of wandering about, Sucre reached Cartagena de Indias. Bolívar, Mariño, and others had reached this city before, planning to launch a new offensive from there. The typical divisive dynamics of communities of exiles developed among them. Because Bolívar found strong internal opposition to his leadership in Cartagena, he and some of his friends left for Jamaica in May 1815.

The development of communities of exiles was difficult in this period. First, they came on a temporary basis, hoping to return as soon as the situation allowed it. Second, their position as strangers placed them in dire prospects of accommodation in their host environment. Many pressures then came to the fore. Because the exiles were usually part of the upper classes at this stage in the history of their countries, they tended to see themselves as prospective leaders. As such, they often got into conflict about leadership, goals, and sectional and personal animosities and sympathies. This made the possibility of accomplishing necessary unified political action much more difficult than if they had remained in their home country.

We see here a pattern that will recur time and again throughout most of the 19th and 20th centuries. The unraveling of social and political groups produced by exile, combined with pressures in alien environments, deepens previous political differences and creates new rifts, thus weakening political capabilities.

The attitude of the host country is crucial in shaping the fate of the exiles. In many cases, suspicion and persecution were the usual lot of translocated individuals. As Bolívar left Venezuela headed to Jamaica, penniless, his intention was to gain support abroad to resume the struggle for independence:

... the events in my homeland, the *Costa Firme* [Venezuelan mainland], forced me to come to this island with the goal of reaching England, in order to make efforts to get support for America, the kind of support that will create an obligation to repay its debts in an advantageous manner for its benefactors.[42]

Jamaican authorities gave him a cold treatment. The governor refused to meet him or answer his letters. Spanish agents tried to kill him. Bolívar then left for Haiti.

De-Sola, *Curazao, escala en el primer destierro del Libertador.* Caracas: Monte Avila Editores, 1992, pp. 23–36 and 67–68; and idem, "La estadía de Simón Bolívar en Curazao," pp. 91–97 in *Los sefaradíes – Vínculo entre Curazao y Venezuela.* Asociación Israelita de Venezuela and Museo Sefardí de Caracas Morris E. Curiel, 2002.

[42] Letter to the Governor of Jamaica, May 1815, in *Cartas del Libertador.* Caracas: Banco de Venezuela and Fundación Vicente Lecuna, 1964, vol. I, p. 189.

The fall of Cartagena made many take refuge in Haiti. Antonio José de Sucre left Cartagena under the royalist siege in 1815, together with other independence leaders such as José Francisco Bermúdez, Mariano Montilla, and Manuel Carlos Piar and military troops and civilians who escaped hunger and the unavoidable defeat. After a long sailing, during which many died or were captured by the Spanish fleet, Sucre and Bermúdez reached Haiti in January 1816. In contrast, Haiti provided a haven for those escaping the wrath of Spanish authorities. Bolívar was already there, organizing a new expedition with the support of then Haitian president, Alexandre Pétion, to resume fights in Venezuela. Pétion supported him with the expectation that Bolívar would abolish slavery in the territories he intended to liberate. This expedition set sail with 250 men in April 1816.[43]

Dissent within the group was a persistent trend, however. Many internal disputes rose in this period, as General Bermúdez and Mariano Montilla both aspired to lead the expedition. With dismay, Sucre decided to move to Trinidad instead. He might have wanted to spare himself the necessity of committing himself openly to one side or the other.[44] In Trinidad, Sucre received a cold treatment by the British authorities, which underestimated the eventual victory of the patriotic cause. Sucre's family was by then dispersed throughout the Antilles and Cuba. When Sucre got notice of Bolívar's fleet arriving on Venezuelan shores, he set sail to join the fight.[45]

These early examples of *tactical translocation* and proto–expatriation illustrate how strongly host countries conditioned the subsequent development of actions on the part of exiles. The possibility of moving away from their places of origin in order to tactically prepare for sustained fighting was conditioned by the attitudes of the host countries. This attitude, ranging from hostility to lack of support and indifference on the part of the British, was rooted in the latter's ambivalent positions toward Spain's role as a foe of the French in the Napoleonic Wars. Very different was the attitude of Alexandre Pétion, whose republican and antislavery ideas favored support for the fellow Americans' patriotic enterprise.

Exile tended to develop in this period through a trifactorial structure. The interests of the translocated individuals interplayed with the interests of the host countries vis-à-vis the pressures exerted by the home countries. This triangular structure of exile changes in detail from case to case, but its formal physiognomy persisted as a major structure as long as the nation-states were the major players in the international arena. It will partially undergo a core transformation in the 20th century, once a fourth increasingly important element enters the exile equation: a global arena preoccupied with humanitarian international law, human rights, and political freedom.

[43] Moacir Werneck de Castro, *El Libertador: Vida de Simón Bolívar*. Caracas: Instituto de Altos Estudios de América Latina, Universidad Simón Bolívar, 1990.
[44] John P. Hoover, *Admirable Warrior: Marshal Sucre, Fighter for South American Independence*. Detroit, MI: Blaine Ethridge Books, 1977, pp. 23–24.
[45] Carlos Héctor Larrazabal, *Sucre, Figura Continental*. Buenos Aires: Talleres de Juan Pellegrini, 1950, pp. 61–65.

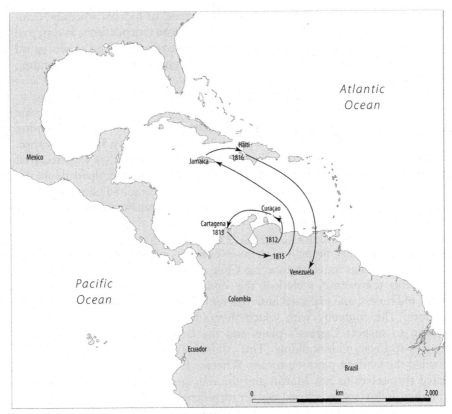

MAP 2. Simón Bolívar's exile and wanderings.

Territorial Identities in Undefined Boundaries

The early stages of struggle over the status of the Spanish-American territories reveal the confrontational yet undefined nature of territorial politics and the cultural underpinnings of banishment, especially with regard to those cases in which the conspirators belonged to the local elites in the early independent period.

An analysis of the case of the Carrera brothers in Chile clearly reveals how personal rivalries, ambitions, and local allegiances played a major role in the configuration of translocation as a *marker of new boundaries and identities*, while it functioned as well as a dissolvent of older ones. In the early 19th century, political networking shaped a rapidly changing scenery, highly unstable and rather anarchic, which led to countervailing attempts of coordination, under the dictatorship of José Miguel Carrera, who headed the government in 1811–1813 and 1814, a period known in Chilean historiography as the 'Patria Vieja' period. Part of an aristocratic family of Santiago, Carrera and his brothers, Juan-José, Luis, and Javiera, soon found themselves opposed to Bernardo O'Higgins and other patriotic figures, which held different views for the future of Chile. The Carrera brothers had a localized vision of Chile and saw themselves as fit to lead as part of the 'crème' of local aristocracy. Contrastingly, O'Higgins and his allies conceived Chilean independence as a step to be taken in the framework of a comprehensive movement aimed at getting rid of the Spanish presence on a continental basis, beginning from Cuyo, liberating Chile, and heading toward the liberation of Peru.

With the disintegration of the Carrera government as a result of the loss to the royalists in the battle of Rancagua in 1814, various anti-Spanish patriotic groups crossed the Andes into Cuyo. The patriots hoped to continue fighting and hopefully to regain control of Chile, while the menace of a Spanish invasion of Cuyo from Chile was perceived as a real threat. In Cuyo, they were received by the local governor, Colonel José de San Martín. Cuyo, later divided into the Argentine provinces of Mendoza, San Juan, and San Luis, had been part of the *Capitanía General* of Chile until 1778, when it was transferred to the recently established Virreynato of the Río de la Plata.

Consequently, the Chileans, especially those with an aristocratic background such as the Carreras, thought of themselves not as exiles but as forced *emigrés* whose destiny was to return to a free Chile as rulers. They viewed San Martín as a plebeian governor, a clerk in the service of the government of Chile (as in the old times), and expected him to defer to his dethroned head, José Miguel Carrera. The contempt with which they addressed him led Governor San Martín to suspect Carrera's plans and the latter's lack of political capacity and strategic understanding. This confrontation with San Martín clearly divided the Chilean patriotic forces. Whereas O'Higgins and others subordinated themselves to San Martín and the *Ejército de los Andes*, the Carreras and their followers recognized neither jurisdiction nor borders. For them, San Martín's authority was recognized only conditionally, as long as it served their own status and objectives. This dynamic reflected the disintegration of former boundaries and the protracted development of new ones in what will soon become the new independent republics of the Spanish-speaking Americas.

As San Martín and O'Higgins managed to consolidate their military forces and to cross the Andes, so as to liberate Chile from the Spaniards, the Carreras and their supporting allies in Chile and Buenos Aires increasingly found themselves on the defensive. Although they continued to oppose the supreme director of Chile, Bernardo de O'Higgins, they were forced to live abroad, and their political machinations were constrained by the authorities of Buenos Aires and their provincial representatives in Mendoza, themselves allies of O'Higgins.

In mid-1817, they tried to organize a plot against O'Higgins, believing they counted with powerful allies who were affected by the antiaristocratic policies of the new Chilean rulers, or those offended by the arrogance of the Argentine commanders in Chile, as well as with the support of former royalists, who saw their lives and properties threatened. The plot was discovered, and brothers Luis and Juan José were brought to trial in both Chile and Mendoza. Whereas a conciliatory approach was adopted in Chile, in Mendoza, the Carrera brothers were imprisoned, with the intention of sending them to a distant land to neutralize them. As the other brother and sister tried to liberate them from prison, a new trial for treason against the local authorities in Mendoza and in Chile was initiated, which led to the capital punishment of Luis and Juan José Carrera. Until 1821, when he himself was executed, José Miguel Carrera led a relentless war against O'Higgins and those responsible for the execution of his brothers.

The death of the Carrera brothers was a measure that San Martín and others initially tried to avoid. It was an extreme measure with unforeseen consequences. According to what was taken for granted at the time, it was more convenient to avoid a spiral of violence that such a measure could trigger. A good counterexample that brings this understanding into relief is the case of Manuel Rodríguez, an uncontrolled guerrilla fighter according to his own description, who conspired together with the Carreras against O'Higgins. Even after they came to know his indomitable personal character, San Martín and O'Higgins opted to spare him punishment and preferred to co-opt him, nominating him to high administrative positions under their command.

Before the August 1817 plot by the Carrera brothers, nobody thought the reaction against the plotters would be any different from the treatment given to Rodríguez and others under similar circumstances. In the words of historian Francisco Encina,

> Doña Javiera, while throwing her brothers into the unsuccessful plot... believed that in the worst of the cases, they risked prison or a *destierro* to Montevideo or Rio de Janeiro, which would be easy to evade. The concept of political crime was not yet born. To conspire against a government, in a war situation, was unacceptable for the members of the same polity. Also, [conspiracy] was a right linked to the concept of freedom, and from the perspective of Andalusian mentality, an act of bravery. Moreover, the Carreras were part of Santiago's aristocracy, which in opposition to what was taking place in the rest of America, showed itself inimical to the political scaffold.... The execution of its members, whatever could be the political distance or the crime committed, was not even conceived as possible.[46]

The typical way of punishing conspiracies in Chile was prison or *destierro* to a place from which the conspiring agents would be unable to remain politically active. Still, beyond the norm inherited from Spanish colonial times, a new concept was being introduced. This new concept, related to the absolute authority of the new republican state, would place physical elimination of plotters as a ready-made though extreme alternative to political exile in the early 19th century, as in other Latin American states.

Paradoxically or not, the execution by firing squad of José Miguel Carrera in Mendoza on 4 September 1821 precipitated Chilean Supreme Director O'Higgins' downfall from power. For years, Chile's aristocracy, discontented with O'Higgins, supported him as a bulwark against the peril of a military dictatorship by Carrera. Although O'Higgins was totally committed to the cause of pan-American independence, widening groups of Chilean society felt tired of the continuing war beyond Chilean boundaries and capabilities. Forced by

[46] Francisco Antonio Encina, *Historia de Chile*. Santiago de Chile: Editorial Nacimento, 1947, vol. 7, pp. 530–531.

circumstances, O'Higgins abdicated power in 1823 and left for Valparaíso, and ultimately to Peru, where he settled down in land donated to him by the Peruvian government.[47]

O'Higgins's party in Chile became disorganized with the leader's expatriation to Peru. Some of his supporters also left the country, such as José Ignacio Zenteno, who remained in Peru between 1823 and 1826. If a few were still loyal and awaited his return and restoration to power, their influence was very limited.[48] During the 1830s, Diego Portales, the father of the 1833 Constitution and the leading political figure of the period, would eliminate the last vestiges of loyalty to O'Higgins, notwithstanding their favorable rally to the Conservative Party. Portales even denied O'Higgins a permit to visit the homeland because his presence was considered disturbing for the political order.[49]

Only with the death of Portales, the end of the war against the Peruvian–Bolivian Confederation, and the stabilization of a constitutional regime in Chile were the greater part of the army officers deposed in 1830 restored to their rank and honors. Special attention was given to O'Higgins. Besides being reestablished in the military rank of captain general previously taken from him, he was allowed and invited to return to the country.[50]

Confrontational Politics and Expatriation

The expatriation of central political figures following independence – and their identification as icons of political exile – starts a tradition in which the absent leader becomes the pole of attraction and political consultation for actors in the home society. Exile kept the leader away from the localized public spheres and projected his figure as the incarnation of an alternative vision that cast a constant shadow on the way in which political actors conducted politics back home. The 'absent leader' used the political capital he amassed in the past to keep aloof of realpolitiks as well as the political prices to be paid by dealing with daily politics. It also created a situation in which the return of the leader remained an open item in the political agenda. The case of O'Higggins and San Martín set this model very early on.

O'Higgins can be considered an expatriate because he left Chile voluntarily, having understood that his presence was a source of internal political strife. While he preferred to leave his homeland in order to contribute to political pacification, the presence of his supporters as an opposition force within Chile transformed him into an exile. The Chilean authorities (basically Portales) would not allow him to return to his homeland. Only shortly before his death were his rights returned. Economic hardship was then the lot of the person

---

[47] Although the Peruvian government treated him with great deference as a hero, the Chilean authorities suspended the payment of his wages and dues.

[48] Luis Galdames, *A History of Chile*. New York: Russell & Russell, 1964, p. 232.

[49] Galdames, *A History of Chile*, p. 239.

[50] O'Higgins could not take advantage of this invitation, for, when he was preparing to do so, he died in Lima in 1842.

who was once the Supreme Director of Chile. The impossibility of returning home did not preclude him from following the Chilean political scene. His followers kept him well informed and visited him from time to time. The eventual economic success of O'Higgins did not diminish his will to return to the homeland, even if only for a short visit.

The other leading figure of pan-American independence in this region, José de San Martín, would opt to leave the countries he had liberated and end his days far away from his homeland, in Europe. He became the prototypical figure of an exile, despite leaving the Americas as an expatriate, in what historians defined as a self-imposed ostracism.

The reasons for San Martín's decision have been debated exhaustively in Latin American historiography and seem to be related to the failed meeting between San Martín and Simón Bolívar in Guayaquil in July 1822. Commanding an army of Argentinean, Chilean, and Peruvian troops, San Martín had managed to occupy great parts of Peru and the capital of Lima, where the independence of Peru was proclaimed on 28 July 1821. San Martín was invested with the highest rank of Protector of Peru, the highest political and military position in the country. In that function, he sent a Peruvian–Argentinean division who assisted General Antonio José de Sucre in the battle of Pichincha, Ecuador (May 1822), which opened the gates of Quito to the independence party. Nonetheless, a large royalist force of 19,000 veterans retained control of parts of Peru and the whole territory of Alto Perú. This army was more than twice as large as the army supporting the independence side. Its presence could menace the independence of Peru and cast doubts on the viability of the whole enterprise of creating an independent South America.

San Martín's success in Peru concerned Bolívar, who was interested in winning the final victory over the Spaniards himself. In early 1822, San Martín, as the Protector of Peru, could not complete the liberation of Peru without help from external sources, which meant help from Bolívar's intervention in Peru. Motivated by this aim, San Martín sailed to Guayaquil to a summit with Simón Bolívar, who had completed the liberation of Great Colombia and occupied Guayaquil. While San Martín wanted the immediate support of the Colombian forces in the final liberation of Peru, Bolívar was reluctant and suspicious of the former's agenda. According to his own testimony, San Martín offered to put his forces and himself under the command of Bolívar and, on lack of agreement, decided to return to Peru and, once there, renounce his positions as high commander and Protector of Peru. The versions surrounding the Guayaquil meeting and the reasons for San Martín's expatriation from the Americas remain, to a large extent, a matter of speculation and debate.[51]

---

[51] Bolívar's account differs notably from San Martín's. In several letters he wrote to his closest allies immediately after the meeting, Bolívar tells that San Martín complained to him about the latter's companions-in-arms in Lima and about internal enemies, all drawn by ambition and a rebellious spirit. Bolívar reports that San Martín came to see him without any clear agenda, just to get assurances of friendship, and that he seemed to have had already made up his mind

Beyond the different interpretations, the move of a supreme leader who opted for exile instead of retaining positions of power at all costs became paradigmatic of the noble and often martyred images associated with the exile of cherished leaders in Ibero-America.

San Martín returned to Peru and then left for Chile, finding waves of animosity inspired by the enmity of Lord Thomas Cochrane, while being received with high honors by the supreme director of Chile, his former companion-in-arms Bernardo de O'Higgins. After retiring to his Mendoza house, San Martín was constantly harassed by a suspicious government that saw in his presence a permanent threat to stability, and his name was used by the opposition without his approval. The opposition thought that San Martín was the only figure able to organize the state and reunite the country, whereas the government highly resented the potential danger that his presence represented. Spies surrounded him; his letters were opened. According to his own vision,

In those circumstances I was convinced that, to my lack of fortune, I have played a more prominent role than the one I wished for myself in that revolution. That precluded me to keep a distanced impartiality between the rival parties. As a result and in order to dissipate any idea about my ambition to any kind of power, I sailed for Europe.... [52]
It was impossible to live in peace in my homeland as long as emotions ran high. It was this lack of certitude which brought me to decide on my departure to Europe.[53]

Following his wife's death in August 1823, isolated and averse to political and military conspiracies in Buenos Aires, San Martín decided to take his daughter with him to Europe to educate her, thinking of distancing himself from his country's turbulent politics.[54] On French territory, he was not allowed to go

on leaving his positions in Peru – which he wanted to be ruled by a scion of a monarchical European family – and retiring to Mendoza. Bolívar did not believe San Martín was sincere on both accounts. The Liberator thought that the Protector of Peru wanted to keep the throne ready for himself. Bolívar, a person who 'resigned irrevocably' and retired so many times only to come back again and again as the savior, did not take seriously his rival's intentions to leave power and retire to private life. The incompatibility of characters, between Bolívar's extroverted and power-oriented personality, and San Martín's introverted ways and resentment of factionalism, precluded each leader from taking his peer's declarations on face value. The mismatch of personalities, expectations, interests, and ambitions will decide the future of South America and be the trigger of San Martín's decision about exile. According to his own account, Bolívar was highly satisfied after the meeting because he had attained several important aims, namely, the incorporation of Guayaquil to Colombia, while keeping San Martín's and Peruvian friendship toward Colombia, and the possibility of sending a Colombian army to Peru, where it would gain glory and the gratitude of Peruvians. All these were instrumental to his 'great plan': the unification of South America. Letters to the Secretary General of the Republic of Colombia and to the Intendente of the Quito Department, General A. J. de Sucre, both dated 29 July 1822, signed by J. G. Pérez and dictated by Bolivar; letters to General F. de P. Santander, on 29 July 1822, and to General Sucre, on 30 July 1822, both signed by Bolívar, in *Cartas del Libertador*. Caracas: Banco de Venezuela and Fundacion Vicente Lecuna, 1965, vol. III, pp. 254–269.

[52] Ricardo Rojas, *El Santo de la espada*. Buenos Aires: Ediciones Corregidor, 1993, p. 399.
[53] Letter to O'Higgins, in Samuel W. Medrano, *El Libertador José de San Martín*. Buenos Aires: Instituto Nacional Sanmartiniano, 1995, p. 128.
[54] Letter to Federico Brandsen, 10 February 1824, in Rojas, *El santo de la espada*, p. 309.

ashore by the police and the authorities. He stayed in England for a few months, but finally settled down in Brussels, motivated by the low cost of living and dreaming of returning one day to his homeland and to his farm in Mendoza.[55] The general had entrusted his funds to a friend, who, uncunningly, lost most of it in the London stock exchange. San Martín was reduced to poverty.

In February 1829, San Martín decided to try to return to Buenos Aires. The move was prompted by the insistent advice of several friends who wanted to see him back and by the assurances of order and tranquility of the Buenos Aires government. On arrival, he realized that reality had changed and that the country was again in a process of civil war between unitarians and federalists. Despite the acts of sympathy of some old friends, he met a cold and suspicious reception and decided to go back to Europe, after a short foray in Montevideo.

San Martín's decision to leave America was based on the incompatibility between his harsh judgment of the political situation and his sense of honorable duty. On the eve of his departure, he said:

The situation in our country is such that the man in command has no alternative but to rely on one faction or resign command. The latter is my option.... There will be those who will claim that the fatherland has the right to demand the sacrifice of life and interests, but not of one's honor.[56]

After his failed visit to Buenos Aires, San Martín established his residence in Paris in 1831. An old companion-in-arms who became a rich banker, Alejandro Aguado, helped him buy the property of Grand Bourg, in which he lived between 1834 and 1848. There his daughter joined him, after having finished her years of studies. His home became a point of attraction for Latin American personalities passing through Paris.

San Martín died in France in August 1850, after 26 years in exile. Despite his dislike of politics and tyranny and his grateful attitude toward French hospitality,[57] San Martín remained a Spanish-American patriot, committed above all to the independence of the countries for which he had fought so hard. Between 1845 and 1849, France and Great Britain were in conflict with the Argentinean Confederacy and its ruler, Juan Manuel de Rosas. In his will of 1844, San Martín left his sword to Juan Manuel de Rosas, who had resisted an earlier foreign blockade of Buenos Aires:

The sabre that was my companion in all the war of independence of South America, as a proof of satisfaction for me – as Argentinean – in witnessing the firm manner in which General Rosas stood by the honor of the Republic against the unjust demands of the foreigners who tried to humiliate it.[58]

55 Letter to O'Higgins, 8 February 1825, in Rojas, *El santo de la espada*, p. 311.
56 Rojas, *El santo de la espada*, p. 338.
57 Enrique Mario Mayochi, *El Libertador José de San Martín*. Buenos Aires: Instituto Nacional Sanmartiniano, 1995, p. 73.
58 From San Martín's will, in Bartolomé Mitre, *Historia de San Martín y la emancipación Lati-noamericana*. Buenos Aires: Editorial Ateneo, 1950, p. 984. Rosas will also be forced to leave

San Martín's move tilts between self-imposed expatriation and exile. It was his own decision to leave the American shores for Europe, but it became an experience of exile on two grounds: in connection with his attempted return in 1829, as well as because of the ways his presence in Peru and Chile had raised strong animosities, forcing him to leave for political reasons.

In terms of political history, San Martín became a Latin American icon of the uncommon victorious leader who decides that his involvement in politics would be extremely detrimental to the cause for which he had fought. His military campaigns were mostly successful, despite a lack of resources and sometimes a lack of solid political support. But it was the tendency of the new polities to drift into factional violence – civil strife, militarization of politics, and civil war – that prompted his decision to leave the countries he had fought so heartily to liberate for the isolation of the self-imposed exile in Europe.

At stake were not only issues of personal inclination and character but rather political visions and ideals. San Martín favored the kind of parliamentary monarchy that seemed unacceptable to most of the Latin American patriots. His reluctance to assume dictatorial powers was evident in the leniency with which he treated conspirators and political foes throughout the war of liberation (e.g., his treatment of the Carrera brothers and Manuel Rodríguez). Similarly, it was also shown in his willingness to pacify Peru and reach an agreement with the royalist forces instead of looking for a total confrontation. This attitude contrasted with the more Jacobine spirits, which proliferated in the wars of independence.

San Martín did not find his place in postindependent political life and did not dare to stay because he felt he would be unable to retire from the power struggles and remain neutral *in situ*. After playing a central role in the struggle for independence, he feared he would not be able to maintain an unbiased position in politics, but that rather his name and prestige would be drawn against his will into internecine fights. Therefore, it seemed natural that a widower and father of a school-age daughter would move as far away as possible, to Europe.

Factionalism and Elites

Factionalism within closely knit elite networks can be seen as one of the most immediate factors in triggering political exile. A 'thick analysis' of early independent Ibero-American cases of translocation indicates that dissent within the ranks of both established elites and countervailing forces was a major factor of centrifugal dispersion across the incipient boundaries of the emergent Latin American polities. The case of General Francisco de Paula Santander in Colombia can be used to further portray the activating role of this factor.

The political system that crystallized in Cundinamarca, Colombia, following independence was conflict-ridden, divided between two major factions. One

---

Argentina in 1852 for an exile in Southampton, UK, where he passed away in 1877. See Juan Manuel de Rosas, *Cartas del exilio*. Buenos Aires: Rodolfo Alonso Editor, 1974.

supported President Bolívar, whereas the other stood behind Vice-President Santander, one of the leading commanders in Bolívar's independence army. The dominant sector behind Bolívar included large landholders and the traditional aristocracy, who endorsed a strong centralized government, a vision akin to the project of the Liberator who decried decentralization as a source of anarchy. Supporting Santander were the federalists and liberals, who endorsed the primacy of Congress as the sovereign representative of the people.

The relations between the two leaders reached a critical point by 1827, when Bolívar was in Caracas after leaving the Colombian troops under the command of officers loyal to him, so as to restrict Santander's powers. Although Santander insisted on subordinating the troops to the constitutional rule of Congress, in July 1827, Bolívar decreed that Páez's jurisdiction in Venezuela was dependent directly and exclusively on Bolívar himself.[59]

In September, Bolívar was back in Bogotá to officially assume office as constitutional president, and many Santanderists fled the capital, fearing persecution. Among them were Senators Francisco Soto, Juan N. Azuero, and Miguel Uribe, who returned after being assured that Bolívar would not persecute them. Nevertheless, in this period, many liberals were harassed in public places by Bolívarists, with no steps being taken by official agents to stop it. The press of the liberal newspaper was violently dismantled, and copies of the paper were burnt publicly.

The estrangement between the two leaders was growing. Vice-President Santander was not invited to government meetings, although he was constitutionally entitled to attend. In February 1828, as rumors were spreading about a royalist expedition arriving on Venezuelan shores, Bolívar decreed a state of emergency, suspending all sorts of constitutional guarantees. He departed from the capital with his troops, leaving in charge a Council of Government to perform all administrative functions, thus bypassing Santander's prerogatives. There was a climate of exaltation in the country during the debates of the National Constituent Convention in Ocaña. A military group in Cartagena planned to revolt under calls of death to the Convention and to Santander.[60] The situation reached a point at which the vice-president came to fear for his life and decided to leave Colombia. He wrote to Bolívar asking to be allowed to leave the country:

In case the government could not guarantee my personal rights against certain aggressions [*vías de hecho*], I implore your Excellency to give me a passport to exit Colombia with guarantees for me, three servants and my luggage, since the natural law dictates me to seek a safe place, in spite of the law and my destiny as vice-president, rather than expose myself to become a fruitless victim of ill will and vengeance.[61]

---

[59] In his letters, Bolívar harshly attacked Santander and "the immoral administration that has reigned in this Bogotá using theft and plunder." Pilar Moreno de Angel, *Santander*. Bogotá: Planeta, 1989.

[60] Moreno de Angel, *Santander*, p. 149.

[61] Letter to the President of the Republic. Ocaña, 17 March 1828. In Roberto Cortázar, *Cartas y Mensajes de Santander*, vol. VII, p. 403, in Moreno de Angel, *Santander*, p. 419.

The personalist character of confrontational politics was fully at work in these settings. Bolívar was unwilling to make things easy for Santander. In a letter to Daniel Florencio O'Leary, he confided that "General Santander asked me for guarantees and even a passport. I won't let this opportunity pass without having him feel his misery."[62]

Bolívar officially assumed the dictatorship in August 1828, after his men ensured the Constituent Assembly's failure to adopt a new constitution. The vice-presidency of Colombia was then voided. On September 11, the minister of foreign affairs communicated to Santander that he had been appointed ambassador to the United States. On Santander's departure, the opposition would be necessarily weakened. Historian Moreno de Angel comments that, at the same time, the appointment had the goal of appeasing Santander, after he had been arbitrarily deposed from office.[63] Santander had been longing for this post since 1826, and accepted it, albeit not without hesitation, because he was well aware of the nature of the appointment:

This is a political decision. Be it that the government considers me harmful here or would like to give me guarantees, the truth is that after eighteen years of continuous services in seeking [to establish] the fatherland, I am forced to leave it. A harsh condition for a citizen always faithful to his duties and principles.[64]

Before he was able to leave, a failed *coup d'etat* took place on 26 September 1828. Even though Santander did not participate, he was imprisoned and sentenced to death on November 7, in a clearly political trial. Notwithstanding the move, it was not an easy task to get rid of Santander because he enjoyed high prestige and had friends and supporters at all levels of society. The public and the Church raised their voices in an intercession for Santander. The archbishop of Santa Fé wrote to Bolívar:

We decided to ask Your Excellency...to alleviate the prison and liberate General Francisco de Paula Santander. This petition notwithstanding, if it fits the public peace, you may [order] that he will not remain in the territories of the State, following the destination conferred upon him before or that he exits Colombia.[65]

The Council of Ministers deliberated on the issue and issued a statement, advising Bolívar to spare Santander's life:

It will be in the interest of the government to commute the death penalty into the cancellation of employment and the translocation [*extrañamiento*] from the Republic, prohibiting him from entering back the territory without a special permit from the Supreme Government; under the condition that if he fails to abide by the terms of this prohibition, any judge or military chief could apply to him the death penalty in the

---

[62] Bucaramanga, April 13, 1828. In Vicente Lecuna, *Cartas del Libertador*, vol. VII, p. 224, in Moreno de Angel, *Santander*, p. 419.

[63] Moreno de Angel, *Santander*, p. 440.

[64] Letter to José Fernández Madrid. Bogotá, September 18, 1828. *Archivo Santander*, vol. XVII, pp. 380–381.

[65] In *Archivo Santander*, vol. XVIII, p. 96. Quoted from Moreno de Angel, *Santander*, pp. 464–465.

place of his capture; and that his properties should be kept as deposit, without any possibility of selling or mortgaging them, to function as a security bond so that he will not break the prohibition and to be confiscated in the future, in case he breaks the prohibition.... The Council is of the opinion that, by taking this road, the vengeance of justice [*sic*] will be satisfied, while the government will get the love, admiration and respect of the governed and thus attain the needed peace and trust of the citizens.[66]

The pressure was effective, and Bolívar commuted the death penalty into exile. Santander was given three days to arrange his departure, under armed custody, to the Atlantic coast. However, on arriving in Cartagena, he was imprisoned for seven months under harsh conditions in the fortress of San Fernando de Bocachica. Protesting, Santander wrote to Bolívar a letter in which he fully acknowledges the background of the rift with the Liberator:

I beg you to order the implementation of my departure outside Colombia, since once far away from the country, I will no longer belong to factions [*partidos*] and only live in peace and my name will not serve as a pretext to hamper public order.[67]

Santander enjoyed high prestige in the United States, and the high circles of that country resented the unjust sentence against the former vice-president of Colombia.[68] Antonio José de Sucre also interceded in favor of Santander, asking Bolívar to release the prisoner and send him to the United States or Europe. Bolívar decided, instead, to transfer Santander to another prison in Venezuela, where he would be more isolated. Santander was accompanied by his brother-in-law, Colonel José María Bricero Méndez, a loyal and good friend of his, an aide, and three servants. The same day of his arrival to Puerto Cabello, Santander notified José Antonio Páez, Venezuela's civil and military commander-in-chief, of his situation, asking him for a passport to leave the country or, if unable to issue it himself, to intercede with the Liberator in that sense.[69] Páez acceded, extending him a passport to leave for any place in Europe.[70]

---

[66] Horacio Rodríguez Plata, *Santander en el exilio*, pp. 77–79, in Moreno de Angel, *Santander*, p. 467.

[67] Letter dated 13 December 1828. Roberto Cortázar, *Cartas y Mensajes de Santander*, vol. VII, pp. 447–461. Quoted by Moreno de Angel, *Santander*, p. 475. See also José M. De Mier, *Complemento a la Historia Extensa de Colombia: Testimonio de una Amistad*. Colombia: Plaza & Janés, 1983, vol. 2, p. 131.

[68] Santander had personally notified President Andrew Jackson of his situation in a letter dated 19 May 1829.

[69] *Archivo Santander*, vol. XVIII, pp. 125–126, in Moreno de Angel, *Santander*, p. 486.

[70] The terms of the passport were the following: "PASAPORTE. José Antonio Páez, Jefe Superior Civil y Militar de Venezuela, etc. De orden del Gobierno Supremo de la República, concedo franco y seguro pasaporte al señor Francisco de Paula Santander, para que pueda transportarse a Europa en el buque y al punto que más le convenga. Puerto Cabello, August 20, 1829. PAEZ." *Archivo Santander*, vol. XVIII, p. 130, in Moreno de Angel, *Santander*, pp. 486–487. Santander was instructed not to disembark at all but rather to remain on board the ship that had brought him to Venezuela until the ship that would take him to Europe arrived. Finally, it was a merchant boat, licensed I Hamburg, that took him on board on August 26.

In societies with deep social cleavages and relatively narrow elite circles, the rulers increasingly adopted exile among commonly used means of political exclusion. The existence of a tradition of colonial translocation and the hierarchical background of these societies were important factors in shaping this tendency. As early as 1951, John Johnson observed that

One of the earliest grounds for upholding asylum and exile stem from the rigid caste system, carried over from the period of Spanish domination. The jails and prisons – poorly constructed and with few provisions for sanitation and comfort – were unfit, or so it was thought, for the elite of society; and it was this group for whom diplomatic asylum was almost wholly reserved.... Coincidental with these considerations was the more widely used defense of saving the most capable manpower.... In ensuing struggles for power, diplomatic asylum and exile served to offer the surest and most economical means of conserving the ruling class. The loser, whether morally right or wrong, was assured a place of retreat so long as asylum was respected.[71]

Elites were interested in avoiding, as long as possible, a situation of total war that could weaken their hold over the whole social matrix. This possibility could become a reality either by launching a cycle of mutual retaliation, creating long-term blood feuds, or by forcing the elites to open the political game to growing numbers of supporters from the lower strata. These developments could endanger the entire position of the elites in the medium and long ranges. Concurrently, because the conditions for imprisonment were seen as unsuitable for members of the elite, a prison sentence was used as a harsher measure than exile and, as such, was used as a threat. Social networks, friendship, family ties, and clientelistic entourages played into the preceding system of power in favor of a nontotalistic solution: political exile.

The thesis of the elitist roots of translocation as a political mechanism and its selective use as a means of punishment of political rivals is further reinforced by looking back at the racial bias of its implementation, which was projected in a continuous line from colonial to independent times. Perhaps paradigmatic is the case of Bolívar dealing with two of his leading opponents in the framework of Great Colombia, the *pardo* [mulatto] General José Padilla and General Santander. Whereas in the latter case, Bolívar would reluctantly acquiesce to the intercessions of elite sectors on Santander's behalf, in the case of Padilla, Bolívar opted for his execution. José Padilla was the leading figure of the independence camp in the predominantly Afro-Caribbean city of Cartagena, an individual who had enjoyed the dual patronage of Bolívar and Santander. In 1828, when the rift between the two patrons was evident, Padilla sided with Santander and launched a constitutionalist coup. Bolívar accused him of inciting to a racial war, a frightening reminder of the Haiti Revolution, and had him executed.[72]

[71] John J. Johnson, "Foreign Factors," in Hugh M. Hamill, Ed., *Caudillos: Dictators in Spanish America*. Norman and London: University of Oklahoma Press, 1992, p. 198. This article was originally published in *Pacific Historical Review*, 20, 2 (1951).

[72] Aline Helg, "Simon Bolivar and the Spectre of *Pardocracia*: Jośe Padilla in Post-Independent Cartagena." *Journal of Latin American Studies*, 35 (2003): 447–471.

In November 1828, a month after the execution, Bolívar confided in a letter to Paez his uneasiness about the different treatment he had reserved for Santander and *pardos* such as Piar or Padilla:

Things have reached a point that keeps me wrestling with myself, with my ideas and with my glory. . . . I already repent for the death of Piar, of Padilla and the others who have died for the same cause; in the future there will be no justice to punish the most atrocious murderer, because [by saving] the life of Santander [I have pardoned] the most scandalous impunities. . . . What torments me even more is the just clamor with which those of the class of Piar and Padilla will complain. They will say with more than enough justice that I have been weak in favor of this infamous white [Santander], who did not have the record of service of those famous [*pardo*] servants of the fatherland. This exasperates me, so that I don't [know] what to do with myself.[73]

One should look beyond the apologetic tone to ground his fears of being accused of racism in the context of Bolívar's attempts to avert the disintegration of Great Colombia into Venezuela, New Granada (Colombia), and Ecuador, which eventually took place in 1830. Concomitantly, Bolívar is fully aware of the social context of race, class, and status, which conditioned the differential use of displacement and translocation among other means of political regulation.

Transregional Political Dynamics

In early independent Latin America, under a situation of fragmentation of political authority and undefined borders, exile was not conceived in terms of modern political asylum. Rather, individuals forced to move to other regions conceived it as a tactical escape of the sphere of influence of their persecutors, the rulers of their home society.

Although beyond these rulers' spheres of control, the translocated individuals did not perceive themselves as foreigners but rather as 'patriots' moving within the borders of the Great American fatherland, or as expatriates waiting to return to the homeland.[74] With the passing of time, the translocation of 'political enemies' beyond the areas directly controlled by the new state became a factor related to the effective definition of borders between the newly formed states.

An outstanding case of such transregional dynamics conditioning translocation and the emergence of exile is that of Peru, Bolivia, and Chile in the 19th century. Connections between Peru and Alto Perú (later Bolivia) had existed since Incan and colonial times. Similarly, in the colony, territorial links connected Peru and Chile, with many instances of individuals from Peru being relocated in Chile, which constituted the outer frontier where the Lima authorities sent troublemakers. The links between Peru and Alto Perú were weakened between 1776 and 1809, when Alto Perú was incorporated into the newly

---

73 Quoted from Helg, "Simon Bolivar and the Spectre," p. 470.
74 David Brading, "Patriotism and the Nation in Colonial Spanish America," in Roniger and Sznajder, Eds., *Constructing Collective Identities and Shaping Public Spheres: Latin American Paths*: 1998, pp. 13–45.

created viceroyalty of the Río de la Plata, with its capital in Buenos Aires, but became relevant again with independence. While the centralist Peruvian Constitution of 1828 required that the president be a Peruvian by birth, in fact, many of the figures who shaped Peruvian history from the 1820s to the 1860s were natives of other regions in what are now Ecuador and Bolivia. Such were Andrés Santa Cruz, Juan José Flores, and José de la Mar, the leading *caudillos* who fought, plotted, expelled each other from power, and ruled Peru during that period.[75]

This transregional political dynamic was reconstituted during independence. In July 1809, a junta in La Paz issued a declaration of independence in the name of deposed Spanish King Fernando VII. Following repression by the royalist forces of Cuzco, the leaders were executed and more than a hundred 'rebels' were banished from the land.[76] Royalist forces continued to struggle to keep control of the urban centers, whereas 'bandits' and guerrilla forces controlled the countryside.

The Peruvian royalists, the supporters of independence in Peru, and the independence movement of Buenos Aires all considered Alto Perú part of their administrative jurisdiction, thus turning the region into a battlefield. It was the royal commander there, Pedro Olañeta, who chose not to collaborate with the royalist army of Peru, which was led by liberals, whom the *criollo* general despised. Once General Antonio José de Sucre defeated the royalists in Ayacucho in December 1824, he managed to also defeat Olañeta's forces a few months later, opening the way for Alto Peruvian elites who chose the route to independence in 1825.

Simón Bolívar was acclaimed as president of the newborn Republic of Bolivia. He spent only a few months there, and returned then to his headquarters in Lima, promising formal recognition of the new state by the Peruvian Congress, without which no Bolivian state could safely exist because its establishment was opposed by most members of the Peruvian elite. From Lima, Bolívar named General Sucre as president of Bolivia, and the decrees and laws issued by both leaders in regard to Bolivia would still keep the heading "Republic of Peru."[77]

In turn, as is well known, Peru, the royalist stronghold, was liberated from beyond its boundaries as part of a continental movement in two stages: first, by the combined efforts of General José de San Martín Cuyo's forces and the Chilean and Peruvian forces that landed by the sea, and second, by the

---

[75] "Se advierte con sumo interés el hecho de que Santa Cruz se mueva entre Bolivia y Perú como Pedro por su casa, como si no tuviera noción de su nacionalidad. Lo mismo ocurre con el general Lamar." Jorge Alejandro Ovando Sanz, "El Surgimiento de la Nacionalidad Charquina y la Formación del Estado Boliviano," in Rosana Barragán, Dora Cajías, and Seemin Qayum, Eds., *El Siglo XIX: Bolivia y América Latina*. La Paz: Coordinadora de Historia e I.F.E.A, 1997, p. 236. Santa Cruz was a native of Bolivia and La Mar was Ecuadoran.

[76] Herbert Klein, *Bolivia*. Oxford: Oxford University Press, 1982, pp. 90–92.

[77] Ovando Sanz, "El Surgimiento de la Nacionalidad Charquina y la Formación del Estado Boliviano."

Colombian forces of Generals Sucre and Bolívar, who defeated the last wave of royalist opposition to independent rule in South America.

After independence, both Peru and Bolivia were ruled by short-term dictatorships led or inspired by Bolívar, followed as in other parts of Spanish America by instability, constitutional debates, turmoil, and civil war. These conflicts revolved around the issue of the relative authority of the executive and parliament, the role and control of the military, personal sympathies and antipathies. States of emergency were declared, which prevented the disintegration of the republics. These dynamics were common to most Spanish-speaking territories. Nonetheless, the lack of national consciousness added its own flavor to the regions under consideration. When in 1828 General Agustín Gamarra invaded Bolivia, claiming it indivisible from Peru, his job was made easier by many Bolivians who defected to his camp:

Since the Bolivian nationality was recently established and there were old ties and sympathies between Lower and Upper Peru [i.e., Peru and Bolivia], nobody thought with guilt nor considered it treason to belong to Peru if the invasion eventually had that aim, or remain in the new Bolivian Republic. The masses in particular ignored the political question stirred by the quarreling parts.[78]

The political game was dominated by *caudillos* who attempted to unite Bolivia and Peru, to append part of Bolivia to Peru or vice versa, as in the attempt by General Andrés Santa Cruz to establish a Peruvian–Bolivian Confederation. The governments of Peru and Bolivia were deeply involved in each other's domestic politics for decades. Many of these 'national' leaders expelled each other or fled from Peru or Bolivia, mainly to Ecuador or Chile, and back. Once abroad, they sought a temporary stronghold from where they planned a return to power, supported or opposed by the political forces in the host societies.[79]

In the 1830s, violent confrontations ensued, and the temporarily prevailing party deported many of the leaders of the defeated party to be displaced, in turn, once the other faction took power. Thus, there were waves after waves of displaced leaders forced to flee with their supporters as they were ousted from power or tried to regain power with the support of neighboring allies. In Peru, President José de la Mar was removed from power by General Agustín Gamarra and died in exile in Costa Rica in 1830. When General Luis José de Orbegoso became president in 1833, it was Gamarra's turn – he had opposed Orbegoso and backed another candidate, Pedro Pablo Bermúdez – to take the road of exile. When the Gamarra faction prevailed for a few months in 1834, many prominent members of the political class were deported, among them Vice-President Armando La Fuente and Speaker of the Senate Tellería. In May 1834, after defeat, Gamarra fled to Bolivia and later on to Chile. With the support of Chile, the Peruvian émigrés managed to oppose the establishment

---

[78] Luis Mariano Guzmán, *Historia de Bolivia*. Cochabamba: Imprenta del Siglo, 1983, p. 78.
[79] Ronald B. St. John, *The Foreign Policy of Peru*. Boulder, CO: Rienner, 1992, pp. 23–43.

of the Peruvian–Bolivian Confederation, led by General Andrés de Santa Cruz as supreme protector and Orbegoso as president of North Peru. Once defeated, Orbegoso abandoned Peru, to return only years later, settling in his hometown to write his memoirs and staying away from active political life.[80]

As measures were taken to consolidate territorial power, political exile crystallized in its modern sense of banishment from state boundaries rather than a mere translocation across traditionally defined administrative sister-territories. Illustrative of this transformation are a series of legal provisions promulgated in Peru. In June 1834, Orbegoso issued an edict, forever prohibiting the return to Peruvian territory of all those who had taken part a few months earlier in an insurrection against his election as president. If they returned, they would be denied any legal protection and would face execution.[81] In nearly simultaneous fashion, he issued a law sanctioning the death penalty to any official – be it a minister or the president himself – who would attempt to change the existing form of government or act "against national independence." In cases of incurring in these offenses indirectly, the sentence would be "to banish the culprits forever from the territory of the Republic." Permanent banishment would also ensue to a minister or president who caused the death of a Peruvian. Another law prohibited the expatriation of any citizen without a proper sentence issued by a competent judge.[82]

The creation of a national imagery – and its tension with transnational trends – took place in tandem with the creation of communities of exiles, who were involved in the pursuit of alternative political projects under the tutelary eyes of the host rulers and subject to their policy priorities. For instance, former Peruvian President Gamarra and his followers, who had taken asylum in Bolivia, kept close contact with their allies in Peru, particularly with those hoping to restore Cuzco to its previous primacy.[83] Despite the Peruvian government's protests, Bolivian President Santa Cruz refrained from taking any action, claiming in response that the conduct of the Peruvians was being watched and professing to maintain Bolivia's neutrality.[84]

Contrastingly, Peruvian émigrés found in Chile a propitious environment for their campaign against the Peruvian–Bolivian Confederation led by Santa Cruz and their fellow countryman General Orbegoso. They led a vocal campaign through publications such as Felipe Pardo's *La Jeta, meditaciones poéticas por*

---

[80] Charles F. Walker, *Smoldering Ashes: Cuzco and the Creation of Republican Peru, 1780–1840*. Durham, NC: Duke University Press, 1999, pp. 121–151; Modesto Basadre y Chocano, *Diez Años de Historia Política del Perú*. Lima: Editorial Huascarán, 1953, pp. 7–20. In his memories, Orbegoso would portray Santa Cruz as somebody who abused Peruvian resources when he granted pensions and sums of money as compensations to those who spent time banished in Europe, such as General Herrera.

[81] Evaristo San Cristóval, *El Gran Mariscal Luis José de Orbegoso*. Lima: Gil S.A. Editores, 1941, p. 54.

[82] Idem, pp. 272, 275.

[83] Walker, *Smoldering Ashes*, pp. 128–138.

[84] St. John, *Foreign Policy*, p. 21.

Monsieur Alphonse Chunca Cápac Yupanqui, alluding to the Napoleonic–indigenous amalgam of the person of Santa Cruz, and the newspapers *El Intérprete* (under the direction of Pardo), *La Aurora, El Popular, La Bandera Bicolor*, and *El Eclipse*.

Nonetheless, Peruvian émigrés in Chile were highly divided, replicating the factionalism of the home country and being exposed to the political support or animosity of policy-makers in Chile. The most important factions were those led by Gamarra and La Fuente, and younger networks led by Manuel Ignacio de Vivanco and by Pardo. The latter group aspired to establish a new regime in Peru, a regime of regeneration, and not just to precipitate a return to the state of affairs that enabled the rise to power of Santa Cruz. Diego Portales, the strongman of Chilean government, had made friends with key individuals in the younger network, manifesting his hostility toward Gamarra. As the followers of Gamarra realized this, they began drawing plans for an invasion of Peru, not counting now on Chilean support, and seeking instead the support of Ecuador for an invasion from the north. Accordingly, Gamarra moved to Guayaquil, and Chilean authorities convinced some of his followers who remained in Chile, led by La Fuente, to join the Chilean expedition to Peru, together with Vivanco's and Pardo's followers, in exchange for the elimination of Gamarra. Seeing the cause in peril, an agent of Gamarra adopted the disloyal attitude of contacting Santa Cruz and revealed to him the details of the planned invasion, which accordingly failed.

After its failure, Agustín Gamarra was able to return to Chile because his enemy Portales had been killed shortly before during a military revolt in June 1837. Gamarra won the support of the emerging Chilean leader, General Manuel Bulnes, under whom Gamarra and La Fuente organized Peruvian troops for the new campaign that set sail in July 1838. After the war, Gamarra was reinstated into power, and he gave eminent posts to those who accompanied him in Chile. The new government of Marshall Gamarra (1838–1841) declared the Peruvians who had lived in exile *"beneméritos en grado eminente"* (i.e., meritorious in the highest degree), rewarding them with key political positions, appointments in the militias and the military, and tax exemptions.[85]

In late 1838, Orbegoso set sail into exile in Ecuador, after declaring that he was "willing to exit the country if this is necessary to ensure complete peace":[86]

I am going to Guayaquil: I think of residing in Cuenca, until my fatherland will become quiet and then I'll come back to live privately with my family. My presence could be harmful [now] to the defense of the country. I'll always make sacrifices for my fatherland, whether they will be recognized or not.[87]

---

[85] Jorge Basadre, *Historia de La República del Perú*. Lima: Editorial Universitaria, 1968, vol. II.

[86] September 1838. San Cristóval, *Gran Mariscal*, p. 131.

[87] Letter to Francisco de Paula Santander, 30 November 1838. San Cristóval, *Gran Mariscal*, p. 159. After the Yungay defeat that signaled the dissolution of the Peruvian–Bolivian Confederation, Santa Cruz himself resigned and on February 1839 also left for exile.

The situation of exile, while providing some measure of immunity from physical aggression by political enemies, did not preclude many other forms of verbal and written aggression against the person who sought shelter abroad.[88] Sometimes, even when the émigrés tried to disengage from politics, those in power in the expelling country suspected them of not being sincere and kept attacking the exiles, thus driving them back into the orbit of politics. To cut the umbilical cord linking the leader in exile to his home country, all factors – the exile, the home country, and the host country (and, later on, the transnational arena as well) – should concur in recognizing that individual's detachment from politics.[89]

The preceding analysis indicates that the recurrent use of banishment and exile took place in dialectical interaction with the process of construction of distinct identities and demarcation of state sovereignties. Long-standing practices of displacement became transformed into a major mechanism of political regulation in the newly established states. By being displaced, these displaced individuals were unwillingly major actors who, while engaging in power struggles, also contributed to the tension-ridden process of definition of nation-state identities, a process closely tied to shaping the boundaries of the emerging states in this part of the Americas.

---

[88] For instance, during his exile in Guayaquil, Orbegoso remained the target of virulent attacks from the Gamarra second administration (1838–1841), which issued decrees condemning him as a traitor and published press notes that blackened him. This strategy led Orbegoso to publish in 1839 a response titled *La Defensa*, in which he refuted the accusations and justified his actions.

[89] In 1839, Perú adopted a more centralized and authoritarian political system, but this did not preclude the struggle over presidential succession. By 1845, the Peruvian state was on the way to consolidation and the frontiers were defined in general terms, even if nationhood and national identity remained embryonic. The political events (e.g., a street attack on President Castilla in 1860) continued to generate political exile, and Chile remained a pole of attraction.

3

The Format of Early Exile

> [D]uring a time of civil discord no impartial man can be found...and this is
> because while the actors live it is impossible to get them to agree with the judgment
> of their fellow men, especially when their own intentions are examined.
>
> Manuel Montúfar y Coronado (1832)[1]

Exile became a major feature of political life, inherent in the specific patterns
of configuration of modern politics and political regimes in 19th-century Latin
America. When the polities reached higher levels of institutional consolidation,
exile was already internalized in the political culture as part of an exclusionary
politics of exit, prevailing over more open and pluralistic politics of voice, in
the terms of Albert Hirschman.[2] In this chapter, we examine the evolution of
exile in the newly formed states, focusing on what we define as a three-tiered
format of early exile, in which displaced individuals and communities played
an increasingly important role in the politics of exit as well as on the formation
of state identities and collective imageries.

The Three-Tiered Format of Early Exile

The crystallization of the new states did not preclude overlapping territorial
claims. The political class of each region continued to exercise extensive influence on the equation of political forces in the neighboring countries. The
intricate connections among Peru, Bolivia, and Chile analyzed in the preceding chapter are not unique. During the dictatorship of Rosas in Buenos

---

[1] Manuel Montúfar y Coronado, *Memorias para la historia de la Revolución de Centro América*
   (*Known as Memorias de Jalapa 1832*). Guatemala: José de Pineda Ibarra, 1963, vol. 1, p. 30.
[2] Albert O. Hirschman, *Exit, Voice and Loyalty*. Cambridge, MA: Harvard University Press,
   1970. See also Hirschman, *Crossing Boundaries: Selected Writings*. New York: Zone Books,
   1998. Seemingly, this contrasted with the institutional pattern that crystallized in the United
   States, even under states of emergency. See Robert G. Caldwell, "Exile as an Institution."
   Political Science Quarterly, 58, 2 (1943): 239–262.

Aires and the rule of federalist *caudillos* in the provinces of Río de la Plata (later Argentina) and Banda Oriental (later Uruguay), individuals favoring centralization and liberalism and members of the young intelligentsia left for exile in both Uruguay and Chile.[3] Many of the leaders of Uruguayan independence, starting with José Gervasio Artigas, went into exile in Argentina, Brazil, and Paraguay. In the Central American Isthmus, the countries that had formed the confederation from 1823 to 1838 continued to interfere in a continuous struggle between conservatives and liberals, using exiles as a political tool. Similarly, political actors moved constantly among Venezuela, Colombia, and Ecuador as well as within the Caribbean area, Central America, and Mexico.[4]

We identify at this stage a three-tiered structure of exile, in which translocated individuals and communities played an increasingly important role. Political classes intervened in the configuration of other countries' political factions, according to their own interests. When the faction they sided with was defeated, neighboring countries might accept the vanquished political actors in their territory, hosting them, and even supporting their plans of return, playing regional politics in spite of, or because of, the exiles' defeat. They acted in such a manner so as to regain control of the neighboring political scene or, at least, exercise their influence by strengthening sympathetic political allies. When the defeated faction was inimical to their political plans or design, the country of reception could still host the expelled individuals and control their freedom of action, thereby curtailing the possibilities of plotting against their ally, the ruling government in the neighboring country. In all cases, the translocated individuals and communities of exiles played an increasingly important role in this three-tiered structure, both as part of the plans of regional hegemony of the host country and interplaying with their home rulers' strategies that put pressure on the states hosting the exiles (see Diagram 3.1).

The presence of exiles was tolerated, and even fostered, as a political tool to be used by the host country relative to the political scene in the exiles' home country. This attitude not only impinged on the country of origin of the exiles but also contributed toward defining the rules of membership in the host political community. Often, although exiles were used in the transregional power games, they were precluded from intervening in the local politics of the host

---

[3] William H. Katrak, *The Argentine Generation of 1837*. London: Associated University Presses, 1996. See also François-Xavier Guerra, "The Implosion of the Spanish Empire: Emerging Statehood and Collective Collectives," in Roniger and Herzog, Eds., *The Collective and the Public in Latin America*, pp. 71–94; Federica Morelli, "Territorial Hierarchies and Collective Identities in Late Colonial and Early Independent Quito," ibid., pp. 37–56.

[4] In parallel, also the United States and Europe became poles of attraction and asylum for the Latin American exiles. European sites such as Paris also attracted other migrants, businesspeople, students, and expatriates, in addition to exiles as part of the diaspora community. See subsequent discussion.

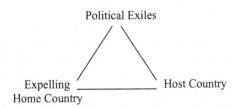

Expelling Country	Political Exiles	Host Country

Exclusion from Public Domain Motivations   Policies of Asylum
* Territorial Banishment   Paths to Exile   * Reception
* Escape Abroad   Displacement   * Support Mechanisms
* Internal Relegation   Political Activity   * Limitations
* 'Insile'   Abroad   * Political Use of Exiles
                             Serial Exile

DIAGRAM 3.1. Format of early exile.

country. Such was the experience of the Argentinean liberal exiles who settled in Chile under the latter's conservative and authoritarian presidential regime, without being able to influence local politics according to their own ideological visions. The exiles were welcome as long as they did not interfere in internal politics or on the condition that they sided with the rulers in power. When the exiles took positions contrary to the government, they were immediately expelled from the country.[5]

While abroad, the exiles and émigrés continued to be deeply divided into factions. They struggled with one another, claiming to represent the collective will and seeking to gain the support of the host governments as they drafted plans for the invasion of their home country. On their part, the host rulers were willing to support such military campaigns whenever they felt it coincided with their geopolitical interests and kept their control over the exiles' leadership.

The exiled leaders were heads of clientelistic networks of followers accompanying them outside the home territory. Once back in power, the returning leaders rewarded those who took the road of exile with them. In a context of deep factionalism, personal allegiance was expected and rewarded, reinforcing a dichotomous view of political forces, which were thought of as divided into friends and foes.

[5] Tulio Halperin Donghi, *Proyecto y construcción de una nación*. Caracas: Biblioteca Ayacucho, 1980, p. 500.

Returning to the Homeland

In tandem with internal strife and translocation, those in power defined the rules of the game of return to the home territory. In general, the sanctuary offered by host countries was respected, but attempts to return prematurely would be severely punished, often with the death penalty.

Accordingly, exiles could never be sure of the possibility of returning to their homeland. In these polities, much depended on power shifts, such as the rulers' demise from power or the death of political contesters. Such shifts could transform exile into a springboard back to power. Paradigmatic is the case of Santander (see Chapter 2), who had been ostracized when Bolívar was alive. After Bolívar's death in May 1830, and following the restitution of all his military grades and honors, Santander returned to become president of the Republic of Colombia in 1832. In his exile years, he traveled extensively in Spain, Italy, Belgium, Austria, Prussia, and later in the United States, assimilating political ideas, especially those that reinforced his own liberal principles.

Following pressures from the Colombian government, the French government warned him that he was granted asylum under the sole condition that he would not be involved in any political activity. Nonetheless, he continued to meet with prominent public figures and politicians. Santander also deepened his cultural knowledge, as he visited libraries and museums, attended theaters and concerts, in search of things that might be of use back in the homeland. Despite his public clout in exile, Santander was fully aware of his condition as an exile.[6] Once back in Colombia, President Santander invested efforts in implementing what he had learned abroad, particularly Jeremy Bentham's utilitarianism, despite a strong opposition by conservative and Catholic circles.

Return from exile in circumstances in which the balance of power did not change radically could produce a tragic end. This was the case of Agustín Cosme Damián de Iturbide (1783–1824), the ruler of the short-lived independent empire established in Mexico. Soon after he was named emperor in May 1822, Iturbide faced growing opposition from those coveting greater political powers. Republican elements led by General Antonio López de Santa Anna, buttressed by federalist forces representing regional interests, rebelled. A tug-of-war ensued as these forces tried to impose new parliamentary elections to force the legal dethronement of the emperor. By March 1823, Iturbide resigned the throne and was allowed to leave Mexico for Europe, with an entourage of 27 members, which included his family, secretary, and servants. He explained his decision as a way to keep social peace and avoid civil war.[7] Once on the Old Continent, he was treated honorably as an exiled monarch. In Mexico, rumors abounded about Iturbide's planning to come back at the head of an army provided by the Holy Alliance. The Republican government enacted regulation

---

[6] Moreno de Angel, *Santander*, p. 506.

[7] Anna Timothy, *The Fall of the Royal Government in Mexico City.* Lincoln, NE: University of Nebraska Press, 1978, pp. 189–215.

allowing the state to send into exile without trial any person suspected of conspiring against the Republic. As Iturbide moved from Livorno to England, the
Mexican Congress blocked his pension payments and ordered the death penalty
if he should return to Mexico. In May 1824, unaware of the latest decision and
ignoring José de San Martín's advice not to return because an act of this kind
would probably trigger a civil war, Iturbide decided to come back. As soon as
he arrived, he was taken prisoner and summarily executed.

Progressively, the return of exiles became linked to policies of amnesty and
pardons aimed at achieving 'national reconciliation,' promising to break away
from policies of institutional exclusion. This trend opened the issue of political
and administrative reincorporation of exiles into the home society, sometimes
even accepting the returnee into the ruling coalitions and centers of power.
Outstanding was the case of Chile, where, under conditions of early state
consolidation, the state looked for ways to diminish the frictions provoked by
civil strife, by reinstating the translocated individuals into formerly abolished
privileges, pensions, and ranks.[8]

In this transitional period, political exile functioned as a mechanism regulating tensions in polities in which the presence of strong opposition leaders
could lead almost by default to a zero-sum political game and civil war. Political factionalism, although widespread, was perceived as extremely dangerous.
The social closeness of elites in tandem with the traditional forms of exclusion
of wider strata conditioned the forms of politics, with exile evolving as an
alternative to imprisonment and execution. The latter had greater social costs
and could lead to civil war and a zero-sum game in politics.[9] By sending away
those who led the defeated faction – what would be considered the opposition
in a more developed political context – the rulers could claim to be moving
in a lenient way toward organic unity, which they claimed to legitimately
embody.

Ideas and interests could not be detached from politics of personalistic leadership, and exclusion turned out to be a major ruling principle that became part
of the institutional model. The opposition could be demonized and stigmatized
as a divisive force conspiring to destroy society, while the rulers claimed to
reestablish the cherished and broken unity of society. As such, exile, a mechanism of political exclusion, could be represented as a source of harmony. All
these processes were carried out without opening windows to a more pluralistic vision of politics. While in exile, the lives and even the properties of the
excluded leaders would be respected, but once the exiled leaders attempted
a comeback into the political game, the odds of a zero-sum game were so
high that many of them paid with their life. Paradigmatic are the cases of
those political actors who continued to cling to the old pan-Central-American

[8] Brian Loveman and Elizabeth Lira, *Las suaves cenizas del olvido: Vía chilena de la reconciliación
    política (1814–1932)*. Santiago: LOM, 1999, pp. 85–95.
[9] Rebecca Earl, Ed., *Rumours of Wars: Civil Conflict in Nineteenth Century Latin America*.
    London: Institute of Latin American Studies, 2000.

vision against the background of configuration of separate states following the disintegration of the Central American Federation in 1838. Francisco de Morazán, president of the Central American Federation in the 1830s, went into exile with some followers in 1840. After returning from Panama, he led some disaffected Costa Ricans in their attempt to depose the local ruler, Braulio Carrillo. The attempt failed, and Morazán was executed in San José de Costa Rica in 1842.[10]

The Construction of Collective Imageries

As politicians and intellectuals took the road of exile, they could not avoid questioning themselves about what went wrong in their strategies of action. Out of necessity, they began a reevaluation of their previous assumptions and compared their current experience with the ideological and utopian images they had nourished before.

This confrontation triggered also questions of identity, not only on a personal level but leading to the rethinking of the collective tenets of their home society as well. They analyzed the problems of nation-building and the possible paths of their nations and states, in terms of the distance and possible combination between the primordial and constructed – political – components embedded in the nation-state. They also broadened their perspectives in exile, and some of them elaborated visions of pan-Latin American fraternity and unity.

These trends can be illustrated with the experience of Benjamín Vicuña Mackenna, a Chilean intellectual whose experience in exile brought him to devote energies to historiography work. Through his books and his public presence in the press and speeches, he aimed to make a major contribution to the construction of a Chilean modern national identity.

As a young liberal, Vicuña Mackenna combined his creative capacity with the activism of a political actor and participated in two failed revolts against the Portalesian conservative regime of the 1850s. He soon found himself forced to leave his home country, first between November 1853 and October 1855, and for a second time between March 1859 and January 1861.[11] As an exile,

---

[10] See Angel Zúñiga Huete, *Morazán*. Tecigualpa: Editorial Universitaria, 1982; and Leslie Bethell, *Central America Since Independence*. Cambridge: Cambridge University Press, 1991, pp. 13–22. One of his lieutenants, Gerardo Barrios, was thrown in prison at that time but continued to follow Morazán's Central-American optic into the late 1850s and early 1860s, when he met a similar fate. A liberal by conviction, Captain General Barrios reached the presidency of El Salvador and in 1863 supported an unsuccessful rebellion against the conservative government of Nicaragua. In revenge, the Nicaraguan rulers supported a rebellion against him in El Salvador. Forced to leave the country, he boarded a ship that went ashore in Nicaragua during a storm. Captured, he was handed over to the new Salvadoran authorities, who executed him in 1865.

[11] El Museo Nacional, *Vicuña Mackenna: Rasgos biográficos*. Santiago: Prensas de la Universidad de Chile, 1946, pp. 7–14.

Vicuña Mackenna traveled through the Americas and Europe. In the words of José Luis Rénique,

Exile will shape the great questions that throughout the decades of 1860 and 1870 will stimulate his intellectual work. [Vicuña Mackenna will ask himself] What possibilities will Chile have in a world increasingly dominated by the *yankee* dynamism? How could this small appendix of the Spanish Empire in the far South Pacific become an effective, competitive and respected member of that emergent globalization? What materials and traditions will allow the elaboration of a national will to be able to overcome the limits attributed to the Chilean idiosyncrasy (*chilenidad*)?[12]

These issues would be drawn as Vicuña Mackenna compared the reality of Chile with the situation in the countries he traveled through while in exile. Visiting Mexico and Brazil, he became very critical of the ethnodemographic composition of these countries that in his ethnocentric view were polluted by the indigenous and African origins of the population. He also came to the conclusion that Chile had to engage in wide colonization in order to overcome the backward trends imbued in the local indigenous population. His views of the United States were equally negative but for other reasons; namely, because of the materialistic leanings and vulgarity he perceived and that he contrasted with the more cultured and aristocratic background of the elites back home. He was also disappointed by Europe, especially the dirt and poverty of Rome – which contrasted with its classic image and its glorious past – and the social distance between the brutalized masses and the omnipotent aristocracy in the UK.

Vicuña Mackenna returned from exile with full confidence that a dynamic and integrated Chile could look forward to the future "without fear or inferiority feelings." As he reflected on Chile, comparing it with larger countries such as Mexico and Brazil, he believed that certain trends embedded in the political and historical development of Chile enabled an outstanding economic and political stability, which could make her a leading country in the Americas. Whereas in the rest of South America, "the neighboring Republics suffer from inner fragmentation and self destruction," in Chile, with a prosperous economy and "the inaccessible crest of the Andes as a protective wall," the Republic was free of the "quarrels and intrigue promoted by the improvised diplomats of our Republics, stupidly imitating the European monarchies."[13]

His exile experience had led him to engage in the historical analysis of the development of Chile. According to Vicuña Mackenna, two revolutions had already taken place: a conservative one in 1829, which placed Portales at the helm of the Republic, and a liberal revolution, a child of its own troubled time.

---

[12] José Luis Rénique, "Benjamín Vicuña Mackenna: Exilio, historia y nación," *Ciberayllu*, 18 October 2005. Available at http://www.andes.missouri.edu/andes/Especiales/JLRVicuna/ JLR_Vicuna1.html, accessed 29 May 2006.

[13] Benjamín Vicuña Mackenna, *Páginas de mi diario durante tres años de viaje, 1853, 1854, 1855.* Santiago de Chile: Universidad de Chile, 1936, vol. 2, p. 327, in Rénique, ibid.

In exile, he learned that both had attained only partial results because of the violence of the past. A third revolution, the revolution of the future, would

lack in blood spilled in battles, scaffold ropes, prisoner chains and neither lists of proscribed individuals. This will be a revolution of the tranquil, hard-working and fruitful mind; of faith and love; of soul and conscience; of the ideas that in a not distant day will carry out the regeneration of humankind.[14]

To accomplish that deed, he engaged in writing the history of Chile in terms of historical justice, reconsidering the harm done by ostracism and the need for reconciliation. He thus engaged in the production of dozens of books, including two on some of the most prominent exiles: the Carrera Brothers and General Bernardo O'Higgins, heroes of the war of independence who were enemies in life, both dying in exile.[15] By writing such books of history on them and on Portales, whose followers were closely related to his own exile, Vicuña Mackenna expressly aimed to reconfigure the political sphere through national reconciliation and a more open game of power. Through the writing of history, this intellectual elaborated a project of historiography aimed to reintegrate those who had been excluded in the past into the collective imagery, so to construct a way to reconcile Liberalism with the Portalesian authoritarian frameworks that, even if creating an outstanding comparative institutional stability in Chile, had to be reframed toward an expanding and more inclusive Republic. Writing on these leaders and others, Vicuña Mackenna tried to show the pitfalls of inner confrontation and violence and suggested a model for Chilean development that had universal significance. According to this model, the factionalism and political violence leading to ostracism and exile was the major hindrance to development. Development had to be based on civilized political dialogue making room for the building of a stable polity and prosperous society. This imagery was closely linked to liberal and positivist ideas and would become integrated in the modernization of Chile in the second half of the 19th century.[16]

Displacement and exile often followed the defeat of political projects of construction of states and national communities, envisioned in the country of origin. Intellectual and political elites elaborated national histories and education programs that projected the idea of national existence back to the early independence period. In this sense, these intellectuals interpreted the past at the time that they aimed to create models of the future (imagined communities, in Benedict Anderson's terms), projecting them as if emerging from the historical

---

[14] Vicuña Mackenna, *Páginas de mi diario*, 1936, vol. 2, p. 386.

[15] Vicuña Mackenna, *El ostracismo de los Carrera: Los jenerales Jose Miguel i Juan Jose, i el coronel Luis Carrera. Episodio de la independencia de Sud-America*. Santiago: Imprenta del Ferrocarril, 1857; idem, *Ostracismo del general D. Bernardo O'Higgins, escrito sobre documentos inéditos i noticias autenticas*. Valparaíso: Imprenta i librería del Mercurio, 1860.

[16] Vicuña Mackenna was major of Santiago in 1872–1875 and, together with other members of the so-called 1842 generation, many of whom had experienced exile, played an important role in this process of modernization.

and political analysis they undertook. In this manner, they contributed to the crystallization of the collective imagery of the nations created out of the demise of colonial territories.

In parallel, exiles and expatriates elaborated pan-Latin American ideas after relocating beyond the borders of their home country. Particularly salient were those who faced broader arenas of discussion and claimed to represent the 'true soul' of the home countries on a transnational scope. One of these 19th-century figures taking pride in the culture and collective identity of Latin America is José María Torres Caicedo, a writer and intellectual who was born in Bogotá in 1830. At the age of 17, he started a career of political journalism but would soon discover the limits of free speech in Colombia. From mid-1849, he was editor of the newspaper *El Día,* in opposition to the government, which incited a riot in the course of which his typesetting equipment was destroyed. His political stands also led to a duel, in which he was shot in 1850. At the age of 20, he left Colombia for Paris, where he intended to recover from his wounds. He became an expatriate who, save for short visits back home, remained abroad until his death in 1889. He came to represent his country in London and Paris, was the Venezuelan consul-general and chargé d'affaires in France and the Netherlands, and later was chargé d'affaires of El Salvador in France and Belgium.[17]

Even more important, Torres Caicedo developed from afar a continental approach to the countries in the Americas. He was among the first to coin, no later than 1856, the term of *Latin America* as a common denominator for the Hispanic, Portuguese, and French Americas. "We love our native country with passion," he said in 1864, "and yet, we consider the beautiful Latin American land as a common fatherland."[18] As a Latin American prolific writer and literary critic in Paris, he came to play an important role in the International Literary Association founded there in 1878 and led by Victor Hugo, where he projected the voice of an entire continent. He supported the idea of a Latin American Union, which he first advanced in a book with that title written in 1864, and even founded an association with that purpose in mind.[19]

Another prominent example is that of Eugenio María de Hostos y Bonilla (1839–1903). He was a native of Puerto Rico, an island under colonial Spanish rule until 1898, who envisioned a federation of Antillean nations, while settling in the Dominican Republic as an adopted homeland. He developed a body of historiography works of liberal inclination that would influence an entire younger generation of Dominican intellectuals and historians, who worked on the study of their society after 1880.

---

[17] Available at http://www.famousamericans.net/josemariatorrescaicedo/, accessed 14 June 2006.

[18] José María Torres Caicedo, *Ensayos biográficos y de crítica literaria.* París, Segunda serie, 1868, p. 274. There is uncertainty regarding the year of coining of the expression, as Torres Caicedo himself mentioned the date of 1851, but researchers have failed to corroborate this in his writings until 1856 for the first time.

[19] Arturo Ardao, *Génesis de la idea y el nombre de América Latina.* Caracas: Centro de Estudios Latinoamericanos Rómulo Gallegos, Consejo Nacional de la Cultura, 1980.

Hostos had been educated in law in Spain, a country he left in 1869, disillusioned with the lack of support of the Spanish Republicans for the independence of Puerto Rico. He did not return to his home country, however, but turned into a sort of wandering expatriate instead. He moved to New York City and became a member of the Cuban Revolutionary Junta. Shortly thereafter, he left for a four-year trip to Colombia, Peru, Chile, Argentina, and Brazil, where he campaigned for the independence of Cuba and Puerto Rico, in favor of a federation of Antillean nations and the reform of a series of evils he saw in the Americas, including the abolition of slavery.

His championing of maltreated Chinese laborers in Peru helped change public opinion, as did his hostility toward the Oruro railway project. His writings in Chile helped women gain admittance to professional schools, and his advocacy of a trans-Andean railway between Argentina and Chile resulted in its first locomotive being named after him. From 1875 to 1888, he devoted his energies to reforming the educational systems in both the Dominican Republic and Chile.[20]

As Hostos settled in the Dominican Republic in 1879, taking advantage of the ascent to power of liberal friends, he was entrusted with the launching and direction of the College of Education. For nine years, he also taught law and wrote extensively in the press, in favor of a *Confederación Antillana* that would include the three Hispanic islands of Cuba, Puerto Rico, and the Dominican Republic in Hispaniola, among other issues. He soon turned into the "maestro," the leading torch of knowledge, the person who introduced Positivism to the local cultured circles, and the leader who did much to replace the Catholic underpinnings of education in the Dominican Republic:

> Hostos conceived the intellectual's mission to be a function of the struggle against the flawed legacies of the past. In the Caribbean world this would mean overcoming forms of personal dependency and achieving self-determination.... He felt historical knowledge was used exclusively to legalize pernicious power because, in the name of progress, it exalted despots. He put forward a contrary view – that the study of history should pursue knowledge of the sources from which morality springs. Morality, being rooted in the common people.[21]

In 1888, he moved to Chile, where his influence was equally felt in the formation of educators and in law, journalism, and literature, second perhaps only to that of Venezuelan-born Andrés Bello. As Spanish rule of Puerto Rico ended in 1898, he campaigned for Puerto Rico's self-determination, founded the *Liga de Patriotas Puertorriqueños*, trying unsuccessfully to convince the U.S. government and the American administration of the island. Disillusioned with the results, he returned to Santo Domingo in 1900 and worked intensely

---

[20] Eugenio María de Hostos y Bonilla, "1839–1903 Biography," available at http://www.loc.gov/rr/hispanic/1898/hostos.html, accessed 13 June 2006.

[21] Roberto Cassá, "Historiography of the Dominican Republic," in B. W. Higman, *General History of the Caribbean, Vol. VI: Methodology and Historiography of the Caribbean*. London and Oxford: Unesco Publishing and Macmillan, 1999, pp. 395.

to improve the educational and cultural level of the country until his death in 1903, and was buried there.[22]

The 'maestro' had an enormous influence, and some of his students developed into leading historians in the early 20th century. Among them is Américo Lugo, who turned to the Hispanic foundations as the unifying force of the nation at the time of the U.S. military intervention of 1916. In the same line as Hoyos's, he saw in these foundations a "vehicle of moral and cultural opposition to imperialism." Lugo was also the most active figure in the Unión Nacional Dominicana, the group that opposed the occupation and later presided over the Partido Nacionalista. Lugo's Hispanism had a popular, democratic foundation. In Trujillo's times, this Hispanic orientation will take a conservative turn, when it becomes embedded in a state-centered approach, according to which "the people became a nation through the emergence of the state."[23]

Exile and New State Identities

Displacement had its own impact on the formation of new states. The most salient case is that of the *Banda Oriental*, the eastern shore of the Uruguay River, torn between the spheres of influence of Buenos Aires, Spain, Portuguese Brazil, and, later on, the independent Empire of Brazil. For reasons of space, we confine our analysis here to the impact of displacement in this case.

The configuration of a separate political entity in Uruguay is a relatively late development in the region. Tulio Halperin Donghi describes this process in the following terms:

Uruguay is the only neo-Spanish country whose territory was not comprised in a single colonial administrative unit. At the start of the crisis of the Spanish imperial system, jurisdiction of the lands between the Atlantic, the Plata and the Uruguay Rivers and the Portuguese borders was divided among the *Intendencia* of Buenos Aires, which had authority on the southern districts of the Eastern Bank of the Uruguay River; the military governorship of the Missions, which ruled from Yapeyú, a town later included in the Argentinean province of Corrientes, the northern districts of that same bank, as well as much larger stretches of land in what are today northeastern Argentina and southern Paraguay; and the navy governorship of Montevideo, which administered the rest.... [T]hese internal boundaries were quickly erased in the wake of the imperial breakdown.[24]

Within such a transregional reality, the action of local patriots overstepped the future boundaries of Uruguay into the littoral regions of Argentina, and the forces of imperial Brazil and republican Buenos Aires considered the East

[22] Available at http://www.rrp.upr.edu/iehostos/biografiaemh.htm, accessed 13 June 2006.
[23] Cassá, "Historiography," pp. 397–399.
[24] Tulio Halperin Donghi, "Party and Nation-State in the Construction of Collective Identities: Uruguay in the Nineteenth Century," in Roniger and Herzog, Eds., *The Collective and the Public in Latin America: Cultural Identities and Political Order*. Brighton, p. 160.

Bank of the Río de la Plata a natural battlefield for their political and military ambitions.

In 1811, supported by Buenos Aires' forces, José Gervasio Artigas led a movement against royalist rule in the Banda Oriental, the name by which Uruguay had been known. Artigas was an officer of the *Cuerpo de Blandengues* that was created by the Spanish authorities of Montevideo in 1797 as part of defensive measures in case of British or Portuguese attacks and mostly used to pacify the interior. By 1810, Artigas shifted his allegiance to the autonomous junta of the River Plate provinces led by Buenos Aires, only to soon become disillusioned and betrayed by the latter's willingness to sacrifice Oriental autonomy for the sake of its own priorities. Fearing the advance of a Portuguese intervention in the Banda Oriental – which added to the pressure of the Spanish stronghold in Alto Perú – Buenos Aires signed a treaty and armistice with Spanish Viceroy Elío stationed in Montevideo. According to the treaty signed in October 1811, Buenos Aires was to withdraw its troops and Elío would try to convince his allies, the Portuguese, to do the same. Both Buenos Aires and Montevideo agreed to unite forces to defend the River Plate region from foreign attacks, thus ensuring "the unity of the Spanish nation." Although Artigas obeyed and withdrew his forces from the siege of a weakened royalist Montevideo, this defeat was clearly perceived as resulting from Buenos Aires' diplomacy, thus leading to the disengagement of Oriental loyalties and to the birth of a sense of separate identity and goals on the part of the *Orientales*. Even if Artigas accepted the move of Buenos Aires' nominating him "Lieutenant Governor, Superior Judge, and Captain of War" of the district of Yapeyú in the territory of the Missions, he accepted it as a recognition of his election by "those worthy sons of Liberty," the Orientals. Moreover, as the patriot armies withdrew, more than 4,000 civilians (four-fifths of the population outside Montevideo) left their houses and took whatever movable goods they could carry, joining Artigas and his 4,000-strong Oriental militia in a two-month trek that would lead them to Entre Ríos, across the Uruguayan river. The massive exodus was triggered by the sound fear of Spanish reprisals and Portuguese depredations and the confidence in Artigas's leadership. Artigas preferred not to take the civilians with him, as he clearly understood that they would hamper his plans to put pressure on the Portuguese troops.[25]

Within Uruguayan historiography, this translocation – known in its time as the *Redota* (a rustic utterance for the Spanish *derrota*, or defeat) – came to be defined as the "exodus of the Oriental people," which signaled the emergence of self-determination and the consolidation of its separate identity. With the passing of time, it has been portrayed as the "national" exile of the Oriental people, unwilling to submit to foreign domination. As supporting evidence, authors cite the October 23 decision of a fleeing assembly at the shore of the

[25] John Street, *Artigas and the Emancipation of Uruguay*. Cambridge: Cambridge University Press, 1959, pp. 136–161; Oscar H. Bruschera, *Artigas*. Montevideo: Biblioteca de Marcha, 1969, pp. 89–96.

River San José, which proclaimed Artigas as their leader and the decision to follow him beyond the Oriental territory, so as to maintain their liberty rather than submitting to the rule of Spain or Portugal. This historic moment, known in Uruguay as the exile to the Ayui camp, has been captured in the memories of Ansina, Artigas's aid, in which verses narrate how they went into exile to save their freedom and the republican ideology.[26]

In 1817, the Oriental province fell to the hands of the Portuguese, who imprisoned many patriot leaders. Of these, several were taken as prisoners to Brazil, such as Manuel Artigas (José's brother, who died shortly after returning to Montevideo in 1822), José Antonio Berdún (who was held in different places in Brazil for four years), and Juan José Aguiar (sent to Rio in 1822 as a political deportee and who managed to return to Montevideo only in 1846, during Oribe's siege). Many others crossed to Buenos Aires and to the adjacent littoral provinces, especially to Entre Ríos. Such migration would continue throughout the years of Portuguese and Brazilian rule. José Artigas left the Uruguayan territory in 1820 to get help for his cause. But, in Buenos Aires he was considered an enemy because he was declared a traitor in 1814 when he withdrew from another siege on Montevideo, intending to spread his influence to the other provinces of the Littoral of the great rivers of Paraná and Uruguay. After being defeated by the forces of Buenos Aires, he signed a truce with the Unitarians of Buenos Aires in February 1820, which was denounced by his lieutenants, the Littoral *caudillos* Estanislao López of Santa Fé and Francisco Ramírez of Corrientes. Shortly after, in August, he requested asylum from Paraguayan dictator Gaspar Rodríguez de Francia and moved to Paraguay in late September 1820. According to Juan Stefanich, Artigas was the first case of an exile in Latin America because he fits the description of a political asylee, because Rodríguez de Francia denied his extradition to Ramírez and provided for all his material needs.[27] Opinions are divided in respect to Artigas's intentions when he crossed to Paraguay. Francia's secretary, Martínez, claimed on the basis of his meetings with Artigas that his original intention was to gather forces there and return to fight with the help of the Paraguayan leader.[28] Artigas had also received an offer of asylum from the Portuguese and the North Americans, who were willing to grant him an allowance to live comfortably in exile. While in Paraguay, Rodríguez de Francia granted him ample economic assistance, land, and clothing but never consented to meet with him in person and did not allow him to leave Paraguay.[29] Rodríguez de Francia may have been motivated by the fact that in 1822 he discovered that in 1815, Artigas

---

[26] Juan Edmundo Miller, *Artigas el Profeta*. Montevideo: Impresora Uruguaya, 1964, pp. 19–25.

[27] Juan Stefanich, "Artigas, Francia y el Paraguay," in *Artigas*. Montevideo: Instituto Histórico y Geográfico del Uruguay, 1952, p. 393.

[28] Daniel Hammerly Duppuy, "Rasgos biográficos de Artigas en el Paraguay," in *Artigas*. Montevideo: Ediciones de El Pais, 1951, p. 288; Miller, *Artigas el Profeta*, p. 149; Antonio Ramos, "El refugio de Artigas en el Paraguay," in *Artigas*. Montevideo: Instituto Histórico y Geográfico del Uruguay, 1952, p. 438.

[29] Duppuy, "Rasgos," p. 288; Ramos, "El refugio," p. 438; Miller, *Artigas el Profeta*, p. 149.

had participated in a conspiracy led by the latter's friend, Fulgencio Yegros, to overthrow Rodríguez de Francia. The Paraguayan leader believed that Artigas participated and had planned to invade Paraguay and decapitate him. This was seen as part of Artigas's plans to encourage a federal democratic revolt in the framework of a Federal League.[30] Accordingly, although Artigas was protected and supported materially, he was kept in isolation, as Rodríguez de Francia feared his political influence in Paraguay.[31] Artigas experienced exile as a lonely man, living only with the company of his aid Ansina and his dog Charrúa. He stayed in Paraguay, in relative isolation, until his death in 1850.

In exile, Artigas went through different phases. At first, he continued to draw great projects of political democracy but, as time passed, he adapted and became resigned to his situation, shifting to help the local poor and dedicating his days to a simple life working on the farm he was given. When advanced in age, he naturally turned to health worries.[32] In later stages, after Francia's death, he could have returned to Uruguay, but desisted. Indeed, in 1841, Rivera, then president of Uruguay, offered him financial help for his return. He decided to stay in Paraguay. According to his aid, Ansina, he did not wish to return until the formation of the Great America. In addition, Artigas did not want to interfere with the internal affairs in Uruguay, then torn by civil war.[33]

Artigas is perhaps the most well known of Uruguayan exiles, but his case is far from being unique. When, in 1822, after a period of anarchy, the Brazilian Empire prevailed and the territory became its Cisplatine province, many took the route of translocation. After his plots against Brazilian rule were discovered, Juan Antonio Lavalleja escaped to Entre Ríos and in 1824 arrived in Buenos Aires, where more than 100 chiefs and officers of Oriental origin had migrated. Among them were figures such as Gabriel Antonio Pereira (who in 1825 became a member of the first provisional government) and Manuel Oribe, who had moved to Buenos Aires in 1817 with his son Ignacio, Rufino Bauzá, and two battalions. By 1821, Oribe was back in the Banda Oriental, supporting the royalist Portuguese against the Empire, but as the Brazilian Empire prevailed, he left again. Many others were imprisoned but managed to escape, finding their way to Buenos Aires (e.g., Juan Francisco Giró, Benito Blanco, José Antonio Berdún). Manuel Freire, brought to trial along with Pantaleón Artigas by the Portuguese authorities in 1823, left the country, joining Lavalleja's troops in Buenos Aires.

The lives of many of these patriots are marked by translocation and transience. For instance, Lucas José Obes, who acted as representative of the Cisplatine province in Rio, escaped from the court in 1826, joining the patriot cause. The government of Buenos Aires was suspicious of him and confined

---

[30] Duppuy, "Rasgos," pp. 287–288.
[31] Ibid., pp. 292–293.
[32] Ibid., p. 289.
[33] Miller, *Artigas el Profeta*, p. 26. On Artigas, see also Alfredo R. Castellanos, *Vida de Artigas*. Montevideo: Medina Editor, 1954; Street, *Artigas and the Emancipation*; Juan Zorilla de San Martín, *La Epopeya de Artigas*. Montevideo: Biblioteca Artigas, 1963, vol. IV.

MAP 3. Early circuits of exile.

him to the city of Buenos Aires. In 1828, when the Republic was established, he returned to Uruguay, where he held high-rank positions until Oribe deposed him in 1836, under the suspicion of being a Riverista. He then went back to Rio, where he led a modest life until his death a few months later. Others, such as the priests Pedro Vidal, José Catalá y Codina, Lázaro Gadea, and Zenón Piedra in March 1824, were given an order of *destierro* and thus were forced to leave their country.

Lavalleja commanded the *Treinta y Tres*, who disembarked in 1825 to organize the uprising of the Banda Oriental. The task force was composed of

Oriental émigrés who had made their way to Buenos Aires during the previous years: Manuel Oribe, Santiago Gadea (an Artiguist who had moved to Entre Ríos with the Portuguese occupation), Manuel Freire, and others. Lavalleja's expedition led to war between Argentina, which sent military support to the Banda, and Brazil. In the patriot army sponsored by Argentina, there were many other Oriental émigrés, such as Juan Francisco Giró, who thus was able to return to the Banda in 1826.

Politics of Exit

In the decades after independence, lack of stability and authoritarian personal rule characterized many of these American polities. *Destierro, ostracismo*, and expulsions of political opponents were widely used. Still, we cannot talk yet of exile in 20th-century terms. The lack of polyarchic political dynamics did not allow the lawful return of the translocated individuals to their homeland. In its stead, the expelled individuals could hope to return only when political fortune favored their parties. On change of government – basically shifts in the ruling groups – the returning party adopted the same modes of exclusion from which they had suffered before. This in spite of higher levels of institutional consolidation, the politics of exit prevailed on a politics of voice and opening. Thus, even in Brazil, where imperial continuity contributed to the attainment of relative stability earlier than in most Spanish-American states, exile was the lot of many of its leading statesmen. To name but some of the most prominent: José Bonifacio, a key figure of Brazilian independence and an early ally of Pedro I, was forced to leave Brazil for exile in Europe (1823–1829) because of his disagreements with the emperor. Joaquim Nabuco, leader of the abolitionist movement, had to choose expatriation following the reaction to his ideas in the early 1880s. Gaspar Silveira Martins had to leave for two years to Europe because of his monarchist leaning, once Pedro II abdicated in 1889. Similar was the fate of Affonso Celso de Assis Figueiredo, the Viscount of Ouro Preto, the head of the last Council of Ministers of Imperial Brazil.[34] This trend, evident in Brazil, was even more notorious in the Spanish-American states. With independence, *destierro, ostracismo*, and expulsion, which during the Colony had basically been used for social and administrative purposes, became major political weapons in the hands of the political elites.

Four basic elements contributed to the configuration of such politics of exit in the newly constituted states. First, political structures were extremely fragile and, therefore, political fighting could lead to pervading violence or disarticulation of the polity in the form of civil war. The authoritarian trends existing in

---

[34] "Dom Pedro off for Lisbon"; "The Emperor doomed for perpetual exile." *New York Times*, 18 November 1889. Available at http://nyt.com/mem/archive-free, accessed 13 April 2008; Osvaldo Orico, *Confissões do exilio JK*. Rio de Janeiro: Francisco Alves, 1977. See also Maria de Lourdes and Monaco Janotti, "The Monarchist Response to the Beginnings of the Brazilian Republic," *The Americas*, 48, 2 (1991): 223–243.

these societies made it very difficult, and often impossible, to envision a state of coexistence between political opponents. Political leaderships were conceived as central in situations in which parties in the modern sense did not exist and political groups coalesced around personalities. Leading political actors and elites could not conceive the likelihood of central figures who held power retiring from politics. In the incipient public spheres of the new independent states, these central figures assumed 'gigantic stature' in the popular imaginary, to an extent that they were expected by others to continue playing a central role in the political sphere. Willing to suppress open confrontations, and fearing civil war, ruling elites opted to 'export' their political opponents as a major mechanism of stability and control. The lack of early institutional development of guarantees for civil and political rights and for citizenship basically left the decision of expulsion to the good judgment of the executive, which used it extensively. Consequently, leading figures of independence opted to become expatriates rather than become enmeshed in internal fighting in the homeland.

Second, in the struggle that followed the dismemberment of the Spanish-American empire, many soldiers of many lands fought for independence far beyond their homeland or rather pursued a conception of homeland far larger and more inclusive than later definitions would encompass in terms of states and nation-states. Important Latin American leaders were viewed with gratitude and seen as 'national' heroes or denigrated and seen with suspicion in the new countries in which they had fought and sometimes established themselves.

Third, there was a lack of clear-cut boundaries and territorial definitions that prompted the back-and-forth moves of natives from one territory to another, and a struggle between those following a localized vision of political autonomy and those with a broader (and even continental) conception of pan-Latin-Americanism. Various regional clusters of historically related territories emerged, which, in terms of politics of banishment, created centers of territorial attraction and expulsion. Among them, the cluster of Chile–Argentina–Bolivia–Peru, the cluster of Paraguay–Argentina–Uruguay–Brazil, the cluster of Venezuela–Caribbean Islands–Colombia–Ecuador, the cluster of Mexico–Central America–the Caribbean–the United States, and, in addition, Europe as a continuing pole of attraction for the whole region.

Fourth, because the crystallization of the new states did not preclude overlapping territorial claims, the political class of each region continued to exercise high measures of influence on neighboring countries. They intervened in the configuration of the other country's political factions, according to their own interests. When the faction they sided with found itself defeated, they often hastily accepted the vanquished political actors in their territory, hosting them, and even supporting their plans of return. They acted in such a manner to regain control of their neighboring political scene or at least exercise their influence by strengthening sympathetic political allies. When the defeated faction was inimical to their political script or design, they could still host the expelled individuals and control their freedom of action, so as to curtail their possibilities of plotting against the ruling government in the neighboring country.

This remained a persistent trend of Ibero-American politics. As late as August 1987, when the leaders of Costa Rica, El Salvador, Honduras, Guatemala, and Nicaragua met in Guatemala City to sign the Arias Plan, aimed at bringing the Sandinistas and the Contras to negotiate a cease-fire and allow democratic elections in Nicaragua, they explicitly incorporated a clause formulated to ban a government's support of rebel forces in adjoining nations.

4

Sites of Exile

Gentle homeland, receive the vows,
Which Chile swore on your altars:
That you either be the tomb of the free
Or the asylum from oppression
    From Chile's national anthem[1]

Although for centuries Latin America received waves of conquerors, colonizers, slaves, and immigrants, it has been also characterized by varied forms of translocation and expatriation, ostracism and relegation, displacement and exile. Persecuted for political reasons, or fearing for their integrity and safety, individuals have been displaced within their countries or forced to move beyond their borders. This chapter analyzes some of the major sites or *lieux d'exil* chosen by the exiles under constrained circumstances.

Selecting Factors

Studies of internal and international migration have identified a series of strategies and chain factors, shaping the waves of transnational migration.[2]

---

[1] These lines of the chorus ("Dulce Patria, recibe los votos/con que Chile en tus aras juró: /Que o la tumba serás de los libres/o el asilo contra la opresión") were written in 1819 by Bernardo de Vera y Pintado, commissioned by Bernardo O'Higgins. De Vera y Pintado (1780–1827) was a Chilean patriot, born in Santa Fe (now a province of Argentina). He moved before independence to Chile and became part of the Chilean political and intellectual elite, in addition to having served as the first diplomatic representative of the Buenos Aires junta in Santiago de Chile.

[2] P. Krishnan and D. Odynak, "A Generalization of Petersen's Typology of Migration." *International Migration* 25, 4 (1987): 385–397; Aristide Zolberg, "The Next Waves: Migration Theory for a Changing World." *International Migration Review* 23, 3 (1989): 403–427; James T. Fawcett, "Networks, linkages, and migration systems." *International Migration Review* 23, 3 (1989): 671–680; Douglas S. Massey, Joaquín Arango, Graeme Hugo, Ali Kouaouci, Adela Pellegrino, and J. Edward Taylor, "Theories of International Migration: A Review and Appraisal." *Population and Development Review*, 19, 3 (1993): 431–466; S. Vertovec and

The dynamic highlighted by these studies also operates in exile, shaping the constrained choices of the persecuted. There is, however, a major difference between voluntary migration and forced relocation. The harsher the persecution, the fewer the options prospective exiles have in selecting a site of asylum. Of particular weight is the immediate or protracted need to escape for one's life. Lack of time and urgency often override other considerations.

There is another significant difference between an undocumented person who, escaping armed persecution, jumps the fence of an embassy to save his or her life and an individual who, sensing persecution, has the time and resources to evaluate alternative routes of escape and asylum and whether and when to leave the home country. And yet, any such decision involves in an unavoidable way the interplay among the expelling circumstances, personal background, and resources, and finally, the receptiveness and attractiveness of the host countries in terms of distance, climate, language, and institutional support as well as economic, professional, and educational opportunities.

Among the personal factors that affect displacement are the personal resources and the human and social capital of the persecuted individual. These include the contacts and networks held abroad and the capacity for enacting them in dire times. Particularly salient among the structural factors are the policies of possible host countries and their variable implementation by diplomats on the spot; along with the support or lack of support provided by transnational organizations, networks of solidarity, and various NGOs. Furthermore, exile communities, networks of *émigrés*, and diasporas may facilitate the access and integration of the newcomers.

These factors interact with one another and vary from case to case. In each case, the interplay of factors creates a highly variable picture, even within waves of displaced individuals from the same country. Although it is therefore hard to generalize, we may suggest some trends reflected in many cases, even if not universally present: the selection of host country is performed under situational constraints and time pressure. Being forced to move away from one's place of residence is conditioned by factors on the ground, most of which are beyond the control of the future exile. For instance, the willingness or reticence of an ambassador to grant asylum on the embassy grounds may determine how many individuals reach a certain host country instead of others. Similarly, the urgency created by impending repression usually determines the fact that individuals will look for the fastest and easiest way of getting out of such a situation. People belonging to political organizations and parties have been more prone to rely on the decisions made by these organizations, whether to go underground, leave politics, or leave the country. Finally, familial constraints such as the possibility or impossibility of leaving relatives behind also factor into the likelihood of escaping into exile.

R. Cohen, Eds., *Migrations, Diasporas and Transnationalism*. Cheltenham, UK: Elgar, 1999; Thomas Faist, *The Volume and Dynamics of International Migration and Transnational Social Spaces*. Oxford: Oxford University Press, 2000; Danièle Jolly, *International Migration in the New Millenium*. London: Ashgate, 2004.

Even if the decision to leave the home country is forced on the exile, the move abroad opens windows of opportunity. Major sites of exile are those in which the exiles are faced with greater alternatives, both of integration and of continuation of previous life projects and political activity. By opening these theoretically available options, these sites of exile exert their lure on the newcomers and yet pose dilemmas that eventually force them to make choices. These choices are set along a continuum that on the one hand imply being politically involved in the plight for defeating the rulers in the home country but, on the other, may lead the exile to part ranks with fellow co-nationals and integrate into the host society. Under this pull, exiles are forced to rethink past choices and identities as they orient themselves toward the future. The longer the exile, the harder these choices become.

With these factors in mind, we analyze hereafter how certain places became recurrent sites of exile, both in early and recent times. Among these poles of attraction since independence were Paris throughout the 19th and 20th centuries, Santiago and cities such as Valparaíso and Copiapó in Chile and Montevideo in the 1830s and 1840s, Mexico and Caracas in the 20th century, Argentina in general and Buenos Aires in particular for Paraguayan exiles in the 20th century, and the United States for those already coming from Cuba in the 19th and early 20th centuries, but particularly after the Revolution. Costa Rica stands out as a site of exile in Central America. Individuals from places as different as Cuba, Chile, and Nicaragua, among others, have found refuge in that country since the late 19th century and in the 20th, especially after the 1948 civil war. In the following sections, we have chosen to analyze several such major sites of exile.

We begin by analyzing the case of Chile, which became an early pole of attraction for exiles within South America at the beginning of the 19th century, a position that it reclaimed in the second half of the 20th century by offering asylum to many victims of political persecution until the onset of military rule in 1973. Next we look at Paris, a city that played a key role in terms of relocation in Europe. We finally discuss the role of postrevolutionary Mexico as a site of exile, in connection with its élan of hospitality, with contrasting effects on the reception of political and intellectual exiles from South America and poor and uneducated refugees and migrants arriving from Central America.

Early Asylum in the Americas: Chile as a Site of Exile

Chile was one of the first new states to stabilize its polity under the aegis of Diego Portales. Portales, who served in various ministerial capacities until his assassination in 1837, was behind the stabilization of the Chilean version of conservative republicanism. It was in this period that the 1833 Constitution was drafted. This document provided an institutional framework for nearly a century. For three decades, beginning in 1831, former generals became civilian presidents and used the authoritarian and conservative but still democratic constitution to build strong powers, military strength, governmental institutions, and economic conditions that were also favorable to the exiles. All this made

Chile, even in the first part of the 19th century, into an island of stability within the Latin American sea of turmoil and civil wars.

The Chilean governments were able to subdue internal rebellions, to defeat the external enemies of the country in the war against the Peruvian–Bolivian Confederation led by Marshall Andrés Santa Cruz, and overcome the tensions with Argentinean neighbors, avoiding war. In terms of internal politics, the governments of Presidents Joaquín Prieto (1831–1841), Manuel Bulnes (1841–1851), and Manuel Montt (1851–1861) supported a policy of translocation of political enemies. Thus, for instance, in the 1830s, General Freire and his supporters were expelled to Peru, from where they tried – with the support of Santa Cruz – to organize forces to recover power in Chile. Manuel Montt, as minister of the Interior of Bulnes, closed down some of the opposition's newspapers and sent members of the opposition into exile.[3] Perhaps Chile's insularity preserved the Spanish precedents of banishment almost intact. Even as late as in the penal code of 1874, Chile recognized various forms of institutional exclusion: *confinamiento* [penal transportation], *relegación* [banishment to an isolated locality], *destierro* [expulsion from the national territory], and *extrañamiento* [exile to a foreign country chosen by the individual].[4]

While it expelled its own opposition forces, at the same time, Chile became a haven for exiles coming from Argentina, Peru, and Bolivia, as well as attracting other Latin Americans because of its stability and prosperity, which were factors of comparative advantage. It seems as if the adage "the enemies of my enemies are my friends" was valid in many of the cases of exile of neighboring countries in Chile. This goes beyond humanitarian considerations, which some of the exiles who found refuge in Chile suggested was essential. For instance, Domingo Faustino Sarmiento eloquently claimed that "Great and noble is the people that gave asylum so generously to those who were until yesterday its more stubborn enemies." On a similar note, Guillermo Billinghurst wrote in a private letter that "in giving protection to refugees [*asilados*], especially the Argentineans, Chile acted with a generosity without precedent or later equivalent."[5]

Argentineans were well received in the 1830s and 1840s on the basis of what was considered a national debt of Chile, owed to those who fought for independence. In this dimension, the name of San Martín always appeared as

---

[3] Ivan Jaksic, "Sarmiento and the Chilean Press, 1841–51," in Tulio Halperin Donghi, Ivan Jaksic, Gwen Kirkpatrick, and Francine Masiello, Eds., *Sarmiento: Author of a Nation*. Berkeley: University of California Press, 1994, p. 33.

[4] "The offenses covered vary from adultery (in the case of the woman taken in adultery) and the ringing of bells to arouse the populace against constituted authority, for which local exile is provided, to such grave political offenses as starting a civil war or restraining the legal president from the due exercise of his functions. Only in these more serious cases could the penalty be foreign exile for as much as twenty years." Robert G. Caldwell, "Exile as an Institition." *Political Science Quarterly*, 58, 2 (1943): 254.

[5] Francisco Encina, *Historia de Chile*. Santiago: Editoral Nascimento, 1949, vol. XII, p. 603.

Liberator and was often deliberately used by the exiles to elicit sympathy for their fate under the rule of Juan Manuel de Rosas in Buenos Aires.[6]

With its long and permeable borders and a stable and prosperous economy, Chile attracted people from the neighboring countries seeking asylum and a decent job. Chilean local authorities were lenient toward foreigners, especially if they were professionals and were able to supply local market demands and development priorities. For Argentinean exiles, Santiago and Chilean society looked like a backwater. In reference to Chile, Quiroga Rosas wrote to Juan Bautista Alberdi in 1841, "This society is feudality itself. Its backwardness, it is the Spain of Cervantes."[7] This enabled the exiles to gain clout and at the same time generated jealousy in a relatively short time. As Victorino Lastarria expressed it,

This was a new and exciting scene for the youth of our learned society. They, who did not dare to express their opinions in the press, partly out of fear for the ire of the authorities, partly due to the lack of periodicals, and partly due to lack of practice, felt dazzled by the audacity and temerity of the Argentineans who did not fear to pose the most difficult political problems without consulting with anybody and even when risking their own interests. The elegant pose and the notorious culture of the sons of the [Río de la] Plata caused a great deal of jealousy, which they themselves provoked and produced by stressing the narrowness of our literary knowledge and opaque spirits, which the most distinguished of our youth owed to their routine education.[8]

One of the reactions of the Chileans toward the flamboyant attitudes of many Argentinean exiles was to ridicule both them and their country of origin. A major figure in this trend was José Joaquín Vallejos, who signed his satirical articles in *El Mercurio* as Jotabeche. Sarmiento suggested that he discontinue such attacks:

I begged Mr. Jotabeche to take into consideration that two thousand Argentineans, victims of terrible evils and who suffered from his writings live in Chile. It is a duty to offer hospitality to those who fell out of grace; it is not their fault if He does not see in the Argentinean Republic but madness and matters of farce.[9]

Settling in the capital of the country and in Valparaíso or Copiapó, the main areas of economic development, the most prominent exiles worked as journalists, lawyers, and teachers. The combination of the interests of the exiles and those of the host country in receiving individuals capable of contributing to local development enabled the flow of seekers of political asylum and economic opportunities, contributing to the establishment of communities of exiles and others. Chilean authorities took advantage of the skills and

[6] C. Galán Moreno, *Radiografía de Sarmiento*. Buenos Aires: Editorial Claridad, 1961, p. 63.

[7] Jorge Mayer, *Alberdi y su tiempo*. Buenos Aires: EUDEBA, 1963, p. 303.

[8] Domingo Amunátegui, *El progreso intelectual y político de Chile*. Santiago: Editorial Nascimento, 1936, p. 65.

[9] Galán Moreno, *Radiografía de Sarmiento*, p. 79.

professional level of the newcomers to benefit their drive for economic development and encouragement of education, culture, and science.

Paradigmatic was the case of Gabriel Ocampo, a jurist and politician born in Argentina, who, after finishing his academic studies in 1819, moved to Santiago de Chile. In 1822, he was elected to the Congress in the Colchagua province. He was commissioned with reforming the Chilean Legal Code, a task that he carried out with success. In 1826, Ocampo moved to Montevideo and the following year to Buenos Aires, where he was appointed attorney general. As he opposed Rosas, his house was assaulted in December 1838, and, in order to save his life, he had to leave the country and set sail on a French boat headed to Chile. Once there, he settled permanently and played an important role in the structuring of the local legal system until his death in 1882. He participated in 1852 in the reform of the Civil Code and later authored the Chilean Code of Commerce, considered to be his masterpiece. Ocampo is only one of many individuals who, while in Chile, contributed significantly to the country that offered them a shelter from the turmoil in the sister-regions from which they had escaped.

Strangely enough, the exiles from Argentina, mostly of liberal background and ideas, became rapidly linked to the conservative ruling elite once in Chile, praising the latter's policies. On the one hand, they may have wanted to erase the bad image that Rosas and his propaganda wanted to disseminate. They showed that they were not 'troublemakers' as depicted by the ruler of Buenos Aires. On the other hand, Chilean liberals did not pose a realistic alternative to the conservative model. Despite Chile's conservative character, from an economic and cultural point of view, the ruling elites of Chile were strong modernizers and therefore close in spirit to those following the liberal credo in the Río de la Plata. In this context, the case of Vicente Fidel López is worth mentioning. Originally from Córdoba, he went into exile in Chile. Early in the 1840s, he and Sarmiento launched their famous polemics in Chile, defending Romanticism and a renovated Hispanic-American language against the followers of Andrés Bello. The important Chilean intellectual, José Victorino Lastarria, shared their philosophical views on history, which were influenced by Chateaubriand, Cousin, and Guizot. They turned away from the strict rationalism of the Enlightenment, attempting instead to define the 'soul' or the 'spirit' behind historical events. Together with Alberdi, Sarmiento, and other young Argentinean militants in Chile, López found in that country's government an admirable model of constitutional authoritarianism. This system, supported by the socioeconomic elites, seemed to work on behalf of civil reforms, the moral improvement of the masses, and material progress.[10]

López and others demonstrated a contradictory ideological baggage: With eminently conservative social values, they were to become the leaders of Argentina's liberal transformation after the fall of Rosas. Their early ideals

---

[10] William H. Katra, *The Argentine Generation of 1837*. London: Associated University Press, 1996, p. 86.

anticipated the conservative brand of liberalism that was to predominate in Argentina well into the next century. By the time Julio Argentino Roca came to power in 1880, Alberdi, Sarmiento, Mitre, and López – all of whom had returned from exile – agreed about the most important Argentinean issues. They took solace in the fact that their society's direction was firmly in the hands of a small elite, whose conservative social and political ideas generally coincided with the perceptions they gained in Chile. William Katra concludes that, whereas previously their criticism targeted the closed system of localism perpetuated by the *caudillos*, now they could applaud the acceptance of a liberal, cosmopolitan, pro-European outlook by the social elites who combined a conservative social vision and a liberal profession of faith.[11]

While in Chile, when the exiles took positions contrary to the host government, they were immediately expelled from the country, as was the case of Bartolomé Mitre, later president of Argentina (1862–1868). Mitre had purchased the newspaper *El Comercio* of Valparaíso, placed it at the disposal of those who opposed the election of Manuel Montt, and supported the liberal uprising of 1851. He was expelled for "disseminating subversive ideas."[12] That is, exiles were welcome as long as they did not interfere in Chilean internal politics or as long as they sided with the rulers in power. This form of institutionalized exclusion relied paradoxically on the Law of Freedom of the Press dating from 1828 that sanctioned four restrictions to what could be published: blasphemy, immorality, libel, and sedition. The most serious of the preceding crimes was sedition, which could be punished with up to four years of exile or imprisonment. As typical of a hierarchical society, these punishments could be commuted for fines, thus clearly differentiating between those who could or could not afford the monetary payment.[13]

Because of the transnational character of politics in the early stages of independent life, in which international borders were not an absolute hindrance to intervention in the neighboring countries, a situation emerged in which states envisaged the possibility of using exiles actually and in the future to forward their territorial claims and interests. While in exile in Chile, Sarmiento supported the Chilean claims of sovereignty of the Magellan Straits, as part of his antagonism to Rosas. According to Chilean historian Francisco Encina, this kind of transnational concerns probably influenced the decisions of Chilean politicians in their policies toward exiles between 1843 and 1879.[14]

Various waves of exiles reached Chile in these decades. The largest group of exiles consisted of the Argentineans escaping from Rosas' dictatorship, and arriving from the provinces of Cuyo, and from Buenos Aires and Montevideo.

[11] Katra, *Argentine Generation*, p. 300.
[12] Tulio Halperin Donghi, *Proyecto y construcción de una nación*. Caracas: Biblioteca Ayacucho, 1980, p. 500.
[13] Ivan Jaksic, "Sarmiento and the Chilean Press, 1841–1851," in *Sarmiento, Author of a Nation*, pp. 35–36.
[14] Encina, *Historia de Chile*, p. 605.

In 1833, a fraction of the federalists rebelled against Rosas and suffered defeat. The vanquished, known as the *Lomos negros* [black backs] were expelled – turned *proscriptos* – and went into exile, mostly in Montevideo and some of them in Chile. Many others arrived in Chile in the early 1840s, after a series of other failed attempts to overthrow Rosas. Some of these exiles belonged to the so-called Generation of 1837 in Argentina, who had fled to Montevideo and some of them subsequently to Chile.[15]

The fate of the exiles in Chile was highly diverse. Some of them used their competitive advantages to obtain positions either in the Chilean public administration or in the press. Such was the case of Juan Bautista Alberdi, who was paid for writing articles in *El Mercurio* on his arrival in April 1844; he later decided to revalidate his title of lawyer and obtain afterward a public job in Concepción. Although the material conditions of life were rather squalid, Alberdi adapted and moved to Valparaíso, where he became partner in a law firm, conspicuously improving his economic situation. Similarly, Sarmiento – who later was president of Argentina (1868–1874) – came to Chile for a second exile in 1840 and also suffered materially before he managed to become a well-known journalist and friend of Manuel Montt.

A different pattern of exile and integration into Chile is that of individuals who had played prominent roles in their home societies, such as Colombians Juan García del Río and Tomás Cipriano de Mosquera; Uruguayan Juan Carlos Gómez; and Venezuelans Luis López Méndez, Francisco Michelena, and Andrés Bello.

The case of Bello is emblematic. After having left his homeland of Venezuela for Europe as a secretary of a diplomatic mission, he resided in England as a representative of his home government and of Bolívar himself, who at this stage admired him and called him "my tutor and guide" [*mi maestro*]. Relationships deteriorated after Bello did not receive due payment, and Bolívar's influence could not work in his favor when the Liberator was engaged in a power struggle with Santander. As Bello had often declared his monarchical beliefs, his ideas stood in dire contradiction to the republican beliefs in Venezuela.[16] Whether the clash of visions or the lack of opportunities precluded Bello from returning to Venezuela, in 1829 he settled in Chile. After fulfilling a series of roles in

---

[15] The Argentinean group in Montevideo was by far larger than that in Chile, with assessments ranging around 30,000 souls, many of them exiles escaping Rosas. Among them were Miguel Cané, Andrés Lamas, Gervasio Posadas, José Mármol, Esteban Echeverría, Florencio Varela, and Valentín Alsina, who would later play an important role in the future of their home society. Comparatively, in Chile, one of the exiles, Benjamín Villafañe, estimated the number of Argentineans as 10,000. The large number of exiles in both Chile and Montevideo during this period was due to a situation in which prison, exile, or death threatened those opposed to Rosas, as depicted by Félix Luna. William H. Katra, *The Argentine Generation of 1837*. Luna, *Historia*, vol. 5, p. 202.

[16] "[Limited] monarchy is the only form of government that suits us," he said. In Domingo Amunategui, *El progreso intelectual y político de Chile*. Santiago: Editorial Nascimento, 1936, p. 44.

the Ministry of Finance and the Ministry of Foreign Affairs, his stature within
Chile grew. But even within conservative circles, his monarchical ideas isolated
him. He thus moved to the domain of culture and higher education, founding
the University of Chile and contributing to the elaboration of the legal codes
of the country.

Similarly, journalist and politician Juan Carlos Gómez arrived in Chile after
opposing *caudillismo* in his home country, Uruguay. He found *caudillismo*
irreconcilable with a civil society, and so he opposed any military ruler, such
as Artigas, Rivera, or Flores. Born to a Portuguese immigrant in 1820, when
he was 23, he was forced to leave for Brazil during the siege of Montevideo. In
Brazil, his liberal ideas earned him a decree of expulsion, and in 1845 he had to
seek refuge in Chile, where he stayed for seven years. Taking residence in Valparaíso, he collaborated on various newspapers and became a renowned publicist, like Alberdi and Mitre. He succeeded Sarmiento as editor of *El Mercurio
de Valparaíso*, always defending the cause of freedom, with no regard for
parties or governments.[17] Gómez enriched the host country with his ideas
of political culture, constitutional rule, and public development. In 1852, he
crossed through Argentina on his way back to his homeland, Uruguay.

The exiles from Peru and Bolivia constitute a third pattern. In this case, their
presence in Chile was conceived as short term and served as a time to prepare
military operations aimed at regaining power in the homeland. The Chileans
who were going to confront Marshall Andrés Santa Cruz in the war against the
Peruvian–Bolivian Confederation were very supportive of these activities on
three accounts. First, they incorporated the exiles' support, enhancing Chilean
military capabilities. Second, they 'tamed' those who would become rulers
after the demise of Santa Cruz. That is, they rallied the future support and
goodwill of these exiles toward the Chilean government and Chilean interests.[18]
Finally, the Chilean government benefited politically from a very active group
of Peruvian exiles, who were highly vocal in their opposition to Santa Cruz
and the Confederation, tilting Chilean public opinion in the direction of war.

The press and publicist activities were also a center of feverish activity for
the exiles coming from the Argentinean territories. Carlos Tejedor published
El Progreso, which, together with *El Heraldo Argentino*, was the spearhead of
a strong anti-Rosas press in Chile.[19]

Inner divisions, public confrontations, and private quarrels characterized
the various groups of exiles. Among the Peruvians and Bolivians, three factions worked against one another. Some supported former President Agustín
Gamarra, who was seen with diffidence by the Chileans. Others sided with
his vice-president, Antonio Gutiérrez de La Fuente, and a third group was led

---

[17] José María Fernández Saldaña, *Diccionario Uruguayo de Biografías*. Montevideo: Editorial
   Amerindia, 1945, p. 583.
[18] Jorge Basadre, *Historia de la República del Perú*. Lima: Editorial Cultura Antártica, 1949, vol. 1,
   p. 184.
[19] Carlos Tejedor had arrived in Chile after serving three years in Rosas' prisons.

by Felipe Pardo and Manuel Ignacio de Vivanco. Argentineans were a more compact group, although not lacking in friction in terms of their opposition to a powerful enemy, Rosas. When General Juan Lavalle organized a revolt from Montevideo against Rosas in 1840, Commander Gregorio Aráoz de Lamadrid – who was exiled in Chile – joined the campaign in Mendoza. As they suffered defeat, General Gregorio Las Heras and Sarmiento crossed into Argentina to rescue the survivors of the battle of Rodeo del Medio. Among those who reached Chile were Chacho Peñaloza, the actor Casacubierta, and General Lamadrid himself. Thanks to Sarmiento's influence with Manuel Montt, the exiles were welcomed into Chile. When in 1842 Peñaloza organized a second ride against Rosas in northern Argentina, he was defeated in Tucumán and he withdrew back to Chile. Anti-Rosas activities did not preclude divisions and frictions among Argentinean exiles in Chile, some of them of a rather menial nature, as judged from the distance of years. For example, while writing for the prestigous *El Mercurio*, Sarmiento introduced grammatical changes into the Spanish script, which were eliminated by its editor Alberdi with the support of Andrés Bello, who was a purist of the Spanish language and despised Sarmiento's romanticism. This scholarly dispute opened a rift that was reinforced by the opposing political views of federalist Alberdi and unitarian Sarmiento.

The journalist and publicizing activity of the Argentineans against Rosas in Chile was intense and became a source of friction between the government of Chile and Rosas', especially under the presidency of Manuel Bulnes. Articles signed by Mitre, Vicente Fidel López, Sarmiento, and Alberdi were extremely harsh with the dictator of Buenos Aires. For his part, Rosas was unable to silence the exiles:

The pampa and the Andes separated Buenos Aires and Santiago. . . . In addition, Rosas did not have an imperialist policy and had many internal problems. This left him no time to deal with the exiles. Rosas had [also] serious problems with Santa Cruz and with the foreign powers.[20]

When Rosas decided to get rid of political opposition, he could not imagine that so many of them would remain active while abroad and generate intense political propaganda against himself and politics. Since 1846, *El Mercurio* had been edited by Alberdi, an exile, who also wrote the *Bases y puntos de partida para la organización política de la República Argentina*, which became the institutional script for the enacting of the Argentinean Constitution of 1853. Sarmiento wrote one of the main anti-*caudillist* works, *Facundo*, in which the historical analysis of the figure of the *caudillo* Facundo Quiroga was a critical indictment of the Rosas regime in general and a call to defeat barbarism in the name of (European-like) civilization. A few years later, the activities by Sarmiento and the others provoked mounted protest by the representatives of Rosas in Santiago. Manuel Montt, although sympathetic to the exiles and

[20] Francisco Encina, *Historia de Chile*, vol. XII, p. 604.

their contribution to Chile's development and culture, felt he had to restrain Sarmiento and finally offered him a study mission to Europe and the United States, in order to appease the Argentineans.

In this period, Chile was a major site of exile for individuals coming from the neighboring countries and even from more remote areas. Despite the authoritarian character of Chilean elitist democracy, beginning in the 1830s, the increasing institutionalization of the country enabled the elaboration of developmental policies. This development also led to a more or less orderly political life. Both trends provided the basis for inner stability and set the ground for the reception of political exiles, whose actions fit the long-term goals of Chilean policies. Witnessing the process of political consolidation and cultural thriving taught the exiles lessons about nation- and state-building that they could not learn while residing in their home country, which were still submerged in a sea of anarchy. This was less effective in the case of the Peruvians and Bolivians, who stayed for shorter periods and used Chile as a basis for overthrowing incumbent governments in their home country.

In the case of the Argentineans who stayed longer because of the resilience of the Rosas government in Buenos Aires, the opportunity to learn and participate in Chilean incipient public spheres provided tools and visions that were instrumental to their future political activities after the fall of Rosas in 1852.

The contrast between Chilean ruling conservatism and the Argentinean exiles' contrasting ideological tenet was elaborated through a twofold practice. First, exiles enjoyed relatively wide freedom to struggle for their principles against Rosas, as long as they did not intervene in Chilean politics. This served Chilean long-range interests in a situation of a developing conflict with Argentina, although the commitment elicited by benign Chilean policies toward the exiles was far from universal once the exiles returned to their home country.

Links between Chile and Argentina had been strained since the beginning of the 1840s.[21] Growing tensions between the countries finally led to an open-ended conflict for the control of the Straits of Magellan and the Tierra del Fuego area that would continue until 1984. In the early 1850s, Chile and Argentina began to argue about the possession of the Straits of Magellan and the lands of Patagonia. In 1856, both countries signed an agreement favoring international arbitration, which would be disregarded, at least until 1874. Sarmiento, Carlos Tejedor, and many others had returned from exile in the early 1850s. Sarmiento was elected to the presidency of Argentina in 1868 and Carlos Tejedor, who had served in diplomatic positions, became minister of Foreign Affairs in his administration. Tejedor was a hardliner regarding the

---

[21] One of the main factors was the attitude of Father Aldao in Mendoza, who treated Chileans in an abusive way. The incidents reached such proportions that, with Bulnes assuming the Chilean presidency, he had to veto a decision of the Chilean Congress to cut economic links with Mendoza. In April 1842, Chile suspended commerce with Cuyo, and Aldao retaliated by forbidding the introduction of Chilean products, newspapers, and Chilean guanaco hunters into Mendoza.

territorial dispute with Chile over Patagonia, and he was of the belief that the arbitration agreement did not apply to that region but was conceived regarding the Andean borderline. During his presidential term, Sarmiento pushed forward a policy of Argentinean hegemony in Patagonia, which did not relinquish sovereignty to the national pretensions of Chile under its Foreign Affairs Minister Adolfo Ibáñez. Sarmiento was also convinced that although Chile had a rightful claim over the Magellan Straits, the Patagonia was part of Argentina, especially because Chile had had no claims over that area until 1853. However, Chile would remain for Sarmiento a cherished country, a kind of second homeland. Accordingly, he used his reputation in Chile in order to try to advance a reasonable and amicable solution and simultaneously appease the Argentinean nationalist faction, which was willing to engage in an open international conflict if necessary. Although accused by his co-nationals of being too lenient, Sarmiento's position, cautious and stern, did much to save the relationships between the two countries. The serious knowledge that Sarmiento and Tejedor had of Chilean politics and interests brought them to conclude that Argentina could settle the Patagonia, whereas Chilean interests rested mainly in the Straits of Magellan, advancing their national interest without risking war in the 1870s.[22]

The experience of exile also triggered changes in the understanding of politics. Chilean policies favored economic development within a framework of political stability and conservative rule. In that framework, many exiles found opportunities to make a living and to integrate into Chilean society. Politically, the obligations and loyalties toward their country of origin had a persistent role, but a new set of obligations and loyalties developed toward the country of shelter.

This dual set of obligations and loyalties created a more open and critical stance among the exiles toward both countries. Part of this change was due to the complex and changing interaction of contractual links of citizenship and emotional ties experienced by the exiles. With the passing of time, relocation enabled them to compare historical experiences of the country of origin and their current place of residence. Thus, exiles went through a process of learning, which in most of the cases created more sophisticated, or at least reflexive, public views. Later on, these views shifted dynamically according to the circumstances enabling or hampering the return of the exiles. In the case of the Argentineans in Chile, although the exile experience did not transform them into conservatives, it provided a patina of conservative pragmatism to their erstwhile liberal ideas, mostly eliminating traces of Jacobinism.

While abroad, exiles underwent transformations of various kinds. In some cases, notably those of leading intellectuals and political figures, these transformations would be fundamental when they returned to their home country

---

[22] *Historia Argentina Contemporánea.* Buenos Aires: Editorial El Ateneo, 1965, vol. 1, pp. 125–129; Galán Moreno, *Radiografía de Sarmiento.* Buenos Aires: Claridad, 1961, 335–336; Encina, *Historia de Chile,* vol. 15, pp. 143–216.

or while finding a new homeland in the Americas. Caracas-born Andrés Bello conceived his ideas about (Latin) American identity and patriotic civic culture during his 19-year stay in England, ideas that would be central in shaping his role as cultural entrepreneur as he arrived in Chile in 1829. Argentinean Sarmiento used his experience in the mission to Europe and the United States to learn about the educational systems there, which enabled him to upgrade the national educational frameworks and contents on his election as president of Argentina in 1868.[23] Chilean Benjamín Vicuña Mackenna elaborated a perspective on nation-building and national reconciliation on the basis of his experiences of exile in the Americas and Europe. Being displaced from Chile after his participation in the liberal revolts against conservative rule, once in exile, he came nonetheless to value the contribution of Portales to the institutional stability and republicanism of Chile. Even as he retained his commitment to modernization on the basis of liberal-positivistic views – which made him resent the deep socioeconomic and cultural gaps he perceived in the countries of exile – he perceived that once back in Chile these views had to be reconciled with the institutional frameworks installed by the conservatives and bring these institutions to the open in liberal directions.[24]

Exiles in Chile and exiles in Europe found shelters in cities characterized by comparative stability and development. In most of the cases of exile, they arrived as strangers who had to struggle to make a living and survive in the new environment. For some, the new situation implied financial insecurity and dire prospects of finding a new purpose in life. Moreover, exiles were expected to abstain from intervening in local politics and, of course, from entering into a collision course with the national and international policies of the incumbent government. Many exiles managed to transform these difficulties into assets. In fact, they were not total strangers in the new location because they had the language and culture (in the case of those arriving in Chile) or shared a similar civilizational–political background (as in the case of those arriving in Paris). As such, they adapted to the local habitus, proceeding to climb positions in the local milieu, as in Chile, or enjoying their closeness to the leading figures of European politics and civilization, as in Paris.

Chile once more became a pole of attraction from the 1960s to Allende's fall, particularly for those individuals of the political Left (e.g., in post-1964

---

[23] Bello began such a cultural journey into the roots of Spanish-American identities during his days-long visits to the British Library, where he studied the poem of *El cid campeador*, which tells the deeds of Rodrigo Díaz de Vivar, "the story of a man banished from his homeland and condemned to live among strangers, a parallel with himself that Bello could not have overlooked." Karen Racine, "Nature and Mother: Foreign Residents and the Evolution of Andrés Bello's American Identity, London 1810–1829," in Ingrid E. Fay and Karen Racine, Eds., *Strange Pilgrimages: Exile, Travel and National Identity in Latin America, 1800–1990s.* Wilmington, DE: Scholarly Resources, 2000, pp. 5–9.

[24] José Luis Rénique, "Benjamín Vicuña Mackenna: Exilio, historia y nación," *Ciberayllu*, 18 October 2005, available at <http://www.andes.missouri.edu/andes/Especiales/JLRVicuna/JLRVicuna1.html>, accessed 29 May 2006.

Brazil) whose countries had already entered a cycle of authoritarian rule and political closure. Many who opposed the military in Brazil went mainly to Uruguay, Chile, and France. The possibility of moving to Paz Estensoro's Bolivia was closed in November 1964, when General René Barrientos overthrew civilian rule there. After the military coup in Brazil in March 1964, around 30 exiles arrived in Chile. In early 1969, there were 70 exiles and, by the end of that year, 280. Their number rose steadily, attracted by the political developments and the centrality of the Chilean Left. Chile became more attractive to Brazilian leftist exiles when Allende was elected president in 1970. In mid-1970, as the Chilean elections were near, their number had reached 600. Many arrived after the 1971 Banzer military coup in Bolivia, whereas others went to Argentina. In mid-1973, the Brazilian exile community in Chile was assessed as consisting of already between 3,000 and 4,000 members. Among some of the renowned individuals were the former Minister of Labor under Goulart, Almino Affonso, who was expelled from Uruguay, and former Minister of Education Paulo de Tarso; former parliamentarians Plinio de Arrunda Sampaio, Adao Pereira Nunes, and Salvador Romano Lozzaco; economist Celso Furtado; sociologist – and, in the 1990s, twice president of Brazil – Fernando Henrique Cardoso; and education theoretician Paulo Freire; among many others.[25] Chile could exert such attraction also because it hosted a series of international institutions of education, research, and development that transformed Santiago into a center for the Latin American intelligentsia:

It was a privileged balcony from which people could participate with a rather unmediated vision of the events taking place [in all places] from the Rio Bravo to Patagonia. For us, Brazilians, who always had lived with the back to our neighbors, separated from them by an ocean – more dense and profound than the other – of Amazonic forest, we had the feeling of having discovered a New World.... Living together and sharing experiences, for instance, with comrades of so many different regions, an amalgamation of political leadership that struggle had led to exile. Or participate in classes, debates, conferences, with leading experts of the problems of the Continent.[26]

In sharp contrast to 19th-century Chilean policies, in 20th-century Chile, foreigners, including Brazilians, were allowed to be active in Chilean politics and Chilean political parties. Internationalist winds were blowing strongly in the leftist wing of the Chilean political spectrum. Many of the Brazilian exiles, especially those coming from armed resistance movements in their home country (the so-called generation of 1968), aligned themselves with the most extreme parts of the Chilean Left. These exiles perceived themselves as a "popular revolutionary vanguard" with much political experience and gave their opinions and advice to their Chilean peers. They even demanded from Allende's government to be paid salaries in order to be able to continue their political work in Chile. Some even thought to take over the Brazilian Embassy in Santiago

[25] Cristina P. Machado, Os exiliados. São Paulo: Editora Alfa - Omeg, 1979, pp. 39–48.
[26] Testimony of José Maria Rabelo, in Pedro Celso Uchoa Cavalcanti and Jobelino Ramos, Eds., Memorias do exilio. Brasil 1964/19??. São Paulo: Livraria Livramento, 1978, pp. 155–156.

and establish a revolutionary government in exile there, but this action was rapidly discarded, due to the political damage it would cause to the Chilean government of Allende.[27]

Undoubtedly, the ideological enthusiasm added to a situation of freedom, and an interesting set of political developments played a role in attracting so many Brazilians to Chile. Still, feelings were mixed. "Forgetting Brazil has been always impossible for our exiles. But the longing of Brazil and the open wounds hurt less in Chile. The great celebration that took place before Allende's death and the end [literally: burial] of the popular movement involved all and made them all drunk."[28]

In September 1973, the situation of the Brazilian exiles became untenable. While exiles from Argentina, Peru, and Uruguay who resided in Chile were offered by their respective governments the possibility of return to their home countries – even to those who had to face trials and prison – the Brazilians lacked that alternative. The gates of the Brazilian Embassy were closed. Ambassador Antonio da Câmara Canto was later honored with an award by the Chilean junta for the services he rendered. Contrastingly, a Brazilian officer of the UN saved hundreds of lives, helping exiles to reach various embassies. As he returned to Brazil, he was sent to prison for his actions against the Chilean Junta.[29] The abrupt end of Allende's administration created a massive phenomenon of Chilean exile and of serial exile for many Latin Americans who had found shelter there, or who had come to Chile motivated by the promise of a democratic socialist revolution. Many of them chose Paris as their next site of exile.

Exiles in the City of Light

> They would spend the nights in La Coupole of Hemingway [*sic*], in the Monmartre [*sic*] of Toulouse-Lautrec, they would see the evening dwindle in the coffee terrace where Sartre wrote, in Saint-German des Près, where Juliette Gréco used to sing... – Do you realize, Ana, that we are not in any city, but in Paris?
>
> Ana Vásquez[30]

During the late colonial period, the Creole elites were strongly influenced by both the example and practice of Bourbon absolutism, which ruled both Spain and France, as well as by the Enlightenment ideas and their political corollary, the French Revolution. The principles of the French Revolution and the political traditions of France were known to Latin American elites before independence and had an impact on the social elites and among political actors and intellectuals in the processes leading to independence from colonial rule.

---

[27] Machado, *Os exiliados*, pp. 98–101.
[28] Ibid., pp. 97–98.
[29] Ibid., p. 110.
[30] Ana Vásquez, *Mi amiga Chantal*. Barcelona: Lumen, 1991, p. 183.

Although the realities of the new American states differed from those in France, the basic principles for legitimating the new polities addressed the ideas of representation, popular sovereignty, civil and human rights, and equality deriving from the French Revolution and its subsequent institutional transformation. Still led by their traditional societies, the newly born polities of Latin America turned to French and other external models. Following the disruption of an earlier administrative imperial model in the territories of the former Spanish Empire, the absolutist organizational and political models of the mother country were rejected, because they were seen as decadent and backward from an international prism.

Beginning with the Enlightenment and following with the Revolution, France provided the ideological discourses and ideas that were influential among the new states' elites as they established new polities, and in thinking about them. Both Latin American conservatives and liberals found in Paris the anchors for their reflection and search of legitimacy for their political positions. Revolution and the *Ancien régime*, people's sovereignty and *volonté générale*, social contract and citizenship, despotism, liberty and egalitarianism as well as conservative and Catholic-integralist ideas, entered into the Latin American public discourse as an indirect reflection of French political discourse. Some of these concepts (like popular will) had existed before but now acquired new meanings. Others, such as citizenship, were entirely new and served to construct reality in ways that differed from their practice in France. Thus, for instance, the very innovative character of the new states prompted a redefinition of citizenship in quasi-primordial and sacred terms as the basis of other entitlements and of membership in a political community. To quote Bernardo de Monteagudo in the *Gazeta de Buenos Aires*: "Who are citizens: to be [a citizen] is a primordial right from which derive all other rights composing that sacred list that appears in the first pages of the code of a free people."[31]

France's influence worked in contrasting directions. French ideas and controversies had a strong impact on Ibero-American liberals. Later on, the founders of Positivism in Mexico, Central America, Venezuela, Brazil and Chile – first learnt about the doctrine both in France and from France.[32] Working against the devoted attitude were those who resented French expansionism in the name of civilization. The Napoleonic takeover in Spain reinforced the themes of the conservatives, who opposed the French Revolution because of its Jacobin trends and its attack on all hierarchies in the name of popular sovereignty and universal rights. Spanish and Latin American Creole conservatives cherished Bourbon absolutism, siding with the French antirevolutionary forces. Francisco Bilbao's *La América en peligro* (1862) and Luis Alberto de Herrera's *La Revolución Francesa y Sudamérica* (1910) are two works representative of the reaction to the paramount place of French models. The French invasion of Mexico provided fire in the opposite direction, as the Mexican

---

[31] *Gazeta de Buenos Aires*, III, 23, 122.
[32] In the Southern Cone, the influence was more Spencerian and Darwinian.

conservatives sided with the French and Maximilian, while the liberals waged war against the foreign invasion in the name of patriotism.

Paris and France were not only the harbingers of the Revolution, but were also envisioned as a major model of modernity. With its *cafés*, salons, effervescent intellectual life, open and discursive public sphere, wide press and pamphlets, and a mecca of fashion and new social mores, Paris appeared before the eyes of the newcomers as the epitome of modern sociability and ideas. Although in Latin America, the economic and political influence of the British Empire and later on, of the United States were at times stronger, Paris was to dominate the cultural horizons of the elites and even of wider groups for a long period:

> As Walter Benjamin famously said, Paris was the capital of the nineteenth century, and thus was no less true for the poets, intellectuals, diplomats and exiles of Latin America's fragmented world, which had great cities, but no natural center, as New York was for the United States or Paris itself for the French.[33]

Paris functioned for two centuries as a pole attracting Latin Americans who arrived there in many capacities, ranging from tourists, big landowners, entrepreneurs and renters to students, artists, intellectuals, and political exiles. Often these categories were blurred and individuals moved from one status to another as time passed and better suited their interests and constrained goals. As many of these residents, tourists, expatriates, and exiles walked about the boulevards of Paris, a community of individuals who began identifying themselves both as nationals of the home country and as 'Latin Americans' evolved into part of the permanent social framework of the city. The following waves of exiles from Spanish and Portuguese America found there an existing foothold of nationals and trans-Latin American fellows.

Francois-Xavier Guerra studied the relationship between Spanish-American elites and France, showing that the process of independence led to an increase in the number of individuals coming to France for studies, especially in the area of medicine. However, many students came to Paris not to complete studies, but mainly to experience the *savoir vivre* of that society. They would live in Paris, the most cosmopolitan European city of the 19th century, and erratically attend classes of the most renowned professors, meet celebrated intellectuals, buy books, and adopt with enthusiasm fashionable ideas and beliefs.[34]

Many of those who lived in Paris as visitors or students brought books and periodicals back with them to the Americas. These works served as a source of inspiration for large groups, even for those who never had been to Paris but for whom the city was the model of civilization. Even before independence, visitors to the Americas such as Alexander von Humboldt noted the growing

---

[33] Roberto González Echevarría, "The Master of Modernismo." *The Nation*, 13 February 2006, available at http://www.thenation.com/doc/20060213/echevarria.

[34] Francois-Xavier Guerra, "La lumiére et ses reflets: Paris et la politique Latino-Americain," in *Le Paris des Etrangers*. Paris; Edition de l'Impremerie Nationale, 1989, pp. 171–182. See also Hebe Pelossi, *Argentinos en Francia. Franceses en Argentina*. Buenos Aires: Civdad Argentina, 1999.

presence of individuals with a tendency "to adopt, often in non-reflexive ways, new modes of behavior and ideas"; who took great joy in instruction; and who knew French and Italian literature, music, and art.[35] Some would become leaders of their countries' independence movements, such as Francisco Miranda and Simón Bolívar in New Granada, Fray Servando de Mier and Lucas Alamán in Mexico, and Bernardino Rivadavia in the Río de la Plata. Among the most prominent Spanish-American personalities who came to Paris was José de San Martín, expatriate and independence hero. His home near Paris in the 1830s and 1840s became a focus for prominent South American visitors.

Through the 19th and 20th centuries, Paris was a center of Ibero-American diaspora. In 1896, there were more than 3,000 Latin Americans registered in Paris, of varied origins: Brazil (1,216), Argentina (488), Mexico (248), Colombia (238), Chile (231), Peru (218), Haiti (181), Venezuela (174), Uruguay (98), and Ecuador (55). Even Cubans and Puerto Ricans, whose lands were until 1898 under Spanish rule, lived then in Paris by the hundreds (ca. 300 in 1896). Indeed, since the middle of the 19th century, Cuban aristocrats began to move to Paris for short periods of time. Members of the sugar-planter elite and the petit-bourgeoisie of liberal professionals formed the core of the Cuban community. Others came to study, especially medicine.[36]

An important segment of this diaspora consisted of political exiles. Since 1868, and especially in 1895–1898, Cuban exiles flowed into Paris and made it the center of European solidarity with the cause of Cuban independence within a network of international contacts and global concern. In practical terms, the Cuban Committee in Paris was subordinated to the main exile command in New York, and a great deal of the funds raised crossed the Atlantic in that direction. But, the Cuban delegation in Paris served as a meeting point for Cubans fleeing Spain, the core of a series of local solidarity committees, and a point of departure for other European destinations. The centers worked at the local level, producing propaganda through pamphlets and the press, organizing public protests, raising funds, and lobbying parliamentarians. Around the publication of the bilingual *La República Cubana/La République Cubaine* there formed a group of French writers and journalists who supported the Cuban cause.

Paris was also important for many Latin Americans for the reason that it was a center for exiles in the era of national movements because of the intellectual climate and the ideological attraction of the French Revolution, a Jacobin center with participative traditions and the Parisian commune. The center for Polish, Czech, and Greek nationalists was in Paris. In Paris, there was a tradition of *proactive* exile.

From its location in Paris, the Cuban Committee sought to extend its contacts far beyond the Americas. The Committee found itself depending on the

---

[35] Alexander von Humboldt, *Alejandro de Humboldt por tierras venezolanas*. Caracas: Fundación de Promoción Cultura de Venezuela, 1983, pp. 137–140.

[36] Paul Estrade, *La colonia cubana de París, 1895–1898*. La Habana: Editorial de Ciencias Sociales, 1984, p. 11.

financial goodwill of the rich Cuban *émigrés*, whereas its support within French public opinion came especially from socialist and anarchist circles. It tried to maintain intellectual and political equilibrium between left and right, attempting to please both sides. Yet, thanks to personal contacts with exiles from other countries, the Cuban question was addressed with sympathy in Russia, the Netherlands, Austria, and Germany. European volunteers from these countries enlisted in the revolutionary army through their contacts with the Cubans there. The Cuban Committee in Paris was also responsible for establishing contacts with other separatist movements, such as the Hong Kong Committee of Philippine Revolutionaries, thus creating a nexus between them and the New York delegation. *La República Cubana* manifested in its articles its support for the Philippine cause, a further indication of the Cubans' global immersion.[37]

As French cultural and social influence grew along the 19th century and into the 20th, a visit to Paris became a rite of passage for many Latin American young men on the road to becoming part of the most select elites. For the members of middle and lower strata, a Parisian journey – even if accidental – was a source of social and cultural capital, in Pierre Bourdieu's terms,[38] which would provide a means of escalating the social ladder in their country of origin. For many Latin Americans, Paris was (and, for some, still is) the cultural capital of the civilized world. Looking from their personal angle, Paris had to be the place in which they could acquire the cultural patina for becoming citizens of the world. As such, when returning to the homeland, the visit to the cultural *capital* and their acquisition of *cultural* capital awarded them a status that confirmed their privileged position vis-à-vis the provincialism of those who lacked such a cultural and social advantage.

For Brazilians, too, Paris had become the uncontested model and mythical reference of many artists, intellectuals, and politicians, for whom it provided a source of aesthetic and political ideas. Brazilians, for example, began to prefer Paris over Coimbra, Portugal, toward the end of the 18th century and more pronouncedly after 1816, when a French mission arrived in Rio de Janeiro. Not only were radical ideas elaborated there, but also monarchist and Catholic ideas were reaffirmed, as in the case of Brazilian Eduardo Prado in the late 19th century. Even before arriving in Paris, the Brazilian intellectuals knew French landscapes by heart, were enthusiastic about French culture and ideas, and admired French heroes. During the late 19th century, the largest group of Latin Americans in Paris was that of Brazilians. In 1822, 1823, and 1842, when the Brazilian Empire experienced periods of political turmoil, the government used deportation as a way of getting rid of the most stubborn parts of the opposition, although it seemed to have allowed the flow of financial support to the exiles.

Roderick Barman, who studied the Brazilians in France, distinguishes two types of exiles. Most of those who found shelter in Paris were "well behaved"

---

[37] Estrade, *La colonia*, pp. 20–61 and 102–115.
[38] Pierre Bourdieu, "The Forms of Capital," in J. G. Richardson, Ed., *Handbook of Theory and Research for the Sociology of Education*. New York: Greenwood Press, 1986, pp. 241–258.

and did not intervene in either French or Brazilian politics and were allowed to return after a period of "cooling off." Such was the case of Pedro Araújo Lima, who returned to Brazil in 1826 after two years of exile in Paris and assumed a place in the Chamber of Deputies; later on, he served as regent of Brazil (1837–1840) and three times as prime minister, invested as the Marquis of Olinda. The aloof character of these exiles was especially salient as the people of Paris revolted against King Charles in 1831, King Louis-Philippe in 1848, and again during the Paris Commune of 1871. Brazilians did not take part in these revolts of republican and revolutionary character. José da Natividade Saldanha was an exception to the rule. After taking part in the uprising of 1824 in the Brazilian northeast, he was exiled and arrived in Paris, where he was closely watched by the police. His foray in Paris was very short, as his radical reputation and African ancestry singled him out for rapid deportation from France in February 1825 after only two weeks there.[39]

Continuing this tradition of benign exile, Emperor Pedro II took the road to exile in France in November 1889, after a coup that ended the Empire and established the First Republic in Brazil. At least three times before exile, in 1871, 1876, and 1887, the emperor handed over the reigns of power and opted to leave his country for long vacations that took him to more sedate and intellectually challenging environments, especially in Europe, and Paris in particular. There, "he was no longer the emperor but simply Dom Pedro de Alcântara, the close associate of leading savants and men of letters."[40] Pedro II considered Brazil his country of birth and emotional homeland, whereas he saw in France an intellectual magnet and his country of reference in the realm of culture. During his first visit, he met with, among others, Adolphe Thiers, and, during his second visit, he enjoyed the company of Victor Hugo and was accepted as a foreign associate to the *Académie de Sciences* of France, one of the most prestigious academic institutions of the world at that time.[41] When he was forced by the republican takeover to go into exile, he naturally opted for France, which he saw as the center of civilization. From the start, he discouraged the monarchical faction who dreamed about his return to power in Brazil and adopted a conciliatory stance of further noninvolvement in Brazilian internal affairs, while following the image of paternal role model for his country while in Europe:

His attitude to the republican regime was kindly but patronizing and, in many respects, paternal. Commenting on April 19 on the draft constitution, D. Pedro noted: "Anyway, the work reveals learning and as I have already said, I would be republican if I judged Brazil sufficiently advanced for that form of government."[42]

---

[39] Roderick J. Barman, "Brazilians in France, 1822–1872: Doubly Outsiders," in Fay and Racine, Eds., *Strange Pilgrimages*, pp. 23–39.

[40] Roderick J. Barman, *Citizen Emperor: Pedro II and the Making of Brazil, 1825–91*. Stanford, CA: Stanford University Press, 1999, p. 364.

[41] Ibid., *Citizen Emperor*, p. 282.

[42] Ibid., *Citizen Emperor*, p. 380.

As an exile, Dom Pedro showed a rare brand of altruistic patriotism, which gave priority to the interests of his country, Brazil, over any personal ambitions. The republican attitude was also of a conciliatory nature and, after a short period, they allowed those banished with Pedro II to return to Brazil. Many in the former emperor's entourage, like the Viscount of Ouro Preto, opted to return to Brazil. Dom Pedro's conciliatory attitude prevented him from becoming a leader of antirepublican activism abroad. On a more practical level, the state of his finances was dire, and yet the emperor disregarded all attempts to convince him to accept a pension from the republican government in Brazil. He continued to lead the way of life of a traveling emperor, who did not concern himself with the prosaic question of how to pay the huge sums required to sustain the costs of his entourage staying at expensive hotels in Cannes, Paris, and other European cities. He showed no inclination to economize on his living expenses, and his relatives, friends, and close advisers shielded him from such concerns, which were supplied eventually by the sale of properties in Brazil. His health deteriorated rapidly after the death of his wife, and he passed away in December 1891.

In the 20th century, Porfirio Díaz and his entourage of relatives, political associates, and close friends found a site of exile in Paris, after he lost power in Mexico. Thanks to the wealth accumulated during his decades-long rule as president of Mexico and the connections he had among Mexican diplomats in Europe, he was still treated with all the honors of a former head of state while abroad between 1911 and 1914. The governments of France and the countries he visited also awarded him all kinds of honors. His wealth and international prominence turned his sojourn into a Golden Exile. He was buried in the cemetery of Montparnasse in Paris.[43]

Living in Paris brought the tension between cosmopolitanism and parochialism into sharp awareness, serving as the background for literary works such as *Los transplantados*, published in 1904 by Alberto Blest Gana (1831–1920), who arrived there as the ambassador of Chile. This novel described how the experience of the Chileans in Paris eroded national identity, with the exposure to modernity and the ethics of subversive dissolution of localized identities in the exposure to the cosmopolitanism of Paris and France. Rubén Darío (1867–1916), a key figure of Ibero-American letters, was drawn as a Nicaraguan expatriate to Paris' cosmopolitanism, and was strongly criticized for that by many in Spain and Latin America:

"I had dreamt of Paris since I was a boy to the point that, when I said my prayers, I prayed to God that he wouldn't let me die without seeing Paris." . . . When he landed at the Saint Lazare station in Paris, he wrote: "I thought I was treading on sacred ground. . . . The atmosphere of Paris, the light of Paris, the spirit of Paris, are unconquerable, and the ambition of 'every man' who comes to Paris is to be conquered."[44]

43 Carlos Tello Díaz, *El exilio: un relato de familia*. México: Cal y Arena, 1993.
44 Jason Weiss, *The Lights of Home: A Century of Latin American Writers in Paris*. London: Routledge, 2003, pp. 15–16.

Contrastingly, it was in Paris that others began a reflective period in their sojourn that would eventually lead to possible changes in their relationship to society and politics. Such was the Brazilian group of Gonçalves de Magalhães and the journal *Nitheroy*, thought to elaborate a "national literature" and launch Brazilian Romanticism. Brazilian Modernism was born in the French Bohemian quarters, and it is from this center of intellectual gravity that creators such as Oswald de Andrade launched an iconoclastic attack on their own society.[45] In the 1960s and 1970s, many exiles began reflecting on society in terms of a long-durée perspective informed by their deconstruction of previous cultural assumptions, as recalled in a testimony by Magno José Vilela, a Brazilian Dominican friar exiled serially in Santiago de Chile, Rome, and Paris:

There are changes that you don't really know how to describe with objectivity as of their impact and effects. For instance, I consider a great achievement that I do not feel tempted to judge the French in a somehow racist way. And instead, to be able to admire and respect their ways and try to learn from them, in a manner that could be useful for me and my country.... Is it likely that we, the post-1964 Brazilian exiles, are living collectively through a historical experience that could reverberate later positively on the ways of our own Brazilian society?[46]

Throughout the last two centuries, Paris attracted Latin American intellectuals, who arrived in search of an atmosphere of cultural effervescence and freedom of thought and expression. One was the Argentine writer Julio Cortázar, who in 1951 became an expatriate, opting to leave Argentina because of the alienation that Peronism had produced in cosmopolitan young intellectuals like him. Benefiting from a French scholarship, he arrived in Paris:

We had a sense of being raped on a daily basis, having to suffer that popular overflow – remembered Cortázar years later. Our position as young intellectuals, reading in various languages, precluded us from understanding the phenomenon. We were harassed by the loudspeakers shouting "Peron, Peron, how Great you are!" They mixed with the last concert of Alban Berg [or Bartok] we were listening to. This created a fatal mistake [in interpretation] and led many of us to run away.[47]

Cortázar arrived willingly in Paris and stayed there until his death in 1984. In Paris, he shifted his early reticence of Peronism and rediscovered the popular movements of Latin America from the optic of cosmopolitan Paris. His growing commitment to Socialism precluded, however, his return to Argentina, as institutionalized repression increasingly targeted political figures and intellectuals in his home country. Expatriation became forced exile. Becoming part of the

---

[45] Mario Carelli, *Cultures croisés: Histoire des échanges culturels entre la France et le Brasil, de la découverte aux temps modernes*. Paris: Nathan, 1993, pp. 149–167.

[46] Testimony of Magno Jose Vilela, in Uchoa Cavalcanti and Ramos, Eds., *Memorias do exilio*. São Paulo: Livraria Livramento, 1978, p. 219.

[47] "Julio Cortázar, Argentino, 1914–1984," *Literatura Latinoamericana*, available at http://www.geocities.com/macondomorel/julio.html, accessed 23 April 2006.

intellectual milieu of Paris, Cortázar broadened his Latin American interests, visited Cuba, sided with the Chilean opposition to Pinochet, and supported the Sandinistas as they reached power in Nicaragua in 1979. He nonetheless was harshly criticized for being a 'far-away' revolutionary, disconnected and ignorant of the 'real' Latin American situation and professing a Parisian kind of Communism, distanced from the armed struggle. And yet, vis-à-vis European intellectuals and political actors, Cortázar stood up in exile as a powerful voice and defender of Latin America.

France became a site of exile for those fleeing the onset of military dictatorship in South America as well as repression in Central America and the Caribbean states. From an incipient beginning in the 1960s, the communities of Latin American exiles, particularly of Chileans, burgeoned in the 1970s. According to the CIMADE (*Comité inter-mouvements auprès des evacués* or Inter-Movements Committee for Refugees), 60 Brazilians had been received in France in 1966 together with 10 Haitians.[48] After May 1968, the French government adopted a policy of banishment of hundreds of foreign students who had been active in the radical riots. Yet, after the coups in the Southern Cone the numbers of exiles rose sharply. Between November 1973 and November 1974, 1,075 Latin American political refugees arrived in France on an emergency basis, among which 70 percent were Chileans, 10 percent Brazilians, 8 percent Bolivians, and 4 percent Uruguayans.[49] According to the French Ministry of the Interior, in 1973–1974, there were 409 political refugees out of 1,218 Chilean residents; in 1979–1980 there were already 3,231 refugees in a community of 6,014, and in 1985–1986, 5,526 refugees among 8,944 Chilean co-nationals. The formal situation of the newcomers varied greatly, from those who kept their passport of origin to those undocumented and others who received residency on the basis of a status of refugee granted by ACNUR (Alto Comisionado de las Naciones Unidas para los Refugiados; ACNUR is the Spanish acronym for UNHCR, the UN High Commissioner for Refugees).[50] Yet, organizationally, the exiles of the different Latin American countries in France

---

[48] This group was part of hundreds who fled Haiti in the 1960s, particularly to the Dominican Republic, Bahamas, Mexico, and Canada. Later on, the flow would increase and become continuous, especially as the island entered a period of anarchy and violence. In 1987, the number of Haitians in exile was estimated at one million or more than 15 percent of the country's population. At that time, between 15,000 and 30,000 of them resided in France, as compared with nearly 450,000 in the United States; between 250,000 and 400,000 in the Dominican Republic; and around 50,000 in French-speaking territories of the Antillas and Guyana (Anick Billard, "Haití: Esperanza, regreso y desilusión." *Refugiados*, March 1987, pp. 15–18).

[49] Erasmo Sáenz Carrete, *El exilio latinoamericano en Francia, 1964–1979*. Mexico: Potrerillos Editores, 1995, pp. 90–92 and p. 100.

[50] Anne Marie Gaillard, *Exils et retours. Itineraires chiliens*. Paris: CIEMI and L'Harmattan, 1997, p. 39; Eugenia Allier Montaño and Denis Merklen, "Milonga de estar lejos. Los que se fueron a Francia," in Silvia Dutrénit Bielous, Ed., *El Uruguay del exilio*. Montevideo: Trilce: 2006, p. 344.

made use of their common interests and identities as they interacted with French authorities and organizations, such as France Terre d'Asile.[51] In the 1980s, the international crisis in Central America transformed Paris, along with London, into a center of political activities against the U.S. intervention and in favor of the defense of human rights. In Paris, there were several committees of Central American exiles, such as Comité Salvador, Comité de Solidarité Nicaragua, and the Collectif Guatemala, which organized demonstrations and published bulletins such as *Amérique Centrale*.[52]

Living in Paris brought the tension between the ideal image and the realities of the site of exile. Although some exiles of the 1970s recall the solidarity of various sectors such as students, professionals, and political activists, others recall being offended by the patronizing attitude of their French hosts, even those in the Left willing to help them in adapting to their new society. Some of the exiles felt treated as inferiors by the arrogance of their hosts:

The reputation of France as a land of asylum is only a varnish. As if they were saying we are doing you a favor. We *may* help you. They never did it on the basis of equality.[53]

To be in France was to move to a country where modernity was evident in the social, educational and health infrastructure. I could not believe my eyes when I went to check the nursery of my children.... Yet, an exile arriving in France had to face the sense of superiority of the French host. Wherever he went he was looked down. Even people with impeccable professional records and valid titles, and whose professions were in high demand, were treated with disdain, suspicion and lack of belief. They could not believe we Chileans were as knowledgeable and professionals as they, the French. Every such encounter gave us a sense of being unwanted.[54]

This tension between the need to be assisted and the sense of being in a situation of dependency on the goodwill of the host society and host government is not unique to Paris or France. Yet, the image of cultural superiority projected by Paris and France and historically incorporated by Latin Americans themselves turned this tension almost unbearable. This was especially evident in the case of those assisted by French institutions such as the Social Security, municipalities, schools, and various ministries, which in return demanded a rather

---

[51] Letter to Dr. Gerold de Wangen, director of France Terre d'Asile, 7 May 1979 by CAIS-Comité Argentin d'Information et Solidarité, Comité France Brasil, Comité de Défense de Prisonniers Politiques Chiliens, Comité Santé Chli, Association de Parents de Disparus Chiliens, Comité Nicaragua Information, Collectif Paraguay, Comité de Défense des Dróits de l'Homme au Perou, Collectif Salvador, Comité Salvador Information, CDPPU Comité de Defense de Prisonniers Politiques Uruguayens, AFUDE Association des Parents des Parents des Disparus en Uruguay, CDRS Collectif Défense Raul Sendic, CLA Comité des Réfugiées Politiques Latinoaméricains, at the International Institute of Social History (IISG), Amsterdam, France Folder 7.1.

[52] "Amérique Centrale," July 1980; "Pour l'autodétermination du people d'El Salvador. Marche Nationale le 28 Novembre," November 1981, at the IISG, Amsterdam, France Folder 7.1.

[53] Testimony of Nana Verri Whitaker, interviewed in Paris, 14 October 1995, in Rollemberg, *Exilio*, p. 137.

[54] Interview with Gustavo Silva, Jerusalem, 15 May 2006.

strict adherence by exiles to a long series of regulations, proper behavior, and controls. This tension was also evident in the domain of social encounters, in which many Latin American exiles felt estranged and some measure of racism, although these attitudes were stronger against Arabs than toward Latin Americans. Related to this sense of social alienation, testimonies report a tendency to create national or Latin American ghettos.[55] This trend is particularly strong in what Ana Vásquez and Ana María Araujo define as the first stage of exile, the stage of traumatism and grief, but remain also in later stages of transculturation and demise of earlier myths.[56]

The situation of the exiles became particularly tenuous in the labor domain, as their legal status forced many of them to work in menial jobs, unrelated to their previous education and professional status in their home country. Denise Rollemberg refers to such downward mobility of the exiles in France and Europe in the 1970s:

Heads of vanguard organizations started making a living taking care of children. Leaders of social movements did floor work in factories. Militants, intellectuals and members of the liberal professions took production jobs, did house cleaning and worked in nurseries, did night watches in hotels or worked in cinema halls, worked as aides in dressing models, unloaded ships in the piers, drove trucks in highways, took care of ill people, cleaned tombs and washed the dead. Students who thought of transforming their country through their actions returned to the classrooms and dedicated themselves to research in archives and libraries. In contrast to the situation in Chile, where professional appreciation opened space for integration, in Europe professional and social devaluation was the fate of the majority and their only way to earn a living. Only a minority [of Brazilian exiles] was able to maintain their previous status, most of them individuals of the 1964 generation having already developed a career.[57]

Typical is the story of Anina de Carvalho, who experienced serial exile in Chile and France. As Anina, a lawyer who had worked in defense of political prisoners in Brazil, arrived in Paris, she confronted serious economic difficulties. Living in dire conditions, she struggled to get student tickets to eat at university restaurants and found lodging in a maid's quarters without toilet and hot water. Occupationally, she could not exercise her profession and found work as an aid to a woman who represented an association of producers of belts and male underwear. As part of her job, she was requested to be a help dresser in fashion shows of male underwear:

In a psychological climate of beginning of exile, in which you lost everything that was of importance, you find yourself in a total abyss, living through economic hardship and often lacking enough money to eat. This way you felt annihilated, having to assist a

55 Albertina de Oliveira Costa, Maria Teresa Porciuncula Moraes, Norma Marzola, and Valentina Da Rocha Lima, *Memorias das mulheres do exilio*. Rio de Janeiro: Paz e Terra, 1980, pp. 63, 97–98, 429.

56 Vásquez and Araujo, *Exils Latino-Americains*, pp. 41–53.

57 Rollemberg, *Exílio*, pp. 124–125. See also Machado, *Os exiliados*, pp. 123–124.

model as he puts on his underwear. . . . It was a short experience as I became ill and had to drop. I could not continue.[58]

A similar tension was also evident in the context of organizing networks of solidarity that would address causes less evident than the *cause célèbre* of Chile after 1973. In the realm of cultural creation, this theme was elaborated by the director Fernando Solanas in his film *El exilio de Gardel, Tangos*, which addressed the tension between the attraction of residing in cosmopolitan Paris and the difficulties of reaching an audience and support in the city. The will of exiled Argentineans to retain their identity – and express it fully in tango performance – alienates them from even the most sympathetic locals. Their tango performance – coined with the neologism of *tanguedía* (i.e., a simultaneous combination of tango, tragedy and comedy) fails to communicate their struggle and retain the broken lines of communication with those back in the homeland, as they face the pressures of Parisian cosmopolitanism. Incomprehension, fragmentation, and loss of direction merge with doubts, despair, and ever-renewed hopes as they color the daily lives of the exiles in France.[59]

Paris exerted a strong influence and transformation, particularly on female exiles, as evidenced in the case of the Brazilian women. Many of these women had lived as exiles in Chile, a country they were forced to leave once Pinochet took power in 1973. In Chile, a strongly traditional society at that time, their social role was that of 'wives of political exiles.' As such, they were expected to remain attached to the private, domestic sphere, taking voluntary roles supporting newcomers within the community of exiles. Notwithstanding, they established in 1972 a *Comitê de Mulheres Brasileiras no Exterior*, with the aim of involving Brazilian exiled women in political activities. Chile did provide an incipient framework for changes in gender roles. Displaced to France, Brazilian women became acquainted with vanguard feminist ideas and trends. Experiencing serial exile, the crisis of values and identity became stronger, which opened the search for wider horizons, in environments where myriad cultural and intellectual alternatives were being discussed. The need to provide for their families while their partners expected them to continue taking care of domestic chores further sharpened the awareness of these women to gender inequalities and their roles and potential in exile and in general. Although Brazilian female exiles were exposed to these ideas in various sites, it was in Paris in 1975 that a *Circulo de Mulheres Brasileiras* was established. This association, initially led by a Trotskyist nucleus, soon opened to wider feminine publics, reaching

---

[58] Testimony of Anina de Carvalho, in Uchoa Cavalcanti and Ramos, Eds. *Memorias do exilio*, pp. 63–64.

[59] Fernando Solanas, *El exilio de Gardel, Tangos* (coproduction of Argentina and France, 1985). Another theme is the difficulties of establishing a bridge between Paris, the city of exile dreamt of before, and Buenos Aires, the home city, forcefully turned into the new focus of the exiles' dreams. References to mythic figures of Argentine history also linked to France, such as Carlos Gardel and San Martín, challenge the taken-for-granted identity of Argentineans and force the viewers to reconsider what happened to Argentina and its citizens during the years of dictatorship.

a membership of nearly 100 Brazilian exiles. The political perspective of these female exiles widened from a concern with government and politics to include a focus on the private realm and gender. The women in this group maintained contacts both with women in Brazil and with feminist groups in France and other European countries. Their first public appearance could not be arranged within the Brazilian community of exiles because they met the opposition of the male leaders who were unsympathetic to gender-related activities and considered feminism to be a 'trick' of developed countries to silence issues of class discrimination and political oppression, which, according to their view, had to be at the center of the struggle in Latin America. The women then had to voice their project and demands in the framework of a French feminist congress under the banner addressing all the "women of Latin America."[60]

The ensuing debates on gender and politics led to a reappaisal of the authoritarian character of Brazilian politics, including the politics of the Left, and to a new perception of human rights and its implications. However, the debates fell short of changing other well-established attitudes (e.g., homosexuality), which the Left preferred to ignore. In those cases in which the idea of discussing the issue was addressed, it showed to be highly divisive, as occurred in the Cultural Group of the CBA (Comitê Brasil pela Anistia, or Brazilian Committee for Amnesty), the Brazilian Committee that worked in the 1970s to achieve an amnesty for the political activists in prison and in exile.

In the framework of the tensions that Paris created between universal and particularist trends, it is significant to observe that the female exiles also created another association, *O clubinho do Saci*, oriented to the projection of the more primordial elements of their collective identity as Brazilians. The club was intended to meet the challenge of a very long sojourn outside of Brazil and to keep the language and image of Brazil alive among the children of the exiles. Accordingly, they celebrated Brazilian festivities, put on theater pieces, arranged for meetings with typical food and drinks, organized a children's library in Portuguese, all these to keep alive the vitality of Brazilian culture among the young generation, who were losing their identity as Brazilians.[61]

Mexico and Its Tradition of Asylum

In colonial times, Mexico attracted many Europeans and Americans, in its role as the seat of the viceroyalty of New Spain and one of the richest Spanish-American territories. Yet, concurrently, its authorities relocated convicted individuals to distant lands at the outskirts of the empire, to places such as Chile and the Philippines.

After independence, the Mexican state lived through a period of undefined and shifting borders, as the result of internal strife, the separation of Central

---

[60] Angela Neves-Xavier de Brito, "Brazilian Women in Exile: The Quest for an Identity." *Latin American Perspectives*, 13, 2 (1986): 58–80.

[61] Rollemberg, *Exílio. Entre raízes e radars*, pp. 220–223.

rica, and the loss of a huge proportion of its colonial territory in the wars with the United States. In the problematic decades after independence, the political turmoil produced many cases of individuals fleeing from their home regions within the country and beyond its borders. In contrast with Chile and, to a lesser extent, Montevideo and Brazil, the institutional instability of Mexico until the late 19th century did not create conditions of attraction for political exiles from other troubled regions of Latin America. However, from very early on, a series of treaties and conventions were drafted to secure the fate of political refugees and exiles. In 1823, Lucas Alamán, foreign affairs minister of Mexico, signed the Treaty of Union and Confederation with Colombia, in which the rights of individuals persecuted politically were recognized. Political asylum was recognized in Article 15 of the 1857 Constitution and in the 1917 Constitution, which forbade extradition of political transgressors.[62]

Similarly, between the 1839 peace treaty that closed the so-called Pastry War with France and the beginning of the civil war in 1854, a French community of nearly 8,000 households was formed. Most Frenchmen were of humble backgrounds. Peasants and artisans were drawn to the country with the hope of improving their life chances, lured by the praise of Mexico as a land of opportunities in the writings of Baron von Humboldt and others; similarly motivated in moving were a few investors and rich merchants. In parallel, yet, many French expatriates decided to escape threats by political opponents and thus crossed the Atlantic to Mexico.[63]

It was only with the stabilization of political order and the beginning of the harsh rule of Porfirio Díaz that, in tandem with the repression of its own citizens and the escape of many of them abroad, Mexico became a pole of attraction for newcomers from other Spanish-speaking regions in the Americas. Díaz, who was president in 1876–1880 and in 1884–1911, ruled Mexico in an authoritarian way, with the support of a positivist entourage and the harsh police methods of his *Guardias rurales*. His economic policies produced the pauperization of the Indians and their loss of lands to the market, thus leading to a concentration of land and increased social gaps. Concomitantly, a measure of modernization and economic progress was reached through the attraction of foreign capital, building of railroads, the development of new mining enterprises, and urban and infrastructural projects. Entire groups such as the Yaqui Indians of Sonora were repressed as they opposed the modernizing capitalistic policies of the center, and found themselves translocated en masse to the henequen farms in the southern region of Yucatán. In the early 20th century, Mexican political activists such as Ricardo Flores Magón and his

[62] Felipe Tena Ramírez, *Las leyes fundamentales de México, 1808–1957*. Mexico: Porrúa, 1957, pp. 608 and 822.
[63] See Chantal Cramaussel, "Imagen de México en los relatos de viaje Franceses, 1821–1862," in Javier Pérez Siller, Ed., *México-Francia: Memoria de una sensibilidad común*. Pueblo: El Colegio de San Luis, 1998, pp. 333–363, esp. pp. 340–344.

followers fled to the southern United States and attempted to fight Díaz's rule from there.[64]

Despite its coercive effects within the country, in another plane, the development and political stabilization of Mexico during the *Porfiriato* created a context favorable to the conditional reception of political exiles, many of elite and upper-class backgrounds. The first major wave of such exiles taking refuge in Mexico came in the second half of the 19th century from Cuba and to a lesser extent from Puerto Rico, both colonial societies affected by intermittent movements struggling to attain independence from Spain.

During the Mexican Revolution, the generation of exile accelerated because of political instability and violence. Followers of defeated factions went into exile, mostly to the United States, especially after the break of World War I in 1914. Thus, to mention but several of these waves of displacement: Under Francisco Madero (1911–1913), followers of Pascual Orozco and Francisco Vázquez fled the country; under Victoriano Huerta's rule (1913–1914), it was the turn of the *maderistas*; the Constitutionalist access to power (1914) prompted the escape of *huertistas*; followers of Pancho Villa and Eulalio Gutiérrez were forced to flee in 1914–1915. Many of them attempted to continue their fight from the United States, even though often their movements were controlled and some of them spent time in prison for violating the rule of neutrality that the United States proclaimed to cherish.[65] Mexico continued to generate exile in later decades. An outstanding case is that of Archbishop Ruiz y Flores, who as late as 1932 suffered such punishment, despite the fact that Mexico did not sanction exile as a penalty for its citizens, and it even forbade extradition of political transgressors. Born in Mexico, he was deported as an undesirable alien after being declared a foreigner because "he owed allegiance to a foreign sovereign," the Pope.[66]

At the same time, postrevolutionary Mexico was becoming a haven for Latin American and other political exiles. A wave of exiles arrived in Mexico

[64] Javier Garciadiego, "Exiliados de la revolución Mexicana." III Jornadas de la historia de las izquierdas, Centro de Documentación e Investigación de la Cultura de Izquierdas en la Argentina, Buenos Aires, 4–6 August 2005; Andrew Grant Wood, "Death of a Political Prisoner: Revisiting the Case of Ricardo Flores Magón," available at http://ncsu.edu/project/acontracorriente/fall_05/Wood.PDF8, accessed 8 July 2007. A forthcoming work on *Los exiliados de la revolución* is about to be published by El Colegio de México.

[65] Later on, further waves included the followers of Venustiano Carranza, Adolfo de la Huerta, Gonzalo Escobar, José Vasconcelos, Plutarco Elías Calles, Juan Andreu Almazan, in addition to the Cristeros. Victoria Lerner Sigal, "Exilio e historia: Algunas hipótesis generales a partir del caso de los Mexicanos exilados por la Revolución Mexicana." Chicago: University of Chicago, Mexican Studies Program, Center for Latin American Studies, Working Paper Series No. 7, 2000. As indicated, a multivolume collective study of the exiles of the Revolution will be published in 2009, under the editorship of Javier Garciadiego of the Colegio de México.

[66] J. Lloyd Mecham, *Church and State in Latin America*. Chapel Hill, NC: University of North Carolina Press, 1934, p. 500.

in the 1920s, when part of the political exiles who fled Venezuela came to the country (others went to such widespread destinations as Cuba, Costa Rica, Peru, Curaçao, the United States, Spain, and France). These individuals were fleeing from the authoritarian rule of Juan Vicente Gómez, who was president of Venezuela intermittently between 1908 and 1935. A former exile himself in Colombia, once in power, Gómez used his country's oil wealth toward infrastructural development, while he built up a strong army and a secret police force to consolidate his rule. Serious dissent was met with swift punishment, exile, or imprisonment.

In that period, as Mexico received some of its citizens who had fled abroad in the last stages of Porfirismo and the early stages of the Revolution, the country also opened its gates to political exiles from Latin America, projecting an image of hospitality and an offer of asylum, which would reach its peaks with the coming of Spanish Republican political exiles in the late 1930s and the reception of thousands from the Southern Cone in the 1970s. Mexico ratified all Latin American treaties and three conventions on asylum, becoming one of the few states in the region to have done so by the late 20th century.[67]

The country had emerged from the Revolution projecting itself as a democratic haven, committed to its population and to the creed of a *mestitzo* nation. Central intellectual figures condemned publicly and harshly Gómez's dictatorship in Venezuela. One of them was the statesman and writer, José Vasconcelos, who had been in exile several times during his revolutionary involvement against Porfirio Díaz, met Venezuelan exiles in New York, and developed awareness to their cause. After the Revolution, in his role of rector of the UNAM (National Autonomous University of Mexico) and, later on, as Minister of Education in the 1920s, Vasconcelos sought to redefine the collective identity of Mexico and Latin America as the melting pot of a new – or, in his words, "cosmic" – race and civilization and the carrier of progressive and democratic ideas. As part of this view, he strongly supported the struggle for democracy in Venezuela and other parts of the Americas. Together with other prominent Mexican intellectuals, such as the poet Carlos Pellicer, Vasconcelos was a most outspoken critic of tyrants such as Gómez:

The year 1920 has been a glorious year in the chronicle of Latin America, as it has witnessed the fall of two tyrannies: Venustiano Carranza's [dictatorship] in Mexico and Manuel Estrada Cabrera's [dictatorship] in Guatemala. Now a cable announces that a Revolution has been launched in Venezuela, against Juan Vicente Gómez, the last of the tyrants of Spanish America, the most horrendous, the most repulsive and the most contemptible of all the despots produced by our unfortunate lineage.[68]

Vasconcelos's rhetoric and criticism, expressed at the highest level, had such an impact that it brought about the mutual withdrawal of diplomats in 1922,

---

[67] We refer to the conventions of La Habana (1928), Montevideo (1933), and Caracas (1954). On these, see Chapter 5.

[68] José Vasconcelos, *Discursos, 1920–1950*. Mexico: Ediciones Botas, 1950, pp. 54–55.

leading in 1927 to the severing of diplomatic relationships, not to be renewed until Gómez's death in 1935.

High-ranking officials and members of top social circles declared their solidarity with the exiles. President Alvaro Obregón himself organized a group of Mexican female friends of Venezuela, which was chaired by his wife.[69] Among the best-known Venezuelan exiles in this period were the former governor of Caracas, Dr. Carlos León, and Miguel Zúñiga Cisneros, a student leader arriving in Mexico in 1921, invited by Vasconcelos to participate in an inter-American congress of students. The governor of the Mexican state of Yucatán, Felipe Carrillo Puerto, not only supported León but also supplied an important number of weapons to be used by the Venezuelan opposition in their fight against Gómez.[70] Gustavo Machado and Salvador de la Plaza, also exiled in Mexico, were strongly influenced by the local Communist Party.

Despite the sympathy of the administrations of Obregón and Calles, until 1925, Venezuelan exiles in Mexico did not have a central position within the Venezuelan diaspora, which was spread in various countries. It was only in 1926, with the foundation in Mexico of the Partido Revolucionario Venezolano (PRV, or Venezuelan Revolutionary Party) and the location of its central committee there, that Mexico gained centrality among the exiles' struggle against Gómez. The PRV incorporated many of the tenets of the Mexican Revolution, such as secularism, a concern for peasants and indigenous people, and attempted various failed revolts against their home ruler.

As a result of the hospitality Venezuelan exiles found there, Mexico gained limited prestige as the antithesis of the dictatorship back home. Mexico turned into a utopian counterimage of the expelling country. The discovery of an old colonial house in which the Liberator Simón Bolívar, founding father of their homeland, reportedly dwelled in while in Mexico added a further mythical dimension to Mexico as a transtemporal locale of asylum. The University also opened a chair position bearing the name of Bolívar in those years. In March 1925, a group of intellectuals, among whom the great revolutionary muralist painter Diego Rivera, lover and married partner of painter Frida Kahlo and friend of another prominent exile in Mexico, León Trotsky, launched a journal that spread the ideas of the *Liga anti-imperialista de las Américas*, under the Bolivarian name of *El Libertador*.[71] In addition, Bolívar's ideal of pan-Latin-American unity seemed to be incarnated in the flow of exiles from various Spanish-American nations, thus lending a true trans-Latin-American character to exile life in Mexico. One of the most colorful individuals in this milieu was

[69] José Vasconcelos, *El desastre (Tercera parte de Ulises Criollo)*. Mexico: Editorial Jus, 1968, pp. 23–25.

[70] When Carrillo Puerto rebelled against the Mexican federal government and was executed, the life of his close Venezuelan friend and ally, Carlos León, also condemned to die, was spared because of his condition of exile. See Guillermo García Ponce, *Memorias de un general de la utopía*. Caracas: Cotragraf, 1992, p. 67.

[71] Ricardo Melgar Bao, "Utopía y revolución en el exilio venezolano en México," paper presented at the LASA annual conference, Guadalajara, April 1997.

perhaps Gustavo Adolfo Navarro, who adopted the name of Tristán Marof, a Bolivian diplomat and writer, who became alienated from the circles of power in his home country and turned radical socialist in the 1920s. Living in exile for many years, he arrived in Mexico after residing in Peru, Panama, and Cuba and before departing for New York and, later on, Buenos Aires.[72]

The image of hospitality and provision of asylum was further reinforced as part of Mexico's self-image in the international arena during the years that followed Franco's victory in Spain. Starting in 1937, and en masse after 1939, Spanish émigrés arrived in Mexico, with an estimated total of 25,000, far above the number of those who moved to Argentina and other locations in the Americas. During the Spanish Civil War, Mexico consistently supported the Spanish Republic on the diplomatic front, at times forcefully upholding its rights in the League of Nations and selling arms to the republican government.[73]

In 1939, Mexico announced that it was willing to accept an unlimited number of refugees, on the condition that the republican government finance their transportation and settlement in Mexico. President Lázaro Cárdenas (1934–1940) was a well-known sympathizer of the republican cause. Nevertheless, some observers claim that Cárdenas had more than altruistic considerations in mind when accepting the Spanish refugees, as some U.S. $50 million (part of the Spanish treasure that had remained in the hands of the republican government) was to be allocated to the refugee resettlement programs. Clearly, the Mexican economy would benefit from the investment.[74] Moreover, as repeatedly stated by the president, the Spaniards who reached Mexico were, by and large, highly qualified in their respective professions. As such, their contribution to the economic development of the country was expected to be considerable. The refugees were expected to settle in locales decided by Mexican officials, mostly in underpopulated regions, and to work either on agricultural cooperatives or on state land, using their own resources. Urban centers were supposedly off-limits for Spanish immigrants. Only the intellectuals were exempt from such restrictions. The government offered to bring Spain's most prominent intellectuals to Mexico and to provide them with the facilities and income necessary for the continuation of their work. For this purpose, it created *La Casa de España*, later renamed *El Colegio de México*, which went on to become a prestigious institution of research and higher education. The Spanish intellectuals, it was thought, would contribute to Mexican intellectual life by lecturing, writing, and tutoring students in scholarly pursuits.[75]

---

[72] Ricardo Melgar Bao, lecture in the workshop on Political Exile in Argentina and Latin America, CEDINCI, Buenos Aires, August 2005. Marof (1896–1979) is one of several key figures of Bolivian letters, who had to spend years in exile. Other prominent figures include Mariano Ricardo Terrazas (1833–1878), Nataniel Aguirre (1843–1888), and Alcides Arguedas (1879–1946).

[73] Patricia W. Fagen, *Exiles and Citizens: Spanish Republicans in Mexico*. Austin: University of Texas Press, 1973, p. 24.

[74] Hans Wollny, "Asylum Policy in Mexico: A Survey." *Journal of Refugee Studies*, 4, 3 (1991): 219–236; mention on p. 222.

[75] Fagen, *Exiles and Citizens*, pp. 27–31 and 47–48.

Cárdenas stressed the similarities between the future immigrants and the Mexican people: a shared culture, a shared language and, no less important, a shared history made them preferable to any other immigrants. In short, Mexico would greatly benefit from the absorption of the refugees. Moreover, because the refugee organizations would provide the funds for transportation and reset-tlement, the benefit would come at a minimum cost. The immigration of the Spanish refugees was strongly opposed by several sectors of the population. The Mexican press was especially vocal in its opposition to Cárdenas's plan. Among the reasons most commonly cited by the opponents of the idea was the danger that these supposedly extremist elements represented. Some saw the Spanish exiles as anticlerical revolutionaries. Even more important was the fear that the refugees would compete with Mexicans in the labor market. The hostility felt toward the possible competitors was by no means the exclusive domain of blue-collar workers. Such professional groups as the medical association and the teachers' syndicate also expressed opposition.

Asylum has been related in Mexico to policies of migration, which were restrictive, especially concerning possible access to citizenship. Mexico's first law of naturalization and foreigners (1886) and the first migration law (1908) both recognized the issue but limited the possible entrance of handicapped individuals and criminals, with the exception of politicians and military perse-cuted on political grounds. In the migration laws of the 1930s, a new category was added: local visitors to border and littoral areas of the country. Hans Wollny, who studied the asylum policies in Mexico, identifies a basic tension between the *raison d'état* that served as rationale for these policies and the interests of the refugees themselves. He observes that Mexico's asylum pol-icy was never based exclusively on purely humanitarian purposes, but that grant of asylum was always heavily influenced by aspects of political affinity, employment policies, national development strategies, and even by aspects of racial prejudice, as in the case of Jewish refugees who were denied entry dur-ing World War II. Indeed, Mexican immigration laws from the 1920s onward acquired a strong xenophobic character. The immigration regulations of June 1932 emphasized the preference of foreigners easily prone to be assimilated into the Mexican environment – described in the document as those of Latin or Western European origin, belonging to the white race, excluding Slavs, Jews, Gypsies, Africans, Mulattos, Hindus, Asians (besides Japanese, Filipinos, and Hawaiians), and any other *mixed color*.[76] The regulations passed in 1933 and 1934 were even more extreme in their discouragement of the immigration of "undesirable foreigners." Starting in 1938, Mexican diplomats were instructed not to consider requests of asylum filed by individuals not applying from their home countries.[77] The impact of these regulations on actual immigration can

---

[76] Gloria Carreno and Celia Zack de Zuckerman, *El convenio ilusorio: refugiados polacos de guerra en México, 1943–1947*. Mexico: Centro de Documentación e Investigación de la Comu-nidad Ashkenazí de México, 1998, p. 87.

[77] Daniela Glazer, "Refugiados judíos bajo el Cardenismo," lecture in the workshop on political exile in Argentina and Latin America, organized by CEDINCI, Buenos Aires, August 2005.

best be illustrated by German immigration to Latin America. Between 1933 and 1945, about 110,000 German refugees – of whom more than 90 percent were of Jewish origin – resettled in Latin America; at least 45,000 went to Argentina, some 25,000 to Brazil, and some 12,000 to Chile. In comparison, Mexico admitted only around 2,250 of them.[78]

This wider context leads to suggest that, in this period at least, the reception accorded to the republican refugees may have constituted the exception rather than the rule in Mexico's refugee policy. The Spanish exiles were the first and only group that was offered the rights of unlimited immigration and almost automatic citizenship following arrival in Mexico. Most of them opted to become Mexican citizens. Accordingly, the absorption of the Spanish exiles was highly successful because of a host of favorable conditions: a common linguistic and historical background combined with the high professional capacity of the refugees and the strong sympathy the host government professed for the republican cause.[79]

Mexico kept its strict refugee policy even after the war was over. Again, a comparison between the number of European refugees absorbed elsewhere in Latin America with the number of those who settled in Mexico illustrates the point: whereas more than 32,000 went to Argentina, 28,000 to Brazil, and 17,000 to Venezuela, the number in Mexico did not reach a thousand. Since the late 1940s, a formal distinction was made between political refugees from countries in the Americas and those fleeing from persecution in other countries and continents. The migration laws introduced at the end of 1947 gave preference to immigrants from the American continent. According to the Mexican Population Law of 1947 (*Ley General de Población*) and the implementing act of 1950, refugees from other places were required to fill their petitions while abroad, whereas individuals escaping from other American states had more chances of being granted the status of refugee, once they entered the Mexican territory. In addition, being granted refugee status did not guarantee a better legal standing than that of other aliens in Mexico. For all migratory categories, even the simple exercise of constitutionally guaranteed rights remained explicitly under permanent reservation of being expelled from the country.[80]

And yet, Latin Americans fleeing from repression in the 1950s, a period of political turbulence throughout Latin America, chose Mexico as one of their first options for exile, motivated by the image of progressive, revolutionary commitment of the Mexican political elite. In that period, Mexico received a host of exiles escaping from the dictatorships of Rafael Leónidas Trujillo in the

---

[78] Wollny, "Asylum Policy in Mexico: A Survey," p. 223. David Bankier, "Los exiliados alemanes en México y sus vínculos con la comunidad judía (1942–1945)." *Judaica Latinoamericana.* Jerusalem: Magnes, 1989, pp. 79–89; Judit Bokser-Liwerant, *Imágenes de un encuentro. La presencia judía en México durante la primera mitad del siglo XX.* Mexico: UNAM, Comité Central Israelita, MBM, 1991.

[79] Cpara Lida, *Inmigración y exilio Reflexiones sobre el caso español* México: Siglo XXI/Colegio de México, 1997.

[80] Wollny, "Asylum Policy in Mexico," pp. 219–236.

Dominican Republic, Francois 'Papa Doc' Duvalier in Haiti, Anastazio Somoza in Nicaragua, Marcos Pérez Jiménez in Venezuela, Carlos Castillo Armas and the subsequent short-term military rulers in Guatemala, and Fulgencio Batista in Cuba. Rooted in the postrevolutionary tradition, Mexico granted hospitality and political asylum to the persecuted antidictatorial and progressive forces of Central and South America, as it had granted shelter to the Venezuelans in the 1920s and to the defeated Spanish Republicans and anti-Fascist refugees from other countries in Europe in the late 1930s.

Besides the common Spanish language, cultural factors, and intra-elite contacts, Mexico's location in the proximity of their homelands could be turned into an asset as these forces tried to regain power in their countries of origin. Paradigmatic is the case of the Cuban exiles, who used Mexico as a point of access to the United States, a source of arms and financial support, and as the place from which they envisioned and eventually succeeded in overthrowing the government of Fulgencio Batista in 1959.

When Batista took power in the military coup of March 1952, ousted President Carlos Prío Socorrás went into exile in Mexico, together with his family, ministers, close associates, and many other political and public figures. Batista did not deter those fleeing from Cuba from reaching their places of exile. On the contrary, he granted them permits [*salvoconductos*] that enabled them to leave, assuming that once abroad, the international treaties of asylum would force the host countries to prevent the newcomers from remaining actively involved in political and military actions against his home government. Although Prío Socorrás soon left Mexico for exile in the United States, his former Secretary of State Aureliano Sánchez Arango organized Cuban exiles' political activities in Mexico. Batista put pressure on Mexico to prevent it, but the political exiles also had powerful contacts and networks. They managed to curb Mexican police pressure against their activities by contacting President Adolfo Ruiz Cortínez several times as their activists were detained or harassed.[81]

A second wave of Cuban exiles reached Mexico in the 1950s as the result of the mounting repression launched by Batista, after the failure of the attack at the Moncada military camp on 26 July 1953 (the origin of the official name of the revolutionary movement led by Fidel Castro). While the leaders of the attack were killed or imprisoned in the Isla de los Pinos, many members of various opposition groups suffered persecution and left Cuba for Mexico. In Mexico, they were able to develop a wide range of anti-Batista activities. Prominent Cuban figures such as Raúl Roa, Sánchez Arango, and Teresa Casuso y Morín published many articles in the magazine *Humanismo*, which spread the ideas of Latin-American exile.[82]

---

[81] Salvador E. Morales Pérez and Laura del Alizal, *Dictadura, exilio e insurrección: Cuba en la perspectiva mexicana, 1952–1958*. Mexico: Secretaría de Relaciones Exteriores, 1999, pp. 179–186.

[82] Morales Pérez and Alizal, *Dictadura*, pp. 188–189. The magazine *Humanismo* published in Spanish the famous interview awarded by Fidel Castro to Herbert Matthews of *The New York Times* in Sierra Maestra in 1957.

In 1955, Batista arranged for elections in which he was elected president and declared a political amnesty, releasing political prisoners and allowing for the return of exiles. The amnesty excluded outlawed communists and the prisoners of the Moncada attack. Following popular pressure, the latter were allowed to regain their freedom. After his release, and feeling the limits of political freedoms in Cuba, Fidel Castro and other political activists left for Mexico in July 1955. In Mexico, Castro met his brother Raúl as well as other exiles, and for the first time met Ernesto Guevara, known as "Che." In the late 1950s, Castro's movement, the *Movimiento 26 de Julio,* turned into one of the most active organizations in the exile community. Many other organizations were formed or flourished there, among them the following: Organización Auténtica, Directorio Obrero Revolucionario, el Partido del Pueblo Cubano (the so-called *Ortodoxo* party), la Juventud del Partido Revolucionario Cubano, and the Club de Exiliados José Martí.

The exiles benefited from their image as fighters for freedom in the homeland. Castro and others traveled to the United States and collected money for anti-Batista activities. Back in Mexico, they initiated a series of military training programs, enrolling both Cubans and Mexicans for the cause. It is in this framework that Castro met Colonel Alberto Bayo Giroud, a Cuban-born Spaniard who had served in the Republican Army in the Spanish Civil War (1936–1939). Bayo, exiled in Mexico after the defeat of the Spanish Republic, was eager to train Cubans in their fight for freedom. With the financial support of Prío Socorrás and the Cuban communities of the United States, Castro and Juan Manuel Márquez purchased local arms and smuggled weapons into Mexico. The military training led to the arrest and interrogation of members of the *Movimiento 26 de Julio* and the danger of deportation. The detention put into motion a series of contacts with exile communities and individuals that Castro had learned to appreciate while in Mexico. Through the intercession of lawyers and local public figures (including former President Lázaro Cárdenas, who contacted Mexican President Ruiz Cortínez on their behalf), the pressures of the Cuban diaspora in the United States, and the wide coverage of the Mexican and American press, the exiles were allowed to remain active in Mexico. The government of Batista continued to put pressure on Mexico by presenting formal complaints and spreading misinformation in an attempt to curtail the activities of the exiles. However, the Cuban exiles managed to continue their underground activities, buying a small ship – the *Granma* – with which Castro and 81 followers launched their invasion of Cuba in late November 1956.[83]

Mexico granted asylum to political exiles through its diplomatic missions in the Americas. Some of the best-known cases of such 'diplomatic asylum'

---

[83] Morales Pérez and Alizal, *Dictadura*, pp. 210–222. The departure of this expedition from Mexico led to new formal complaints by Batista that, in turn, forced the Mexican authorities to advise the Cuban exiles to be careful not to violate the laws of asylum. Still, material support for the rebels continued to be mobilized in the country and forced the authorities to expel one exile to Miami and reprimand the others.

occurred in Guatemala in 1954, when 318 persons were granted asylum in the Mexican Embassy after the overthrow of the government of Jacobo Arbenz, and in 1964 after the *coup d'etat* that deposed Brazilian President João Goulart, when more than a hundred individuals were able to leave Brazil for Mexico after obtaining diplomatic asylum. In postrevolutionary Cuba, especially after 1964 when the Mexican delegation became the only Latin American diplomatic mission that remained open, Mexico granted asylum even to those who had sought refuge in other Latin American embassies and whose governments had severed their diplomatic relations with Cuba. Unsurprisingly, a substantial number of Cuban refugees reached Mexico. However, for the majority, Mexico was an intermediate stop on the way to their final destination: the United States.

The experience of the Mexican authorities with exile activities, as well as other international considerations, led to the introduction of changes in the legislation of asylum, aimed to better control the political activities of exiles. Truly enough, the legal limitations that regulated the presence of foreigners in Mexican territory already were in existence in the Mexican Population Law of 1947 (*Ley General de Población*), which in its Article 33, allowed for the expulsion of foreigners whose presence was 'inconvenient' to the national interest. The general phrasing would lead to more concrete references in Article 42 of the New 1974 Law of Population, which established political asylum with temporary, nonimmigrant status:

In order to protect his freedom or his life from political persecution in his or her country of origin, a person subject to political asylum is authorized to remain [in Mexico] for the period that the *Secretaría de Gobernación* sees fit or judges convenient, according to the circumstances of each case. If the person subject to political asylum violates national laws, s/he will lose his/her migration status without diminishing sanctions applicable to his or her case. The same *Secretaría* will be free to change his status while in the country. The person subject to political asylum cannot leave the country without permission from the *Secretaría*, otherwise he or she may lose their status.[84]

Mexican migration authorities have maintained since the 1970s a monopoly over the interpretation of political asylum. Trivial reasons, such as getting involved in street fights or even a car accident could be sufficient reason to threaten a newcomer with deportation.

According to the Inter-American Commission of Human Rights, during the 1970s there were between 8,000 and 10,000 refugees fleeing from Bolivia and more than a half million each from Chile and Argentina, after these countries' *coups d'état* in 1971, 1973, and 1976, respectively. The number of those who had left Uruguay was also estimated at a half million, although not all cases had been politically motivated, but rather there was a mixture of political and economic motivations behind the exit of the Uruguayans. Many South American refugees had to change asylum countries several times, especially after the

---

[84] *Ley General de Población y Reglamento de la Ley General de Población*. Mexico: Consejo Nacional de Población, 1987. Cecilia Imaz, *La práctica del asilo y del refugio en México*. Mexico: Potrerillos Editores, 1995.

over in Argentina, and when their personal safety was no longer gainst secret police activity from Chile and Uruguay. Estimations nes widely. The most reliable figures about the exiles in Mexico seem to be those of the 1980 census, as reported by Pablo Yankelevich, which speaks of 5,479 Argentineans, 1,106 Brazilians, 3,345 Chileans, and 1,553 Uruguayans.[85] These numbers coincide with those provided by the UNHCR, according to which, at the beginning of the 1980s, there were about 10,000 South American refugees in Mexico. On the other hand, unofficial sources report the presence of about 11,000 Argentines, 10,000 Chileans, and 2,000 Uruguayans in Mexico.[86] Carlos Ulanovsky estimates the number of Argentines alone to be more than 5,000 (he also mentions the number 12,000) in Mexico City in this period, based on unofficial statistics.[87] Mario Margulis puts their numbers between 8,000 and 8,800.[88] Out of this number, about 800 Chileans, 400 Uruguayans, and 65 Argentineans were granted the status of beneficiaries of political asylum. In the case of the Argentineans, out of the 65, 26 were part of the family of Fernando Hugo Vaca Narvaja, one of the leaders of the Montoneros. Relocating to Mexico were also leaders and activists of the Bolivian Movimiento Nacionalista Revolucionario de Izquierda (MNRI, or the National Revolutionary Leftist Movement), the Unión Democrática de Liberación of Nicaragua, and the Partido Socialista Revolucionario of Peru.[89]

Mexican diplomatic missions played an important, though variable, role in the rescue of those persecuted by the military regimes of South America. This was especially the case in Chile, after the overthrow of the government of Salvador Allende in 1973. President Luis Echeverría (1970–1976) instructed the diplomatic mission in Santiago to offer diplomatic asylum whenever deemed necessary. Between September 1973 and November 1974, more than 700 citizens left Chile after being granted asylum at the Mexican Embassy. The refugees were subsequently joined by their families.[90] The Mexican ambassador to Chile, Gonzalo Martínez Corbalá, personally looked after prominent members of the Allende administration hidden around Santiago to offer them the protection of the Mexican government.[91] In addition, the Mexican embassy interceded with the Chilean junta on the behalf of well-known politicians and

---

[85] Pablo Yankelevich, "Memoria y exilio. Sudamericanos en México," in Bruno Groppo and Patricia Flier, Eds., *La imposibilidad del olvido*. La Plata: Ediciones al Margen, 2001, p. 233.

[86] Wollny, "Asylum Policy in Mexico," pp. 225–226.

[87] Carlos Ulanovsky, *Seamos felices mientras estamos aquí*. Buenos Aires: Ediciones de la Pluma, 1983.

[88] Mario Margulis, "Argentines in Mexico," in Alfredo E. Lattes and Enrique Oteiza, Eds., *The Dynamics of Argentine Migration (1955–1984). Democracy and the Return of Expatriates*. Geneva: UNRISD, 1987.

[89] Informe de la misión de la Internacional Socialista a América Latina, 15–25 March 1978. Socialist International Archives (1951–1988) at the International Institute of Social History, Amsterdam, files 1125–1129.

[90] Yankelevich, "Memoria y exilio. Sudamericanos en México," p. 232.

[91] Ibid., p. 237. In 1992 González Corbalá was awarded the Orden al Mérito de Chile by the democratic government of that country.

intellectuals. Moreover, as an expression of its principled stance, Mexico broke off diplomatic relations with Chile as soon as the last political refugee left the country.

Among the Chileans who sought diplomatic asylum in Mexico were prominent figures such as the widow of Salvador Allende, Hortensia Bussi de Allende, their daughters and grandchildren; former ministers of the UP (Unidad Popular, or Popular Unity coalition) government such as Lisandro Cruz Ponce, head of the Ministry of Justice, and Pedro Vuskovic, former head of the Ministry of Economy and president of CORFO (Corporación de Fomento, or Development Corporation); Adolfo Ortega, former president of the national airline; senators such as the socialist Alejandro Chelén; and key figures of the state-related mass media and politics.

The role played by Mexican diplomatic missions in other South American capitals was significant as well. In Bolivia, some 200 people took refuge in the Mexican Embassy, whereas the numbers in Uruguay in the 1970s were around 400.[92] The Mexican ambassador in Montevideo, Vicente Múñiz Arroyo, is remembered by numerous political exiles as someone who went beyond his diplomatic duties to help the *asilados*, even fighting the Uruguayan security forces to save potential refugees.[93]

In Buenos Aires, the granting of political asylum by the Mexican Embassy was less frequent than in the Uruguayan case, covering only 65 cases. This was due to a much stricter interpretation of the rules pertaining to diplomatic asylum. A comparison between the conduct of the embassy in Buenos Aires with those in Montevideo and Santiago illustrates the point: In the latter two cases, citizens of other South American countries found refuge in the Mexican diplomatic missions. The one in Buenos Aires refused to grant asylum to non-Argentineans, even though there was evidence of cooperation between the South American juntas in the persecution of political opponents. Moreover, those seeking asylum in the Mexican Embassy in Buenos Aires had to wait for periods of up to six years before they were given a pass [*salvo*] [*conducto*] by the military government allowing them to leave the country. One of the best-known cases was that of the Argentinean ex-President Héctor J. Cámpora, who in April 1976 entered the Mexican Embassy with his son and with Juan Manuel Abal Medina, the young secretary-general of the Movimiento Nacional Justicialista (Peronism) and brother of the late Fernando Abal Medina, founder of the Montoneros. Cámpora remained in the Mexican Embassy for more than 3.5 years because of the refusal of the military government to grant him a safe conduct. He was allowed to leave only after the terminal nature of his

---

[92] Silvia Dutrénit-Bielous, "Recorriendo una ruta de la migración política del Río de la Plata a México." *Estudios Interdisciplinarios de América Latina*, 12, 2 (2001): 67.

[93] Muñiz Arroyo and a second Mexican diplomat, Gustavo Maza, physically fought members of the security forces to rescue a student and political militant, Federico Falkner, who was captured while trying to enter the embassy. Silvia Dutrénit and Guadalupe Rodríguez de Ita, *Asilo diplomático mexicano en el Cono Sur.* Mexico: Instituto Mora and SRE, 1999, p. 5.

illness was established. His son left a year later to attend the funeral of his father. Abal Medina was allowed to leave only in May 1982, after spending more than six years in the diplomatic mission. Comparatively, this delay contrasts with the case of Uruguayans seeking asylum at the Mexican Embassy in Montevideo. There, the candidates for asylum waited for up to a maximum of eight months before being allowed to leave their country. The Mexican government granted visas to Uruguayan communists and others on the condition that they would move forward from Mexico to other destinations. Although the USSR and the German Democratic Republic had offered entry visas to members of the Partido Comunista de Uruguay, the latter insisted on obtaining political asylum in Mexico, creating an administrative conundrum around the quota for Uruguayan refugees.[94]

The activism of Mexican diplomatic missions also might have had to do with the personal disposition of the ambassadors as much as with official policy. The appointment of a new ambassador to Uruguay in June 1977 was followed by a drastic decrease in the granting of asylum. In Argentina too, the small number of individuals who were granted asylum might have been related to the personal stance of the ambassador who, unlike the Mexican ambassador to Chile at the time of the *coup*, made asylum conditional on the potential beneficiary arriving at the embassy by his or her own means. Because diplomatic missions were heavily guarded by the Argentinean security services in an attempt to prevent political dissidents from seeking asylum, a trip to the embassy involved the risk of being arrested and even killed.[95]

Mexican asylum policy was neither disinterested nor one of 'open gates.' Former Mexican ambassador to Argentina, Roque González Salazar, pointed out that President Luis Echeverría had more than altruistic reasons in mind when he decided on a policy of steadfast support of political exiles. González Salazar explains that the implementation of a generous refugee policy, especially in the case of intellectuals, brought Mexico considerable prestige in the international political arena; this advantage was a major consideration, in particular, after the student massacre of Tlatelolco in 1968 had badly damaged Mexico's international image.[96] Moreover, in Uruguay at least, the *asilados* were encouraged by Mexican diplomats to emigrate to countries of the socialist bloc. This was part of a strategy pursued by the Mexican government, its

---

[94] Guadalupe Rodríguez de Ita, "Experiencias de asilo registradas en las embajadas Mexicanas," in Silvia Dutrénit and Guadalupe Rodríguez de Ita, Eds., *Asilo diplomático Mexicano en el Cono Sur*, 1999, p. 138; and Silvia Dútrenit Bielous, "Recorriendo una ruta de la migración política del Río de la Plata a México," *EIAL*, 12, 2 (2001): 71–74. This information is based on documents of the Archives of the Foreign Affairs Ministry of Mexico (AHDSREM).

[95] Dútrenit Bielous, in Dútrenit and Rodríguez de Ita, *Asilo diplomático*, pp. 5–7.

[96] Despite this understanding, González Salazar denied asylum to many individuals attempting to escape repression in Argentina. Pablo Yankelevich, "Asilados sudamericanos en México: luces y sombras de la política de asilo del estado mexicano durante la década de 1970," paper presented at the LASA XXVII Internacional Congreso in Montreal, September 2007.

intention being to adopt quotas for the entry of political refugees into Mexico. The Uruguayan community of exiles and the Mexican officials had reached an understanding according to which Mexico would grant visas to the *asilados* in the diplomatic mission in Montevideo on the condition that some of the Uruguayans already residing in Mexico would opt for a third country.[97]

Thus, Mexico's asylum policy during the 1970s was shaped by diverse and sometimes contradictory factors. Humanitarian concerns, domestic and foreign strategies, all played a role in the configuration of Mexico's handling of asylum petitions.

The wave of armed conflicts that destabilized Central America in the late 1970s and early 1980s sparked a severe refugee crisis. Civil wars in Nicaragua and El Salvador and major counterinsurgency operations by the Guatemalan military created an unprecedented flow of refugees. For the first time, Mexico was confronted with a major refugee crisis in its territory. Salvadorans made up the largest group of refugees, followed by Guatemalans and Nicaraguans. The case of Salvadorans is particularly acute as the number of refugees reached around 750,000, or 16 percent of the country's population in the mid-1980s – of them, 175,000 in Nicaragua, 120,000 in Mexico, 70,000 in Guatemala, 20,000 in Honduras, 10,000 in Costa Rica, 7,000 in Belize, and 1,000 in Panama. The number of political refugees was estimated to be 245,000 in 1984. In addition, there were internal refugees [*desplazados*] forced to flee within El Salvador.[98] According to Wollny, the total number of refugees alone surpassed the 1.3 million. Of these, Salvadorans comprised more than a million, whereas the number of Guatemalans and Nicaraguans was estimated to be around 200,000 and 63,000, respectively.[99]

The number of refugees in Mexico was estimated to be at least a half million.[100] Nevertheless, only 46,600 had received UNHCR assistance by the end of 1987. Beginning in 1983, the Mexican government stopped recognizing Salvadorans as refugees. Mexican authorities claimed that Salvadorans were economic migrants and refused to grant them asylum status or otherwise legalize their presence in Mexico. If caught, Salvadorans had to provide documented proof of employment or face deportation. Although Salvadorans were, by and large, well-educated young people belonging to the urban middle

---

97 Dutrénit Bielous, *Asilo diplomático*, p. 6.
98 Celio Mármora, "Hacia la migración planificada interlatinoamericana. Salvadoreños en Argentina." *Estudios migratorios latinoamericanos*, 1, 3 (1986): 275–293. See also Marina Pianca, "The Latin American Theater of Exile." *Theater Research International*, 14, 2 (1989): 174–185.
99 Hans Wollny, "Asylum Policy in Mexico: A Survey." *Journal of Refugee Studies*, 4, 3 (1991): 228. However, Wollny warns that all estimates need to be handled with some reservation.
100 In 1987, the number of Salvadorans residing illegally in Mexico was estimated to be at least a half million by the Mexican coordinator for Salvadoran refugees (Yundt, 1988: 139). More than 110,000 Guatemalans and a few thousand Nicaraguans must be added to this number. UNHCR estimates for May 1986 indicated that at least 1 million, or perhaps twice as many, had been displaced by the generalized violence afflicting the region. Keith W. Yundt, *Latin American States and Political Refugees*. New York: Praeger, 1988, p. 135.

classes, government officials portrayed them as a problematic and undesirable population.[101]

Guatemalan refugees had to confront even harder obstacles: An indigenous rural population who had been the subject of discriminatory policies in the home country, they were mostly illiterate and lacked economic means. Moreover, even though Guatemalans shared a common ethnic background with the inhabitants of southeast Mexico, many of them did not speak Spanish but rather their own languages, a fact that greatly impaired their ability to integrate.

In 1980, the Mexican government created a special interministerial body, the Mexican Commission for Aid to Refugees (Comisión Mexicana de Ayuda a Refugiados, or COMAR) to deal with the mass influx of refugees. COMAR proposed to recognize most Central American refugees as *asilados políticos*. However, this proposal was not implemented. Mexican migration authorities defined the mass of Central American refugees as economic migrants rather than victims of political persecution and implemented a policy of deportation and, at times, harassment. Between 1980 and 1982, at least 70,000 Salvadoran refugees were deported from Mexico to Guatemala or directly to El Salvador. Some estimates put the number of Central Americans deported annually to their home country at more than 46,000.[102]

A number of reasons may be cited to explain the restrictive Mexican attitude toward the Central American refugees, such as the country's economic situation, the complex relationship with the United States, and, last but not least, the country's fear of a spillover of the Central American wars into its territory, becoming an indirect victim of political turbulence in the region.

Among those moving to Mexico in the early 1980s were many indigenous Mayans from Guatemala. Most of them entered Mexico as refugees, escaping counterinsurgent campaigns by the Guatemalan Army and paramilitary groups. Most tended to settle in improvised camps near the border, mainly in Chiapas and, to a lesser extent, in the states of Campeche and Quintana Roo, sharing cultural and linguistic ties with the local population and hoping to return when possible. In this case, Mexico was forced to confront a novel situation in a relatively short time: Tens of thousands of Guatemalan peasants crossed the border. Whereas in the earlier waves of exile (e.g., from the Southern Cone in the 1970s), exiles came from the middle and upper strata, the refugees from Guatemala were of lower-class origins, adding pressures to the problems of access to land, already in existence in Southern Mexico. Resulting from this situation, a change in foreign policy took place in this period. Mexico pursued the pacification of Central America, both in order to stop the flow of refugees and to facilitate the return of those refugees already settled in its territory. In parallel, as already indicated, the Mexican government attempted to expel illegal migrants in the thousands, while granting asylum to few individuals.

[101] Yundt, *Latin American States*, p. 139.
[102] Wollny, "Asylum Policy," p. 231.

In a 1984 survey of Guatemalans in Mexico City, 80 percent of the sample declared having left their country for political reasons, 73 percent did not possess any kind of document, 13.6 percent had tourist visas, and only 3 percent had received political asylum. Within Chiapas, the Mexican government put forward a policy of resettlement into neighboring states, but by 1987 managed to convince only about 18,200 peasants to move. Many others refused to abandon the state of Chiapas. The government granted them documents as border visitors or agricultural workers, and the dioceses of San Cristóbal de las Casas and UNHCR provided them with support and recognized many of them, thus precluding the possibility of expulsion.[103]

The arrival of successive waves of refugees and exiles turns a certain host country into a pole of attraction. Once there is such a community in a site of exile, interacting with the local society, learning mutually to understand their cultural practices and ideas, knowing how to move around vis-à-vis employers and the local authorities, and how to go to the market and how to interact socially, it will be easier for further waves of fellow co-nationals to find their way around. The old-timers may also become a bridge for the newcomers. One of the crucial factors is the formation of a critical mass of exiles and refugees. For the newcomers, the presence of 'old-timers,' both prior exiles and other fellow countrymen, can be a bridge to lessen alienation and in constructing more rapidly a certain sense of normalcy and community in the diaspora. Nonetheless, for the host authorities and locals, such a critical mass forces the recognition of a major problem and imposes the need to address the problem of exiles and refugees in a more comprehensive way, resulting in the generation of paradoxical implications, as analyzed by Sarah Lischer for the cross-national and international arena.[104]

Conclusion

Sites of exile present various advantages and disadvantages for those seeking shelter, from both a material and a cultural perspective. In its insularity, Chile was probably an atypical site for those escaping repression and civil war in sister-countries. Distance and lack of accessibility could impair contacts with the home countries but, at the same time, granted a measure of security, especially under the strong centralist administrations since the 1830s. Chilean political stability and Conservatism further provided a workable model whose advantages were perceived by the exiles, who could then try to apply them once back in the home countries. Constitutionalism and respect for the law were key elements experienced by the exiles, difficult to be disregarded as

---

[103] Laura O'Dogherty, "Mayas en el exilio: Los refugiados guatemaltecos en México," in *Memorias del Segundo coloquio internacional de Mayistas*. Universidad Autónoma de México, Centro de Estudios Mayas, 17–21 August 1987, pp. 213–217.

[104] Sarah Lischer, *Dangerous Sanctuaries: Refugee Camps, Civil War, and the Dilemmas of Humanitarian Aid*. Ithaca, NY: Cornell University Press, 2005.

political lessons. On the other hand, such an environment forced the exiles to refrain from participating in Chilean political life by following the ideas and conceptions that brought them into exile.

Moving to Paris and France involved leaving the home country far behind, especially in earlier times. Shifting to a different language was no minor task, especially for those intellectuals for whom linguistic expression is a main tool. Furthermore, keeping home standards of living in Paris required no minor economic effort and sources of income, often unavailable to exiles. Nonetheless, the advantages of cosmopolitan Paris and the image of living in the cultural capital of the West provided compensation. Learning opportunities, social contacts, meeting fellow Latin Americans and other exiles, ideological and political discussions, and the mere immersion in the French world of culture were highly valuable assets for any aspiring political and intellectual figure in the countries of origin.

Mexico turned into a major site of exile partly because of its practices of providing asylum to persecuted individuals in Latin America and beyond. Alejo Carpentier once said that when political repression turned violent, persecuted individuals almost naturally thought of finding refuge in Mexico. Under such circumstances, he said, "the only solution is to look for asylum in an embassy of a Latin American country. You think of the Mexican [Embassy]."[105] The postrevolutionary ethos presented exiles with a paradox. Being accepted as fellow revolutionaries from other countries of Latin America, they were constrained by the institutional tenets of the Mexican state. Benefiting from solidarity and a welcoming administration that provided study, research, and employment opportunities, they could maintain their previous ideological positions as long as they refrained from intervening in Mexican politics. They would enjoy the support of large segments of Mexican society and politicians, motivated by the latter's causes within the framework of a Latin-American ethos, but could not support radical causes within the host society.

Because of the combined effects of these factors, Chile, France, and Mexico turned into major sites of exile. These sites are far from being the only *lieux d'exil* for Latin-American exiles. In the Caribbean area, Venezuela became a pole of attraction for exiles especially since its democratization in 1958. In this case, the image of a stable, pluralistic, and democratic political system was important in bringing politically persecuted individuals from countries ruled by dictatorship. The Venezuelan oil prosperity made the relatively swift labor insertion of the newcomers possible. Contrastingly, revolutionary Cuba officially received activists from the Left escaping repression in other countries, as did later on Nicaragua under Sandinista rule. After the 1964 coup, Brazilian politicians and activists found shelter in Uruguay and Chile. Allende's Chile became a pole of attraction for Left forces between 1970 and 1973. After

---

[105] So oyen varios disparos... Tomas la calle aledaña. Tu única solución es buscar asilo en alguna embajada de país latinoamericano. Piensas en la de México. Alejo Carpentier, *El derecho de asilo*. La Habana: Arte y literatura, 1976.

the military takeovers in Uruguay and Chile, Argentina received many exiles who later were forced to escape once again, following the Argentinean coup of 24 March 1976. Paraguayan exiles traditionally found shelter in Argentina, suffering the consequences of the military repression during the Operation Condor.[106]

Established democracy has not been a *sine qua non* for the attraction and reception of exiles. Ideological and interest considerations as previous personal relations could open the gates of host countries to individuals escaping from their home country. Polities with authoritarian traits, such as Chile in the 19th century and postrevolutionary Mexico, may favor policies of asylum and reception of exiles. The creation and survival of major long-term sites of exile hinges on the receptivity of governments and local elites supporting administrative steps and regulation easing or hampering the presence of exiles in their midst.

Beyond the continent, many other countries provided a shelter for those fleeing from the last wave of repression in Latin America, starting with European countries such as Italy, Sweden, both Germanys, Spain, the UK, Switzerland, the USSR, the Eastern European countries, and including more uncommon sites such as Australia, Israel, Angola, and South Africa. Some of these are analyzed in the following chapters.

---

[106] J. Patrice McSherry, "Tracking the Origins of State Terror Network: Operation Condor." *Latin American Perspectives*, 29, 1 (2002): 36–60.

5

Widening Exclusion and the Four-Tiered Structure of Exile

In polities of restricted political participation, exile was mostly a privilege reserved for a segment of the political elite ostracized by those in power. By the late 19th and early 20th centuries, however, a process of 'massification' of exile was manifest, as growing numbers of exiles with a middle- or lower-class background were affected by their purposeful or unwilling involvement in politics and the public arena. Widening exclusion led to a dynamic of dispersion of exiles, allowing them to increasingly focus the attention of an evolving international public sphere, in which former themes of internal politics found an echo on the basis of growing awareness and care about human-rights violations, political persecution, and exile. The transformation of the early three-tiered structure of exile into a four-tiered structure constitutes the core of this chapter.

Massive Exile: The Counterface of Political Inclusion

This process of massification of exile occurred in tandem with the changing nature of the political and social conflicts in the region. Latin American countries underwent processes of population growth, modernization, migration, and urbanization at different paces. Within each of them, the uneven pace of transformations was replicated, shaping strong internal asymmetries. Still, beyond differences, the entire region was a scenario of changes in the 20th century: from traditional into modern lifestyles, from rural into urban settings, and from Catholicism into religiously diversified and, at times, secular frameworks. From both socioeconomic and political perspectives, these societies were transformed under the aegis of population growth, immigration, and internal migration. With improved transportation and the introduction of new communication and other technologies, a sudden incorporation of peripheries into mainstream social and political trends was operated. As they became a part of nation-states, the broader strata were subject to the prospects and often unforeseeable perils of political participation.

In the context of polities tainted with authoritarianism or outrightly authoritarian, inclusion and political access have implied the likelihood of forceful exclusion. As inclusion was, in most cases, a product of sociopolitical pressures resulting in crises and instability, the possibility existed of excluding individuals and groups who were detrimental to the political control of those in power. In many cases, the prospects of routinized public order were perceived as contingent on the manageable exclusion of parties and sectors seen as the opposition. Rhetorically transformed into a threat to the national existence, these groups and individuals were often persecuted and expelled with the tacit support of manipulated public opinion. Arrests, torture, extrajudicial killings, and exile were widely used in order to deal with those portrayed as dangerous opponents. The move could be portrayed as instrumental to crisis resolution and as a contribution to public stability and orderly development. Brian Loveman's research has indicated that, institutionally, emergency legislation was widely applied to suppress social and political turmoil, providing a halo of legitimacy to policies conceived out of political expediency.[1]

Whenever political participation and mobilization widened and threatened the control of those in power and their supporting coalitions, excluding 'troublemakers,' 'dangerous enemies,' or 'triggers of instability' became highly beneficial. Although comparatively, Latin America as a whole experienced a limited number of international wars, internal conflicts have long characterized the region.[2] In the late 19th and early 20th centuries, inclusive pressures increased in the form of political and revolutionary groups that often adopted violent and anarchical forms of action. Facing these pressures, governments and social elites adopted repressive mechanisms of control and regulation. As countries modernized, pressures for political democratization grew and in some countries, were projected through populist leaders. In the post–World War II period, the entire subcontinent was increasingly touched by the processes of mobilization subsumed in the terms of the Cold War.[3]

Therefore, it was only natural to witness how exile – already encoded into the political culture of these countries during the first century of independent life – was activated as a major mechanism of institutionalized exclusion, not only by and against members of the old political classes but also increasingly by and against the leaders, activists, and rank-and-file sympathizers of those sectors that were newly incorporated into politics.

The middle classes entered politics mostly through some interweaving of an enlarged franchise and corporatist unionization. Along with social and

---

[1] Brian Loveman, *The Constitution of Tyranny: Regimes of Exception in Spanish America*. Pittsburgh, PA: University of Pittsburgh Press, 1993.

[2] Miguel Angel Centeno, "War in Latin America: The Peaceful Continent?," in Julio López-Arias and Gladys M. Varona-Lacey, Eds., *Latin America. An Interdisciplinary Approach*. New York: Peter Lang, 1999, pp. 121–136. See also Arie Kacowicz, *The Impact of Norms in International Society: The Latin American Experience, 1881–2001*, Notre Dame, IN: University of Notre Dame Press, 2005.

[3] Leslie Bethell, Ed., *Latin America since 1930*. Cambridge: Cambridge University Press, 1998.

economic modernization, there was increased political activism and membership in movements, parties, or politically linked organizations such as trade unions, newspapers, and professional organizations, as well as intellectual and academic groups. The larger countries of the region also went through processes of industrialization and diversification of their social structures, including a growing urban working class directly involved in production and related services. Concurrently, state bureaucracies expanded at the national, provincial, and municipal levels. These sectors increasingly entered the public domain, initially backing inter-elite struggles as part of differentiated sets of alliances, which mobilized them by promoting and supporting their sectorial demands.

The extent of the socioeconomic pressures, political confrontation, and repressive violence can be traced through the long series of bloody confrontations, falling short of revolutionary changes such as those attempted in Mexico, Bolivia, Cuba, or Nicaragua. Repressive violence was endemic but had its peaks, such as the massacre of Canudos in 1897 and the Contestado War in 1912–1916 in Brazil; the massacre of Santa María de Iquique in Chile in 1907; the Tragic Week anarchic revolts and pogroms in Argentina in 1919; the various U.S. interventions in Central America; the civil war in Costa Rica in the late 1940s; the assassination of Jorge Eliécer Gaitán in 1948 that emboldened the decade-long period of *La Violencia* in Colombia; the cycles of guerrilla war and repression in Guatemala from the 1950s to the 1990s; the Peruvian Shining Path [*Sendero Luminoso*] in the 1980s; the Colombian complex of narcotrafficking, criminality, guerrillas, and counterguerrillas since the 1960s; and the tense situations in Chiapas and the Andes during the 1990s and 2000s, in which the spillover of violence was mostly avoided. The magnitude of violence permeating these varied instances of protest, mobilization, and repression was modulated by the exacerbated use of political rhetoric coupled with the development of the mass media.

Whereas the first half of the 20th century was a transitional period in terms of mass exile, the subsequent decades turned into the most tragic period relative to mass exile, as the countries of the region faced failing and changing development models, mass mobilization, political polarization, and the dilemma of carrying out reforms or exposing themselves to revolutionary threats. These trends were entrapped in the antinomies of the Cold War, the resilience of powerful conservative sectors to relinquish power, and the development of doctrines of national security, which transformed the whole area into a scene of violent political exclusion.

With the intensification of the Cold War confrontations in the 1960s and 1970s, the use of political exile both as a means of escaping repression and death and as a mechanism of forced exclusion became more and more common. Latin-American political exiles spilled all over Latin America and reached the United States, Canada, Western Europe, the Communist bloc and, to a lesser extent, countries as far away as Israel, Algeria, Sierra Leone, and Australia.

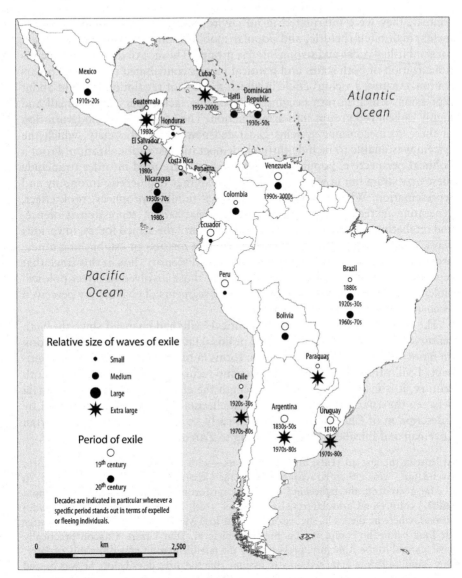

MAP 4. Expelling countries.

Paradoxically, a main factor lying beyond the widening use of political exile as a major mechanism of exclusion was the development of many features of modern civil society in various parts of Latin America. Functioning civil societies meant not only the emergence of bases for democracy but also increased political involvement and growing demands of social and political rights, redistribution, and transparency. In more stable environments, all of these could perhaps be channeled into strengthening democracy. Yet, in the Latin-American

context, they were interpreted in an environment of revolutionary developments, high-pitch rhetoric, and popular mobilization as a destabilizing threat
for established order and strong interest groups. The lack of democratic institutionalization of both states and political parties contributed to political polarization, creating a vicious circle in which the fear of revolution brought about
repression, which in turn became a convincing factor that pushed small and
highly radicalized groups into armed action. The very drive of modernization
of these socioeconomic systems generated new forces in society, which the
system was unable to include through democratic institutionalization. From a
political perspective, populism and clientelism were used in order to include
these new strata but in ways that did not encourage democratic autonomy and
representation. When populism failed, a 'self-fulfilling prophecy' took effect,
generating increasing political and social polarization, repression, violence,
and retaliations, decreasing levels of stability, until the armed forces, in various
ways, took over power with the self-attributed mission of establishing a new
order on the basis of their doctrines of national security. It is at this stage that
repression exceeded the limits of persecuting those involved in direct political
violence, and those in power began to target segments of civil society perceived
as enemies or bedrocks of subversion.

The processes behind the use of political exile had changed since the 19th
century. Confrontational politics and political factionalism continued but took
on more institutionalized and modern forms in many of the states of the continent. To illustrate the persistent impact and recurrence of elite exile in the 20th
century, it is instructive to quote at length the characterization of Guatemala
between the 1920s and the 1960s by intellectual Isidoro Zarco, followed by
a description of Chile in the 1920s and early 1930s by social scientists, Brian
Loveman and Elizabeth Lira. According to Zarco,

At least in the last 40 years, all former rulers – with the exception of Colonel Flores
Avendaño – were either led with honors to the General Cemetery or had (or have) to
live far away from the fatherland due to the misfortunes of politics. After suffering a
military coup, Don Carlos Herrera had to travel "freely by force" [*forcivoluntariamente*]
abroad, where he died. His successor, General José María Orellana, passed to a better
life long before he completed his presidential term. Don Lázaro Chacón practically
gave his soul to the Almighty, pressured by the terrible load of governing this country.
Don Baudilio Palma managed only to assume rule for three days before he was ousted
and he later died in exile. General Manuel Orellana left with a consular position to
Barcelona and was not allowed to die in his beloved fatherland. After 14 years of iron
rule, General Ubico died in exile and only under Colonel Peralta's rule were his remains
repatriated to Guatemalan lands. The only one who was permitted to return when dying
was General Ponce Vaides. Of those still alive, Arévalo, Arbenz and Ydígoras are forced
to stay far from their homeland. Some live with the threat of prison. Others must fear
death.[4]

[4] Isidoro Zarco, "El exilio: ingrato destino de nuestros ex-gobernantes," in Cesar Brañas, Ed.,
   El pensamiento vivo de Isidoro Zarco. Guatemala: Editorial José de Pineda Ibarra, 1973,
   pp. 125–126.

The options to exile were even harsher, as clearly stated by former Bolivian President Germán Busch (1904–1939) in an interview with political scientist Robert Caldwell. Referring to the opposition, he candidly said, "If I had not thrown them out, I would have had to shoot them."[5]

The situation in Chile in the early 20th century was not so dissimilar to that of other countries in terms of the uses of exile:

> Beyond overseeing and spying on trade union leaders, politicians and others, by governments since WWI, the administration of Ibáñez [1927–1931] imprisoned, relegated and sent to exile hundreds of opposition individuals of all political colors and also media representatives. Among them President [Arturo] Alessandri, General Enrique Bravo, Colonel Marmaduque Grove, Senators Luis Salas Romo and Luis Alberto Cariola, Deputies Pedro León Ugalde, Ramón and Luis Gutiérrez Alliende, Ernesto Barros Jarpa and future minister of Interior of the Popular Front and later founder of the anti-Communist group *Acción Chilena Anticomunista* (ACHA) [Chilean Anti-Communist Action] Arturo Olavarría.[6]

By the 20th century, exiles were both members of the political elite as well as rank-and-file political activists, union activists, intellectuals, students, and even persons detached from any public or political involvement. The new logic of demobilization affected members of all social segments. Factionalism was no less harsh than in the 19th century, although it was embedded in the process of institutionalization of party politics and the establishment of more participatory public spheres. All these were being forcefully limited by authoritarian governments that had a very negative view of politics and its impact on their countries. The military, while professing to be neutral in political terms, saw themselves as the saviors of the 'nation' and the moral reservoir of its perennial values. In this context, exile came to be conceptualized as a mechanism for the complete exclusion of those portrayed as the 'enemy.' This enemy was not one who, when circumstances allowed, would return to the homeland and resume its former social and political roles. It was an enemy to be totally excluded, either by physical elimination or through permanent exile. At this stage, exile served as a regulatory mechanism for nation-states centered on their own political and public spheres.

Military and authoritarian rule reformulated the criteria of inclusion and exclusion according to their own ideological tenets. From the start, they created whole categories of individuals and organizations to be excluded institutionally, as alien to the nation, its spirit, tradition, well-being, and future. Marxism, Leninism, Trotskyism, Socialism, Communism, Left-Wing Liberalism, the Christian Left, some forms of Populism, and whoever promoted these ideologies or merely sympathized with them had to be marginalized and/or eliminated because of the threat posed to the nation and its 'values.' Doctrines

---

[5] Testimony of Germán Busch to Robert G. Caldwell as reported in "Exile as an Institution." *Political Science Quarterly*, 58, 2 (1943): 246.

[6] Brian Loveman and Elizabeth Lira, *Las ardientes cenizas del olvido: vía chilena de reconciliación política, 1932–1994*. Santiago de Chile: LOM, 2000, p. 9.

of national security determined clear-cut criteria of inclusion and exclusion. These criteria were applied with varying degrees of autonomy of interpretation by the different mechanisms of repression.

The enemies were marked from the start. They included such varied targets as a professor who taught Marxism and other 'alien doctrines'; trade union leaders and members who fought for greater benefits; high school students who contested the established authorities in their demand for reduced fares for public transportation; a priest who defended the poor in his parish; a lawyer committed to the cause of human rights; a security officer who refused to shoot students in a demonstration; members of some academic disciplines, especially in the social sciences and humanities, such as psychology, sociology, and political science, and – briefly in Argentina – even modern mathematics, which were perceived as critical to the established order; artists and forms of art that expressed protest against social injustice and oppression; and all types of organizations – from political parties to professional and neighborhood associations – that were committed to 'antinational,' anti-Western, anti-Christian ideas. Various degrees of exclusion were applied in each of the countries, finding expression in the intervention into academic life, the destruction of several professional career tracks, the proscription and sometimes burning of 'dangerous' books and artistic creations, and prohibition against broadcasting 'subversive' music.[7]

Displacement ceased to be perceived by both persecutors and escapees as a tactical move. Truly enough, in some cases such as Chile, especially in the 1980s, those in power used internal exile [*relegación*] as a tool of punishment and political exclusion.[8] In this case, the move was less radical in terms of displacement and loss of contact with the home habitat but no less dramatic from a personal persective, as reflected in Carlos Guzmán's film, *La frontera* (Chile, 1991), and in personal testimonies gathered by FASIC (Fundación de Ayuda Social de las Iglesias Cristianas, or Social Aid Foundation of the Christian Churches).[9] Moreover, the very fact that a person was 'relegated' became a form of social stigma and occupational punishment. On their release, many of the internal exiles found themselves expelled from work or banished from continuing their university studies.

The rupture was usually even sharper in the case of those forced to move abroad. In a line of continuity with the more elitist forms of exile that prevailed in earlier times, the exiles knew that those in power would not tolerate their return, and if they could enter their country of origin, their mission would be

---

[7] Luis Roniger and Mario Sznajder, *The Legacy of Human-Rights Violations in the Southern Cone* 1999, pp. 249–250.

[8] In Chile, this mechanism was used following Decree Law 3,168 of 1980, which sanctioned internal exile for those found to be disturbing public peace. Between 1980 and 1985, 1,277 individuals were displaced to internal exile, with a peak of 733 in 1984. See *Programa de reunificación familiar: Reencuentro en el exilio*. Santiago: FASIC, 1991, Anexo No. 1.

[9] FASIC, *Exilio Interno, Relegación I, 1980*. Santiago: FASIC, 1981, Documento de trabajo No. 2.

to remove from power those responsible for the repression and their own exile. Concomitantly, a transformation was effected under the impact of views leading to zero-sum strategies, such as the doctrines of national security that called for the cleansing of society of subversive elements, coupled with the equally totalistic revolutionary views of some of the exiles, which were projected onto the entire political opposition as a means of disarticulating the 'old' forms of politics. Under this set of characterizations, political exile became a comprehensive means of exclusion, intended by those in power to have a long-lasting effect in the public arena. From the point of view of the authoritarian rulers holding power in various Latin-American countries during the Cold War, those who went abroad or were expelled for political reasons would be forever relegated to permanent exclusion. In other words, instead of denoting a politics of exit that might have implied regaining the status quo ante, as in the past, exile was orchestrated into a mechanism of total exclusion from politics. It is in this framework that Shain's definition of a political exile does not cover the entire gamut of political exiles. For Shain,

a political exile is that who engages in political activity, directed against the policies of a home regime, the home regime itself or the political system as a whole, and aimed at creating circumstances favorable to his return.[10]

When policies of long-term and unconditional exclusion are applied systematically and on a massive scale, cutting the links between the exile and his home-country politics, the will of the exile to act politically abroad and to return to the home country ceases to be the *sine qua non* requirement for defining exiles. Truly enough, a small group of displaced individuals continued to be politically active while abroad and were not only denied citizenship rights but also were attacked verbally and sometimes targeted physically by agents of their country's rulers. But these politically active exiles were only part of a much larger set of people suffering territorial exclusion following their identification as targeted enemies, whether or not they had played a political role in the past and whether or not they were engaged in politics in the present.

The triangular structure of exile had changed as well. Such a triangular structure was predicated on the interplay between the interests of the exiles, those of the host countries, and the pressures exerted by the home countries. Among these factors, the latter two assumed greater centrality as the states consolidated their borders and promoted national symbols and consciousness through education and civil and military services. This triangular structure of exile, present since early independence, persisted as the nation-states continued to be the main players in the international arena. The concept of the 'Patria Grande,' rooted in Bolivarianism, while persisting in the margins of the Left and the Right, had somehow given place to clear-cut distinctions sustaining the collective identities of Argentines, Mexicans, Brazilians, Colombians,

[10] Yossi Shain, *The Frontier of Loyalty.* Middletown, CN: Wesleyan University Press, 1989, p. 20.

Peruvians, and the other nationalities of the region. It would be in exile that the transnational identities would be regained, albeit only partially, in the framework of campaigns of solidarity, cross-national movements favoring regional integration, and the rediscovery of the common fate shared with the nationals of other Latin-American countries.

This structure underwent a core transformation in the second half of the 20th century, once the global arena entered the exile equation as a fourth factor (see Diagram 5.1). The global arena turned increasingly important in the exile equation as it became preoccupied with humanitarian international law and the protection of human rights. It is at this stage that, in the words of Saskia Sassen,

citizenship becomes a heuristic category through which to understand the question of rights and subject formation and to do so in ways that recover the conditionalities entailed in its territorial articulation and thereby the limits or vulnerabilities of this framing.[11]

In part, at least from the perspective of Latin America, this trend was the result of the increasingly transnational character of opposition and repression. In some outstanding cases, this confrontation reached the point of assassination in settings far removed from the home country; *vide* the murder of former Chilean Minister of Foreign Affairs Orlando Letelier and his secretary, a U.S. national, Ronnie Moffitt, on 21 September 1976 in Washington, D.C., orchestrated by the Chilean DINA (Dirección Nacional de Inteligencia, or National Intelligence Directorate). The Condor Operation, reaching far beyond each Latin-American country, was the logical development of the impossibility of containing political opposition by their exclusion from domestic public spheres. The counterface of this wave of institutionalized exclusion and political persecution was the internalization of principles of human rights by organizations at the international and global arena. Instrumental in such shifts were organizations such as the United Nations, Amnesty International, Human Rights Watch, and, particularly, Americas Watch, the World Council of Churches, the Catholic Church, the UNCHR, the International Organization for Migration, the Red Cross, the European Parliament and human rights parliamentary commissions across the globe, international associations of political parties such as the Socialist International and the International of Popular (Demo-Christian) parties, confederations of trade unions at the national and international levels, and myriad NGOs concentrated on the defense of human rights. This multilayer infrastructure enabled the rapid creation of a dense network of committees of solidarity with the victims of institutionalized repression fleeing persecution.

The crystallization of an international public sphere attentive to what once were considered 'internal matters' wrapped in the nation-state mantle

---

[11] Saskia Sassen, *Territory, Authority, Rights*. Princeton, NJ: Princeton University Press, 2006, p. 278.

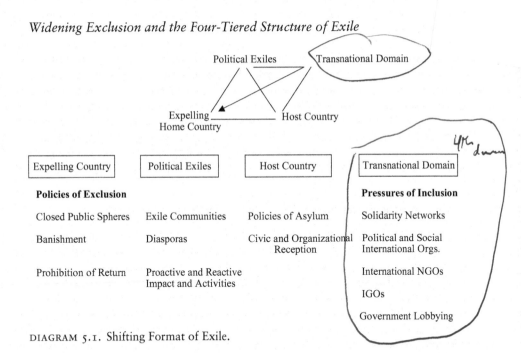

DIAGRAM 5.1. Shifting Format of Exile.

of sovereignty publicly unraveled the character of authoritarian repression, projecting the plight of the exiles in terms of human rights and debordering its treatment. In the last stages of the Cold War, the work of transnational solidarity networks and international agencies echoed cases of autocratic abuse, making them politically costly, strengthening the cause of democracy and opposition to authoritarianism.[12] This generated pressures in multiple directions, unforeseen by the rulers of the Ibero-American states until then.

The fourth tier of exile – the transnational dimension – emerged as a crucial aspect of the tug-of-war among political exiles, their supporting networks, and the repressive rulers of their home country. Theoretically, the fourth tier has operated against the supposed monopoly of the nation-state over domestic public spheres and politics by empowering exiles in terms of transnational influence and resonance for their voice in the global arena. As such, they contributed from the bottom up toward the construction of what will be theorized starting in the late 20th century as the formation of a global civil society. In John Keane's terms, such a concept implies

[A]n unfinished project that consists of sometimes thick, sometimes thinly stretched networks, pyramids and hub-and-spoke clusters of socio-economic institutions and actors who organise themselves across borders, with the deliberate aim of drawing the world together in new ways. These non-governmental institutions and actors tend to pluralise power and to problematise violence.[13]

[12] Laurence Whitehead, "Three International Dimensions of Democratization," in Whitehead, Ed., *The International Dimensions of Democratization: Europe and the Americas*. Oxford: Oxford University Press, 1996.

[13] John Keane, *Global Civil Society*. Cambridge: Cambridge University Press, 2003, p. 8.

The roots of this transformation can be traced back to the second half of the 19th century, as states began developing a normative framework of treaties and conventions, increasingly binding for individual signatory countries as they faced issues such as diplomatic and territorial asylum, a normative figure evolving since ancient times. In parallel, as terror and fear of persecution expanded well beyond national borders, exiles were able to capitalize on international solidarity networks, projecting the issue of repression and exile into the general public awareness and helping develop an arena for transnational activism.

Asylum and the Protection of Persecuted Individuals

Since ancient times, societies recognized the existence of inviolable space, in which persecuted individuals could find asylum. In ancient Israel, special towns and altars were designated as locales of asylum. In Greece, some of the major temples served as similar places of asylum. In Rome, too, there were locales for those seeking the rights of asylum, who were commonly "slaves who had been maltreated by their masters, soldiers defeated and pursued by the enemy, and criminals who feared a trial or who escaped before sentence was passed."[14] Churches soon provided sanctuaries for threatened individuals because it was customarily recognized that these individuals were not to be dragged from the altar. Asylum thus turned into a "sanctuary or inviolable place of refuge and protection for criminals and debtors, from which they cannot be forcibly removed without sacrilege."[15] And yet, the right of asylum was considered to be a prerogative that states had to recognize rather than the simple "right of a fugitive to demand protection."[16]

With the passing of time, the right of asylum was transferred from religious centers to diplomatic sites, a trend reflected in the modern concept of asylum granted on the grounds of persecution. The Spanish *Enciclopedia Universal Ilustrada* compares the right of immunity of the churches or temples and the right of extraterritoriality of ambassadors and diplomatic agents of foreign nations. The latter originated in the use of *jus quarteriorium* by virtue of which the places surrounding diplomatic dwellings or embassies served as refuge, at the beginning, for common criminals escaping police or court actions.[17] In absolutist Europe, common criminals enjoyed the protection of asylum, whereas political offenders, were likely to be extradited on the basis of a conception of the complete authority of the rulers over the life and possessions of their subjects.[18]

From the point of view of political asylum, the French Revolution constituted the watershed. As it proclaimed "The Rights of Man and of the Citizen,"

[14] *Encyclopædia Britannica*, 1953, p. 593.
[15] *The Oxford English Dictionary*, 1933, p. 528.
[16] *Encyclopædia Britannica*, 1953, p. 594.
[17] *Enciclopedia Universal Ilustrada Europeo Americana*. Madrid: Espasa-Calpe, n.d., p. 675.
[18] David Alejandro Luna, *El asilo político*. San Salvador: Editorial Universitaria, 1962, p. 20.

it recognized resistance to oppression as a "natural and impresceptible right," and by doing so, it tacitly laid the groundwork for the development of political persecution as a distinct category, which serves as a basis for the modern concept of political asylum. Since 1815, the UK rejected the extradition of people persecuted on political grounds. The figure of political asylum soon became a focus of juridical interpretation and legislation. In 1829, Hendrik Provó Kluit in his *De deditione profugorum* defended the rights of political asylum and the exclusion of politically persecuted persons from treaties of extradition. European nations such as Belgium, France, and the Scandinavian countries enshrined political asylum in official treaties.[19] The right of political asylum spread in parallel to processes of democratization in Europe and beyond. Still, violent anarchist activities constituted a singular problem for those states that recognized the right of asylum at the end of the 19th century and the beginning of the 20th century. These states were still unwilling to receive individuals involved in proactive violence into their territories. The U.S. Immigration Act of 1924 declared anarchist and other political extremists as "unwanted," barring their entry into the country. In the same period, Soviet Russia declared its willingness to provide asylum to any foreigner persecuted on political or religious grounds.[20]

Fascism and its allies further constrained the use of political asylum. Most notorious are the cases of the Republican Spaniards who sought asylum in France after the 1939 defeat of the Second Republic and, once France was overtaken by Nazi Germany, were sent back to Spain, where they faced long-term imprisonment or capital punishment by death squads.

Latin America began very early to deal with the problem of political asylum. This early development is rooted in the contradictory context of political instability: On the one hand, instability generated exclusion and exile throughout the sister-nations of the Americas. On the other hand, the politics of exit could be hampered by the difficulties of transport and communications, even in neighboring countries. Moreover, those in power could use exile as a means of harassment of political enemies in neighboring countries. And even when reluctant to concede asylum to 'troublemakers' from neighboring countries, they could not ignore that eventually they themselves may need that mechanism if ousted from power by a coup. Accordingly, this issue turned into a much discussed subject in negotiations and meetings on diplomatic asylum, making Latin America a pioneer region on that matter.[21]

In 1867, diplomatic representatives of the different states discussed in Lima the issue of diplomatic asylum, without reaching agreement. The first document on this legal figure was produced by the First South American Conference on International Private Law in Montevideo in 1889. A Treaty of Peace and

---

[19] Luna, *El asilo político*, pp. 20–21.
[20] "Asile." *Larousse au XXᵉ siècle*. Paris: Librarie Larousse, 1928, vol. I, p. 384.
[21] Jaime Esponda Fernández, "La tradicíoon latinoamericana de asilo y la protección de los refugiados," available at http://www.acnur.org/biblioteca.pdf/3392.pdf, accessed 10 July 2007.

Friendship was signed on December 1907 by the representatives of Costa Rica, Guatemala, Honduras, Nicaragua, and El Salvador in Washington, D.C., aimed to achieve stability in the Isthmus. The contracting parties undertook the commitment not to allow the leaders and activists of political émigrés "to reside in the border regions of the countries, the peace of which they could disrupt." In 1911, the Andean countries reached agreement on extradition in a congress in Caracas. The Central American countries reached a parallel agreement in Guatemala in 1934. Inter-American treaties on asylum and political refuge were signed in La Havana (1928), Montevideo (1933), and Caracas (1954). The 1928 treaty denied the right of asylum to common delinquents, and the 1933 agreement clearly defined the legal framework of political asylum. Most American nations adhered to the treaty and ratified it, with the exception of Venezuela, Bolivia, and the United States. In 1939, these understandings found their way into the most comprehensive regional treaty, reached in Montevideo by the countries in the region. The 10th Inter-American Conference produced an agreement on political asylum in 1954. It declared in its Article 2 that "every state has a right to concede asylum; but cannot be forced to concede it, neither to explain the reasons why it denies it."[22] This reflected the consensus shaped during the interwar period in Europe, as elsewhere, concerning the perception of asylum as a state prerogative, to be granted by individual states as they take into consideration the gravity and nature of the political crime committed.[23]

Whereas the 1928 and 1933 treaties dealt with asylum mainly in diplomatic terms, the 1954 treaty devoted concurrent attention to the territorial aspect of asylum. The Caracas Congress dealt with this aspect explicitly following the renowned case of Víctor Raúl Haya de La Torre, founder of the APRA (Alianza Popular Revolucionaria Americana, or American Popular Revolutionary Alliance) movement in Peru. With his party outlawed in 1948, he spent five years caught in diplomatic asylum at the Colombian Embassy in Lima.

Both Colombia and Peru brought the case before the International Court of Justice, which recognized in a November 1950 ruling that the protection had been improperly granted. Yet, as Peru further requested the Court to order Colombia to surrender Haya de la Torre to Peruvian authorities, the Court ruled in June 1951 that although Peru was legally entitled to claim that the asylum should cease, there was no obligation on the part of Colombia to surrender

---

[22] Unión Panamericana, *Convención sobre asilo diplomático suscrita en la X Conferencia Interamericana. Caracas: 1–28 marzo 1954*. Washington: OEA, 1961. On the legal aspects of political asylum in the region, see also Leonardo Franco et al., "Investigación: El asilo y la protección de los refugiados en América Latina. Acerca de la confusión terminológica 'asilo-refugio.' Informe de progreso,' in *Derechos humanos y refugiados en las Américas: lecturas seleccionadas*. San José de Costa Rica: ACNUR-IIDH, 2001 (www.acnur.org); and Luis Miguel Díaz and Guadalupe Rodríguez de Ita, "Bases histórico-jurídicas de la política mexicana de asilo diplomático," in Silvia Dutrénit-Bielous and Guadalupe Rodríguez de Ita, Eds., *Asilo diplomático mexicano en el Cono Sur*, pp. 63–82.

[23] See, for instance, the entry on 'Asile.' *Larousse au XXe siècle*. Paris: Librarie Larousse, 1928, vol. I, p. 384.

Haya de la Torre, as this would be opposed to "the Latin American tradition in regard to asylum, a tradition in accordance with which a political refugee ought not to be surrendered." The Court recognized in its ruling the deadlock.

According to the Havana Convention, diplomatic asylum, which is a provisional measure for the temporary protection of political offenders, must be terminated as soon as possible. However, the convention does not give a complete answer to the question of the manner in which an aylum must be terminated. As to persons guilty of common crimes, it expressly requires that they be surrendered to the local authorities. For political offenders, it prescribes the grant of a safe conduct for the departure from the country. But a safe conduct can be claimed only if the asylum has been regularly granted and maintained and if the territorial state has required that the refugee be sent out of the country.[24]

The Court opted not to give a practical solution but only suggested the parties to seek guidance "from those considerations of courtesy and good neighborliness which in matters of asylum, have always held a prominent place in the relations between the Latin American Republics." Only in 1954 did the Peruvian government finally grant Haya de la Torre safe conduct after years of bitter denunciations from liberals throughout the Western Hemisphere and after the case had been brought before the International Court of Justice in 1950 and 1951.[25]

Latin-American countries had debated also territorial asylum even before the issue reached global attention following World War II. Within the international arena, the creation of the United Nations High Commissioner for Refugees (UNHCR or, in its Spanish acronym, ACNUR) in 1949 signaled the diffusion of such concern for identifying the problem and dealing with it in the framework of refugee support. According to the UNHCR charter, even if contemplating concrete historical circumstances, a political refugee is any person who

owing to well-founded fear of being persecutred for reasons of race, religion, nationality or political opinion, is outside the country of his nationality and is unable or, owing to such fear or for reasons other than personal convenience, is unwilling to avail himself of the protection of that country; or who, not having a nationality and being outside the country of his former habitual residence, is unable or, owing to such fear or such reasons other than personal convenience, is unwilling to return to it.[26]

---

[24] International Court of Justice, Haya de la Torre Case, available at http://www.icj-cij.org/icjwww/idecisions/isummaries/ihayasummary510613.htm.

[25] Luna, *El asilo político*, pp. 39–40. Although APRA was legalized in 1956, Haya de la Torre remained mostly abroad until 1962, when he returned to campaign for the presidency in Peru. This was not the first time that de la Torre and his movement were persecuted. Haya de la Torre had founded APRA, a pan-Latin American movement, in 1924, while in Mexican exile. As he returned in 1931 to run for the presidency, he was imprisoned for 15 months. APRA was then outlawed until 1934 and again from 1935 to 1945.

[26] Statute of the Office of the United Nations' High Commissioner for Refugees. See http://www.unhcr.org, accessed 12 July 2007; and "Convention related to the status of refugees (1951)," art. 1, in Office of the UNCHR, available at http://www.unhchr.ch/html.menu3/b/o_c_ref.htm, accessed 28 April 2006.

In the 1960s, following the beginning of massive entry of Cuban political refugees to the United States and the parallel exit of Haitians, Paraguayans, Bolivians, Dominicans, Nicaraguans, and Hondurans, the Interamerican Commission of Human Rights issued a report in which it recognized that their escape from the home countries was putting high pressure on possible countries of asylum and threatened to change traditional views on political refugees and exiles.[27]

In parallel, the regulatory norms evolving out of these international fora became increasingly binding in the 1960s. Specifically, with the Declaration on Territorial Asylum adopted by the General Assembly of the UN in December 1967, Article 14 of the Universal Declaration of Human Rights was enforced, as the Declaration recognized that the grant of asylum by a state "is a peaceful and humanitarian act and that, as such, it cannot be regarded as unfriendly by any other state."[28]

The process of formalization of these provisions went even further in the 1980s and 1990s. It was then that, following the displacement of hundreds of thousands of refugees in Central America, a series of Latin-American meetings organized by UNHCR brought together government officials, UN agents, professional experts, and NGOs to discuss the humanitarian and legal problems of asylum and refugees. Starting with a program of cooperation between the OAS (Organization of American States) and the UNHCR signed in 1982 and the 1984 Declaration of Cartagena on Refugees, resulting from a colloquium on the international protection of refugees in Central America, Mexico, and Panama, numerous inter-American meetings and summits have further endorsed the normative framework for the protection of refugees in the Americas. This framework, sanctioned once again in the San José Declaration of 1994, stresses the humanitarian and apolitical character of their treatment, the rejection of forced repatriation, and the need to reinforce legality.[29]

The UNHCR, which was charged with the task of helping refugees in the late 20th century, distinguished two subgroups of refugees: the statutory and the displaced. Statutory refugees include individuals who fled their country because of well-founded fear of persecution, whereas displaced refugees are

[27] María Claudia Pulido and Marisol Blanchard, "La Comisión Interamericana de Derechos Humanos y sus mecanismos de protección aplicados a la situación de los refugiados, apáatridas y solicitantes de asilo," available at http://www.acnur.org/biblioteca/pdf/2578.pdf, accessed 10 July 2007.

[28] "Declaration on Territorial Asylum," available at http://www.UNHCR.ch/html/menu3/b/o_asylum.htm, accessed 10 July 2007.

[29] Franco et al., "Investigación: El asilo y la protección de los refugiados en América Latina," pp. 176–177. The major meetings were those of Tlatelolco in 1981, the declaration of Cartagena in 1984, the meetings of Guatemala in 1989 (CIREFCA), San José de Costa Rica in 1994, Tlatelolco in 1999, Rio de Janeiro in 2000, Asuncion in 2005, and Montevideo in 2006. Alberto D'Alotto, "El sistema interamericano de protección de los derechos humanos y su contribución a la protección de los derechos de los refugiados en América Latina," available at http://www.acnur.org/biblioteca/pdf/3186.pdf, accessed 10 July 2007.

those who can be determined or are presumed to be without or unable to avail themselves of the protection of the government of their state of origin. As students of these phenomena have emphasized, the determination of eligibility for the refugee status remained in the hands of the country in which asylum was being sought.[30]

International organizations have based their work on several international agreements that protected exiles. Authorities grant asylum in virtue of the principle of nonrefoulement provided by Article 33 of the 1951 UN Convention on the status of refugees and Article 22 (8) of the American Convention of Human Rights. According to the former, "no contracting state shall expel or return [*refouler*] a refugee in any manner whatsoever to the frontiers of territories where his life or freedom would be threatened on account of his race, religion, nationality, membership of a particular social group or political opinion."[31] It has been observed that in many cases, states have also applied this principle to asylum seekers, which exceeds the expectation of this norm but has been instrumental in preventing deportation. This normative framework is not lacking in contradictions and tensions, as Niklaus Steiner has pointed out while discussing Western European cases:

The strength of this international norm has led states into the uncomfortable (and perhaps untenable) position of declaring that most asylum-seekers are not in enough danger at home to be granted asylum, yet they are in too much danger to be returned home. Deportations of rejected asylum-seekers are relatively rare and rejected asylum-seekers instead are often allowed to remain, but with only limited status and rights.[32]

Because of the massive and complex character of the problem, especially in Central America, the legal and normative frameworks elaborated in the 1980s and 1990s in Latin America have increasingly incorporated the international normative of political refugees, broadening the scope of political asylum as a characteristic of the regional normative shaped originally in the framework of elite politics. Thus, the legal frameworks endorsed in the region have increasingly conflated the categories of refugees, persons devoid of citizenship ('apatrides'), and asylees.[33]

---

[30] Dennis Gallagher, "The Evolution of the International Refugee System." *International Migration Review*, 23, 3 (1989): 579–598.

[31] Office of the UNHCR, *Convention relating to the state of refugees*, adopted by the UN on 28 July 1951, entry into force 22 April 1954.

[32] Niklaus Steiner, *Arguing about Asylum: The Complexity of Refugee Debates in Europe*. New York: St. Martin's Press, 2000, pp. 15–16. On the same problems in Latin America, see Jorge Santistevan de Noriega, "ACNUR e IIDH, Una relación para el refugio," (2001), available at http://acnur.org/biblioteca/pdf/0267.pdf, accessed 8 July 2007.

[33] Pulido and Blanchard, "La Comisión Interamericana de Derechos Humanos"; Cesar Walter San Juan with the participation of Mark Manly, "El asilo y la protección de los refugiados en América Latina: Análisis crítico del dualismo 'asilo-refugio' a la luz del Derecho Internacional de los Derechos Humanos," available at http://acnur.org/biblioteca/pdf/3418.pdf, accessed 10 July 2007.

The Emergence of a Four-Tiered Structure of Exile

The triangular structure of exile was built on the connections and tensions between the agenda of the exiles, the political considerations of the host countries, and the pressures exerted by the home governments, rooted in a framework of political and administrative fragmentation. This formal structure remained a major characteristic as long as states were the central players in the international arena. The promise of the French Revolution in terms of rights accorded to "man and citizen" underwent transformations and suppressions under Napoleonic rule and the Restoration of the *ancien regime* norms carried out by the Holy Alliance. Liberal resurgence in 1848 in Europe, heavily tainted with nationalism, was concentrated in the internal public arenas of the old and new nation-states. Although this enhanced sovereignty, it basically put aside a serious concern with the consequences of state politics in terms of expulsion of political opponents into exile.

Countries used exiles as pawns in their international strategies. Illustrative is the situation as late as World War I, when the role of political exiles comes together with [*revoluzionirung*][*politik*]; that is, with internal politics being played by one country against another by using political exiles, émigrés, and other agents, and by exiles using spaces in the host countries to bring about a certain result in the home country. The most famous European cases of this triadic structure are perhaps those of Roman Dmowski of the Polish National Movement and Thomas Masaryk of the Czech National Movement, as they led movements in Paris and legions against the Central Empires; and Vladimir Ilyich Lenin, the leader of the Bolsheviks, being sent by the Germans in a sealed wagon to Russia, through Sweden and Finland, in order to propel the fall of the Romanovs and take Russia out of the war.

In the Americas, one of the most notable cases is that of the Cuban exiles who started relocating to the United States as early as the 1820s. Even though exiles were part of a larger diaspora of Cubans, many of them workers in the tobacco industry, the former played an increasingly influential role in policy-setting, along with U.S. economic and political interests. Illustrative is the progressive move of the United States to press for the resignation of President Gerardo Machado in the early 1930s. By then, the economic crisis and the hardships it produced had led to widespread protest, met with increasing repression by the Machado administration. Institutionalized violence sent hundreds of exiles to the United States, mainly to Florida and New York, where they forcefully campaigned against the *caudillo*, with a minority advocating direct U.S. intervention. The presence of a Cuban oppositionary voice in the U.S. press played an important role in the decisions taken by the Roosevelt administration to refrain from further supporting Machado, thus hastening his escape from Cuba and the series of events that would soon lead to Fulgencio Batista's ascent to power.[34] Beyond the details of this and other cases of exile

---

[34] Ramón Eduardo Ruiz, *Cuba: The Making of a Revolution*. Northampton: University of Massachusetts Press, 1968, pp. 76–95; "The Machado Dictatorship," available at http://www. cubafacts.com/History/history_of_cuba7.htm, accessed 14 June 2006.

politics in the Americas and elsewhere, the principal point is that as influential as exiles were in this triangular structure, there were almost no institutional arenas on the international level that could serve as effective frameworks for the discussion and regulation of issues concerning political exile and constitute, as a fourth tier, a source of pressure on individual states.

With the evolution of a global arena with transnational networking, communications, and forums within which problems of international law and international human rights could be aired, this structure of exile underwent a core transformation. Once this fourth element entered the exile equation, the political exiles abroad were increasingly able to condition local politics from afar by playing in a transnational arena.

This structure of exile emerged progressively in Latin America, acquiring at first a regional physiognomy and shifting increasingly to transnationalism. Perhaps one of the earliest indications occurred in the 1950s in the Caribbean and Central American subregion, when a series of dictatorships generated waves of exiles that spread all over the region. Consequently, an intense activity of exile groups from the states in this region, particularly Guatemala, Nicaragua, Cuba, Venezuela, and the Dominican Republic, took place. By 1952, virtually the entire Spanish Caribbean was dominated by dictators persecuting and suppressing internal opponents so that political opposition in the area came almost exclusively from exiles and the networks they managed to create and sustain abroad. The principal centers for Caribbean exile activity were at that time Mexico City, San José de Costa Rica, San Juan (Puerto Rico), Miami, and New York.

Venezuelan Acción Democrática (AD, or Democratic Action, the Social Democratic Party of Venezuela) was heavily concentrated in Mexico, probably a thousand strong and closely knit around the figure of former President Rómulo Gallegos. Gallegos, deposed by a military coup in November 1948, was a prominent writer and popular speaker, whose reputation and salience in Mexico and throughout the Americas gave prestige to the exile cause. Dominicans were found throughout the Central American and Caribbean areas, with their largest numbers concentrated in San Juan and New York. Miami was the traditional stronghold for Cubans, but they were also active in Mexico, San Juan, and New York. The Nicaraguans and Hondurans still preferred Mexico and, depending on circumstances, San José de Costa Rica. The more militant exiles of all nationalities were in Arbenz's Guatemala, until the *coup d'état* deposed him and forced him into exile in 1954.[35]

Besides their political activities, the exiles engaged in writing, teaching, lecturing, and public speaking, partly because this was their way to make a living. Yet, these activities projected their cause into the Caribbean and Central and North America. The activities of the exile politicians were important

---

[35] The analysis of the political exiles in Central America and the Caribbean in this period is based mainly on Charles D. Ameringer, *The Democratic Left in Exile: The Anti-Dictatorial Stuggle in the Caribbean, 1945–1959*. Miami: University of Miami Press, 1974, especially "The Diaspora," pp. 161–221. On the Venezuelans in Mexico, see also Rafael José Neri, *La embajada que llegó del exilio*. Caracas: Academia Nacional de la Historia, 1988.

enough to provoke the reaction of local dictators and generate sympathy in democratic countries, generating international pressure. Democratic dialogue and alliances cemented transnational cooperation among democratic leaders and exiles throughout the Americas. Physical exclusion from domestic public spheres was increasingly not equivalent to political exclusion. Through their international impact, exiled individuals could affect the equation of power in their home country while far away from them. The attempts of assassination of exiles abroad are a clear indication of the increasing importance of this fourth tier as part of the structure of exile in the region. The activities of the agents of Trujillo, Batista, Somoza, and other dictators, although largely uncoordinated, signaled a move to radicalizing tactics of dealing with important leaders of the exile oppositions, as will be typical of Operation Condor nearly two decades later. The fourth tier was becoming more central for both expellers and exiles.

The better organized exile parties (the Venezuelan AD, the Dominican Revolutionary Party [Partido Revolucionario Dominican, or PRD] and the Cuban Auténticos) supported their militants. Parties managed to raise funds through voluntary contributions and occasionally through activities and raffles. A number of Cuban exiles lived 'in princely fashion' in Miami and Miami Beach, in what some defined as a Golden Exile. Two of the wealthier co-nationals, Carlos Prío Socorrás and José Alemán, used their personal assets to support other exiles and promote their cause. Toward the 1950s, the U.S. government also helped finance the exile movement, although indirectly and covertly.

No exile was fully beyond the reach of the dictators of the Caribbean. The Dominicans, particularly, were carefully watched through Rafael Trujillo's efficient espionage system, which used the diplomatic and consular services to harass and even liquidate his enemies. After 1956, Fulgencio Batista and Trujillo plotted together the assassination of Costa Rican President José Figueres, who supported the Democratic Left in exile. By 1957, Trujillo's agents were directing numerous intrigues in Mexico and Central America. Trujillo had friends in the U.S. Congress, attracted by his anti-Communist policy and the extensive lobby he maintained, and was able to foment close scrutiny of the exiles' activities. On the other hand, Trujillo occasionally bribed his antagonists with money or promises of amnesty. In 1955, the Dominican Congress passed an amnesty bill, and Trujillo announced that the government would help financially those exiles seeking repatriation. Marcos Pérez Jiménez also reached out to deal with enemies, especially attempting to eliminate Rómulo Betancourt and putting pressure on host countries to expel him and constrain his movements.

Although countries respected the right of asylum, they watched the activities of exiles carefully in order to avoid radicalizing influences in the domestic arena and, at the same time, avoid international friction and embarrassment with peer governments. Students, in particular, were a category not always welcome, as they tended to be politically active. In 1956, the Honduran government was reported to be trying to persuade Guatemalan student exiles to depart for

Costa Rica because it did not want them to stir up the local student body. Similarly, in Mexico in 1953, when it was discovered that Mexican arms had been used in Castro's assaults in Cuba, Mexican authorities undertook efforts to prevent arms smuggling to Cuba and expelled two Cuban exiles. In 1956, Castro, Che Guevara, and others were arrested on charges of plotting a revolutionary action against Batista. Nevertheless, before the year ended, Castro had invaded Cuba; the area of Yucatán had served as his jumping board. Probably as a result of this experience, Mexico ousted 550 'undesirable aliens' in 1957, some of whom were engaged in political actions considered dangerous or embarrassing to the Mexican government. For this reason, and because Marcos Pérez Jiménez had been ousted in Venezuela, Cuban exiles began 'flocking' to Caracas in 1958. The United States followed a similar policy toward Cuban exiles; it provided a haven but would not tolerate violations of its laws.

AD (Venezuela) was the largest of the exile parties and the best organized, with Rómulo Gallegos as its spokesman in Mexico and Luis Augusto Dubue presiding over affairs in Costa Rica. Liaison was maintained by the Coordinating Committee, which Dubue also administered in Costa Rica. By far, the largest number of activists was in Mexico, where they maintained the party structure and activity. Here, the Confederation of Workers of Venezuela in exile, under the direction of AD militants, collaborated closely with the international free-trade union movement. Special focus was given to youth and student affairs by the Juventud of AD. The most important exile newspaper, *Venezuela Democrática*, was edited in Mexico between 1955 and 1957. Periodic public meetings were held, principally in Mexico and Costa Rica, energized by the commemoration of the martyrs who had died in exile and in the underground of Venezuela. During the first four and a half years of exile, AD leaders were preoccupied with securing a reliable communication network with those in the underground, directing their activities from abroad and promoting their cause before the UN. The closing of penal colonies in 1949 and 1952, as well as the release of Valmore Rodríguez and others from prison in 1949, stemmed from denunciations of human-rights violations made by exiles before the UN. The exiles were also successful in organizing a boycott of the Conference of the Petroleum Committee of the International Labor Organization held in Caracas in 1955, as important unions refused to send representatives. AD also led a strategy of cooperation with other opposition parties, inspired by the belief that the tide was turning against the dictators and the pending expiration of Pérez Jiménez's term of office at the end of 1957. Agitation for free elections became the basis for unifying the Venezuelan opposition groups. Following an orchestrated plebiscite that would enable Pérez Jiménez to stay in power, the political arena entered into turmoil. A military revolt against Pérez Jiménez in January 1958 seemed to fail, and although it would trigger riots that resulted in more than 300 dead and the eventual ousting of Pérez Jiménez, the Venezuelan military officers implicated in the revolt fled to Colombia aboard a stolen plane. After being captured by Colombian intelligence in

Baranquilla, the government decided in favor of their release. The press reported that

Carlos de Santamaría, Colombia's Foreign Minister, said yesterday that the eighteen Venezuelans would be released shortly and would be "free to live anywhere they liked in Colombia, expect in towns on the Venezuelan border." The Foreign Minister also noted that it was only proper that Colombia provide asylum for the Venezuelans since "at least 10,000 Colombians" who fled from the dictatorship of General Gustavo Rojas Pinilla between 1953 and early 1957 were still living in Venezuela.[36]

During the years in exile, AD effectively opposed the dictatorship and maintained a party structure, so that it quickly became a major political factor in Venezuela after the deposition of Pérez Jiménez. The party eventually reached power and continued cooperating in the struggle against the other dictators of the Caribbean. Few parties of the Democratic Left enjoyed the same success in exile, probably because none was as well organized.

The Cuban exiles were deeply divided. A number of rival parties existed, including the People's Party or Ortodoxo, and the Communist Popular Socialist Party. The Auténticos were torn by personalist factionalism and found it difficult to arouse sympathy, with many Cubans disillusioned by their previous leadership. Therefore, they, as well as other Cuban exile groups, tended to rely on conspirational activity. Most of their energy and resources were spent in active and violent forms of opposition. The Dominican exiles had been scattered the longest, some since 1930. By the time Germán Ornes went into exile in 1955, he complained that he found an "aristocracy of exiledom," in which those who had been in exile the longest looked down on the recent arrivals and regarded them with suspicion as collaborationists.

These political organizations were creatures of exile. In the Dominican Republic, there were no true political parties before Trujillo; afterward, none were tolerated. The closest that the Dominicans came to a political party in the modern sense was the PRD, founded in Havana in 1939 by Juan Bosch and Angel Miolan, with branches in Puerto Rico and New York. Other groups, all founded in exile, were at best splinter parties and at worst a handful of followers of a single leader. Aside from the communists, only one of these organizations lasted beyond the exile years, the Vanguardia Revolucionaria Dominicana founded in Puerto Rico in 1956, with branches in Mexico and New York. Despite the Batista dictatorship, it maintained headquarters in Cuba until 1958, when it moved to Caracas. Owing to the contacts of Bosch with democratic leaders and organizations, it managed to elicit strong denunciations of the Trujillo regime internationally.

Loose coalitions characterized the activities of the Dominican exiles in New York. With their protests and demonstrations, they seemed puny in comparison with the dictatorship of Rafael Leónidas Trujillo, but their activities had important effects. They rejected Trujillo's demands of total submissiveness.

[36] Ted Szulc, "Venezuela Quiet After Rebellion." *The New York Times*, 4 January 1958, p. 6.

They contributed to an atmosphere that facilitated a shift in U.S. policy. Trujillo himself overreacted to the exile activities, which produced additional scorn against his government. Despite factional differences, the PRD developed a party structure and acquired sufficient prestige, so that when the time came, it could try to provide a democratic alternative. By going into exile, the PRD was free from any collaborationist taint.

When a country lived through a democratic period and projected an image of being committed to popular causes, it could become a haven for political exiles, such as Guatemala between 1944 and 1954, Costa Rica after 1948, and redemocratized Venezuela after 1958. In the 1940s, exiled communist leaders were conspicuous in Guatemala. They were active in Guatemalan political affairs. Cuban communist leaders were frequent visitors to Guatemala, aiding the local Marxists in their rise to control organized labor. Venezuelan communists were also frequent visitors, but the most active were the Salvadorans. The Dominican Popular Socialist Party was the Communist Party of the Dominican Republic in exile, but they also belonged to the Guatemalan Labor Party. In 1952, they undertook to organize all Dominican exiles under a Committee of Dominican Exiles, and in June their "Solidarity" broadcast claimed a favorable response from Dominicans everywhere. Other national groups in exile established similar united fronts in Guatemala. These included the Asociación Democrática Salvadoreña, the Movimiento de Nicaragüenses Partidarios de la Democracia, and the Partido Democrático Revolucionario Hondureño. The Spanish Republican exiles were also active, and they joined these groups to form the Frente Democrático de Exilados Americanos y Españoles. In the 1953 May Day parade, the exiled groups marched with 70,000 partisans demonstrating loyalty to President Arbenz. At the same time, Guatemala campaigned actively against the Caribbean dictators. With the fall of Arbenz in June 1954, the exiles fled Guatemala. After they were gone, Castillo Armas placed their names on a list of communist agents forbidden to return to Guatemala. The list included noncommunists, such as Venezuelan AD leaders and the PRD leader, Juan Bosch.

Anastasio Somoza García's dictatorship in Nicaragua was another factor in the creation of resistance groups in exile, foremost in Costa Rica. In 1953, Nicaraguan leader Pablo Leal used Costa Rica as a base for collecting support for a revolutionary movement against Somoza. He traveled to Miami, where Cuban President Prío Socarrás pledged to support him and instructed him to get in touch with his representatives in Mexico City. With their help, arms were shipped to Costa Rica, which eventually were smuggled into Nicaragua. Leal went to Guatemala next, where he recruited Nicaraguan revolutionaries. By the end of 1953, these elements departed Guatemala for Costa Rica. Leal made the final preparations in Costa Rica, including the formation of the Partido Nacional Revolucionario. He next met with figures such as Dominican leader Bosch and Venezuelan politician Betancourt, and, together with Cuban Sergio Pérez, they helped in the acquisition of weapons. Of the 21 comrades who finally accompanied Leal, 16 were Nicaraguans and 5 of various nationalities.

This failed expedition resulted in the death of many, among them Amadeo Soler, a Dominican friend of Juan Bosch. Romulo Betancourt was depicted as the mastermind behind the plot and forced into serial exile.

Somoza was finally killed in 1956 by Rigoberto López Pérez, a young Marxist Nicaraguan poet who had previously been exiled in El Salvador. This, added to the sympathy demonstrated by Salvadorans to Somoza's killer, made Nicaraguan–Salvadoran relations tense. Especially sharp demands were put on El Salvador regarding the control of exiles, including the extradition of certain Nicaraguan exiles. El Salvador refused to extradite exiles for political reasons, thus reiterating its policy of asylum, provided the displaced individuals refrained from political activities in the host country. In similar fashion relative to their compatriots in Costa Rica, Nicaraguan exiles in Honduras were gathering near the border and enjoying a freedom never before experienced, under the umbrella of Honduras' Democratic Left government of Ramón Villeda Morales. Because Villeda Morales' situation was too precarious for foreign adventures, the activities of anti-Somoza exiles were not in the best interests of their host. Finally, the Honduran government interned the would-be invaders and took steps to deport them to Guatemala, to preclude their engagement in a planned insurgency.

Central America and the Caribbean countries entered the Cold War with many of its polities in a state of agitation. Political dynamics were characterized by recurrent shifts between democracy and dictatorship, redefining lines of alignment and generating streams of political exiles. For different reasons, Mexico and Costa Rica had become traditional sites of exile. Guatemala, up to the 1954 coup, and Venezuela, after the return to democracy in 1958, also attracted large numbers of exiles, and Colombian Embassies were instrumental in granting asylum to many would-be exiles, despite the violence that erupted in that country in the late 1940s. Cuba played an ambiguous role, serving as a host country for Latin-American exiles while generating waves of exiles from among its own citizens. Similarly, while persecuting his own political opposition and spearheading anticommunism, the dictatorship of Trujillo in the Dominican Republic hosted exiles as varied as the refugees from the Spanish Civil War (1936–1939), Jewish refugees escaping Nazi Europe who were unable to find shelter almost anywhere,[37] and the well-known case of Peron in the 1950s. Rafael Trujillo even proudly played the card of being the architect of a doctrine of diplomatic humanitarian asylum, thus reflecting – within the limits of his

---

[37] At the 1938 Conference on Refugees in Evian, the Dominican Republic offered to accept up to 100,000 refugees. Trujillo's generous offer contrasted with the indifference of the other participant countries and was connected to his vision of racial improvement of the population, through the arrival of white immigrants, which would preclude the country from becoming a mulatto or black nation. The first 400 Jewish refugees arrived in 1940. However, an unfavorable report by the Brookings Institution seems to have hampered the full use of this quota. See *Capacity of the Dominican Republic to Absorb Refugees. Findings of the Commission Appointed by the Executive Power of the Dominican Republic.* Ciudad Trujillo: Editora Montalvo, 1945. Kaplan, Marion. *Dominican Haven: The Jewish Refugee Settlement in Sosúa, 1940–45.* New York: Museum of Jewish Heritage, 2008.

ideological view and combined with his repressive policies – the increasing importance of humanitarian themes as part of foreign policy.[38]

This ambiguity was not only found in the polities where democratic contestation was banned. Truly enough, most of the countries forcing exiles abroad were under dictatorial rule, with exile resulting from closed public spheres and proscribed political participation. However, even formal democratic administrations, such as those of Costa Rica and Chile that provided a haven for political exiles from other Ibero-American countries, used expulsion as a means of settling accounts with their political oppositions. In Costa Rica, José Figueres, a prominent politician and economic entrepreneur, who criticized democratically elected President Rafael Angel Calderón, found himself expelled to Mexico between 1942 and 1944. In Mexico, Figueres joined a group of Latin American politicians who formed the Caribbean Legion that plotted against the ruling governments of the Dominican Republic, Venezuela, Nicaragua, and Costa Rica. The policies of Calderón, expropriating German assets in the framework of World War II, alienated coffee growers and bankers of German descent and many conservatives, who backed Figueres. In 1948, a situation of political polarization and a short but bloody civil war resulted from contested electoral results. When Figueres took power at the head of a junta, Calderón was forced to flee into exile to Nicaragua and later to Mexico, where he stayed for nearly a decade.[39]

The fourth tier further developed following the *coup d'état* in Brazil in 1964, as analyzed by James N. Green with a focus on the solidarity movement in the United States. The ups and downs of this movement were closely linked to the main issues central to U.S. politics. The interest in supporting the plight of exiles in the late 1960s was high, especially among intellectuals, students, and the clergy, and was intimately connected to the opposition to the American involvement in the Vietnam War. In the early 1970s, with the electoral defeat of George McGovern and the beginning of U.S. withdrawal from Vietnam in 1973, the consequent loss of steam of the antiwar movement was also reflected in the loss of interest in the Brazilian case. The movement of solidarity with Chile after the Pinochet coup would rekindle the interest in Latin America. According to Green, the Watergate hearings and Senator Frank Church's investigations on Washington's efforts to destabilize the Allende government revealed the depths of corruption and depravity of the Nixon administration and provided a broader political space for a policy discussion about human rights in Latin America. The work around Brazil had laid the groundwork for the Chilean solidarity movement.[40]

[38] Henry Helfant, *La doctrina Trujillo del asilo diplomático humanitario*. Mexico: Editorial Offest Continente, 1947; Kaplan, *Dominican Haven*, 2007.

[39] Charles D. Ameringer, *The Caribbean Legion Patriots, Politicians, Soldiers of Fortune, 1946–1950*. University Park: Pensylvannia University Press, 1996.

[40] James N. Green, "Clergy, Exiles and Academics: Opposition to the Brazilian Military Dictatorship in the United States, 1969–1974." *Latin American Politics and Society*, 45, 1 (2003): 87–117.

Chile was a country that had stabilized politically by the end of 1932 and followed formal democratic procedure until the coup of September 1973. Nonetheless, inner exile [*relegación*] and exile abroad [*destierro*] had persisted and were used massively by democratic administrations. Even under formal democracy, Chilean political culture contained strong authoritarian and exclusionary elements enshrined constitutionally and reflected in the recurrent use of emergency laws promulgated whenever there was a political crisis. The use of emergency legislation created a situation of constitutional dictatorship that did not preclude the electoral game but constrained participation and excluded those considered dangerous to the political system.[41]

As a matter of fact, Chile was the only country in Latin America to lack extraconstitutional changes of government between 1932 and 1973. In this, Chile was exceptional. But institutional continuity, lack of *coups d'état*, and democracy are not synonymous:

In the 27 years after 1930 there were 16 laws or decree-laws of exceptional powers that imposed restrictions to freedom and allowed for a kind of "institutional dictatorship" during almost a total of four years, i.e. close to 20 percent of the time. When the country was not under a "regime of exception," the possibility existed for the government of issuing such measures, integrating into the political culture the implicit menace of demanding extraordinary faculties, declaring a state of siege or a state of emergency.[42]

Costa Rica was another case in which formal democracy did not preclude the use of institutional exclusion as a central political tool. After the 1948 Civil War, the Junta government imprisoned thousands of political activities, expropriated personal assets, dismissed civil servants linked to the previous administration, and sent nearly 1 percent of the population into exile.[43] There is a transnational dynamic evident in the spread of individual leaders throughout the region, the emergence of political parties in exile, the establishment of cross-national political alliances, and counteralliances and transnational repressive operations targeting the oppositions in exile. On a regional level, one witnesses in Central America and the Caribbean Basin the incipient formation of a four-tiered structure of exile, which, beyond the individual countries'

---

[41] Many laws of exception were enacted between 1933 and 1973, the most notorious being the Law of Internal Security of the State (Law 6026 of 1937) that proscribed both communists and Nazis, and the Law of Defense of Democracy (Law 8987 of 1948), used to exclude communists from work and political participation, forcing thousands to be relegated or forced into exile, among them, later to be Chile's Nobel Laureate, Pablo Neruda.

[42] Brian Loveman and Elizabeth Lira, *Las ardientes cenizas del olvido: Vía chilena de reconciliación política, 1932–1994*. Santiago de Chile: LOM, 2000, pp. 27–28.

[43] James Dunkerley, *Power in the Isthmus: A Political History of Modern Central America*. New York: Verso, 1988, p. 131; in Deborah J. Yashar, *Demanding Democracy: Reform and Reaction in Costa Rica and Guatemala, 1870s–1950s*. Stanford, CA: Stanford University Press, 1997, pp. 179–190. Bowman defines the Costa Rican system between 1948 and 1958 as a "semi-democracy" (Kirk S. Bowman, *Militarization, Democracy and Development: The Perils of Praetorianism in Latin America*. University Park: Pennsylvania State University Press, 2002).

preoccupation with their own exiles and the exiles they hosted, started developing international networks trying to appeal to international organizations and states beyond the region to affect policies and regain power.

A generation later, the fate of persecuted citizens of individual countries turned increasingly to be of concern for the international community, debordering the nation-state–contained treatment of political exile. The coup by Pinochet against the constitutional government of Salvador Allende was a major focus of concern, especially driven by the massive plight of Chileans looking for asylum in Santiago's embassies and, once relocated throughout the world, rekindling the banner of solidarity with the exiles in their fight for the restoration of democracy and against the human-rights violations of the dictatorship. No less fundamental in reconstructing the international arena was the effect of the Argentine military administration's policies of denial and persecution of its citizens. While Argentine authorities embarked on a policy of systematic disinformation and denial of human-rights violations, claiming it was the result of conspiratorial webs linked to international Communism, the increasing evidence shaped a dense web of critics on the transnational and international arena, which would radically change the discursive and political balance in favor of the exiles.[44]

Among the concerned organizations and networks instrumental for this transformation into a dense organizational scenario defending human rights were civil associations and committees of solidarity in Europe and the United States; officers in these countries' administrations concerned with flagrant violations; political networks such as the Socialist International supporting persecuted political activists; domestic human-rights organizations; transnational organizations like Amnesty International and Americas Watch that gained heightened profile and respectability as they contested the dubious explanations of targeted states about their record of humanitarian violations; powerful representatives of the international media such as the *Washington Post* and *The New York Times*; and concerned international bodies such as the Inter-American Commission of Human Rights centered in San José de Costa Rica and the UNHCR and its domestic representative agencies supporting the flow of refugees in European and other countries.

The *de facto* rulers were increasingly forced to argue and counterargue in terms of human rights, thus paradoxically reinforcing the hold of such discourse as the normative discourse that was about to supersede the previous hegemonic discourses of national sovereignty, at least on the declarative level. This transformation, also under effect in the intellectual arena, re-created the terms under

---

44 David Sheinin, "How the Argentine Military Invented Human Rights in Argentina," in Carlos H. Waisman and Raanan Rein, Eds., *Spanish and Latin American Transitions to Democracy*. Brighton, UK: Sussex Academic Press, 2005, pp. 190–214; Roniger and Sznajder, *The Legacy of Human-Rights Violations in the Southern Cone*, pp. 38–49.

which the plight of the exiles would be examined.[45] Exiles would henceforth find greater political space for their long-term activism in favor of the end of authoritarian rule, the restoration of democracy, and a full inquiry about the record of human-rights violations of the dictatorships. In the short term, however, many of them were forced to escape for their lives, sometimes even serially as the region plunged into a domino process of breakdown of civilian rule and instauration of authoritarian military or civilian–military dictatorships. In this sense, the last wave of repression will exacerbate trends already evident in the late 19th and early 20th centuries.

Patterns of Exile

Those who moved abroad did not follow a single pattern of expatriation, exile, and escape. There were many who managed to enter a foreign embassy, where they received diplomatic asylum, to leave later to a host country according to interregional and international norms of asylum. Others escaped the home country and sought territorial refuge in a foreign country. There were also those who, fearing for their lives, left with the support of human-rights or international refugee organizations. There were those who were pushed into exile after they were excluded from any possibility of finding employment, after being fired and included in a black list of 'troublemakers.'[46] Finally, there were individuals who left the home country after spending time in prison, freed by the repressive government under the condition of being received by another country.[47]

Often, exile began as the voluntary displacement of people who, without having been part of the ousted government, sympathized with it or were activists. In an authoritarian traditionalist pattern of rule, such individuals are usually forfeited persecution. By simply ceasing any political involvement, they are often spared repression and may be able to continue their routine life, now depleted from any political involvement. In this situation, the political realm is closed, but domains are still left open in the public spheres, as long as what occurs here does not interfere with the rulers' understanding of politics, and as long as the masses are effectively depoliticized and demobilized. Such

---

[45] On the transformation of such discourses and the role of the intellectuals in the Southern Cone, see Luis Roniger and and Leandro Kierszenbaum, "Los intelectuales y los discursos de derechos humanos: La experiencia del Cono Sur." *Estudios Interdisciplinarios de América Latina y el Caribe*, 16, 2 (2005): 5–36.

[46] In the case of Argentina, there was a law (*Ley de prescindibilidad*, no. 21260/76) that allowed firing public employees under suspiscion of connections with 'subversive' activities. This law was as ambiguous as the Law of State Security, which targeted people considered enemies of the state or of the nation. Similar legislation had existed in other countries as well since independence, as analyzed by Brian Loveman, *The Constitution of Tyranny*.

[47] Maria Luisa Tarrés, "Miradas de una Chilena," p. 23; Pablo Yankelevich and Silvina Jensen, Eds., *Exilios: Destinos y experiencias bajo la dictadura militar*. Buenos Aires: Ediciones del Zorzal, 2007.

was the case of Brazil from the 1964 coup until the institutional change that took place in December 1968. In this period, while the political system was controlled from above by the armed forces and the deposed civilian rulers fled the country into exile, it was still possible to conduct intellectual and academic life in a more-or-less open way, with Marxist texts and thriving public debates, even though the most radical elements of the Left still pursued the path of armed rebellion and guerrilla.[48]

In political situations in which the rulers took a more totalistic approach in their fight against the Left, such as Argentina between 1976 and 1983 and Chile between 1973 and 1990, the penetration and 'cleansing' of civil society from Marxist influence and mobilization came together with a high measure of closure of the public spheres. In these situations, the repressive government aimed to redefine the basic tenets of society in a manner that demonized a wide spectrum of social and political forces, defined as 'enemies of the nation.' Even certain disciplines and professions were considered subversive 'by nature' and supporters of guerrilla insurrection, as in the case of psychology and psychoanalysis in Argentina. The changes undergone by these professions in the 1960s and 1970s were the grounds for their persecution:

Psychoanalysis was widely adopted by the Argentinean middle classes in the 1960s. By then, mental health in Argentina was confronting important changes. There was a "revolution" in psychiatry and psychology and hospitals incorporated services of psychopathology. In parallel, processes of insurgency and revolution in Latin America and the impact of the French May [of 1968] gave new meaning to the relationships of professional practice and politics in the framework of the authoritarian dictatorship of Onganía. Psychologists and psychoanalysts began to perceive themselves more as workers than as liberal professionals and, at the same time, favored treatments for free to the working classes. They were persecuted, their offices were invaded and they had to flee to exile because they had treated patients with social, political and armed militancy. For the military, these professionals were not only a possible source of information about the activities of the "subversive," but they were also considered to be supporters of the guerrilla due to the professional help they provided to those in the underground.[49]

All those falling into one of the 'dangerous' categories were liable to become victims of persecution and repression. This pattern generated a very strong incentive for displacement. In such a manner, many individuals coming from all parts of the political spectrum and civil society opted to leave – as if it were voluntary – making it difficult to trace a dividing line between expulsion and escape. Thus, even indirectly, the closure of the public spheres in these latter situations

---

[48] Parameswara Krishnan and Dave Odynak, "A Generalization of Petersen's Typology of Migration." *International Migration*, 25, 4 (1987): 385–397; Roberto Schwarz, "Culture and Politics in Brazil, 1964–1969," in Schwarz, *Misplaced Ideas: Essays on Brazilian Culture*. London: Verso, 1992, pp. 126–159.

[49] Silvina Jensen, "Política y cultura del exilio argentino en Cataluña," in Pablo Yankelevich, Ed., *Represión y destierro*. La Plata: Editorial Al Margen, 2004, p. 125.

revived the old 19th-century options of *encierro, destierro, o entierro* – that is, to be in jail, in exile, or facing death.

In despair, many persecuted individuals did not have the possibility of choosing their destination but had to leave through the first available embassy or to the first country that would let them in. Here, sometimes ethnic and national origins played a role. Resorting to ethnic and national origins in order to obtain documents and the possibility to enter the ancestral country of origin was a possibility. Persecuted and threatened individuals turned in the plight to the representatives of Spain, Italy, Germany, the UK, Switzerland, and other European countries. Striking was the case of Israel, whose representatives were addressed by Latin-American persecuted persons of Jewish origins, who, in most of the cases, were ideologically opposed to Zionism and the policies of the government of Israel.[50]

But, in principle, while constrained to the same extent as past exiles in their decisions, 20th-century exiles had more open avenues. In particular, the framework of a global arena divided by ideological convictions determined that the question of asylum became intimately connected to foreign policy considerations and to the struggle for vilification of the opposite ideological camp:

Granting asylum to a refugee is an implicit critique of another state's treatment of its citizens, so that states are often quick to accept refugees from foes, but hesitant to accept them from friends. Such an asylum policy was common during the Cold War.... The US in the 1980s generally admitted Nicaraguans and Cubans, but rejected El Salvadorans and Haitians.[51]

This framework, which facilitated the exiles' move to countries with a value system close to their own, was replicated in the opposite end of the political spectrum by leftist exiles and refugees who went to Cuba and communist countries in Eastern Europe, as in the case of members of the Chilean Communist Party moving to East Germany.[52]

With the increased development of means of transportation, many more individuals than in the past could move to locations a great distance from their homeland, thus highlighting pull factors such as the political and socioeconomic opportunities in settling in European or North American countries. Many Latin Americans went into exile in Sweden, the UK, France, Italy, West Germany, Holland, Belgium, Canada, and the United States.

Sweden, which became a pole of reception of political exiles for various reasons, deserves special attention. Since 1968, the Social–Democratic government of Olof Palme developed a policy of active neutrality oriented to the

---

[50] The links between escape and exile deserve special analyis and are analyzed in a later section of this chapter, especially in connection with the cases of Israel and Italy, on which there is more documentation.

[51] Niklaus Steiner, *Arguing about Asylum*. New York: St. Martin's Press, 2000, pp. 3–4.

[52] Testimony of José Rodríguez Elizondo in Jerusalem, March 2000; and idem, *La pasión de Iñaki*. Santiago: Editorial Andrés Bello, 1996.

Third World and sympathetic to the movements of liberation. Sweden had been a country of immigration since the eve of World War II but had increasingly restricted its reception policies. In 1972, Sweden made the decision to allow entry and residence to political refugees only for humanitarian reasons or for reasons of family unification. Accordingly, the infrastructure developed to facilitate the absorption of immigrants, which involved social workers, teachers of Swedish, occupational assessors, and a framework of well-provided-for refugee camps could be redirected to attend the needs of the political refugees arriving from South America in the wake of the military takeovers. The country was particularly receptive to the victims of Pinochet's persecution, who arrived after 1973. Sympathy toward Allende's experiment in Democratic Socialism touched a sensible chord in the context of Swedish Social Democracy and had brought about the establishment of a committee of solidarity with Chile in 1971, later replicated in similar committees of solidarity with other Latin-American countries. This committee greatly enlarged its activities after the September 1973 coup. It published a bimonthly bulletin, which published 20,000 copies in its prime. The committee was dissolved 20 years after its foundation, in 1991, once Chile returned to democracy. Chilean exiles and migrants became the largest community of Latin Americans in Sweden, reaching a total of 27,841 out of 47,980 individuals registered by the Central Bureau of Statistics of Sweden (SCB) in 1990.[53] Besides labor and study opportunities, freedom and stability, the core countries of the developed West also provided access to the international public sphere and the main domains in which not only politics but also human-rights violations were discussed and action could be taken against their authoritarian home governments.

Geographical or cultural proximity, especially if linked to democratic rule, were highly important factors as well. For example, many Chileans – among them the later Nobel Laureate, Pablo Neruda – left for Argentina in the late 1940s, when the Communist Party was outlawed. Once again, after the 1973 military coup in Chile, another wave of exiles, including General Carlos Prats, the constitutionalist commander of the Chilean Army under Allende, crossed the Andes. In 1974, there were already 15,000 Chilean exiles in Argentina and 1,500 in Peru. In 1976, the military takeover in Argentina endangered the Chilean exiles and refugees there. The UNHCR intervened and relocated as many as 30,000 Chilean refugees and exiles to other Latin American countries, Europe, and Australia.[54] Accordingly, the figures indicated a progressive dispersion as many of the countries in Latin America slipped into military control. Partial data for 1984 reflect this trend in relation to Chilean expatriates:

[53] In 1989, there were 26,292 Chileans in Sweden but only, 2,396 Uruguayans, 2,341 Argentineans, and 1,907 Bolivians. Daniel Moore, "Latinoamericanos en Suecia," in Weine Karlsson, Ake Magnusson, and Carlos Vidales, Eds., *Suecia-Latinoamerica: Relaciones y cooperación.* Stockholm: LAIS, 1993, pp. 161–183.

[54] Alan Angell, "La cooperación internacional en apoyo de la democracia política: El caso de Chile." *Foro Internacional*, 30, 2 (1989): 215–245.

nearly 47 percent of them were still in Latin America, now mainly in Venezuela (hosting 44 percent of them); 37 percent in Western Europe (Spain 10 percent, France 8.3 percent, Italy 6.6 percent, and Sweden 5.5 percent); and 8 percent in North America (of them 6.7 percent in Canada). Even Australia received 5 percent and Eastern Europe and Africa 3 percent. By then, Chilean exiles were established in nearly 120 countries.[55]

Similarly, throughout the century, most exiled Paraguayans left for Argentina as they sought to escape political persecution in their home country. Nonetheless, after 1954, General Alfredo Stroessner built an intricate network of spies and collaborators to infiltrate this community of exiles and émigrés in an attempt to control the oppositionary activities of the most politically active elements among them.

The case of Uruguay under military rule is also illustrative of the combined effects of exiles choosing neighboring countries as locales for their escape, subsequently superseded by expanding paths of dispersion. Around 1973, many Uruguayan political refugees and exiles went to Argentina, where they found shelter until local anti-Left groups and the military who took power persecuted them. Uruguayan exile was accompanied by a wave of migration of mixed socioeconomic and political motivations, composed of hundreds of thousands of people. By the late 1970s and 1980s, around half of the number had migrated to Argentina, but the United States and Australia had attracted a significant number of Uruguayan expatriates.

Another case of relocation in terms of geographical and cultural proximity involved the relocation of activists from the Caribbean Basin and Central America to Mexico in the 1950s, a period of political turbulence throughout those areas. As previously analyzed, Mexico granted hospitality and political asylum to the antidictatorial and progressive forces persecuted there.

After the Cuban revolution, in addition to fleeing to the United States, large groups of Cubans, many of them exiles, resettled in Costa Rica, Colombia, Mexico, and Panama, engrossing some of the earlier networks of co-nationals established in these countries. The case of Cuban exiles has been thoroughly analyzed in such a vast number of excellent works, especially for those relocating to the United States and Spain, that we have consciously refrained from addressing it in full in this book.

The across-the-border pattern of refuge becomes even more pronounced in situations of civil war, as illustrated by those who fled from El Salvador or Guatemala in the 1980s. The number of Salvadorans living abroad in 1980 totaled 750,000, a number that represented 16.2 percent of the country's population. The early 1980s migration further added to that number. According to UNHCR, Salvadoran refugees were living in all the countries of the region: 175,000 in Nicaragua, 120,000 in Mexico, 70,000 in Guatemala, 20,000 in

[55] Jaime Llambias-Wolff, "The Voluntary Repatriation Process of Chilean Exiles." *International Migration*, 31, 4 (1993): 579–597.

Honduras, 10,000 in Costa Rica, 7,000 in Belize, and 1,000 in Panamá.[56] Many of them moved on in further search of economic opportunities for livelihood, one million settling in the United States.[57]

The proximity factor also weighed heavily in the case of exiles from Haiti, which was reinforced by the modest resources of most refugees. Even though they had been viewed with distrust and animosity since their early 19th-century invasion and spoke a different language than the Dominicans, many Haitians moved to the Spanish-speaking Dominican Republic when they had to leave the homeland because of political persecution or oppression. Over the course of the 20th century, between 250,000 and 500,000 Haitians settled in the Dominican Republic. A more reduced number moved to the affluent United States, but moving to France was beyond the pale for most, even if there was a linguistic affinity and France was economically stable. Only about 4,500 Haitians lived in France in the 1980s, according to OFPRA (Office Français de protection des réfugiées et des apatrides, or French Office of Protection of Refugees and State-less Persons), an agency responsible for determining refugee status. It is hard to discriminate how many of the translocated Haitians were driven by political instability rather than by concerns with economic subsistence, but certainly the choice of the Dominican Republic reflects the weight of proximity. Other locations would be more attractive in terms of economic prospects alone, as the parallel move of many Dominicans leaving illegally to Puerto Rico, looking for jobs and possibly a ticket to the United States, seems to indicate.

Perhaps the most important intervening variables in selecting paths of exile have been the political environment and cultural setup in the prospective host countries. Most exiles escaping persecution by dictatorial rulers preferred to settle in democratic countries. A country close to their homeland, qualifying more or less as 'free' and 'democratic,' would rank high. Manuel Jirón, a Nicaraguan who had to flee his home country both under the Somoza dictatorship and later under the Sandinistas, recalls how a community of co-nationals in exile formed in Somoza's times in San José de Costa Rica, with its members – among them Pedro Joaquín Chamorro, his spouse Violeta Chamorro, the "tormented poet" Manolo Cuadra, Teño López, and the intellectual, Gonzalo Rivas Novoa – plotting and discussing Nicaragua's problems aloud in San José's coffeehouses.[58]

Yet, even if the country of reception was not democratic, as was the case of Nicaragua in the late 1940s and 1950s, it could provide a hospitable environment for exiles fleeing Costa Rica after the 1948 civil war. Somoza welcomed

---

[56] Celio Mármora, "Hacia la migración planificada inter-Latinoamericana: Salvadoreños en Argentina." *Estudios Migratorios Latinoamericanos* 1, 3 (1986): 275–293.

[57] Segundo Montes, "Migration to the United States as an Index of the Intensifying Social and Political Crises in El Salvador." *Journal of Refugees Studies*, 1, 2 (1988): 107–126.

[58] Manuel Jirón, *Exilio S.A. Vivencias de un nicaragüense en el exilio.* San José: Ediciones Radio Amor, 1983.

into Nicaragua those persecuted by the government of José Figueres, primarily individuals associated with former President Rafael Angel Calderón Guardia and his followers, the labor movement associated with the Communists, and parts of the oligarchy. Anastasio Somoza, who had backed Calderón in the civil war, hosted the exiles. When, in 1954, Figueres let the Nicaraguan exiles launch an invasion of their home country to overthrow Somoza, the Nicaraguan president retaliated by launching an invasion of Costa Rica in January 1955, integrating Costa Rican exiles in the attack that almost cost Figueres his presidency, but for the intervention of the OAS and the United States.[59] As in the past, proximity to the home country was a plus because it built up the hope of a prompt return.

If relocated far away, say in Europe, cultural affinity would weigh heavily in favor of Spain over other destinations. Although it was relatively underdeveloped compared with other European destinations at the time of the onset of repression in the 1970s, the sharing of the Spanish language was a major factor of attraction, even before democratization and even more so after Franco's death and the democratic opening. Testimonies of Latin American exiles in Sweden and Israel bear witness to the pull that Spain and Mexico exercised on them despite the better conditions provided them by the Swedish or Israeli authorities.[60]

Spain increasingly attracted the largest numbers of Latin American exiles and refugees within Europe, in parallel to the arrival of many migrants motivated by economic reasons. Among Latin Americans, the most numerous groups in Spain by the mid-1980s were Argentineans (42,358), Chileans (28,717), Uruguayans (10,966), and Dominicans (8,818). Other estimations put those numbers even higher. The Argentinean consulate in Madrid estimated 25,000 co-nationals resided in the city. Nearly 9,000 Argentines had permanent residency and more than 3,000 had temporary residence. Another estimated 25,000 were undocumented. The consulate in Barcelona estimated that more than 25,000 Argentines had settled in Catalunya, and 5,000 to 6,000 were thought to reside in Southern Spain and some thousands more in the Balearic Islands. In the same period, 2,809 Chileans had obtained Spanish citizenship, 4,031 held residence permits, and 1,877 were permanent residents. Around 20,000 Chileans were estimated to be in Spain as undocumented persons, most of them in the areas of Madrid (more than 15,000) and Barcelona (around 5,000). In the same period, most Uruguayans in Spain were in the area of Barcelona (more than 5,000). These figures, which include those naturalized and those undocumented, are an indication of the attraction of Spain for exiles, represented

---

[59] G. Pope Atkins, *Encyclopedia of the Inter-American System*. Westport, CT: Greenwood, 1997, p. 106.

[60] Interview with Elda González, Madrid, 26 June 1998; Diana Guelar, Vera Jarach, and Beatriz Ruiz, *Los chicos del exilio*. Buenos Aires: País del nomeolvides, 2002; Orit Gazit, *"No Place to Call Home." Political Exile, Estrangement and Identity. Processes of Identity Construction Among Political Exiles from Latin America to Israel, 1970–2004*. Jerusalem: Shaine Working Papers No. 11, 2005.

mostly by Argentineans, Chileans, and Uruguayans, as well as for migrants, represented mostly by Dominicans. It is hard to distinguish between the cultural affinity and the economic and political attraction, which became increasingly important in the case of Spain. And yet, personal recollections and memories bear testimony to the weight of the first factor, even before Spain turned into an economically or politically open country. The pull factors overwrote distances for prospective exiles from South America, thus reversing the late 19th-century and early 20th-century pattern of relocation to the Americas.[61]

Other European destinations such as Sweden or France received a much smaller number of exiles and refugees. When the preceding factors played a secondary role in shaping the routes of escape political connections affected the differential number of relocated individuals from various Latin-American countries. Thus, as we have seen, many more Chileans than other South Americans arrived in Sweden because of the connections of the Chilean Social Democracy (SD) and the SD in power in the host country. Other Scandinavian countries also received Latin-American exiles, although a less significant number. For instance, until August 1987, Denmark had received only 800 Chileans.[62]

Escape and Exile

When there is institutionalized repression, state terror, and generalized violence, as in the 1970s in South America and in the 1980s in Central America, there is a flow of individuals fleeing for their lives and looking, often desperately, for asylum. In such situations, there is no certainty that possible host countries will come forward and save those willing to escape political persecution. Escape is often enabled by the personal decisions and vision of individuals representing potential host countries, sometimes taking action on behalf of politically persecuted people, helping far beyond their formal instructions. Being guided by their concern for fellow human beings and humanitarian values, these representatives of foreign governments and international organizations may take risks inspired by human-rights values that had become enshrined in the international and transnational arena in recent generations. The existence of a fourth tier clearly influences attitudes that facilitate escape and exile.

Such situations, clouded by political violence, imprisonment, torture, disappearance, and assassinations, are dramatic:

Whoever decides to come to the [Italian] consulate, knows that, in the best of the cases, s/he will have to leave Argentina, the family, the house, the work, all the things that s/he has built or fought for until then. They will have to start again from zero in Italy,

[61] The source for these figures is the Spanish government, UNHCR, and NGOs, as cited in CISPLA, *Latinoamericanos: Refugiados políticos en España*, Valencia, 1982. See also Chapter 6.

[62] Daniel Moore, Olsen Frykman, and Leonardo Rossielo, "La literatura del exilio Latinoamericano en Suecia (1976–1990)." *Revista Iberoamericana*, 59 (1993): 164–165.

a country they know only through the fables told by their parents. This is a country in which they will find themselves without a house and without money, isolated and where it will be hard to find work. Such a step involves a kind of laceration accepted only by those who know they are being looked for – generally after the kidnapping of someone close, who probably had given away a name, since nobody resists torture – and having spent all the money and with no shelters, has no alternative but to wander around the city, expecting to be abducted at any moment and taken away amidst the indifference of onlookers.[63]

The decision to escape and go into exile became a major decision for many who might or might not become victims of repression and had to decide on a step that would affect their lives and the lives of thousands of co-nationals for years to come.

In this section, we analyze cases of escape and exile in the 1970s, specifically those cases in which individuals feeling the angst of persecution resorted to the aid of foreign diplomats to exit the home country. One generation after World War II and the Holocaust, a minority of diplomats and foreign representatives in Latin America had a special sensibility to persecution, probably sharing the values of the UN Declaration of Human Rights.[64] The cases selected here are those of the individuals who contacted the Italian and the Israeli representatives in two South American countries: Chile and Argentina.

The abrupt onslaught of the military *coup d'état* in Chile created a sudden and massive wave of escapees entering the grounds of the various embassies and diplomatic residencies in Santiago, in search of diplomatic asylum. Following the coup in September 1973, several gestures of solidarity by diplomats took place. A key figure in mobilizing the diplomats stationed in Chile was Swedish Ambassador Harald Edelstam, who became known as "the Raoul Wallenberg of the 1970s" for his commitment to help refugees. "Ambassador Edelstam was credited with single-handedly preventing troops from storming the Cuban embassy and with providing protection for about 20 Chileans, Brazilians and other political refugees who had sought asylum there. When Mr. Edelstam protested the breach of the normal diplomatic safe-conduct affairs, he was beaten by Chilean soldiers and armed police."[65] Socialist International resolved to ask governments led by member parties to provide asylum quotas to those who were currently escaping from Pinochet.[66]

---

[63] Enrico Calamai, *Niente asilo politico. Diario di un console italiano nell'Argentina dei desaparecidos.* Rome: Editori Riuniti, 2003, p. 160.

[64] See Micheline Ishay, *The History of Human Rights.* Berkeley: University of California Press, 2004.

[65] Edelstam was expelled from Chile in December 1973. "1974 Legislative Session: 4th Session, 30th Parliament, Wednesday, 27 March 1974, Afternoon Seating," available at http://www.legis.gov.bc.ca/HANSARD/30th4th/30p_04s_740327p.htm, accessed 5 June 2006.

[66] "Reserved" message from the [Israeli] Embassy in Santiago to the South American desk at the Foreign Ministry in Jerusalem, on the subject of the situation of the radical elements after the

Israeli diplomats in Santiago, surprised by the violent character of the military coup, confronted a situation in which persecuted leftists approached them in search of asylum. They lacked coherent directives from the Ministry of Foreign Affairs in Jerusalem, as Israeli law did not contemplate the possibility of granting asylum to political refugees. Nevertheless, Israeli Ambassador Moshe Tov and his second-in-command, Benjamin Oron, began to assist victims of military persecution on their own initiative. In the first stage, they redirected those individuals to the Swedish Embassy, providing financial support to help feed the increasing number of asylees. Later on, when the Swedish could not shelter any more persecuted people on their premises, they received political refugees in the Israeli Embassy located in an apartment building in central Santiago. The Israelis, different from the Italians and the Mexicans, for instance, were not perceived by the military authorities as providing asylum and, accordingly, their embassy was less targeted by police, trying to preclude the access of potential refugees. Moreover, most of the 'guests' at the Israeli Embassy were not interested in reaching Israel as their place of exile and were assisted by the Israeli diplomats in obtaining safe conducts and asylum in other embassies. Often, the Israeli diplomats moved these individuals in their own cars, taking advantage of their diplomat license plates and immunity. Soon, the Israeli diplomats moved to a third stage of looking for the release of political prisoners and trying to find information about people whose whereabouts were unknown. After long negotiations with the Chilean Air Force, the Israeli Embassy managed to liberate some prominent political prisoners, among them Benjamín Teplizky, secretary-general of the UP coalition, and Luis Vega, a high official of the Ministry of Interior under Allende.[67] The Labor Party, which governed Israel until 1977 and was a member of the Socialist International, complied with the resolution by the latter and took about 50 Chilean political refugees, Jews and non-Jews, who were granted residence in Israel and were received through acts and expressions of solidarity.[68]

Similarly, and to a much larger extent, the Italian authorities had to deal with a substantial number of Chileans and foreigners seeking asylum in the residence of the ambassador in Santiago. Between 1973 and 1975, several hundreds of refugees managed to smuggle themselves into the grounds. According to the testimony of Brazilian exile in Chile, José Serra, who found shelter there, there was a time between October 1973 and May 1974 that the embassy hosted more than 600 asylees, men, women, and children, both Chilean nationals and

---

coup and the intervention of the Social Democrats and the Socialist International," in Israel's National Archive, doc.5376/22 no. 717, dated 8 October 1973.

[67] Interview with Benjamin Oron, Jerusalem, 9 August 2000.

[68] Interview with lawyer Nahum Solán, Jerusalem, 12 August 2003. Solán, who at the time was a functionary of the Absorption Ministry, mentioned various cases, among them that of the Chilean writer Manuel Rivano, who years later relocated from Israel to Sweden.

foreigners who were exiled in democratic Chile.[69] The diary of Enrico Cala-mai, who served in a diplomatic position on the grounds for two months in late 1974, attests to the organizational capacity of the refugees who had taken shelter in the Italian diplomatic residence. They had organized themselves democratically in committees with representatives of the Chilean parties, dealt with all aspects of daily life in the dire conditions in which they lived, negotiated with the Italian representatives, and even defied the Pinochet government by commemorating the first anniversary of the military coup with black flags and a mass mourning.[70]

This mass of asylees would need the intercession of the diplomatic representatives of Italy before the Chilean military administration to obtain safe conducts to leave Chile, while the Christian Democratic government of Italy had not recognized the government of Pinochet. In parallel, the Chilean government could not force its way into the diplomatic grounds but did create a security belt to preclude the exit of the asylees and the access of others seeking asylum, while it refused to grant the safe conducts. In particular, the Chilean military were after Humberto Sotomayor, second-in-command in the hierarchy of the MIR (Movimiento de Izquierda Revolucionaria, or Revolutionary Leftist Movement), who had entered the diplomatic residence with his family.[71] Eventually, after many months of negotiations, the Chilean government granted safe conducts allowing the asylees sheltered in the foreign embassies to exit the country for Italy and other countries. Until May 1974, the Chilean government let thousands of those who had taken refuge in the diplomatic missions – both 1,265 nationals and 4,949 aliens radicated in Chile – exit the country. By early April 1975, all those who had taken refuge in the Italian diplomatic residence had left Chile. The Italian diplomats had made efforts to find them asylum in other countries, primarily non-Communists to Australia and Communists to Romania.[72] Italy preferred to be selective in granting asylum to leftists coming from Chile, especially because of the influence of right-wing circles close to those in power (P-2) and in the context of the Cold War. Asylum was accordingly restricted. An October 1974 report by the OAS indicates that only 228 such individuals (aliens and Chileans) had been received by Italy until mid-1974, far behind the number of individuals finding asylum elsewhere[73] (see the following list).

---

[69] José Serra, "The Other September 11." *Dissent*, Winter 2004, available at http://www.dissentmagazine.org/article/?article=411, accessed 5 June 2006.

[70] Calamai, *Niente asilo politico*, p. 90.

[71] Calamai, *Niente asilo politico*, pp. 95–97, 100.

[72] Interamerican Commission of Human-Rights, Organization of American States, "Report on the Status of Human-Rights in Chile: Findings on the Spot. Observations in the Republic of Chile, 22 July–2 August 1974." OEA/Ser.L/V/II.34, doc. 21, corr.1, 25 October 1974, available at http://www/cidh.org/countryrep/Chile74eng/chap13.htm, accessed 4 June 2006; Tomaso de Vergottini, *Cile: diario di un diplomatico, 1973–1975*. Rome: Koinè, 2000, pp. 118 and 238–241.

[73] OEA, "Report on the Status of Human-Rights in Chile," note 10.

Country	Number of Asylum-Seeking Individuals
Argentina	902
France	854
Mexico	805
Sweden	649
Federal Republic of Germany	594
Panama	436
Cuba	374
Russia	263
Venezuela	249
Italy	228
Netherlands	201
Peru	189
Spain	162
Colombia	156
Austria	152

The pattern of repression in Argentina was different, with a spiral of increasing violence taking place in tandem with the politicization and polarization of the public domain in the democratic interregnum of 1973–1976. The coup of March 1976 did not diminish violence but rather obliterated the institutions and legal mechanisms that could operate as countervailing weights to the onslaught of institutional – yet partially uncoordinated – violence against those suspected of leftist leanings. Individuals started escaping in the last stages of the democratic downfall and, with the deepening of generalized violence and disappearances, sought ways of escape, often desperately. Embassies were told by the authorities to take measures to avoid letting escapees seeking asylum enter their premises. Analyzing the cases of the Italian and Israeli displomatic envoys and representatives, one cannot but stress the key role played by individual foreign officials, often in clear defiance of hierarchical administrative rules or in advance of the regulations decided by their central authorities, be they ministries of foreign affairs or agencies of immigration.

The Italian Ministry of Foreign Affairs opposed any intervention in favor of those seeking asylum, especially having the precedent of their embassy in Chile flooded with asylees. Enrico Calamai, who had been stationed as Italian consul in Buenos Aires since 1972, was sent in late October 1974 to Santiago, where he was exposed to the misery of the Chilean asylees in the embassy there. Once back in Argentina and facing the plight of Argentinean activists on the run – most of them of Italian descent – who sought a way to escape the tightened circle of repression, Calamai made the decision to help many of these individuals to escape, even defying the directives:

Clearly, the Argentineans expect the full cooperation of the Italian diplomats, in order to avoid the repetition of what happened in Santiago and not to make public what was about to occur in the country. The Italian Ministry of Foreign Affairs had the same expectations of us. It was a coincidence of points of view that since the beginning was unacceptable and impossible to understand. Any behavior outside this line would carry serious consequences for a diplomatic career.[74]

Being approached by relatives and friends of the individuals on the run, Calamai opted to build an 'underground' network with Filippo di Benedetto, a representative of the Italian trade unions in Argentina, and Giangiacomo Foà, a journalist of the *Corriere della Sera* to help the persecuted individuals, using one of the offices of the Italian consulate in Buenos Aires as a shelter. The latter cooperated through their intimate knowledge of hundreds of associations of Italians in Argentina to send individuals in need to Calamai. Foà, well aware of the extent of repression in Argentina, used information he received from Calamai to publicize the plight of the persecuted and condemn the Argentinian military in the most widely read Italian newspaper. These activities eventually led to his expulsion from the country. Calamai used his diplomatic prerogatives and issued passports and visas to hundreds of individuals, and he even accompanied some of the escapees to the border in order to facilitate their exit from the country. The decision to help those in flight involved both a personal and an institutional risk. Although the consul was willing to receive whoever arrived, he had to personally examine each case in order to ensure that the person was not a provocateur or an informant sent by the military authorities. Many were sent through Uruguay, even if they knew that the Argentinean security forces operated in that country too. Still, the intense traffic between the two countries on the River Plate and the requirement of only a personal ID instead of passports led them to use this path of escape.[75] Until 2000, Calamai's dedicated work in favor of the fleeing individuals was kept secret, as it obviously ran against the directives of the Italian Foreign Ministry.[76]

Even more convoluted was the role played by the Israeli diplomats and representatives in Argentina during the peak of repression in the late 1970s, which affected many individuals of Jewish origins, who in their plight contacted the former as they sought ways of escape.[77]

The relationships between Israel and Argentina, which had sunk to a nadir during the period following Adolf Eichmann's kidnapping in 1960 and his transferal to Jerusalem for trial there,[78] had improved notoriously. At the onset of military rule, they could even qualify as cordial and close. On the international level, Israel had turned into a clear ally of the United States, thus

---

[74] Calamai, *Niente asilo politico*, pp. 139–140.

[75] Calamai, *Niente asilo politico*, pp. 161, 250–251.

[76] Maria Adriana Bernardotti and Barbara Bongiovanni, "Aproximaciones al estudio del exilio argentino en Italia," in Pablo Yankelevich, Ed., *Represión y destierro*. La Plata: Ediciones al Margen, 2004, pp. 53–55.

[77] The following analysis is based on Mario Sznajder and Luis Roniger, "From Argentina to Israel: Escape, Evacuation and Exile," *Journal of Latin American Studies*, 37, 2 (2005): 351–377.

[78] Raanan Rein, *Argentina, Israel and the Jews: Perón, the Eichmann Capture and After*. Bethesda, MD: University Press of Maryland, 2003.

confronting the USSR and the Soviet bloc in the Middle East both directly and indirectly. Israel was considered to have a strong influence in Washington, an idea that prevailed both in military circles and among other elites as well, and prompted the view that it was convenient to maintain good relations with Israel in this regard. Additionally, the Argentinean military commands were impressed by the Israeli Defense Forces military prowess and its capacity to ensure the survival of a country in hostile surroundings. Ensuing commercial relationships developed and involved the sale of Argentinean meat to Israel and the sale of Israeli arms to Argentina.[79]

Paradoxically, however, this admiration was mixed with apprehension and mistrust because parts of the military high ranks feared a presumed Zionist plan to infiltrate Argentina and take over Patagonia. According to this imagined scheme, known as the Andinia plan, and much in concordance with the doctrine of national security, parts of the local Jewish community were seen as collaborators of the Zionists, and their loyalty to Argentina was to be suspected. Needless to say, this mistrust of co-nationals was imbued with open anti-Semitism in sectors of the armed forces.[80]

Ambiguity thus dominated this set of relationships. The military junta strongly emphasized that it did not carry out anti-Jewish policies and stressed their good relationships with Israel as part of the anti-Communist front led by the United States, while they simultaneously mistrusted the loyalty of the Argentine Jews. Furthermore, the military could not fully follow the nuances of Jewish identity, on the basis of their conceptual confusion regarding who was "Jewish," "Israelite," or "Israeli." This confusion would be used tactically by the Israeli diplomats and representatives of the Jewish Agency (JA) so as to attempt to help those fearing persecution and repression.

Israel did not possess a special statute for refugees or political exiles but, throughout the years, had received thousands of Jews escaping persecution by

[79] In 1977–1981, Israel provided 14 percent of Argentina's military purchases. Germany led the list, providing 33 percent, the United States 17 percent – despite the embargo of 1978 – France 14 percent, and the UK 12 percent. Behind were other providers of arms such as Switzerland, Belgium, Spain, and Austria. Israeli sales rose after 1982, when the Western countries imposed the embargo effectively. Bishara Bahbah, "Israel's Military Relationships with Ecuador and Argentina." *Journal of Palestine Studies*, 15, 2 (1986), pp. 76–101; and Joel Barromi, "Israel frente a la dictadura argentina: El episodio de Córdoba y el caso Timerman," in Leonardo Senkman and Mario Sznajder, Eds., with the cooperation of Edy Kaufman, *El Legado del Autoritarismo*. Buenos Aires: GEL, 1995, p. 348.

[80] Even in 2003, 20 years after the fall of the military government, versions of the Andinia plan still surface. In August 2003, different sources attributed to the chief of the army, General Roberto Bendini, a statement – made at the high military academy, the Escuela Superior de Guerra – in the sense that alien interests were trying to steal Patagonian resources. According to the source, Bendini claimed that "for now there is no definitive enemy," although he added that the activities of "small Israeli groups," and NGOs are being closely observed. In the case of these "small Israeli groups," Bendini explained that they arrive inadvertently under the "guise of tourism" (http://www.radio10.com.ar/interior/home.html). In light of the reactions generated by his comments, General Bendini denied he had singled out any specific groups (Clarín, 13 September 2003).

different governments.[81] Israel took in such individuals within the framework of its basic constitutional laws, primarily the Law of Return that entitled every Jew who immigrated to automatically receive Israeli citizenship on arrival, enjoying full civil and political rights. When facing a threat to the lives of individuals of Jewish origin in any place in the world, Israel could thus use the legal–institutional mechanisms that allow and favor their immigration and integration as citizens. The JA was the institutional mechanism in charge of regulating Jewish immigration from countries with which Israel had diplomatic relations. The representatives of the JA were those charged with processing applications of those who wished to immigrate to Israel legally and were able to do it openly, through the regular immigration procedures.

Under the PRN (Proceso de Reorganización Nacional, or National Reorganization Process) in Argentina, a situation with few precedents came about. Jews whose family members had been detained and disappeared desperately appealed to representatives of the JA, consular representatives, and Israeli diplomats. People of Jewish origin who felt threatened by the wave of terror and the persecution taking place there began to rapidly apply for help through these channels.[82] The high number of cases largely surpassed expectations. The question was how to proceed, and which policies to adopt concerning cases of individuals under severe fears or life-threatening danger, and who had often gone underground and were sought after by the local authorities and security forces of Argentina.

A process of pragmatic decision-making was initiated by the Israeli representatives stationed in Argentina, which involved the representatives of the JA as well as the Israeli diplomats. These representatives stationed on the ground found themselves on the spot and had to deal with the pleas for help coming from the persecuted. The persecution, evacuation, and exile of these individuals from the countries of the Southern Cone were not objects of discussion

---

[81] Among these were the Holocaust survivors, expatriates of their native lands, who were persecuted and annihilated by Nazism and rejected by many countries during World War II; many of the Jews escaping Arab countries in the Middle East and North Africa, who were forced to leave their countries of origin with almost no resources, as a consequence of the Arab–Israeli conflict and the establishment of the state of Israel; and, more recently, the Jews from the former Soviet Union.

[82] According to testimonies by Ran Curiel and Dany Recanati, they immediately began receiving family members of detainees and *desaparecidos* following their arrival in Argentina in 1976 at the Israeli Embassy and as head of the JA delegation, respectively. Yet, according to Curiel, at first many of the Jews who were persecuted did not appeal solely to the Israeli representatives, and only later, when the Israeli delegation received permission to make "consular" visits to Jewish prisoners, an option not available to other diplomatic missions, did the family members appeal mainly to the Israeli Consulate. This seems to have been buttressed by a diplomatic initiative of Allen ("Tex") Harris of the American Embassy in Buenos Aires to orientate the relatives of Jewish background to the Israeli consulate for assistance. Testimony of Ran Curiel, Jerusalem, 12 September 2003, and interview with Dany Recanati, 20 April 1990, available at the Section of Oral Interviews, Institute of Contemporary Jewry [henceforth: ICJ], Jerusalem, no. 216 (2).

or factors in the process of decision-making and had no priority in the agenda of high-level politicians, governmental officials, or the Israeli Parliament. In theory, the lower-level representatives were merely in charge of carrying out the policies of the government and Israeli institutions but, in fact, they became the initiators of policies that were formalized through practice.

Nonetheless, some of the Israeli representatives stationed in Argentina felt it was their duty to stand against anti-Semitism, to help persecuted Jews to escape and send them to Israel, where they would be safe. These diplomats shared an ethos that depicted the State of Israel as a shelter for persecuted Jews. In very wide terms, the Zionist ethos saw Jews in the diaspora as "exiles" and the process of their ingathering in Israel as a "dis-exile" – that is the return of descendants of a people expelled and dispersed from the home country almost 2,000 years ago. The persecuted Argentineans of Jewish origin could rely on this ethos to find a way of escaping the trap set by the military, but they did not share it. On the contrary, motivated by radical leftist positions, many of them were highly critical of the Israeli position in the international scene and saw Israel only as a temporary shelter, a site of exile, perhaps to be left shortly after escaping Argentina or once the situation in the home country returned to democracy. These contrasted visions could be reconciled only because of the seriousness of their plight.

Both leftist and rightist governments in Israel were willing to receive the individuals of Jewish origins who had to flee for their lives in Argentina, even if the latter's political visions were antithetical to the Israeli official strategies in the Cold War and the Israeli–Palestinean conflict. Even before the 1976 *coup d'état*, efforts were made to 'save' young Jews who had joined revolutionary movements, either of Peronist leanings or other orientations, and who, in some cases, were becoming part of the guerrillas.[83] Both the foreign minister as well as leading political figures expressed an uncompromised commitment to rescuing those individuals who feared for their physical integrity in the

---

[83] Nahum Solán, representing the Zionist Youth Organization and belonging to the Zionist-Socialist MAPAM (Mifleguet Poalim Meuhedet, or United Workers Party), remembers his journey to Argentina in 1975 as an envoy of the JA. Once there, he tried to contact the young men and women who had shifted from the Zionist–Socialist groups toward Argentinean leftist groups, such as the ERP (Ejército Revolucionario del Pueblo, or People's Revolutionary Army) and the Montoneros, motivated by the desire to participate in the revolutionary struggle. Nonetheless, many of them had doubts after discovering anti-Semitic prejudices, which prevailed in such groups formed by many Catholics. But, as they were already 'inside' the underground movements, they saw no other options but to remain there. Desertion would be considered as treason to the cause and could even bring about the death penalty. At one point, Solán remembers traveling to the hills in the province of Córdoba and managing to meet with a score of young people who were living through that experience. They belonged to a left-wing Zionist organization that had lost dozens of members to 'subversive' leftist movements such as the ERP. Among these former members, six individuals had returned to Argentina from Israel to join the guerrilla movement. Solán reportedly managed to convince 12 of them to abandon the local leftist movements and leave for Israel. Interview with Solán, Jerusalem, 12 August 2003.

atmosphere of repression and terror. Emblematic is Menahem Begin, leader of the Israeli National Right opposition that within months would win the elections and the government after overthrowing Yitzhak Rabin's Labor coalition, who voiced this view as he visited Argentina in August 1976. In a closed meeting with the Zionist representatives in Argentina, Begin reportedly said that "Israel has to help every persecuted Jew. This should bear no regard to his/her political ideas, whatever these may be." Interpolated by one of the Israeli envoys who held that a great part of the young persecuted individuals belonged to the extreme Left and that, on arriving in Israel, they would join the extraparliamentarian anti-Zionist groups, Begin responded: "They can associate with Matzpen [anti-Zionist, extreme Left] in Israel for all I care. Israel is obliged to save them."[84] Begin embodied a point of view widely found in Israel and shaped by the vision of the Holocaust, which predicated a historical role for Israel as a Jewish state with a mandate to help any Jew in distress. This became especially crucial in cases in which elements of political persecution were being mixed with anti-Semitism, as was the case in Argentina. And yet, once in power as prime minister in 1977, Begin failed to shape the course of agenda setting because of the weight carried by the positions of the Israeli ambassador, the local Jewish leadership, and other diplomatic and commercial interests.[85]

The view of the need to evacuate the persecuted individuals was shared by the head of JA representatives in Argentina, Dany Recanati, who tried to assist in the escape of the persecuted individuals, other diplomatic and consular representatives in Argentina, along with figures such as Rabbi Roberto Graetz and Rabbi Marshall Meyer.[86]

Recanati began receiving appeals for help and processed them, being aware that the local authorities considered many of these individuals to be subversives and terrorists. This does not mean that these representatives did not consult with their superiors in the JA or the Ministry of Foreign Affairs (henceforth,

[84] Aryeh Dayan, "Thanks to Menahem Begin." *Kol Hair*, 9 September 1987, p. 34 (in Hebrew). Matzpen was a small Trotskyist and anti-Zionist extraparliamentary group, ostracized by most political forces in Israel. Various Israeli figures visited Argentina during those years, including former prime minister Itzhak Rabin, Yigal Alon, and the president of the JA, Arie Dultzin. The Israeli diplomats who received and accompanied them in Buenos Aires repeatedly brought up the problem of the persecuted and missing individuals. In light of reactions such as Begin's during his visit to Argentina in 1976, it is difficult to understand how the issue was not projected to the center of public concerns in Israel.

[85] Despite the identification of these factors, it is hard to evaluate the relative weight of each one on the official agenda setting. This is not possible before a full opening of archives in the future, on 'sensitive' issues like the arms industry, probably not before 2016.

[86] Rabbi Marshall Meyer and Rabbi Roberto Graetz were key figures in the defense of those who were politically persecuted. Without enjoying diplomatic immunity and often endangering themselves and their families, they undertook a huge effort in the area of human-rights preservation. This was publicly recognized when Argentina returned to democracy, especially in the case of Marshall Meyer, who not only was nominated to the CONADEP (Comisión Nacional Sobre la Desaparición de Personas, or National Commission of Inquiry on the Disappeared) but who also received the highest Argentine decoration, the Order of General San Martín.

MFA) in Jerusalem in order to receive precise instructions, establish the limits of what was permissible, and approve whatever was being practiced *in situ*. Yet, the modules of escape, evacuation, and exile were shaped on the spot rather than derived from the framework of high-level politics and administration. In fact, it was the contrasting attitudes and, sometimes, clashes between Ambassador Ram Nirgad and senior JA representatives such as Dany Recanati and Itzhak Pundak that seem to have led to upper-level meetings in Jerusalem and to the formalization of the procedures and their rerouting to the JA and MFA representatives in South America. Beyond the personal level, the confrontation reveals the crucial role played by competing interpretations of issues and problems and the alternative worldviews that underlie the positions of individuals who were expected to act in unison.[87]

The confrontation was shaped by the cautious position of the ambassador, who in 1976 was willing to intercede only on behalf of Israeli citizens in trouble, as against the representatives of the JA and some of the junior staff of the embassy, who followed a broader mandate that included helping Argentine citizens of Jewish background. This case, which led to the liberation and evacuation of eight individuals, was the first case of open recognition by the Argentinean authorities of the *locus standi* of Israel regarding Argentine Jews.[88] It was also the first case of an ongoing, but tense, cooperation between the Israeli ambassador and the JA representatives.[89]

As there was a growing consciousness of the problem, and as the tensions generated in Argentina required adjudication, a series of meetings took place in Jerusalem around June–July 1976, aimed at coordinating the stands of the MFA, the JA, and other agencies (the Ministry of Interior and the Immigration Absorption Ministry). JA officials discussed with the Israeli MFA the issue of the families of the persecuted individuals, specifically those families within which some of the members were not Jewish. They decided to assist any such individual – whether Jewish or not – in escaping the country because it was assumed that the arrival of any such family member to Israel would accelerate the rescue process of those left behind.[90] Instructions were similarly drafted

[87] Documentation on this confrontation abounds in the archives, in the form of reserved reports (e.g., by Itzhak Pundak to Avraham Argov, 14 February 1977); to Almogi and Dulzin, 6 September 1977; and to Almogi, 12 October 1977), Central Zionist Archives, C85/199, and a telegram of protest by Dr. Reznicki of the DAIA to Almogi (with copy to Israeli Foreign Minister Moshe Dayan) against the declarations of Pundak aired on Israeli radio on 30 June 1977, regarding the situation in Argentina. We are grateful to Dr. Leonardo Senkman who made available copies of these still undisclosed documents.

[88] See Barromi, "Israel frente a la dictadura," pp. 325–335; and the testimony by Israel Even Shoshan, 11 November 1990, ICJ, no. 216 (1).

[89] Ambassador Nirgad and JA director's representative Yitzhak Pundak had serious differences of opinion concerning the labeling of the military rulers as anti-Semitic, images that Pundak had circulated in Israel. See Senkman, "Israel y el rescate"; and Marcel Zohar, *Free my People to Hell. Betrayal in Blue and White; Israel and Argentina: How the Jews Persecuted by the Military Were Neglected*. Tel Aviv: Zitrin, 1990 (in Hebrew).

[90] Secret memorandum sent by Joshua Wolberg, chief of the Latin American section of the Department of Immigration of the JA in Latin America, 11 June 1976; this document was endorsed

regarding the possible treatment and evacuation of individuals whose lives were at risk in South America.[91]

The instructions were intended to be rerouted to South America – not only to Argentina – and specified the procedures to be followed with regard to individuals in danger, defined as "those who were persecuted for their Judaism, their participation in Zionist activities or their political activity in general, and who were under physical threat due to their personal background or their relatives' activities." The instructions explicitly excluded individuals who were fleeing the authorities for having committed financial offenses, terrorist acts, or petty crimes. Leonardo Senkman sums up the prescriptive norms:

> It was the functionary's task to carefully interrogate the individual with regards to his/her personal history in order to test the authenticity of the motives of persecution.... The Israeli Embassy, the Jewish Agency in Jerusalem, and a local security official [at the Jewish Agency], were to receive a synopsis of the investigation. Following the ambassador's consent, the immigration emissary was to organize the evacuation via neighboring countries or directly to Israel. Under precise instructions, the Department of Immigration was to be on the side but unnoticed during the immigration procedure and the escaping individual was not to carry compromising documents mentioning Israel as the final destination; only in outstanding cases, when there was no other alternative, could the Jewish Agency offer Israeli transit documents [_laissez passer_] subordinated by the approval of the local [Israeli] Ambassador. When possible, it was recommended that the individuals should travel on their own to neighboring countries after receiving financial aid from the Jewish Agency [and once abroad they would receive an Israeli _laissez passer_].[92]

In addition to being a compromise in the tug-of-war between the representatives of the different agencies, the instructions formalized the operating procedure already tried on the ground by the JA delegates.[93]

The attitude of the Israeli ambassador was cautious and reflected a more generalized attitude of some Israeli circles, which advised discretion concerning the provision of help to people persecuted by their home governments. Such an attitude was shaped by diverse factors, from commercial and material interests to diplomatic caution. A series of arguments was put forward to justify diplomatic caution, primarily (a) the intent not to endanger the work of the JA in the realm of legal immigration; (b) the wish not to affect the relationships with the military junta at a time when Israel was being censored in the UN and its diplomatic connections were being reduced internationally; and, finally, (c) the claim that discretion was required for helping the politically

with the signature of Jehuda Dominitz, vice-director general of the JA for Immigration (personal archive of Dany Recanati, representative-in-chief of the JA in Buenos Aires; in subsequent references, PADR).

[91] "Procedures for the treatment of people escaping from South America" (in Hebrew: Nohal tipul benimlatim me-artzot Drom America), PADR, Jerusalem, no date, probably June 1976.

[92] Leonardo Senkman, "Israel y el rescate," in Senkman and Sznajder, _El legado del auteritaritmo_. Buenos Aires: GEL, 1995, pp. 302–303.

[93] In April 1990, Recanati recalled that "we had built an operational framework we defined as evacuation." Testimony in ICJ, 216 (2).

persecuted individuals in escaping Argentina. A fourth argument, often used by the local Jewish community, was that an open confrontation with or criticism of the policies of the military junta, to be launched in Israel or in international forums, would produce an increase in anti-Semitism, which in turn would affect Jewish institutions and the community at large. Behind the scenes, especially in Israel, were also interests connected to the armaments industry, the impact of which can be guessed at but will remain undocumented until the Israel National Archives release such documentation in the future.

What is clear is that there was ambiguity in the highest circles. On the one hand, any public expression against the ruling junta and any condemnation of its repressive policies were cast aside in Israel. Members of the Israeli Parliament, the Knesset, presented eight urgent motions regarding the issue between 1976 and 1981, the critical period of human-rights violations in Argentina. The Parliament's secretary did not approve any of these motions and, consequently, they went down before even reaching the stage of debate. In their later testimonies, Geula Cohen, Dror Zeigerman, and Menahem Hacohen, members of Parliament, claimed that this lack of approval was because the president of the Knesset, Menahem Savidor, yielded to the pressure of the Israeli MFA that demanded that the issue not be discussed openly.[94] This case was clearly one of agenda denial, in which problem identification did not lead to the issue's gaining agenda status and, therefore, sidelining it in the short term, albeit maximizing the chances of criticism and issue expansion in the long run.[95]

The provision of help consisted of several venues, from visits to political prisoners held in prison to the benefits of the so-called Option Law and the covert evacuation of individuals who felt seriously threatened in the wave of repression. Through these various paths, between 350 and 400 individuals were assisted in escaping Argentina and arriving in Israel.

In Israel, the fleeing individuals found themselves in different environments, from universities to Hebrew language learning centers, cities, and kibbutzim. There, the new environments forced them to test previous assumptions and reshape their various identities. Who were the newly arrived from Argentina? Persecuted Jews willing to integrate into Israeli society? Were they exiles? Or, rather, were they leftist individuals from Latin America who used Israel as a bridge to less compromising *lieu d'exil*? Argentinean expatriates? Many of the newly arrived individuals found a source of political affinities to their leftist leanings in the kibbutz structure. The testimonies of dozens of people who arrived indicate that the fleeing individuals did not develop into a community

94 Testimonies by Geula Cohen (ICJ-216/42); Dror Zeigerman (ICJ-216/40); and Menahem Hacohen (ICJ-216/23); Appel and Bachrach, "The Politics of the Israeli Governments Regarding the Jewish Detainees-Disappeared in Argentina." Hebrew University of Jerusalem, Seminar Paper, 2002, p. 28.
95 On these aspects of agenda setting and agenda denial, see, among others, Roger W. Cobb and Marc Howard Ross, *Cultural Strategies of Agenda Denial*. Lawrence: University Press of Kansas, 1997, esp. pp. 3–4; and David Dery, "Agenda Setting and Problem Definition." *Policy Studies*, 21, 1 (2000): 37–47.

with its own identity and political agenda. Moreover, they dispersed throughout the entire country. Left-wing movements such as MAPAM's Youth, tried to 'convert' or 'reconvert' them into Socialist Zionism. Although some became active on the margins of Israeli politics, many refrained from any political activism. Indeed, their experience contrasted with that of Chilean exiles in Israel and elsewhere, who worked tirelessly in the political and international arena to keep Pinochet's record of human-rights violations in the news and to pave the way for the eventual restoration of democracy in their homeland.[96] The presence of the Argentinean newcomers did not have a notable impact on Israeli public life and did not affect the political debate on state terror and forced disappearance of Argentinean citizens, at least until the early 1980s, close to democratization.[97]

Many continued to experience the syndrome of 'living with the suitcases packed,' in a situation of suspended reality, of living neither in the homeland nor in the host country, which compounded the challenges of exile. With the passing of time, most of the escaped individuals left Israel for Europe, Spain in particular, or else for Latin America, where language and cultural affinity existed. Others returned to Argentina in the period of democratization initiated in 1983. A minority remained in Israel, adding on to the other Argentineans and Latin Americans who had immigrated voluntarily. Like many of those other immigrants, the fleeing individuals became 'invisible' in Israeli society as they integrated into the different spheres of everyday life and spread their residence throughout the entire country, rather than forming a cohesive community.[98] Their past remained a living memory and constitutive trait of their multifaceted, and at times fractured, personal identity, and their collective experience went unnoticed until recently, as part of the multiple paths of individuals and groups of the Latin-American diaspora generated by the military repression.

This analysis reveals that even countries without explicit or with restrictive policies of asylum faced the plight of individuals persecuted and requesting diplomatic assistance. In the cases that we analyzed, reluctance toward asylum was evident on the part of high governmental circles in Italy and Israel. Diplomatic representatives and immigration agents in Chile and Argentina, imbued

---

[96] Thomas C. Wright and Rody Oñate, *Flight from Chile: Voices of Exile*. Albuquerque: University of New Mexico Press, 1988. There were organizational moves by relatives of the victims of disappearance, foremost Memoria, led by Luis Jaimovich, father of Alejandra, abducted and disappeared, but their impact was limited.

[97] Appel and Bachrach, "The Politics."

[98] On Latin Americans in Israel, see Luis Roniger, "The Latin American Community of Israel: Some Notes on Latin American Jews and Latin American Israelis." *Israel Social Science Research*, 6, 1 (1989): 63–72; and Luis Roniger and Deby Babis, "Latin American Israelis: The Collective Identity of an Invisible Community," in Judit Bokser Liwerant, Eliezer Ben-Rafael, Yossi Gorny, and Raanan Rein, Eds., *Identities in an Era of Globalization and Multiculturalism: Latin America in the Jewish World*. Leiden and Boston: Brill, 2008, pp. 297–320. The assessment of processes of reconstruction of identity in Israel deserves separate analysis. On these, see Orit Gezit, 'No place to call Home'. Jerusalem: Shaine Working Papers, No. 11, 2005 (in Hebrew).

with a humanitarian ethos increasingly recognized internationally, were sensible to the plight of the persecuted and responded with personal initiatives that saved the lives of many. On the ground, they confronted a similar problematique. Caught between the scope of domestic repression and the unwillingness of their governments to generate positive policies toward the persecuted, they took the initiative in granting asylum, assisting escape, getting safe conducts, and finding locales of exile.

These initiatives likely brought institutional responses and eventually turned into systemic directives for treating the political exiles. The collective identities of the persecuted – among whom were many individuals of Italian and Jewish descent but full members of Chilean and Argentinean societies and persecuted as such – were tested by extreme circumstances that forced them into looking for diplomatic help in escaping. The personal decisions of individual diplomats and representatives were under such circumstances as crucial as formal directives in shaping the routes of escape and ultimately saved many human lives by making their exile possible. This problematique reveals how the human-values characteristic of the transnational and international arena by the late 20th century had subsumed considerations based on narrower collective identities or *realpolitik* of interests. Once abroad and safe, the escapees could decide to integrate into the host society, continue their political activity in the host country and return to the home country when conditions allowed, or continue into serial exile.

Serial Exile

The political will of exiles to continue the struggle against dictatorship at home is a major factor shaping the phenomenon of serial exile. We define *serial exile* as the subsequent and sometimes recurrent displacement from one site of exile to another, as the countries the displaced individuals settled in restrict their freedom of action.

Such restrictions are often due to policies of asylum, to pressures from the home country, or the case of a host country entering a period of political repression and dictatorship. These factors existed already in the 19th century, as exemplified in cases as renowned as those of Simón Bolívar and José Martí, and were intensified in the 20th century. In the 1970s, Peru, Mexico, and Venezuela were considered stable and safe places of refuge. Thus, for instance, after the 1973 military coup by Pinochet, Chilean leftists crossed the Peruvian border. Many, such as the exile Hugo Alvarez, thought that Peru "was one of the few possible places [of refuge] that were near and safe."[99] But Peruvian authorities restricted the exiles' political activities, and many, including Alvarez, felt pressured to relocate to a second *lieu d'exil*, in his case to Sweden. Redemocratized Venezuela, and especially Caracas, attracted exiles from all

[99] Ana Barón, Mario Del Carril, and Albino Gómez, *Por qué se fueron*. Buenos Aires: Emecé Editores, 1995, p. 410.

over Latin America. Among those settling there were leaders from the Bolivian Partido Revolucionario de Izquierda Nacionalista (PRIN, or the Nationalist Leftist Revolutionary Party) and of the MIR, Brazilian Partido Trabalhista leader Leonel Brizola, Curaçao and Aruba political activists, leaders of the Panamanian Social Democratic Party (PSDP), and the Paraguayan Febreristas. Representatives of different political parties from the Southern Cone, living in exile in Caracas, created a coordinating committee of the Democratic Forces, the Junta Coordinadora de las Fuerzas Democráticas del Cono Sur. Bringing together Aniceto Rodríguez of the Socialist Party of Chile, Adolfo Gass of the Radical Party in Argentina, Oscar Maggido of the Frente Amplio of Uruguay, Elpidio Yegros of the Febrerista Party of Paraguay, Erwin Moller of the PRIN of Bolivia, and Mario Astorga of the Radical Party of Chile, they vowed to coordinate their actions against the dictatorships in the home countries.[100] Venezuelan democracy developed in the late 1990s a situation of political polarization that prompted thousands to leave their home country for exile. Alongside Venezuelan citizens were some of the families of an estimated number of 30,000 Cubans who had relocated to the country after Castro's revolution and who now feared the repeat of Fidel Castro's policies by Chávez. Paradoxically, daughters and sons of former Cuban exiles in Venezuela have recently flocked to the Cuban consulates in Caracas and Valencia looking for ways to prove their Cuban origins in order to benefit from the Cuban Adjustment Act, a law that allows any person who can prove that s/he was born in Cuba or to Cuban parents to become a legal resident of the United States.[101]

Going into exile often implies being the victim of circumstances because of the need to relocate even in the absence of choice and a clear mindset of the range of alternatives. Typical is the case of the Brazilian exiles and expatriates who moved out of Brazil as their home country was taken by a military coup in 1964. Many of those who found shelter in Chile and participated in ideologically similar organizations and supported Allende's political project were forced to flee Chile with the onset of military rule in September 1973. They joined Chilean exiles, finding temporary refuge in Mexico. The Mexican authorities, however, clearly discriminated between Chilean and Brazilian exiles arriving in the aftermath of the Chilean coup. Whereas the Chileans were granted the benefits of political asylum, the Brazilians and other nationals coming from Chile were given some support but were not allowed to work or study. Because their situation was precarious in terms of residential status, these exiles looked for possibilities of asylum and relocation away from Mexico. "We tried all [the embassies] that could be imagined: Pakistan, India, Luxemburg, always receiving negative answers."[102] Some were granted tourist

[100] *Informe de la misión de la Internacional Socialista a América Latina*, 15–25 March 1978. Socialist International Archives (1951–1988) at the International Institute of Social History (IISG), Amsterdam, files 1125–1129.

[101] "Double Exile," *Miami Herald*, 28 October 2007, available at www.archives.econ.utah.edu/archives/cubanews, accessed 12 June 2008.

[102] Testimony of Marijane Lisboa, in Rollemberg, *Exílio*, p. 123.

visas for a year to Yugoslavia, and the Mexican authorities were prepared to cover the costs of the flight tickets. In their layover in Belgium, waiting for the next-day flight to Yugoslavia, many stayed. Again, in Belgium, the local authorities were helpful toward the Chilean exiles but declined to give such status to the Brazilians and other serial exiles. Accordingly, they tried to have their condition as refugees recognized by the local office of the UNHCR. Many remained there and in other European countries unregistered. Their main pre-occupation shifted from collective political action to personal survival. While in Chile, they kept alive their orginal revolutionary ideals because, owing to their serial relocation, they were forced to concentrate on finding menial work and making a bare living. The host countries did not contemplate the need of serial exiles to find political asylum. From a psychosocial and political perspective, the Chilean coup of 1973 was the *cause célèbre*, whereas the Brazilian military takeover of 1964 had been long forgotten. Chilean exiles were seen as 'legitimate' seekers of asylum, whereas the Brazilians were relegated to a gray area of undocumented migrants. Their only way out of this condition would be an international recognition of their status as refugees. This case helps explain why many refugees have wandered through several countries before reaching the receiving country, following troublesome trajectories seeking asylum and working opportunities.[103]

In many cases, exiles were forced to relocate from place to place because of pressures from the home rulers on the host country, met with the latters' lack of political will to create an imbalance of power with the country of origin. Well-known cases of pressures leading to relocation and serial exile are those of Raúl Haya de la Torre, Juan Domingo Perón, and Rómulo Betancourt.

Raúl Haya de la Torre was the founder of APRA. The pace of his displacement was rather hectic and was motivated and conditioned by the development of his continental, pan-Latin-American ideas. Because of his political activity, Haya de la Torre was banished from Peru and deported to Panama in 1919. In Panama, he developed his anti-imperialist and Bolivarian ideals and went to Cuba, where he took an active part in organizing the student union and spreading revolutionary ideas. He traveled through Mexico in the aftermath of the revolution, and, after founding APRA in 1924, he traveled to the United States and the USSR. Because of an illness, he moved to Switzerland, but was soon expelled from there. Following the intercession of the Peruvian government, the Swiss authorities considered him to be a danger to public order. In 1925, he visited Florence, London, and Paris. In the latter city, he was active in the community of Peruvian émigrés, intellectuals, workers, artists, and students and founded a chapter of APRA within the Asociación General de Estudiantes Latinoamericanos (AGELA, or General Association of Latin American Students). He then went back to Oxford, where he divided his time between political activism and anthropological studies. His continental views became further refined, and he elaborated his third position against both Western imperialism and Communism, a position that granted him the animosity of the

---

[103] Anne Marie Gaillard, *Exiles et retours: Itineraires chiliens*. Paris: CIEMI-L'Harmattan, 1997.

Latin American Communist Parties, among others. After completing his studies
in London, he returned to New York and from there went to Mexico, where he
was involved in some revolutionary activities. He then went to several Central
American countries, where he was jailed in Guatemala and El Salvador. After
international pressures, he was liberated and moved to Berlin, where he made
a living by writing for the international press. In 1930, there was a 'revolution'
in Arequipa against Augusto Leguía, and General Luis Miguel Sánchez Cerro
became president of Peru. Haya de la Torre wanted to go back but could not
obtain official approval, so he stayed in Europe, further developing the "Indian
doctrine" of his ideology. After two years in Berlin and after many years in
exile, he was finally able to return to Peru in 1931 as the candidate of APRA
for the presidency of Peru.[104]

In the case of Perón, he left Argentina in October 1955, after being forcefully
removed from power by the armed forces. He first arrived in Paraguay, invited
by President General Stroessner, and was welcomed warmly by the population
that recalled Perón's symbolic decision to hand back the trophies taken by
Argentina in the 1864–1870 War of the Triple Alliance. Following pressures
from the Argentinean government on Paraguay, Perón was asked to leave the
country. Invited by Anastasio Somoza to settle in Nicaragua, he was flown in
Stroessner's personal plane but decided to reside in Panama for nine months.
He was under constant protection and surveillance, receiving threats from anti-
Peronist elements. He then traveled to Venezuela, where Marcos Pérez Jiménez
sheltered him from August 1956 until January 1958. The Argentine authorities put constant pressure on the Venezuelan administration to curtail Perón's
freedom. He himself refrained from open attacks on Argentine authorities in
order to respect the asylum regulations. Nonetheless, he was targeted in several attempts on his life, which failed. Following the fall of Pérez Jiménez's
government, Perón found asylum with Isabelita and six close associates in the
Embassy of the Dominican Republic. In late February 1958, he got a safe
conduct to leave Venezuela for the Dominican Republic, where he maintained
excellent relations with local ruler, Rafael Trujillo. He received a Spanish visa
and moved to Spain in January 1960, settling there for close to 13 years. In
Spain too, despite his very positive image and good connections with General Franco since 1946, when Perón had provided free agricultural produce
to famished Spain, he had to be very careful not to exceed the terms of asylum and was forced to refrain from openly targeting Argentinean rulers, which
could lead to strained relationships between the two countries. His residence
was nonetheless the center of political pilgrimage for Argentine union leaders,
politicians, and activists looking for his directives and advice. In December
1969, Perón had tried to secretly travel back to Argentina, in what has become
known as "Operation Return." This attempted return took place following
declarations by President Arturo Illia that there were no exiles from Argentina
but only expatriates unwilling to come back. Perón snuck out of Madrid. The

---

[104] F. Cossio del Pomar, *Haya de la Torre: El Indoamericano*. México: Editorial América, 1939.

plan was to fly to Montevideo and then move to Asunción, where the general would establish his headquarters until a popular uprising in Argentina would force his return. However, the Iberia flight was forced to land in Brazil. Franco was outraged and ordered the ousting from Spain of those asylees who had traveled with Perón, while Perón himself was put under greater surveillance and pressure to refrain from openly engaging in politics. Only in 1972, following political developments in Argentina, was the aging leader able to visit Argentina and then to permanently return in 1973, elected to run his home country as president until his death in July 1974.[105]

Rómulo Betancourt is perhaps the most exemplary case of a serial exile among 20th-century political leaders forced to flee their home countries for long periods. In 1928, Betancourt left Venezuela for the first time, for seven years, after being involved in a failed military–student insurrection against President Juan Vicente Gómez. Resembling Simón Bolívar, he first moved to Curaçao, where he was actively involved with the community of exiles and workers; then to the Dominican Republic, where he conceived a strategy of class alliance to fight against dictatorship; to Colombia, where he created a Revolutionary Alliance of Left Forces (Alianza Revolucionaria de Izquierda, or ARDI); and finally to Costa Rica, from where he was able to return only after Gómez died in December 1935. Having returned in late 1936, Betancourt soon found himself implicated in protests against a draconian Law of Public Order and was expelled for one year by the new Venezuelan administration of Eleazar López Contreras, together with 36 other political leaders and activists. Betancourt went underground to evade displacement, but in 1939, the police located him and he was forced to leave for Chile, where he was in contact with socialist activists, among them Salvador Allende. He returned in 1940 to Venezuela and became a key figure in the AD Party, reaching an understanding with Marcos Pérez Jiménez to launch a coup and becoming head of the Revolutionary Junta of Government in 1945. After the coup by Pérez Jiménez and other military officers against elected President Rómulo Gallegos of the AD, in November 1948, Betancourt was forced to seek asylum and leave Venezuela for a third exile.

Already a well-known political leader, Betancourt sought asylum in the Colombian Embassy and was allowed to leave for Cuba in 1949. In Havana, he was the victim of an attempt on his life, perhaps ordered by Pérez Jiménez or by Rafael Leónidas Trujillo, dictator of the Dominican Republic. He then moved to Costa Rica, where his presence was severely monitored because of pressures laid on by Venezuela and also by Nicaragua, where there had been a plot against the government. Betancourt was depicted as the mastermind behind the plot and, under Nicaraguan demands, he was ordered to leave Costa Rican territory in 1954, along with other exiles, foremost the Dominicans Bosch, Pompeyo Alfaro, and Sergio Pérez; the Honduran Marcial Aguiluz; and a long list of

---

[105] *Perón, el hombre del destino.* Buenos Aires: Abril Educativa y Cultural, 1975, vol. III: 107; Tomás Eloy Martínez, *Las memorias del general.* Buenos Aires: Planeta, 1996, pp. 116–126.

Nicaraguans. Betancourt had become anathema to all the Caribbean dictators. Venezuela, in particular, resented the asylum granted AD exiles in Costa Rica. The United States managed to dispel the crisis by arranging Betancourt's move to the United States and his settling in Puerto Rico. Here too, Venezuelan government representatives pressured U.S. Congressmen for his deportation. Only a year after the fall of Pérez Jiménez in 1958, he returned to Venezuela and was elected president for the period 1959–1964.[106]

At work here is the character of the political and institutional environment of host countries, which, while providing asylum in the spirit of Latin-American brotherhood, are willing or pressured to monitor the political activities of the exiles in their midst. Personal considerations may play a role in the mechanics of serial exile. Friendships or enmities with those in power; love affairs, marriages, and marriage disruptions; personal assets or lack of them; all those are extremely of weight in facilitating or discouraging the exile to seek accommodations in a certain host country. In general, the host countries are adamant about allowing exiles' interference in their internal politics, while sometimes tolerating their activities, as far as they are restricted against the governments of the home countries. This policy is enforced, unless coincidence of interests between the host country's and the home country's governments creates a context that forces a new displacement. In extreme cases, the haven may become a trap for the exiles, as the host government is unable or unwilling to guarantee their personal security.

Of similar effect is a radical political change in the host countries or the creation of governments that resemble repressive rule in the expelling home country. We have already referred to the case of the Brazilian expatriates who had moved out of Brazil in 1964. Let us focus on one paradigmatic case of serial exile, that of Mauricio Paiva.

Following the 1964 coup, Paiva found his first shelter in Argelia. He later moved to Cuba because many members of the political organization he was part of were there, and he felt close ideological ties to the Cuban Revolution. After becoming disappointed with the Cuban lifestyle, he moved to Chile during Allende's government. With Pinochet's coup, he moved to Buenos Aires under the sponsorship of the UNHCR. There, under increasing political polarization, the Federal Police pressured many asylum seekers to leave Argentina. By the end of April 1974, as the Portuguese authoritarian regime of Salazar-Caetano fell, Paiva arranged his documents to move to Portugal. To facilitate his entry, he got in touch with old friends of the Portuguese Socialist Party who had been exiled in Brazil and were already back in Lisbon. He thought that after entering Europe through Portugal, he could easily move to another European

---

[106] Robert Jackson Alexander, *Romulo Betancourt and the Transformation of Venezuela*. New Jersey: Transaction, 1982. After leaving the presidency, he traveled to the United States and Asia and settled in Europe, remaining an influential figure but refraining from direct involvement in his country's politics until his death in 1981.

country. In the end, he got a tourist visa for Norway that allowed him to stay there for a short period of time. Finally, he went to Portugal in mid-August. He traveled through the Pacific so as to avoid going through Brazil in case the plane would be forced to land there in case of an emergency. In spite of Portugal's coup at the end of 1975, Paiva stayed in that country until the end of September 1979, when he returned to Brazil. He is an exile who moved serially to countries with governments close to his ideological mindset and was forced to relocate because of military coups.[107]

This dynamic can be further illustrated in detail as one follows the case of João Goulart. Brazilian President João Goulart was deposed from power by a military coup in 1964 and had to leave his country. As with many others in his situation, his preferred locale of exile was then Uruguay because of its proximity to Brazil and an administration still democratic and sympathetic to the plight of the exiles.[108] The alternative choice of Bolivia was somehow downplayed at that time because of the problems that the government of Paz Estenssoro, fearing for its stability, posed for the Brazilian exiles whose moves were surveilled by the political police. For a few months, Bolivia hosted a small group of exiles such as José Serra, president of the national student forum; Colonel Emanuel Nicols; journalist Carlos Olavo da Cunha Pereira; and former parliamentarian, Nieva Moreira. They even founded a newspaper that supported the progressive branch of the Bolivian MNRI. Shortly after the Bolivian coup of November 1964, some moved to Chile until 1974, when they were forced to move again, this time mainly to France.[109]

Goulart moved to Uruguay, where he lived for nearly a decade as an asylee. His presence in Uruguay, close to the Brazilian border, as well as that of other politicians such as Leonel Brizola, was a further focus of attraction for other escapees. In 1967, Goulart created, together with Carlos Lacerda, a former governor of Guanabara (and foe of both Vargas and Goulart), a bloc aimed at restoring free elections and democracy in Brazil. The movement was able to mobilize demonstrations supported by labor and political leaders but was soon banned in April 1968. During his stay in Uruguay, Goulart established a farm for rice production using artificial irrigation and contributing to making that industry the leading nontraditional export of the host country. His economic situation was better than that of many of the other exiles, whom he assisted financially as the main contributor to a collective fund of assistance and, politically, through his high-level contacts in the Uruguayan administration. Many union leaders and politicians stayed temporarily at his farm in Tacuarembó.[110]

[107] Mauricio Paiva, *O sonho exilado*. Rio de Janeiro: Achiamép, 1986.
[108] Cristina P. Machado, *Os exiliados*. Sao Paulo: Editora Alfa-Omega, 1979, pp. 29–31.
[109] Uchoa Cavalcanti, Pedro Celso, and Javelino Ramos, *Memórias do exílio*. Sao Paulo: Livraria Livramento, 1976, vol. 1, pp. 153–156.
[110] José de Hebert Souza, in *Memórias do exílio*, pp. 35–37.

However, especially after the shift to authoritarianism with Bordaberry's government in June 1973, his situation was far from secure. Once the Brazilian authorities did not renew his passport, both Stroessner and Perón offered him assistance. Eventually, he left Uruguay for democratic Argentina in 1974, settling in Buenos Aires. In December 1976, nine months after the military takeover in Argentina, Goulart was found dead in his apartment. Whereas the official version was that he died of a heart attack, the mysterious parallel deaths of oppositionary leaders such as Marcos Freire and Carlos Lacerda contributed to the credibility of conspirational theories.[111]

In addition to proximity, as was the case of Uruguay, the other major factor of attraction was the political setup of the host country. The case of Chile clearly reflects that trend for the Brazilian exiles. As previously analyzed, Brazilians and other foreigners were permitted to be active in Chilean politics and Chilean political parties. Internationalist winds were blowing strongly in the domestic political process. Many of the exiles, coming from armed resistance movements in their home country, aligned themselves with the most extreme parts of the Chilean Left. These exiles perceived themselves as a popular revolutionary avant-garde with political experience and freely expressed their views and extended their advice to their Chilean friends. They demanded wages from Allende's government that would allow them to continue their political work in Chile. There was even an attempt to take over the Brazilian Embassy in Santiago and establish a revolutionary government in exile, but this action was rapidly suppressed by the Chilean police and politically rejected by the Chilean government of Salvador Allende.

Once there was a radical break in the host political environment, as in Chile in 1973, exiles considered it wise to move again. There were also Brazilians who sought asylum at various embassies. Whereas Argentina, Peru, and Uruguay considered taking back their co-nationals, the Brazilian Embassy in Santiago refused to consider such a possibility.[112] Some of them moved to democratic Argentina, only to find themselves two-and-a-half years later in need of a new relocation as that country fell under military rule. There, they were joined by many Chileans who had taken shelter in Argentina after the military coup. The

---

[111] Jorge Otero, *João Goulart, lembranças do exilio*. Rio de Janeiro: Casa Jorge, 2001. Goulart was only one among many prominent Brazilian politicians and intellectuals forced into exile. Among those moving to Uruguay were Renato Acher, Amaury Silva, Ivo Magalhaes, Claudio Braga, Darcy Ribeiro, and Leonel Brizola. Brizola lived in Uruguay from 1964 until 1977, when he was deported for "violating the norms of political asylum." The increasingly authoritarian character of Uruguay forced exiles to relocate. While Goulart moved to Argentina, Brizola found refuge at the U.S. Embassy and moved to the United States and later Portugal, before returning to Brazil in 1979.

[112] The Brazilian ambassador to Chile, Antonio da Camara Canto, was awarded recognition by the Chilean government, whereas a Brazilian officer of the UN who managed to find diplomatic refuge for his co-nationals was detained once he returned to Brazil. Machado, *Os exiliados*, p. 110.

majority were successful in escaping thanks to international groups that organized outlets to Europe when Latin-American countries refused to accept them.
There were also Brazilians who asked for and obtained asylum at the Embassy
of Panama. The coup in Chile thus significantly altered the distribution of the
Brazilian diaspora by forcing exiles to relocate to more remote sites, in countries such as France, Sweden, Belgium, and West Germany because many of
the Latin-American countries did not accept them anymore. The UNHCR was
instrumental in obtaining refugee visas for some of them in Europe, Australia,
or other Latin-American countries. The number of persons relocated under
such conditions according to one estimate stands at 30,000.[113]

This situation was paradigmatic also of the paths taken by many Chileans.
A couple, Manuel and Ana María, sought refuge first in Argentina because
it was her country of birth and where relations enabled him to find a job
equivalent to the one he held back in Chile. But, Chileans arriving at that time
were considered communists *a priori*. After two years of residence and still
under a fragile civilian rule, the police issued an order of expulsion for Manuel
because he was considered to be a threat to national security. His wife, being
Argentine born, could not be legally expelled. Manuel had written to various
universities in France, Mexico, and the United States in search of a job, and once
a French university accepted his candidacy, the couple left, with a promise of
professional security, rather rare among exiles and refugees. In most cases, the
formal procedures of international transference of escaping individuals from
one country to another were complicated enough to deter those without good
reasons and a fierce will.[114]

Prompting relocation and serial exile has been also the fear by the host
government of the economic impact of exiles and refugees on the local society and economy. This case was especially true in the case of the Haitian
refugees in the Dominican Republic and the politically motivated dislocation
of populations and forced mass displacement of Central Americans during the
civil wars in Nicaragua, El Salvador, Guatemala, and Honduras. The exiles
and refugees were perceived as a heavy burden on the structures of already
pressured countries faced with the residence of these groups.[115] In most cases,
however, political factors have been central, with massive serial exile shaped
mainly by the changing political circumstances of a host country interplaying
with the persisting will of many of the displaced individuals to continue fighting
the governments that forced them into exile.

Massive exile heightened the likelihood that the diaspora of Latin Americans would include communities of co-nationals, in some of which the exiles

---

[113] Angell, "La cooperación internacional," pp. 215–245.
[114] Gaillard, *Exils et Retours*.
[115] Relief Web, "Central America: Main Refugee Flows during the 1980s," available at http://
www.reliefweb.int/rw/RW.NSF/db900SID, 8 July 2007; NCHR Refugee Program, "Beyond
the Bat Eyes," available at http://www.nchr.org/reports/bateyes.pdf, accessed 8 July 2007.

played a major role as proactive actors in the mobilization of other sojourn-ers, the activation of networks of transnational solidarity, and the contacts with national and international agencies with an increasing presence in the global arena. This transnational dimension, which transformed the structure of political exile, worked against the claimed monopoly of the nation-state over domestic public spheres and politics. It empowered exiles in terms of influence and resonance for their voice in the global arena, affecting the policies of the expelling countries and redefining the role and impact of communities of exiles.

6

Exile Communities, Activism, and Politics

In this chapter, we trace the strategies and dynamics of exile communities, analyzing the plurality of collective experiences by focusing on the most recent waves of exile. As thousands of individuals moved abroad to escape political persecution between the 1960s and the 1980s, communities of exiles developed throughout the Americas, Europe, and as far away as Australia, Asia, and Africa. Although in some places only minor concentrations found asylum, other locations attracted thousands of co-nationals, among them political exiles, turning from mere *lieux d'exil* into *milieux d'exil*, which in turn would attract new waves of politically persecuted individuals and groups.

Often, political exiles are but a minor part of the entire community of co-nationals in a certain host country and of diaspora politics. However, communities of Latin-American migrants, students, and sojourners were often politically activated and radicalized by incoming exiles. Under conditions of mobilization of the host country's public opinion and new connections with international organizations and transnational social–political spaces and networks of solidarity, the presence of exiles often constituted a catalyst for the formation of an *image* of an influential community of exiles.

Communities of Exiles

There is immense variance in this regard across communities of exiles, which can be analyzed through two key elements; namely, the degree of politicization and political activism of the exiles, and their capacity to become the core vectors of a community of translocated co-nationals through their ability to organize the newcomers and *represent them as exiles* vis-à-vis local, national, and international organizations and networks. We analyze this capacity in terms of the relative quietist or *proactive* engagement of various exiles.

Following this perspective, we have selected four South American cases that reflect the variable centrality of the 'political' in the constitution of the various communities. Analysis reveals that political manifestations of exile vary from the survival of political parties abroad to political participation among co-nationals abroad; from publicist and journalist activity to the creation of new political fronts against dictatorial rule in the home country; and from the myriad networks of solidarity established with parties, civil society groups, human-rights organizations, and individuals in the host countries, to activities vis-à-vis foreign governments and international forums and institutions. In the framework of such a gamut of activities, a central analytical question is the extent to which the political exiles become key vectors of collective mobilization in the various domains and spheres in which they are active and participate, working for political change and a full enforcement of human rights in the home countries.

The cases analyzed are those of, first, the Brazilian exiles who moved out of their country starting with the military coup of 1964. The length of the dictatorship – 21 years – and the subsequent onset of military rule in South American countries created a situation of serial exile. There were two waves of exile, which led to internal differentiation in the communities of exiles, according to ideological, generational, and class backgrounds. The continued recourse to exile as an institutionalized mechanism of exclusion by the military shaped clear stages, from an initial phase of confidence in their rapid return to later phases of reconsideration of such assumptions. Although in the first stage, Brazilian exiles managed to keep their political identity and projects – both reformist and revolutionary – alive, the subsequent relocation of exiles fragmented their identity as a community and prioritized their individual struggle for subsistence in the diaspora. Moreover, as they were torn by generational, class, and other distinctions, these divisions further impaired their mobilization capacity while abroad. In the long run, the exiles joined the Brazilian domestic mobilization in favor of political amnesty in 1979, which would open the gates for return even before the end of military rule. It is difficult to assess the impact of the Brazilian exiles on political opening and redemocratization, even if it is rather evident that they played a role secondary to that of the military and the political forces within the home country.

The second case is that of the Chilean exiles, in the Americas and especially in Europe, who managed to become early vectors of resistance to the Pinochet dictatorship and the core representatives of all Chileans in a diaspora fighting with a very effective political activism. Although military rule in Chile lasted for 16½ years, the political activism of the Chilean exiles and their organizational capacity managed to mobilize forces in many countries and the international public spheres both benefiting and projecting the case of Chile as the *cause célèbre* of the Left and the Social Democrats in the 1970s.

The third is the case of the Argentine exiles in Mexico and other countries, who were intensely involved in discussing reflexively their recent political defeat and their own existence as exiles. Torn between isolation and adaptation, they invested time and energies among their co-nationals and managed to become leading actors in the communities of co-nationals. In Mexico, they projected themselves as exiles in a country that prided itself on a long tradition of acceptance of persecuted individuals. There, as elsewhere, debates were nonetheless more endogenous than effective vis-à-vis the host country, and the international community, and even within the community of co-nationals abroad, it provoked divisions and a gradual decline in political activism.

Finally, we analyze the Uruguayan diaspora, created before the dictatorship with the dispersion of hundreds of thousands because of the socioeconomic and political crisis. Following the onset of the civil–military dictatorship in Uruguay in 1973, political exiles joined many of these migrants but failed to mobilize them massively into political action against the dictatorship. The inner composition of these groups precluded the projection of an image of Uruguayans being a massive community of political exiles.

Brazilian Exiles: Between Elite Exile and Revolutionary Activism

Following the 1964 *coup d'état* against the democratic government of President João Goulart, a military dictatorship of 21 years was established in Brazil. Military rule lasted far longer in Brazil than in the later dictatorships in Argentina, Uruguay, and even Pinochet's Chile. In the long period of military rule in Brazil, there were stages of deeper repression and stages of distension and relative opening. Nonetheless, the publication of Elio Gaspari's *A ditadura derrotada* revealed almost 30 years after the events that even General Ernesto Geisel, who was considered to be the moderate *de facto* ruler who initiated a period of distension, was – on the eve of assuming the presidency in 1974 – prone to support the extrajudicial killing of 'subversives,' much like the type of repression widely used in the other countries of the Southern Cone.[1] According to Gaspari's text, in the meeting with General Dale Coutinho inviting him to serve as minister of the army in his government, Geisel confided:

I am of the opinion that subversion did not end. That is a damned virus for which there is no antibiotics to liquidate it easily. It is abated. It is dissolved. [Yet] you can see from time to time its articulation, people die or people are imprisoned, it continues to mobilize.... Things have improved much. It improved, between us, when we started killing. We started killing, declared the future Prime Minister. The future President of the Republic added:... In ancient times one captured the individual and he went outside [was sent abroad, into exile].... Look Coutinho, this business of killing is a barbarity, but I find it necessary.[2]

It seems that like the military rulers who took power in the other Southern Cone countries in the 1970s, even the less extreme sectors of Brazil's military commands, were motivated by the same organicist ideas, which were expressed in the neighboring countries' doctrines of national security and the commitment to eradicate the "virus of Communism," safeguarding the social and political

---

[1] Luis Roniger and Mario Sznajder, *The Legacy of Human-Rights Violations in the Southern Cone*.

[2] Elio Gaspari, *A ditadura derrotada*. São Paulo: Companhia das Letras, 2003.

order, while defending military institutions and promising in March 1964 a prompt return to democracy.[3]

The military takeover did not provoke a significant immediate armed resistance, contrary to early expectations. Nonetheless, the military government took measures meant to proceed immediately toward its objectives, issuing the first "Institutional Decree" (AI-1) that, among other extraordinary prerogatives, legalized the power of the Brazilian executive to suppress the political rights of any citizen for 10 years.[4] While the military rulers maintained the parliamentary framework, by this first institutional decree, 41 politicians had their political rights suspended, among them three former presidents, João Goulart, Juscelino Kubitschek, and Jânio Quadros; the ministers, Almino Affonso, Paulo de Tarso Neto, and Darcy Ribeiro; the Communist leader, Luis Carlos Prestes; Leonel Brizola; Celso Furtado; the governor of Pernambuco, Miguel Arraes; and 29 labor leaders. More than 120 officers were expelled from the armed forces. More than 10,000 civil servants were expelled (i.e., became *exonerados*) because of their identification with the ousted administration. Opposition political parties were banned. Unions and student organizations were closed and strikes prohibited. Between 10,000 and 15,000 Brazilians took the road to exile.

Five days after the military coup of 1964, Goulart held a press conference in a Uruguayan resort near Montevideo. He explained the background that led him to leave Brazil:

JG: I would not have felt forced to leave the country if Congress would have behaved as it should, in a legal manner [according to the Constitution]. Congress deviated from the proper line of conduct and forfeited its authority. [Congress had declared the Presidency vacant and was willing to approve the nomination of the speaker of the Lower House to that position, despite the fact that Goulart was still in Brazil.]

–Why did you not resist?

JG: In Porto Alegre I felt cut off from the rest of the country and desolated as I contemplated the only perspective: a fratricidal war.[5]

As in other cases of expatriation going back to the founding of the Ibero-American Republics, Goulart opted for exile, seemingly to avoid civil war. He declared he was a nationalist patriot, alien to the specter of Communism he was accused of proselytizing to, and, paradoxically, resembling in his positions the same nationalist rhetoric of those who ousted him from power.

[3] Maria Celina D'Araujo, Gláucio Ary Dillon Soares, and Celso Castro, *Os anos de chumbo: A memória militar sobre a repressão*. Rio de Janeiro: Relume Dumará, 1994; Roniger and Sznajder, *The Legacy of Human-Rights Violations*, pp. 18–20, 60–61, and 122–123.

[4] Thomas E. Skidmore, *Five Centuries of Change*. New York: Oxford University Press, 1999, pp. 160–161. Until 1978, the number of *cassados* was 4,877, out of which 1,069 were politicians and political activists (Roberto Ribeiro Martins, *Liberdade para os Brasileiros: Anistia ontem e hoje*. Rio de Janeiro: Civilização Brasileira, 1978, 2nd ed., p. 147).

[5] Jorge Otero, *João Goulart: Lembranzas do exílio*. Rio de Janeiro: Casa Jorge, 2001, p. 173.

In Brazil, the military administration launched repressive operations, which included the persecution, imprisonment, torture, killing, or concealing of arrested subversives and censorship of the public media. The following step was the purge and arrest of thousands of leaders and members of the oppositional left-wing organizations, in an operative euphemistically called "Operação Limpeza" [Cleaning Operation]. Many of the detainees were tortured in special centers of torture located across the country, first mostly in the northeast and later also in Rio, São Paulo, and other Brazilian cities. Starting in 1969, the armed and security forces launched Operação Bandeirantes (OBAN) to coordinate repression within Brazil.

Since 1964, and starting with the community of Brazilians in Uruguay, exiles abroad were under the increasing surveillance of the local security services, who worked in coordination with their peers in Brazil, and the U.S. officers of the security services, who registered all visitors to the residences of Goulart and key Brazilian politicians in exile in Uruguay, posed as security personnel supplied by the local authorities, supposedly to protect the exiles. This mechanism – known as Operação Yakarta – was later reproduced in other sites of exile, leading also to the infiltration of groups of political activists working against dictatorial rule in the home countries. By the mid-1970s, the cooperation between the security services of the various countries was formalized in the framework of Operation Condor, aimed at coordinating repression against the opponents of the South American military governments on a continental basis. In the cases of prominent exiles, such as Bolivian General Juan José Torres and Chilean General Carlos Prats, both in Argentina, Bernardo Leighton in Italy, and Orlando Letelier in the United States, surveillance was only a first step, followed by attempts against the lives of the exiles and assassination.[6]

Normal political activities were banned as the military shut down the parliament by their fifth institutional decree (AI-5), and repression intensified along the lines of the Law of National Security, which punished those involved in revolutionary warfare with death or exile.[7] Armed struggle groups were active prior to the enactment of the preceding laws, carrying out bank assaults and arms expropriation. But, in 1969, their actions took center stage as the ALN (*Ação Libertadora Nacional*, or National Liberation Organization [Brazil]) and MR-8 (*Movimento Revolucionário 8 de Outubro*, or Revolutionary Movement 8th October) kidnapped U.S. Ambassador Charles Burke Elbrick in Rio de Janeiro, in September. This led to a harsh wave of repression, with armed guerrilla warfare continuing until 1974, when the defeat of the group of Araguaia signaled the end of the armed struggle. Many of the members of the guerrilla groups that emerged in this period and other militant opposition members were young people coming from the elite and middle sectors of Brazilian

---

[6] Jorge Otero, *João Goulart: Recuerdos de su exilio Uruguayo*. Montevideo: Tradinco, 2003, pp. 8–9; J. Patrice McSherry, "The Undead Ghost of Operation Condor." *Logos*, 4, 2 (2005), available at http://www.logosjournal.com/issue_4.2, accessed 11 May 2006.

[7] The AI-5 is of 13 December 1968 and the Law of National Security is of 18 September 1969.

society. Thus, in addition to low-class individuals and marginals at whom were directed the traditional forms of repression (involving arbitrary detentions, violence against detainees, and brutality within prisons), members of the higher-income sectors also became victims of severe human-rights violations. The repressive apparatus was directed against all enemies of the state, yet members of privileged sectors were arrested and with few exceptions (e.g., journalist Vladimir Herzog and politician Rubens Paiva) did not undergo torture, whereas lower-strata activists suffered it.[8] The systematic use of torture during the interrogations was directed toward everyone, irrespective of age, gender, physical, and psychological situation of the suspects, affecting even minors and pregnant women.[9] Still, within the framework of the Southern Cone, repression was comparatively more selective, partly because of the high levels of infiltration of the armed leftist groups by the security forces.[10]

Repression was thus concentrated in two phases: the first, between 1964 and 1966, during the presidency of Humberto Castelo Branco (in spite of its democratic discourse), and the second one during the mandate of Emílio Garrastazú Medici between the years 1969 and 1974, following the rise of contestation and violence in 1968 and the truncated attempt of liberalization by Costa e Silva.[11]

In these two periods, a total of 2,127 and 4,460 citizens were prosecuted, respectively.[12] According to official reports, 184 individuals were executed within Brazil in the 1964–1983 period, 8 died abroad, and there remains a residual category involving another 14 deaths. Another unsolved issue is that of the 'disappeared' people. According to the report *Brasil: Nunca Mais*, the number of disappeared in Brazil is estimated at 138, and another 13 Brazilians disappeared abroad, as part of Operation Condor.[13] Beyond these extreme cases of concealed murders and disappearances, the majority of the victims suffered imprisonment and torture. There are estimates that put the number of prisoners in the Tiradentes prison of São Paulo alone at 2,800 between 1968

---

[8] We are grateful to one of the anonymous readers for this hindsight. See also Archdiocese of São Paulo, *Brasil: Nunca Mais*. Petropolis: Vozes, 1990, 25th ed.; and Wolfgang S. Heinz and Hugo Frühling, *Determinants of Gross Human Rights Violations by State and State-Sponsored Actors in Brazil, Uruguay, Chile, and Argentina 1960–1990*. The Hague: Martinus Nijhoff, 1999, pp. 8–16.

[9] *Brasil: Nunca Mais*, pp. 43–48.

[10] This is assessed by the testimonies of former prisoners themselves. See Alipio Freire and Izaías Almada e J. A. de Granville Ponce, orgs., *Tiradentes, um presídio da ditadura*. São Paulo: Scipione, 1997; and Mari Cecilia Loschiavo, org., *Maria Antonia - Uma Rua na Contramao*. São Paulo: Studio Nobel, 1998.

[11] The detailed process is far more complex. See Ronaldo Costa Couto, *História indiscreta da ditadura e da abertura*. Rio de Janeiro: Record, 1999; and idem, *Memória viva do regime military, Brasil 1964–1985*. Rio: Record, 1999.

[12] Couto, *Memória viva*, p. 85. Another estimate places the number of prosecuted individuals between October 1965 and November 1977 at a total of 6,196, 32 percent of whom were convicted.

[13] J. Patrice McSherry, "Tracking the Origins of a State Terror Network: Operation Condor." *Latin American Perspectives*, 29, 1 (2002): 38–40. See also http://www.torturanuncamais-rj.org.br.

and 1973, the majority of whom underwent torture in the DOPS (Delegacia de Ordem Política e Social, or Department of Political and Social Order), where they were officially placed, and by the OBAN, the major clandestine center of torture in Sao Paulo.[14] The *Relatorio Azul*, a paper produced by the Commission of Human Rights and Civility of the Legislative Assembly of Rio Grande do Sul, described 283 different forms of torture used by the security forces during the years 1964–1979. The paper also indicated that 1,918 political prisoners testified about having been tortured during that period.[15] The categories of victims often overlap, as torturers sometimes evaded the tribunals by killing prisoners or making them disappear before any lawyer could confirm their place of detention.[16]

Denise Rollemberg, who studied Brazilian exile, identifies two waves of exile resulting from military rule, which developed in parallel to the stages in the policies of the military and that she defines as the "1964 generation" and the "1968 generation." The first wave included those identified with the reformist policies of Quadros and Goulart, basically members of parties such as the PTB (Partido Trabalhista Brasileiro, or Brazilian Workers' Party) or the Communist Party. Politically active in the ranks of the system, these individuals were already established in their careers and positions. Many went into exile in Uruguay, following Goulart and other political leaders, envisioning their sojourn abroad as a short interregnum on the way back to the homeland. Others went to Chile, Mexico, and Bolivia, and a small group relocated to Algiers and France. Most of them contemplated an imminent return to Brazil with the hoped-for fall of military rule.

Exile turned out to be a long sojourn, with the military holding power until 1985 and exiles precluded from returning at least until the amnesty of 1979. In 1968, the military entered a second phase in their 'revolution.' Following a series of kidnappings of diplomats in the late 1960s, the urban guerrillas managed to negotiate the banishment of 128 imprisoned political leaders and activists, who went into exile between September 1969 and January 1971. For instance, as part of a swap with the U.S. ambassador kidnapped in 1969, 15 leaders were released from prison and allowed to leave Brazil for Mexico. Among them were Gregório Bezerra, a veteran of the Brazilian Communist Party (PCB) who had been instrumental in the organization of rural workers; union leader, José Ibraim; guerrilla member, Onofre Pinto; and student leaders, Luis Travasso and Vladimir Palmeira. In addition and in reprisal, the military managed to kill Carlos Marighella, a radical revolutionary theoretician and leader of the guerrillas of the ALN.[17]

---

[14] Personal communication, Mauricio Frajman (frajman@amnet.co.cr), 3 December 2003.
[15] http://www.dhnet.org.br/inedex.htm.
[16] Thomas Skidmore, *The Politics of Military Rule in Brazil 1964–1985*. New York: Oxford University Press, 1988, pp. 132–133.
[17] Thomas Skidmore, *Brasil: De Castelo a Tancredo*. Rio de Janeiro: Paz e Terra, 1988, pp. 203–207.

Generalizing, this second wave of exiles consisted of activists who were more extremist in their political positions than those who had followed Goulart and who despised reformism and the compromising vision of the Communist Party. Whereas the goal of those in the first wave was to redress the end of democracy and defend reformism, for those in the '1968 wave,' the central goal was revolution. They felt contempt for most of the political elites exiled in 1964. In turn, those in the first wave regarded the latecomers as leading to a dead end. Many of these exiles had been active in the student movement and endorsed revolutionary ideas and armed struggle. When they went into exile – primarily to Chile and France – most were just beginning their professional lives, and the years of exile were those in which they developed individually and professionally, and, with the forced prolongation of exile, many ultimately changed their initial political visions.

The estimates of the number of Brazilian exiles vary greatly. In February 1978, the Commission of Peace and Justice of the Archbishopric of São Paulo estimated that the number of exiles who left in these waves had reached 10,000. The Brazilian government contested the Church's statement, claiming that these were not exiles but rather mere expatriates, moving abroad 'for convenience.' The UNHCR put the number at 5,000, of whom 1,800 had received diplomatic asylum in various countries signatory of the Convention.[18] Even though these numbers are rather reduced in comparison with the number of inhabitants of Brazil at that time (more than 90 million),[19] the exiles' backgrounds as members of the political, intellectual, academic, and professional elites give special weight to the vacuum that was created by their move abroad and underline the future institutional impact of their return.

According to Denise Rollemberg, the two waves of exiles were parallel lines that did not meet, with just a few – like Arraes, Apolonio de Carvalho, and Rolando Frati – crossing the lines from the first 'generation' to the other. However, Brizola, who was a prominent member of the first wave, acted as a political bridge to the second wave. Teotonio dos Santos, Rui Mauro Marini, and hundreds of other exiles of the later wave participated in the rebuilding of the PTB in Lisbon, led by Brizola. Beyond this, it should be stressed that the inner variability of exiles was enormous, cutting across the preceding distinctions:

There were those affected by banishment. There were those who decided to leave, sometimes with legal documentation as they rejected the political climate in the country. There were those who, without being targeted by the political police, went into exile accompanying their spouse or parents. There were others persecuted by being involved in confrontation with the military regime. There were those who went to live abroad for non-political reasons, but [once there] through contacts with exiles, were integrated in the campaigns of denunciation of dictatorship and thus could not return easily to the country.... In this universe, there were all exiles. We could fall into a senseless abyss

---

[18] Martins, *Liberdade para os Brasileiros*. There is no agreed-on figure about the number of Brazilian exiles; some estimates place the number at 30,000.

[19] In 1970, Brazil had 93,139,037 inhabitants (http://countrystudies.us/brazil/26.htm).

by pretending to establish who was or who was not an exile in the strict sense of the word.[20]

This inner variability was reinforced by tensions generated as the newcomers arrived and had to combine their political activities with the need to adjust to living in exile. A source of tension and inner animosity was created by the unequal commitment of the exiles to continued political activism against the dictatorship. Whereas some insisted on the short demise of the military government prompted by the revolutionary impetus of the Brazilian people, and thus they prepared themselves to lead an armed struggle – even traveling to Cuba and Algiers to take guerrilla training[21] – many others considered the days of the revolution to be over and they were identified as deserters of the cause, being ostracized accordingly. The latter were seen with disdain and arrogance by the former, augmenting tensions and disarticulating rather than projecting the presence of the exile community as a whole.

Another major source of divisiveness was social class. Theoretically, exile involved a loss of social status and economic solvency, harder to bear for those individuals used to the amenities of the higher classes. Whereas individuals of the lower classes could feel integrated whenever their status and economic situation improved, exiles of higher class could find it difficult to live in exile. At the same time, however, the majority of people of higher status arrived – for instance, in Chile – with greater social capital, higher education, language skills, and networks, which created better chances for accommodation in the host country.

In March 1964, shortly before the military coup, Fernando Henrique Cardoso was accused of subversive activities. As an order of preventive arrest was issued, Cardoso flew to exile in Chile. With a background in social sciences, he was hired by the ILPES (Instituto Latinoamericano de Planificación Económica y Social, or Latin American Institute of Social and Economic Planning), the research center set up by the UN in Santiago, and enjoyed the preferential employment benefits of UN employees at that time in Chile. Cardoso himself referred to this period in his life as a Golden Exile, to be projected into France, where he moved for a short sojourn in 1967.[22] As in many previous experiences, such as those of Argentinean Domingo Faustino Sarmiento and Cuban José Martí, the forced relocation provided professional and public opportunities for personal growth and political positioning. In the case of Cardoso, this experience broadened his professional horizons and international contacts:

Exile allowed Fernando Henrique Cardoso to focus on his research work, extend his field of knowledge to all of Latin America, and be invited to visit institutions of international prestige, such as the Institute of Advanced Studies at Princeton or the College de

[20] Denise Rollemberg, *Exilio*, pp. 49–52. Quotation from p. 52.
[21] José Dirceu and Vladimir Palmeira, *Abaixo a ditadura. O movimento de 68 contado por seus lideres.* Rio de Janeiro: Garamont, 1998.
[22] Interview of the authors with President Cardoso in the Palacio da Alvorada, Brasilia, 24 September 2000.

France. Even before arriving in Chile, he received an invitation from Spanish sociologist José Medina Echavarría, a director of ILPES . . . to hold the chair of Developmental Sociology. Exile led him to take a direct part in debates on the transformations in the field of power in Latin America and on their economic and social effects. The dependency theory that provided him with international renown was developed during this period, in collaboration with Chilean sociologist Enzo Faletto. . . . Exile in Chile, in addition to allowing him to become acquainted with Latin American elite – Isabel Allende worked under his guidance – made it possible for him to return to Paris as visiting professor at the University of Nanterre, thanks, once again, to Alain Touraine's intervention. He took advantage of this time to draft his analysis of the research he had carried out at ILPES and to prepare the thesis that was part of the selection process for the Chair of Political Science at USP, which would cut short his exile.[23]

Class distinctions weighed heavily in some communities, where they created tensions. It is interesting to see how this tension was perceived by the exiles, many of whom belonged to the higher social classes, denoting the elitist character of Brazilian politics. Whereas exile leaders proclaimed solidarity among the people, exiles of a lower social class felt the rejection of the exile 'establishment.' This contradiction manifested itself particularly in the Brazilian community in Chile. In Chile, the exiles arrived in several distinct waves, all of them with clear internal socioeconomic differences. In 1969, when the second wave of exiles arrived, the majority were upper-class and middle-class students, uncertain about their job prospects and with no experience, only more extreme in their political ideas than the first wave.[24] The first wave created a collective fund to provide newcomers with their immediate basic needs as well as university scholarships. However, the majority of the exiles did not take advantage of this fund because their families in Brazil sent them small allowances in U.S. dollars that, because of a very favorable rate of exchange in the local foreign currency black market, allowed them to live comfortably before and during Allende's period.[25] Contrastingly, the exiles of lesser means did not adapt in Chile. Not only did they face greater economic hardship, but they also were the target of prejudice: "There was open discrimination against those who worked. Working in Chile was ugly. It meant to be poor; to be ignorant; to lack political capacity."[26] The majority of the Brazilian colony studied and did not work because of their bourgeois background. Instead, they received money from their families and could live in upper-class neighborhoods. Some testimonies are highly critical of the lack of solidarity among the Brazilians.[27]

---

[23] Afrânio Garcia Jr., "A Dependence on Politics: Fernando Henrique Cardoso and Sociology in Brazil," in *Tempo sociológico*. São Paulo, 2005, 1: 8, available at ⟨http://socialsciences.scielo.org/pdf/s_ts/v1nse/scs_a01.pdf ⟩, accessed 23 April 2006.

[24] Cristina P. Machado, *Os exiliados*. São Paulo: Editora Alfa-Omeg, , 1979, p. 53.

[25] Machado, *Os exiliados*, p. 99.

[26] Albertina De Oliveira Costa, Maria Teresa Porciuncula Moraes, Norma Marzola, and Valentina Da Rocha Lima, *Memorias das mulheres do exilio*. Rio de Janeiro: Paz e Terra, 1980, vol. 2, p. 179.

[27] De Oliveira Costa et al. *Memorias das mulheres*.

This contrasts with the trends among Brazilian exiles in Uruguay, who mainly arrived in the first wave. Yolanda Avena Pires, Waldir Pires' wife and member of the Brazilian political elite in Uruguayan exile, reconstructs communal life of Brazilians differently. The exiles, she recalls, were always aware of the new displaced individuals arriving in Montevideo, and had organized a financial aid cooperative effort to which each one contributed according to his or her capacity. The main contributor was former President João Goulart.[28]

Demography and the socioeconomic background can become clear differentiating factors within a community of exiles. These differences are especially important for understanding the internal dynamic of the exile communities. The Brazilian exile reproduced the character and class and ethnic distinctions of the home society. When social differences are large and class concepts figure prominently, as was the case of the Brazilians abroad, the amalgamation of the exiles into a community with clear-cut political strategies is more difficult.

Another variable is the ethnocultural affiliation of the exiles. This aspect was very important not only in the adaptation of the exiles to the receiving society but also in the selection of the host country, as exemplified by the exiles in Sweden, where many felt secluded because of cultural differences despite the warm welcome and facilities provided to the newcomers.[29] The latter explains the pull of Sweden, whereas the former prompted their move to other *lieux d'exil*. At first, Sweden had the second biggest colony of Brazilians living in Europe, consisting of around 200 people.[30] After a few years, however, many of them left, mostly because of the difficulties they recognized in the host environment. The lack of similarities in the professional field, the culture, and language led many professionals such as lawyers, journalists, and teachers to work as blue-collar employees. In social terms, domiciliary segregation was the norm, with most exiles living in ghettos of Latin Americans and other émigrés. With the passing of time, many Brazilians – like other Latin Americans as well – opted to leave the social democratic receptiveness of Sweden, choosing to join the Brazilian diasporas elsewhere (e.g., in Portugal or France). The exiles also mentioned climate as a factor in their decision to move southward in Europe.[31]

Other Latin Americans shared this experience with the Brazilians. In a testimony, Argentine historian Elda González spoke of her exile experience in Sweden, emphasizing the cultural difficulties that exiles had integrating into that country:

I believe we are different. The cultural differences weigh heavily. Even if one is provided all the economic and material support, one feels the pressure of the system.... When

---

[28] Machado, *Os exiliados*, p. 34. .
[29] De Oliveira Costa et al. *Memorias das mulheres*, p. 63.
[30] Machado, *Os exiliados*, p. 126. The Brazilian community grew with the years, especially through migration, to reach a total of 2,162 inividuals in 1990. See Daniel Moore, "Latinoamericanos en Suecia," in Weine Karlsson, Ake Magnusson, and Carlos Vidales, Eds., *Suecia-Latinoamerica: Relaciones y cooperación*. Stockholm: LAIS, 1993, p. 166.
[31] Machado, *Os exiliados*, p. 129.

I mention cultural differences I mean the way people behave. Not only the language, which one can master eventually. But rather the way people act and react. I always remember seating for the first time at the University and watching the tempos of speaking and questioning, so slow. We are different.[32]

Many Brazilians in Europe would go during their holidays to Portugal, not only because it was an affordable choice but also because they would have the sensation of visiting their grandparents' home. In addition to the nostalgic feeling, they had the comfort of speaking the same language and having the same culture. These similarities led many exiles to stay in Portugal despite the economic problems they met there.[33]

France was the country that absorbed the largest number of individuals and had the largest community of Brazilians living abroad, which reflected the historical links between both countries and the image of cultural Mecca that Paris projected. In the 1960s, of the 6,000 exiles in France, several hundred were from Brazil. In particular, Brazilian exiles arrived from Greece, followed by a large number of co-nationals from Portugal and Latin America.[34] Because France traditionally welcomed exiles, it offered the UN the biggest quota to receive exiles from Chile following Pinochet's takeover. The timing of the arrival of the Brazilians was fundamental to their integration in Europe. The exiles who arrived prior to 1968 settled better than those who arrived during the 1970s. According to Professor Luiz Hildebrando, before 1970,

there were few people that found themselves in Europe with some cultural and financial support and in a period of expansion of universities and research institutes, thus facilitating their professional insertion. Even the few students who arrived could expect to get a scholarship, due to the reduced number of exiles. Starting in 1970 the situation changed. The various hundreds of Brazilians in search of asylum were now part of a wave of thousands of Chileans, Uruguayans and Argentineans, competing in the labor market. Europe was no longer in a period of prosperity. In France as in the other countries, the rate of unemployment was on the rise constantly. For the Brazilians [coming from Chile] there was the additional problem of the lack of documentation. The Chilean military government, even if employing violence as it reached power, provided passports for their exiles [but not for us].[35]

While in Chile, Brazilian exiles – members of a Committee of Indictment of Repression in Brazil – had met Italian socialist Senator Lelio Basso in October 1971, while he participated in a seminar on the Transition to Socialism. This encounter led to the idea of launching a Russell Tribunal II, modeled on the one on American war crimes of Vietnam, to be focused on the Brazilian situation,

[32] Interview with Elda González, Madrid, 26 June 1998.
[33] Mauricio Paiva, *O sonho exiliado*, Rio de Janeiro: Achiamép, 1986, p. 175.
[34] Machado, *Os exiliados*, p. 124.
[35] Luis Maira, "Claroscuros de un exilio privilegiado," in Pablo Yankelevich, Ed., *En México, entre exilios: Una experiencia de sudamericanos*. Mexico: SRE, ITAM, Plaza y Valdés, 1998, pp. 127–128.

later to be expanded to cover repression in Chile and other South American countries.[36] Basso had taken part as rapporteur in the Vietnam Russell Tribunal, and he embraced the idea enthusiastically. Basso served as president, with leading figures of the intellectual and political world as part of the 25-member jury, among them Yugoslav historian, Vladimir Dedijer; Colombian writer, Gabriel García Márquez; Belgian professor of International Law, François Rigaud; French Sorbonne Professor, Albert Soboul; former Dominican Republic President, Juan Bosch; Argentinean writer, Julio Cortázar; French Nobel Prize Winner of Physics, Alfred Kastler; and Greek PASOK Secretary-General, Andreas Papandreu. In April 1974, the Russell II Tribunal issued a verdict, after meeting on March 30–April 5, to evaluate the extent of repression and human-rights violations in Brazil, Chile, Uruguay, and Bolivia. In its verdict, it declared "the authorities that exercise power in Brazil, Chile, Uruguay and Bolivia to be guilty of serious, repeated and systematic violations of human rights" and that "these constitute a crime against humanity." The Tribunal called all democratic forces in the world to publicize the extent of repression in Latin America, to raise funds, to ask governments to stop all economic and military assistance to the condemned countries, to launch a massive campaign for the liberation of political prisoners there, and to exercise pressure on the Chilean junta so that it provides safe conducts to political activists who found asylum in embassies, and finally to conduct a boycott on sales of arms to the repressive governments. The Russell II Tribunal decided to transmit its hearings and conclusions to a wide array of international organizations and individuals: the Secretary General of the United Nations, the UN Educational, Scientific and Cultural Organization (UNESCO), the UN International Labor Organization (ILO), WHO, OAS, the Non-Aligned States, the Justice and Peace Commission, the World Council of Churches, the International Red Cross, leagues of Defense of Human Rights, all governments, and members of the U.S. Congress. Exiles, particularly in Chile, managed in this way to rekindle their cause in the transnational arena, from where it will reverberate back into their home country.[37]

In 1974, the military decided to adopt an initiative for a change. General Geisel assumed the presidency and, together with his political advisor, General Golbery Couto e Silva, started negotiations concerning the fate of the missing Brazilians with the Catholic Church, the most important and strongest opponent at that time, along with other opposition leaders, and made some approaches to union leaders in São Paulo. This political maneuvering,

---

36 The Bertrand Russell Tribunal on Repression in Brazil was renamed the Bertrand Russell Tribunal on Repression in Brazil, Chile, and Latin America after the 1973 coup in Chile.

37 The Verdict of the Second Russell Tribunal on Latin America, Tribunale Russell II per la repressione in Brasile, Cile e America Latina. Rome, accompanied by a letter of Lelio Basso, 22 April 1974, and Russell Tribunal Brazil, no. 1 (February 1973). Archives of the International Institute for Social History (IISG), Amsterdam. Earlier campaigns against torture in Brazil started in 1970 and reached a peak in 1971 and 1972.

accompanied with an easing of censorship and police surveillance in 1974–1975, increased confidence among opposition groups. Nonetheless, assassinations continued unabated and even crescendoed in 1974, as compared with 1964–1970. Human-rights associations demanded guarantees for the physical integrity of detained individuals, the recognition of habeas corpus, and a general amnesty for political prisoners. Campaigns against torture in Brazil took place in the early 1970s, reaching a peak in 1972–1973. The *Movimento Feminino pela Anistia* led by Teresinha Zerbini and Helena Grecco was founded in 1975 to work in favor of prisoners and exiles and was supported by prisoners and ex-prisoners who were members of the revolutionary movements and their families. Exiled Brazilians, too, supported this call for amnesty, portraying the rebels as the defenders of democracy.[38]

Adopting a 'legalist' line of action and heading toward democracy, Golbery had to restrict the use of torture or any other illicit activity, even if these could not be completely curtailed. And yet, the rulers had to secure that no punishment would be inflicted on those who served in the security forces. Nonetheless, in contrast with the situation in the other countries under military government, the main civilian political institutions in Brazil had not been entirely repressed, a fact that contributed to the process of redemocratization. Another important influence stimulating the process was the international criticism coming from North American and Western European churches, politicians, and intellectuals concerning the use of torture and the abuse of human rights. Following Geisel's retirement in 1979, João Baptista Figueiredo continued the process of relaxing authoritarian rule by keeping the hard-liners at bay while mediating between them and the moderate sector of the military forces.[39] The problems faced by Figueiredo's government in the economy and with the workers' strikes in 1979 were also accompanied by the incapacity of the military hard-liners to discredit the social movement calling for amnesty. The call for a "wide, general and unrestricted amnesty" [*anistia ampla, geral e irrestrita*] became more and more persistent. The movement gathered public presence and momentum through massive demonstrations in all major cities, which contributed, in turn, to regaining the right of free speech. Consequently, the government was forced to shift its initial offer of a limited amnesty and broaden its scope. In August 1979, the Congress approved Justice Minister Petronio Portella's amnesty bill, which covered all those imprisoned or exiled for political crimes since September 1961, excluding those guilty of "acts of terrorism" and of armed resistance.

This amnesty enabled both the effective liberation of political prisoners and the return of exiled politicians and activists. On the return of many of the exiled activists and leaders, the Brazilian political system increasingly assumed a more open character. The amnesty movement was not content with the legislation because it did not include any accounting for the 197 to 240 Brazilians

---

[38] http://www.dhnet.org.br/denunciar/tortura/ textos/aarao.htm; personal communication, Mauricio Frajman, 3 December 2003.
[39] Skidmore, *The Politics*, p. 210; *Five Centuries*, p. 186.

believed to have died at the hands of the security forces. The reason for this handling of the subject was the fear of the military that a judicial inquiry might someday lead to an attempt to attribute responsibility for the torture and murder of prisoners. Another reason for the discontent was the fact that the amnesty also included the military agents involved in the perpetration of crimes against humanity. Actually, this was a kind of feasible trade-off with which the opposition cooperated, hoping that someday the subject might be reopened and investigated. But even to a greater extent than the other countries with similar constellations of forces, in Brazil there was a wide consensus on upholding the amnesty, despite the fact that it did not address the issue of the responsibility of those who had been involved in human-rights violations.

The conditions of transfer of power from military to civilian rule downgraded the military's apprehensions concerning their future. The elections of 1985, held under the Electoral College system, elected Tancredo Neves from the Brazilian Democratic Movement Party (Partido Movimento Democrático Brasileiro, or PMDB) as incumbent to the presidency. Neves was known for his honesty and good judgment and was acceptable to the military. Secret talks were conducted, involving the elected President Neves, ex-President Geisel, and then-President Figueiredo. The three reached a series of understandings, which were not an official pact but gave Neves the needed leverage for entering the final stages of transition. Because of its secretive nature, and much like the Uruguayan case, the agreement lacked an institutional foundation and apparently was never displayed in writing. Yet, its terms can be discerned clearly: Civilians committed themselves to upholding the 1979 amnesty protecting the military against prosecution and to respect the high degree of autonomy and functions of the military in various realms, such as internal security and the development of military technology.[40] Securing the amnesty law was crucial for shielding the military from prosecution for most of the human-rights violations committed during their rule. Especially after the initiation of trials against the military commands in Argentina, the unwritten pact alleviated Brazilian military anxieties about relinquishing power. When José Sarney assumed the presidency following Neves's death in March 1985, the military felt confident that the new civilian president would respect the agreement and safeguard the core interests of the armed forces.

The Argentine Diaspora: Debating Political Strategies and Struggle

Between 1955 and 1973, the Argentinean political system existed under the shadow of the ban imposed by the military on the major political force, Peronism. The key political figure of Argentina, General Juan Domingo Perón, was in exile, forcefully precluded – as was his movement – from participating

---

[40] Wendy Hunter, *Eroding Military Influence in Brazil*. Chapel Hill: University of North Carolina Press, 1997, pp. 38–39.

208

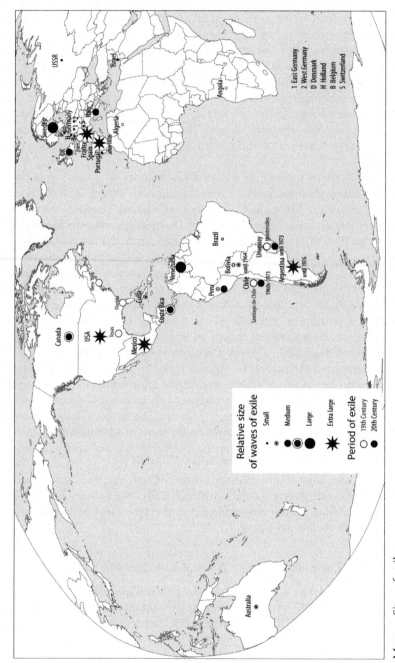

MAP 5. Sites of exile.

openly in politics but still remaining the most influential actor in the Argentine public arena.

Argentina lived through a period of political instability and intermittent military uprising and interventions. By the end of the 1960s, under military rule, the country entered a spiral of popular mobilization and increasing unrest, which culminated in the *Cordobazo* in May 1969, an uprising of industrial workers and students that was harshly repressed by the police and the armed forces. In parallel, guerrilla activities of the Trotskyist and later Guevarist ERP (Ejército Revolucionario del Pueblo, or People's Revolutionary Army) and the left-wing Peronists, known as the Montoneros, increased. By the early 1970s, the *de facto* ruler, General Alejandro Agustín Lanusse, recognized the lack of feasibility relative to precluding Peronism from participating in politics and called for elections in March 1973. Peronism won and elected President Héctor Cámpora, paving the way for a new election and Perón's return from exile. In September 1973, the ticket of Juan D. Perón and María Estela ("Isabelita") Martínez de Perón won the election with an absolute majority. Perón's return raised expectations in all quarters, yet social tension and unrest increased as well as guerrilla activities and repressive violence by anti-Leftist paramilitary groups, primarily the so-called Triple A (Anti-Communist Argentine Alliance). Left-wing and right-wing Peronists resorted to open violence against each other.

The death of Perón in July 1974 only added to the institutional decay of Argentine democracy, with the military being granted emergency powers already in 1975 to fight the urban and rural guerrillas. Repression had an enormous spillover onto society in general, leading to escape and exile. When the military took power in March 1976 and began the so-called National Reorganization Process (PRN) based on forced political demobilization, enforced consensus, and systematic persecution of opposition forces and intellectuals, the number of those who went into exile increased notoriously, greatly adding to the Argentinean diaspora both in Latin America and on other continents, particularly in Europe.[41] Equally, if not more, vulnerable was the situation of Latin-American refugees who had settled in Argentina and were left without legal protection and could fall prey to repression. According to one estimate, there were around 100,000 Latin Americans living in Argentina in 1976, out of which about 300 had been granted formal refugee asylum and another 1,100 were accepted as *de facto* refugees by the UNHCR. Following the coup, the UNHCR moved 5,500 such refugees out of Argentina.[42]

There are studies on the waves of Argentinean exiles settling abroad, some of them ground-opening in terms of specific communities.[43] Similarly, in recent

---

[41] Noé Jitrik, *Las armas y las razones. Ensayos sobre el peronismo, el exilio y la literatura*. Buenos Aires: Sudamericana, 1984.

[42] Ian Guest, *Behind the Disappearances*, Philadelphia: University of Pennsylvania Press, 1990, pp. 63–64, and p. 464, note 1.

[43] See for instance Pablo Yankelevich and Silvina Jensen, Eds., *Exilios. Destinos y experiencias bajo la dictadura militar*. Buenos Aires: Ediciones del Zorzal, 2007, and Yankelevich's edited book *México, país refugio*. Mexico: Plaza y Valdés, 2002.

years, fascinating books of testimonies have been published.[44] Finally, Ian Guest's *Behind the Disappearances* provides very useful information on the tug-of-war between the exiles and human-rights activists, on the one hand, and the junta diplomatic representatives, on the other, over the formation of international public opinion and the adoption or rejection of initiatives against the repressive policies of those in power in Argentina.[45] Still, information on some communities and other aspects of exile is partial, and a systematic study on the entire diaspora is still to be conducted. The analysis that follows is only a first step in that direction.

Thousands of individuals left Argentina, a few thousand to other Latin-American countries, primarily Mexico and Venezuela, and many others to host countries in Europe, especially Italy, Spain, France, and Sweden; to North America; and even to less common sites of asylum such as Australia and Israel. For most of them – contrasting with the early case of the Brazilians or the latter case of the Chileans displaced by the onset of Pinochet's rule – it would become more difficult to project the plight of the Argentinean people in terms easy to comprehend in the sites of exile. Argentina had been bleeding for years because of inner dissent and spiraling violence. Institutional decay and state violence had preceded the breakdown of democracy. It was harder to convey what Peronism was or was not, when even Peronists fought one another in terms of left and right and when the history of that country had been a continuous succession of military and civilian rule since the 1930s. Moreover, the fact that the right wing of Peronism led by López Rega was supportive of repression whereas the other extreme – Montoneros – was at the core of insurgency, but both referred to the same leader and symbols, added ambiguity:

The problem of Argentinean political exile was that there was no parallel to the Peronist guerrilla [Montoneros], in Spain. Peronism was perceived in Spain as a semi-Marxist movement.... This was different than for instance the Chilean [wave of] exile in which Socialists met Socialists, Communists met Communists. From a political point of view, Argentina was an extremely confusing country, since instead of political parties there were political movements... and within them, a mixture of Left and Right, of secular and clerical activists. To convey what Peronism signified was extremely difficult. Moreover, the Peronists could not agree about the "nature" of Peronism... and those who killed the guerrillas were also Peronists.[46]

Exiles from Chile and Uruguay, coming from countries with well-established party systems, could almost automatically establish links with the sister parties in Europe. These political parties could easily relate to the drama in the country of origin of the newcomers, reading the distant events in the same keys of interpretation they applied to their home polities. In the case of Argentina, the

[44] Jorge Luis Bernetti and Mempo Giardinelli, *México, el exilio que hemos vivido.*
[45] Ian Guest, *Behind the Diasppearances.*
[46] Interview with Blas Matamoro, Madrid, 28 June 1998.

dominance of Peronism as a Populist political movement with no comparable equivalent in Europe in the 1970s, together with the relative weakness of the traditional Communist and Socialist Parties, made it difficult in Europe to find parallels and energize solidarity in the mainstream political parties.

The beginning of massive Argentine exile in the 1970s coincided with the oil crisis that affected some countries and an oil bonanza that benefited others. As oil-exporting countries, Mexico and Venezuela enjoyed a wave of prosperity as the oil prices rose. Argentine professionals, academics, and intellectuals arriving there would find occupational insertion easier than those who, for different reasons, sought asylum in host countries affected by the oil crisis. Moreover, in the case of Mexico, the PRI (Partido Revolucionario Institucional, or Revolutionary Institutional Party) regime supported a vision of providing a shelter for those suffering political persecution. Starting in October 1974, a number of prominent Argentine expatriates – which included professionals and intellectuals – began arriving in Mexico, driven out of the homeland by threats to their lives initiated by the Triple A. It should be stressed that the exiles moved from a society governed by a formally democratic rule to another country where the limits of formal democracy were narrower. Many of the prospective exiles were vocal intellectual figures related to radical organizations in the country of origin, where a spiral of violence threatened their lives and freedom of speech and action, whose move abroad was made possible by the supportive strategy of welcoming them in the host country. The three-tiered structure operated here by providing an ideal site of exile for highly visible intellectual and political individuals, prone to becoming victims of repressive violence, who opted to escape from Argentina to Mexico, despite the more authoritarian character of the host society and politics at that time.

The flow of exiles from Argentina increased in 1975, with that country still under democratic rule. Following the military coup of March 1976, a group of between 5,500 and 8,400 individuals arrived in Mexico, the majority settling in the Federal District and its metropolitan area.[47] Of those who went into exile, only a small minority was granted diplomatic asylum in Buenos Aires. The majority reached Mexico by their own means, as tourists, and once there, they tried to legalize their status as exiles and refugees, receiving formal asylum. The exiles from Argentina were treated in a completely different way from that of the mass of hundreds of thousands of refugees arriving later on from Guatemala and El Salvador in Mexico as a result of civil war in Central America. The Argentinean exiles received preferential treatment because of a combination of factors: their socioeconomic profiles, the intellectual capital they brought with them, their clear status as political activists, and the favorable economic circumstances of their early arrival in Mexico.

Among those arriving in Mexico were a large number of highly qualified professionals, including academics and intellectuals, whose escape was linked

---

[47] According to the 1980 census, 82.1 percent of the Argentinean population of Mexico lived in Mexico City and its metropolitan area.

to the expulsion of faculty members from the University of Buenos Aires in late 1974, soon to be followed by persecution and attacks on those dismissed.[48] Among them were intellectuals and activists such as Rodolfo and Adriana Puiggrós, Ricardo Obregón Cano, Esteban Righi, and Ana Lía Payró, who arrived in the first wave of newcomers. The educational and professional level of the exiles – in a country in which close to 30 percent were virtually illiterate – and the economic expansion greatly facilitated their integration into the Mexican labor market.[49] In the mid-1970s, Mexico enjoyed an economic bonanza related to sharp increases in oil prices, resulting from the 1973 Israeli–Arab war. Market expansion and fiscal surplus allowed the Mexican government and economy to generate new employment openings. At the same time, this growth enabled the host society to benefit from the integration of highly qualified professionals. In this case, economic circumstances combined with Mexican political tradition and self-images to provide structural slots in which the newcomers did not pose an open threat in employment terms. However, with the exception of psychologists and psychoanalysts who were given great latitude, the labor insertion of many liberal professionals was difficult. Precluded from exercising their professions independently, they had to enter into association with Mexican professionals and work under their guise and patronage or become employed by the government.

Overall, many of the Argentinean professionals and experts in the humanities reached important positions in universities and scientific institutions, as well as in journalism, public administration, and the liberal professions. Interesting is the case of the CIDE (*Centro de Investigación y Docencia Económica*, or Center of Economic Research and Teaching), opened by the Mexican administration in order, among other reasons, to incorporate professional newcomers, experts in economics and the social sciences, while creating a high education pole for capacitating local elites and forming skilled individuals for the public administration and the private sector.[50] Thus, many Argentinean exiles became upwardly mobile, acquiring a higher professional and economic status in Mexico than had been the case in their home country. The traditional association of exiles with loss of social status was actually reversed in this case.

For those moving to Spain, it was relatively easy to enter the country, when possessing travel documents:

In that period [1976] anybody born in Latin America could enter into Spain and could attain citizen status after two years.[51]

[48] Mario Margulis, "Argentines in Mexico," in Alfredo E. Lattes and Enrique Oteiza, Eds., *The Dynamics of Argentine Migration (1955–1984): Democracy and the Return of Expatriates*. Geneva: UNRISD, 1987, p. 85.

[49] Lucia Sala, "Los frutos de una experiencia vivencial," in Pablo Yankelevich, Ed., *México*, p. 81.

[50] http://www.cide.edu.

[51] Interview with Arnoldo Liberman, Madrid, 28 June 1998.

I would not say that the reception before the Law of Foreigners [*Ley de Extranjerı* was automatic, but it was almost automatic. Once you arrived, you could ask for a permit of residence, you did not need a labor permit. Then, with the permit of residence, you could stay for two years, opting afterwards for the Spanish nationality.... I think that in the case of Spain, if one had [some initial] documentation, it was possible to move through the [bureaucratic] loopholes that the permit of residence allowed.[52]

Estimations on the numbers of Argentineans who entered Spain, settling mainly in Madrid and Barcelona, vary greatly. This range is probably due to the disparity between the number of legal residents and the overall number of exiles and sojourners, as well as the different agencies reporting them (e.g., the General Directorate of Police or the INE [Instituto Nacional de Estadística, or National Institute of Statistics]). The range is enormous, from[53] 8,506 (1980) to[54] 15,000 (1982) to[55] 42,000 (1984). One source[56] mentions 37,799 Latin Americans in Spain in 1975 and 36,244 in 1980, whereas others indicate[57] 43,392 Latin Americans for 1980 or put that number at[58] 75,000 for 1985.

Once in Spain, exiles had to face the problems of occupational insertion into the domestic labor markets. By 1976, Spain – together with most Western European countries – was only starting to recover from the oil crisis. In Spain, the economic situation was also accompanied by the start of a process of uncertain democratization and rapprochement into Europe after the death of Franco. Many exiles testify that their reception was therefore problematic:

The economic problem, lack of political definition, the terrorism Spain already had, the rejection by Europe (there was the problem of the French veto on Spain's entry to the European Community) – all these made Spaniards adopt a very defensive position towards the *sudacas* [a pejorative term defining the newcomers from the Southern Cone] with their problems and this added further complications. There were some rather aggressive reactions against South American emigration. They published terrible notes in the press, although there were also some in favor. It was another problem added to the many issues that Spain already was facing. I recall people saying:... they are bringing migrants?! People that need work when we have unemployment, that wish to share when we don't have what to distribute. It was not a good timing to come to Spain.[59]

---

[52] Interview with Elda González, Madrid, 26 June 1998.
[53] Antonio Izquierdo Escribano, *La inmigración en España 1980–1990*. Madrid: Ministerio de Trabajo y Seguridad Social, 1992, p. 36.
[54] CISPLA, "Latinoamericanos refugiados políticos en España." Valencia: CISPLA, 1982, pp. 9–24.
[55] IOE, "Los inmigrantes en España." *Revista de Estudios Sociales y Sociología*, 66 (1985): 138.
[56] Yolanda Herranz Gómez, *Formas de incorporación laboral de la inmigración Latinoamericana en Madrid*. Ph.D. thesis, Universidad Autónoma de Madrid, 1996, p. 84.
[57] Izquierdo Escribano, *La inmigración en España 1980–1990*, p. 36.
[58] Olga Lutz and Pilar Walker, "Los exiliados latinoamericanos en España." *Estudios del CESERAD* (Madrid), 3 (1985): 22.
[59] Interview with Blas Matamoro, Madrid, 28 June 1998.

In the framework of a restricted labor market, political exiles had difficulties finding work and suffered from downward mobility. Many were employed in menial jobs as peddlers, repairmen, underpaid translators, salespersons, and in the underpaid black job market. For instance, renowned writer Clara Obligado mentions the hardship of her first years in Spain:

Here I worked, cleaned, did all sorts of menial jobs. At the beginning more, as I was not myself.... The three first years were awful, crazy. I believe I was then mentally deranged, defenseless.... Only after three years I got a replacement job at a Ministry....[60]

To begin with, union leaders and workers were not proportionally represented among exiles in Spain, even though they constituted a third of the victims of repression, primarily of the 'disappeared.' Silvina Jensen claims that exile in Catalonia and perhaps in Spain in general was not an option for the working and lower classes:

Differing from the Chilean exile, the proportion of union leaders and workers was low. There was first a screening posed by the possibility to pay for the trip or get family support or having personal, political or professional contacts in order to prepare the escape. It is not that in order to leave the country you have to be part of the cattle-raising oligarchy. But yet the option [of leaving] was available mostly to wide sectors of the middle classes.[61]

Moreover, there was a vicious circle between the loss of status of many new-comers and their recourse to semilegal, and even illegal, means of survival on the part of some, which were magnified and projected as the basis of prejudice and stigma. It reached the point in which signs indicated that Argentineans should abstain from trying to rent a house, or the derogative '*sudaca*' or the pejorative '*latinoché*' coined to stereotype the group.[62]

In certain occupational niches, however, Argentine exiles filled voids that the domestic working force could not supply. This was especially true for dentists (a profession that was not taught as separate from medicine in Spain, whereas Argentinean universities offered dentistry at the highest professional level), psychologists and psychoanalysts, and to some extent even journalists, who seem to have integrated relatively well:

There are personalities that have reached very high: Enrique García-Lupo, an Argentinean attorney specialized in penal law, has become a judge of the Supreme Court of Spain.... This is also the case of the psychoanalysts, who arrived in flocks and stayed, creating the discipline. More than anything, they introduced the school of Lacan.... Also, journalism.... One of the most salient professionals in this country

---

[60] Interview with Clara Obligado, Madrid, 26 June 1998. There are testimonies that speak even of living on the verge of hunger.

[61] Silvina Jensen, "Política y cultura del exilio argentino en Cataluña," in Pablo Yankelevich, Ed., *Represión y destierro*. La Plata: Editorial Al Margen, 2004, p. 123; *Comisión Argentina de Derechos Humanos (CADHU)*, "Argentina: Proceso al genocidio." Madrid: Elías Querejeta, 1977, p. 147.

[62] Horacio Salas, "Duro oficio el exilio." *Cuadernos hispanoamericanos*, 517–519 (1993): 558.

[Spain] is an Argentinean: Ernesto Ekaizer, a colleague of mine in [the newspaper] La Opinión, who left Argentina after receiving threats. He has become one of the directors of "El País", the most influential daily in Spanish.[63]

Also, political factors played a crucial role in the way Argentinean exiles were received, as shown in the case of Italy. Many of those Argentine exiles who moved to Italy were of Italian descent and managed to escape thanks to the work of Italian consul Enrico Calamai.[64] However, the Italian government was reluctant to receive these exiles. The previous experience of the flood of asylum seekers in the embassy in Santiago de Chile in 1973 had produced diplomatic problems. Moreover, the Christian Democracy (Democracia Cristiana, or DC) – which historically had been the stronghold of anti-Communism – was facing a very complex political situation. The Italian PC was reaching an electoral zenith and, at the same time, had launched the idea of a 'historical compromise' by which they renounced class war, revolutionary violence, and their previous commitment to abolish private property. Having learned the lesson of Chile's defeat, the communists were contemplating becoming a legitimate and central partner of government, perhaps allied with the left-wings of the ruling Christian Democrats. The right-wings of the DC, seemingly penetrated by the notorious anti-Communist Masonic lodge P2 (Propaganda Due), were against receiving leftists from Latin America. The domestic urban guerrilla of the *Brigate Rosse* [Red Brigades] and other groups had a strong and menacing presence between 1968 and the early 1980s, and the arrival of Latin-American revolutionaries was suspected as potentially reinforcing political violence. The P2 was highly influential in Italian politics because it had members in the magistracy, the Parliament, the army, and the press. It also had Latin American members, particularly in Argentina, but also in Brazil and Uruguay. Among them were extreme right-wing figures in Argentina such as José López Rega, founder of the Argentine Anticommunist Alliance, and Emilio Massera and Carlos Suárez Mason, who became key figures in the repressive military administration. Unsurprisingly, the P2 was against granting asylum to leftist exiles escaping the assassination campaign of the anti-Communist A and later military repression in Argentina. They were not able to preclude completely the arrival of escapees, but they certainly narrowed their flow.

Once in Italy, Italian society and especially the Italian Left were welcoming to exiles. In the context of Italian administrative 'openness,' the exiles were not persecuted or expelled. Among the exiles were leading figures such as Oscar Bidegain, former governor of the province of Buenos Aires, and respected writer and poet, Juan Gelman, both friends of Italian socialist Senator Lelio Basso (of the Partito Socialista Italiano di Unità Proletaria [PSIUP], or the Italian Socialist Party of Proletarian Unity), who was instrumental in supporting the newcomers and promoted the establishment of the Russell Tribunal II. Armed

[63] Interview with Blas Matamoro, Madrid, 28 June 1998.
[64] See Chapter 5.

organizations like the Montoneros and the ERP chose Italy as one of their centers of influence, with core figures such as Fernando Vaca Narvaja and Mario Eduardo Firmenich of Montoneros and PRT (Partido Revolucionario de los Trabajadores, or Workers' Revolutionary Party); activists Fernando Chávez, Ana María Guevara (the sister of Che Guevara) Luis Mattini, Enrique Gorriarán Merlo, and Julio Santucho, brother of the late leader of the organization, Mario Roberto Santucho. Between 1974 and 1983, the exiles established the CAFRA (Comité Anti-Fascista contra la Represión en Argentina, or Anti-Fascist Committee against Repression in Argentina), whose name was explicitly tailored to awaken strong historical connotations and attain the solidarity of the Left and the trade unions with the plight of the exiles. Its initial reduced impact in intellectual circles was bolstered by the arrival of thousands of exiles. Trade unions and the Communist Party were especially supportive of their activities.

There was another aspect in moving from Argentina to Europe, particularly to Spain or Italy, as opposed to moving within Latin America, to a country such as Mexico. This dimension was especially at work for the descendants of immigrants who crossed the Atlantic Ocean westward in the late 19th and early 20th centuries, in search of freedom and a land of opportunities in Argentina:

Many of us were grandchildren of European immigrants and many times we had sung their deeds as a story of heroism. By dictate of history, we their grandchildren had to take the road of return. Then to be an Argentinean in Europe implied to have taken a return ticket. Spaniards and Italians, Arabs and Jews had thought of Argentina as the "promised land" or had escaped a hostile European setting. We were going back to Europe to continue loving freedom and life.... Spain began to be the body we needed to drown our strangeness and the fears we carry with us. The sense of lacking a shelter was played through a series of shared themes: the brothers and sisters who disappeared, the old nostalgia of our grandfathers, the daily pauses where fear habits, the streets of sadness of a sun abandoned in Europe and met again through our eyes. Such confusion, such sense of strangeness, such disorientation – all had at the same time the non-repairable sweetness of being alive.[65]

In Mexico, the occupational and professional success of the exiles strengthened the will to integrate into Mexican society and fostered feelings of gratitude and identification with the host country. In the testimonies subsequently quoted, a political scientist and a journalist relate how their professional success influenced their experience in Mexico:

To teach, to write, start research. All this enabled my identification with Mexico [*armarme identidariamente en Mexico*]. This is what Mexico represented to me. I spent eighteen years here. My work is to me a very strong framework of reference. I write here, I think here.... I must confess that I like my work. I have an enormous freedom and great support. I like what I do. I like the country.

[A]gainst all odds I survived, mostly due to the reservoir of energy that was available there... in that remarkable [work] place that pulls me up, as I had all the occupational conditions to function in an excellent way. It has been the best work I had in my

---

[65] Arnoldo Liberman, "Rememoración del exilio," p. 547.

entire life. I never had such margins of maneuver, of freedom and pleasure as I enjoyed working in that journal [*Uno más uno*] between 1977 and 1982.[66]

Professional success was only one of the factors that contributed to the incorporation of the Argentinean exiles in Mexico. The relative measure of cultural compatibility was another. Doubtless, the fact that the exiles spoke the language of their hosts was of critical importance in the process of their integration. In a linguistically foreign environment, most exiles experienced a stronger sense of isolation, which in turn could lead to deep feelings of alienation from the host society. In Mexico, the common Spanish heritage, as well as the insertion in the environments of the Mexican middle class – as evidenced in their sending the children to private progressive schools at the primary and secondary levels and to the public universities – played a significant role in reducing feelings of alienation. In the words of Néstor García Canclini,

The common language and traditions we shared helped us to integrate into Mexico more than to Europe or the USA. They also created a sense of solidarity among Mexicans for the political causes that brought us to come. It also was of great help to share the same cultural characteristics with other Latin Americans that were there in exile.[67]

The importance of similar cultural surroundings should not be overestimated. This affinity does not ensure automatic integration when resettling. It does mean that those settling in a country that culturally resembled their own will be spared the traumatic experience of finding themselves unable to comprehend their surroundings. In fact, many newcomers felt cultural and psychological resistance, which hampered a full adaptation. Exile unavoidably generates a deep psychological strain, in which – beyond differences of personality, gender, and age – the preservation of known points of reference such as language, values, traditions, religion, and interpersonal relations is of major significance.

Thus, even though the Argentineans and the Mexicans spoke the same language, their Spanish was imbued with different inflexion and tonality, different expressions and connotations:

To speak means an intertwined approximation and a definite distance. Our pronunciation is embedded in language. And at the same time conveys what we tried to conceal, our strangeness.[68]

Broad cultural similarities aside, Mexicans and Argentineans differed in many other crucial aspects, which demanded from the exiles a shift in mindset and social codes.[69] Indeed, Argentina had developed with its back to the indigenous elements in its society and culture, as a society praising its European orientation and its immigrant character. Contrastingly, living in Mexico, one could not but

---

[66] In Pablo Yankelevich, *México, país refugio*, pp. 246–247.
[67] Néstor García Canclini, "Argentinos en México: una visión antropológica," in Pablo Yankelevich, Ed., *En México, entre exilios*, p. 63.
[68] In Jorge Boccanera, *Escritores Argentinos en el exilio*. Buenos Aires: Ameghino, 1999, p. 100.
[69] Cavalvanti, in Pablo Yankelevich, Ed., *En México, entre exilios*, pp. 40–43.

confront almost daily the social, cultural, and political significance of the ever-present indigenous components of the hybrid and *mestitzo* cultural identity the country professed to endorse.

There were mutual prejudices between Argentineans and Mexicans. Argentineans claimed that Mexicans did not accept them, and Mexicans claimed that Argentineans lived in ghettos. Argentineans were perceived as arrogant, with a direct approach that made them aggressive in Mexican eyes. Argentineans saw Mexicans as submissive, slow, unpunctual, and irresponsible. By professional training, many sought and found employment within universities and academic centers. Phrases like "this faculty is infested with Argentineans" could be heard, although by legal standards only a maximum of 10 percent of foreigners were allowed in any working place. Letters were sent to newspapers, denouncing the usurping presence of Argentineans at the expense of national Mexicans.

The differences between the culture of the home country and that of the host country demanded a shift in cultural codes and patterns of interaction and interpretation on the part of exiles, partly leaving behind traces of chauvinism, local patriotism, and near-racist prejudice and disdain for the Indo-American population of Mexico.[70]

These ambiguities and tensions were also replicated and magnified in the case of the community of Argentine co-nationals in Spain. For them, arriving in a country where Spanish was spoken was attractive. Even after exiles had been accepted and settled in Sweden, receiving all the benefits provided by that Nordic welfare state, still many of them decided to move to Spain, as they envisioned greater cultural and social compatibility in the latter country:

I believe that the Spanish cultural presence was pervasive, whether you were of Spanish descent or not. Spanish culture influenced all dimensions of life, to the extent that Spain turned a natural destiny for anybody [among us, exiles], even for those who had moved to another country, as was the case of Sweden. To seek asylum in Spain was a little bit of a need, the need not to feel a stranger [while abroad].[71]

Language and culture were key factors in diminishing the sense of alienation that many exiles felt abroad. Blas Matamoro insisted that language "makes things easier, if one arrives to a country and does not need to learn but certain nuances of a language. That is the case particularly if you make a living from writing or speaking. Then, this [language proficiency] facilitates life."[72]

And still, once again in Spain, a country that shared its home language officially, there were vocabulary and accent differences that marked the difference between the locals and the newcomers. The former made a point of stressing them and the latter felt them as well, in their case, as both markers of identity and vectors of exclusion, a tension evident in the following testimonies:

---

[70] In Boccanera, *Escritores Argentinos*, p. 110.
[71] Interview with Elda González, 26 June 1998.
[72] Interview with Blas Matamoro, 28 June 1998.

This is a living metaphor of our experience in Spain: the use of *ustedes* in the second person plural. There is no disguise as feeble as language. *Ustedes* is for us – metaphorically and in reality – what the unattainable *vosotros* and at the same time a verdict on the eternal distance [that separates us]. By the second connotation we erase months of effort [to integrate].... [After years in Madrid] my language is a *made in exilio* mixture of Spanish and Argentinean. Only the *ustedes* cannot be bribed, it is like the signs of smallpox that have left forever their mark of past existence [on our skin].... We have crossed many frontiers save for one: the inner one.[73]

Even if the exile managed to master the local dialect and sometimes lost his or her original accent, there remained a sense of loss, of having lost with it part of his or her identity. This, again, seems especially crucial in the case of writers and intellectuals, whose creativity is predicated on the maintenance of intimate ties with the homeland:

I cannot write in Argentina even one line, since I already lack that sort of malleable Spanish of the porteño [resident of Buenos Aires]. I have a very basic Argentinean. Then, the collision is constant. I write in peninsular Spanish, in the Castilian of Spain. So they tell me: you are a *gallega* [literally, born in Galicia; by implication, any Spaniard]. I am not. But they insist. So, whenever I teach and conduct seminars on writing in Argentina, I have to change the inner chip and speak the Spanish as spoken there.[74]

In Mexico, in tandem with the solidarity expressed toward the plight of the exiles by the authorities and powerful circles, major sectors of Mexican society exhibited distrust and xenophobic attitudes toward the newcomers and their self-professed complacency and self-complacent wit, a reaction that surprised many and in some cases led to anger and personal depression among the newcomers.[75]

Part of the mutual reticence and social distrust was due to an absence of shared cultural codes and a lack of shared understanding of what things stand for, which are particular to every society: "In Mexico one cannot intuitively guess the fourth reply as we pose the first question. We ignore the biographical foundations of the things."[76] Nicolás Casullo concurs: "Mexico is like Latin America, many different things. Yet one does not live from regional abstractions but from the rhythms of one word, from the meanings of one phrase, from the names of foods and the smell of the neighborhoods."[77]

For most Argentineans, this awareness of difference sharpened the feeling of being a foreigner. It is the absence of what is one's own and its replacement with

---

73 Arnoldo Liberman, "Rememoración del exilio," p. 550. The Uruguayan writer Cristina Peri Rossi similarly speaks of the humiliation of a writer facing Spaniards correcting with authority and arrogance apparent linguistic errors, while in fact the speaker was using expressions rooted in her home society instead of the parallel terms adopted in Spain; cited in Claude Cymerman, "La literatura hispanoamericana y el exilio," *Revista Iberoamericana*, 46, 164–165 (1993): 523–550.
74 Interview with Clara Obligado, 26 June 1998.
75 Jorge Luis Bernetti and Mempo Giardinelli, *México: El exilio que hemos vivido.*, pp. 37–40.
76 Bernetti and Giardinelli, *México*, p. 109.
77 Bernetti and Giardinelli, *México*, pp. 100–101.

something foreign. Pedro Orgambide, a novelist who spent time in Mexico, stated:

> Being a stranger [*la extranjería*] . . . there was no single day in which I could fail to think about it. In spite of the solidarity of many Mexican friends to whom I will forever be grateful, being a stranger was an irreversible condition and conviction [*una condena*].[78]

Thus, unlike in the professional sphere, the social integration of the Argentinean exiles – even when successful – retained a halo of transience. With few exceptions, the exiles entered the road of accommodation over assimilation – that is, to become integrated while retaining their distinctive lifestyles and identities.

A crucial line of inner differentiation in the communities of exiles and migrants from Argentina was determined by the background of the relocating exiles, which affected the composition of the community of co-nationals and its internal dynamics and political impact. In general, one could identify exile communities reflecting the various waves of repression, with the first arrivals starting with the deepening of political violence in 1974, when the Triple A targeted many political, intellectual, and professional figures, and spreading later to the armed organizations and to relatives of the victims of repression. For instance, beyond a somehow constant annual flow of between 2,000 and 3,000 Argentineans who relocated to Italy in the 1970s, according to the annual publications of the Istituto Nazionale di Statistiche, research has identified several distinct waves:

> The first [was the exile] of intellectuals, politicians, lawyers, journalists, university teachers, union leaders, the categories targeted by repression decluched by the Triple-A following Peron's death. They settled in the big cities and founded CAFRA, launching a campaign of solidarity and denouncing repression that will concentrate their efforts in the following years. The second wave, from the end of 1976 to the end of 1978, is characterized by the exile of leaders and activists of the armed organizations. In most cases, it is an organized exile: Montonero leaders and middle cadres and activists of the Montoneros and of the PRT arrive in Italy. Leaders and cadres built in Italy the bases for political action designed to renew [armed] struggle in Argentina. The PRT established schools [of cadre formation] in Northern Italy. The Movimiento Peronista Montonero was launched as an international organization in Rome, which approved a plan of counteroffensive [in Argentina]. . . . Activists of these organizations became members of CAFRA, revealing the capacity of overcoming the initial shock and moving into solidarity work above internal divisions. The last wave is that of the exile of family members of the disappeared, who moved from late 1978 to the end of dictatorship. These exiles will enjoy CAFRA's support for initiatives led by the Mothers, Grandmothers and family members of the prisoners and the disappeared.[79]

---

[78] Bernetti and Giardinelli, *México*, p. 153.

[79] Maria Adriana Bernardotti and Barbara Bongiovanni, "Aproximaciones al estudio del exilio Argentino en Italia," in Pablo Yankelevich, Ed., *Represión y destierro*, pp. 50–51.

The harshening of repression in Argentina forced debate on the ways of confronting the events back home. Exiles were divided. The key issue was whether to continue armed struggle expecting to generate popular uprising and bring down the military, or to act in political ways, putting aside armed resistance that was portrayed by its critics as an immolation of idealistic youth by those directing them to follow the counteroffensive war against the military in power.

Jorge Masetti, another militant of the PRT-ERP has written a book of memoirs in which he evokes his Italian exile between 1977 and 1978. Beyond underlining Italian solidarity, especially at the popular level and in the trade unions, Masetti recalls that those months devoted to study, thought, and discussion produced political divisions, especially on the feasibility and wisdom of continuing armed struggle. General Secretary Luis Mattini was in favor of abandoning it, whereas Enrique Gorriarán Merlo led the militarist position, proposing to return immediately to Argentina to continue fighting.[80]

Toward 1979 the division was complete, with many ERP and Montonero activists leaving the armed struggle and joining other avenues of political activity in the framework of CAFRA. In the case of the ERP, the remaining leadership advised militants in 1980 to move to Mexico in order to arrange an organized return to Argentina. In Italy, the impact of the exiles was moderate. While they sensitized Italian public opinion to the issue of repression in Argentina and hosted for short periods the leading figures of the armed guerrillas of the home country, the Italian context exerted a strong influence on the exiles, while they were unable to establish more than a marginal presence. The radical leaders left, whereas those acting in the framework of CAFRA adapted to the rhetoric and transformative principles of the evolving Italian democracy.

A somehow similar dynamic of internal differentiation developed in France and other locations. Between 1973 and 1983, at least 1,600 Argentineans arrived in France as legal newcomers, out of which 921 were recognized as political refugees. Probably the number of political migrants was larger, because many arrived with a European passport or as illegal residents, unaccounted for the statistics of the Institut national de la statistique et des études économiques, or National Institute for Statistics and Economics (INSEE) and the Ministry of Interior Affairs.[81] The exiles activated in a large number of organizations, within which they projected their various political commitments and tried to reflect the political problematique of Argentina, fighting the repressive regime in the home country. While in Argentina they engaged in political and violent revolutionary activism, in France – and in other sites of exile – action

---

[80] Bernardotti and Bongiovanni, "Aproximaciones al estudio del exilio Argentino en Italia," p. 67. Years later Masetti fled to Cuba and later fled Cuba. While he professed to be a revolutionary, he was accused in the 2000s of being a CIA agent committed to spreading disinformation against revolutionary movements in Latin America. Masetti's book is called *El furor y el delirio*. Barcelona: Tusquets, 1999.

[81] Marina Franco and Pilar González Bernaldo, "Cuando el sujeto deviene objeto: La construcción del exilio Argentino en Francia," in Pablo Yankelevich, *Represión y destierro*, pp. 17–47, especially p. 22.

turned increasingly to nonviolent discursive, public, and networking activities, even if some circles retained the revolutionary rhetoric. Exiles established and joined organizations driven by universal ideas such as the defense of human rights and persecuted persons, promoted by CADHU[82] (Centro de Abogados por los Derechos Humanos, or Lawyer's Center for Human Rights) and COSOFAM (Commission de solidarité des parents des prisonniers, disparus et tues en Argentine). Others were of a domestic projection, such as the CAIS (Centre Argentine d'Information et Solidarité, or Argentinean Center Information and Solidarity), the largest organization of Argentine exiles in France. Finally there were others of more corporate character, like union and professional organizations: TYSAE (Travailleurs et syndicalistes argentines en exil, or Argentinean Workers and Syndicalists in Exile) GAAEF (Groupe d'avocats argentines exilés en France, or Group of Argentinean Lawyers Exiled in France) and UPARF (Unión de Periodistas Argentinos Residentes en Francia, or Association of Argentinean Journalists Living in France).

These organizations were instrumental in promoting the banner of human rights, discrediting the propaganda of the junta, and in launching campaigns of solidarity with the victims of institutionalized repression:

[R]egular demonstrations denouncing [repression took place] in front of the Argentine Embassy in Paris every Thursday at noon, symbolically walking at the same time as the Mothers of Plaza de Mayo in Argentina and with the participation of a large number of French human rights organizations and prominent public figures in the arts, the intellectual milieu and particularly the French Socialist party, the Socialist League for Human Rights, the Christian Association for the Abolition of Torture and figures such as François Mitterand, Yves Montand, Simone Signoret, and others.[83]

The most politicized activists were seen with reticence by many who participated in the public acts of protest but declined to adhere to the discrete political organizations, which they considered part of an 'Argentine ghetto.'[84]

Still, the impact of these organizations was aimed at affecting public opinion in France. Particularly active in CADHU was Argentinean lawyer Rodolfo Matarollo, who had defended political prisoners and had been a leading member of the ERP political wing in Argentina.[85] Matarollo and his colleagues were effective in their denunciations of gross human rights violations committed by the Argentinean armed forces and in their political attacks against military rule. CADHU scored a major success, when two of its leading members, Gustavo

---

[82] The CADHU was formed in Argentina in 1975 by members of a revolutionary group, joined later by individuals related to Mothers of Plaza de Mayo and the Centro de Estudios Legales y Sociales (CELS). CADHU moved abroad in 1976, after two of its founding members disappeared. Soon the organization became a most vocal critic of the junta from its center in Paris and other branches in Mexico, Rome, Madrid, and Geneva and also the one that functioned in Washington, D.C., between 1976 and October 1978.

[83] Marina Franco and Pilar González Bernaldo, "Cuando el sujeto deviene objeto," p. 31.

[84] Marina Franco, *El exilio argentino en Francia*. Buenos Aires: Siglo XXI.

[85] Ian Guest, *Behind the Disappearances*. 90, pp. 66–69.

Roca and Lucio Garzón Maceda, were invited to the U.S. House Subcommittee on Human Rights to give testimony. This provided an opportunity to establish a CADHU branch in Washington, D.C., in December 1976, coinciding with the election of Jimmy Carter to the presidency and imminent changes in U.S. policy toward Latin America.

In Buenos Aires, the junta understood the potential danger of exiles abroad, who could mobilize the international public sphere against them. A slander campaign against Matarollo and other exiles was initiated, portraying them as dangerous subversives. The junta launched a counteroffensive from its embassy in Paris, where a pilot office was established in June 1977. Elena Holmberg, the press attaché and career diplomat, led the effort, trying to stress the positive effects of the PNR in Argentina. Very soon, however, Holmberg was sidelined and a more aggressive line was adopted, following the arrival of several under-cover ESMA (Escuela de Mecánica de la Armada, or Navy Mechanics School) operatives, members of Task Force 3/32, who were sent to Paris to infiltrate exile circles.[86]

As time passed, CADHU, CAIS, COSOFAM, and TYSAE cooperated in launching activities of protest.[87] In late January 1981, a colloquium on "Policies of Forced Disappearance of People" was convened in the Medici Hall of the Senate of France in Paris. Presided over by Nobel Prize Laureate, Adolfo Pérez Esquivel, at that time one of the most well-known Argentineans, it attracted such a public that forced the conveners to shift the venue to the National Assembly. Messages of support arrived from King Juan Carlos I, the International Commission of Jurists, the International Union of Lawyers, and the Christian Association for the Abolition of Torture, as well as from Venezuelan former President Carlos Andrés Pérez and the Cardinal of Chile Raúl Silva Enríquez. Participants included human-rights activists Eduardo F. Mignone and the Mothers of Plaza de Mayo, former Argentine President Arturo U. Illía, writer Julio Cortázar, and journalist Jacobo Timerman. The representative of the UNCHR attested that Argentina, Bolivia, Brazil, Chile, El Salvador, Guatemala, Mexico, Nicaragua, Peru, and Uruguay had conducted systematic policies of forced disappearance of persons.[88]

---

[86] This task force [*grupo de tareas*] of the Argentinean Navy had rounded up, captured, and killed the Montoneros leadership in Argentina and had its headquarters in the infamous ESMA, the largest center of detention, torture, and disappearance. The leader of the task force, Jorge "Tigre" Acosta, seconded Admiral Emilio Massera in repression and in his attempts to launch a populist party, modeled after the Peronist movement. Holmberg, aware of the contacts between Massera and the exiled Montoneros that Massera tried to co-opt, was assassinated in Argentina in 1978. See Guest, *Behind the Disappearances*, pp. 70–75.

[87] See, e.g., "Argentine, Cinq ans de dictadure militaire" (March 1981), "Campagne pour un Noel sans prisoniers ni disparus en Argentine (December 1981), in International Institute of Social History (IISG), Amsterdam.

[88] COSOFAM-Barcelona (Casa Argentina), Boletin No. 2, March 1981. IISG, Amsterdam, folder no. 1398.

The continental character of the 'antisubversive' struggle had displaced exiles to Europe and North America, where they were positioned to attempt influencing the public spheres and even branches of government. The Cold War was not to be conducted there on the brutal terms used in Argentina. The Argentinean military rulers would soon realize the impact of the fourth tier of the late 20th-century international arena, discovering the limits of their repressive actions abroad, as the Chileans had realized before them following the spree of attacks on prominent co-nationals in exile, such as Orlando Letelier, who was assassinated in the U.S. capital. While leading the Cold War, the Western democracies could not accept that their allies in Latin America would disregard the rules of the democratic game they publicly endorsed and export the violent and illegal strategies to their own countries.[89]

In Mexico, most exiles kept a separate Argentinean identity nurtured by a strong will to return. They formed a closely knit community and a significant – if not the most important – part of their social life centered on the activities promoted by the exiles' organizations. The Argentinean community in Mexico congregated around two organizations: the Argentinean Committee of Solidarity with the Argentinean People (Comité Argentino de Solidaridad con el Pueblo Argentino, or COSPA), led by Rodolfo Puigróss and Ricardo Obregón Cano, and the Argentinean Solidarity Commission (Comisión Argentina de Solidaridad, or CAS), in which Noé Jitrik played a fundamental role. The Mexican authorities recognized both organizations as the official representatives of the Argentinean exiles, enabling them to negotiate vis-à-vis the Mexican government. Both received support from the Mexican government. COSPA was initially established in February 1976 by a core of Montonero exiles, later joined by others such as the PRT related to the ERP. As an organization nucleating exiles, it grew initially to several hundred activists, until around 1978, when the extremist and acritical tone of the Montoneros and ERP core activists alienated many other exiles, who increasingly left it. Many of those who left became active in a group committed to human rights, the *Coordinadora de Derechos Humanos*. The CAS, organized by Peronists close to Cámpora and by leftists somehow distanced from their home organizations, was established in early 1975, functioning in a house rented and furnished thanks to the personal involvement of former President Luis Echeverría.[90] Because it operated democratically, it increasingly turned into the most representative association of Argentine exiles, with a peak in the early 1980s of nearly 600 activists coming from a broad spectrum of political affiliations – Peronists, leftists, socialists, and some

---

[89] In June 1976, in a meeting with the Foreign Affairs Minister of the military Junta in Argentina, Kissinger told Admiral César Augusto Guzzetti in Santiago de Chile that "if there are things that have to be done, you should do them quickly. But you should get back quickly to normal procedures." Memorandum of conversation, 6 June 1976, available at http://www.gwu.edu/~nsarchiv/NSAEBB133/index.htm, accessed 8 July 2007.

[90] Pablo Yankelevich, "Memoria y exilio. Sudamericanos en México," p. 242.

radicals. Even if not disclosed in the public arena, there were constant frictions among the different organizations of the Argentine exiles, which reduced the effectiveness of the work in favor of human rights.[91] These groups promoted a wide range of activities. Among these activities were political assemblies, cultural events, nursery facilities, medical services, legal counseling, and help with the handling of migratory procedures.[92]

The close social interaction of the Argentinean exiles nurtured a ghetto culture that was, at once, highly productive from an intellectual perspective and insular in its approach to Mexican society. Writer Mempo Giardinelli describes the situation thus:

> Obviously, [the culture] was one of ghetto and we were conscious about it. What was the key concern in exile? How it relates to Argentina: of utmost importance was to have points of reference in Argentina.[93]

Contrasting with the situation within Argentina, information about the homeland flowed freely into Mexico, triggering discussion, self-reflection, and criticism, the harbingers of conceptual and political change. The Argentine exiles were intensely involved in discussing reflexively their recent political defeat and their own existence as exiles. Torn between isolation and adaptation, they invested time and energies among their co-nationals and managed to become leading actors in the communities of co-nationals. The major political debates that divided the exile community of Argentines in Mexico were, first, the role of violence in the process leading to the dictatorship back home, and, second, the need for violence in the continuing fight against military rule there. The lack of self-criticism of the guerrillas was met by an increasing reflexivity and recognition of the defeat by most exiles. The latter began to be increasingly skeptical of what they considered the protracted elitism and voluntary endorsement of violence by the Montoneros and ERP leadership. Debates were often endogenous and not always effective vis-à-vis the host country and the international community, and even within the community of co-nationals, they provoked divisions and a gradual decline in political activism. On the other hand, it would take many years for political exiles to rightly evaluate the potential of the fourth tier. At first, they were unconvinced of the impact of denouncing human-rights abuses and arising international solidarity for their cause.

---

[91] Bernetti and Giardinelli, *México*, p. 26. A similar dynamic can be traced in the case of the Argentinean community in Madrid, where the Casa Argentina provided legal support and medical, social, and educational services and served as a meeting ground for exiles, and the Centro Argentino was a center of political activism against the dictatorship. See Guillermo Mira Delli-Zotti, "La singularidad del exilio Argentino en Madrid: entre las respuestas a la represión de los '70 y la interpelacion a la Argentina post-dictatorial," in Pablo Yankelevich, Ed., *Represión y destierro*, pp. 87–112.

[92] Pablo Yankelevich, *México, país refugio*. Mexico: Plaza y Valdés, 2002.

[93] Interview with Mempo Giardinelli by Mario Sznajder and Luis Roniger, Jerusalem, 11 May 2001.

In his first years in exile, Pedro Orgambide reflected on his partial skepticism of centering efforts on international campaigns:

To be sincere: I do not expect much from these relatively interconnected and solidarity world, to which you refer. Let me explain, I believe in the importance of international forums and in revolutionary solidarity, especially that of the Liberation movements of Latin America. However, the change we wish for our country will not come from abroad, only from inside.[94]

Increasingly, the cause of human rights and the fate of the *desaparecidos* as central to the struggle became the focus of interest. In the early 1980s, the major debate was triggered by the Malvinas–Falkland war, which split the community of exiles between a minority that accused the move as a cynical distractive policy, and all those who supported the national idea of recovering the Malvinas, even if many of them continued to condemn the Argentine dictatorship for its human-rights record.[95] Among the latter was a delegation of exiles that traveled to Argentina "in order to support the Argentine nation against the imperialist Anglo-North American aggression."[96] Another polemical debate followed the preparation of a documentary on the Argentine exile in Mexico, produced by María Seoane and others. Finally, an ongoing debate led to the reevaluation of democracy in lieu of the old forms of hierarchical and paternalistic control that had been used in the revolutionary camp.[97]

The intensity of the communal life of the Argentineans was a reflection of their relative closure. Nicolás Casullo explains:

I felt the break. I lived among Argentineans and among Mexicans. I lived without immersion in the Mexican ways, every day I walked and was fully within the Argentinean ways that turned increasingly into a land of perimeters.[98]

And yet, the Argentinean exiles were never isolated completely. According to some testimonies, with the passing of time, the group organized in CAS opened itself to other Latin Americans:

The exile in Mexico, at least in its militant flank, was conceived as a Latin American exile. Our house, the CAS [Comisión Argentina de Solidaridad], was home to

---

94 Alejandro Dorrego and Victoria Azurduy, *El caso argentino: Hablan sus protagonistas*. Mexico: Editorial Prisma, 1977, p. 221.

95 This is a general trend in communities of Argentine exiles elsewhere as well (e.g., in Brazil). See Ana Baron, Mario del Carril, and Albino Gómez, *Porqué se fueron*. Buenos Aires: Emecé, 1995, p. 78.

96 Important political activists were part of this delegation, led by Dr. Ricardo Obregón Cano, former governor of the province of Córdoba, joined in Lima by Dr. Oscar Bidegain, former governor of the province of Buenos Aires, who was exiled in Spain. Press release: "Retorno de opositores argentinos exiliados," distributed in Mexico and Spain, 8 May 1982. Archives of the IISG, Amsterdam, Spain folder no. 7.1.

97 Bernetti and Giardinelli, *Mexico*, pp. 80–83, 140–144.

98 Boccanera, "Escritores Argentinos," p. 110.

Nicaraguans, Salvadorans, Paraguayans, Uruguayans, that is, all those who lacked their own house, as they were few. We maintained also relations with the *Casa de Chile*, even if the Chileans had their own House.[99]

The large majority of Argentineans as well as other exiles of the South were involved in Mexican affairs and made a contribution to Mexican society and culture:

In Mexico, Latin American exiles left a salient mark in the areas of teaching, research, art and culture, in which they integrated and enriched with their talent and daily performance.... They joined the middle strata and some of them the elites. Their presence also was instrumental in the settling of other co-nationals (family, friends or co-citizens), who arrived to work in trade and services. Unintentionally, the old exiles became a support and bridge between local society and their co-nationals who arrived to Mexico for economic reasons.... Beyond their specific contributions, these foreigners arriving due to military coups and dictatorships in the second half of the 20th century left a most profound and emotional impact. In Mexico [they left an imprint on] family, friends, neighbors, loves, broken loves and children.[100]

Following democratization, many opted to stay or return intermittently to Mexico, and many children of exiles turned Mexican or 'Argen-mex,' carrying hybrid identities that related strongly to both the home country of their parents and the country of their growth.[101]

This dialectic of accommodation of Argentinean exiles in Mexico fed continuously into a strong will to return to the homeland as soon as the political conditions would allow it. By and large, for the exiles, the decision to leave Argentina had been forced on them by the spiral of violence; rather, they had never intended to settle permanently in this host country and regarded their residence in Mexico as purely temporary. Indeed, when the opportunity presented itself with Argentina's return to democracy, the overwhelming majority of the exiles chose to return. Their life experience in Mexico, with all its contradictions and social and cultural difficulties, led almost naturally to this decision taken by most of them.

In the framework of the four-tiered structure of exile, by late 1983, the options of the relocated exiles had been broadened to include their home country in a transition toward democracy. In this situation, social, cultural, and material factors were superseded by the political expectations of joining the process of renewed democratization in Argentina.

---

99 Interview with Mempo Giardinelli, Jerusalem, 11 May 2001.
100 Mónica Palma Mora, "Destierro y encuentro. Aproximaciones al exilio latinoamericano en México, 1954–1980." *Amerique Latine, Histoire et memoire*, p. 16, available at http://www.alhim.revues.org/document636.html, accessed 10 July 2007.
101 Yankelevich, *En México, entre exilios*, p. 132; and the documentary film *Argen-Mex, 20 Años*, Director, Jorge Denti, 1996.

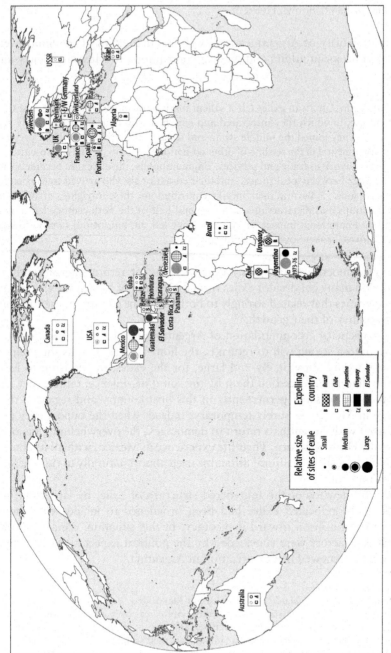

MAP 6. Selected communities of exiles and diasporas, 20th century.

The Chilean Diaspora: Political Mobilization and Openness to Global Trends

Historically, Chileans perceived their country as a site of asylum for others, yet already in the 19th century, as we have previously analyzed, it expelled part of its own elites or transferred them into internal exile to remote parts of the country while accepting exiles from other countries. In the early 20th century, well-known members of society and politics were forced into external or internal exile. Arturo Alessandri Palma was exiled in Italy in 1924–1925 as a result of a military coup. Emilio Bello Codecido spent the period between 1925 and 1936 in exile. Eliodoro Yáñez was exiled in Paris between 1927 and 1931, during Carlos Ibáñez del Campo's dictatorial rule. Ibáñez himself escaped to Argentina twice. The first time was in 1931, when he lost power as a result of the demonstrations related to the economic crises of that time, and again in 1938 after the failed coup by the Movimiento Nacional Socialista de Chile that wanted to place him in power, skipping the national elections. Later, in 1948–1958, the outlawing of the Communist Party of Chile forced many of its members, among them Pablo Neruda, to move abroad.[102]

Yet, it was mainly during the last wave of dictatorship that the Chilean phenomenon of exile acquired a distinctive, transformative character, both in terms of the country and its political realignment. Law Decree 81, enacted by the military junta in November 1973, legalized administrative exile as an executive procedure to be used at the discretion of the rulers.

By that decree, the military government required citizens who had left the country after the coup to obtain permission from the Ministry of Interior to reenter Chile. Thus, no exile considered dangerous was allowed to return. When they renewed their passports at Chilean consulates, many exiles had the letter L stamped on them, indicating that the bearers were on the list of those prohibited from returning. Having portrayed exile as a humane alternative to prison for "enemies of the nation," the military government had no intention of changing its policy on return. When foreign correspondents covering the plebiscite on the 1980 Constitution asked Pinochet whether exiles would be allowed to return, he replied: "I have only one answer: No" (Comité Pro Retorno de Exiliados 1980: 10).[103]

Furthermore, by way of Law Decree 604, the government precluded the reentrance of Chileans who had left the country for any reason. In practice, these regulations were enforced by the Ministry of Interior and the border police of Chile through the use of 'blacklists' of nationals and former

---

[102] Simon Collier and William F. Sater, *A History of Chile*. New York: Cambridge University Press, 1996; Brian Loveman and Elizabeth Lira, *Las ardientes cenizas del olvido: Vía Chilena de reconciliación política, 1932–1994*.

[103] Thomas Wright and Rody Oñate, "Chilean Political Exile," *Latin American Perspectives*, 34, 4 (2007): 31–49.

residents who had left, were banished, or were not permitted to return to Chile.[104]

The estimated number of Chileans who left Chile between 1973 and 1990 ranges from a few hundred thousand to nearly 2 million.[105] With democratization, the National Office of Return in Chile estimated 700,000 Chileans abroad, of whom 200,000 had left the country for political reasons[106]:

At the beginning, international organizations in charge of assisting those in exile estimated that about 4,000 individuals had requested political asylum or had been expelled from the country. Some years later the estimate had increased to 10,000 (30,000 with family members). If we add to the political exile *sensu stricto* the other exile motivated by "political" unemployment, this number increases to 200,000 [Esponda Fernández 1991: 21–27]. However, the number of people who have suffered expatriation has always been difficult to determine because motivation for emigration has varied and no data are available to provide an objective follow-up. We estimate that another 100,000 persons should be added to this number. Without doubt, this has been the greatest emigration in Chilean history.[107]

The latest estimate of the Chilean Commission for Human Rights in its 1982 annual report is 163,686, whereas an article appearing in a Chilean weekly, *Hoy*, in January 1984 gave a total of 179,268. Also in 1984, a study was carried out in Chile and abroad by the CIDE, which gave a total of 200,250.[108]

There are even larger estimates, such as Jorge Arrate's, who places the number of exiles and migrants at 1,800,000. Even deducting natural emigration figures caused by nonpolitical factors (e.g., traditional Chilean migration to Argentina, especially in periods of economic prosperity there and economic difficulties in Chile), the figures are very high for a country with a population just above 10 million at the beginning of the period and under 14 million at the end of it.[109] Adding the fact that Chile lived through two periods of

---

[104] These lists of individuals still included 4,942 names in 1984 and 3,878 in 1985. *Chile: Country Reports on Human Rights Practices for 1985.* Washington, D.C.: Department of State, 1986, p. 452. By December 1987, according to the Chilean government, 338 cases of exiles precluded from return remained pending. The Vicariate of Solidarity claimed that the number was 561. *Chile: Country Reports on Human Rights Practices for 1987.* Washington, D.C.: Department of State, 1988, p. 412.

[105] According to CELADE – Centro Latinoamericano de Demografía – there were around 500,000 Chileans living abroad in the 1980s; that is, nearly 5 percent of the population. See J. Pizarro, *Situación y tendencias de la migración internacional en Chile.* UNESCO, CELADE, mimeo, 1997, p. 20.

[106] Fernando Montupil, Ed., *Exilio, derechos humanos y democracia. El exilio chileno en Europa.* Bruselas and Santiago: Coordinación Europea de Comités Pro-Retorno, 1993, p. 10.

[107] Jaime Llambias-Wolff, "The Voluntary Repatriation Process of Chilean Exiles." *International Migration*, 23, 4 (1993): 580–581.

[108] Alan Angell and Susan Carstairs, "The Exile Question in Chilean Politics." *Third World Quarterly*, 9, 1 (1987): 153.

[109] Jorge Arrate, *Exilio: Textos de denuncia y esperanza.* Santiago: Ediciones Documentas, 1987, pp. 90–91. The second is Jorge Gilbert, *Edgardo Enríquez Frödden, Testimonio de un destierro.* Santiago: Mosquito Editores, 1992, p. 122.

prosperity under military rule – between 1978 and 1981 and between 1985 and 1990 – the strength of political repression as an expelling factor becomes even more evident. Political repression was not only exerted directly against a single political activist, who might be directly persecuted and haunted, but also against groups as a whole, such as the left-wing parties and organizations in Chile.

The closure of all forms of political expression, with the exception of those favoring military rule and military-sponsored ideas, placed a heavy burden in a highly politicized society and especially on its political class. All those who were not inclined to support ideas such as those of the *gremialistas* of Catholic integralist leaning, the corporative nationalists, the authoritarian neoliberals, and all others connected to various versions of the Doctrine of National Security felt the rarified atmosphere. To some extent, this explains why many of the leaders and activists of Chile's Christian Democratic Party (Partido Demócrata Cristians, or PDC), who actively opposed Allende's government before the 1973 military coup, left for exile. Many of them moved to Italy, where they were well received by their political counterparts of the ruling PDC – and acted abroad in total opposition to military rule. Among them were not only the haunted activists but also many former members of the administrative state apparatus who had been 'exonerated' (i.e., fired) because their loyalty to military rule was dubious, because of cuts in government size, or a combination thereof. Others were individuals freed from prison under the expressed purpose of expelling them from the country by an authoritarian legal mechanism of expulsion that included a nonreturn clause. In 1987, about 800 people were still affected by such a ban, precluding them from entering Chile.[110] Many others had to leave Chile because they simply could not find a livelihood in a rapidly changing socioeconomic setup devoid of any kind of political freedom and dominated by an unbound version of free-market economics. Fernando Montupil, whose estimate of the number of Chilean political exiles for the whole dictatorial period reaches 1 million people, believes that even around 1993, about a fifth of them, or close to 200,000 of those who had left the country for politically related reasons, stayed abroad after redemocratization.[111]

This number and spectrum of exiles, spread across many countries, constituted a potent diaspora disputing the legitimacy claimed by the Pinochet regime and struggling to energize the international campaign against its rule. Chilean exiles formed "nuclei of *Chilehood*" [*núcleos de chilenidad*] aimed at giving international projection to the plight of Chile. The parameters of their activity were shaped by the high level of politicization of Chilean society in the period prior to military rule and by the length and strength of the dictatorship. Many Chilean exiles, looking back at their country with a political vision, adopted voluntarist attitudes that stressed the need for political activism, the organization of committees of solidarity, and the dissemination of information

---

[110] Gilbert, *Edgardo Enríquez Frödden*, p. 122.
[111] Montupil, *Exilio, derechos humanos y democracia*, p. 10.

about the Chilean cause, in order to confront the dictatorship while abroad. This attitude, seen as closely related to the struggle against dictatorship being led by different political actors inside Chile at different levels during different periods, resulted in a view of exile as a transitional phenomenon, which could be activated to accelerate the fall of military rule. In a certain sense, the attitudes of many Chilean exiles could be summarized in Bertolt Brecht's dictum on exile: "Do not even put a nail on the wall, throw your jacket on the chair. Is it worthwhile to worry about four days? Tomorrow you will return."[112]

Political activism abroad fed a sense of transience and was, in turn, perceived through such lenses. But the dictatorial period was long and harsh. From another angle, confronting life in exile brought up the problems of integration. These extended from fulfilling basic needs to becoming a full member of the host society. There was a basic contradiction between leading the political struggle that would allow going back and integrating into the new environment, especially in Europe. From the beginning, exile was marked by the constant tension between the need to accommodate to the host society and the tendency to remain attached to the homeland. As with other exiles, a certain level of accommodation was universally required, even if the basic intention was to be politically active as an exile and return to the home country as soon as possible.

Until that wave of exile, Chile assumed its insularity. The country was perceived by its own citizens as a very far-away country, perceived as *Finis Terrae*, as if at the End of the World, and, as such, rather isolated from the international scene. Salvador Allende's accession to power, as the first freely elected Marxist president in a democratic framework, projected the Chilean experience into a special place in the framework of the Cold War, awarding a strongly universal meaning to the defense of the values of Chilean democracy, soon to be crushed by the military. The Chilean experience was well known in the international public sphere, because of the novelty and the many questions raised by the experience of democratically elected Marxists in power. And yet, it was only with the arrival of the Chilean exiles that a new bond of solidarity was created that both energized the political scene in the host countries and served as a powerful instrument in breaking Chilean insularity or historical isolation.[113]

Chilean exile was a corollary of the political and social project imposed on Chile by military rule. Because it exiled virtually the entire leadership of the Left who were not assassinated or imprisoned during the first stage of state terror, and prevented those considered dangerous from returning at least until 1984, Pinochet managed to consolidate his hold on Chile. And yet, the creation of a Chilean diaspora proved dysfunctional for Pinochet's project in the long run, as subsequently discussed.

Immediately after the military coup, a National Commission of Aid to Refugees (Comisión National de Ayuda a Refugiados, or CONAR) was formed,

[112] Arrate, *Exilio*, p. 34.
[113] Arrate, *Exilio*, p. 33.

led by Lutheran Bishop Helmut Frenz. Its main role was to help persecuted Chileans reach and enter foreign embassies where they would receive asylum and save their lives. In 1974, an agreement was reached among the Inter-European Committee for Migration, the International Red Cross Committee, CONAR, and the Chilean government to facilitate the exit of those individuals placed under administrative detention but not scheduled to stand trial. In 1975, another agreement was signed that made it possible also for people who suffered from political persecution and were serving sentences to leave Chile. Three thousand Chileans were freed from prisons in order to leave the country. In addition, since 1974, large numbers of detainees who were held in concentration camps without convictions, under the provisions of the State of Siege Law, were expelled from the country by decree. On 30 April 1975, Decree Law 504 established that a sentence dictated by the military courts (i.e., prison, internal exile [or *relegación*], or conditional sentences) could be exchanged for an *extrañamiento* (i.e., the expulsion from the country without right to return).

In Latin America, the greater concentrations of Chilean exiles were in Argentina (especially before 1976), Venezuela, Brazil, and Mexico. Important, although more reduced, was the number of Chileans who moved to Cuba and later Nicaragua. Others went to Canada and the United States. In Europe, Chileans spread all across the continent but many went to the UK, Sweden (who helped especially in many urgent cases), Italy, Spain, France, and Denmark. In 1992, there were nearly 28,000 Chileans in Sweden, of which 13,900 were political refugees in 1987 (6,500 of these had arrived in 1968–1977, 3,800 in 1978–1984, and 3,600 in 1985–1987).[114]

According to Jaime Llambias-Wolff,[115] the distribution of Chilean expatriates in 1984 was as follows (in percentage):

Venezuela	44.0%
Other Latin-American countries	3.0%
Spain	10.0%
France	8.3%
Italy	6.6%
Sweden	5.5%
Other Western Europe countries	6.6%
Canada	6.7%
United States	1.3%
Australia	5.0%
Eastern Europe and others	3.0%

---

[114] Danièle Joly and Robin Cohen, Eds., *Reluctant Hosts: Europe and its Refugees*. Aldershot, UK: Avebury-Gower, 1990, p. 198; and Daniel Moore, "Latinoamericanos en Suecia," in W. Karlsson, A. Magnusson, and C. Vidales, Eds., *Suecia-Latinoamérica*. Stockholm: Latin American Institute of Stockholm University, 1992. According to Joly and Cohen, until August 1987, 800 Chileans had been received as refugees in Denmark (*Reluctant Hosts*, p. 43).

[115] Llambias-Wolff, "The Voluntary Repatriation," p. 581.

A group of members of the Communist Party received asylum in East Germany and a few in the USSR.[116] Not only communists arrived in the Eastern bloc. After being detained and tortured during military rule, later President Michelle Bachelet left Chile in 1975 with her mother to go to Australia. Later on, she moved to East Germany, where she studied German and continued studying medicine at the Humboldt University in Berlin. In 1979, she returned to Chile, finished her studies, and resumed political activism.[117]

As a group, the Chileans were no less diverse than others in terms of age and gender, occupational and class backgrounds, and regional or ethnic composition. In terms of class background, workers were underrepresented versus individuals of middle- and upper-class backgrounds, who were overrepresented. A relatively large group of Mapuches, 500-strong and particularly targeted by the military, found its way into Western Europe, where they founded their own organization, the *Comité Exterior Mapuche* that coordinated actions with other organizations and networks of Chilean exiles.

The common denominator of the exiles was the banning of the political organizations back home, in which they had activated or sympathized, and the brutal state repression that drove them into exile. This commonality led to the reestablishment of the political parties abroad: the Socialist Party, the Communist Party, MAPU (Movimiento de Acción Popular Unitaria, or Movement of United Popular Action), MAPU-OC (MAPU Obrero Campesino, or Workers-Farmers MAPU), the Radical Party, the Christian Left, MIR, and all associated with the former coalition of Allende and reconstituted in exile, mainly in Europe.[118] Thus, the majority of exile organizations belonged to leftist parties, although there were also nonpartisans and a group of Christian Democrats, who, after their initial support of the coup, opposed the ensuing policies of Pinochet and found themselves on the run.[119]

Political action through parties, committees of solidarity, NGOs, and local and international organizations took place almost immediately with the arrival of the Chilean exiles. In the UK, committees of Solidarity with Democratic Chile were established in London, Birmingham, Sheffield, Oxford, Swansea, Edinburgh, Liverpool, Manchester, and Durham. Although at the beginning the initiative was taken by British leftist groups and the Labor Party, the arrival of almost 3,000 exiles gave further impetus to the committees.[120] Already by January 1974, a Chile Committee for Human Rights (CCHR) was established, under the chair of Joan Jara, the widow of folksinger Víctor Jara, assassinated in the first wave of repression. The local sponsors included members of both houses of the British Parliament, religious dignitaries, and prominent public

---

[116] Arrate, *Exilio*, pp. 95–96.
[117] Biografia, Presidencia de la Republica, http://www.presidencia.cl.
[118] Montupil, *Exilio, derechos humanos y democracia*, pp. 14–15.
[119] Wright and Oñate, *Flight from Exile* (1998) and "Chilean Political Exile" (2007).
[120] Montupil, *Exilio*, p. 59.

figures. The CCHR set among its goals to promote the adoption of political prisoners by individuals and groups, work with exiles, do research, and provide information, in addition to fund raising.[121] Political activity was often hectic, with leaders participating in numerous meetings and intensely defining the methodologies of working in unison with the local networks of solidarity generated by the September 1973 events. The Labor government of Harold Wilson was very supportive of Chilean exiles, who enjoyed what one exile defined as a widespread net of "effective solidarity," involving the British government, the Labor Party, trade unions, students, academics, human-rights groups, and the Communist Party of the UK.[122]

The Chilean case became a *cause célèbre* for Europeans and found strong echoes with public officials, parliamentarians, party activists, trade union activists, human-rights associations, Catholic and Protestant Churches, and student federations:

Many exiles were politicians with links with sister parties... Chilean Socialists, Communists, Christian Democrats and Radicals – all found receptive communities outside Chile.... International sympathy for the Chilean opposition was widespread and strong – much more so than for the exiles from other military regimes in the Southern Cone. The international community felt that it understood and could relate to what was happening in Chile, whereas the politics of Argentina, or Brazil or Uruguay were so different from the experience of most developed countries that military coups in those countries evoked little response.[123]

Massive marches of protest and popular demonstrations were organized in front of Chilean Embassies. Stevedores' unions in Anvers, Liverpool, and Marseilles boycotted Chilean ships. In Israel and Spain, public protests managed to block the entry to port of the *Esmeralda*, the training ship of the Chilean Navy that in 1973 had served as a prison and torture center. In the UK, the Chilean Solidarity Movement published a long list of British firms trading with Chile, calling the trade unions to boycott them.[124] Fearing for the safety and lives of those in Chilean prisons, exiles led hunger strikes, which had an impact on public opinion in Europe. Folkloric *peñas* were organized to collect monies to support the families of political prisoners, widows and sons of the 'disappeared' in Chile. Chilean music and theater were major keys in keeping spirits high. Exiled groups such as the Quilapayún located in Paris and the Inti Illimani based in Rome traveled incessantly from community to community in

---

[121] Chile Committee for Human Rights, "Our Work in Britain," ca. 1976. Archives of the IISG, Amsterdam, UK folder 7.1: movements of solidarity.

[122] Testimony of Ingrid Hecker-Perry, member of the Chilean MIR exiled in the UK, 23 May 2004.

[123] Alan Angell, "The Chilean Coup of 1973 – A Perspective Thirty Years Later," available at http://www.lac.ox.ac.uk/coup.pdf, accessed 17 June 2008.

[124] Jimmy McCallum, "A Trade-Unionist Guide to the Chile Issue: Does Your Firm Trade in Torture?" no date (ca. 1974). Archives of the IISG, Amsterdam, UK folder 7.1.

order to energize the struggle against the dictatorship and keep their culture of resistance alive.[125]

Chilean exiles created in Europe a series of organizations that combined politics and cultural collective identity and promoted networks of solidarity with a wide array of organizations and political forces; among them, Chile Democrático in Rome, the Instituto para el Nuevo Chile and the Centro Salvador Allende in Rotterdam, SEUL-Casa de América Latina in Brussels, the Comité Salvador Allende in Laussane, the Comité Salvador Allende in Stockholm, the Centro de Estudios Salvador Allende in Madrid, the Comité Chileno Anti-Fascista y Chile Democrático in London, and Chile Democrático in Paris. These committees established transnational networks that organized major conferences and hearings in support of Chile such as in Frankfurt in April 1974; Caracas in November 1974; Copenhagen in June 1974; Paris in July 1974; Berlin in July 1975; Mexico, Caracas, and Athens in November 1975; among many others, especially in the 1970s and early 1980s.[126] The conferences and hearings provided meeting grounds for the Chilean opposition in exile to engage in focused cooperation with the European and Latin American Left against the dictatorship back home.[127]

The passing of time in exile, however, took its toll. In the first stage, all these activities were believed to articulate and support the consolidation of a strong and effective opposition that supposedly would lead to the demise of the dictatorship in Chile. However, the margins for antimilitary political action in Chile were nearly closed by repression and persecution. The consolidation of Pinochet's rule in Chile led to a phase of questioning and reevaluation of the political tactics. Concurrently, the enthusiasm for the Chilean *cause célèbre* waned. International solidarity shifted to other causes. As distance and time took their toll in a long, protracted process, Chilean political activism decreased and was replaced with social activism in the communities of exiles: tapestries, greeting cards, sales of records and cassettes, festivals, concerts, new books, calls to affiliation, all these as means of revitalization of local committees.[128] Indeed, besides strict party political organizations, Chilean exiles had also reconstituted trade unions and women's organizations abroad and created

[125] Ana Maria Cobos and Ana Lya Sater, "Chilean Folk Music in Exile," in Liliana Sontag, Ed., *Intellectual Migration: Transcultural Contributions of European and Latin American Emigres. Papers of the 31st Annual Meeting of SALAM.* Madison, WI: SALAM Secretariat, 1986, pp. 295–339.

[126] The Archives of the International Institute for Social History, in Amsterdam, contain a huge number of documents, pamphlets, and reports that reflect this intense organizational effort; e.g., "Chile Fights/Chile Lucha" published for years since September 1973, Latin American Front (London), and the IUSY archives (IISG, Amsterdam).

[127] For instance, among the conveners of the Conference Pan-Européenne de Solidarité avec Chili on 6–7 July 1974 were Francois Mitterand, first secretary of the Socialist Party, as well as leading members of the PCF, PSU, MRG, CFDT, FEN, and CGT of France (IISG, Amsterdam, Folder no. 1412).

[128] "Chile Lucha." Magazine of the Chile Solidarity Campaign No. 43 (Winter 1983). IISG Amsterdam, Folder no. 1421, 30 pp.

cultural centers and football teams. In many European cities, they established associations of family members of the disappeared and prisoners, as well as institutions dedicated to the treatment of specific problems of exiles. Such initiatives and frameworks sprung up in France, Sweden, Italy, and other countries. In the mid-1970s, the Chileans who arrived in the first wave of exile had already established social organizations aimed at easing the landing and adaptation of new arrivals. In Brussels, COLAT (Colectivo Latinoamericano de Trabajo Psicosocial, or Latin American Collective of Psychosocial Work) was founded, later renamed EXIL. In Copenhagen, a Centre for Psychosocial Assistance to Refugees and Migrants (Center for Psykosocialt Arbejde med Flygtninge og Indvandrere, or CEPAR) was established. The University of Hamburg held a series of symposia on culture and psychosocial pressures in Latin America, with the participation of exiled academics and mental health professionals. In a third stage, pro-return committees were established, becoming part of a pan-European network.[129]

There are differences among the various communities of Chilean exiles. All exiles had problems of adaptation, but those settling in Latin-American countries felt a sense of belonging that was mostly absent among those settling in Europe, Canada, Australia, Asia, or Africa, where they had to adjust to different cultures, food, and lifestyles. In some cases, the difficulties led to closure of the exile community. Osvaldo Puccio, son of President Allende's secretary, was 20 when he arrived in Germany. Years after his arrival, in a testimony, he was highly critical of many Chileans who created cultural and social *ghettos*, turning inward to their music, their food, wine, and sadness. He noted with regret that some lived in Germany for 10 or 15 years without learning the language and thus were secluded from communicating within their environment.[130]

Also in terms of their composition, the various communities of exiles differed. For instance, Mexico received a large group of exiles, close to 10,000. Four-fifths of them arrived after receiving asylum at the embassy in Santiago. Some of them were professionals and technicians, in addition to individuals connected to the high echelons of the former government and public administration. Among them were the widow of Salvador Allende and his two daughters, Clodomiro Almeyda, Pedro Vuskovic, ministers and subsecretaries of state, senators and deputies, leaders of political parties, important academics, and core cultural figures, who found occupational opportunities and were warmly welcome by the Mexican administration and the population. Once there, Chilean exiles established close relationships with their Mexican counterparts and were active politically and socially as a community, influencing the strong position of Mexico against the Pinochet regime in the international arena and keeping alive their connections to Chile. They also made major contributions to the host society, including those of Miguel Littín in cinematography, José de Rocka in

---

[129] Montupil, *Exilio, derechos humanos y democracia*, pp. 13–16.
[130] Mili Rodríguez Villouta, *Ya nunca me verás como me vieras*. Santiago: Ornitorrinco, 1990.

the arts, Luis Enrique Delano in literature, Angel Parra in music, Fernando Fajnzylber in economics, and Edgardo Enríquez in medicine.[131] Contrastingly, the communities in Sweden, the UK, and Canada included larger percentages of individuals of popular backgrounds.[132]

The greater difficulties in adjusting to countries beyond Latin America were somehow compensated for by the existence of governmental programs of assistance in the developed countries that provided means of subsistence through welfare programs. Wright and Oñate mention the case of union leader, Isidro Carrillo, executed six weeks after the coup. His widow Viola Carrillo and their 10 children moved to the Soviet Union and were provided housing, jobs, and educational opportunities through the university level.[133] Similarly, in Western Europe, Canada, and Australia, exiles were offered language classes, occupational training, scholarships, and even subsidized housing. The case of Sweden is paradigmatic. Most Chilean exiles were of middle-class extraction; on average, 35 to 40 years of age, students, professionals, individuals with technical backgrounds, artists and artisans and labor leaders, with a substantial number of political activists. In Sweden, the government of the Social Democratic Party felt sympathy toward the cause of Latin-American political exiles. It is important to note that another factor allowing an open reception policy is the ethos of the country that always helped refugees and political exiles of the Third World. Public opinion in Sweden identified itself with the Chilean political plight. Many young people visited South America through NGOs or IGOs. Some were imprisoned, others killed, and others expelled, such as Ambassador Harold Edelstam, who saved many lives and gave asylum to the persecuted. There were numerous committees of solidarity with Chile, and the main image of the Latin Americans was very positive. In the 1960s, Swedes were a source of inspiration for radical ideas, and they were also imbued with a missionary Lutheran spirit. Until the 1980s, all Latin-American immigrants were seen in Sweden as synonymous with political refugees, perceived as 'heroes' or 'martyrs.' The combination of a receptive ethos and a supportive governmental action was a constant that was maintained even as the Social Democrat government fell from power in September 1976.[134]

Still, many found themselves alienated from their new environment and in a process of mourning defeat, feeling guilt for the dead, jailed, or disappeared left behind, which produced high rates of depression, divorce, alcoholism, and suicide. But most worked to adapt, developing new occupational skills,

---

[131] Maira, "Claroscuros de un exilio privilegiado," pp. 136–137.
[132] Maira, "Claroscuros," p. 129.
[133] Wright and Oñate, "Chilean Political Exile," p. 38.
[134] Daniel Moore, "Latinoamericanos en Suecia," pp. 161–183; Fernando Camacho Padilla, "La diáspora chilena y su confrontación con la embajada de Chile en Suecia, 1973–1982," in José del Pozo Artigas, Ed., *Exiliados, emigrados y retornados Chilenos en América y Europa, 1973–2004*. Santiago: RIL Editores, 2006, pp. 37–62.

learning in higher education, projecting their culture onto the new generations and keeping alive the spirit of resistance:

Exile as a whole is, according to my perception, a painful and complex process, regardless of the experience lived through. Learning, in any area and when it takes place, comes also with pain. It may be less or more alienating, for different people, but the opportunities offered by the host country are always interpreted from the condition of exile, of an "alien" as the British say, which reflects so well the way they feel about. From the English "alien", stranger, foreigner...comes also "alienation".[135]

The crackdown of Pinochet on the UP leadership and the failed attempt by socialists, communists, and the MIR to resist as clandestine organizations, which were decimated and crushed, transformed exiles into the most effective front for fighting the dictatorship, at least until 1982. Pinochet used exile to suffocate political action but, once abroad, the exiles reconstructed a dense network, replicating their former political organizations on the local, regional, national, and international planes.

The socialists and the UP established their headquarters in Berlin. The communists opted for Moscow, and the MIR selected Havana and Paris. As a result, the exile community created several transnational networks, following former ideological divisions and commitments.[136] Every Leftist Party of Chile was reconstructed abroad: the Socialists, Communists, MAPU, MAPU-OC, Radicales, Izquierda Cristiana, MIR, and, in the first years, even the youth movements of each of these parties. Also established were the Movimiento Democrático Popular (Popular Democratic Movement) or MDP; the Convergencia Socialista; the Bloque Socialista; and later on, the MIDA (Movimiento de Izquierda Democrática Allendista, or Pro-Allende Leftist Democratic Movement) and the PPD (Partido por la Democracia, or Party for Democracy). Exiles worked with their parallel political parties and student, labor, church, and human-rights associations in the host countries, and they formed numerous committees of solidarity with Chile. In some cases, as in the German Federal Republic or Canada, there were more than a hundred committees of solidarity. Exiles were also active in the framework of the union organizations (CUT [Central Única de Trabajadores, or Workers' Union Organization] the Comité Sindical Chile) and women's organizations linked to the UP, which they established in close to 35 countries, as well as cultural centers, football teams, and other associations. Moreover, the magnitude and brutality of the repression ignited the emergence of new associations such as the Asociaciones de Familiares de Detenidos y Desaparecidos, Comité Exterior Mapuche, Pastoral Católica del Exilio, youth centers, and childrens' ateliers.

---

[135] Personal communication of Ingrid Hecker-Perry, member of the MIR (Chile) exiled in the UK, 23 May 2004.

[136] Ana Vásquez,, "The Process of Transculturation: Exiles and Institutions in France," in Danièle Joly and Robin Cohen, Eds., *Reluctant Hosts: Europe and its Refugees*, pp. 125–132; Arrate, *Exilio*, pp. 100–101.

Political activities were combined with and carried out by cultural, trade union, sport, and other group activities. Accordingly, the organizational impetus also led to the establishment of many civil organizations and committees of solidarity that crystallized during exile.[137] Through these organizations, exiles lobbied host-country governments to condemn the Pinochet regime at the UN and other international forums and organized campaigns for the release of political prisoners and the banning of Chilean imports. "These efforts were crucial to countering the influence of powerful business interests that supported the dictatorship for reopening Chile to international capital and, through the neo-liberal policies it imposed, creating an ideal investment climate."[138]

Along with this impressive organizational impetus, the exiles replicated their traditional political rivalries while abroad, although they were able to combine efforts and collaborate for the sake of their common goal, which is the key to the Chilean exiles' effectiveness in keeping the plight of their homeland as a top-priority issue in the international agenda.

The exiled leaders of the UP, who lived on subsidies from host governments or political organizations or received well-paid jobs, traveled among exile populations and worked with world political and government leaders to gather support for their cause. Some of them turned into figures with international clout. Anselmo Sule, president of the Radical Party, was elected vice-president of the Socialist International in 1976, a reflection of the high priority the Chilean case had for this organization. The Socialist International lobbied governments and the UN and supported think tanks and publishing houses active in the campaign for the 1988 plebiscite. Similarly, the cross-party organization, Chile Democrático, which received financial support from governments in Western Europe, lobbied at the highest levels, published a very influential periodical (*Chile América*) with information about Chile, and monitored the human-rights situation there, while it also supported financially the Chilean movement of human rights related to the Vicaría de la Solidaridad in the home country.

The socioeconomic profile of political exiles included rank-and-file activists of the parties, student and professional organizations, and labor unions. In exile, political solidarity and activism erased, to a large extent, class and rank differences that were salient in Chile. Activism and political solidarity went together, especially between members of the same political party in the home and the host countries. José Rodríguez Elizondo, a writer and later diplomat, coming from the higher ranks of the Communist Party and Chilean UP administration, went with many of his 'comrades' to exile in East Germany. He recalls the beginning of his sojourn in Leipzig, as a local committee of solidarity invited all the Chilean exiles to a welcome party in the Democratic Republic of Germany. Speeches in German and Spanish were made, which spoke highly of international brotherhood, of the common bonds of Communism, of the

---

[137] Montupil, *Exilio, derechos humanos y democracia*.
[138] Wright and Oñate, "Chilean Political Exile," p. 41.

anti-Fascist struggle. Food and alcoholic drinks were served in a lavish manner. After the formal speeches and reception, the party began. The Chileans, still somewhat shy, were drawn into dancing. Rodríguez Elizondo was standing by a short, stocky Chilean trade union member from Valparaíso. The man enjoyed so much the food, drinks, and dancing with a tall, statuesque blonde and blue-eyed East German female comrade who had invited him to dance. In the heat of the party, rhythms of dance changed into slower, romantic tunes. Soon the man found himself dancing with his nose buried in the bosom of the German lady. In a break, the comrade from Valparaiso came back to Rodríguez Elizondo and declared: "Comrade, as I always believed . . . The Socialist paradise exists. It is here."[139]

While the leading politicians worked at the supraorganizational level, it was the localized and social support of the myriad organizations of the exile that kept the sense of confidence and direction alive and created domestic networks and committees of solidarity with Chile:

> The political groups carried out organizational activities, disseminated information on Chile, organized marches and demonstrations, and collected used clothing to be distributed among the poor in Chile, whose ranks multiplied under the Chicago Boys' economic policies. They held *peñas* and made and sold *empanadas*, the traditional meat and onion pies, to raise money and consciousness.[140]

Even in countries with greater structural constraints for the Chileans, the political activism of the exiles kept the cause of Chile alive. On the basis of interviews with former exiles, Wright and Oñate reconstruct how the exiles worked under such conditions in Costa Rica and Brazil:

> [In] countries with fewer nongovernmental organizations, exiles used lower profile approaches to cultivate the support of their host countries. Frustrated by the divisions among the UP parties in Costa Rica, a group of exiles established a bi-national solidarity organization, *Por Chile*, to influence the media and the Costa Rican government in quiet but effective ways. In Brazil, the military government prohibited open political activity such as street demonstrations or leafleting but tolerated political events in private spaces such as churches[141]

The Chilean Left underwent a profound transformation, especially under the impact of reconfiguration of the European Left around its debates on Euro-Communism, the struggle of Solidarity in Poland, and the disillusion with the Soviet Union. In many cases, the contact with *real*-Communism in the socialist countries brought about early disenchantment and the will to go back to the

---

[139] Chilean Ambassador José Rodríguez Elizondo, in a class lecture at the Hebrew University of Jerusalem, March 2000. Mili Rodríguez Villouta brings also testimonies about similar cases of 'opportunities' that European society offered to Chilean exiles. See *Ya nunca me verás como me vieras. Doce testimonios vivos del exilio.* Santiago: Ornitorrinco, 1990, pp. 100–106.

[140] Wright and Oñate, "Chilean Political Exile," pp. 38–39.

[141] Thomas Wright and Rody Oñate, manuscript version of "Chilean Political Exile," 2006, pp. 8–9.

West, provoking some to break from the ranks of the Communist Party.[142] Although the Sandinista victory in Nicaragua in 1979 could still be interpreted within the framework of the Cold War, events in Europe – the transformation of Euro-Communism into a new kind of Social Democracy and the process of parallel rigidity, weakening, and disintegration of the Eastern bloc and the USSR – went far beyond. All these collective and personal transformations contributed to the reconfiguration of the Chilean Left, especially as they followed self-reflection and reassessment among its ranks and as they established a series of think tanks to study ways to modernize Chile. These trends of transformation were also part of a process of redefinition of the political positions and horizons of other exiles in the Chilean diaspora.

Ricardo Lagos, who was close to Allende and set to become the Chilean ambassador to Moscow at the time of the military takeover in 1973, went into exile in the United States and returned to Chile only in 1978. In an interview in May 2002, President Lagos reflected on the impact of exile on the reformulation of his political ideas and attitudes toward democracy:

Never in the history of Chile had so many Chilean women and men with varied degrees of cultural exposure – social leaders, politicians, heads of local associations, and many more – moved into the world [*se asoman al mundo*] and begun to see the world from the new reality they witness. This produces a change, especially in the Left-wing and most progressive thought of Chile. I recall my participation in a meeting of the Chilean PS in Bordeaux.... Someone would stand up and say: "We, the Socialists of Milan think." Another would declare: 'We, the Socialists of Stockholm, say....'" One could sense a cultural renewal in the way of thinking of the delegate from Milan and a Scandinavian worldview in the exile from Stockholm. I believe that exile left its imprint, leading us to recognize the value of democracy, the higher value of human-rights... abandoning the classic [ideological] tools of the Left in the 1960s and '70s, to be replaced by the revalorization of democracy, of human-rights, of the place of the market, of the role of the means of production and service. In other words, there is a great *aggiornamento*, moving and preceding the move to globalization.[143]

The Chilean communists, who had been a moderating force in the UP government, found themselves not supported in their idea of leading a broad anti-Fascist front of the UP parties and the DC. By 1980, they decided to support all forms of struggle, including armed struggle and popular insurrection. In 1983, they supported the creation of the guerrilla group known as the Frente Patriótico Manuel Rodríguez. The experience in exile changed the socialists, leading them progressively to embrace political democracy in a principled way. At first, the socialists split in 1979 into a radical and a more moderate wing.

---

[142] Such were the cases of high-ranking officials of the UP administration such as José Rodríguez Elizondo, a well-known Chilean who spent part of his exile in East Germany, and Gustavo Silva, member of the PCCH, who visited Eastern Europe while in French exile. Interviews with Gustavo Silva, Santiago, August 2001, and with Rodríguez Elizondo, Jerusalem, March 2000. See also Rodríguez Elizondo, *La pasión de Iñaki*. Santiago: Editorial Andrés Bello, 1996.

[143] Interview of Mario Sznajder with President Ricardo Lagos in the Palacio de la Moneda, Santiago de Chile, 2 May 2002.

While the latter became closer to the DC, the hard-liners attempted to join the communists and use the mass protests of 1982–1986 to topple the regime. With the return of exiles into Chile, the shifts also influenced the domestic front. After failing to defeat Pinochet through mass insurrection, the hard-liners joined the renovated wings of the Party in an alliance with the PDC to contest Pinochet in the 1988 plebiscite on the dictator's extended rule. Their success led to the *Concertación* of 17 parties that defeated Pinochet a year later and opened the way for the return to civilian rule.[144]

The four-tiered structure of exile is clearly reflected in the experience of the Chilean communities of exiles. These communities were caught between a strong military government that created a mass phenomenon of expulsion and precluded their return, despite their willingness to do so, and the presence of host societies and wide networks of political and social solidarity supporting their activism abroad. The increased politicization characteristic of Allende's period evolved and crystallized in the form of exile communities that fought against repression by constituting themselves into a living bridge to the international public sphere and many networks of solidarity that eventually affected Chilean politics and the transition to democracy.

The Uruguayan Diaspora: Blending Economic and Political Motivations

The Uruguayan diaspora crystallized precociously and was as widespread as the Chilean. Yet, it lacked the organizational strength and political presence of the latter, primarily because it was formed by a greater component of economically motivated expatriates, but also because of four political factors: the revolutionary character of the leftist activists both in terms of rhetoric and action; the experience of the political Left in the opposition, being harassed and persecuted already before the onset of military rule; the factionalist trends of the Left; and the belated move of the leftist political exiles to a strategy of action already envisaged by Zelmar Michelini before his assassination – namely, a strategy connected to the rising discourse of human rights. In addition, because Uruguay had lived under democratic governments until the 1970s – with the exception of Gabriel Terra's dictatorship in the 1930s – there was no tradition of political exile, unlike in Argentina and many other countries in Latin America. Analyzing these factors, we attempt to explain the distinctive character of the relationships between the exiles and the communities of Uruguayans in the diaspora.

Unsurprisingly, the composition of the Uruguayan diaspora has led to an approach following mainly demographic, quantitative terms, which reveal its

---

[144] The think tanks and periodicals disseminated the renovated ideas. ASER in Paris, the Instituto para el Nuevo Chile in Rotterdam, and Chile Democrático in Rome were leading think tanks. *Plural*, published in Rotterdam, *Convergencia Socialista* in Mexico City, and *Chile-América* in Rome were major factors and expressions of this transformation. See Carlos Orellana, "Revista a las revistas Chilenas del exilio 1973–1990," available at http://www.abacq.net/imagineria/revistas.htm, accessed 4 June 2008.

magnitude and patterns of formation. Although we pay attention to this aspect of the composition of the diaspora, we turn subsequently to the relative weight of the political exiles within it. Studies by Adela Pellegrino, Silvia Dutrénit-Bielous, César Aguiar, Israel Wonsewer, and Ana María Teja portray the patterns of formation of the Uruguayan diaspora. In parallel, they highlight and stress how difficult it is to disentangle the political from the economic motivations of hundreds of thousands of co-nationals who moved abroad.[145]

The flow of Uruguayans to neighboring countries, primarily Argentina, started very early on and reached a peak in the 1970s. On the basis of censuses and estimations, by 1914 Argentina had already attracted a large number of Uruguayan migrants. According to the preceding analyses, 88,650 Uruguayans were living then in Argentina, representing 7.2 percent of the Uruguayan population at that time. Even though theories of chain migration could have predicted the growth of that community, the number of Uruguayans in Argentina went down progressively until it was reduced to 58,300, or 2.1 percent of the Uruguayan population, by 1970. Between the years 1963 and 1975, about 7 percent of the Uruguayan inhabitants left the country. According to the census of 1981, the emigration before 1963 was 33,000 (9.8 percent); between 1963 and 1975, it went up to 200,000 (54.7 percent), and between 1976 and 1981, it consisted of 133,000 migrants (36.3 percent). Standing out in particular was the period 1970–1975, when 88.3 percent of the total of émigrés for the period of 1960–1975 left Uruguay. The peaks were found in 1974 with 64,687 emigrants and in 1975 with 40,984. The number of Uruguayans who settled abroad grew exponentially.[146]

Uruguay had lived under democracy for most of the 20th century but, by the end of the 1960s,

economic decline coupled with inflation and labor unrest fuelled political activism and urban guerrilla activities, primarily of the Movimiento de Liberación Nacional-Tupamaros, founded in 1962. The response of the government of President Pacheco Areco was to impose martial law in 1968, to which the Tupamaros responded by increasing their actions. In a political system characterized until then by the search for consensus and power sharing, Pacheco Areco introduced non-party technocrats to the cabinet, used the military to repress strikes, limited media coverage of terrorism, and in September 1971 suspended the right of habeas corpus on the basis of a declaration of internal war. The old system of power-sharing between the two major political parties (the Colorados and the Blancos) was shattered.[147]

[145] Adela Pellegrino, *Informe sobre la migración internacional en Uruguay en el período 1950–1985*. Montevideo: Facultad de Ciencias Sociales, 1996; Silvia Dutrénit-Bielous, *El Uruguay del exilio*. Montevideo: Trilce, 2006; César Aguiar, *Uruguay, país de emigración*. Montevideo: Ediciones de la Banda Oriental, 1982; Israel Wonsewer and Ana María Teja, *La emigración Uruguaya 1963–1975: Sus condicionantes económicas*. Montevideo: Ediciones de la Banda Oriental, 1983.
[146] Pellegrino, *Informe sobre la migración internacional*, 1996.
[147] Roniger and Sznajder, *The Legacy of Human-Rights Violations*, p. 13.

With authoritarianism, Uruguay witnessed massive arrests conducted mostly in the open; long-term reclusion of political prisoners; and torture, disappearance, and assassination of political opponents. Many believed that Uruguay had in this period the highest record of political prisoners in Latin America.[148] Once known as the 'Switzerland of Latin America,' Uruguay had become in the words of Uruguayan essayist, Eduardo Galeano, a vast "torture chamber." In the following years after 1973, large numbers of Uruguayans left the country, driven out by the combined pressure of economic decline and a level of repression that made it necessary to have a political permit to celebrate a birthday.[149] Estimations put the number of exiles among those leaving Uruguay during the dictatorship and the years of violence that preceded it in a range between 28,000 and 62,000.[150]

Buenos Aires became the center of Uruguayan political exile. Thousands of political activists flew to Argentina as repression in the home country increased. Argentina was driving in the opposite direction: The military, which tried unsuccessfully to preclude Peron's participation in political life since 1955, had finally acknowledged the lack of governability of the country without Peronism. Héctor Cámpora was elected president in March 1973, and the road for the return of Peron had been paved. Argentina was then in a state of political effervescence, contrasting hopes of radical and reformist change and revolutionary rhetoric. For the Uruguayan exiles, the trends of political change in Argentina seemed to reassure them of the correctness of their radical revolutionary ideals, which could become a reality in Uruguay as well. The survival in power of the democratically elected Marxist President of Chile, Salvador Allende, further contributed to this sense of confidence. They also maintained contacts with the Tupamaros back home, as well as with revolutionary groups in Argentina and other South American nations.

Following the June 1973 civil–military coup, thousands of Uruguayans moved to Argentina. Among them was former Senator Enrique Erro, founder of the Leftist Frente Amplio, who had enjoyed the electoral support of the Tupamaros. In Buenos Aires, he founded in October 1974 the UAL (Unión Artiguista de Liberación, or Artigas Liberation Union) that proclaimed total war on the Uruguayan dictatorship, sharing with other associations – such as the ROE (Resistencia Obrero-Estudiantil, or Workers' and Students' Resistance), established by other exiles in April 1974 – the revolutionary optimism of earlier times more than a year after the onset of Pinochet's rule in Chile. In March 1975, Erro was arrested by the democratic government of Argentina, accused of violating the asylum laws. He became a political prisoner who was

---

[148] Roniger and Sznajder, *The Legacy of Human-Rights Violations*, p. 25.

[149] William Rowe and Teresa Whitfield, "Thresholds of Identity: Literature and Exile in Latin America," *Third World Quarterly*, 9, 1 (1987), p. 230.

[150] Juan Carlos Fortuna, Nelly Niedworok, and Adela Pellegrino, *Uruguay y la emigración de los 70*, Montevideo: Ediciones de la Banda Oriental, 1988; Fernando Klein, "La emigración de los uruguayos o el "otro" excluido," pp. 1–2, available at http://www.liceus.com/cgi-bin/ac/pu, accessed 27 November 2008.

relocated from Buenos Aires to prisons in Ushuaia and in Chaco, to be later expelled to exile in France, from which he traveled all across Europe, Mexico, and Venezuela in an effort to denounce the Uruguayan dictatorship.[151] Many other Uruguayan activists met even worse fates: they were abducted, tortured, and made to disappear, even before the military takeover of March 1976.

The trends of movement reflect sociopolitical shifts in South America. Until 1976, 54.2 percent of the emigrants went to Argentina. As anti-Leftist violence increased and democracy broke down, Buenos Aires – the 'classic' site of relocation for Uruguayans across the Rio de la Plata – became a trap for political exiles. Increasing repression combined with cooperation between the security forces of both countries in 'depuration campaigns' proved deadly for many Uruguayan leftists who were abducted, tortured, and made to disappear in Argentina.[152] After 1976, the number of persons migrating to Argentina lessened because of the local coup and the economic crisis. The United States became the second choice as host country for the emigrants, with a total of 11 percent, followed by Australia with 7.4 percent, and Brazil with 7.1 percent.[153] Yet, according to the various censuses conducted in the 1970s, the Uruguayans in Argentina still numbered 58,300, in Brazil 13,582, in the United States 5,092, and in Paraguay 2,310. Under the dictatorship, Uruguay lost 25 percent of its professionals and technicians, 10 percent of its doctors, 15 percent of its architects, and 9 percent of its engineers.[154] Between 1967 and 1975, Uruguay lost 8 percent of its population, who departed because of forced exile or migrated. From 1976, the phenomenon declined, but it worsened again in 1981 and 1982 as a result of the economic crisis generated by the rupture of the famous "*tablita*."[155] In the 1980s, there were 109,724 Uruguayans in Argentina, 21,238 in Brazil, 13,278 in the United States, 9,287 in Australia, 7,007 in Venezuela, and 4,160 in Canada.[156]

The format of the Uruguayan diaspora thus shifted with political and economic changes in the host countries. As Argentina sunk itself into its own repression by the mid-1970s, the attractiveness of Brazil heightened because of the latter's prosperity and policies of technological and scientific development. Concentrations of Uruguayans also moved to Venezuela and Mexico, which were attractive because of their labor opportunities and a demand for qualified personnel. Venezuela attracted many migrants, refugees, and exiles from

---

[151] Senator Erro died in exile in 1985, shortly before the return of democracy in Uruguay. Nelson Caula, "Un hombre de espíritu volcánico, al decir de Zelmar." *La Fogata Digital*, available at www.lafogata.org/05latino/latino10/uru_3-4.htm, accessed 11 May 2006.

[152] Roniger and Sznajder, *The Legacy of Human Rights Violations*, pp. 24–25.

[153] Jorge Notaro, Agustín Canzani, Agustín Longhi, and Estela Méndez, *El retorno de emigrantes y las respuestas de la sociedad uruguaya.* Montevideo: CIEDUR, 1987.

[154] Mónica Bottero, "Yo no me voy; este país me echa," *Brecha*, Montevideo, 21 August 1987.

[155] A fiscal mechanism aimed to secure monetary stability through a preestablished scale of valuation.

[156] Adela Pellegrino, *Informe sobre la migración internacional*, p. 18.

other Southern Cone countries, which made Uruguayans the smallest group of newcomers from that area.[157]

Other Uruguayans went to the United States, driven by prospects of occupational training and higher salaries, even for those without special skills. Smaller numbers moved to a varied range of countries, including Sweden, Switzerland, Spain, and Cuba. According to Pellegrino, by 1980, the percentages of Uruguayan professionals in the United States and Canada were nearly 12 and 10 percent, respectively, far behind representation in the communities of Uruguayans in Venezuela and Mexico, whereas the percentage of workers was more than 40 percent, more than double the case in the latter communities.[158] In the United States, many Uruguayans worked in blue-collar and service jobs. Even if we cannot draw a line between the various motivations of newcomers, it seems that the pull of economic prospects was combined in most cases with the attraction of moving to a less oppressive political environment.[159]

Political exiles sustained their previous revolutionary positions and rhetoric in terms of class struggle and revolutionary war against the bourgeoisie and its henchmen, the military. They did not believe in the 'humanitarian lamentations' and purely informative activities of the human-rights groups and organizations.

It is important to point out that Erro and radical leftist activists were in contact with human-rights organizations but did not seem to consider them as playing a crucial role against the regime. They still believed in the short-term success of their ways of fighting and traditional resistance in Uruguay.[160]

This position was coherent with a belief in total confrontation between the people and the repressive structures and the need for violence, total dedication, and sacrifice while engaged in class war. Addressing human-rights

---

[157] In 1981, according to DIEX (*Direccion Nacional de Identificación y Extranjeria*) of Venezuela, 6,747 Uruguayans held work permits as against 11,541 Argentineans and 23,185 Chileans. G. Bidegain, "Democracia, migración y retorno: los Argentinos, Chilenos y Uruguayos en Venezuela." *International Migration*, 25 (1987): 299–323.

[158] Pellegrino, *Informe sobre la migración internacional*, Table 10.

[159] In the late 20th century, the drainage of co-nationals continued. The preferred countries for emigration were Argentina (24 percent), Spain (18 percent), United States (16 percent), and Australia (13 percent). According to data reported by the newspaper *El Observador* in 2000, there were 18,111 Uruguayans in the United States and 133,453 in Argentina (other estimates put the number around 250,000), 43,000 in Brazil, 20,000 in Paraguay, 17,000 in Australia, 1,500 in Sweden, 8,2000 in Spain, and between 1,500 and 2,000 in France. In Cataluña, there were 6,400 Uruguayans registered, and it was estimated that another 1,800 lived there. During the last few years, in comparison with the emigration of the 1970s, which was mainly toward the regional countries, the move became increasingly motivated only by economic considerations and shifted accordingly to the United States and Europe. The strongest communities were located in Buenos Aires, Rio Grande do Sul, Sydney, Toronto, and Miami. Ana Inés Cibils, "Donde fueron a parar," *El Observador*: Fin de Semana, Montevideo: 29 de julio de 2000, pp. 2–4.

[160] Vania Markarian, "From a Revolutionary Logic to Humanitarian Reasons: Uruguayan Leftists in the Exile and Human Rights Transnational Networks," *Cuadernos del CLAEH*, vol. 1, special edition, Montevideo, 2006, translated by María Cristina Cafferatta, available at http://socialsciences.scielo.org, accessed 12 May 2006.

NGOs, international organizations, and groups of humanitarian and charitable activists in the developed world was perceived as a sign of revolutionary weakness and possibly falling into the many traps set by Western imperialism. It also implied a profound lack of belief in the workings of civil society and liberal democracy. It would take years for them to slowly open to the rising transnational discourse of human rights, a process that operated similarly among other South Americans.[161]

Contrastingly, Senator Zelmar Michelini, also an exile in Buenos Aires, supported the strategy of denouncing the human-rights violations in the international arena. Michelini understood that the adoption of the human-rights discourse in terms of liberal democracy could be used to put pressure on the Uruguayan military government through international organizations and governments. Michelini did not abandon his leftist political position and contacts, but the concern for human rights led him to reframe the meaning of the experience of political imprisonment, torture, and murder of activists, to be instrumentally used to contest the claims of legitimacy of the military rulers in the very centers of Western hegemony. His approach stressed the international domain, where links should be fostered with Amnesty International and the Red Cross, aimed at defining mechanisms of punishment for human-rights violators. He believed that international human-rights organizations could be used by Western imperialism but could also be effective in the opposite direction as a stage for denunciation of institutionalized repression and for raising support for its victims. For Michelini, the United States – which was responsible for the installation of military rule in Latin America – was susceptible to support the plight of the victims in terms of the defense of their human rights. By addressing international fora or the U.S. Congress with these issues, he thought, he and his fellow political exiles could create pressure on the Uruguayan administration. Michelini thus shifted to the language of universal human rights. He led a trend of using this discourse within a historical narrative that stressed the Uruguayan civil tradition and its attack by the military, thus reformulating the importance of individual human rights to the detriment of earlier class struggle.[162]

As he was scheduled to present the case of Uruguay at the U.S. Congress, he was abducted – together with Speaker of the Chamber of Deputies Héctor Gutiérrez Ruiz and two activists of the Tupamaros – and assassinated. Michelini's murder focused public attention on the gross human-rights violations by the dictatorship and led many exiles to understand the importance of supporting the first wide campaign of Amnesty International against torture in Uruguay, launched in February 1976 in New York. Wilson Ferreira Aldunate, leader of the Blanco Party and the opposition in exile, had escaped a fate similar to Michelini's while in Buenos Aires, joined efforts with Edy Kaufman, an

---

[161] Luis Roniger and Leandro Kierszenbaum, "Los intelectuales y los discursos de derechos humanos en el Cono Sur." *Estudios Interdisciplinarios de América Latina*, 16, 2 (2005): 5–36.

[162] Markarian, "From a Revolutionary Logic to Humanitarian Reasons," pp. 7–9.

Argentine–Israeli scholar holding a leading position in Amnesty International at that time, and who had been instrumental in saving Ferreira Aldunate's life.[163] Kaufman and Ferreira Aldunate testified before the U.S. Congress and were echoed, especially by Democratic Senators Edward Kennedy, James Abourezk, and Frank Church and Congressmen Edward Koch, Tom Harkin, and Donald Frazer, all of whom challenged the policies of Secretary of State Henry Kissinger on Latin America.[164] In September 1976, Congress passed and submitted to the president a foreign-aid appropriation bill that prohibited military assistance, international military training, and weapon credit sales to the government of Uruguay for its violations of human-rights standards.[165]

This strategy was effective following the assassination of Orlando Letelier in Washington, D.C. – which sensitized public opinion to political persecution and repression in the Americas – and on the eve of a political shift that would bring Jimmy Carter to the White House. The lack of relative weight of Uruguay in overall U.S. foreign policy was probably also instrumental. Yet, even though effective, the strategy followed was not based on the massive mobilization of the Uruguayan diaspora, thus contrasting with the strategies carried out by the political organizations of the exiles in the Chilean diaspora. The crucial discriminating factors in this case seem to have been the different insertion of the Uruguayan exiles among their co-nationals, their limited organizational structure abroad, and their origins in a society with almost no tradition of political exile in the 20th century. All these explain the distinctive character of the relationships between the exiles and the communities of Uruguayans in the diaspora.

Internal fragmentation characterized the Uruguayan communities abroad. A sociological study of two such communities in the state of Massachusetts by Abril Trigo, although not focusing explicitly on exile, reveals a high extent of divisions and tensions among the Uruguayans, which may explain the low degree of political mobilization. The first Uruguayans arrived there in 1967, and by the 1970s they had reached 300. Most arrived through personal and family contacts, in a sort of chain migration, that followed until the mid-1980s, partly coinciding with Uruguay's political transition and the economic crisis of the so-called Fall of the *Tablita*. The immigrants of the first wave felt driven by a strong and honest ethic that motivated them to succeed through hard work, and they viewed the later expatriates as degraded, driven by greed into faking work accidents, filing faulty insurance claims, and contracting debts they did not intend to repay.[166] The disdain shown to the uneducated immigrants seemed rooted in the self-identification of old-timers with the image of a 'cultured

[163] Edy Kaufman, personal communication, January 2002.
[164] Juan Raúl Ferreira, *Con la patria en la valija. El exilio, Wilson y los años trágicos*. Montevideo: Linardi y Risso, 2000.
[165] Markarian, "From a Revolutionary Logic to Humanitarian Reasons," p. 12.
[166] Abril Trigo, "Memorias de migrancia: Una comunidad de Uruguayos en USA," Ohio State University, typescript, 2006.

nation' spread during the heyday of the Battle model in Uruguay. Accordingly, some old-timers described the new immigrant wave as 'horrendous' and as comprising "people of marginal living, without families, men who come as single and join... obscure dealings."[167]

This trend is replicated in other communities, particularly the Cubans in the United States. When the *balseros* arrived, the old-timers were ambivalent. Some favored supporting them in order to prevent their move into robbery or the drug business, something that would discredit the Cuban community. Others were fearful of the newcomers and their competition.[168] Despite the willing help of many in the Cuban community, many others exhibited a defensive prejudice against the newcomers, "who are not the same as we are." The exiles who arrived in the 1970s and 1980s found themselves converted into a work force often exploited by those who had arrived first, thus adding tensions to an already complex interaction of exiles and migrants.[169] Returning to the Uruguayans in the United States, although in fact many of the old-timers lacked more than a primary education, they still praised their cultured background as an asset enabling them to project themselves into a path of upward mobility:

I do believe we have one hundred percent more education than here. Perhaps we are more intelligent. What we lack is English. If I knew English, I would be teaching at school now.[170]

Part of this self-image was buttressed by the exile of prominent Uruguayan intellectuals, who joined other exiles throughout the world during the heyday of repression.

An important community of Uruguayans existed in Venezuela, with 7,000 migrants, most of them arriving in search of a living.[171] Mexico had granted asylum to 300 individuals in the 1970s and, by the early 1980s, there were between 1,500 and 2,000 Uruguayans in Mexico.[172]

The most active community of exiles from Uruguay was perhaps that of Spain, where exiles exhibited a high degree of self-help and organization, having their own Casa del Uruguay, Colectivo de Mujeres Uruguayas, and other institutions. Most active individuals were disciplined members of the leftist Frente Amplio. Although they tried to retain control of the organizations over

---

[167] Testimony of Daniel Di Pierro, quoted by Trigo, "Memorias de migrancia: Una comunidad de Uruguayos en USA," Ohio State University typescript, 2006.

[168] José Luis Martínez, *La Cuba disidente*. Montevideo: Fin de Siglo, 1996.

[169] Rafael Hernández, "Fallacies Regarding the Cuban Community in the United States," in *Cuba and the United States: Will the Cold War in the Caribbean End?* Boulder, CO: Lynne Rienner, 1991, p. 136.

[170] Testimony of Susana Bregua in Abril Trigo, "Memorias de migrancia."

[171] Venezuela was hosting also 25,200 Chileans and 11,451 Argentines in 1981. Gabriel Bidegain, "Democracia, migración y retorno." *International Migration*, 25 (1987): 299–323.

[172] Hans, Wollny, "Asylum Policy in Mexico: A Survey," *International Migration*, 25 (1987): 219–236.

those activists who remained in Uruguay, they did not show the party cleavages and divisions that characterized Argentine and Chilean exiles in Spain.[173] Important for political mobilization were the committees of solidarity with Uruguay, which disseminated information about the repression back home and denounced the dictatorship. Still, the impact of Uruguayans was rather limited, with many co-nationals lacking the epical prestige of being labeled 'an exile,' even though Spanish intellectual and academic circles felt rather close to the presence of leading Uruguayan intellectuals who had moved into their midst: Mario Benedetti, Carlos Rama, Eduardo Galeano, Juan Carlos Onetti, and Cristina Peri Rossi.[174]

Uruguayans were also active in France, especially in Paris, where, toward the late 1970s, there were already between 1,000 and 1,800 persons.[175] This number included individuals who left their country with a legal passport; others who had been expelled as a condition for their release from prison – defined as the "constitutional option" – and received a status of 'refugees' accredited by ACNUR (Alto Comisionado de las Naciones Unidas para los Refugiados, the Spanish acronym for UNHCR); and, finally, those who entered France illegally, including some coming from Cuba and Eastern Europe.[176] The political activists linked to the Tupamaros had established already in October 1972 a *Comité de Défense de Prisonniers Politiques en Uruguay* (CDPPU, or Committee for the Defense of Political Prisoners in Uruguay), supported by young French sympathizers led by Alain Labrousse. The goals of the committee included work of solidarity with the political prisoners in Uruguay, denouncing violations of human rights in the home country, and helping Uruguayan exiles and refugees arriving in France. French members of the CDPPU also wanted to energize the French Radical Left through the presence of the Uruguayan Tupamaros guerrilla members, a trend that was resented by the latter. The committee established links with the UNCHR in Geneva as well as with French political parties, particularly the socialists. Political divisions rose in the community of Uruguayan exiles after 1976, when a substantial number of communist activists arrived in France and joined the ranks of *France-Amerique Latine*. The CDPPU put an end to its activities on 14 March 1985, the day when the

[173] Jorge Ruffinelli, "El exilio, solidaridad sin fronteras." *Brecha*, 5 June 1987; Carlos María Gutiérrez, "Adentro y afuera." *Brecha*, 30 January 1987, p. 11.

[174] Cynthia Vich Florez, "Entrevista a Cristina Peri Rossi." *Scriptura* 8–9 (1992): 229–230, Universidad de Lérida; Cristina Peri Rossi, *Escritora del exilio*. Buenos Aires: Galerna, 1998; Rubén Svirsky and Guillermo Waksman, "La diversidad de los de afuera," *Brecha*, 13 February 1987, p. 12. Other well-known exiles were Fernando Ainsa and Angel Rama in France and Emir Rodríguez Monegal, who resided in the United States.

[175] Before June 1973, there were 60 to 70 Uruguayans in France. That number rose to 100 to 150 in early 1976, a number enlarged by a hundred co-nationals fleeing Argentina. Beyond the capital, minor groups of Uruguayans stayed in Marseilles, Lyon, and Toulouse. Eugenia Allier Montaño and Denis Merklen, "Milonga de estar lejos: Los que se fueron a Francia," in Silvia Dutrénit Bielous, Ed., *El Uruguay del exilio*. Montevideo: Trilce, 2006, pp. 345–346.

[176] Eduardo Esteva Gallicchio, "Libertad personal, seguridad individual y debido proceso en Uruguay." *Ius et Praxis*, 5, 1 (1999): 187–210.

last of the political prisoners were freed in Uruguay. In terms of the fourth tier contextualizing the political action of exiles, the activities of the *Secretariado Internacional de Juristas por la Amnistía en Uruguay* (SIJAU, or International Secretary for Amnesty in Uruguay), was particularly important. This organization, founded in 1976 by Uruguayan and French lawyers, applied international pressure to bring the Uruguayan government to release political prisoners, to obtain information on the disappeared, to restore political freedoms, and to allow the return of exiles. Their activities, which included the organization of academic and public colloquia in cooperation with international agencies and the coordination of missions of inquiry to Uruguay, produced great awareness to the political situation in that country.[177]

On the social front, the Uruguayans in France maintained between 1976 and 1978 a Uruguay House in Paris that served as a community focus for the entire network of exiles and other co-nationals. Uruguayans met there on a regular basis for social meetings with newcomers from the homeland; activities such as soccer, games, and *asados*; and, last but not least, to serve as a child care center.[178]

These trends were projected after the return to democracy. With democratization in 1985, months of euphoria accompanied the arrival of hundreds of exiles as visitors in Uruguay in order to assess the possibilities of return. However, in parallel, the national census of 1996 identified between 60,000 and 70,000 Uruguayans who emigrated between 1985 and 1996.[179] In 1997, on the contrary, for the first time a decrease in the emigration numbers was noticed, but it did not last long. According to a report by *Crisis Económicas*, between 1995 and 1999, 218,000 Uruguayans had left the country. In contrast to other nationals living in the United States, such as Guatemalans and Salvadorans, most Uruguayans did not send foreign remittances to their families back home, as many migrants either took their families abroad or disengaged themselves after leaving at a relatively early age. In addition, Uruguay, for lack of demand and means, did not take advantage of the skills and education the returnees had acquired abroad.[180]

The Exile Communities and the Centrality of the Fourth Tier

All exiles face individual constraints and openings as they are forced to shift their residences to a new place. The ways in which individual exiles face these limitations and make use of these opportunities are not only the result of

---

[177] Eugenia Allier Montaño and Denis Merklen, "Milonga de estar lejos," pp. 353–354.

[178] "Cinco años de actividad del Comité de Défense de Prisonniers Politiques en Uruguay." Casa de Uruguay-Francia, *Espacio*, no. 4, 5 December 1977, p. 18, IISG Amsterdam, Documents France folder 7.1. Later on, this center was replaced with the so-called Parrilla, which has remained active into the 2000s.

[179] Adela Pellegrino mentions these figures in a study devoted to an earlier period ("Informe sobre la migración internacional").

[180] Marcelo Pereira, "Portada: Bajón Uruguayo." *Brecha*, 18 August 2000, pp. 2–3.

personal skills and capital. They are also connected dialectically to the previous existence of a community of co-nationals and the possible constitution of a group of exiles playing a central role among the gamut of these co-nationals and vis-à-vis the home and the host countries.

In the period preceding the consolidation of state boundaries and national identities, exile played into a three-tiered structure, in which the translocated individuals and the communities of exiles were important in the definition of interregional politics, becoming political tools for both host and home countries and thus contributing to defining the boundaries of membership, loyalty, and political obligations.

Along with the consolidation of national borders and identities, a series of norms and agreements about diplomatic and political asylum were elaborated. This precocious trend was strengthened when the international arena turned to drafting regulations and legislation, which rapidly became the basis of a framework recognizing the rights of asylum. The triangular structure of political exile in early independent times shifted in connection with the transregional dynamics of Latin America, contributing both to the international awareness about the problem of exile and later on to the elaboration of new norms linked to international law and human rights.

A crucial factor affecting the capacity of the exiles to impinge on the global arena and indirectly affect the fate of the home country is thus the formation and centrality of the political exiles within the community of co-nationals. In relation to the expelling country, the range of possibilities varies between the formation of a community of exiles and the creation of a diaspora composed primarily of migrants. The formation of a community of exiles hinges on the emergence of a critical mass of individuals with a proactive attitude and focus on the home country. In the case of a diaspora community, the critical mass of individuals tends to be proactive economically vis-à-vis the host country.

There is nothing natural in the process of crystallization of these two types of communities of sojourners. Preconditions create a propensity toward either one. In the case of Uruguay, the recurrent economic crises of the model of development had already created a series of migration waves that later combined with military repression. However, those Uruguayans who escaped repression were unable to shift the center of power in their diaspora toward a politically proactive attitude that would increasingly become hegemonic among the sojourners. The impact of Uruguayans was limited because of this predominance of economic migrants, who had a different perspective than the politically proactive exiles. Still, Zelmar Michelini and other Uruguayan exiles perceptively understood the importance of promoting the discourse of human rights in the developing arenas of the international domain.

Chileans abroad further projected such a constant presence in the public spheres of the host countries and the global arena. They came from a political system with strong political parties that actively projected themselves into the host countries and international organizations. The military takeover in Chile did constitute a breakdown of the democratic constitutional tradition of the country and ended the first experiment that brought to power a Marxist–Socialist administration through the ballots. The clear-cut terms of the process of military takeover and the magnitude and harshness of repression transformed Chile into the *cause célèbre* of the Left and later of democratic forces in general. Chilean exiles were thus able to find resonance for their cause everywhere, both in Western democracies and in communist countries. Because the Chilean military rulers banned the political parties, alienating many Christian Democrats and members of other nonrevolutionary and center parties, they created a situation that transcended the divide of the Cold War and unwillingly became a *bête noire* in the East as well as in the West. The Chilean diaspora had a critical mass of politically proactive exiles that disseminated a strong moral image of their fight against the military dictatorship and Pinochet. The projection of the DINA's activities outside Chile to Latin America, the United States, and Europe and Operation Condor were ineffective, not in targeting political opponents but in silencing the opposition. Pinochet would soon have to face the political implications of this transnationalization of the war against the opposition, which damaged Chilean military rulers at the center of Western democracies. It is the combination of all these factors that explains how Chilean exiles had such an impact on the redefinition of international human rights and the struggle for the return of democracy. Politically, it seems that exile has been politically instrumental in the consolidation of united opposition fronts to dictatorships that affected the transnational arena and the internal realignment of political forces in the home countries. In the case of Chile, the reconstitution of political parties in exile and the configuration of solidarity networks with Chile abroad shaped the establishment of an alliance of 17 parties that finally defeated Pinochet's candidacy in the October 1988 plebiscite. There have been other cases of creation of united opposition fronts against dictatorships, such as the APE (*Acuerdo Paraguayo en el Exilio*, or Paraguayan Accord in Exile), established in 1979 to fight Stroessner's continued rule. In the 1980s, the APE managed to create some momentum for political unity among the Partido Revolucionario Febrerista, the Partido Liberal Radical Auténtico, (PLRA, or the Authentic Liberal Radical Party), the PDC, and the Movimiento Popular Colorado (MOPOCO, or the Red Popular Movement), the democratic wing of the ruling Colorado Party supporting Stroessner, which had seceded and fought the home dictator since 1959, five years after his access to power. The APE galvanized political forces demanding general amnesty, the return of exiles, and the derogation of repressive legislation. Yet, contrasting with the case of the Chilean exiles, the late emergence of the front both reflected the decade-long fragmentation of the Paraguayan community and indicated its only partial transnational impact.[181]

---

[181] Comité Ejecutivo Central, "Estatuto del Acuerdo Paraguayo en el Exilio (A.P.E.)," Suiza, Diciembre de 1981; Fernando Vera, "La situación política del Paraguay." Madrid: Fundación Pablo Iglesias, Jornadas por la democracia en el Paraguay –PSOE, ca. 1987. Archives of the IISG, Amsterdam.

The Argentinean communities were formed by waves of intellectuals, militants, and relatives who managed to create their own organizations of exile, active both in politics and communal solidarity. In Mexico, they acquired a critical mass of proactive exiles because of a specific constellation of circumstances that enabled their reception and occupational accommodation in relatively high positions from which they were on speaking terms with the local elites. While there, and in other host countries, exiles were able to establish links with networks of solidarity. The very nature of the Argentine political process and the centrality and divisions of Peronism projected an unclear image that reduced the attractiveness of the political platforms aimed at centralizing armed struggle in fighting dictatorship. On the other hand, it would take time for Argentinean exiles to work in the international arena. These individuals saw international solidarity as important but not decisive. Debates ensued that would divide the communities of exiles and eventually shift the center of the exile community to the discourse of human rights and the struggle against those who so blatantly violated such principles.

The Brazilian exiles, although important individually, did not manage to assume a strong voice as a community that was politically proactive in the fight against the military government in their home country. Although as individuals, many acquired prestige and a voice in their sphere of activity, as a community of exiles, their presence was feeble, partly because of the internal divisions but also because of a lack of political articulation in facing a military administration that claimed to be committed to national development, internal stability, and the eventual reconstruction of the democratic political game. The second wave of exiles, many of whom had supported the ideology and practice of armed struggle, clashed with the first wave that had arrived after 1964, making it difficult to construct a united front.

These distinctions are analytical. In practice, they were blurred on the ground according to a series of factors such as the political culture of the newcomers, the timing of their arrival, the previous organizational experience, and the social and educational capital of individual exiles.

The tiered model we advance identifies major factors explaining how different communities developed in such distinctive ways. Rather than implying that there is some intrinsic tendency that is due to their national character, we claim that the differences pointed out were due to the organizational format in which these communities had to put forward their plight as groups of individuals forced to leave their countries of origin. The first are the background factors of exile, such as the extent of incorporation of strata in politics and the organizational strength of parties, unions, and professional associations. These factors determined the extent to which the exiles had a capacity to reconstitute as a proactive political force while abroad. The second are the ways in which the exclusion of exiles from the public spheres and politics was operated. The relative magnitude and pace of repression determined the pace of arrival and the chances that a community of exiles would be set in a specific host country to welcome new waves of escapees. The third, and most crucial, are the background and measure of political commitment of the exiles themselves.

Finally, communities of exiles have varied space for political proactivism, depending on the attitude of the host government; the networks of solidarity on the part of international, transnational, and local political, social, and professional organizations; and the extent to which the theme of exile retains a prestigious presence in the public sphere. Diasporas may provide an environment and support for the exiles and their political activities. In the Cold War, political exile played into the polarization between East and West, Left and Right, Communism and Capitalism. This dichotomy created a situation in which some groups of persecuted individuals were granted the label of exiles while others were denied it, with all the consequences in terms of asylum, benefits, and possibilities to continue operating politically. In tandem, ideological polarization produced a situation in which expelling societies broadened the scope of repression, expanding it to cover liberals as well as other groups in the political center. Thus, whether in Cuba or under military rule in the Southern Cone, the scope of the 'enemy' became so wide that large groups were forced into exile, even if unconnected or not clearly connected to the so-called subversive activities because of a critical stance toward authoritarian rule.

The fourth tier of international organizations and transnational networks granted a wide projection to the plight of the exiles and a wider voice to their political activism. This global tier echoed in a more effective way the situation of the exiles, as part of the opposition to policies of human-right violations. It contributed to constraining the choices of the host repressive governments and forced them to redo their policies, at least by acknowledging they could no longer silence the voice of the opposition forces by expelling them beyond the borders of the state. The expelling states had to increasingly recognize that politics was, in fact, projected by the presence of the co-nationals abroad, turning exile into a less effective tool to close the vernacular political arena than it had been in previous waves of dictatorship. Attentive to the rising hegemony of the discourse of human rights, exiles managed to relate to that discourse and promote it in ways that connected their personal and political demands of democratization to a moral claim that could not be disregarded in the international arena.

7

Presidents in Exile

In this chapter, we analyze the specific case of presidential exile. The exile of incumbent and past presidents is quantitatively only the 'tip of the iceberg' of exile, but qualitatively its significance for the political systems of Latin America is major. In this part of the globe, heads of state have been central vectors of politics and often defined the patterns of authority, developmental models, limits of public spheres, and range of rights and constraints for entire nations.

Ibero-American political systems inherited from colonial times a tradition of executive predominance, while republicanism and a formal division of powers were adopted. In the 19th century, most independent states assumed a presidential form of government and formally endorsed some of the ideals of the French and North American revolutions as well as elitist Liberalism, much influenced by British thought. In practice, presidents enjoyed a status far above crisscrossing institutional controls, even though in certain cases heads of state accepted limits on their power and agreed to the constitutionalization of opposition rights, such as primarily in mid-19th-century Chile and somehow also in imperial Brazil.[1] In most cases, however, the U.S. practice of checks and balances, the French conception of separation of powers, and the British form of parliamentarian controls were constrained in practice. Far more important than constitutional provisions was, in practice, the president in his character as

---

[1] This is a topic of wide significance and debate, and we do not pretend to offer a comprehensive analysis of presidentialism here. We do not make any essentialist claim, being fully aware of the continuous fluctuations in the relative salience of executive power vis-à-vis other branches of government and political parties in all Latin-American countries, with peculiarities such as those indicated for Chile and Brazil. On the latter, see Julio Heise González, *150 años de evolución política institucional*. Santiago: Editorial Andrés Bello, 1989; Timothy Scully, *Rethinking the Center: Party Politics in Nineteenth and Twentieth Century Chile*. Stanford, CA: Stanford University Press, 1992; Richard Graham, *Patronage and Politics in Nineteenth Century Brazil*. Standford, CA: Stanford University Press, 1989.

Primer magistrado and *Jefe de Estado*, becoming in many cases supreme judge
and ultimate guide over public affairs and, in extreme cases, even over the lives
and fortunes of individual citizens. Presidential elections have been generally
far more decisive than parliamentarian, regional, or local elections.

While analyzing presidentialism, Bolivar Lamounier reviewed some of
the prerogatives that have reinforced presidential power in Latin America: a
"plebiscitarian aura" that weakens the effectiveness of the political party system; the "Caesaristic right" to issue provisional measures and use legislation of
emergency to pursue political goals; and the historical tendency of these countries to maintain, until recently, large state apparatuses that have often been
used as a tool of political maneuvering by presidents.[2] Similarly, José Murilo
de Carvalho builds on a historical analysis of Brazilian citizenship to draw
a rather pessimistic diagnostic of citizenship in an elitist–hierarchical polity.
According to him, the different path of access to civil, political, and social
rights that took place in Brazil – and in other Latin-American countries – has
created a series of traits that die hard. Among them: an excessive valorization
of executive power rather than a system of checks and balances; expectations of
state paternalism; politics oriented to entice the government to concede rights
rather than gain entitlements through citizen activism; impatience with the
slow functioning of democratic institutions; a corporatist vision of collective
interests; and, in tandem with low institutional trust, the proliferation of
clientelistic networks 'colonizing' the formal structure of the state, and, under
special circumstances, the emergence of populism led by charismatic leaders.[3]

In cases in which real power resided in the hands of military commanders,
juntas, or other elites, the latter took great care not to dismiss the figure of
the president. Actual power-holders felt the need to nominate designated presidents, even if the real decisions remained theirs. Illustrative are the cases of
Panama under Omar Torrijos and Manuel Noriega and of revolutionary Cuba
between 1959 and 1976. In October 1968, Arnulfo Arias Madrid was elected
for a third time as president of Panama. After 10 days in office, he was ousted by
the armed forces, and Colonel Omar Torrijos became the strongman of a country with a democratic facade and *de facto* dictatorship. Torrijos ruled without
assuming formal power. He first designated another army officer, Colonel José
María Pinilla Fábrega, as president and chair of a provisional junta. The latter's
disloyalty to Torrijos brought him to establish the Partido Revolucionario

---

[2] Bolivar Lamounier, "Brazil. The Hyper-Active Paralysis Syndrome," in Jorge Luis Domínguez
and Abraham Loventhal, Eds., *Constructing Democratic Governance: Latin America and the
Caribbean in the 1990s*. Baltimore, MD: Johns Hopkins University Press, 1996, pp. 185–186.
On 'democratic Caesarism,' see Maxwell A. Cameron, "Citizenship Deficits in Latin American
Democracy." Paper presented at the 2006 meeting of LASA, San Juan de Puerto Rico, 15–
18 March 2006. See also the analysis by Laurence Whitehead, "The Alternatives to 'Liberal
Democracy': A Latin American Perspective." *Political Studies*, 40 (1992): 146–159.

[3] José Murilo de Carvalho, *Cidadania no Brasil. O longo camino*. Sao Paulo: Civilização Brasileira,
2001. See also Mario Sznajder, "Il populismo in America Latina." *Ricerche di Storia Politica*, 7,
3 (2004): 347–366.

Democrático (PRD), whose candidates were subsequently elected as figurehead presidents of the country. Similarly, following Torrijos's death in an airplane accident in 1981, Colonel – later General – Manuel Antonio Noriega, who ruled Panama from 1983 onward, did not contemplate the abrogation of the presidential office and continued to designate and remove presidents until his arrest and deportation to the United States in 1989. Similarly, in Cuba after the 1959 revolution and for the next 17 years, the figure of the president was retained as separate from the revolutionary elite, who were the real power-holders. Osvaldo Dorticós Torrado fulfilled that role until Castro himself assumed the presidency in December 1976.

In Latin-American narrative too, the encompassing significance of the figure of the president was immortalized in different works such as *Yo el supremo* by Augusto Roa Bastos; on the origins of the Paraguayan state; and *La silla del águila*, by Carlos Fuentes, on Mexico.[4]

The practical and symbolic centrality of heads of state has not passed unnoticed by scholars working from various disciplinary perspectives, among which we may mention such works as Claudio Lomnitz's symbolic anthropological–historical analysis of the Mexican presidency, and the political–sociological seminal works by Guillermo O'Donnell, Scott Mainwaring, Matthew Shugart, Juan José Linz, Arturo Valenzuela, Arendt Lijphart, Carlos Waisman, and José Antonio Cheibub.[5]

Electoral procedure was a clear conditioning factor for presidential power and a source of continuous political strife. Despite the democratic profession of faith of political regimes in Latin America, the recurrence of dictatorship, civil wars, crisis of governance, and emergency legislation shaped irregularity as one of the major traits of presidential terms. The rule of institutionalized uncertainty encoded in electoral systems was often broken. Likewise, in Ibero-America, it was more difficult than in the United States to predict the form of conclusion of a presidential term. This created a paradoxical mixture of heads of state leaving office before the end of their terms or even very shortly after assuming power, along with others who stayed in power for long periods, either in continuous or serial ways, such as Porfirio Díaz in Mexico, Juan Vicente Gómez in Venezuela, Alfredo Stroessner in Paraguay, or Fidel Castro

---

4 Claudio Lomnitz, "Passion and Banality in Mexican History: The Presidential Persona," in Luis Roniger and Tamar Herzog, Eds., *The Collective and the Public in Latin America*. Brighton, UK: Sussex Academic Press, 2000; Augusto Antonio Roa Bastos, *Yo el supremo*. Buenos Aires: Siglo XXI, 1975; Claudio Fuentes, *La silla del águila*. Mexico: Alfaguara, 2003.

5 Guillermo O'Donnell, "Delegative Democracy." *Journal of Democracy*, 5, 1 (1994): 55–69; idem, "In Partial Defense of an Evanescent Paradigm." *Journal of Democracy*, 13, 2 (2002): 6–12; Scott Mainwaring and Matthew Shurgart, Eds., *Presidentialism and Democracy in Latin America*. Cambridge: Cambridge University Press, 1997; Juan José Linz and Arturo Valenzuela, *The Failure of Presidential Democracy: The Case of Latin America*. Baltimore, MD: Johns Hopkins University Press, 1994; Arendt Lijphart and Carlos Waisman, Eds., *Institutional Design in New Democracies: Eastern Europe and Latin America*. Boulder, CO: Westview, 1996; José Antonio Cheibub, *Presidentialism, Parliamentarism and Democracy*. New York: Cambridge University Press, 2007.

in Cuba. Returning to Panama, we see that its independent political history since 1903 has been dotted with unfinished terms and a long list of interim and designated presidents (constituting 23 out of 56 presidencies), despite the absence of military coups until 1968.

Assessing the impact of exile on the political life of heads of state reveals some basic characteristics of Latin-American politics. Exile could enhance the legitimacy and image of an ousted politician. In 1977, while in exile, João Goulart met President Carlos Andrés Pérez of Venezuela and complained to him that he was on the verge of despair from his hope of returning to Brazil, still under military rule after 13 years: "You should know better, Jango," Pérez said, "I spent years in exile and as you can see, now I am the President."[6]

What the Venezuelan president in the 1970s hinted at is that contrary to the belief of authoritarian nationalists that sending people into exile meant the elimination of political enemies, exile could operate differently, conferring a halo of legitimacy on the ousted politician. Indeed, often exile served as a springboard to higher positions in politics, as an interregnum for learning and reflection, and as a moratorium for political maturity. Furthermore, ostracism could certainly enhance the international networks and prestige of the exile back home. Exclusion from the domestic public spheres of the nation, painful and traumatic though it might be, could provide political resources to better confront the public game of power in the home country.

Many key political figures who shaped the destinies of Latin-American countries in recent and contemporary times experienced exile or expatriation, either before or after holding power, for different reasons and with different results. From Cuba's Fidel Castro to Brazil's Fernando Henrique Cardoso; from Haiti's Jean-Bertrand Aristide to Chile's Michelle Bachelet; from Ecuador's Abdala Bucaram to Mexico's Carlos Salinas de Gortari; from Ecuador's Jamil Mahuad to Paraguay's Raúl Alberto Cubas Grau; from Nicaragua's Anastasio Somoza Debayle to Ecuador's Lucio Gutiérrez; from Argentina's María Estela Martínez de Perón to Venezuela's Pedro Carmona; from Peru's Alberto Fujimori to Paraguay's Alfredo Stroessner; all of them have experienced exile.

Many exiles died outside their home country, among them some of the most well-known political figures of Latin-American countries. Death in exile is a testimony to the lack of capacity of the home countries to include the ousted individuals again during their lifetime and an open issue at the center of historical national narratives, always reverberating in connection with contemporary political issues and debate. This is why the return of the remains of those prominent public individuals who died while in exile has been a mechanism of reforming the body politics.

The Return of the Dead

Countries found it hard to address the political causes of exile in the framework of their historical narratives and collective memory. The projection of political

[6] Abelardo Jurema, *Exilio*. Paraiba: Acauá, 1978, p. 16.

actors beyond the boundaries of domestic collective life and public spheres has marked the collective identity of these states and societies with a denial of pluralism, lack of respect of human rights, and dearth of justice. In many cases, it will be a later generation that will have to address such ostracism and attempt to change the ground rules of politics and self-organization, so as to incorporate at least a measure of historical justice by including those who were forced out of the country. Later redress involved the return of remains but also was geared to historical reconstruction.

By advancing the return of their dead bodies for burial or organizing state funerals for their remains in a display of state equanimity and power, rulers and governments often promoted a reevaluation of the past and tied their own position of political legitimacy to a discourse of reconciliation and national unity. Thus, they often gained ascendancy over those in the opposition by claiming and showing themselves as the true representatives of the nation, welcoming to the homeland the dead bodies of those who, while alive, had been excluded through exile. Sometimes close to their death and sometimes many years afterwards, the return of the dead bodies acquired new political life, as analyzed by Katherine Vedery.[7] Their projection as part of national cults of heroes, surrounding the repatriation of their remains, was geared to politics of memory connected to current political events and interests. In situations of dissent, the repatriation of remains played a central role as a building block of reconciliation and attempts to encourage 'national unity' under the aegis of those currently in power.

An interesting case is that of Mexico under Porfirio Díaz's rule, as analyzed by Matthew Esposito. From 1877 to 1889, the government financed 16 such funerals, 8 of them with major state burials, only 2 of which were of Porfiristas. Díaz promoted burials for heroes of the Mexican independence, as well as for liberal leaders of the wars of Reform and the French intervention, who had once been ostracized. Particularly striking was the spectacular funeral of former President Sebastián Lerdo de Tejeda, deposed by Díaz and sent into exile in 1876. Lerdo died in New York in 1889, after 13 years of exile. Díaz had, in the meantime, married the eldest daughter of Manuel Romero Rubio, a leading Lerdista who had returned from exile and later served as Díaz's Minister of the Interior. The matrimony had cemented a political alliance between former adversaries. On the death of Lerdo de Tejeda, the family was approached by Romero Rubio, Lerdo's former ally and now Díaz's father-in-law, and gave its agreement to the repatriation of the remains to Mexico for a state burial, a move also supported by the United States. Lerdo's body was sent by train from New York to Mexico City and was honored along the journey through ceremonial acts that, organized on regional and local bases, helped to generate national enthusiasm and to serve as a mechanism of patriotic worship, linking state officials and regional elites to the political center that had instrumented the move. Porfirio Díaz used such major dramaturgical events – in which the

---

7 Katherine Verdery, *The Political Lives of Dead Bodies.* New York: Columbia University Press, 1999.

upper classes played a major ceremonial role but also in which the lower and marginal classes participated, albeit sometimes with their own funeral ceremonies or through acts of crowd misbehavior regulated by the political center – to gain adherents and consent to his rule.[8]

In Argentina, the remains of José de San Martín were brought back in 1880, at a moment in which Argentina was leaving behind factionalism and civil war. As the country was moving toward the consolidation of its political institutions, his remains had to be repatriated because, although he had been neither a head of state nor an active participant in internal politics, San Martín acquired the status of a founding father as liberator of Argentina and other South American countries. Whereas in life he had been a member of the *Logia Lautaro*, when repatriated, he was laid to rest in a chapel mausoleum in the National Catholic Cathedral, a further sign of national reconciliation.[9] Similarly, in April 1888, the Venezuelan government repatriated the remains of another founding father of the early independent period, José Antonio Páez, who had died in New York in 1873, during his fourth exile.[10] Among other renowned cases are those of the repatriated remains of Bernardo O'Higgins in Chile, Porfirio Díaz in Mexico, José Artigas in Uruguay, and Dom Pedro II and the Infanta Isabel in Brazil.

This trend of repatriation of remains and their symbolic projection in terms of a contemporary political agenda has been a recurrent feature of public affairs in Latin America since the 19th century and up to contemporary times, as revealed by the cases of Juan Manuel de Rosas in Argentina and Cipriano Castro in Venezuela. Bringing back the remains of Rosas was particularly controversial. Historians and politicians in Argentina wrangled over the interpretation of Rosas. Whereas the Liberals considered him a tyrant who suffocated early democracy, nationalists considered him a leading hero in the defense of the country's borders and resources against British and French imperialism. In 1989, President Carlos Menem brought back the remains of Rosas from the UK as part of a policy of symbolic reassertion of national reconciliation, which was to be combined with the pardons of the principal figures of the violent 1976–1983 era who were serving sentences in prison after being put on trial during the democratic administration of President Alfonsín. The measure also implied a connection to a historical figure emblematic in the defense of national sovereignty, at a moment in which Menem's administration was about to depart from the traditional protectionist policies of previous governments and embark on neoliberal policies of privatization,

[8] Matthew D. Esposito, "The Politics of Death: State Funerals as Rites of Reconciliation." *The Americas*, 62, 1 (2005): 65–94.

[9] Beatriz Celina Doallo, *El exilio del Libertador*. Buenos Aires: Instituto de Investigaciones Históricas Juan Manuel de Rosas, 1997, pp. 137–142.

[10] Another case is that of José María Vargas, who had experienced exile while serving as president in the 1830s and had left for the United States in 1853, dying a few months later in New York. His remains were repatriated to Caracas in 1877.

which would affect the public control of resources and assets by the political center.[11]

The Venezuelan case of repatriation of Cipriano Castro's remains, like the Argentine case, is tied to contemporary political strategies and symbolic redrafting of historical interpretation and historiographical debate. On 14 Feburary 2003, President Hugo Chávez presided over the relocation of the remains of President Castro into the National Pantheon in Caracas, on the same grounds where Simón Bolívar had been interred:

The Constitution grants this honor to illustrious Venezuelans by recommendation of the President or the agreement of two thirds of the states' governors [of the Venezuelan federation].... The Official Gazette indicates the reasons for this act: "Considering that the General led the Restoring Revolution that closed the historic cycle of warlord *caudillismo*, that restored national unity, that restored political stability, independence and security for the country, all honors of National Pantheon are granted to General Cipriano Castro."[12]

General Castro had ruled over Venezuela between 1899 and 1908. His administration was characterized by corruption, embezzlement, and repression. Castro had lived as a libertine, which eventually led to his departure in 1908 for Paris to seek medical treatment for syphillis. He left the government in the hands of his lieutenant and Vice-President Juan Vicente Gómez, who became a dictator and ruled Venezuela until 1935. In addition, Castro's government had defaulted on the international debt owed to European countries, resulting in a naval blockade by Great Britain, Italy, and Germany to pressure payments or face the foreign occupation of the country. In 1902, the United States intervened as part of President Theodore Roosevelt's decision to implement the Monroe Doctrine, preventing the European invasion and mediating in the transference of part of the collected custom monies to the creditors. The fact that Venezuela had faced an international imperialist intervention in the early 20th century could be seen at the root of Hugo Chávez's decision to honor Cipriano Castro, in a way that reasserts the fight for autonomy, albeit downplaying Castro's autocratic and whimsical ways of ruling Venezuela. Later generations wrangle with the image of previous waves of exile and may write historical analyses motivated by contemporary political concerns. As political figures develop a public career, they often search for legitimacy in the historical mirror and the collective memory of the nation. In this mutual impact of discursive strategies, power relations, and practice of citizenship, the great absentees or 'victims' of national politics – the exiles – have often played a central role.

---

[11] Jeffrey M. Shumway, "Sometimes Knowing How to Forget Is Also Having Memory: The Repatriation of Juan Manuel de Rosas and the Healing of Argentina," in Lyman L Johnson, Ed., *Death, Dismemberment and Memory: Body Politics in Latin America*. Albuquerque: University of New Mexico, 2004, pp. 105–140.

[12] "Cipriano Castro," available at http://efemeridesvenezolanas.com/html/castro.htm, accessed 18 June 2006.

Circumstances of Exile

It is important to stress that circumstances of both prepresidential and post-presidential exile are highly variable. Fernando Henrique Cardoso and Michelle Bachelet went into exile before becoming well-known political leaders. With the Brazilian coup of 1964, Cardoso moved to exile in Chile, where he worked at ILPES (CEPAL) and other institutions. In exile, he developed international networks through an academic career in Santiago de Chile, Buenos Aires, Mexico, and Paris, where he researched and taught at institutions of higher learning. Once back in Brazil with well-established academic credentials, he was reinstated at the University of São Paulo for several months in 1968 before being dispossessed of his political rights in April 1969. In the following decade, Cardoso moved increasingly into national politics, being elected to the federal senate in 1978 and reaching the presidency of the country for a first term in 1994.

The combination of academic work and politics projected through exile can be found also in the case of Ricardo Lagos, who in 1973 – after serving as Allende's ambassador to Moscow – became an exile. He had a Ph.D. from Duke University and in exile he served as secretary-general of the Latin American Faculty of Social Sciences (Facultad Latinoamericana de Ciencias Sociales, or FLACSO) in Buenos Aires and then as a professor of Latin American studies at the University of North Carolina, in addition to a consultancy with the United Nations Development Programmes (UNDP). Upon return to Chile in 1978, he worked for the UN Employment Regional Program for Latin America and the Caribbean (PREALC) and turned into one of the leaders of the opposition to Pinochet. He increasingly influenced the move of the Chilean Left to abandon Marxist positions in favor of Social Democratic views, which will allow the *Concertación* to become the pivotal political force of Chile in the transition to democracy and its consolidation.

His co-national and presidential successor, Michelle Bachelet, was the daughter of Chilean Air Force General Alberto Bachelet, who was arrested in the aftermath of Pinochet coup and died in prison in 1974, after refusing to leave Chile. Bachelet had been involved in the Socialist Youth Underground movement and was forced into exile with her mother in January 1975, after both had been arrested and tortured. After their release, they went into exile to Australia and East Germany. During her exile and on her return to Chile in 1979, her energies were initially focused on becoming and working as a physician. Only years later did she return to play an increasingly central role in the administration and politics. She served in the Lagos administration, first as Minister of Health (2000) and later as Minister of Defense (2002), the first female to serve in this position in Latin America. It is her success in this role, as she refrained from revenge and showed commitment to civil principles, that propelled her to a successful bid for the presidency of Chile, which she won in January 2006.

Very different are the cases of Carlos Salinas de Gortari, Alberto Fujimori, and Alfredo Stroessner, who chose the road of expatriation after serving as heads of state. Salinas escaped from Mexico to Ireland in 1995, after ending his presidency, fearing persecution by the Ernesto Zedillo administration th accused him of mismanagement of the economy that had led to the steep devaluation of the Mexican currency, triggering a crisis of unprecedented scope. Moreover, his brother and some of his closest staff were accused of implication in politically motivated criminal actions, primarily the assassination of José Francisco Ruiz Massieu, PRI secretary-general and Salinas' former brother-in-law. Fujimori's meteoric political career in Peru ended as he was about to start his third presidential term in the wake of a scandal involving his close associate and head of the National Intelligence Service (Servicio de Inteligencia Nacional, or SIN), Vladimiro Montesinos. In November 2000, Fujimori arrived unexpectedly in Japan after participating in an Asia–Pacific summit in Brunei. Three days later, he faxed his resignation to the Peruvian Congress, which opted to reject it and dismissed the president instead, on grounds of his being morally unfit to govern. Years later, as he left his Japanese refuge and tried in November 2005 to return to Peru and take part in the national elections, Fujimori was arrested in Chile. He was later freed on bail and requested to refrain from talking publicly on Peruvian politics while in Chile. The Supreme Court of Chile faced a Peruvian demand to have him extradited to stand trial on charges of corruption and human-rights violations. On 22 September 2007, the request was granted and the former president stood trial as he landed in Peru. Fujimori's eldest daughter, Keiko, as leader of the *Fujimorista* Alliance for the Future in Congress, organized a warm welcome for her father, in her own words "as a former president deserves." Keiko Fujimori has declared that if she is elected to the presidency in future elections, she will pardon her father.[13]

Even Alfredo Stroessner, one of the longest ruling heads of state in the Americas in the 20th century, who served as president of Paraguay for eight consecutive terms (1954–1989), ended his career as an exile in Brazil, where he died in 2006. An Argentine court issued an international warrant for his arrest on charges of human-rights violations committed under his aegis during Operation Condor in the 1970s and 1980s. Stroessner was also wanted by the Paraguayan courts on charges of disappearances of persons and other atrocious acts committed under his rule.

The Impact of Presidential Exile

The variation in the circumstances of presidential exile is enormous. In some cases, politicians and political activists grew into figures of national stature during their exile. In these cases, the popularity of the exiles was amplified in popular opinion, launching even expectations of a kind of Messianic return of the exiled leader. In others, exile and expatriation was the lot of presidents who fell from power. Sometimes exile had an expanding effect on future political careers. In others, it signaled the closure of political life and the beginning of

---

[13] "Fujimori's daughter faces criticism for saying she would pardon him if elected president," *Peruvian Times*, 10 June 2008, available at http://www.peruviantimes, accessed 15 June 2008.

·idents by Country and Number of Times in Exile

		Three Times	Four Times	Five Times	Six Times	Total
	8	5	0	0	0	0	13
..ia	24	7	1	0	0	0	32
Brazil	8	0	0	0	0	0	8
Chile	12	5	0	0	0	0	17
Colombia	10	3	0	0	0	0	13
Costa Rica	16	0	0	0	0	0	16
Cuba	10	2	1	0	0	0	13
Dominican Rep.	4	5	0	1	0	0	10
Ecuador	15	5	0	0	1	0	21
El Salvador	20	0	0	0	0	0	20
Guatemala	13	3	0	0	0	0	16
Haiti	11	5	1	0	0	0	17
Honduras	13	3	0	0	0	0	16
Mexico	24	3	1	0	0	0	28
Nicaragua	12	2	1	0	0	0	15
Panama	4	1	0	0	0	0	5
Paraguay	11	5	0	0	0	0	16
Peru	14	11	1	0	0	0	26
Uruguay	5	2	0	0	0	0	7
Venezuela	20	10	0	0	0	0	30
Total	254	77	6	1	1	0	339

judicial procedures in national or international courts. The conditions of exile and the possibility of return to public life and politics have been shaped by the interaction between the personal resilience and personality of the émigré, on the one hand and, on the other, the impact of the four-tiered structure of exile. Likewise, in some cases, former rulers and politicians had their movements constrained by the host governments, whereas in others the host countries provided a most propitious jumping board for access to power or a political comeback. Similarly, the international arena became less tolerant of former rulers if they were implicated in human-rights violations or in money laundering, reducing the room for political maneuvering of some of the exiled political leaders.

To test the magnitude and effects of exile for those who reached the highest positions of power in these political systems, we constructed a database of slightly more than 1,500 ruling terms since the early 19th century. With independence, most Latin-American countries adopted a presidential system, although there were a few cases of emperors and more frequent cases of a collective executive in the form of a ruling council or junta. Because we look at exile as a political phenomenon that affects heads of states, with symbolic and pragmatic implications, we included in the database all such cases, covering both the presidential positions as well as the heads of juntas and emperors. We analyzed postpresidential exile as well as prepresidential exile, the latter in order to assess the relationship between the experience of ostracism and the accession to power as heads of state.

Before we enter into the analysis, let us indicate the methodological decisions we adopted. The units of analysis are the terms served by heads of state, mostly presidents, regardless of the length in their exercise of power and taking into account all cases of exile, whether they occurred within a term or after it ended regularly or otherwise. Political actors serving as heads of state for more than one term were counted once for each of the administrations, unless otherwise indicated in the subsequent specific analyses. A measure of stability of a country was defined as the average duration of presidential terms across the years, expressed in months. We used this measure to adjust for 'baseline' differences between countries. All terms shorter than one week were omitted from the analyses. Prepresidential exile was counted once – before the first presidential term – whereas all other exiles were counted as 'postpresidential' exile.

The first finding is that as of early 2008, there were 339 cases of heads of states who experienced exile either before becoming presidents or following their mandate (Table 1). Table 2 shifts to presidential terms, which will be the unit of statistical analysis in the remainder of the chapter, except for Tables 3 and 4, which use the person as the unit of analysis. According to Table 2, there have been 435 cases of presidential terms preceded or followed by the exile of incumbents, out of them 158 cases of prepresidential exile and 277 cases of postpresidential exile.

To assess the relative salience of the phenomenon of such displacement, we suggest an index of exile representing the ratio between the number of exile cases following presidential terms and the number of presidential terms on a country-by-country basis. The index ranges from zero to one, with a larger number reflecting a greater extent of exile (see Table 2, third column). From the vantage point of the index, out of the 20 Latin-American countries examined, in more than a third of them – 7 out of 20 – the index is 0.25 or more. Leading the list are Peru (0.43), Venezuela (0.36), Bolivia (0.33), Cuba (0.32), Mexico (0.28), and Haiti and Ecuador (both with 0.27). Surprisingly, Costa Rica, a country considered contemporarily as a stronghold of democracy, follows with 0.22, closely followed by Guatemala (0.21). The midrange consists of a set of countries with an index of 0.17–0.12 of presidential exile: Paraguay, Argentina, El Salvador, Brazil, Honduras, Nicaragua, and the Dominican Republic. The countries with a lesser extent of presidential exile are Chile, Colombia, Uruguay, and Panama.[14]

In many cases, exile preceded access to presidential power. In 158 cases in the database, people reached the presidency for the first time after experiencing exile (being defined as 'prepresidential' exile). A notorious example is that of

---

[14] If we were to build an index based on the ratio between exiled presidents and the number of individuals who served as presidents, the results would have been higher. For instance, Venezuela would reach an index value of 0.66 instead of 0.36 and Mexico a value of 0.38 instead of 0.28.

TABLE 2. *Presidential Exile – Index of Exile, by Countries*

Country	Numbers of Post-presidential Exile[a]	Post-presidential Exile Index[b]	Numbers of Prepresidential Exiles	Pre-presidential Exile Index[c]	Stability Index[d] (Months)
Peru	24	0.43	15	0.35	36
Venezuela	25	0.36	15	0.33	30
Bolivia	28	0.33	13	0.20	27
Cuba	8	0.32	9	0.47	57
Mexico	26	0.28	7	0.11	24
Haití	17	0.27	7	0.13	39
Ecuador	23	0.27	7	0.11	25
Costa Rica	14	0.22	2	0.04	35
Guatemala	13	0.21	6	0.11	36
Paraguay	10	0.17	11	0.21	39
Argentina	9	0.16	9	0.17	37
El Salvador	16	0.15	4	0.05	23
Brazil	6	0.15	2	0.05	54
Honduras	12	0.13	7	0.10	24
Nicaragua	11	0.12	8	0.12	24
Dominican Republic	11	0.12	7	0.12	20
Chile	7	0.10	15	0.28	33
Colombia	7	0.10	9	0.15	33
Uruguay	7	0.09	2	0.04	30
Panama	3	0.06	3	0.07	26
Total	277		158		30

[a] Only terms with complete exile information and duration longer than one week are included.
[b] Proportion of presidents with any postpresidential exile.
[c] Proportion of presidents who experienced exile before their first presidency.
[d] Average effective term duration in months.

Mexican politician Benito Juárez, who became one of the most important public figures and symbols of the Mexican nation. Of humble Zapotec origins, Juárez was educated in a Franciscan seminary in Oaxaca and was destined to become a priest. Having studied Aquinas and other Catholic philosophers, he decided to go into law and became acquainted with the rationalist philosophers of the Enlightenment and their secular ideas. He soon entered politics. He started defending Indian rights at the municipal level in the 1830s, later to become a judge and ultimately governor of Oaxaca (1847–1852). When Antonio López de Santa Anna regained power in 1853, he drove Juárez into exile, together with such prominent figures as Melchor Ocampo and José Guadalupe Montenegro. After a short and penurious sojourn in Cuba, he moved to New Orleans. Because he did not have any money, he disguised himself as a sailor and mixed himself among the third- and fourth-class passengers. In the United States, he was discriminated against because of his skin color and lived in extreme

TABLE 3. *Number of Presidential Terms by Number of Times in Exile*

Number of Terms	Number of Times in Exile				Total
	0	1	2	>2	
One Term					
Frequency	455	177	51	0	683
Percentage	51.88	20.18	5.82	0.00	77.88
Row Percentage	66.62	25.92	7.47	0.00	
Column Percentage	84.42	70.24	65.38	0.00	
Two Terms or More					
Frequency	84	75	27	8	194
Percentage	9.58	8.55	3.08	0.91	22.12
Row Percentage	43.30	38.66	13.92	4.12	
Column Percentage	15.58	29.76	34.62	100.00	
Total	539	252	78	8	877
	61.46	28.73	8.89	0.91	100.00

poverty, working in a cigar factory. He lived in cheap houses and hostels and did not have the money to get medical treatment when he got sick with the 'black vomit' and yellow fever. Juárez nonetheless emerged as a key figure in the network of liberal émigrés, initially headed by Melchor Ocampo. He joined others in setting a revolutionary group aimed at overthrowing Santa Anna, who accused them of conspiracy. The morale of the exiles was low because of nostalgia, abatement, doubts; because of their financial situation and diseases. The situation turned even more critical when Santa Anna confiscated Ocampo's goods. In its attempt to darken the exiles' reputation, however,

TABLE 4. *Number of Presidential Terms by an Indicator of Prepresidential Exile*

Presidential Terms	Prepresidential Terms		Total
	No Exile	Exile	
One Term			
Frequency	532	110	642
Percentage	64.33	13.30	77.63
Row Percentage	82.87	17.13	
Column Percentage	79.52	69.62	
Two Terms or More			
Frequency	137	48	185
Percentage	16.57	5.80	22.37
Row Percentage	74.05	25.95	
Column Percentage	20.48	30.38	
Total	669	158	827
	80.89	19.11	100.00

Frequency missing = 50.

Santa Anna's government achieved the contrary effect, giving Juárez and his allies an acknowledgment and projecting their name in Mexico among many who never had heard about them. On his return to Mexico, Juárez assumed high positions such as that of president of the High Court of Justice. Following the vacancy of the presidency, he took the role of president of Mexico, fighting the conservatives and, later on, the French intervention that placed the Habsburg prince Maximillian in power. Juárez's image of public sacrifice and unrelenting fight for his ideals and defense of Mexican sovereignty were buttressed by exile, not only through his political activities but also in terms of his personal suffering and endurance.[15]

Exile did not hamper the chances of a politician to reach the presidency. Analysis indicates a strong association between the number of terms served and times in exile. For statistical analysis, a category of 'no exile' was added, assessing the association between the number of presidential terms and times in exile for all exiles (Table 3) and for prepresidential exiles in particular (Table 4). In both cases, the association was found to be highly significant. For all exiles, a chi-square test was highly significant ($p < 0.001$). In tracing the association between prepresidential exile and terms served, we found a clear association between being in exile before the first term and presidents who served more terms, with a chi-square test that is highly significant ($p = 0.005$).

In other words, there is a positive association between the times politicians spent in exile and the number of terms they served as presidents; exile before the first presidency seems to be an indicator of likelihood of serving in the presidency for more than one term. Even if this may hinge on political longevity, it indicates the weight of exile in political careers in Latin America. Among many such cases, we may cite the exile experience of José María Velasco Ibarra in Ecuador. Five-time President (1934–1935, 1944–1947, 1952–1956, 1960–1961, 1970–1972) Velasco Ibarra was an important populist and popular leader who was overthrown time and again by the military, experiencing many exiles and serial exiles. An outstanding speaker and essayist, author of philosophical, political, legal, and historical works, and an academic, in exile his figure gained stature as a leader seen popularly as suffering ostracism for the sake of his country. Following the defeat of Ecuador by Peru in 1941, he strongly advocated and influenced the resignation and forced exile of President Carlos Alberto Arroyo del Río and was able to return in 1944. Considered a 'messiah' by the people who took the streets by revolt, he assumed power by force and was soon elected formally to the presidency for a second term. This pattern of intermittent truncated presidencies and repeated exile periods was to be repeated three more times. In the case of Velasco Ibarra, as well as many others, such as Fernando Belaúnde Terry in Peru, Rómulo Betancourt in Venezuela, Carlos Ibáñez in Chile, and Víctor Paz Estenssoro and Hernán Siles Suazo in Bolivia, the experience of exile not only did not hamper the prospects of a new presidency but, on the contrary, seem to also

[15] Ralph Roeder, *Juárez y su México*. Mexico: Fondo de Cultura Económica, 1972; Charles Allen Smart, *Juárez*. Barcelona: Grijalbo, 1969; Jorge L. Tamayo, *Epistolario de Benito Juárez*. Mexico: Fondo de Cultura Económica, 1957.

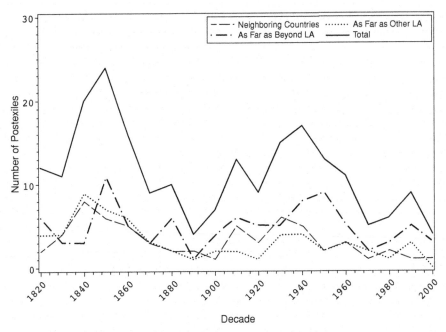

GRAPH I. Sites of postpresidential exile by geographical proximity.

have contributed to the national projection of the stature of the ostracized leaders.[16]

The exiles' selection of a host country is often decisive for their subsequent fate. Usually, a site of exile close to the home country in terms of language, cultural background, and relative proximity would be preferable with an eye on political activism, provided the host government has similar interests or is sympathetic to the cause of the exile. This decision is compounded by existing political networks, common ideological background, the political importance of the host country, and the extent and fear of persecution by the home rulers, which could bring exiled presidents to choose a country far away from home. Whereas João Goulart chose neighboring Uruguay as his main site of exile, Perón chose friendly and ideologically akin countries but most of them were more remote countries. Indeed, he moved beyond Stroessner's Paraguay to Pérez Jiménez's Venezuela, Guardia Navarro's Panama, finally relocating to Franco's Spain as site of exile.

When we move beyond the level of individual cases, systematic quantitative analysis reveals changes in the long-term patterns of relocation during the last 200 years. In assessing the selection of sites of presidential exile, we started from the descriptive level (Tables 5 and 6) and then included the effect of century, region, as well as the interaction term between the two, analyzing the logarithm of the number of postpresidential exiles (Table 7).

---

[16] Gobierno nacional de la República del Ecuador, "Historia constitucional," available at http://www.presidencia.gov.ec, accessed 29 July 2006.

TABLE 5. *Sites of Relocation of Postpresidential Exile*

Area	Cases	Percentage
Neighboring Countries	64	25.00
Other Latin American Countries	52	20.31
Beyond Latin America	62	24.22
Neighboring and Other LA Countries	11	4.30
Neighboring and Beyond LA	14	5.47
Other LA and Beyond LA	15	5.86
Neighboring, Other LA, and Beyond LA	6	2.34
Missing	32	12.50
All	256	100.00

TABLE 6. *Sites of Exile, According to Three Categories*

Region	Frequency	Percentage
1. Neighboring countries	62	29
2. At least one location in other Latin American countries	60	28
3. At least one site of exile is beyond Latin America	93	43

TABLE 7. *Results of a Repeated Measure Analysis for Sites of Postpresidential Exile by Region, Century, and Their Interaction*

Effect	Region	Estimate	Std Err	DF	t Value	Pr > |t|
Intercept		1.1750	0.1283	19	9.16	<0.0001
Century		−0.2864	0.1028	19	−2.78	0.0118
Region	Neighboring countries	−0.5509	0.2267	19	−2.43	0.0252
Region	As far as other LA	−0.5825	0.1781	19	−3.27	0.0040
Century × Region	Neighboring countries	0.3448	0.2258	19	1.53	0.1434
Century × Region	As far as other LA	0.4712	0.1970	19	2.39	0.0273

The transformation of analysis to a logarithm scale was required for satisfying the normality assumptions of the model. In the analysis, if an exile moved among several regions, she or he was assigned to the most remote area.

Repeated-measures analysis included six measurements for each state: three region categories by two centuries. The reference categories are the 20th century and the region category, 'beyond Latin America.' The results indicate significant interactions between centuries and regions. The mean number of exiles is lower significantly in the categories of 'neighboring' and 'as far as other Latin

American countries' in the 20th century as compared with the 19th century, whereas presidential exiles tend to relocate more to sites that are beyond Latin America in the 20th century as compared with the 19th century.

The estimates of Table 7 sum up as follows:

20th century, Beyond	Estimate = 1.1750, approx. 1.18
20th century, Neighbor	Estimate = 1.1750 − 0.55 = 0.63 (approx.)
20th century, LA	Estimate = 1.1750 − 0.5825 = 0.60
19th century, Beyond	Estimate = 1.1750 − 0.2864 = 0.89
19th century, Neighbor	Estimate = 1.1750 − 0.2864 + 0.3448 = 1.23
19th century, LA	Estimate = 1.1750 − 0.2864 + 0.4717 = 1.36

Thus, North America, Europe, and other locations beyond Latin America became increasingly relevant as choices for presidents forced to leave or choosing to take the road of expatriation after leaving power. The development of transportation and communication technologies, added to the strengthening of transnational networks and, in the 1970s, the process of democratization of the Iberian countries may have contributed to these results.

Timing, Duration, and Trends of Presidential Exile

The next set of findings refers to the timing of exile and the time spent in exile. Regardless of the way presidential terms ended in Latin America, an immense majority of cases of postpresidential exile – more than 85 percent in our database – have taken place within one year after the end of the term (see Table 8). Well-known examples are those of Juan Manuel de Rosas and Juan Domingo Perón in Argentina, Andrés de Santa Cruz and Hilarion Daza in Bolivia, Washington Luis Pereira de Souza and João Goulart in Brazil, Carlos Prío Socorrás and Fulgencio Batista in Cuba, Maximiliano Hernández Martínez and Carlos Humberto Romero Mena in El Salvador, Jacobo Arbenz and Carlos Herrera y Luna in Guatemala, Jean-Claude Duvalier and Jean-Bertrand Aristide in Haiti, Pedro Varela and Manuel Oribe in Uruguay, and Rómulo Gallegos and Marcos Pérez Jiménez in Venezuela, among many others.

A review of the time spent in exile by individuals who eventually became presidents in Latin-American countries shows that the largest set is that of those who were exiled for periods of 1 to 5 years, followed by those who spent between 5 and 10 years. A chi-square test for the categorized 'duration' variable

TABLE 8. *Duration from End of Presidential Term to Exile*

Time	Frequency	Percentage
Up to 1 year	138	85.71
1–5 years	18	11.18
>5–10 years	3	1.86
>20 years	2	1.24

[handwritten margin note: Lack of tolerance for opposition]

TABLE 9. *Length of Prepresidential and Postpresidential Exile*

Length	Pre-exile		Postexile		First Postexile		All	
	N	%	N	%	N	%	N	%
Up to 1 year	12	9	13	6	12	6	25	7
1–5 years	73	54	97	44	87	43	170	48
>5–10 years	33	25	60	27	54	27	93	26
>10–20 years	9	7	38	17	35	17	47	13
>20 years	7	5	14	6	13	7	21	6
Total	134	100	222	100	201	100	356	100

(Table 9) indicates significant association between duration and whether the exile was before or after the first presidential term ($p < 0.001$). A t-test for the continuous variable 'duration' also indicates significant differences. The t-test was carried out in a log scale to comply with the normality assumption. The number of exiles in this table does not include those cases of presidential exile of unknown duration. The mean difference (1st post–pre) for the log (duration) is 0.1597 (std = 0.4801).

The exile periods following presidential rule were, on average, longer than the exile periods that preceded the exile's reaching presidential power. The comparatively longer time spent as a postpresidential exile may have been related to the clientelistic and personalistic character of Latin-American political systems, in which networks formed around the figures of acting presidents have been salient, to the extent that opposition leaders have tried to weaken them by expelling the leaders beyond the borders of the country. In this sense, often, acting presidents ousted from power shortly found themselves on the way to exile, secluded from the domestic public arena, hopefully to hamper their reconfiguration of political networks and diminish their capacity to regain power in the future. Exiles seem to regain presidential power more often in the year after their return or in the next five years (Tables 10, 11, and 12).

As we differentiate the extent of exile by decades, we find that certain periods witnessed more exile than others. After a country gained independence, the number of exiles increased until reaching a peak in the 1850s, descending

TABLE 10. *Time from Prepresidential Exile to Presidency*

Time	N	%
Up to 1 year	26	18.98
1–5 years	32	23.36
>5–10 years	29	21.16
>10–20 years	24	17.52
>20 years	26	18.98
Total	137	100.00

TABLE 11. *Time from Postpresidential Exile to Presidency*

Time	Frequency	Percentage
Up to 1 year	20	46.51
1–5 years	17	39.53
>5–10 years	2	4.65
>10–20 years	4	9.30

rapidly to a nadir in the 1890s. The period between 1870 and 1930 is a period of comparative decline in exile, with two minor upsurges in the 1880s and 1910s. Starting in 1930, exile increased once again, a trend that continued until the end of the 1960s, albeit not reaching the levels of postindependence. The decades of the 1970s and 1980s – in which military dictatorships implied a lack of presidential turnover – represent another nadir (despite the fact that this period produced waves of political exile of individuals active in politics), with a new rise in the 1990s (see Graph 2).

On a continental level of analysis, we do not find a simple correlation between authoritarianism and presidential exile and between democracy and lack of presidential exile. In parallel, it seems that exile seems to drop under two sets of circumstances. One, when there is stable authoritarian rule accompanied by a measure of economic prosperity, as during 1870–1930, a period of economic insertion in the international division of labor. The only exception is in the 1910s, because of the political destabilization of Mexico during the Revolution. The second set of circumstances occurred in the 1970s and 1980s, when most of Latin America was under authoritarian and/or military rule, and despite massive repression and human-rights violations, which generated huge waves of exiles and refugees fleeing these countries, there was a drop in the exile of former presidents.

A review of exile in long-term rates confirms these trends. Exile has been a constant presence from the early 19th century to the early 21st century. Overall, as we compare the 19th-century rates of postpresidential exile with the 20th-century levels, we do not see a significant change, despite the higher institutionalization of the political systems and of the presidential role. Up to the late 20th century and early 21st century, presidents have fled their countries

TABLE 12. *Time to Presidency Since Prepresidential and Postpresidential Exile*

Together	Frequency	Percentage
Up to 1 year	46	25.70
1–5 years	48	26.82
>5–10 years	31	17.32
>10–20 years	28	15.64
>20 years	26	14.53

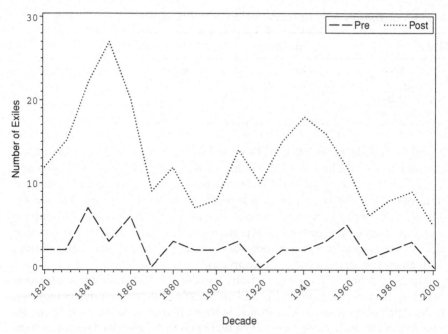

GRAPH 2. Presidential exile – a long-run view.

or have been exiled, even under democracy. Among them are Alfredo Stroessner and Raúl Alberto Cubas Grau leaving Paraguay; Jean-Bertrand Aristide fleeing Haiti; Alberto Fujimori, self-exiled from Peru; Abdala Bucaram Ortiz, Jamil Mahuad, and Lucio Gutiérrez leaving Ecuador; and Carlos Salinas de Gortari, expatriating himself from Mexico.

A quantitative analysis of postpresidential exile comparing the 19th and 20th centuries reinforces this observation. As can be seen in Table 13, with the 20th century as reference, the raw/crude mean difference between the number of postpresidential exiles in the 20th century and in the 19th century is −7.3 (std = 2.9). A repeated-measures analysis similar to the previous analysis indicates significant century effect ($p = 0.02$) as well as significant interaction between century (c) and the stability measure (x, mean term duration, $p = 0.02$).

The estimated model is given by

$$y = 6.20 + 7.26c + 0.0044x - 0.22xc.$$

The fact that the interaction is significant means that the association between postpresidential exiles and the stability measure is different in the two centuries. There is a level as well as slope difference. Plot 1 shows a clear difference in the association between the number of cases of postpresidential exile and their average term duration in the 19th and 20th centuries. In the 19th century, shorter presidencies are associated with a higher number of

TABLE 13. *Results of a Repeated Measure Analysis for Postpresidential Exile by Century, Stability, and Their Interaction*

Effect	Estimate	Standard Error	DF	*t* Value	Pr > |t|
Intercept	6.1692	3.0591	18	2.02	0.0589
Century	7.2599	2.9316	18	2.48	0.0234
Stability Index	0.0040	0.0902	18	0.04	0.9650
Stability Index × Century	−0.2246	0.0865	18	−2.60	0.0182

postpresidential exile and longer terms are associated with a lower number of exiles. In the 20th century, the average duration of terms is not associated with the number of cases of postpresidential exile. We interpret these findings as indicating the internalization of political exile to the point at which, in the 20th century, even formally democratic systems have produced postpresidential exile (see Plot 1).

An analysis by countries and centuries in Graph 3 indicates striking differences between countries in the extent of postpresidential exile, reinforcing what we presented in Table 2. It identifies a continuous presence of postpresidential exiles along the 19th and 20th centuries, with six countries exhibiting more than 13 cases of exile: Bolivia (26), Venezuela (25), Mexico (24), Peru (24), Ecuador (20), and Haiti (13). When the number of cases are differentiated by their occurrence in the 19th and 20th centuries, two subsets of countries clearly

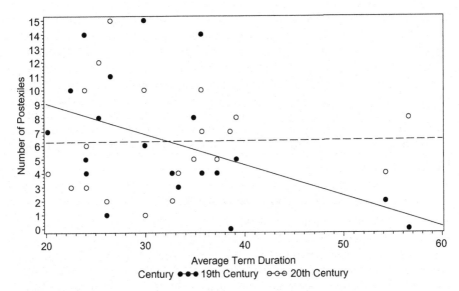

Regression Equation:
n_post (century: 19th century) = 13.42912 - 0.220534 ‡ oy_term_dur_tr 1w
n post (century: 20th century) = 6.169191 + 0.004018 oy term dur tr 1w

PLOT 1. Association Between Number of Postpresidential Exiles and Century.

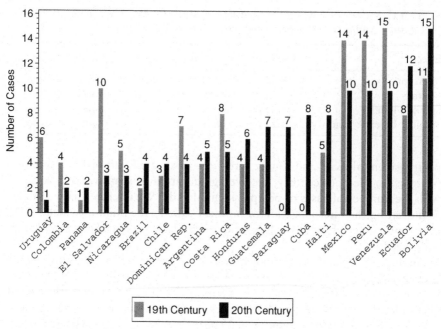

GRAPH 3. Postpresidential Exile by Countries and Centuries (sorted by 20th-century frequencies).

emerge. The subset of Venezuela, Mexico, and Peru – which evince a larger number of presidents exiled in the 19th century – is also shared on a smaller scale by five other countries (i.e., El Salvador, Costa Rica, Dominican Republic, Uruguay, and Colombia). The second subset, led by Bolivia, Ecuador, and Haiti and shared by eight other countries, has a larger number of postpresidential exile in the 20th century. Also noted is the difference between countries such as Uruguay, El Salvador, and Colombia – in which the incidence of postpresidential exile drops significantly in the 20th century – and countries such as the Dominican Republic and Costa Rica, for which the same tendency is less pronounced.

Exile and Expatriation, Expulsion and Reception

The term *exile* includes both presidents forced to abandon their countries and heads of state leaving voluntarily. Hereafter, we refer to the former as exile and define the latter as expatriation. To a large extent, presidential expatriation has been lower than forced presidential exile. Graph 4 reflects this general trend, with the cases of Chile, Argentina, and Mexico exhibiting a rate of expatriation of slightly more than 40 percent out of the total number of former presidents who left their countries for political reasons. Moreover, more than 40 percent of all cases of voluntary postpresidential exile are concentrated in Mexico,

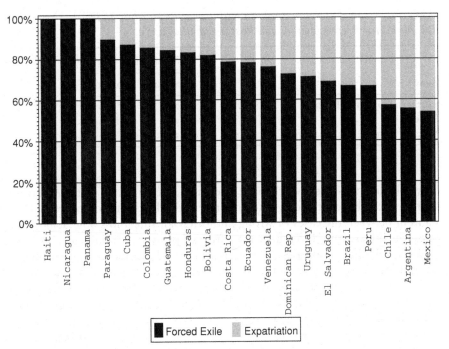

GRAPH 4. Postpresidential Exile and Expatriation by Country.

Peru, and Venezuela, with Mexico alone providing 17 percent of all postpresidential expatriation.

The cases of Paraguay, Brazil, and Chile deserve separate consideration. During the entire 19th century – with the exception of the case of Brazilian Emperor Pedro II in 1889 – these countries did not experience forced exile of heads of state, and almost no expatriation following their holding of the reigns of power. These countries lived under long-term stable rulers. In the case of Brazil, there was imperial continuity, and although in the 1830s and 1840s the country witnessed some regional revolts, they did not affect the central rule. In Paraguay, the succession of strong presidents after 1811 – José Gaspar Rodríguez de Francia, Carlos Antonio López, and Francisco Solano López – and the subsequent rule of the Colorado Party between 1870 and 1904 created a constellation of power that made exile of presidents superfluous. In Chile, after the exile of Bernardo O'Higgins and Ramón Freire in the 1820s, the stabilization of the country according to the constitutional model of Diego Portales started a long period of stable rule, again leading to the sidelining of presidential exile. In Argentina, after the fall and exile of Rosas, the combined effects of institutionalization and economic prosperity nullified forced presidential exile until the 1930s. Other countries with lack of forced presidential exile are Uruguay since 1880; the Dominican Republic for almost the entire 20th century, with the exception of Juan Bosch, who was deposed and exiled in 1963; Mexico after 1930; and Costa Rica after the 1950s. We infer that weak democracies

TABLE 14. *Mean Difference Between Number of Expulsions and Receptions for Prepresidential and Postpresidential Exile*

Zone	N	Mean Difference	
		Pre-exile	Postexile
Southern Cone and Brazil	5	2.0	5.0
Andes	3	−3.3	−10.0
Mexico, Central America, and Caribbean	12	−2.9	−7.1

or weak dictatorships, which have been the rule in many Latin-American countries, can be identified as sending former presidents into forced exile. They stand in between the cases of strong authoritarian rule and stable democratic rule, which were found to reduce the extent of postpresidential exile.

We checked the countries of reception of exiled presidents in Latin America and looked at the association between host countries and the number of their own heads of state expelled. We ran regression analyses of the difference between the number of expulsions and number of receptions, after aggregating countries into three broad geographic categories – Andean countries; Mexico, Central America, and the Caribbean; and the Southern Cone and Brazil – and the stability measure, which revealed no significant association. Table 14 summarizes the data. It seems that the outcome here is associated with the covariate number of exiled terms. A regression model adjusting for the stability index indicated a p-value of 0.10, with the difference decreasing (slope −0.18) as the percentage of prepresidential exiles out of first presidential terms increased. The association between the difference between expulsion and reception of postpresidential terms and geographical categories proved to be of only borderline significance of geographical zones ($p = 0.0965$). Only the model of the difference on the percentage of exiled terms out of all terms indicates high significance ($p < 0.001$), with a slope estimated as −0.69.

Country-by-country graphs (Graphs 5 and 6) show the trends in both expulsion and reception of prepresidential and postpresidential exiles. We may start by reviewing prepresidential relocation in exile; that is the cases of individuals who would become heads of state after experiencing exile before their access to power. The countries with the largest number of such political actors receiving shelter are Argentina (24), Chile (18), Peru (15), and Mexico (13). In the cases of Argentina, Chile, and Peru, these places of exile were selected by the individuals on the run due to their proximity to the home country, from where they could reorganize themselves and launch political initiatives. In the case of Mexico, the picture is more varied: out of the 13 exiled politicians, 4 came from Cuba and 3 from Guatemala, but the others came from Colombia, Costa Rica, El Salvador, Haiti, Nicaragua, and Peru.

As we shift to postpresidential exile, a review of the database indicates that the majority of the presidents settling in Latin-American countries arrived from

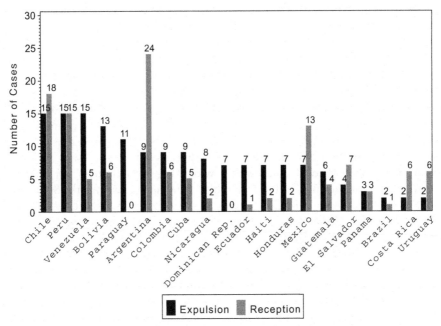

GRAPH 5. Expulsion and Reception of Prepresidential Exile by Countries.

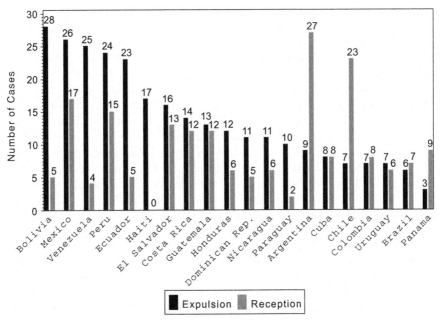

GRAPH 6. Expulsion and Reception of Postpresidential Exile by Countries.

neighboring states. For instance, in Argentina, out of the 27 cases of registered former presidents in exile, 4 came from Bolivia, 1 from Brazil, 3 from Chile, 8 from Paraguay, and 3 from Uruguay. The remaining nine times of exiled presidents choosing Argentina were from Ecuador and Peru. Similarly, out of the 23 postpresidential exiles finding shelter in Chile, 10 came from Bolivia, 7 from Peru, 1 of Venezuela, and 1 from Argentina. Out of the remaining four, three came from Ecuador. Guatemala received exiled presidents from Central America, the Caribbean area, and Colombia. Peru was host country primarily to presidents from the Andean area. The exception to the rule of exiled presidents finding a host country close to the expelling home country applies to Mexico. Those arriving in Mexico came from a wide range of countries not only in Central America and the Caribbean but also from as far away as the Southern Cone. The self-image of Mexico as a country of asylum, especially following the adoption of its postrevolutionary ethos, clearly affected such choices, attracting a wide range of heads of state: in descending order, former presidents from Guatemala – the only Latin-American country with a land border with Mexico – (5), Nicaragua (3), Cuba (2), Costa Rica (1), Colombia (1), Venezuela (1), Paraguay (1), Bolivia (1), Panama (1), and Argentina (1).

Argentina, Chile, and Mexico have been the countries most likely to serve as host settings for former heads of state in exile, whereas Haiti, Paraguay, and Venezuela have been the less likely countries of shelter in Latin America. Santiago Mariño, who took power by force in Venezuela in 1835, was deposed in 1836 and expelled from the country into a long exile that took him, among other lands, to Haiti, the single case of a former head of state moving to that country.[17] Especially in the case of Venezuela, this finding is surprising, because Venezuela hosted many exiles, although apparently was not a chosen place for heads of states in Latin America. The three atypical cases are those of Antonio López de Santa Anna, Juan Domingo Perón, and Jean-Bertrand Aristide. The leader of early Mexican independent life, Antonio de Padua María Severino López de Santa Anna y Pérez de Lebrón (1794–1876) was in and out of power in Mexico between 1833 and 1855, spending close to 336 months in intermittent exile, staying, among other places, for two years in Venezuela. Another unlikely locale of exile was Paraguay, where only Perón and Anastasio Somoza found shelter under the protective shield of Stroessner. These former presidents could rely on the heads of state carrying anti-Communist policies such as Stroessner or Pérez Jiménez in Venezuela and Trujillo in the Dominican Republic. The shelter provided by the authoritarian rulers could not save the exiles from attempts against their lives. In the case of Perón, it was the leadership of the armed forces in Argentina that attempted to assassinate him after he relocated to exile in Caracas in 1956, whereas in the other case, it was Enrique Gorriarán Merlo

[17] Santiago Mariño's exile took him to Curaçao, Jamaica, Haiti, and finally to Colombia, only to return to Venezuela in 1848. On his return, he became head of the army under President Tadeo Monagas, so as to be able to confront General José Antonio Páez, his former leader and also president of Venezuela.

of the Argentinean Trotskyist group ERP who succeeded in 1980, assassinating the exiled Nicaraguan dictator Anastasio Somoza Debayle in his Paraguayan exile.

Comparing prepresidential exile with postpresidential exile, we can identify two basic patterns. In most cases, there are many more instances of postpresidential exile than prepresidential exile. This set of countries includes Bolivia, Mexico (especially in the 19th century), Venezuela, Peru, Ecuador, Haiti, El Salvador, Costa Rica, Guatemala, Nicaragua, Honduras, Uruguay, and Brazil. We interpret this pattern as reflecting the incapacity of the political system to accommodate former presidents in the public arena. The second pattern, which includes only Chile, the Dominican Republic, Cuba, Paraguay, Argentina, and Colombia, is predicated on a larger number of prepresidential cases of exile in comparison with the number of postpresidential cases. Compared with the previous set, these countries show higher tolerance toward previous heads of state remaining in their public arena after leaving office. Yet, the political system retained at times some strong authoritarian features, prompting the displacement of politicians before their access to the presidency.

Contrasting with the positive democratic image that Venezuela acquired since its return to democratic rule in 1958, this country stands out in terms of the extent to which heads of state have taken the road of exile, during both dictatorial and democratic periods. Since independence, out of 72 terms – some of which were extremely short, especially in the days of military coups in the 19th century and some of which were extremely long, such as that of Juan Vicente Gómez (1908–1935) – 27 presidents spent time in exile, with 21 of them spending an accumulative time of more than five years in exile. Venezuela lived through long periods of power struggle and periods of dictatorship, reaching long-term democracy in 1958. Internalized as a common practice in the 19th century, postpresidential exile remained also valid in the changed framework of democracy. Whereas in the authoritarian and/or unstable periods, exile was a direct result of power struggles, generally violent, in the democratic period it followed accusations of corruption processed through the court system. Still, even when the heads of state were brought to trial on corruption charges, such as Marcos Pérez Jiménez, Carlos Andres Pérez, Raúl Leoni, and Jaime Lusinchi, they found it difficult to remain in Venezuela and moved to exile after their sentence and the conclusion of the time in prison or under house arrest. Paradigmatic of the inability of democratic rule in Venezuela to open the public spheres instead of excluding leading opponents perceived as dangerous is the case of Marcos Pérez Jiménez. A member of the military junta presided over by Carlos Delgado Chalbaud (1948–1952) and later military president following the annulment of the 1952 elections, Pérez Jiménez was deposed by a general uprising and riots in January 1958. He then moved to the United States, a country that had supported him and awarded him the Legion of Merit in the past. In 1963, the Venezuelan democratic government obtained his extradition from the United States to face charges of corruption and embezzlement of hundreds of millions of dollars. He spent five years in prison and, following his release, he left Venezuela for exile in Spain. His election, in absentia, to the Venezuelan Senate in 1968 was annulled by the Supreme Court on technical grounds. In 1973, his presidential candidacy was again nullified by a Constitutional amendment that proscribed him politically, thus signaling the end of his political career. Carlos Andrés Pérez, twice president of Venezuela (i.e., 1974–1979 and 1989–1993) ended his second term abruptly after charges of misappropriation of public funds were brought against him in the Supreme Court and he was impeached by the Senate. After two years and four months under domiciliary arrest, he left for Santo Domingo and later for Miami and New York, and has stayed abroad since then. This high rate of presidential exile, which was paralleled by the exile of many rank-and-file political actors, has been a mark of the Venezuelan state since the 19th century, with a central component of institutionalized exclusion. Under formal democracy, the profound changes that occurred since 1958 did not eradicate the deeply instilled tradition of exclusion from the political system. With the decline in the threat of authoritarian military coups, the political pact of the Fourth Republic (1958–1998) enabled the growing colonization of state agencies and positions, according to clientelistic considerations. In this scheme, membership in or loyalty to AD or COPEI was considered a requisite for appointment to the judiciary, senior levels of the armed forces, posts within the electoral administration, and promotion in key sectors such as higher education. In a recent work, Julia Buxton analyzes the lines of institutional continuity, which we found have shaped a tradition of exclusion reflected in the wide recurrence of imprisonment and ostracism of political oppositions:

While critics argued that the approach followed by the . . . Chávez government to achieve its Bolivarian revolution was authoritarian in nature, this masked parallels between the so-called Fourth Republic and the Fifth Republic installed by the Chávez administration. Rather than undermining an established democracy, Chavismo was characterized by continuity with the illiberal Punto Fijo state rather than change. The distinction between the two was determined by access. The Fourth Republic excluded the radical left and the poor. The Fifth Republic [of Chávez] excluded the politicians and beneficiaries of the Fourth Republic. Both relied on the politicization of the state to maintain authority and both were hegemonic projects, which denied the voice of opponents on the basis that this was contrary to the national interest. Crucial to the development of this tendency in both regimes was the initial fear of revanchist actions by supporters of the preceding regime.[18]

At the other extreme end of the scale, we find Colombia, a country with a contemporary image of violence, which generated a huge wave of more than 300,000 dead and fugitives during the decade of La Violencia, but which overall generated comparatively low levels of presidential exile. Out of 60 presidencies, only five heads of state spent an accumulative period of more than five years in exile, four of them in the 19th century (i.e., José María Obando, José María

[18] Julia Buxton, "Venezuela's Contemporary Political Crisis in Historical Context." *Bulletin of Latin American Research*, 24, 3 (2005): 328–347, quote from p. 345.

Melo, Pedro Nelo Spina, and Mariano Ospina Rodríguez) and only one (i.e., Alfonso López Michelsen) in the 20th century. Since 1952–1953, no political figures who were or would be presidents of Colombia went into exile. The last to flee into exile were Carlos Lleras Restrepo and Alfonso López Michelsen, who fled because of the attacks on liberals under the Gómez administration in 1952, and Laureano Gómez who left for exile at the beginning of the dictatorship of Rojas Pinilla (1953–1957). The consociational arrangements of power sharing reached in 1956–1957 by Laureano Gómez in exile and Alberto Lleras Camargo would imply a radical change in the patterns of political turnover in Colombia, thus obviating the political use of exile.

The recurrence and diversity of cases of presidential exile and expatriation in independent Latin-American countries show the complexities of its study from a comparative perspective. By combining quantitative and qualitative analysis, we have evaluated the weight of presidential exile on a continental basis through the vantage points of periods, country-by-country differentiation, and categorization of the diverse types of exile. Analysis has revealed the dynamic character and changing scope of exile while attesting to the ubiquity of the phenomenon throughout the two first centuries of independent Latin-American states. Institutional exclusion has been a recurrent experience for rising politicians and presidents. Exile became a recurrent mechanism of political exclusion and power control, applied by political figures to solidify their position and to squelch dissent by force or the threat of force. Presidents and future incumbents have suffered ostracism as the result of the limited and exclusionary character of most Latin-American politics, regardless of formal provisions. Located at the highest echelons of power, many of these individuals nonetheless went through exile for engaging in politics, like hundreds of thousands of other citizens displaced from their home societies in Latin America. The macrocomparative perspective followed here enabled tracing this collective experience beneath the individual lot of so many heads of state who experienced political exile.

8

Is Return the End of Exile?

This final chapter is programmatic rather than conclusive. At its core is a tentative assessment of how exile had an impact on the lives of thousands and the question of whether return means the end of exile, an issue that is multidimensional and open to interpretation. Here, we touch on some of its personal and collective dimensions, examining the multiple effects of exile on the lives of individuals and on the home countries, especially as changes of government and democratization in recent decades created conditions for the return of hundreds of thousands of individuals who had fled abroad.

Living abroad and interacting with host societies, exiles experienced significant personal changes and ideological shifts in the way they conceived issues such as political activism, gender, race, ethnicity, and national unity. With the crystallization of new perspectives, the experience of exile affected political and social processes in the home countries, especially as part of the communities of exiles' attempted return and home countries and international organizations supported the move. Some of these effects and impacts of prospective and actual return are presented hereafter, opening issues that will constitute the basis of future research.

In parallel, as we review these aspects, we claim that democratization cannot close the book on either the effects of exile or on the possibility of new cases of exile. Although democracy is substantially more inclusive and allows political dissent and does not tend to generate massive waves of exile as those experienced under authoritarian rule, it still does not eliminate the occurrence of current and future exile and cannot undo all the evils of past exile. And, although the transformed international setting does constrain the former use of exile by home governments, new forms of ostracism have emerged following recent political transformations in some Latin American countries.

The Impact of Exile

Displacement is often hard. Working conditions do not usually meet the professional and occupational experiences of most exiles; there are financial insecurity and psychological hardships; relationships disarticulate under the pressures of new environments, as shown by the typically steep rate of divorce in exile communities. For many, it may be hard to find a new purpose in life. Political involvement for the cause of the home country can ameliorate the feelings of estrangement by creating networks of solidarity, but even such activity cannot fully overcome the sense of alienation that often is the lot of the displaced. Often, exiles were confronted by host societies reminding them that they were strangers unable to understand domestic realities and, therefore, they were precluded from attempting to influence local politics and public spheres. This dynamic has been aptly portrayed by Elsa Triolet, the wife of poet Louis Aragon, reflecting on her exile in France:

All people who find themselves away from their place of origin are always suspect to somebody – or everybody. . . . It is really the existence of a poor relation, forced into humility, into a marginal life and deep shame – someone who is reduced to sleep in a camp-bed in the corridor, trying not to disturb his hosts, adapting himself to their habits, eating at their usual mealtimes, partaking of their tastes and interests, in order not to upset the routine of their days and nights.[1]

The feeling of being a stranger was felt even as exiles crossed the borders of 'sister' Latin-American countries. The reader may recall the case of the early 19th-century émigrés from Argentina and Uruguay who arrived in Portalesian Chile, fleeing their home countries and attracted by Chile's political stability and economic openings, analyzed in Chapter 3. Some of them used their competitive cultural advantage to obtain positions in the host country's public administration and the press. But, even after they gained professional stature in Chile, they had to suffer attempts aimed at disqualifying their learned arguments because – so went the argument – they were strangers. One of them, Domingo Faustino Sarmiento, demanded that his arguments should be judged on their intrinsic value and not in terms of primordial identities.

Exile poses such constraints, but it also can have expanding effects, both in terms of social capital and broadened perspectives. Edward Said observed that

While it perhaps seems peculiar to speak of the pleasures of exile, there are some positive things to be said for a few of its conditions. Seeing "the entire world as a foreign land" makes possible originality of vision. Most people are principally aware of one culture, one home; exiles are aware of at least two, and this plurality of vision gives rise to

---

[1] Paul Tabori, *The Anatomy of Exile*. London: Harrap, 1972, pp. 16–17.

an awareness of simultaneous dimensions, awareness that – to borrow a phrase from music – is *contrapuntal*.[2]

The experience of exile may prompt such critical awareness, projected even to new generations through emotions, behavior, and daily practices by displaced grownups as they interact with their children who relocated at an early age or were born abroad.[3]

From this perspective that emphasizes both constraining and expanding effects, exile should be analyzed in terms of the series of personal and collective challenges each experience of exile poses while opening opportunities to reach out – occupationally, educationally, and socially. Testimonies from Chileans who went into exile in Sweden attest that while arriving in the host country forced them to accept any possible job in order to survive, once they returned to Chile their attitude had changed and they strove to obtain an occupation according to the education and status they had eventually attained abroad.[4] Their European exposure and know-how changed their self-perception about the place they deserved and expected in society following return.

In parallel, the exilic experience may force – or enable – overcoming well-entrenched 'markers of certainty' and 'provincialism' and trigger self-questioning and awareness of one's own views and identities. José Carlos Mariátegui, one of the leading figures of Latin-American thought in the 20th century, reflected on such widening of horizons as he spent years abroad, "departing for a foreign country not in search of the secret of others, but in search of our own secret." José Luis Rénique, who studied Mariátegui, has suggested that it was the move abroad that shaped in Mariátegui and others the drive to overcome borrowed and limiting visions of modernism or skepticism, to attain a wider vision of humanity reconciled with their particular understanding of themselves as Peruvians and "children of the Andes."[5]

---

[2] Edward Said, "Reflections on Exile," in R. Ferguson, M. Gever, T.T. Minh-ha, and C. West, Eds., *Out There: Marginalization and Contemporary Cultures.* Cambridge, MA: MIT Press, 1994, p. 366.

[3] Gabriela Fried-Amivilia, "Exile and Return, Nostalgia's Captives," in "The Dynamics of Memory Transmission Across Generations in Uruguay. The Experiences of Families of the Disappeared, Political Prisoners, and Exiles, After the Era of State Repression, 1973–1984," Ph.D. Dissertation, University of California at Los Angeles, August 2004, Chapter 4.

[4] Raimundo Heredia Vargas, "El retorno: Una perspectiva de los que volvieron desde Suecia." Universidad de Chile: Instituto de Ciencia Política, 1994, documento de trabajo no. 40.

[5] José Carlos Mariátegui, "Siete Ensayos de Interpretación de la Realidad Peruana," in *Mariátegui Total.* Lima: Empresa Editora Amauta, 1994, vol. I, pp. 6–157; and José Luis Rénique, "De *literati* a socialista: el caso de *Juan Croniqueur*" ("Vicuña Mackenna"), in *Ciberayllu*, available at http://www.andes.missouri.edu/andes/Especiales/JLRCroniqueur/JLR_CroniqueurNotas.html, accessed 15 July 2008. See also Karen Racine, "Introduction: National Identity Formation in an International Context," in Ingrid E. Fey and Karen Racine, Eds., *Strange Pilgrimages. Exile, Travel, and National Identity in Latin America, 1800–1990s.* Wilmington, DE: Scholarly Resources, 2000, pp. xi–xx.

In this framework, to talk of some of the advantages of exile may be a balanced corrective to a bias recognizing only loss and forceful displacement.[6] The experience of exile leads to unforeseen opportunities to upgrade skills, learn languages, discover one's strengths and weaknesses, and develop new relationships and understanding of roles, including gender roles. Often, exile widens the sojourners' perspectives of personal identity, national identity, and, in the cases under consideration in this work, also pan- Latin-American identity.

Indeed, the experience of exile has brought individuals to confront their nurtured conceptions with their experience in the host countries. This often forced them to reconsider truisms, as they wrangled with experiences and new ideas in their host environment. A variety of paths can be identified, ranging from individuals who cling to their separate and more localized visions and identities, to others shifting to more transnational or even global attitudes. Across the continuum, however, exiles have been forced to reconsider what went wrong in the home country in terms that went beyond circumstantial explanations. The experience of exile brought Sarmiento to predicate tolerance and to suggest open discussions and the possible coexistence of differing views and plural public spheres.[7] Similarly, in 1832, politician and historian Manuel Montúfar y Coronado from Guatemala advised tolerance to his co-nationals in a historical treaty published after two years in exile. In this work, he proposed to the liberal-dominated government of Central America that the competing parties unify on the basis of shared interests, because

[N]o administration composed exclusively of one of the two parties can be national, nor cease to be vengeful and persecutory; at the individual level just, impartial, and generous sentiments can be found; but the group fosters exclusivity and exclusive sentiments cannot be national nor produce the peace and order sought by all.... In order to remain in power, those who at present dominate the republic need to reform the laws, be truthfully tolerant, and not pretend that what has never endured in any country is in fact eternal – that is, a party that, by democratic means, hopes to exclusively govern a nation full of diverse opinions and interests.... This would truly be the triumph of reason over passion.[8]

Exile provides a crossroad of processes of fundamental importance for rethinking politics and for the renewal of politics. Exile offers learning opportunities

---

[6] Typical is Julio Cortázar's dictum that "exile and sadness always go together" [el exilio y la tristeza van siempre de la mano]. Julio Cortázar, *Argentina: Años de alambradas culturales.* Barcelona: Muchnik Editores, 1984, p. 13.

[7] Ivan Jaksic, "Sarmiento and the Chilean Press, 1841–51," in Tulio Halperin Donghi, Ivan Jaksic, Gwen Kirkpatrick, and Francine Masiello, Eds., *Sarmiento: Author of a Nation.* Berkeley: University of California Press, 1994, p. 45.

[8] Manuel Montúfar, *Memorias para la historia de la Revolución de Centro América (Memorias de Jalapa of 1832),* (Guatemala: Joséde Pineda Ibarra: 1963), vol. 2, pp. 296–9; in Timothy Hawkins, "A War of Words: Manuel Montufar, Alejandro Marure, and the Politics of History in Guatemala." *The Historian,* 64, 3–4 (2002): 526.

for political actors forced to live through and learn about political agendas and projects with which they were unacquainted. Illustrative is the case of German Bosch of the Dominican Republic. His 26 years in exile, starting in 1935, were a period of political learning and ideological transformation. As he returned to the Dominican Republic in 1961, he tried to implement these ideas in his home country, before becoming president in February 1963:

During his seven months in office Bosch sought to set a model for democratic government. He encouraged wide organization of the labor and peasant movements, sponsored passage of an agrarian reform law, and financed an extensive program for training local leaders of cooperatives, unions, and municipalities. The Bosch government also maintained the fullest civil liberties.[9]

A generation later, some Latin-American leftists who witnessed experiences of 'real Socialism' while in exile in communist countries, including Cuba, reevaluated the feasibility or applicability of their former ideological positions. Experiences of exile in liberal democratic countries brought other leftist exiles to a better understanding of the welfare state and of social democratic and Christian democratic ideas and practices. The international public sphere, more conscious of human-rights violations in Latin America, provided a dimension for political action that proved instrumental in the facilitation of processes of democratization and, in many cases, material and discursive support for those fighting authoritarian rulers. Moreover, the process of transformation of authoritarian rule in Southern Europe, particularly in Spain, made a strong impression on the exiles, especially those witnessing the process firsthand. In parallel, these experiences triggered a process of reevaluation of the political processes that had led to the institutional crises generating their own exile.

The combination of such introspection and awareness of wider processes of transformation served as a basis for a new generation of politicians for whom exile has been a catalyzing factor in the reshaping of political creeds. In cases such as Chile and Brazil, the joint experience of massive displacement of political elites and the transformation of the global arena moved political parties toward the center of the political spectrum, abandoning extreme radical and revolutionary ideals and rhetoric:

The experience of state terrorism was the primary learning experience driving this change. As José M. Insunza put it, before the coup "We gave less importance to democracy because we have (had) never experienced dictatorship and human rights violations were sporadic.... Representative democracy and socialism are integrated in our discourse; in the old discourse they were antagonistic terms."... Renovation proceeded both at home and abroad, but the renovating current was stronger among exiles, particularly those in Europe. Exiles cited a number of experiences that pushed them toward renovation. Jorge Arrate, a leader in the renovation movement, emphasized that firsthand exposure to international developments and intellectual currents was decisive

---

[9] Available at http://www.bookrags.com/biography-juan-bosch/index.html, accessed 22 June 2006.

(1987: 101). The exiles were influenced by Gramsci, the debates over Euro-communism and Perestroika, and developments such as the Polish workers' movement Solidarity and its suppression and the Soviet invasion of Afghanistan.... Many Chileans were particularly impressed by the work of Felipe González and the Spanish Socialist Party in the post-Franco era.... Exiles in Western Europe and many other host countries were able to discuss, meet, and disseminate their ideas freely – opportunities completely lacking in Chile until the small opening of 1984.[10]

In an analysis of the varied experiences of the various Chilean political parties in exile, Alan Angell indicates that the process involved a dual transformation: a debate on the lessons of the Chilean experience, which led – at least in Western Europe – to a rethinking of political strategies of the Left, and a transformation of the way of thinking of the exiles, who were deeply affected by the political discussions around them:

The debate over Eurocommunism helped to produce a more moderate and pragmatic Chilean left. The European left developed ideas on the desirability of the mixed economy and the need for cooperation between capital, labor, and the government that profoundly affected the Chilean exiles, especially those in the socialist parties. Chileans exiled in Venezuela also seem to have been persuaded of the virtues of political compromise as a means of consolidating a stable democracy. Exiles in countries which stressed the virtues of revolution rather than democracy – such as Mexico, Cuba, or Nicaragua – seem to have maintained more firmly their beliefs in the essential correctness of the aims of the Popular Unity government.[11]

As Angell indicates there, the party most affected by exile and repression was the Socialist Party. Indeed, when exiled socialists begun returning to Chile in the mid-1980s, they brought their experiences and organizations with them and had a strong influence on the renovation of the Socialist Party at home. Without abandoning the commitment to the resolution of socioeconomic problems, leaders and activists – including many influenced by their experience and learning in exile – led to the reconfiguration of the Left in pragmatic terms, endorsing new models of market economy and political pluralism. Building on the experience of returnees, Denise Rollemberg similarly evaluated that exile had a profound transformative effect on the political and life projects of many Brazilian exiles:

A reassessment of daily life took place. Women reconsidered their role in society, questioning *machismo* and the oppression of traditions. A transition was operated from an authoritarian political culture to value democracy as never before. Brazil was perceived now from the outside. The narrow [mental] borders of the country were widened. Cosmopolitanism replaced provincialism. Individuals, who, at the beginning, so proudly showed off their condition of exiles, began to accept the status of refugees.... The

---

[10] Wright and Oñate, "Chilean Political Exile, pp. 42–43.

[11] Alan Angell, "International Support for the Chilean Opposition, 1973–1989: Political Parties and the Role of Exiles," in Laurence Whitehead, Ed., *The International Dimensions of Democratization: Europe and the Americas.* Oxford: Oxford University Press, 1996, p. 180.

diversity and intensity of experiences led to unforeseen changes. . . . The traditional concepts of revolution were rethought and other questions replaced them at the center of the agenda: that of democracy. Between roots and radars, the exiles re-evaluated the project that had been defeated. They abandoned some of its central aspects, added others, built paths and worldviews again, redefining themselves as they looked to what they left behind and what they perceived ahead, the contradictions of the past and the novelties of the present, [facing] the future.[12]

One should not expect, however, to witness a generalized transformation but rather progressive, partial, and often complex shifts of positions and views. In a study of the last wave of Uruguayan exiles, Vania Markarian stresses that participating in the work of human-rights networks "required revising the traditional heroic language of the left that made repression and abuses part of their expected political experience and eluded legalistic references and denunciations in order to stress social and economic claims." Her research reveals that the Uruguayan leftist exiles did not totally replace their worldview, as most maintained their ideology; and yet, their exposure abroad and perception of the changing global and domestic politics in the 1970s brought them to become active in the transnational human-rights network in order to denounce the repressive government of the homeland in the new global setting. Their very success in raising awareness to human-rights violations caught them – as well as the denounced governments – by surprise, leading them to interpret the isolation of the Uruguayan regime not as the result of change in U.S. or OAS policies but rather as the result of their own political activism. Truly enough, the lobbying experience achieved by the exiles was a major factor in this development but, in internal circles, it was still rhetorically constructed in revolutionary terms, which contradicted the 'external' discourse of protection of human rights that they used to convince European lawyers and American congressmen to cooperate against the authoritarian home government.[13]

Another aspect refers to the transformation of identities into more hybrid and reflexive. It has been away from the home environment that generation after generation of exiles have recognized their own identities as nationals of one country while, at the same time, rediscovering themselves as 'Latin Americans,' who share cultural and historical roots of continental scope with others in the Americas. Writing about the Latin-American writers who became exiles in the last wave of authoritarianism, literary critic Florinda Goldberg estimates that

[N]ational "provinciality" is replaced with a comprehensive view of Latin America as a whole, achieved either by living in another country within the continent, or elsewhere with other continental expatriates. [Tununa] Mercado says that, after her intellectual gains in France, "in Mexico I became aware of the difference [between Latin American countries]: Pre-Hispanic culture, modern art, the different literatures of the country, but above all the manners of the people, how they use their Spanish, how they move." "We learned that we were not the world's navel," says [Hugo] Achúgar; [Noé] Jitrik

---

[12] Rollemberg, *Exílio*, p. 302.
[13] Vania Markarian, *Left in Transformation: Uruguayan Exiles and the Latin American Human Rights Networks, 1967–1984.* New York: Routledge, 2005; quote from p. 7.

speaks of overcoming 'omphalocentric' fallacy.... [For many exiled critics] going into exile widened perspectives that until then had been almost exclusively circumscribed by their national literatures.[14]

Finally, human capital shifts while in exile, often developing skills and aware-ness that are transferable on a more extensive spatial basis. According to Ger-man Wettstein, the Uruguayan experience of exile of the 1970s made possible a cultural capitalization with clear implications, thanks to the receptor countries and the human quality of the Uruguayan sojourners and migrants. Exile enabled better access to goods than in their homeland; prompted a rupture with inher-ited bonds; brought about a reinforcement of the importance of labor; proved that subordination affects not only third-world countries; enhanced social secu-rity; created less dependency on parents; less social pressure; solidarity toward different people; diffusion of the Latin-American lifestyle around the world; more access to training workshops; and, overall, a fruitful confrontation with their own stereotypes and prejudices.[15]

The experience of exile has marked the lives of many with a long-lasting impact on shifting attitudes, norms, and practices. Particularly important in the late 20th century was the change experienced by many women who fled their home countries and, once abroad, adopted new visions of gender, partnership, and parenthood.

Exiled Women and Gender

The intention of authoritarian rulers to demobilize the populations of South and Central America involved women as victims of repression and therefore as exiles. With mass politics, women participated in armed struggle and rev-olutionary organizations and, because of repression, many of them went into exile. Many others were forced to depart for exile because of the risks involved in the political activism of their male spouses and partners.

The processes of cultural and material globalization opened sites of asylum and exile throughout sister Latin-American nations, in Europe, North Amer-ica, Australia, and even Asia and Africa. Often, displacement carried out an unavoidable questioning of cultural assumptions and viewpoints. The new envi-ronments put the exiles' personal resources and relationships under pressure and challenged them to rethink the markers of certainty embedded through years of childhood, adolescence, and adulthood. A major dimension of this transformative process took the form of reformulation of gender perceptions and roles.

[14] Florinda Goldberg, "Latin American Migrant Writers: 'Nomadic, Decentered, Contrapuntal,'" in Luis Roniger and Carlos H. Waisman, Eds., *Globality and Multiple Modernities. Compar-ative North and Latin American Perspectives.* Brighton, UK: Sussex Academic Press, 2002, p. 303.
[15] José Pedro Díaz and German Wettstein. *Exilio-Inxilio. Dos Enfoques.* Montevideo: Instituto Testimonios de las Comarcas y del Mundo, 1989.

Family relationships became highly strained as a result of exile. In those cases in which one of the members of the family went into exile, partners and families met in exile. These included cases in which separation was imposed by the need for one of the partners to flee immediately or because of the delayed departure of that partner who, while persecuted, could not find asylum or an easy road of escape. The women also faced a huge dilemma, whether to promote a drive for integration in their children or to nurture the connection with the country they left with the 'mythical' remembrance of their family.[16]

Almost immediately, families faced the impact of exile. To function in the new environment, they had to adapt, follow different cultural expectations, and assess their own attitudes, including those related to family life and the domestic division of roles. They also had to confront new challenges, after losing previous resources, contacts, and finding their know-how only partially effective. Networks, status, money, security of employment, language proficiency, knowledge of procedural ground rules − all these had to be rebuilt under the emotional shock of the move abroad, made under pressure.

In an analysis of Chilean exiles in Glasgow, Diana Kay found that the experience of exile had brought dramatic changes for both men and women. For many men, the overwhelming experience of exile was one of loss of power. The attempt to reconstruct a Chilean political front in exile in the UK was fraught with difficulties. The exiles were cut off from the semiclandestine political activities in Chile and placed in the unfamiliar British context. Therefore, their political stature was restricted. For many middle-class exiles, this involved diminishing personal influence and autonomy compared with their positions in Chile. Stripped out of public positions, the men also lost the structural basis underlying their role as heads of families.[17]

In many cases, women had to take care of income, dealing with unemployment, harsh labor conditions, exploitation by employers, lack of documentation, and the challenges of adaptation to the new environment, as well as with crises of identity, depression, and nostalgia not only of themselves but also of their spouses and children. It is the women who, in most cases, took care also of the problems of the children, confronting uprooting, the need of adopting local norms and behavior, and the possibility of return, with a new crisis of identity and uprooting again.[18]

All this posed strenuous challenges and created a background for redefining − willingly or not − gender, parental, and partnership roles. Unsurprisingly, the rate of separation and divorce became extremely high in most exile communities.

---

[16] María Angélica Celedón and Luz María Opazo, *Volver a empezar*. Santiago: Pehuén, 1987.
[17] Diana Kay, "The Politics of Gender in Exile: Chileans in Glasgow," in Danièle Joly and Robin Cohen, Eds., *Reluctant Hosts: Europe and its Refugees*, pp. 104–124.
[18] Equipo Praxis, "Aproximación a la situación de la mujer inmigrante y exiliada en España," in *Jornadas sobre Emigración, exilio y mujer*. Madrid: Editorial IEPALA, 1987, pp. 21–37.

Women were particularly prone to meet these pressures and undergo a trans-formation of roles and life assumptions. In exile, many women were forced to take employment in conditions that were below their aspirations, and yet, they took an entrepreneurial stand, as they had to provide for their fami-lies. In parallel, often their traditional roles as mothers quickly brought these women in contact with a series of practitioners and professionals, promoting language proficiency at a faster pace than among unemployed males. The new circumstances of exile duress centralized the various roles of women within the family, prioritizing and empowering women, creating an incentive for the redefinition of gender domains and roles both within and beyond the family:

I lived exile as a loss of status, not only materially. It took me long to build a sense of belonging, of being a citizen in Chile. And suddenly I was cut out of the roots that I had created with so much effort. I was desperate leaving an airport where tens of people bid me farewell and arrive at another airport, where my husband – in a matrimony that was not functioning – was waiting for me alone. Even if I eventually found work in France as behavioral psychologist, the exile for me represented a loss of space, of human contacts and networks. I left Chile voluntarily. I followed my husband who was arrested and expelled. I did not receive any support as those who were granted asylum, like my husband. I arrived exhausted, with a child and without any knowledge of French. My husband, who knew the language, threw me into the water without any support. The next morning I had to take my child to a nursery and went right away to look for work. French society was sensitized to the plight of the Chileans. I contacted the committee of Chilean women in exile. Most marriages were in crisis, and this was also the heyday of feminism in France. In a strange land, I went through a long and sad separation, with a sense of loneliness and lack of protection. My first identity in France was that of a woman.[19]

In many countries, Latin-American women in exile showed a strong tendency to organize themselves in solidarity organizations, some of them entirely com-posed of women. In a first stage, they joined political associations but became increasingly disappointed and later shifted to a wide span of feminine-and human-rights associations. The political consciousness transformed during exile brought them increasingly to use their assets to develop a new conscious-ness that, in parallel with some of the transformations of public debate in the home countries, turned them into an avant-garde of the new feminist movement in Latin America.[20]

It was mainly in France that the transformation of women's activism, increas-ingly focusing on gender and feminism, took place. The Brazilians were among the first exiled women to undergo this shift, as epitomized in the transition during the 1970s from the *Comitê de Mulheres Brasileiras* founded in Chile to the *Circulo de Mulheres Brasileiras* established in Paris, which we analyzed in Chapter 6. It is instructive to follow Denise Rollemberg's evaluation of how this transformation operated in France:

[19] Interview with Fanny Muldman. Santiago de Chile, 19 August 2000.
[20] Praxis, "Aproximación a la situación de la mujer inmigrante y exiliada en España."

They questioned the submission of women to domestic chores; the wage inequality between men and women when performing the same work; the double workday women were subjected to; the culture that represses women sexuality, identifying exclusively with procreation, inhibiting the knowledge of the own body; the relationship between men and women; the imposition of a certain standard of beauty, disqualifying those who do not fit; a society that encourages rivalry among women, producing a lack of female solidarity; the consumerism that uses the feminine image to sell; the different education for girls and boys that reproduces these biases; the tradition of justice that sees the rapist as a victim of women; the banning of abortion imposing unwanted maternity and condemning to death many women of the lower classes who resort to clandestine abortion; the moral that blames those who decide to interrupt pregnancy; the campaigns of birth control by the Brazilian governments that did not inform about contraception methods and sterilize massively the poorest strata, while they endorse the use of those contraceptives discarded in developed countries.... Women established contact with an universe completely different from past political activism once they opened – and favored – a space for the individual. Glória Ferreira commented: "If Chile had a historical dimension, the *Círculo* was an opening in relation to the world, to the individual."[21]

The ensuing debates on gender and politics led to a review of conscience about the authoritarian character of the home society and the political domain, including the politics of the Left, while triggering a new perception of human rights, as analyzed in previous chapters.

The intimate connection between exile and the emergence of women's movements in general and women's activism in particular was replicated at different rhythms and paces in other exile communities, progressively becoming a generalized phenomenon throughout the continent. For Guatemalan women, for instance, this is one of the major impacts of their displacement in Mexico. A major drive took the form of the organization Mama Maquin, founded in 1990 and named after an old woman who had died in 1978 defending land rights of a Mayan community attacked by the Guatemalan army. The organization soon acquired a feminist and egalitarian character and despite initial male opposition, grew exponentially to reach more than 8,000 members:

In our country, as women, our work was that of the kitchen and having children. Living in Mexico has been an education, like school for us. Our eyes were opened and we learned to organize.[22]

... As a result of the Organization, women realize that they have rights. Now no one says: we can't talk because we are women. Now we know that women are equal to men.[23]

[21] Denise Rollemberg, *Exilio*, pp. 214–215.
[22] Kathleen Sullivan, "Constructing La Casa de la Mujer: The Guatemalan Refugee Women and the Midwives of Monja Blanca in El Porvenir Border Camp, Mexico," in Wenona Gilles, Hellen Moussa, and Penny Van Esterik, Eds., *Development and Diaspora: Gender and the Refugee Experience*. Dundas, Ontario: Artemis Enterprises, 1996, p. 273.
[23] Patricia R. Pessar, "Women's Political Consciousness and Empowerment in Local, National and Transnational Contexts: Guatemalan Refugees and Returnees." *Identities*, 7, 4 (2001): 462.

In the liminality of the exilic condition, many women discovered their skills and capacity for survival, as well as their comparative strength vis-à-vis their male partners:

... Women allowed their partners the personal space they need to start recovering the old self and restructuring or "reinventing" the new self, while women themselves, in general, do without that kind of support.[24]

Similarly, Salvadoran women learned in exile the advantages of communitarian solidarity, sharing with their peers, labor issues, security, education of children, food. Although many of those relocating in Central America were supported by ACNUR with basic needs, their participation developed into a process of gender empowerment. The skills they acquired in exile were instrumental in the process of reinsertion, on return to the home society.[25]

Through these experiences, many women reconsidered gender relations and life practices, with a long-term impact on their empowerment in the home society, evinced as women members started returning from exile.

Undoing Institutional Exclusion

According to the UNHCR, once the fears that prompted the search for asylum away from the home country are overcome, the displaced individuals are expected to return to their country of origin. Yet, many of the difficulties created with the move abroad cannot be easily undone because of the time lag and to the complexities and varied forms of exile and asylum. A multiplicity of legal, social, economic, and cultural problems affects the dreamt-of return of those who had been displaced.

With the transition to democracy, Latin-American countries and international organizations tried to facilitate return. In Chile, the military government used exile as a political tool, unaware that the displacement and dispersal of co-nationals would only exacerbate the international opposition to Pinochet and his administration. The proactive presence of the mobilized Chilean political diaspora sensitized international public opinion to human-rights violations and eventually put great pressure on the military government in Chile. This international pressure led to an attempt by the latter of disinformation, though not only within Chile, to convince public opinion that the Chilean opposition had been sent into a 'Golden Exile' rather than harsher punishment for their 'antinational' deeds such as keeping them in concentration camps, prisons, or worse. Moreover, the military orchestrated disguised killings of exiles such as

---

[24] Marlinda Freyre, "The Latin American Exile Experience from a Gender Perspective: A Psycho-Dynamic Assessment." *Refuge*, 14 (1995): 14–25, esp. 21. See also the excellent analysis of this dynamic in France by Vásquez and Araujo, *Exils Latino-Americains*, pp. 129–162.

[25] *Las mujeres refugiadas y retornadas. Las habilidades adquiridas en el exilio y su aplicación a los tiempos de paz*. San Salvador: Editorial Las Dignas, 2000.

Operation Colombo, intended to discredit the antimilitary opposition, present-ing it as carrying out internal strife in exile, seemingly fighting and killing one another by the dozens.[26] Also, as part of this strategy, the DINA carried out a policy of targeted assassinations and attempts of assassination of key exiled figures, which reached Buenos Aires, Rome, Madrid, and Washington, D.C. As is well known, this strategy backfired, leading to further discredit and institu-tional changes in Chile. Without being fully aware, the government of Pinochet had transformed the issue of exiled opposition into a major focus of interna-tional concern, intimately connected with human-rights violations in Chile and abroad.[27] Under the growing impact of the fourth tier of international and transnational public opinion, institutions, and networks, the military finally had to recognize the limited effectiveness of the old-fashioned strategy of exile to control Chile in an authoritarian pattern.

According to the 1978 Decree-Law of Amnesty, all those sentenced to exile by a civil or military court could return. Still, to return, they needed the explicit authorization of the Ministry of Interior, which was extremely reluctant to grant this 'privilege.' By then, the problem of exile could already be conceptual-ized as a major form of human-rights violations, conceived in terms of Article 11 of the UN Universal Declaration of Human Rights, which established in 1948 the "right to live in one's homeland." A Committee for the Return of Chilean Exiles (*Comité Pro-Retorno de los Exiliados Chilenos*) was formed by human-rights activists linked to the Vicaría de la Solidaridad.

Thomas Wright and Rody Oñate portray the initial steps of this association:

Nothing was accomplished, however, until the Chilean economy entered a severe crisis in late 1981 which sparked the first domestic opposition movement since the coup. Emboldened by the crisis, regime opponents began fielding street demonstrations by 1982. In September 1982, demonstrators protested the Supreme Court's refusal to permit the return of the expelled president of the Chilean Commission on Human Rights, Jaime Castillo Velasco. Since Castillo Velasco, a Christian Democrat, could not be portrayed as a dangerous radical, his case served to broaden support for the return movement beyond the families of UP exiles and, by uniting the left and the Christian Democrats around a common cause, posed a significant challenge to the regime. In a clear attempt at preemption, the government convened a commission to study return policy in October 1982, and on Christmas day of that year issued the first of ten lists of persons authorized to return. This cosmetic concession quickly proved to be a hoax. The monthly lists contained a total of only 3,562 names – a minuscule proportion of the exiles – and when duplications, the deceased, and persons who had previously returned were subtracted, fewer than 2,000 individuals were authorized to return – and certainly

---

[26] One hundred nineteen activists were detained and disappeared in Chile between May 1974 and February 1975. Later on, such a number of cadavers was found in Argentina, probably disappeared, who were killed by the local armed forces. The Argentine authorities denied that any of these were their victims, whereas the Chilean authorities and a censored press indicated these were the bodies of the disappeared co-nationals who died in intestine fighting abroad. See the Rettig Report (*Informe de la Comisión Nacional de Verdad y Reconciliación*. Santiago: Secretaría de Comunicación y Cultura, Ministerio Secretaría General de Gobierno, 1991).

[27] Roniger and Sznajder, *The Legacy of Human-Rights Violations*, pp. 121–145.

none was considered a dangerous enemy of the regime. [At this rate, it would take approximately one hundred years for all exiles to be repatriated.][28]

In the following years, internal and international pressures mounted, and the military began to reverse the process of exclusion by admitting back a limited number of exiles. Petitions to the courts, publications by human-rights organizations, reports in the press, and attempts by exiles not included in the lists to openly return in spite of the ban, raised a generalized awareness about the magnitude and seriousness of the problem:

Beginning in mid-1984, the regime's return policy came under more direct attack as prominent opposition figures began flying into Santiago without authorization to enter the country. In July, two members of the popular exile musical group Inti Illimani flew into Santiago's international airport and were denied entry. On September 1, six UP leaders arrived on an Air France flight from Buenos Aires. Chilean agents entered the airplane, roughed up and handcuffed the six, and after the French ambassador visited them on the airplane and denounced Pinochet's policy on return, re-embarked them to Buenos Aires. The six leaders returned the following day on an Avianca flight; denied entry again, they were flown to Bogotá, where they conducted a hunger strike and were received by President Belisario Betancur. Covered extensively by the international press, these events, occurring as Chile's South American neighbors were emerging from their own repressive regimes, created a public relations embarrassment as well as a serious enforcement problem, as the international airlines had begun openly defying the regime's long-standing threat to cancel the landing rights of any airline that failed to deny passage to Chileans lacking documentation authorizing their return.[29]

By 1 September 1988, the restrictions on the return of all exiles were lifted as the military aimed at legitimizing the oncoming plebiscite called on Pinochet's possible continuing rule. Still, the progressive lifting of restrictions between 1982 and 1988, obtained as concessions from the military, did not create a welcoming environment toward the exiles. Returning exiles faced many difficulties and were directly caught in the struggle between the human-rights organizations that tried to support them and the government that unwillingly allowed their return. This may have been a major consideration in individual decisions of return because, under such conditions, entering Chile would imply a major commitment to political activism, irrespective of personal prospects of reinsertion. The ingathering of exiles would be a factor of importance in the results of the plebiscite.[30]

The case of Paraguay further underscores the political considerations and difficulties surrounding the change of policy allowing the return of exiles. Under the decades-long dictatorship of Alfredo Stroessner, tens of thousands

[28] Thomas Wright and Rody Oñate, "Chilean Political Exile." *Latin American Perspectives*, 34, 4 (2007): 43, and also idem, *Flight from Chile: Voices of Exile.* Albuquerque: University of New Mexico Press, 1988, pp. 171–175.

[29] Wright and Oñate, "Chilean Political Exile," pp. 44–45. There were other failed attempts to enter Chile by land, crossing the Andes from Argentina. See "Chile Forces 21 Exiles Back to Argentina." *New York Times*, 22 December 1984, available at http://www.nytimes.com, accessed 12 June 2008.

[30] Maria Rosaria Stabili, *Il Cile, della repubblica liberale al dopo Pinochet.* Firenze: Giunti, 1991.

of exiles moved abroad, particularly to neighboring Argentina, where also a huge number of Paraguayan migrant workers had settled, especially in Buenos Aires and Posadas. Stroessner maintained a policy of cooperation with other Latin-American dictatorships, of infiltration of exile communities, and the banning of return. With the fall of military rule in Argentina, the situation of the Paraguayan opposition in exile changed radically. Well aware of the danger of having the opposition in free democratic Argentina, Stroessner made the decision to allow the return of exiles in December 1983. Freedom of expression could give new voice to the opposition, composed by political activists of a long list of organizations, ranging from the liberal – such as the MOPOCO, the PLRA, and other minor forces – to the Marxist MPL (Movimiento Patria Libre, or Free Fatherland Movement). Recentralizing the issue of Paraguay, moreover, could affect the beginning of the work on the Yacyretá binational dam, an extremely important economic venture of $10 billion, that was about to start that month. Stroessner preferred to have the exiles return to Paraguay, where his security forces could control their activities. Return had to follow individual notices of date and place of arrival in Paraguay. All political exiles were allowed to return, with the exception of Domingo Laíno and Luis Alfonso Resck, considered to be subversive.[31]

Although denouncing the anticonstitutional aspect of the conditions of return, the major opposition parties who had formed the National Accord in 1979, under the leadership of Domingo Laíno, in exile since 1982, declared to support the return, in order to continue the struggle against the dictatorship.[32] A press release published in Argentina denounced the motives of the dictator for this "false aperture." On the one hand, the exiles interpreted the change of policy as a result of internal crisis, which affected the capacity of the regime to continue subjugating the Paraguayan population, but in tandem claimed for themselves great political agency in the changed international context:

The dictator was forced to dismantle the ticking bomb of Paraguayans in Argentina, which threatened to explode, thanks to the democratic spark of solidarity lighted with Alfonsín. If this would have happened, it would have turned into even more fragile the already tense relationships between a dictatorship and a democracy that have in its hands no less than the keys to Yacyretá.[33]

A third case is that of Brazil, where the ban on return was lifted in 1978. Between 2,000 and 3,000 exiles would return following the 1979 amnesty, many by their own means or supported by their families.[34] There are hard

[31] Epifanio A. Moyas Cobos, Ed., *Exilio y resistencia: Los movimientos políticos de exiliados Paraguayos en Argentina. Declaraciones y crónicas desde 1983 hasta la caída de Stroessner.* Buenos Aires: Alberto Kleiner editor, 1989; "Crónica sobre el retorno de los exiliados al Paraguay," *Revista Ñe-Engatú*, Buenos Aires, Year II, No. 12, January–February 1984.

[32] The parties were the PLRA (Partido Liberal Radical Auténtico), the PDC, the MOPOCO, and the Febreristas.

[33] Moyas Cobos, Ed., *Exilio y resistencia*, p. 20, "Crónica sobre el retorno...."

[34] Teresa Sales, *Brasileiros longe de casa*. Brasil: Cartez Editora, 1999, p. 13.

data on those who returned from exile in Europe, assisted by the UNHCR and the Intergovernmental Committee for European Migrations (later, the International Migration Organization). In 1979, 203 came back, and another 124 returned in the following five years. Denise Rollemberg interprets the little use of the international financial assistance by the many exiles in Europe to return to Brazil in a set of circumstances: the reluctance to accept the condition of refugees as they arrived in Europe with ideas of continued armed struggle and political action, which were not allowed if they were to assume that status; the incapacity to prove the claim of being a refugee after they left Brazil by their own decision; the unwillingness of individuals of a high social class to rely on institutional support and their preference for familial or party financial assistance; and finally, the relocation of exiles from other countries in which they had received first asylum.[35]

Returning from Exile

With democratization, or during the late stages of the *de facto* governments, many exiles considered the pros and cons of returning after a long absence to the countries of origin. During their years abroad, they dreamt of returning home, driven by nostalgia and a will to recover what was lost: "Return was thought as the 'cure' that would make them 'whole' again by integrating in their community of origin."[36]

Countries that expelled people on political grounds created, on democratization, frameworks of return that facilitated the move but were unable to eliminate the difficulties involved in reintegration to a home society that sometimes had changed dramatically during the exiles' absence. In the Chilean case, 15,363 individuals had registered by 1992 at the National Office of Return (*Oficina Nacional del Retorno*, or ONR). The agency was created by Congress in August 1990 to function until September 1994, taking care of returnees, who were supposed to register no later than August 1993. A law amendment in 1993 prolonged benefits until August 1994.[37] The agency was supposed to be instrumental in facilitating the reintegration of exiles to their home society, with a wide range of benefits such as legal support; occupational training; recognition of educational achievements abroad; scholarships; duty-free imports of domestics, cars, and professional apparel; loans; and credit. The programs were supported by the Chilean government, friendly governments, international organizations (International Organization for Migration, World University Service), and NGOs (primarily FASIC, which since 1976 has operated a program of family reunification for exiles).[38]

---

[35] Denise Rollemberg, *Exilio*, pp. 278–281.
[36] Fried-Amilivia, "The Dynamics of Memory Transmission Across Generations in Uruguay."
[37] Biblioteca del Congreso Nacional, http://www.bcn.cl/leyes/pdf/actualizado/30362.pdf, accessed 17 June 2008.
[38] FASIC, *Programa de reunificación familiar. Reencuentro en el exilio.* Santiago: Ediciones FASIC, 1991.

The support included help in the integration of foreign spouses and children. Sixty-eight percent of those who returned before 1992 were professionals, 15.6 percent were workers, 13 percent white-collar employees. After their return, 42 percent were unemployed, 35.67 were employed, and 12 percent were visiting Chile to evaluate their work prospects.[39] By August 1993, the director of the ONR, Jaime Esponda Fernández, presented a balance of the activities of the agency, according to which 11,500 families with a total of 40,000 persons had received benefits, 64 percent of them under Aylwin's government. Thanks to the office, 19,834 persons (or 2,857 families) of those who arrived obtained jobs; 1,300 were professionals educated abroad and incorporated into the Chilean market. Among those, many were involved in arts and culture.[40]

After 11 years of exile in Belgium, Rosa Moreno visited Chile in 1986. Rosa, aka Anaí, confronted the hard prospects of returning to the homeland in the last stages of Pinochet's dictatorship, not only in terms of official policies but also in terms of the general attitude of the population, both in the Right and in the Left:

Another aspect of authoritarian culture: a member of the family who belongs to the political Right [supporters of Pinochet] reassures me: "You can return as you are not demanding." Militants of the Left tell me the same.... The political exile is "allowed" to return as long as he will continue to be an exile here.[41]

Like many other exiles visiting the home country after a long absence, Moreno found that since her departure into exile, Chile had lived through a process of modernization but remained divided by sharp socioeconomic disparities, and poverty was widespread. In some circles, she perceived much superficiality, whereas in others she met a nostalgic and emotional connection to the symbolic figures of the Left, such as Violeta Parra or Salvador Allende. The expectations of the exile – which, even if changed, kept alive a discourse that existed in Chile prior to the military intervention – were not met. The local Chilean society had changed forever. With return, both sides could feel the impact of the chronological and geographical distance that had separated the exiles from the home society.

In Uruguay, return was supported by major parts of society, and its impact was perceived as positive. The receptivity of the population was broadened during the last phases of military rule and had its symbolic landmark during the flight of the children of the exiles and the return of various celebrities, with massive public demonstrations along the road that links the airport and Montevideo. The subject was incorporated into the political agenda through the activities of the Commission for Reuniting Uruguayans, comprising mostly

[39] Jaime Llambias-Wolff, "The Voluntary Repatriation Process of Chilean Exiles." *International Migration*, 23, 4 (1993): 579–597.

[40] Jaime Esponda Fernández, speech of the Director of the ONR, Santiago, 20 August 1993, typescript.

[41] Fernando Montupil, *Exilio, derechos humanos y democracia. El exilio chileno en Europa.* Brussels and Santiago: Coordinación Europea de Comités Pro-Retorno, 1993, p. 94.

political and labor organizations and created in December 1983, prior to formal democratization. Various NGOs began to design and implement support programs for the prospective returnees. The PIT-CNT – the labor union – did not ignore the plight of return and worked for the restitution of exonerated workers and employees to their former jobs. A majority of returnees were reinstated in their former workplace with the exception of those whose organizations went through major organizational changes.[42] Among other important initiatives was the establishment in 1984 of the Servicio Ecuménico de Reintegración (SER, or Ecumenical Reintegration Service) by the Bishops of Montevideo, the Methodist Evangelical Church, the Evangelical Church of the Río de la Plata, and the Christian Youth Association. Later on, SERPAJ (Servicio de Paz y Justicia, or Peace and Justice Service) and the Valdense Evangelical Church joined, with ACNUR serving as an observer. Its objective was to work for the return of those ostracized by military rule, facilitating their reintegration into the Uruguayan society. They organized a program designed to respond to the daily needs of the former prisoners and returnees, attempting to offer immediate assistance in critical situations. Their main priorities were education, health, housing, work, and food.

In March 1985, with the reestablishment of a democratic government, all policies restricting the return of the exiles were banned. In that same month, the parliament enacted a law that sanctioned a political amnesty, creating the National Commission of Repatriation (Comisión Nacional de Repatriación, or CNR) (Law No. 15.737 of 11 March 1985). Other laws recognized the right of public workers to return to their former jobs. The goals of the CNR were to elaborate programs to facilitate return, channel foreign assistance, and articulate between private and governmental efforts in this area. Its resources were aimed toward employment and scholarships. It also financed transportation back to Uruguay; a savings program for housing from the mortgage bank; health insurance through social security institutions; educational assistance to children and youth; facilitated customs paperwork; gave away loans; and enforced minimum wage to those families without any income. The main sources of funding came from the Swedish government and the European Community. In 1987, the CNR closed its doors.[43]

The initiatives undertaken facilitated the return of exiles, leading to rising numbers of returnees in the 1980s, with a peak following the formal return of democracy in 1985. The returnees had the same socioeconomic composition as the emigrants in terms of age, education, and occupation. Yet, although in terms of location most Uruguayan émigrés did not relocate to Europe, among the returnees of 1984–1986, 40 percent came from European countries and

---

[42] Jorge Notaro, Agustín Canzani, Augustín Longhi, and Estela Méndez, *El Retorno de Emigrantes y las Respuestas de la Sociedad Uruguaya.* Montevideo: CIEDUR, September 1987.

[43] Ibid., pp. 69–70. See also Lelio Mármora and Jorge Gurrieri, *Return to Rio de la Plata: Response to the Return of Exiles to Argentina and Uruguay.* Washington, D.C.: Georgetown University, Center for Immigration Policy and Refugee Assistance, 1988, pp. 16–19.

only 20 percent from neighboring countries such as Brazil and Argentina. In addition, the sojourn abroad had contributed to their comparatively higher educational capital, with at least one-third having completed graduate studies. Until the end of 1986, 23,542 employees returned to their workplace. Some of them were assisted by the Unidad Técnica para la Reinserción Laboral (UT, or Technical Agency for Labor Reinsertion), established in June 1985 with the support among others of SER and the Swedish Diakonia.[44]

Nonetheless, nostalgic attitudes that propelled return as a means of recovering the past often turned into a source of disillusion as the returnee confronted the changed reality in her or his home country. Years passed by and left their marks. Expectations were not fulfilled, as often family, friends, and workmates did not show the levels of interest and solidarity the former exiles expected on the basis on their subculture of activism and support abroad. As part of a study of Uruguayan returnees, Gabriela Fried relates the case of a couple who returned from years of exile in Cuba:

... Raquel and Máximo's long awaited return from Cuba, where Raquel had felt very isolated. Long letters with her brother had kept Raquel and Beatriz full of expectation for their "reencounter." Raquel's brother came alone to get them at the airport, and already on the way to town, he had told them that they couldn't stay in what had been their apartment (Raquel had by necessity given him a power of attorney before leaving) because his wife didn't want to live all together. He had, in fact, put the apartment illegally under his name and forced them to stay elsewhere. Beatriz was speechless with pain and disbelief:

"I don't think I can still talk about it today, it just hurts me too much. I had a dear brother, with whom we were very close, I thought. You should have seen the love letters when we were away and possibly not coming back! He adored us! But the moment we came back, he did the worst thing I could have ever imagined: left me in the street." (Testimony by Beatriz's daughter, given in a broken voice).[45]

The children of exiles were especially vulnerable on return, after growing up abroad with the idealized images of the parental home country and a vicarious sense of duty not to forget and return when circumstances will allow it. For them, the gap between the ideal image and the reality was even wider, as they confronted their parents' difficulties of reinsertion coupled with their own alienation in the new environment.

---

[44] Estimations put the number of returnees benefiting from this program at a couple of thousands, ibid., pp. 78–79.

[45] Gabriela Fried-Amilivia, "The Dynamics of Memory Transmission across Generations in Uruguay," in "The Transmission of Traumatic Memories across Generations in Uruguay: The Experiences of Families of the Disappeared, Political Prisoners, and Exiles after the Era of State Repression (1973–1984)." Ph.D. dissertation, University of California at Los Angeles, Summer 2004.

Partially contrasting with the preceding account, the general atmosphere in Brazil was of receptivity. The first exiles returned to the country in late 1970, producing celebration and enthusiasm. The image of the exile acquired a halo of glory, to some extent becoming the epitome of Brazilians' wish to be attuned to global developments:

Exile soon became fashionable. But it was more than that. There was curiosity among those who stayed about learning what they did not live through. There was a proliferation of autobiographies and they sold well. Some were best sellers. The interviews of exiles turned frequent, most of them aimed at creating conciliatory versions, while privileging the folkloric, colorful, funny cases. Eventually, many interviews related the other dimensions of exile. However ... there was a mystification of the exile, as a figure that was becoming known – and constructed – as a sojourner of other lands, who arriving after being away for a long period, sits at the center of a circle and relates what he has seen. All of the sudden, it became glorious to have a kin or a friend who had been in exile or, at least, somebody exiled invited to dinner.[46]

Exiles had to contemplate the danger implicit in a situation in which the structure of repression remained intact, as well as the fact that the military dictatorship had not yet ended. The state apparatus, at every level, remained closed for the exiles. The intelligence services prevented their entry into public life at places such as federal universities. At the same time, because of the economic crisis, the private sector offered few opportunities to the returnees. Hence, the exiles found themselves facing unemployment and many felt like strangers in their own country.

Initially, the returnees did not participate in politics. This changed with the elections of 1982, as some of the exiles gained governorships as part of the electoral victory of the opposition in many states. Important former political exiles such as Leonel Brizola and Darcy Ribeiro were elected as governor and vice-governor of Rio de Janeiro. Others were integrated through the opening up of the state apparatus at state and municipal levels to trained people in the liberal professions and to intellectuals. After the indirect election of Tancredo Neves in 1984, and the direct elections of mayors in 1985, new ground was gained. The consequences of the amnesty did finally extend to offices of state and the universities, and this fact was very important because the majority of Brazilian exiles were party leaders, members of political organizations, and intellectuals, who had traditionally made their careers in the state apparatus or in academic research institutions. By 1986, returnees seemed to have been reintegrated into the political and institutional life of the country.[47]

In countries of large-scale and long-term exile, redemocratized governments confronted this legacy of authoritarianism through legal and administrative mechanisms. In the case of Paraguay, immediately after the demise of Stroessner's long dictatorship (1954–1989), Parliament enacted Law No. 40/89 and Law No. 92/90, creating the Consejo Nacional de Repatriación de

---

[46] Denise Rollemberg, *Exilio*, p. 16.
[47] Herbert d'Souza, "Return Ticket to Brazil." *Third World Quarterly*, 9, 1 (1987): 206–208.

Connacionales with the purpose of fomenting the return of Paraguayans living abroad and encouraging their permanent residence in the country. The Consejo Nacional de Repatriación de Connacionales offered legal aid for prospective returnees, helping them to obtain the needed documentation. It also provided scholarships for short-term studies in technical fields aimed at easing the integration of the exiles into the local labor market. This project was sponsored by the Misión de la Amistad, an ecumenical institution of social character. Among the governmental organizations that encouraged and supported the returns were the Ministry of Interior, in charge of documentation with special privileges to Paraguayan exiles and their families; the Ministry of Foreign Affairs that could provide tax exemptions during repatriation; and so forth. In a country beleaguered by many bureaucratic procedures and a variety of taxes, a decision was taken to grant exemptions in order to ease the reentry of the exiles. In addition to governmental agencies, there were many NGOs willing to support the returnees. The International Organization for Migration (Organización Internacional de Migración, or OIM) also cooperated by offering some financial support for those who wanted to return. The Conferencia Episcopal Paraguaya (CEP, or Episcopal Conference of Paraguay) provided advice on documentation, labor orientation, and institutional support dealing with varied domains such as health, studies, and training of children of returnees.[48]

In Argentina, the Office of Solidarity with Argentine Exiles (Oficina de Solidaridad para Exiliados Argentinos, or OSEA) was created in mid-1983 by leaders of various human-rights organizations such as CELS (Centro de Estudios Legales y Sociales, or Center of Legal and Social Studies), SERPAJ, the Ecumenical Movement for Human Rights, Movement for Life and Peace, and World University Service. Following democratization, in July 1984, a National Commission for Return of Argentines Abroad (Comisión Nacional de Retorno de Argentinos en el Exterior, or CNRAE) was established as a body overseeing the unprecedented return of exiles and acting as a mediating body with the UNHCR, which managed various programs and was funded by international sources. Contrasting with the case of the CNR in Uruguay, the CNRAE did not play an operational role in the reinsertion of the returnees. Many unforeseen problems, such as the issue of the nationality of the children of the exiles, the proper recognition of foreign documentation, and the cases of loss of previous Argentine documentation, were eventually solved, even though the process took longer and was more burdensome bureaucratically than in the case of Uruguay. Mármora and Gurrieri attribute it to the lack of proper awareness and recognition of the Argentine public relative to the plight of the exiles.[49]

The issue of the return of exiles has posed numerous problems at various levels. The oppositions to military rule and long-term dictatorships had clearly committed themselves to undertake the treatment of political exile under the

---

[48] Comité de Iglesias para Ayudas de Emergencias (CIPAE) en el Paraguay, *El retorno – Manual guía para repatriados.*

[49] Mármora and Gurrieri, *Return to Rio de la Plata.*

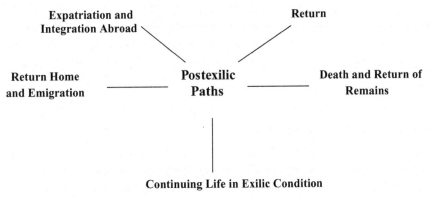

DIAGRAM 8.1. Postexilic paths.

banner of the human-rights cause. In the period of transition to democracy, especially in the 1980s, international and internal pressure mounted and opened windows of opportunity for the reception of exiles in countries still under authoritarian rule. Many of the returnees integrated into local political action favorable to the transition to democracy. NGOs, churches, and IGOs began acting on behalf of the prospective returnees into the home societies. Formal democratization made possible the enacting of legal and administrative mechanisms geared to facilitate return, dealing with many of the concrete aspects of reintegration with the financial support of international and foreign aid. In the wake of the enthusiastic support of democratization, societies were symbolically receptive toward political exiles. Still, the reality on the ground for those returning from exile was extremely complex and difficult. The dual change that took place during dictatorship both in local society and in the life of the exiles abroad created a situation of possible estrangement and mutual alienation. In this respect, some experiences were more successful than others, especially when organizational networks provided channels of reintegration, and the personal capital of the returnees proved an asset that was visible and effective in the process of reintegration into the home society, economy, culture, and politics.

Postexilic decisions are multiple and return is only one among many options (see Diagram 8.1). Many exiles chose not to return and remained in the countries of asylum, while maintaining links with the society of origin. For example, nearly 50 percent of the Argentinean community in Spain did not return after democratization. On the contrary, Argentine economic instability produced a further flow of translocation to Spain[50] in the 1980s and again at the beginning of the 2000s. Many returnees did not find their place in the home countries for myriad factors, among them occupational and familial difficulties, economic hardship, problems in the adaptation of children, including language barriers,

---

[50] In 1987, there were 14,130 registered Argentineans in Spain and many more undocumented residents. Antonio Izquierdo Escribano, *La inmigración en España 1980–1990*. Madrid: Ministerio de Trabajo y Seguridad Social, 1992, p. 36.

counternostalgia for the lifestyle of the host society abroad. This produced among some of them a phenomenon of migration back to the host countries or into other locations. Because of differences in income and standards of living, some of the former exiles were able to develop a 'double residential standard,' living part of the year back in the home country and partly in the host country.[51]

The Possibility of Undoing Exile

The hope of returning to the home country is embedded in the experience of exile, ensconced in the very moment of displacement. For many of the exiles, pining for home turns into a nostalgic dream of reencounter with the loss of life projects and social networks, of childhood habitats and landscapes. The impaired yet persistent will to return can be considered one of the key traits in defining exile as a distinctive category of displacement, as discussed in Chapter 1.

Notwithstanding some of the openings living abroad provides, as analyzed earlier, exile is a traumatic experience, and no less traumatic is the decision to return or stay in the host country, once circumstances enable such return. The way individuals and communities confront the challenges of exile influences the eventual decision of returning to the homeland. Although all exiles can return (e.g., with democratization), only some do actually return. Those who have overcome the initial hardships of exile and retained agency over their lives, becoming somehow entrepreneurial, are better prepared to face the probable difficulties of a new displacement, this time to the dreamt-of-yet-expelling home country. In fact, to return means relocating to a setting only partially known, a fact that may transform the return into a new exile. The home country has changed in the passing years, and these changes were only partially followed from afar, especially when the home dictatorships ruled out the possibility of an early return.

When home countries transited to democracy, exiles faced the dilemma of return in highly tense personal and social terms. Argentinean psychiatrist Arnoldo Liberman, after years in Madrid, reflected critically on the options open once democracy was restored in his home country:

Never again we would meet again our entire body. Without being able to follow the daily changes [in the home country] we are condemned to face just sudden transformations. If the friend I meet upon my return has more gray hair or wrinkles, s/he did not share with me these shifts. If many have died with the passing of years, they all have died on the same day. If my nephews and nieces grew up, I did not witness their coming of age. Forever, nothing could be entirely reinserted in our internal world. That installed a fragmentary character [in our existence].[52]

---

[51] Clara Obligado, interview in Madrid, 26 June 1998; Abrasha Rotenberg, interview in Jerusalem, November 2000.

[52] Arnoldo Liberman, "Rememoración del exilio." *Cuadernos hispanoamericanos*, nos. 517–519 (1993), p. 551. Liberman is a well-known psychoanalyst and prolific writer and poet, born in Argentina and living in Spain since the 1970s.

Those who had been involved in the political struggle for long years were forced to make a hard decision that sometimes threatened to shake them for long weeks, months, and even years. The banners of their identity as political exiles abroad led to defining the return as a political decision and the alternative decision to stay as an individual act of dissociation from the common ideals and goals. Whenever exiles remained politically, culturally, and socially tuned to the home country, this connection might ease the decision to go back. However, these connections and ties can only ease, not obliterate, the difficult decision. Even without acknowledging it consciously, exiles had developed local roots, becoming connected in manifold ways to the host society through personal and social bonds of marriage, parenthood, work, education, friendship, and local mores and routines. Every individual, family, and group was torn by the tensions between their previous experiences and the contemporary habitat, with mixed personal and political considerations. All these brought about decisions that ranged from an immediate return to relegating return to an undefined future.

Many would be forced to recognize the gap between the dreamt-of homeland and the real world of return, discovering the difficulties of reinsertion back home. Eugenia Allier Montaño and Denis Merklen elaborate these tensions on the basis of a story by Uruguayan writer Leo Harari:

Uruguay remained static as a youth memory, as [a memory of] a first girl friend whom one would like to see again. Yet, mature and beaten woman, you are not anymore that young girl of [my] revolutionary dreams. Your eyes reflect the tired image of the man I became. As I return I must confront the image of the defeated man I am. I prefer to keep the Uruguay of streets and utopia young rather than to tiredly walk the worn tiles of the [home] country of today.[53]

In a recent book, José Luis Abellán elaborates three modes of '*desgarro*,' of individual sense of being torn apart by forced displacement. Abellán suggests distinguishing among the refugee, the displaced individual (the *desterrado*), and the exile. Whereas the refugee adopts the logic of survival pulling toward accommodation to the host environment, the displaced lives the new environment in terms of what she or he left behind. According to the author, the third type, the exile – represented by the writer and philosopher, María Zambrano – moves into a more radical position. She or he perceives her or his forced wandering as an ultimate destiny. Once ostracized, return will not heal the wounds. In fact, the condition of exile may come to an end, and yet, for the returning individual, the exile has no end, it is a state of being completely orphaned, having lost forever a taken-for-granted place in the world.[54]

In a sense, the tragedy is that – having changed in parallel – both the exiles and those who stayed in the homeland often become strangers to one another.

---

[53] Eugenia Allier Montaño and Denis Merklen, "Milonga de estar lejos. Los que se fueron a Francia," in Dutrénit Bielous, Ed., *El Uruguay del exilio*, p. 351. See also Allier Montaño, "La (no) construcción de memorias", 2007.

[54] José Luis Abellán, *El exilio como constante y como categoría*. Madrid: Editorial Biblioteca Nueva, 2001, pp. 45–57.

Literary critic Hugo Achúgar has reflected on this double dynamics of estrangement and reencounter with co-nationals:

Uruguayans of exile and disexile...we are beings [torn] between two waters, the marginals of yesterday and tomorrow...strangers...both in exile and back....To return is, somehow, to state the obvious: "the impossibility of returning home," as Thomas Wolfe said...the mythical place was real in its potentiality. Once achieved, it becomes the place of encounter and disencounter. The picture is moved...back home, or at least with the illusion of having really come back home...we find that everything and everybody has changed: in the first place, we who left. We got the country back and we lost it. If the temporary marked part of our exile, what we had to live through upon returning was also frail, unsure, and transitory. We are in a process of disexile, because disexile is not achieved all at once and forever. Disexile is not a noisy, one-time performance....It is a lasting wound that may or may not heal.[55]

Returning from exile is beleaguered with so many problems that it often turns into a new form of exile, an inner exile, in the eyes of the returnee. These problems are found all across the social ladder, from upper-class intellectuals to lower-class workers. Illustrative is the case of María, who went from Chile into exile in Peru and later Cuba. She and her husband had been housekeepers of the Cuban Embassy in Santiago during Allende's government. Following the coup, they felt threatened, even though they were not politically involved. The story and testimony of her experiences in Cuba and return to Chile are worth quoting at length:

In Cuba, everything was granted them and she did not have a problem with language. They received an apartment earmarked for the Chilean exiles. Both she and her husband worked. The children were pampered. The neighbors helped with the children when they were at work.

...They decided to go back. They hesitated – but knew that, as time passed, it would be harder to take off with the children. The children pressed for the return, without imagining the hardships they will encounter. Only when the tickets arrived, they became more ambivalent. Her daughter had only three years to go to be a professional but the mother did not want to leave her behind.

María felt "a moral duty" to return. She had a sense of being guilty towards those who stayed. For her, the return was so hard, "more anguishing than exile itself." Nobody waited for them in Chile – the letter they sent did not arrive in time. She had to live with a cousin, with her mother, without money for food or for the children. Now she had to carry on with the stigma of coming from a Socialist country.

---

[55] Hugo Achúgar, "Entre dos orillas, los puentes necesarios," in Saul Sosnowski, Ed., *Represión, exilio y democracia: La cultura Uruguaya*. College Park and Montevideo: University of Maryland and Ediciones de la Banda Oriental, 1987, pp. 242–43. Tununa Mercado once said that "the expatriate that finally returned...found the places perforated and lived through the vertigo of falling into those holes." Both quotes can be found in Florinda Goldberg, "Latin American Migrant Writers: 'Nomadic, Decentered, Contrapuntal,'" in Luis Roniger and Carlos H. Waisman, Eds., *Globality and Multiple Modernities*. Brighton, pp. 299–300.

... Eventually they opened a convenience store. The daughter suffered immensely and tried to commit suicide three times. "The problem is she never lacked anything. And now, she lacks many things. She has suffered from hunger. She has felt ashamed when she goes out and has no shoes." She also suffered as she defended Cuba and was accused of being a subversive. She wants to go back to Cuba. The younger son failed at school – the teacher did not accept the way of behavior that the child had learnt in Cuba. "My children blame us for having brought them back. I feel guilty. I feel very humiliated."

Nobody helps them. Everybody in the poor environment they live and work thinks that, as they come from abroad, they have enjoyed life. When they suggest improvements, everybody rejects them and "they react in terms of the exiles willing to rule here." "No – they tell me – you come back with children well learned, chubby, with money in your pockets, while our children suffer from malnutrition, we are hungry and are badly off. *Pucha!* In this very poor neighborhood, we cannot even talk with our former friends."[56]

From the first moment, exile is modeled as an act of institutional exclusion imposed by the expelling country on the exiles, depriving them of citizenship rights, and of any possibility of participation in the domestic political arena. Once abroad, the host country, and probably the international public sphere, begin to play roles in the exile equation. In this scheme, return supposes a reversal of both exclusion from the home country and partial inclusion in the host country. A continuum can be traced between, on the one hand, the attempt by the political exiles to enter the expelling country surreptitiously and affect the political process, and, on the other, the return of exiles after being allowed to do so by the expelling country. Any such move will imply a changing equilibrium in the four-tiered structure of exile, accompanying decisions taken initially either by the exiles or the expelling authorities.

The experience of exiles, typically vacillating between their present situation and the remembrance of the past, hopefully to be reencountered in the future, led to new reviews of conscience and redefinition of identity as the home country was about to emerge from the repressive interregnum. With the return of democracy, they would have to face a poignant choice between returning or remaining abroad, recognizing they would no longer be able to claim the label of exiles.

In *Made in Argentina*, a film directed by Juan José Jusid, an Argentinean couple exiled in the United States comes for a visit after many years away, on the occasion of a family wedding. The couple is torn between the consideration of a possible return to the homeland and the thought of taking the wife's brother and his family with them to the United States. Whereas Argentina pulls a wide gamut of emotional chords – from nostalgic meetings with figures of the past and reviving one's youth to the remembrance of betrayals and rejections

[56] María Angélica Celedón and Luz María Opazo, *Volver a empezar*. Santiago: Pehuén, 1987, pp. 41–59.

that led them to flee the country – the U.S. prospects are equally imposing. The attraction there is of a modern, dynamic, and economically prosperous society, prevailing over the grim economic situation of their relatives in Argentina. And yet, the Argentineans in North America are fully aware that they are strangers in a foreign land and they lack the feeling of home they have in Argentina. This contradictory pull of factors does not lead to either return or emigration. Each couple follows its own way. The exiles return to the United States knowing that they have become migrants in the host society, unable to engage in a return to the home country. The local relatives opt to stay in the homeland, despite the allure of a better economic future in a strange environment.[57]

Redressing the Evils of Exile

The evils of exile are numerous and difficult to redress. Forced displacement creates problems that have an impact not only on the lives of individuals while abroad but also create difficulties to be faced by those willing to return. Although political changes may revert institutional exclusion and formally allow the reinclusion of those displaced from the home countries, the possibility of return demands not only administrative and material mechanisms to help the returnees but also the capacity of the exiles themselves to overcome some of the psychological and subjective damage inflicted by institutionalized exclusion. Besides contemplating reparations, compensations, reintegration into the labor market, housing, and the educational system, exiles have many more subtle aspects to be addressed. In this latter respect, the main difficulty lies in the fact that lives have been deviated from what should have been their 'normal course.' A sense of rupture, wound, or cut has been encrypted forever in the bodies and minds of the exiles.

The psychosocial aspects of return, whether consciously or not, imply an attempt to heal the open wound in many different forms, according to the stage in life and conditions in which exile took place. Older exiles, who were grown adults when they left for exile, often had to confront difficult problems of adaptation into host societies. On return, they had to attempt recovering the gap created by their absence. Comparatively, the problem is even harsher for younger returnees. Many young people who went into exile formed their universe of signification abroad and, on their return, they must face a reality in which they did not participate in shaping its contours.[58] Although the identity

---

[57] *Made in Argentina* (also known as *Made in Lanús*), Director, Juan J. Jusid, Argentina, 1987.

[58] Héctor Maletta, Frida Szwarcberg, and Rosalía Schneider, "Exclusión y reencuentro: Aspectos psicosociales de los exiliados a la Argentina," in Patricia R. Pessar, Ed., *Fronteras permeables*. Buenos Aires: Planeta, 1991, pp. 219–221; Vásquez and Araujo, *Exils Latino-Americains*, pp. 83–128; Juana Kovalsky, "Exilio y desexilio: Una experiencia más de violencia," in Adrianne Aron, Ed., *Fuga, Exilio y Retorno. La salud mental y el refugiado*. San Francisco: Committee for Health Rights in Central America, 1988, pp. 83–95. The systematic treatment of these psychosocial aspects is beyond the scope of this work and has been analyzed in brilliant ways by other researchers.

of the former is stronger in terms of the domestic 'markers of certainty' they grew up with, for younger exiles the prospects are that uncompleted markers of certainty were partially condensed within the terms of their experiences abroad, creating a more complex interweaving of cultural codes, opening their minds to new hybrid codes of behavior and visions but simultaneously narrowing their primordial anchors of identity.[59]

Another major issue is the possibility of recovering a sense of shared identity and collective purpose once the destinies of those who stayed and those who went into exile meet again following the end of proscription and institutionalized exclusion. Paradigmatic, even if extreme somehow, is the case of the Argentinean intellectuals and professionals after democratization in 1983. Professor Saúl Sosnowski of the University of Maryland arranged a meeting in Washington bringing together a wide range of participants: a sociologist, a journalist, a philosopher, a theater critic, four literary critics, four writers, a politician, and two historians to discuss Argentinean culture after military repression. Sosnowski had to overcome unforeseen difficulties when convening the seminar for both those who stayed in Argentina and those who left for exile:

The answer was surprisingly unanimous. On the one hand, they told me, there were more urgent needs. On the other hand, they would not sit around the same table with those who had defied [the military rule] with their words and actions from far away, beyond boulevards, rivers and oceans.[60]

The agenda of the meeting was ample, and yet, the subject that dominated it was that of personal accountability, focusing on the opposition of the exiles versus those who had remained in the country during the military government. Mutual recrimination and claims of agency in bringing down the dictatorship took over discussion. Those who remained in Argentina accused exiles of desertion. The counterexperience was that of the exiles, who, after realizing the impossibility of carrying out internal opposition to the military in power and in order to save their lives, left the country and declared a total war against military rule in Argentina. The new exiles joined the Argentinean diaspora, displaying a potent voice sensitizing international public opinion to human-rights violations in their home country. Liliana Hecker, who stayed in Argentina, replied that the role of those who stayed in the country was even more valuable than that of those who went into exile. Moreover, Hecker considered that Argentina was far from having turned into a 'Zombieland,' as some of the exiles assumed, and that an authentic commitment to its people meant contributing to their culture while living with them. Those who went into exile failed, according to Hecker, to live

---

[59] See "Oblivion and Memory in the Redemocratized Southern Cone" and "The Transformation of Collective Identities and Public Life in Argentina, Chile and Uruguay," in Luis Roniger and Mario Sznajder, *The Legacy of Human-Rights Violations in the Southern Cone*, pp. 182–266.

[60] Saúl Sosnowski, "Introducción," in *Represión y reconstrucción de una cultura. El caso Argentino.* Buenos Aires: Universidad de Buenos Aires, 1984, p. 7.

through the experience that the Argentinean people bore during those years. The experience of exile thus opened deep controversies into the reshaping of collective identity and the possibilities of redressing the evils of institutionalized exclusion with the demise of authoritarianism and the newly opened prospects of reintegration into the home society and culture.[61]

Present and Future Exile

Restored democracies take political inclusion seriously. Still, they generate new forms of social and political exclusion, including exile. In recent years, there have been many cases of political actors and intellectuals feeling harassed and forced to leave their home countries. Even though many of those escaping prosecution under democracy might be defined as expatriates, as they leave their country out of free will, these individuals often define their move as a forced displacement, and many of their sympathizers and supporters consider them exiles.

Particularly open to harassment are journalists and intellectuals who, under democracy, dare to criticize public officials and dignitaries. Among well-known cases is that of Chilean writer and journalist Alejandra Matus, escaping abroad in April 1999, after she had published *The Black Book of Chilean Justice*. Chief Justice Servando Jordán presented charges against Matus, claiming, on the basis of the Law of State Security inherited from military rule, that the book's criticism was a "crime against public order." Her book was confiscated, and Matus, who had received death threats in the 1980s, fled to Buenos Aires and later settled in the United States, where she was granted asylum until her home country adopted a new press law:[62]

New legislation introduced in 2001 allowed her to return from exile in the United States and resume her career as a journalist in Chile. However, she is still fighting for freedom of the press. In 2003, she resigned from the newspaper *La Nación* when it refused to run her story about alleged corruption involving the government Institute of Agriculture and Livestock Development.[63]

Similar is the case of Baruch Ivcher Bronstein, chairman of the Board of Directors and majority shareholders of the Peruvian TV station *Frecuencia Latina – Canal 2*. Ivcher, an Israeli-born attorney, legally became a naturalized citizen in 1984, a status that enabled him to enter the communications domain, because by Peruvian law foreigners are precluded from owning radio or TV stations. In 1996, Channel 2 began reporting irregularities and suspicions of corruption in government agencies, including the involvement of top figures

---

[61] Sosnowski, *Represión y reconstrucción*, p. 221.

[62] "La interminable batalla legal de Alejandra Matus," available at www.libertad-prensa.org/matusletter.html, accessed 25 May 2006; and Human Rights Watch World Report 2001, available at www.hrw.org/wr2k1/appendix/index.html, accessed 25 May 2006.

[63] "Chilean investigative journalist Alejandra Matus," The International Development Research Center, available at http://www.edrc.ca, accessed 10 June 2008.

such as Vladimiro Montecinos Torres, a close advisor of President Fujimori and member of the SIN, the National Intelligence Service of Peru. After broadcasting these stories, a number of parliamentarians promoted a congressional inquiry, while *Frecuencia Latina* came under harassment and investigations by tax authorities and other government agencies. In May 1997, Ivcher was accused by the joint command of the armed forces of using the media to wage a campaign of slander against them. They indicated that they would not accept the "tendentious and malicious campaign waged, because it was an abuse of freedom of expression and an attempt to alienate the public from the Armed Forces." Five days later, on 28 May 1997, the government cancelled the naturalized citizenship of Ivcher by a Supreme Decree because of what were described as "acts that could be detrimental to the national security and interests of the state."[64] As he lost the TV network, he went into exile in Miami and continued to fight the proscription before international organizations such as the Inter-American Commission of Human Rights and the World Bank, which blocked a loan to Peru for its curtailment of freedom of the press. The Peruvian government retaliated by arresting close collaborators and bringing Ivcher to trial, together with a brother, on charges of tax evasion going back to 1992–1995. While the Peruvian government placed an order of arrest with Interpol, the suspicion of political persecution precluded its enforcement. Eventually, after the fall of Fujimori and Montecinos from power and the revocation of pending trials by the Peruvian Congress, Ivcher returned to Lima in late 2000 to join his wife and daughters left behind and resume his position in the TV network.

During the early 1990s, political tensions in Peru were on the rise. Heavy-handed repressive policies were undertaken against the Shining Path and other organizations defined as terroristic as well as against those who criticized Fujimori's government for its socioeconomic policies of stabilization. Some members of the opposition took the road of exile, among them more than 200 who found shelter in redemocratized Chile. In Chile, there was already a large community of Peruvian migrants; yet, in the early 1990s, official and public sensibilities of Chileans with their own experience of exile created a favorable environment to help the newcomers. Chilean NGOs such as CODEPU and FASIC that treated problems of human-rights violations and displacement were helpful to those escaping Peru.[65] The Peruvian exiles in Chile, organized by the Peruvian Refugee Committee, presided over by Raul Paiba, were active particularly when former President Alberto Fujimori reached Chile and was arrested, facing extradition procedures to Peru on

---

[64] "Report No. 20/98. Case 11.762 Baruch Ivcher Bronstein Peru. 3 March 1998, Inter-Am.C.H.R., OEA/Ser.L/V/ii.95 doc 7 rev.at 164 (1997). Available at http://www1.umn.edu/humanrts/cases/1997/peru20-98.html, accessed 10 June 2008.

[65] José Luque, "Género, memoria y ciudadanía en un contexto post-nacional. El caso de los peruanos y peruanas refugiados en Santiago de Chile," unpublished manuscript (April 2008); Roniger and Sznajder, *The Legacy of Human Rights Violations in the Southern Cone.*

charges of corruption and human-rights violations during his rule in the home country.[66]

Since the onset of the Bolivarian Revolution in Venezuela, many citizens and residents chose the road of exile. Some of them were journalists who, according to their own reports, had been harassed by progovernment circles. A salient case of an opposition journalist and actor is that of Orlando Urdaneta, a very vocal critic of President Hugo Chávez, who had produced in 2002 a theater play, *Orlando en cadena,* which was sabotaged by Bolivarian circles that attacked those attending the performances. In 2004, Urdaneta decided to move to exile in Miami. While interviewed there for TV by anchorperson María Elvira Salazar, herself daughter of a Cuban exile, Urdaneta called for the assassination of President Chávez as the solution to the political situation in his home country.[67]

This trend of people fleeing Venezuela was further reinforced as the government tightened the grip on the country's political institutions and threatened to deepen the socialist trends in the Revolution. Journalists fled as the government did not renew the license of the main opposition communication network, RCTV (Radio Caracas Televisión).

New communities of Venezuelan exiles have thus been formed recently. Thousands of Venezuelans found refuge in South Florida, many of them supporting ORVEX (Organización de Venezolanos en el Exilio, or Organization of Venezuelans in Exile) and organized in committees protesting political arrests in the home country. They include also a group of Venezuelan military officers in exile, led by Brigadier-General (ret.) Henry José Lugo Pena and Vice-Admiral Oscar Betancourt Patiño, who on February 2008 called their co-nationals to resistance to the home government, while denouncing the ties between Chávez's government and the Colombian guerrillas.[68]

These groups are part of a larger wave of Venezuelans who have almost doubled the size of the Venezuelan diaspora in the United States and who, according to U.S. census data, numbered 91,507 in 2000 – a year after Chávez took office – and 177,866 in 2006. Manuel Corao, director of one of several Venezuelan newspapers published in South Florida, declared that the main factor beneath the rising tide of exile is "fear of change daily, the loss of private property, loss of independence from the government, fear of the loss of constitutional rights and individual liberties."[69]

Similarly, yet for different reasons, the violent political environment of Colombian democracy has generated massive exile. Among others, journalists,

---

[66] Gustavo González, "Chile: Peruvian Refugees Fear Fujimori Will Slip Through the Cracks," available at http://ipsnews.net/news, accessed 15 June 2008.

[67] "Urdaneta llama al magnicidio desde Miami, 1 November 2004," available at http://www.rnv.gov.ve/noticias, accessed 10 June 2008.

[68] http://sociedadcivilvenezuela.blogspot.com/2008/02/militares-venezolanos-en-el-exilio.htm, accessed 12 June 2008.

[69] Kirk Semple, "Rise of Chavez Sends Venezuelans to Florida." *New York Times*, 23 January 2008, available at http://www6.miami.edu, accessed 12 June 2008.

trade union leaders, intellectuals, and fearful members of the upper and middle classes have fled their country for years because of insecurity, political persecution, forced displacement, or death threats coming from various directions, which include right-wing paramilitary organizations, left-wing guerrillas, and narcotraffickers. Large diasporas have been formed, especially in the United States, Canada, Brazil, Costa Rica, and Venezuela. In Europe, the two largest communities are in Spain and the UK. Many others live in Germany, Italy, France, Germany, and Sweden. The Administrative Department of Security (Departamento Administrativo de Seguridad, or DAS), which is in charge of migration control in Colombia, registered 1,600,000 Colombians who left the country and did not return; nearly half of them migrated between 1999 and 2001. These peak years correspond to a period of deep internal crisis.[70] A study conducted by the Florida International University in 2001 estimated 200,000 to 300,000 as the number of Colombians who migrated to the United States in 1998–2000, fleeing political violence and economic turmoil, joining previous waves of émigrés who brought the total number of Colombians in that country to 458,000 in the early 2000s.[71] Paradigmatic is the case of Priscilla Welton, a ballet teacher and spouse of writer and journalist, Fernando Garabito, who fled Bogotá to escape the death squads targeting him for his articles linking Colombia's government to drug traffickers. Welton and her family were granted asylum in the United States.[72] Exile associations and committees of solidarity with the Colombian Left have been established in European cities (Bristol, Gijón, Paris, Rome, and Stockholm), some under the guise of the REDHER (Red de Hermandad y Solidaridad Colombia, or Network of Brotherhood and Solidarity) and others more localized, such as the Asociación Pardo Leal in Stockholm, as well as others in Washington, Buenos Aires, and Montreal.[73] These associations of exiles have organized protests against the government of President Alvaro Uribe, accusing him of state terrorism or at least of incapacity to halt the wave of death attempts and demanding conditions for the return of the exiles.

Also under democracy, leading politicians and former presidents have felt compelled to flee their countries after the end of their terms, fearing charges of corruption or political persecution under the guise of such charges. Relatively recent cases include Carlos Salinas de Gortari, who left Mexico for Ireland and, in Ecuador, many of the recent heads of state, who found themselves in exile to avoid facing charges after political shifts. Thus, Abdala Bucaram left for Panama in 1997; Jamil Mahuad left for the United States in 2000; Gustavo Noboa left for the Dominican Republic in 2003; and Lucio Gutiérrez left in

---

[70] Myriam Bérubé, "Colombia in the Crossfire." *Migration Information Source,* November 2005, available at http://www.migrationinformation.org/profiles, accessed 12 June 2008.

[71] Paul Brinkley-Rogers, "Colombian Exiles Face Uncertain US Future." *Miami Herald,* 6 June 2001, available at http://www.latinamericanstudies.org/colombia/colombian-exiles.htm, accessed 12 June 2008.

[72] http://www.santafenewmexican.com, accessed 12 June 2008.

[73] http://www.redcolombia.org, accessed 12 June 2008.

2005 for a short sojourn in Brazil, the United States, Peru, and Colombia, before returning to his home country.

Similarly, former Bolivian President Gonzalo Daniel Sánchez de Lozada, (1993–1997, 2002–2003) and his former Defense Minister José Carlos Sánchez Berzaín fled to the United States in October 2003 after the Bolivian security forces harshly repressed the demonstrators who protested the economic policies of that administration. Once in residence in the United States, they are facing trials initiated by human-rights groups for their roles in the killing of 67 Bolivian citizens and injuring of 400 mostly indigenous individuals.[74]

Peruvian leaders also felt compelled to leave after their presidential bid failed or after the conclusion of their term. Writer and presidential candidate, Mario Vargas Llosa, moved to Spain in the early 1990s; President Alberto Fujimori left Peru in late 2000 to attend an Asia–Pacific Economic Cooperation (APEC) summit in Brunei and then continued to Japan, from where he resigned the presidency; and President Alejandro Toledo and his spouse, Eliana Karp, left the country for the United States in 2006:

When the current president, Alan García, was elected, the Toledos went into voluntary exile in America's Silicon Valley. A commission of inquiry appointed by the Peruvian Parliament to investigate Karp-Toledo's conduct while her husband was in office revealed she had squandered huge sums of public money on clothing, shoes, dog food, flowers for the presidential mansion and alcohol.[75]

On the basis of polarized public spheres and divisive situations of crisis, some Latin-American democracies have continued to generate conditions in which individuals and segments of the population feel threatened or are actually targeted, thus taking the road of exile. The dynamics of exile have changed much since the 1970s and 1980s, and institutionalized exclusion is no longer fashionable or practical on a large scale. However, a series of factors such as the lack or personal and collective security, the lack of tolerance between political opponents and critics, and spiraling polarization of public rhetoric aimed at the delegitimization of political enemies create conditions that prompt the exile of those who feel endangered. This situation does not result from institutionalized exclusion as in the past but rather from a lack of enforcement of legal guarantees expected in any democracy. The results are, however, similar: Citizens and residents find themselves in exile, engrossing the ranks of substantial communities of co-nationals spread beyond the borders of the home country as the result of previous repressive periods and socioeconomic circumstances.

---

[74] "Human Rights Lawsuits Brought Against Former Bolivian President and Minister of Defense for Complicity in Attacks on Civilians." Human Rights Program of the Harvard Law School, available at http://www.law.harvard.edu/programs/hrp/index.html, accessed 16 July 2008; Janine Zacharia, "US Forced to Confront its Bolivian Problem." *The Global Edition of the New York Times*, 2 July 2008, p. 2.

[75] Efrat Neuman and Sami Peretz, "The Prodigal Son Returns." *Haaretz*, 27 March 2008.

Conclusions

The research design of this work combines theoretical analysis and empirical findings, with information gathered from primary and secondary sources. Building on these sources and analyses, it follows a continental approach that combines country studies, individual testimonies, topical studies, archival work, and historical research. We have followed the itineraries and perils of political exiles inside the countries, throughout Latin America and beyond, into Europe and the rest of the world, and back. Attention has been given to lines of continuity and transformation of exile from colonial times to the 21 century.

There is general hindsight emerging from this study. For one, this study casts some doubts on the truism that in Latin America exile is typical only of authoritarian rule and that there has been no use of exile under democracy. Expatriation, a recurrent phenomenon, has characterized periods of authoritarian exclusion but has widely occurred also in formally democratic periods. Exile has taken place even in recent and contemporary democratic settings. Truly enough, there is a major difference between these contexts affecting exile: authoritarian exile became a massive trend in the 20th century under the impact of broadening franchise and political participation and mobilization. In democratic setups, exile remains a phenomenon specifically tied to individuals critical of administrations, as well as in cases of corruption, or of former authoritarian rulers and top officials, once their administration ends. Some of the Latin-American democracies have entered a stage of increased polarization and political confrontation, using aggressive rhetoric, in which parts of the opposition feel menaced and leave for exile. Another major difference is the purposeful use of exile as a tool of political exclusion in authoritarian circumstances vis-à-vis situations generating personal and group insecurity, aggravated under politically polarized systems. Despite these differences, the persistent practice of exile as a mechanism of political regulation both under authoritarian and democratic systems indicates the inability of some of these political systems to abide by a pluralistic and inclusive model of participation.

We have identified the lines of emergence of political exile in the transition from colonial to independent rule, as this form of institutional exclusion crystallized as a major constitutive feature of Latin-American politics. The roots of this phenomenon go deep into colonial times, when translocation and expulsion were widely used against social offenders, outcasts, rebels, and criminals as a means of administration and relocation according to the imperial policies of Spain and Portugal. In the early 19th century, after independence, the phenomenon of exile began developing the special political profile and role that, although transformed, persisted into the 20th and 21st centuries.

Analysis has traced exile as contributing to the definition of both collective identities and the rules of the political game on a transregional basis, before and following the consolidation of the states. It has related exile to the tension between the hierarchical structure of these societies and the political models that predicated equal participation and republicanism; the tension between the ideas of continental unity and the realities of fragmentation and conflictive territorial boundaries leading to the consolidation of different nation-states; and the evolution of factionalism into modern politics, spurring civil wars, political violence, and polarization.

In this period, the format of early exile was constituted around a three-tiered structure. We identified such a structure, shaped by the dynamic interplay of translocated individuals and communities of exiles, the host country and the home country to which they strived to return as victors destined to rule. In this format, exiles played an increasingly important role in transregional and continental politics, as well as in the definition of the borders of the new collective identities and nation-states.

The major poles and sites of exile that attracted displaced individuals fleeing repression in the home countries were examined, showing that the harsher the persecution, the fewer the options prospective exiles had in selecting a site of asylum. Particularly salient was the difference between the exiles escaping persecution and jumping the fence of an embassy to save their lives, and individuals who, sensing persecution, had the time and resources to evaluate alternative routes of escape and asylum and whether and when to leave the home country. Analysis indicated that decisions involved the interplay between the expelling circumstances; the personal background; and the receptiveness and attractiveness of the host countries in terms of their projected image, distance, climate, language, and institutional support as well as economic, professional, and educational opportunities. Analyzing also the policies of the host countries in terms of asylum, we have paradoxically found that advanced democracy has not been a *sine qua non* for the attraction and reception of exiles. Ideological and interest considerations, as well as previous personal relations, have sometimes opened the gates of host countries to individuals escaping repression in their home country. Highly limited democracies that have exercised authoritarian controls over their own populations favored parallel policies of asylum and reception of exiles, for reasons of *realpolitik* or ideology.

The analysis also identified the transformation of exile from a selective elite phenomenon in the 19th century to a widening mass phenomenon, leading to the creation of communities of Latin-American exiles and expatriates in the 20th century. At this stage, political exile becomes the counterface of political inclusion. In circumstances in which politics and mobilization widened and threatened the control of those in power and their supporting coalitions, rulers often resorted to excluding the political opposition, qualified as 'troublemakers,' 'dangerous enemies,' or 'triggers of instability' to be ostracized and expelled from the country.

The continued reliance on massive exile as a tool of institutionalized exclusion brought about, against the expectations of authoritarian rulers, the emergence of another tier conditioning its development. In the post–World War II period, the counterface of the wave of institutionalized exclusion and political persecution was the internalization of principles of human rights by organizations at the international and global arena, such as the United Nations'

General Assembly and its other agencies, Amnesty International and other IGOs, various churches and religious institutions, the Red Cross, the European Parliament, human-rights parliamentary commissions across the globe, international associations of political parties, confederations of trade unions, and NGOs concentrated on the defense of human rights.

These multiple organizational structures and networks, which emerged as a fourth tier that conditioned exile, enabled the rapid creation of a dense network of committees of solidarity with the victims of institutionalized repression fleeing persecution. As terror and fear of persecution expanded well beyond the national borders, exiles were able to link and operate within international solidarity networks, projecting the issue of repression and exile into the general public awareness, helping develop an arena for transnational activism. The fourth tier emerged as a crucial aspect of the tug-of-war between political exiles, their supporting networks, and the repressive attempts of the home countries. Theoretically, the fourth tier has operated against the logic of the nation-states by debordering visions of rights and protecting exiles, creating resonance for their plight in the global and international arena.

To analyze the relative salience of presidential exile in 20 Latin-American countries since independence, a database of presidential terms was constructed. We focused on the exile of incumbent and past presidents, monarchs, and heads of juntas of government. Heads of state have played a major constitutional and symbolic role in all these countries. Presidential electoral processes were, and still are, far more decisive in Latin America than are parliamentarian, regional, or local elections. Political ideologies and systems of interest have been incorporated with the access of presidents to power and fought through their destitution, assassination, or exile. Inquiring into the weight of presidential exile has revealed that more than a quarter of all those who served as presidents in Latin America experienced exile before and/or after their terms. Although the detailed analysis of the database helped identify countries of larger and lesser extents of presidential exile as well as periods saturated and others almost devoid of presidential displacement, we found a positive correlation between the experience of exile and access to the highest positions of power in these countries.

Finally, we inquired whether return is the end of exile and referred to the process of 'disexile' and its impact on the home society and politics. Redressing the evils of exile has had both material and psychosocial dimensions, mutually implicating a very difficult treatment. Undoubtedly, the process of return has much to do with undoing the effects of institutional exclusion and opening new avenues for reinsertion, anchored in the establishment of institutional frameworks facilitating return, and at the same time creating a collective environment positive toward the return of exiles, a difficult task for societies suffering from economic constraints and crises, and sometimes ideologically divided about their recent past. We selected some areas in which, during the last wave of transition to democracy, exile had a broad impact on these societies and polities, such as the empowerment of women. Exile has had a profound effect on the reconfiguration of political spheres, in which the experience of living abroad had a moderating effect, marginalizing high-pitch rhetoric and radical political factions.

The analysis of political exile opens a long series of retrospective and prospective issues in the research agenda. The uprooting experience of living in unfamiliar social territories in many cases has opened up new forms of relating the personal to the political. Although we began inquiry into some of these issues, more research is needed on the following: In what ways did exile offer political activists innovative ways to think about political and social change beyond renewed activism in political parties and left-wing movements? How did the exposure to shifting ideologies and political events affect the ways in which these activists engaged in the reconstitution of political alliances and projects? How did the new ideas about race, gender, class, and identity, which the exiles encountered abroad, change during the process of reintegration as returnees renewed their links with their countries of birth? The mere fact of having seen home societies from abroad during the years of exile and the possibility of comparing them (and their remembered images) with the host countries adds reflexivity. Overarching these various questions, future research may assess how the experience of exile did contribute to the pluralization of the domestic cultural arena and public spheres, opening the possibilities for the discussion and practice of multiple models of modernity.

Similarly, one of the main questions that this study opens for the research agenda is the extent to which political exile is seen today in Latin America as a human-rights violation. These societies have internalized basic principles of human rights following the last wave of authoritarianism and repression. Nonetheless, the measures taken to address political exile in all facets of legislation, compensation, and incorporation into the historical memory have been partial. Therefore, we should ask what still has to be done in order to consolidate a kind of democracy that should not tolerate institutionalized exclusion and exile anymore. This is especially important because we have found that some of the contemporary democracies still generate exile. In Latin America, the link between democracy and inclusion has been compounded by ethnic, socioeconomic, religious, ideological, and other migratory factors. The consideration of this question is central if these polities, which are still strongly factionalist and contain strong tendencies toward polarization even under democratic rule, are to overcome situations such as those that produced political exile; namely, situations in which individuals and groups feel menaced enough to leave the country as a result of the radicalization of the political rhetoric, discourse, and decisions of those in power.

The implications of this issue go beyond the mere analysis of past political exile. Latin America has witnessed wide waves of migration driving individuals away from their home societies for a variety of socioeconomic and political constraints. There is growing awareness, and many studies, on the problems created by international migration in host countries, and yet these studies could profit by relating to the analysis of exile. Studying migration and exile within a shared framework of exclusion – whether institutional or informal – may prepare us better to understand processes that disrupt normal life and shape varied situations of illegality, which in post 9/11 days may tilt on networks of terrorism, narcocriminality, and modern forms of human slavery and prostitution as well.

Political exile has changed the character of both the diasporas and the home countries. Whereas Latin-American political exiles imagined their rapid return, in fact, the protracted nature of authoritarian rule forced them to stay abroad for relatively long periods of time. In most cases, this opened a process of learning of new experiences and the progressive creation of new networks, which turned into an increased social and cultural capital. The use of such human capital can be extremely important, particularly in tandem with the process of globalization that has accelerated since the 1980s. Although in some areas, such as Mexico, Central America, and Cuba, the remittance of capital by migrants is a well-known factor of great weight in the economies of the home countries, the parallel existence of connections and know-how by former exiles seems to have been neglected from a macropolitical and institutional perspective in most cases. Understanding and incorporating the personal and collective gains of political exiles while abroad constitutes a valuable path to be followed by the new democracies, along with their professed faith in democratic inclusion. It may also be of great value for reconciliation and especially for the mutual recognition of the exiles and those who stayed in the home countries during repressive phases. Recognition is an intrinsic element on the way to attaining a full-fledged inclusion.

Bibliography

Abellán, José Luis. *El exilio como constante y como categoría.* Madrid: Editorial Biblioteca Nueva, 2001.

Academia Nacional de Historia. *Historia Argentina Contemporánea.* Buenos Aires: Editorial El Ateneo, 1965, Vol. 1.

Achúgar, Hugo. "Entre dos orillas, los puentes necesarios." In *Represión, exilio y democracia: La cultura uruguaya,* edited by Saúl Sosnowski. College Park and Montevideo: University of Maryland and Ediciones de la Banda Oriental, 1987.

Adler, Cyrus, Joseph Jacobs, and Elkan Adler. "South and Central America." http://jewishenclyclopedia.com/ (accessed 13 April 2008).

Aguiar, César. *Uruguay, país de emigración.* Montevideo: Ediciones de la Banda Oriental, 1982.

Alexander, Robert Jackson. *Romulo Betancourt and the Transformation of Venezuela.* New Jersey: Transaction, 1982.

Allier Montaño, Eugenia and Denis Merklen. "Milonga de estar lejos. Los que se fueron a Francia." In *El Uruguay del exilio,* edited by Silvia Dutrénit Bielous. Montevideo: Trilce: 2006.

Allier Montaño, Eugenia. "La (no) construcción de memorias sobre el exilio político uruguayo," in Eduardo Rey Tristán, ed. Memorias de la violencia en Uruguay y Argentina, Santiago de Compostela.

Almada, Izaías, Alipio Freire, and J.A. de Granville Ponce, orgs. *Tiradentes, um presídio da ditadura.* São Paulo: Scipione, 1997.

Alonso, Ana María. "The Effects of Truth. Representations of the Past and the Imagining of Community." *Journal of Historical Sociology* 1, 1 (1988): 35–57.

Ameringer, Charles D. *The Democratic Left in Exile. The Anti-Dictatorial Struggle in the Caribbean, 1945–1959.* Miami: University of Miami Press, 1974.

Ameringer, Charles D. *The Caribbean Legion Patriots, Politicians, Soldiers of Fortune, 1946–1950.* University Park: Pennsylvania State University Press, 1996.

"Amérique Centrale," July 1980; "Pour l'autodétermination du people d'El Salvador. Marche Nationale le 28 Novembre," November 1981, France Folder 7.1, International Institute of Social History, Amsterdam.

Amunategui, Domingo. *El progreso intelectual y político de Chile.* Santiago: Editorial Nascimento, 1936.

Angell, Alan. "La cooperación internacional en apoyo de la democracia política: El Caso de Chile." *Foro Internacional* 30, 2 (1989): 215–245.

Angell, Alan. "International Support for the Chilean Opposition, 1973–1989: Political Parties and the Role of Exiles." In *The International Dimensions of Democratization. Europe and the Americas*, edited by Laurence Whitehead. Oxford: Oxford University Press, 1996.

Angell, Alan. "The Chilean coup of 1973 – a perspective thirty years later." http://www.lac.ox.ac.uk/coup.pdf (accessed 17 June 2008).

Angell, Alan, and Susan Carstairs. "The Exile Question in Chilean Politics." *Third World Quarterly* 9, 1 (1987): 166.

Anino, Antonio. "Soberanías en lucha." In *De los imperios a las naciones – Iberoamérica*, edited by Antonio Anino, Luis Castro Leiva, and Francois-Xavier Guerra. Zaragoza: Ibercaja, 1994, pp. 229–253.

Appel, Avital, and Yifat Bachrach. "The Policies of the Israeli Governments Regarding the Jewish Detainees-Disappeared in Argentina." Hebrew University Seminar paper, 2002.

Arango, Joaquín, Graeme Hugo, Ali Kouaouci, Douglas S. Massey, Adela Pellegrino, and J. Edward Taylor. "Theories of International Migration: A Review and Appraisal." *Population and Development Review* 19, 3 (1993): 431–466.

Archdiocese of São Paulo. *Brasil. Nunca mais.* Petropolis, Brazil: Vozes, 1990.

Ardao, Arturo. *Génesis de la idea y el nombre de América Latina.* Caracas: Centro de Estudios Latinoamericanos Rómulo Gallegos, Consejo Nacional de la Cultura, 1980.

Arendt, Hannah. *The Origins of Totalitarianism.* Cleveland, OH: Meridian, 1968.

Arrate, Jorge. *Exilio: Textos de denuncia y esperanza.* Santiago: Ediciones Documentas, 1987.

Artigas, José del Pozo, Ed. *Exiliados, emigrados y retornados chilenos en America y Europa, 1973–2004.* Santiago: RIL Editores, 2006.

Así buscamos rehacernos. Represión, exilio y trabajo psico-social. Santiago: COLAT-CELADEC, 1980.

Azurduy, Victoria, and Alejandro Borrego. *El caso Argentino: Hablan sus protagonistas.* Mexico: Editorial Prisma, 1977.

Bachmann, Susana. *Topografías del doble lugar. El exilio literario visto por nueve autoras del Cono Sur.* Lausanne-Zaragoza: Hispanica Helvetica, 2002.

Bahbah, Bishara. "Israel's Military Relationships with Ecuador and Argentina." *Journal of Palestine Studies* 15, 2 (1986): 76–101.

Bankier, David. "Los exiliados alemanes en México y sus vínculos con la comunidad Judía (1942–1945)." In *Judaica Latinoamericana.* Jerusalem: Magnes, 1989.

Banton, Michael. "Modeling Ethnic and National Relations." *Ethnic and Racial Studies* 17, 1 (1994): 1–19.

Barahona, Marvin. *Honduras en el siglo XX: Una síntesis histórica.* Tegucigalpa, Honduras: Guaymuras, 2005.

Barman, Roderick J. "Brazilians in France, 1822–1872: Doubly Outsiders." In *Strange Pilgrimages: Exile, Travel and National Identity in Latin America, 1800–1990s*, edited by Ingrid E. Fay and Karen Racine. Wilmington, DE: Scholarly Resources, 2000, pp. 23–39.

Barman, Roderick J. *Citizen Emperor. Pedro II and the Making of Brazil, 1825–91.* Stanford, CA: Stanford University Press, 1999.

Baron, Ana, Mario Del Carril, and Albino Gomez. *Por qué se fueron.* Buenos Aires: Emecé Editores, 1995.

Basadre, Jorge. *Historia de la República del Perú*. Lima: Editorial Cultura Antártica, 1949, Vol. 1.

Basadre, Jorge. *Historia de La República del Perú*. Lima: Editorial Universitaria, 1968, Vol. 2.

Basadre y Chocano, Modesto. *Diez Años de Historia Política del Perú*. Lima: Editorial Huascarán, 1953.

Battaglia, Salvatore, Ed. *Grande dizionario della lingua Italiana*. Torino: Unione tipográfica editrice Torinese, 1968.

Benedetti, Mario. *Andamios*. Madrid: Alfaguara, 1997.

Bernardotti, María Adriana, and Barbara Bongiovanni. "Aproximaciones al estudio del exilio argentino en Italia." In *Represión y destierro*, edited by Pablo Yankelevich. La Plata: Ediciones al Margen, 2004.

Bernetti, Jorge Luis, and Mempo Giardinelli. *México: El exilio que hemos vivido*. Buenos Aires: Editorial de la Universidad Nacional de Quilmes, 2003.

Bérubé, Myriam. "Colombia in the Crossfire." *Migration Information Source*, November 2005. http://www.migrationinformation.org/profiles (accessed 12 June 2008).

Bethell, Leslie, Ed. *Latin America Since 1930*. Cambridge: Cambridge University Press, 1998.

Bethell, Leslie. *Central America Since Independence*. Cambridge: Cambridge University Press, 1991.

Bidegain, Gabriel. "Democracia, migración y retorno: los Argentinos, Chilenos y Uruguayos en Venezuela." *International Migration* 25 (1987): 299–323.

Billard, Anick. "Haití: Esperanza, regreso y desilusión." *Refugiados*, March 1987: 15–18.

Boccanera Jorge, *Escritores argentinos en el exilio*. Buenos Aires: Ameghino, 1999.

Bokser-Liwerant, Judit. *Imágenes de un encuentro. La presencia Judía en México durante la primera mitad del siglo XX*. Mexico: UNAM, Comité Central Israelita, MBM, 1991.

Bonilla, Emma. *Continuismo y dictadura*. Tegucigalpa: Litográfica Comayagüela, 1989.

Bottero, Mónica. "Yo no me voy; este país me echa." *Brecha*, Montevideo, August 21, 1987.

Bourdieu, Pierre. "The Forms of Capital." In *Handbook of Theory and Research for the Sociology of Education*, edited by J. G. Richardson. New York: Greenwood, 1986, pp. 241–258.

Bowman, Kirk S. *Militarization, Democracy, and Development: The Perils of Praetorianism in Latin America*. University Park: Pennsylvania State University Press, 2002.

Brading, David. *The First America, The Spanish Monarchy, Creole Patriots and the Liberal State, 1492–1867*. Cambridge: Cambridge University Press, 1991.

Brading, David. "Nationalism and State-Building in Latin American History." *Ibero-Amerikanisches Archiv* 20 (1994): 83–108.

Brading, David. "Patriotism and the Nation in Colonial Spanish America." In *Constructing Collective Identities and Shaping Public Spheres: Latin American Paths*, edited by Luis Roniger and Mario Sznajder. Brighton, UK: Sussex Academic Press, 1998, pp. 13–45.

Brinkley-Rogers, Paul. "Colombian Exiles Face Uncertain US Future." *Miami Herald*, June 6, 2001. http://www.latinamericanstudies.org/colombia/colombian-exiles.htm (accessed 12 June 2008).

Bruschera, Oscar H. *Artigas*. Montevideo: Biblioteca de Marcha, 1969.

Buxton, Julia. "Venezuela's Contemporary Political Crisis in Historical Context." *Bulletin of Latin American Research* 24, 3 (2005): 328–347.

Cabrera Infante, Guillermo. "The Invisible Exile." In *Literature in Exile*, edited by John Glad. Durham, NC: Duke University Press, 1990.

Caetano, Marcelo. *Historia do Direito Portugues*. Lisbon: Verbo, 1981.

Cahill, David. "After the Fall: Constructing Incan Identity in Late Colonial Cuzco." In *Constructing Collective Identities and Shaping Public Spheres: Latin American Paths*, edited by Luis Roniger and Mario Sznajder. Brighton, UK: Sussex Academic Press, 1998, 65–99.

Calamai, Enrico. *Niente asilo politico. Diario di un console italiano nell'Argentina dei desaparecidos*. Rom: Editori Riuniti, 2003.

Calandra, Benedetta. *L'America della solidarietà l'accoglienza dei rifugiati cileni e argentini negli Stati Uniti (1973–1983)*. Rome: Nuova Cultura, 2006.

Caldwell, Robert G. "Exile as an Instititution." *Political Science Quarterly* 58, 2 (1943): 254.

Camacho Padilla, Fernando. "La diáspora chilena y su confrontación con la embajada de Chile en Suecia, 1973–1982." In *Exiliados, emigrados y retornados chilenos en América y Europa, 1973–2004*, edited by José del Pozo Artigas. Santiago: RIL Editores, 2006, 37–62.

Cameron, Maxwell A. "Citizenship Deficits in Latin American Democracy." Paper presented at the 2006 meeting of LASA, San Juan de Puerto Rico, 15–18, March 2006.

Cansani, Agustín, Agustín Longhi, Estela Méndez, and Jorge Notaro. *El retorno de emigrantes y las respuestas de la sociedad uruguaya*. Montevideo: CIEDUR, September 1987.

Capacity of the Dominican Republic to Absorb Refugees. Findings of the Commission Appointed by the Executive Power of the Dominican Republic. Ciudad Trujillo: Editora Montalvo, 1945.

Carelli, Mario. *Cultures croissés: Histoire des échanges culturels entre la France et le Brasil, de la découverte aux temps modernes*. Paris: Nathan, 1993.

Carpentier, Alejo. *El derecho de asilo*. La Habana: Arte y literatura, 1976.

Carreno, Gloria, and Celia Zack de Zuckerman. *El convenio ilusorio: refugiados polacos de guerra en México, 1943–1947*. Mexico: Centro de Documentación e Investigación de la Comunidad Ashkenazí de México, 1998.

Carvalho, José Murilo de. *La formación de las almas. El imaginario de la República en el Brasil*. Buenos Aires: Universidad Nacional de Quilmes, 1997.

Cassá, Roberto. "Historiography of the Dominican Republic." In *General History of the Caribbean, Vol. VI: Methodology and Historiography of the Caribbean*, edited by B.W. Higman. London and Oxford: Unesco Publishing and Macmillan, 1999.

Castellanos, Alfredo R. *Vida de Artigas*. Montevideo: Medina Editor, 1954.

Castro, Celso, Maria Celina D'Araujo, and Gláucio Ary Dillon Soares. *Os anos de chumbo. A memória military sobre a repressão*. Rio de Janeiro: Relume Dumará, 1994.

Castro, Moacir Werneck de. *El Libertador. Vida de Simón Bolívar*. Caracas: Instituto de Altos Estudios de América Latina, Universidad Simón Bolívar, 1990.

Caula, Nelson. "Un hombre de espíritu volcánico, al decir de Zelmar." *La Fogata Digital*. http://www.lafogata.org/05latino/latino10/uru_3-4.htm (accessed 11 May 2006).

Cavalcanti, Pedro Celso Uchôa, and Jovelino Ramos. *Memórias do exilio: Brasil 1964/19??*. São Paulo: Editora Livraria Livramento, 1978.

Celedón, María Angélica, and Luz María Opazo. *Volver a empezar*. Santiago: Pehuén, 1987.

Centeno, Miguel Angel. "War in Latin America: The Peaceful Continent?" In *Latin America. An Interdisciplinary Approach*, edited by Julio López-Arias and Gladys M. Varona-Lacey. New York: Lang, 1999, pp. 121–136.

Chiaramonte, José Carlos. *El mito de los orígenes en la historiografía Latinoamericana*. Buenos Aires: Universidad de Buenos Aires: Cuadernos del Instituto Ravignani, 1991.

Chiaramonte, José Carlos. "Modificaciones del pacto imperial." In *De los imperios a las naciones*, edited by Antonio Anino, Luis Castro Leiva, and Francois-Xavier Guerra. Zaragoza: Ibercaja, 1994, pp. 107–128.

Chile Committee for Human Rights. "Our work in Britain," ca. 1976. Archives of the UK Folder 7.1: Movements of solidarity. International Institute for Social History (IISG), Amsterdam.

Chile. Country Reports on Human Rights Practices for 1985. Washington, D.C.: U.S. Department of State, 1986.

Chile. Country Reports on Human Rights Practices for 1987. Washington, D.C.: U.S. Department of State, 1988.

"Chile Forces 21 Exiles Back to Argentina." *New York Times*, December 22, 1984, http://www.nytimes.com (accessed 12 June 2008).

"Chile Lucha." *Magazine of the Chile Solidarity Campaign No. 43* (Winter 1983). Folder No. 1421, Internacional Institute of Social History (IISG), Amsterdam.

Cibils, Ana Ines. "Donde fueron a parar." *El Observador*, Fin de Semana, Montevideo, 29 July 2000, pp. 2–4.

"Cinco años de actividad del Comité de Défense de Prisonniers Politiques en Uruguay," Casa de Uruguay-Francia, *Espacio*, No. 4, December 5, 1977, 18, Documents France Folder 7.1, International Institute for Social History (IISG), Amsterdam.

Cipriano, Castro. http://efemeridesvenezolanas.com/html/castro.htm (accessed 18 June 2006).

CISPLA. *Latinoamericanos: Refugiados políticos en España*. Valencia: CISPLA, 1982.

Claudio Lomnitz. "Passion and Banality in Mexican History: The Presidential Persona." In *The Collective and the Public in Latin America*, edited by Luis Roniger and Tamar Herzog. Brighton, UK: Sussex Academic Press, 2000, pp. 238–256.

Clavijero, Francisco Javier. *Capítulos de Historia y Disertaciones*, Mexico: Imprenta Universitaria, 1943.

Cobb, Roger W., and Marc Howard Ross. *Cultural Strategies of Agenda Denial*. Lawrence: University Press of Kansas, 1997.

Cobos, Ana María, and Ana Lya Sater. "Chilean Folk Music in Exile." In *Intellectual Migration: Transcultural Contributions of European and Latin American Emigres. Papers of the 31st annual meetings of SALALM*, edited by Liliana Sontag. Madison, WI: SALALM Secretzrizt, 1986, pp. 295–339.

Cohen, Robin, and Danièle Joly. *Reluctant Hosts: Europe and its Refugees*. Aldershot, UK: Avebury-Gower, 1990.

Collier, Simon, and William F. Sater. *A History of Chile*. New York: Cambridge University Press, 1996.

Comisión Argentina de Derechos Humanos (CADHU). *Argentina: Proceso al genocidio*. Madrid: Elías Querejeta, 1977.

Comité Ejecutivo Central, "Estatuto del Acuerdo Paraguayo en el Exilio (A.P.E.)." Suiza, December 1981.

Comité Pro-Retorno de Exiliados. "Documento presentado a las Naciones Unidas." Santiago, Chile, 1980.

"Convention related to the status of refugees (1951)," art. 1, in Office of the High Commissioner for Human Rights. http://www.unhchr.ch/html.menu3/b/o_c_ref.htm (accessed 28 April 2006).

Cortázar, Julio. "América Latina, exilio y literatura." *Eco* 205, November 1978, and reprinted in *Araucania de Chile* 10 (1980): 60.

Cortázar, Julio. *Argentina: Años de alambradas culturales*. Barcelona: Muchnik Editores, 1984.

Coser, Lewis A. *Refugee Scholars in America*. New Haven, CT: Yale University Press, 1984.

COSOFAM-Barcelona (Casa Argentina), Boletín No. 2, March 1981, Folder No. 1398, International Institute of Social History (IISG), Amsterdam.

Costa Couto, Ronaldo. *História indiscreta da ditadura e da abertura*. Rio de Janeiro: Record, 1999.

Costa Couto, Ronaldo. *Memória viva do regime militar, Brasil 1964–1985*. Rio: Record, 1999.

Costa, Albertina de Oliveira, Maria Teresa Porciúncula de Morales, Norma Marzola, and Valentina da Rocha Lima, orgs., *Memórias das mulheres do exílio*. Rio de Janeiro: Paz e Terra, 1980.

Covarrubias Orozco, Sebastián. *Tesoro de la lengua castellana*. Barcelona: S.A. Horta, 1943.

Cox, David. *En honor a la verdad. Memorias desde el exilio de Robert Cox*. Buenos Aires: Colihue, 2002.

Cramaussel, Chantal. "Imagen de México en los relatos de viaje Franceses, 1821–1862." In *México-Francia. Memoria de una sensibilidad común*, edited by Javier Pérez Siller. Pueblo: El Colegio de San Luis, 1998, pp. 333–363.

"Crónica sobre el retorno de los exiliados al Paraguay." *Revista Ñe-Engatú*, Buenos Aires, Year II, No. 12, January–February 1984.

Cunha-Gabbai, Gloria da. *El exilio: realidad y ficción*. Montevideo: ARCA, 1992.

Cymerman, Claude. "La literatura hispanoamericana y el exilio." *Revista Iberoamericana* 46, 164–165 (1993): 523–550.

D'Alotto, Alberto. "El sistema interamericano de protección de los derechos humanos y su contribución a la protección de los refugiados en América Latina." http://www.acnur.org/biblioteca/pdf/3186.pdf (accessed 10 July 2007).

D'Souza, Herbert. "Return Ticket to Brazil." *Third World Quarterly* 9, 1 (1987): 206–208.

Dayan, Aryeh. "Thanks to Menahem Begin." *Kol Hair*, 9 September 1987: 34 (in Hebrew).

"Declaration on Territorial Asylum." http://www.UNHCR.ch/html/menu3/b/o_asylum.htm (accessed 10 July 2007).

Dejbord, Parizad Tamara. *Cristina Peri Rossi, Escritora del exilio*. Buenos Aires: Galerna, 1998.

Dery, David. "Agenda Setting and Problem Definition." *Policy Studies* 21, 1 (2000): 37–47.

Descalzi, Ricardo. *La Real Audiencia de Quito. Claustro en los Andes*. Barcelona: Seix Barral, 1978.

Díaz, José Pedro, and German Wettstein. *Exilio-Inxilio. Dos Enfoques*. Montevideo: Instituto Testimonios de las Comarcas y del Mundo, 1989.

Díaz, Luis Miguel, and Guadalupe Rodríguez de Ita. "Bases histórico-jurídicas de la política mexicana de asilo diplomático." In *Asilo diplomático Mexicano, en el Cono-Sur*, edited by Silvia Dutrénit-Bielous and Guadalupe Rodríguez de Ita. Mexico: Instituto Mora and SER, 1999, pp. 63–85.

Dicionário da Lingua Portuguesa de Candido Figueroa. Lisbon: Livraria Bertrand, 13th ed., Vol. 1.

Dirceu, José, and Vladimir Palmeira. *Abaixo a ditadura. O movimento de 68 contado por seus lideres*. Rio de Janeiro: Garamont, 1998.

Doallo, Beatriz Celina. *El exilio del Libertador*. Buenos Aires: Instituto de Investigaciones Históricas Juan Manuel de Rosas, 1997.

Domínguez, Jorge Luis, and Abraham Loventhal. *Constructing Democratic Governance. Latin America and the Caribbean in the 1990s*. Baltimore: Johns Hopkins University Press, 1996.

Dorfman, Ariel. *Heading South, Looking North: A Bilingual Journey*. New York: Farrar, Straus and Giroux, 1998.

"Double Exile." *Miami Herald*, October 28, 2007. http://www.archives.econ.utah.edu/archives/cubanews (accessed 12 June 2008).

Dunkerley, James. *Power in the Isthmus: A Political History of Modern Central America*. New York: Verso, 1988.

Dutrénit-Bielous, Silvia. "Recorriendo una ruta de la migración política del Río de la Plata a México." *Estudios Interdisciplinarios de América Latina* 12, 2 (2001): 71–74.

Dutrénit-Bielous, Silvia, Ed. *El Uruguay del exilio. Gente, circumstancias, escenarios*. Montevideo: Trilce, 2006.

Dutrénit, Silvia, and Guadalupe Rodríguez de Ita. *Asilo diplomático Mexicano en el Cono Sur*. Mexico: Instituto Mora and SRE, 1999.

Duviols, Pierre. *La destrucción de las religiones andinas*. Mexico: UNAM, 1977.

Duviols, Pierre. *Cultura andina y represión: Procesos y visitas de idolatrías y hechicerías. Cajatambo, siglo XVII*. Cuzco: Centro de Estudios Rurales y Andinos Bartolomé de las Casas, 1986.

Earl, Rebecca, Ed. *Rumours of Wars: Civil Conflict in Nineteenth Century Latin America*. London: Institute of Latin American Studies, 2000.

Eisenstadt, Shmuel N. "The Reconstitution of the Realm of the Political in Modern Societies." Unpublished typescript, 2006.

Eisenstadt, Shmuel N., and Berhard Giesen. "The Construction of Collective Identity." *Archives Européennes de Sociologie* 36 (1995): 72–102.

Eisenstadt, Shmuel N., Wolfgang Schluchter, and Björn Wittrock, Eds. *Public Spheres and Collective Identities*. New Brunswick: Transaction, 2001.

El Museo Nacional. *Vicuña Mackenna. Rasgos biográficos*. Santiago: Prensas de la Universidad de Chile, 1946.

Encina, Diego de, Ed. *Cedulario Indiano*. Madrid: Ediciones Cultura Hispánica, 1945.

Encina, Francisco Antonio. *Historia de Chile*. Santiago de Chile: Editorial Nacimento, 1947, Vol. 7.

Equipo Praxis. "Aproximación a la situación de la mujer inmigrante y exiliada en España," in *Jornadas sobre Emigración, exilio y mujer*. Madrid: Editorial IEPALA, 1987, 21–37.

Escribano, Antonio Izquierdo. *La inmigración en España 1980–1990*. Madrid: Ministerio de Trabajo y Seguridad Social, 1992.

Esponda Fernández, Jaime. "Diagnóstico del exilio – retorno chileno," in *Religión y Exitio–Retorno*. International Seminar Organized by the Episcopal Conference of Caile, 1991.

Esponda Fernández, Jaime. Speech of the Director of the Oficina Nacional del Retorno, Santiago, 20 August 1993, typescript, available at IISG.

Esponda Fernández, Jaime. "La tradición latinoamericana de asilo y la protección de los refugiados." http://www.acnur.org/biblioteca.pdf/3392.pdf (accessed 10 July 2007).

Esposito, Matthew D. "The Politics of Death: State Funerals as Rites of Reconciliation." *The Americas 62*, 1 (2005): 65–94.

Esteva Gallicchio, Eduardo. "Libertad personal, seguridad individual y debido proceso en Uruguay." *Ius et Praxis 5*, 1 (1999): 187–210.

Estrade, Paul. *La colonia cubana de París, 1895–1898*. La Habana: Editorial de Ciencias Sociales, 1984.

Eugenio, María de Hostos y Bonilla 1839–1903. Biography. http://www.loc.gov/rr/hispanic/1898/hostos.html (accessed 13 June 2006).

Fagen, Patricia W. *Exiles and Citizens: Spanish Republicans in Mexico*. Austin: University of Texas Press, 1973.

Faist, Thomas. *The Volume and Dynamics of International Migration and Transnational Social Spaces*. Oxford: Oxford University Press, 2000.

FASIC. *Exilio Interno, Relegación I, 1980*. Documento de trabajo No. 2. Santiago: FASIC, 1981.

FASIC. *Programa de reunificación familiar. Reencuentro en el exilio*. Santiago: FASIC, 1991.

Fawcett, James T. "Networks, linkages, and migration systems." *International Migration Review 23*, 3 (1989): 671–680.

Fay, Ingrid E. and Karen Racine, Eds. *Strange Pilgrimages: Exile, Travel and National Identity in Latin America, 1800–1990s*. Wilmington, DE: Scholarly Resources, 2000.

Fernández Saldaña, José María. *Diccionario Uruguayo de Biografías*. Montevideo: Editorial Amerindia, 1945.

Ferreira, Juan Raúl. *Con la patria en la valija. El exilio, Wilson y los años trágicos*. Montevideo: Linardi y Risso, 2000.

Fortuna, Juan Carlos, Nelly Niedworok, and Adela Pellegrino. *Uruguay y la emigración de los 70*. Montevideo: Ediciones de la Banda Oriental, 1988.

Franco, Leonardo. "Investigación: El asilo y la protección de los refugiados en América Latina. Acerca de la confusión terminológica 'asilo-refugio'. Informe de progreso." In *Derechos humanos y refugiados en las Américas: lecturas seleccionadas*. San José de Costa Rica: ACNUR-IIDH, 2001.

Franco, Marina. *El Exilio Argentina dur ante la dictadura*. Buenos Aires: Siglo XXI.

Franco, Marina and Pilar González Bernardo. "Cuando el sujeto deviene objeto: La construcción del exilio Argentino en Francia." In *Represión y destierro*, edited by Pablo Yankelevich. La Plata: Ediciones al Margen, 2004.

Fraser, Nancy, Ed. *Redistribution or Recognition? A Political-Philosophical Exchange*. London and New York: Verso, 2003.

Freyre, Marlinda. "The Latin American Exile Experience from a Gender Perspective: A Psycho-Dynamic Assessment." *Refuge 14* (1995): 14–25.

Fried-Amilivia, Gabriela. "The Transmission of Traumatic Memories Across Generations in Uruguay: The Experiences of Families of the Disappeared, Political Prisoners, and Exiles after the Era of State Repression (1973–1984)." Ph.D. dissertation, University of California at Los Angeles, 2004.

Frühling, Hugo, and Wolfgang S. Heinz. *Determinants of Gross Human Rights Violations by State and State Sponsored Actors in Brazil, Uruguay, Chile, and Argentina 1960–1990*. The Hague: Nijhoff, 1999.

Frykman, Olsen, Daniel Moore, and Leonardo Rocíelo. "La literatura del exilio Latinoamericano en Suecia (1976–1990)." *Revista Iberoamericana* 59 (1993): 164–165.

Fuentes, Claudio. *La silla del águila*. Mexico: Alfaguara, 2003.

"Fujimori's daughter faces criticism for saying she would pardon him if elected president." *Peruvian Times*, 10 June 2008. http://www.peruviantimes (accessed 15 June 2008).

Furlong, Guillermo. *Los Jesuitas y la escisión del Reino de Indias*. Buenos Aires: Amorrortu, 1960.

Gaillard, Anne Marie. *Exiles et Retours: Itineraires chiliens*. Paris: CIEMI-L'Harmattan, 1997.

Galdames, Luis. *A History of Chile*. New York: Russell & Russell, 1964.

Gallagher, Dennis. "The Evolution of the Internacional Refugee System." *International Migration Review* 23, 3 (1989): 579–598.

García Canclini, Néstor. "Argentinos en México: Una visión antropológica." In *En México, entre exilios. Una experiencia de sudamericanos*, edited by Pablo Yankelevich. Mexico: SRE, ITAM, Plaza y Valdés, 1998.

Garcia Jr., Afrânio. "A Dependence on Politics: Fernando Henrique Cardoso and Sociology in Brazil." *Tempo sociológico* 1 (2005). http://socialsciences.scielo.org/pdf/s_ts/v1nse/scs_a01.pdf (accessed 26 April 2006).

García Ponce, Guillermo. *Memorias de un general de la utopía*. Caracas: Cotragraf, 1992.

Garciadiego, Javier. "Exiliados de la revolución mexicana." Paper presented at the III Jornadas de la historia de las izquierdas, Centro de Documentación e Investigación de la Cultura de Izquierdas en la Argentina, Buenos Aires, 4–6 August 2005.

Garciadiego, Javier, Ed. *Los exiliados de la revolución*. Mexico: El Colegio de México, forthcoming.

Gaspari, Elio. *A ditadura derrotada*. São Paulo: Companhia das Letras, 2003.

Gazit, Orit. *'No Place to Call Home.' Political Exile, Estrangement and Identity. Processes of Identity Construction among Political Exiles from Latin America to Israel, 1970–2004*. Jerusalem: Shaine Working Papers No. 11, 2005 (in Hebrew).

Gerbi, Antonello. *O novo mundo. Historia de uma polemica (1750–1900)*. São Paulo: Companhia das Letras, 1996.

Gilbert, Jorge. *Edgardo Enríquez Frödden, Testimonio de un destierro*. Santiago: Mosquito Editores, 1992.

Gilman, Bruce. "Times of Gal." http://www.brazzil.com/cvrdec97.htm (accessed 4 May 2008).

Giménez López, Enrique, Ed. *Expulsión y exilio de los Jesuitas españoles*. Alicante: Universidad de Alicante, 1997.

Gisbert, Teresa. "Situación jurídica de la Audiencia de Charcas y primeros levantamientos." In *Historia de Bolivia*, edited by José de Mesa, Teresa Gisbert, and Carlos D. Mesa Gisbert. La Paz: Editorial Gisbert, 1999.

Glazer, Daniela. "Refugiados judíos bajo el Cardenismo." Paper presented at the workshop on political exile in Argentina and Latin America, CEDINCI, Buenos Aires, August 2005.

Gobierno Nacional de la República del Ecuador. "Historia constitucional." http://www.presidencia.gov.ec (accessed 29 July 2006).

Goldberg, Florinda. "Latin American Migrant Writers: 'Nomadic, Decentered, Contrapuntal.'" In *Globality and Multiple Modernities*, edited by Luis Roniger and Carlos H. Waisman. Brighton, Sussex UK: Academic Press, 2002, pp. 285–312.

Gómez, Albino. *Exilios (Por qué volvieron)*. Rosario: Homo Sapiens Ediciones, 1999.

González Echevarría, Roberto. "The Master of Modernismo." *The Nation*, 13 February 2006. http://www.thenation.com/doc/20060213/echevarria.

González, Gustavo. "Chile: Peruvian Refugees Fear Fujimori Will Slip Through the Cracks." http://ipsnews.net/news (accessed 15 June 2008).

González, Mike. "Exile." In *Encyclopedia of Contemporary Latin American and Caribbean Cultures*, edited by Daniel Balderston, Mike González, and Ana M. López. London and New York: Routledge, 2000, Vol. 2, pp. 539–540.

Graham-Yooll, Andrew. *A Matter of Fear: Portrait of an Argentinian Exile*. Westport, CT: Hill, 1982.

Grant Wood, Andrew. "Death of a Political Prisoner: Revisiting the Case of Ricardo Flores Magón." http://ncsu.edu/project/acontracorriente/fall_05/Wood.PDF8 (accessed 8 July 2007).

Green, James N. "Clergy, Exiles and Academics: Opposition to the Brazilian Military Dictatorship in the United States, 1969–1974." *Latin American Politics and Society* 45, 1 (2003): 87–117.

Grinberg, León and Rebeca Grinberg. *Psicoanálisis de la migración y del exilio*. Madrid: Alianza Editorial, 1984.

Guelar, Diana, Vera Jarach, and Beatriz Ruiz. *Los chicos del exilio. Argentina (1975–1984)*. Buenos Aires: Ediciones el País de Nomeolvides, 2002.

Guerra, François-Xavier. "La lumière et ses reflets: Paris et la politique Latino-Americain." In *Le Paris des Etrangers*. Paris: Edition de l'Imprimerie Nationale, 1989, pp. 171–182.

Guerra, François-Xavier. "The Implosion of the Spanish Empire: Emerging Statehood and Collective Identities." In *The Collective and the Public in Latin America*, edited by Luis Roniger and Tamar Herzog. Brighton, UK: Sussex Academic Press, 2000, pp. 71–94.

Guest, Ian. *Behind the Disappearances*. Philadelphia: University of Pennsylvania Press, 1990.

Guillén, Claudio. *Múltiples moradas*. Barcelona: Tusquets, 1998.

Gutiérrez, Carlos María. "Adentro y afuera." *Brecha*, 30 January 1987: 11.

Guzmán, Luis Mariano. *Historia de Bolivia*. Cochabamba: Imprenta del Siglo, 1983.

Halperin Donghi, Tulio. *Proyecto y construcción de una nación*. Caracas: Biblioteca Ayacucho, 1980.

Halperin Donghi, Tulio. "Party and Nation-State in the Construction of Collective Identities: Uruguay in the Nineteenth Century." In *The Collective and the Public in Latin America. Cultural Identities and Political Order*, edited by Luis Roniger and Tamar Herzog. Brighton, UK: Sussex Academic Press, 2000.

Hammerly Dupuy, Daniel. "Rasgos Biográficos de Artigas en el Paraguay." In *Artigas*. Montevideo: Ediciones de El País, 1951.

Haslip, Gabriel. "Crime and the Administration of Justice in Colonial Mexico City 1696–1810." Ph.D. dissertation, Columbia University, New York, 1980.

Hawkins, Timothy. "A War of Words: Manuel Montúfar, Alejandro Marure, and the Politics of History in Guatemala." *The Historian* 64, 3–4 (2002): 526.

Hechter, Michael. *Principles of Group Solidarity.* Berkeley: University of California Press, 1987.

Hecker, Liliana. "Polémica con Julio Cortázar." *Cuadernos Hispanoamericanos* 519–520 (1993): 591–595.

Helfant, Henry. *La doctrina Trujillo del asilo diplomático humanitario.* Mexico: Editorial Offest Continente, 1947.

Helg, Aline. "Simon Bolivar and the Spectre of *Pardocracia:* Jose Padilla in Post-Independent Cartagena." *Journal of Latin American Studies* 35 (2003): 447–471.

Heredia Vargas, Raimundo. "El retorno: Una perspectiva de los que volvieron desde Suecia." Universidad de Chile: Instituto de Ciencia Política, 1994, documento de trabajo No. 40.

Hernández, Rafael. "Fallacies Regarding the Cuban Community in the United States." In *Cuba and the United States: Will the Cold War in the Caribbean End?* Boulder, CO: Rienner, 1991.

Herranz Gómez, Yolanda. "Formas de incorporación laboral de la inmigración latinoamericana en Madrid." Ph.D. dissertation, Universidad Autónoma de Madrid, 1996.

Herzog, Tamar. *La administración como un fenómeno social. La justicia penal de la ciudad de Quito, 1650–1750.* Madrid: Centro de Estudios Constitucionales, 1995.

Hirschman, Albert O. *Exit, Voice and Loyalty.* Cambridge, MA: Harvard University Press, 1970.

Hirschman, Albert O. *Crossing Boundaries: Selected Writings.* New York: Zone Books, 1998.

Hollis, Christopher. *The Jesuits: A History.* New York: Macmillan, 1968.

Hoover, John P. *Admirable Warrior: Marshal Sucre, Fighter for South American Independence.* Detroit: Blaine Ethridge Books, 1977. http://acnur.org/biblioteca/pdf/0267.pdf (accessed 8 July 2007).

Human Rights Program of the Harvard Law School. "Human Rights Lawsuits Brought Against Former Bolivian President and Minister of Defense for Complicity in Attacks on Civilians." http://www.law.harvard.edu/programs/hrp/index.html (accessed 16 July 2008).

Human Rights Watch World Report 2001. www.hrw.org/wr2k1/appendix/index.html (accessed 25 May 2006).

Humboldt, Alexander von. *Alejandro de Humboldt. Por tierras venezolanas.* Caracas: Fundación de Promoción Cultural de Venezuela, 1983.

Hunter, Wendy. *Eroding Military Influence in Brazil.* Chapel Hill: University of North Carolina Press, 1997.

Imaz, Cecilia. La práctica del asilo y del refugio en México. Mexico: Potrerillos Editores, 1995.

Informe de la misión de la Internacional Socialista a América Latina, 15–25 March 1978. Socialist International Archives (1951–1988), files 1125–1129, International Institute of Social History (IISG), Amsterdam.

Interamerican Commission of Human Rights. *Report of the Situation of Human Rights in Panama, June 22, 1978.* http://www.cidh.org/countryrep/Panama78ang/chap.7.htm (accessed 3 August 2006).

Interamerican Commission of Human Rights, Organization of American States, "Report on the Status of Human-Rights in Chile: Findings on the Spot. Observations in the Republic of Chile. July 22–2 August 1974." OEA/Ser.L/V/II.34, doc. 21 corr.1, 25 October 1974. http://www.cidh.org/countryrep/Chile74eng/chap13.htm (accessed 4 June 2006).

International Court of Justice, Haya de la Torre Case. http://www.icj-cij.org/icjwww/idecisions/isummaries/ihayasummary510613.htm.

IOE. "Los inmigrantes en España." *Revista de Estudios Sociales y Sociología* 66 (1985): 138.

Ishay, Micheline. *The History of Human Rights*. Berkeley: University of California Press, 2004.

Iwańska, Alicja. *Exiled Governments*. Cambridge, UK: Schenkman, 1981.

Izquierdo Escribano, Antonio. *La inmigración en España 1980–1990*. Madrid: Ministerio de Trabajo y Seguridad Social, 1992.

Jaksic, Ivan. "Sarmiento and the Chilean Press, 1841–51." In *Sarmiento: Author of a Nation*, edited by Tulio Halperin Donghi, Ivan Jaksic, Gwen Kirkpatrick, and Francine Masiello. Berkeley: University of California Press, 1994.

Jensen, Silvina. "Política y cultura del exilio argentino en Cataluña." In *Represión y destierro*, edited by Pablo Yankelevich. La Plata: Editorial Al Margen, 2004.

Jensen, Silvina. "Representaciones del exilio y de los exiliados en la historia argentina". *EIAL*, 20,1 (2009), forthcoming.

Jitrik, Noé. *Las armas y las razones. Enszyos sobre el peronismo, el exilio y la literatura, 1975–1980*. Buenos Aires: Sudamericana, 1984.

Jirón, Manuel. *Exilio S.A. Vivencias de un Nicaragüense en el exilio*. San José: Ediciones Radio Amor, 1983.

Johnson, John J. "Foreign Factors." In *Caudillos. Dictators in Spanish America*, edited by Hugh M. Hamill. Norman and London: University of Oklahoma Press, 1992. Originally published in *Pacific Historical Review* 20, 2 (1951).

Joly, Danièle. *International Migration in the New Millenium*. London: Ashgate, 2004.

"Julio Cortázar, Argentino, 1914–1984." *Literatura Latinoamericana*. http://www.geocities.com/macondomorel/julio.html (accessed 23 April 2006).

Jurema, Abelardo. *Exilio*. Paraiba, Brazil: Acauá, 1978.

Kacowicz, Arie. *The Impact of Norms in International Society: The Latin American Experience, 1881–2001*. Notre Dame, IN: University of Notre Dame Press, 2005.

Kaminsky, Amy K. *After Exile. Writing the Latin American Diaspora*. Minneapolis: University of Minnesota Press, 1999.

Kaplan, Marion. *Dominican Haven: The Jewish Refugee Settlement in Sosúa, 1940–45*. New York: Museum of Jewish Heritage, 2008.

Katra, William H. *The Argentine Generation of 1837*. London: Associated University Press, 1996.

Kay, Diana. *Chileans in Exile. Private Struggles, Public Lives*. London: Macmillan, 1987.

Kay, Diana. "The Politics of Gender in Exile: Chileans in Glasgow." In *Reluctant Hosts: Europe and its Refugees*, edited by Danièle Joly and Robin Cohen. Aldershot, UK: Avebury, 1989.

Keane, John. *Global Civil Society*. Cambridge: Cambridge University Press, 2003.

Kennedy, J. Gerald. *Imagining Paris, Exile, Writing and American Identity*. New Haven, CT: Yale University Press, 1993.

Klein, Fernando. "La emigración de los uruguayos o el "otro" excluido," available at http://www.liceus.com/cgi-bin/ac/pu (accessed 27 November 2008).

Klein, Herbert. *Bolivia*. Oxford: Oxford University Press, 1982.

Kohut, Kart. *Escribir en Paris*. Frankfurt am Main: Klaus Dieter Vervuert, 1983.

Kovalsky, Juana. "Exilio y desexilio: Una experiencia más de violencia." In *Fuga, Exilio y Retorno. La salud mental y el refugiado*, edited by Adrianne Aron San Francisco: Committee for Health Rights in Central America, 1988, pp. 83–95.

Krishnan, Parameswara, and Dave Odynak. "A Generalization of Petersen's Typology of Migration." *International Migration* 25, 4 (1987): 385–397.

Kristeva, Julia. *Strangers to Ourselves*. New York: Columbia University Press, 1991.

Lagos-Pope, María Inés, Ed. *Exile in Literature*. Lewisburg: Bucknell University Press, 1988.

"La interminable batalla legal de Alejandra Matus." www.libertad-prensa.org/matusletter.html (accessed 25 May 2006).

Lamónaca, Julio C. and Marcelo N. Viñar. "Asilo político: perspectivas desde la subjetividad." In *Asilo diplomático mexicano en el Cono Sur*, edited by Silvia Dútrénit Bielous and Guadalupe Rodríguez de Ita. Mexico: Instituto Mora and SRE, 1999.

Lamounier, Bolivar. "Brazil. The Hyper-Active Paralysis Syndrome." In *Constructing Democratic Governance. Latin America and the Caribbean in the 1990s*, edited by Jorge Domínguez and Abraham Lowenthal. Baltimore: Johns Hopkins University Press, 1996.

Larrazabal, Carlos Héctor. *Sucre, Figura Continental*. Buenos Aires: Talleres de Juan Pellegrini, 1950.

Lefort, Claude. *Democracy and Political Theory*. Minneapolis: University of Minnesota Press, 1988.

Legislative Assembly of British Columbia, Canada. "1974 Legislative Session: 4th Session, 30th Parliament, Wednesday 27 March 1974." http://www.legis.gov.bc.ca/HANSARD/30th4th/30p-04s-740327p.htm (accessed 5 June 2006).

Lerner Sigal, Victoria. "Exilio e historia: Algunas hipótesis generales a partir del caso de los Mexicanos exilados por la Revolución Mexicana." Chicago: University of Chicago, Mexican Studies Program, Center for Latin American Studies, Working paper series No. 7, 2000.

"Letter to the Governor of Jamaica," May 1815, in *Cartas del Libertador*. Caracas: Banco de Venezuela and Fundación Vicente Lecuna, 1964, Vol. I, p. 189.

Ley General de Población y Reglamento de la Ley General de Población. México: Consejo Nacional de Población, 1987.

Liberman, Arnoldo. "Rememoración del exilio." *Cuadernos hispanoamericanos* (1993), 517–519: 544–551.

Liberman, Arnoldo. *Exodo y Exilio*. Madrid: Sefarad, 2006.

Lida, Clara. *Inmigración y exilio: Reflexiones sobre el caso español*. Mexico: Siglo XXI/Colegio de México, 1997.

Lijphart, Arendt and Carlos Waisman, Eds. *Institutional Design in New Democracies: Eastern Europe and Latin America*. Boulder, CO: Westview, 1996.

Linz, Juan José and Arturo Valenzuela. *The Failure of Presidential Democracy: The Case of Latin America*. Baltimore: Johns Hopkins University Press, 1994.

Lischer, Sarah. *Dangerous Sanctuaries: Refugee Camps, Civil War, and the Dilemmas of Humanitarian Aid*. Ithaca, NY: Cornell University Press, 2005.

Llambias-Wolff, Jaime. "The Voluntary Repatriation Process of Chilean Exiles." *International Migration* 31, 4 (1993): 579–597.

Lloyd Mecham, J. *Church and State in Latin America*. Chapel Hill: University of North Carolina Press, 1934.

Loschiavo, Mari Cecilia, org. *Maria Antonia – Uma Rua na Contramao*. São Paulo: Studio Nobel, 1998.

Lourdes, Maria de and Monaco Janotti. "The Monarchist Response to the Beginnings of the Brazilian Republic." *The Americas* 48, 2 (1991): 223–243.

Loveman, Brian. *The Constitution of Tyranny. Regimes of Exception in Spanish America.* Pittsburgh, PA: University of Pittsburgh Press, 1993.

Loveman, Brian and Elizabeth Lira. *Las ardientes cenizas del olvido: via chilena de reconciliacion politica, 1932–1994.* Santiago de Chile: LOM, 2000.

Lovera De-Sola, Roberto J. "La estadía de Simón Bolívar en Curazao." In *Los sefaradíes – Vínculo entre Curazao y Venezuela*, 91–97. Caracas: Asociación Israelita de Venezuela and Museo Sefardí de Caracas Morris E Curiel, 2002.

Lovera De-Sola, Roberto J. *Curazao, escala en el primer destierro del Libertador.* Caracas: Monte Avila Editores, 1992.

Luna, David Alejandro. *El asilo político.* San Salvador: Editorial Universitaria, 1962.

Luna, Félix. *Historia general de la Argentina.* Buenos Aires: Planeta, 1995, Vol. 5.

Luque, José. "Género, memoria y ciudadanía en un contexto post-nacional. El caso de los peruanos y peruanas refugiados en Santiago de Chile." Forthcoming in *Estudios Interdisciplinarios de América Latina y el Caribe*, 2009.

Lutz, Olga and Pilar Walter. "Los exiliados latinoamericanos en España." *Estudios del CESERAD* (Madrid), 3 (1985).

Machado, Cristina P. *Os exiliados.* São Paulo: Editora Alfa – Omeg, 1979.

Mainwaring, Scott and Matthew Shurgart, Eds. *Presidentialism and Democracy in Latin America.* Cambridge: Cambridge University Press, 1997.

Maira, Luis. "Claroscuros de un exilio privilegiado." In *En México, entre exilios. Una experiencia de sudamericanos*, edited by Pablo Yankelevich. Mexico: SRE, ITAM, Plaza y Valdés, 1998.

Maletta, Héctor, Frida Szwarcberg, and Rosalía Schneider, "Exclusión y reencuentro: Aspectos psicosociales de los exiliados a la Argentina." In *Fronteras permeables*, edited by Patria R. Pessar. Buenos Aires: Planeta, 1991.

Margulis, Mario. "Argentines in Mexico." In *The Dynamics of Argentine Migration (1955–1984). Democracy and the Return of Expatriates*, edited by Alfredo E. Lattes and Enrique Oteiza. Geneva: UNRISD, 1987.

Mariátegui, José Carlos. "Siete ensayos de interpretación de la realidad Peruana." In *Mariátegui Total.* Lima: Empresa Editora Amauta, 1994, Vol. I, pp. 6–157.

Markarian, Vania. *Left in Transformation: Uruguayan Exiles and the Latin American Human Rights Networks, 1967–1984.* New York: Routledge, 2005.

Markarian, Vania. "From a Revolutionary Logic to Humanitarian Reasons: Uruguayan Leftists in the Exile and Human Rights Transnational Networks." In *Cuadernos del CLAEH*, Vol. 1, special edition, Montevideo, 2006, translated by Maria Cristina Cafferatta http://socialsciences.scielo.org (accessed 12 May 2006).

Mármora, Celio. "Hacia la migración planificada inter-latinoamericana: Salvadoreños en Argentina." *Estudios Migratorios Latinoamericanos* 1, 3 (1986): 275–293.

Mármora, Lelio, and Jorge Gurrieri. *Return to Rio de la Plata: Response to the Return of Exiles to Argentina and Uruguay.* Washington, D.C.: Georgetown University, Center for Immigration Policy and Refugee Assistance, 1988.

Martínez, José Luis. *La Cuba disidente.* Montevideo: Fin de Siglo, 1996.

Martínez, Tomas Eloy. *Las memorias del general.* Buenos Aires: Planeta, 1996.

Masetti, Jorge. *El furor y el delirio.* Barcelona: Tusquets, 1999.

Maxwell, Kenneth R. *A Devassa da Devassa: A Inconfidência Mineira: Brasil–Portugal – 1750–1808.* São Paulo: Paz e Terra, 1985.

Mayer, Jorge. *Alberdi y su tiempo.* Buenos Aires: EUDEBA, 1963.

Mayochi, Enrique Mario. *El Libertador José de San Martín.* Buenos Aires: Instituto Nacional Sanmartiniano, 1995.

McCallum, Jimmy. "A Trade-Unionist Guide to the Chile Issue: Does Your Firm Trade in Torture?" No date (ca. 1974). UK Folder 7.1, International Institute for Social History (IISG), Amsterdam.

McClennen, Sophia A. *The Dialectics of Exile: Nation, Time, Language and Space in Hispanic Literatures.* West Lafayette, IN: Purdue University Press, 2004.

McSherry, J. Patrice. "Tracking the Origins of a State Terror Network: Operation Condor." *Latin American Perspectives* 29, 1 (2002): 38–40.

McSherry, J. Patrice. "The Undead Ghost of Operation Condor." *Logos* 4, 2 (2005). http://www.logosjournal.com/issue_4.2 (accessed 11 May 2006).

Medrano, Samuel W. *El Libertador José de San Martín.* Buenos Aires: Instituto Nacional Sanmartiniano, 1995.

Melgar Bao, Ricardo. "Utopía y revolución en el exilio venezolano en México." Paper presented at the LASA Annual Conference, Guadalajara, April 1997.

Melgar Bao, Ricardo. Lecture in the workshop on Political Exile in Argentina and Latin America, CEDINCI, Buenos Aires, August 2005.

Mendez-Faith, Teresa. *Paraguay, novela y exilio.* Sommerville, NJ: SLUSA, 1992.

Mier, José M. de. *Complemento a la historia extensa de Colombia: Testimonio de una amistad.* Colombia: Plaza & Janés, 1983, Vol. 2.

Millar, Juan Edmundo. *Artigas el Profeta.* Montevideo: Impresora Uruguaya, 1964.

Miller, Kerby A. *Emigrants and Exiles. Ireland and the Irish Exodus to North America.* Oxford: Oxford University Press, 1985.

Miller, Martin A. *The Russian Revolutionary Emigrés, 1825–1870.* Baltimore: Johns Hopkins University Press, 1986.

Mira Delli-Zotti, Guillermo. "La singularidad del exilio Argentino en Madrid: Entre las respuestas a la represión de los '70 y la interpelación a la Argentina post-dictatorial." In *Represión y destierro*, edited by Pablo Yankelevich. La Plata: Ediciones al Margen, 2004.

Mitchell, David. *The Jesuits: A History.* New York: Franklin Watts, 1981.

Mitre, Bartolomé. *Historia de San Martín y la emancipación Latinoamericana.* Buenos Aires: Editorial Ateneo, 1950.

Moerner, Magnus. *The Expulsion of the Jesuits from Latin America.* New York: Knopf, 1965.

Montes, Segundo. "Migration to the United States as an Index of the Intensifying Social and Political Crises in El Salvador." *Journal of Refugees Studies* 1, 2 (1988): 107–126.

Montúfar, Manuel. *Memorias para la historia de la Revolución de Centro-América.* Vol. 2 (Jalapa: Aburto y Blanco, 1832), Guatemala: José de Pineda Ibarra, 1963.

Montupil, Fernando, Ed. *Exilio, derechos humanos y democracia. El exilio chileno en Europa.* Bruselas and Santiago: Coordinación Europea de Comités Pro-Retorno, 1993.

Moore, Daniel. "Latinoamericanos en Suecia." In *Suecia-Latinoamerica. Relaciones y cooperación*, edited by Weine Karlsson, Ake Magnusson, and Carlos Vidales. Stockholm: LAIS, 1993, pp. 161–183.

Morales Pérez, Salvador E., and Laura del Alizal. *Dictadura, exilio e insurrección: Cuba en la perspectiva mexicana, 1952–1958.* Mexico: Secretaría de Relaciones Exteriores, 1999.

Morelli, Federica. "Territorial Hierarchies and Collective Identities in Late Colonial and Early Independent Quito." In *The Collective and the Public in Latin America*, edited by Luis Roniger and Tamar Herzog. Brighton, UK: Sussex Academic Press, 2000, pp. 37–56.

Moreno de Angel, Pilar. *Santander*. Bogotá: Planeta, 1989.

Moreno, C. Galván. *Radiografía de Sarmiento*. Buenos Aires: Editorial Claridad, 1961.

Moyas Cobos, Epifanio A., Ed. *Exilio y resistencia: Los movimientos políticos de exiliados Paraguayos en Argentina. Declaraciones y crónicas desde 1983 hasta la caída de Stroessner*. Buenos Aires: Alberto Kleiner editor, 1989.

Murilo de Carvalho, José. *Cidadania no Brasil. O longo camino*. São Paulo: Civilização Brasileira, 2001.

Naficy, Hamid, Ed. *Home, Exile, Homeland*. New York and London: Routledge, 1999.

NCHR Refugee Program. "Beyond the Bat Eyes." http://www.nchr.org/reports/bateyes. pdf (accessed 8 July 2007).

Neri, Rafael José. *La embajada que llegó del exilio*. Caracas: Academia Nacional de la Historia, 1988.

Neuman, Efrat, and Sami Peretz. "The Prodigal Son Returns." *Haaretz*, 27 March 2008.

Neves-Xavier, Angela de Brito. "Brazilian Women in Exile: The Quest for an Identity." *Latin American Perspectives* 13, 2 (1986): 58–80.

Nussbaum, Martha. *Cultivating Humanity*. Cambridge, MA, and London: Harvard University Press, 1997.

O'Dogherty, Laura. "Mayas en el exilio: Los refugiados guatemaltecos en México." In *Memorias del Segundo coloquio internacional de Mayistas*, Universidad Autónoma de México, Centro de Estudios Mayas, 17–21 August 1987.

O'Donnell, Guillermo. "Delegative Democracy." *Journal of Democracy* 5, 1 (1994): 55–69.

O'Donnell, Guillermo. "In Partial Defense of an Evanescent Paradigm." *Journal of Democracy* 13, 2 (2002): 6–12.

Oñate, Rody, and Thomas Wright. *Flight from Chile. Voices of Exile*. Albuquerque: University of New Mexico Press, 1988.

Oñate, Rody, and Thomas Wright. "Chilean Political Exile." *Latin American Perspectives* 34, 4 (2007): 31–49.

Orellana, Carlos. "Revista a las revistas chilenas del exilio 1973–1990." http://www. abacq.net/imagineria/revistas.htm (accessed 4 June 2008).

Orico, Osvaldo. *Confissões do exilio JK*. Rio de Janeiro: Francisco Alves, 1977.

Otero, Jorge. *João Goulart, lembranças do exilio*. Rio de Janeiro: Casa Jorge, 2001.

Otero, Jorge. *João Goulart. Recuerdos de su exilio uruguayo*. Montevideo: Tradinco, 2003.

Ouditt, Sharon. "Introduction: Dispossession or Repositioning?" In *Displaced Persons: Conditions of Exile in European Culture*, edited by Sharon Ouditt. Aldershot, UK: Ashgate, 2002.

Ovando Sanz, Jorge Alejandro. "El Surgimiento de la Nacionalidad Charquina y la Formación del Estado Boliviano." In *El Siglo XIX: Bolivia y América Latina*, edited by Rossana Barragán, Dora Cajías, and Seemin Qayum. La Paz: Coordinadora de Historia e I.F.E.A, 1997.

Paiva, Mauricio. *O sonho exiliado*. Rio de Janeiro: Achiamép, 1986.

Palma Mora, Mónica. "Destierro y encuentro. Aproximaciones al exilio latinoamericano en México, 1954–1980." *Amerique Latine, Histoire et memoire*, p. 16. http://www.alhim.revues.org/document636.html (accessed 10 July 2007).

Pedraz, Martín Alonso. *Enciclopedia del idioma*. Madrid: Aguilar, 1958.

Pellegrino, Adella. *Informe sobre la migración internacional en Uruguay en el período 1950–1985*. Montevideo: Facultad de Ciencias Sociales, 1996.

Pelossi, Hebe. *Argentinos en Francia Franceses en Argentina*. Buenos Aires: Ciudad Universitania, 1999.

Pereira, Marcelo. "Portada: Bajón uruguayo." *Brecha*, Montevideo, 18 August 2000, 2–3.

Perón, el hombre del destino. Buenos Aires: Abril Educativa y Cultural, 1975, Vol. 3.

Pessar, R.P. "Women's Political Consciousness and Empowerment in Local, National and Transnational Contexts: Guatemalan Refugees and Returnees." *Identities* 7, 4 (2001): 462.

Peters, J.D. "Exile, Nomadism and Diaspora. The Stakes of Mobility in the Western Canon." In *Home, Exile, Homeland*, edited by Hamid Naficy. New York and London: Routledge, 1999, 19–21.

Pianca, Marina. "The Latin American Theater of Exile." *Theater Research International* 14, 2 (1989): 174–185.

Pieroni, Geraldo. *Os excluídos do Reino*. Brasilia: Editora da Universidade Nacional de Brasilia, 2000.

Pieroni, Geraldo. *Vadios e ciganos, heréticos e bruxas – os degradados no Brasil colonia*. Rio: Bertrand, 2000.

Pizarro, J. *Situación y tendencias de la migración internacional en Chile*. Santiago de Chile: CELADE, 1997.

Pomar, F. Cossio del. *Haya de la Torre. El Indoamericano*, Mexico: Editorial América, 1939.

Pope Atkins, G. *Encyclopedia of the Inter-American System*. Westport, CT: Greenwood, 1997.

"Procedures for the treatment of people escaping from South America" (in Hebrew: Nohal tipul benimlatim me-artzot Drom America). Personal Archive of Daniel Recanati, Jerusalem, no date, probably June 1976.

Pulido, María Claudia, and Marisol Blanchard. "La Comisión Interamericana de Derechos Humanos y sus mecanismos de protección aplicados a la situación de los refugiados, apátridas y solicitantes de asilo." http://www.acnur.org/biblioteca/pdf/2578.pdf (accessed 10 July 2007).

Quattrocchi-Woisson, Diana. *Los males de la memoria. Historia y política en la Argentina*. Buenos Aires: Emecé, 1995.

Queiroz, Maria José de. *Os males da ausência ou a literatura do exílio*. Rio de Janeiro: Topbooks, 1998.

Racine, Karen. "Introduction: National Identity Formation in an International Context." In *Strange Pilgrimages: Exile, Travel, and National Identity in Latin America, 1800–1990s*, edited by Ingrid E. Fey and Karen Racine. Wilmington, DE: Scholarly Resources, 2000.

Ramos, Antonio. "El Refugio de Artigas en el Paraguay." In *Artigas*. Montevideo: Instituto Histórico y Geográfico del Uruguay, 1952.

Real Academia Española. *Diccionario de la lengua española*. Madrid: Espasa Calpe, 1984.

Rein, Raanan. *Argentina, Israel and the Jews. Perón, the Eichmann Capture and After*. Bethesda, MD: University Press of Maryland, 2003.

Relief Web. "Central America: Main Refugee Flows during the 1980s." http://www.reliefweb.int/rw/RW.NSF/db900SID (accessed 8 July 2007).

Renique, José Luis. "Benjamín Vicuña Mackenna: exilio, historia y nación." *Ciberayllu*, 18 October 2005. http://www.andes.missouri.edu/andes/Especiales/JLRVicuna/JLR_Vicuna1.html (accessed 29 May 2006).

Report No. 20/98. Case 11.762 Baruch Ivcher Bronstein Peru. 3 March 1998, Inter-Am.C.H.R., OEA/Ser.L/V/ii.95 doc 7 rev.at 164 (1997). http://www1.umn.edu/humanrts/cases/1997/peru20-98.html (accessed 10 June 2008).

"Retorno de opositores argentinos exiliados," press release distributed in Mexico and Spain, May 8, 1982. Spain Folder No. 7.1. International Institute of Social History (IISG), Amsterdam.

Rettig Report: Informe de la Comisión Nacional de Verdad y Reconciliación. Santiago: Secretaría de Comunicación y Cultura, Ministerio Secretaría General de Gobierno, 1991.

Ribeiro Martins, Roberto. Liberdade para os brasileiros. Anistia ontem e hoje. Rio de Janeiro: Civilizacao Brasileira, 1978.

Rights and the United Nations. Philadelphia: University of Pennsylvania Press, 1990.

Roa Bastos, Augusto Antonio. Yo el supremo. Buenos Aires: Siglo XXI, 1975.

Roca, Pilar. Ismael Viñas. Ideografía de un mestizo. Buenos Aires: Dunken, 2005.

Rodríguez de Ita, Guadalupe. "Experiencias de asilo registradas en las embajadas Mexicanas." In Asilo diplomático Mexicano en el Cono Sur, edited by Silvia Dutrénit and Guadalupe Rodríguez de Ita. Mexico: Instituto Mora and SRE, 1999.

Rodríguez Elizondo, José. La pasión de Iñaki. Santiago: Editorial Andrés Bello, 1996.

Rodríguez Villouta, Mili. Ya nunca me verás como me vieras. Santiago: Ornitorrinco, 1990.

Roedor, Ralph. Juárez y su México. Mexico: Fondo de Cultura Económica, 1972.

Rojas, Ricardo. El Santo de la espada. Buenos Aires: Ediciones Corregidor, 1993.

Rollemberg, Denise. Exílio: Entre raízes e radares. Rio de Janeiro: Record, 1999.

Roniger, Luis. "Citizenship in Latin America. New Works and Debates." Citizenship Studies 10, 4 (2006).

Roniger, Luis and Deby Babis. "Latin American Israelis: The Collective Identity of an Invisible Community." In Identities in an Era of Globalization and Multiculturalism. Latin America in the Jewish World, edited by Judit Bokser Liwerant, Eliezer Ben-Rafael, Yossi Gorny, and Raanan Rein. Leiden and Boston: Brill, 2008, pp. 297–320.

Roniger, Luis and Tamar Herzog, Eds. The Collective and the Public in Latin America. Brighton: Sussex Academic Press.

Roniger, Luis and Leandro Kierszenbaum, "Los intelectuales y los discursos de derechos humanos: La experiencia del Cono Sur." Estudios Interdisciplinarios de América Latina y el Caribe 16, 2 (2005): 5–36.

Roniger, Luis and Mario Sznajder. The Legacy of Human-Rights Violations in the Southern Cone. Oxford: Oxford University Press, 1999.

Roniger, Luis and Carlos H. Waisman, Eds. Globality and Multiple Modernities. Comparative North American and Latin American Perspectives. Brighton: Sussex Academic Press, 2000.

Rosas, Juan Manuel de. Cartas del exilio. Buenos Aires: Rodolfo Alonso Editor, 1974.

Rowe, William and Teresa Whitfield. "Thresholds of Identity: Literature and Exile in Latin America." Third World Quarterly 9, 1 (1997): 232–255.

Ruffinelli, Jorge. "El exilio, solidaridad sin fronteras," Brecha, 5 June 1987.

Ruiz, Ramon Eduardo. Cuba. The Making of a Revolution. Northampton: University of Massachusetts Press, 1968. http://www.cubafacts.com/History/history_of_cuba7.htm (accessed 14 June 2006).

Rumazo González, Alfonso. 8 grandes biografías. Caracas: Ediciones de la Presidencia de la Republica, 1993, Vol. II.

Sáenz Carrete, Erasmo. El exilio Latinoamericano en Francia, 1964–1979. Mexico: Potrerillos Editores, 1995.

Said, Edward. "The Mind of Winter: Reflection on Life in Exile." Harper's Magazine, September 1984.

Said, Edward. "Reflections on Exile." in *Out There: Marginalization and Contemporary Cultures*, edited by R. Ferguson, M. Gever, T.T. Minh-ha, and C. West. Cambridge, MA: MIT Press, 1994.

Salas, Horacio. "Duro oficio el exilio." *Cuadernos hispanoamericanos* (1993), 517–519: 555–559.

Sales, Teresa. *Brasileiros longe de casa*. São Paulo: Cartez Editora, 1999.

San Cristóbal, Evaristo. *El Gran Mariscal Luis José de Orbegoso*, Lima: Gil S.A. Editores, 1941.

Sánchez Bella, Ismael, Alberto de la Heray, and Carlos Díaz Rementeria. *Historia del Derecho Indiano*. Madrid: Mapfere, 1992.

Santistevan de Noriega, Jorge. "ACNUR e IIDH, Una relación para el refugio." (2001). http://acnur.org/biblioteca/pdf/0267.pdf (accessed July 8, 2007).

Sassen, Saskia. *Territory, Authority, Rights*. Princeton, NJ: Princeton University Press, 2006.

Scardaville, Michael C. *Crime and the Urban Poor. Mexico City in the Late Colonial Period*. London: University Microfilms International, 1977.

Schäfer, Ernesto. "La Casa de la Contratación de las Indias de Sevilla durante los siglos XVI y XVII." *Archivo Hispalense* 13–14 (1945): 149–162.

Schwarz, Roberto. "Culture and Politics in Brazil, 1964–1969." In *Misplaced Ideas: Essays on Brazilian Culture*, edited by Roberto Schwarz. London: Verso, 1992, pp. 126–159.

Semple, Kirk. "Rise of Chavez Sends Venezuelans to Florida." *New York Times*, January 23, 2008. http://www6.miami.edu (accessed 12 June 2008).

Senkman, Leonardo, and Mario Sznajder, Eds. *El Legado del Autoritarismo*. Buenos Aires: GEL, 1995.

Serra, José. "The Other September 11." *Dissent*, Winter 2004. http://www.dissentmagazine.org/article/?article=411 (accessed 5 June 2006).

Shain, Yossi. "In Search of Loyalty and Recognition." Ph.D. dissertation, Yale University, 1988.

Shain, Yossi. *The Frontier of Loyalty: Political Exiles in the Age of the Nation-States*, Middletown: Wesleyan University Press, 1989.

Shaw, Christine. *The Politics of Exile in Renaissance Italy*. Cambridge: Cambridge University Press, 2000.

Sheffer, Gabriel. *Diaspora Politics: At Home and Abroad*. Cambridge: Cambridge University Press, 2003.

Sheinin, David. "How the Argentine Military Invented Human Rights in Argentina." In *Spanish and Latin American Transitions to Democracy*, edited by Carlos H. Waisman and Raanan Rein. Brighton, UK: Sussex Academic Press, 2005, pp. 190–214.

Shnookal, Deborah, and Marta Muñiz, Eds. *José Martí Reader: Writings on the Americas*. Melbourne and New York: Ocean Press, 1999.

Shumway, Jeffrey M. "Sometimes Knowing How to Forget is also Having Memory: The Repatriation of Juan Manuel de Rosas and the Healing of Argentina." In *Death, Dismemberment and Memory: Body Politics in Latin America*, edited by Lyman L. Johnson. Albuquerque: University of New Mexico, 2004, pp. 105–140.

Simpson, John. "Driven Forth." In *The Oxford Book of Exile*. Oxford: Oxford University Press, 1995.

Skidmore, Thomas. *Brasil. De Castelo a Tancredo*. Rio de Janeiro: Paz e Terra, 1988.

Skidmore, Thomas. *The Politics of Military Rule in Brazil 1964–1985*. New York: Oxford University Press, 1988.

Skidmore, Thomas E. *Five Centuries of Change.* New York: Oxford University Press, 1999.

Smart, Charles Allen. *Juárez.* Barcelona: Grijalbo, 1969.

Sosnowski, Saúl, Ed. *Represión y reconstrucción de una cultura. El caso Argentino.* Buenos Aires: Universidad de Buenos Aires, 1984.

St. Clair Segurado, Eva Maria. *Expulsión y exilio de la provincia jesuítica Mexicana 1767–1820.* Alicante: Universidad de Alicante, 2006.

St. John, Ronald B. *The Foreign Policy of Peru.* Boulder, CO: Lynne Rienner, 1992.

Stabili, Maria Rosaria. *Il Cile, della repubblica liberale al dopo Pinochet.* Firenze: Giunti, 1991.

Statute of the Office of the United Nations' High Commissioner for Refugees. http://www.unhcr.org (accessed 12 July 2007).

Stefanich, Juan. "Artigas, Francia y el Paraguay." In *Artigas.* Montevideo: Instituto Histórico y Geográfico del Uruguay, 1952.

Steiner, Niklaus. *Arguing about Asylum: The Complexity of Refugee Debates in Europe.* New York: St. Martin's Press, 2000.

Street, John. *Artigas and the Emancipation of Uruguay.* Cambridge: Cambridge University Press, 1959.

Sullivan, Kathleen. "Constructing La Casa de la Mujer: The Guatemalan Refugee Women and the Midwives of Monja Blanca in El Porvenir Border Camp, Mexico." In *Development and Diaspora: Gender and the Refugee Experience,* edited by Wenona Gilles, Hellen Moussa, and Penny Van Esterik. Dundas, Ontario: Artemis Enterprises, 1996.

Svirsky, Rubén y Guillermo Waksman. "La diversidad de los de afuera." *Brecha,* Montevideo, 13 February 1987, p. 12.

Sznajder, Mario. "Il populismo in America Latina." *Ricerche di Soria Politica* 7, 3 (2004): 347–366.

Sznajder, Mario and Luis Roniger. "From Argentina to Israel: Escape, Evacuation and Exile." *Journal of Latin American Studies* 37, 2 (2005): 351–377.

Szulc, Ted. "Venezuela Quite After Rebellion." *New York Times,* 4 January 1958, p. 6.

Tabori, Paul. *The Anatomy of Exile. A Semantic and Historical Study.* London: Harrap, 1972.

Tamayo, Jorge L. *Epistolario de Benito Juárez.* Mexico: Fondo de Cultura Económica, 1957.

Tanzi, Héctor José. "El derecho penal indiano y el delito de lesa majestad." *Revista de Historia de América* 84 (1977): 51–62.

Tavares, Flavio. *Memorias do esquecimento.* São Paulo: Globo, 1999.

Teja, Ana María and Israel Wonsewer. *La emigración Uruguaya 1963–1975: sus condicionantes económicas.* Montevideo: Ediciones de la Banda Oriental, 1983.

Tello Díaz, Carlos. *El exilio: un relato de familia.* Mexico: Cal y Arena, 1993.

Tena Ramírez, Felipe. *Las leyes fundamentales de México, 1808–1957.* Mexico: Porrúa, 1957.

The International Development Research Center. "Chilean investigative journalist Alejandra Matus." http://www.edrc.ca (accessed 10 June 2008).

Timothy, Anna. *The Fall of the Royal Government in Mexico City.* Lincoln: University of Nebraska Press, 1978.

Torres Caicedo, José Maria. *Ensayos biográficos y de crítica literaria sobre los principales poetas y literatos hispano americanos.* Paris: Baudry, 1868, Segunda serie.

Trigo, Abril. *Memorias migrantes. Testimonios y ensayos sobre la diáspora uruguaya.* Buenos Aires and Montevideo: Beatriz Viterbo Editora and Ediciones Trilce, 2003.

Turner, Victor. *The Ritual Process: Structure and Anti-Structure.* New York: Cornell University Press, 1974.

Tweed, Thomas A. *Our Lady of the Exile. Diasporic Religion at a Cuban Cathlolic Shrine in Miami.* New York: Oxford University Press, 1997.

Ulanovsky, Carlos. *Seamos felices mientras estamos aquí.* Buenos Aires: Editorial Sudamericana, 2001.

Unión Panamericana, *Convención sobre asilo diplomático suscrita en la X Conferencia Interamericana. Caracas: 1-28 marzo 1954.* Washington: OEA, 1961.

"Urdaneta llama al magnicidio desde Miami," 1 November 2004. http://www.rnv.gov. ve/noticias (accessed 10 June 2008).

Urquijo, José María Mariluz. *Ensayo sobre los juicios de residencia indianos.* Seville: Escuela de Estudios Hispanoamericanos, 1952.

Vargas Araya, Armando. *Idearium Maceista. Junto con hazañas del General Antonio Maceo y sus mambises en Costa Rica, 1891–1895.* San José: Editorial Juricentro, 2001.

Vasconcelos, José. *Discursos, 1920–1950.* Mexico: Ediciones Botas, 1950.

Vasconcelos, José. *El desastre (Tercera parte de Ulises Criollo).* Mexico: Editorial Jus, 1968.

Vásquez, Ana. "The process of transculturation: Exiles and institutions in France." In *Reluctant Hosts: Europe and its Refugees*, edited by Daniele Joly and Robin Cohen. Aldershot, UK: Avebury, 1989, pp. 125–132.

Vásquez, Ana. *Mi amiga Chantal.* Barcelona: Lumen, 1991.

Vásquez, Ana, and Ana María Araujo. *Exils Latino-Americains. La malediction d'Ulysse.* Paris: CIEMI and L'Harmattan, 1988.

Vásquez, Ana, and Ana María Araujo. *La maldición de Ulises.* Santiago: Sudamericana, 1990.

Vásquez, Ana, and Angela Xavier de Brito. "La situation de l'exilée: essai de génèralisation fondé sur l'exemple de réfugiés latino-américains." *Intercultures* 21 (1993): 51–66.

Vázquez, Norma. *Las mujeres refugiadas y retornadas. Las habilidades adquiridas en el exilio y su aplicación a los tiempos de paz.* San Salvador: Editorial Las Dignas, 2000.

Velasco, Juan de. *Historia del reino de Quito en la América Meridional.* Caracas: Biblioteca de Ayacucho, 1981.

Vera, Fernando. "La situación política del Paraguay." Madrid: Fundación Pablo Iglesias, Jornadas por la democracia en el Paraguay – PSOE, ca. 1987. Archives of the International Institute of Social History (IISG), Amsterdam.

Verdery, Katherine. *The Political Lives of Dead Bodies.* New York: Columbia University Press, 1999.

Vergottini, Tomaso de. *Cile: Diario di un diplomatico, 1973–1975.* Rome: Koinè, 2000.

Vertovec, S., and R. Cohen, Eds. *Migrations, Diasporas and Transnationalism.* Cheltenham, UK: Elgar, 1999.

Vich Florez, Cynthia. "Entrevista a Cristina Peri Rossi." *Scriptura* 8–9 (1992): 229–230.

Vicuña Mackenna, Benjamín. *El ostracismo de los Carrera. Los jenerales Jose Miguel i Juan Jose, i el coronel Luis Carrera. Episodio de la independencia de Sud-America.* Santiago: Imprenta del Ferrocarril, 1857.

Vicuña Mackenna, Benjamín. *Ostracismo del general D. Bernardo O'Higgins, escrito sobre documentos inéditos i noticias autenticas.* Valparaíso: Imprenta i librería del Mercurio, 1860.

Vicuña Mackenna, Benjamín. *Páginas de mi diario durante tres años de viaje, 1853, 1854, 1855.* Santiago de Chile: Universidad de Chile, 1936, Vol. 2.

Walker, Charles F. *Smoldering Ashes: Cuzco and the Creation of Republican Peru, 1780–1840.* Durham, NC: Duke University Press, 1999.

Weiss, Jason. *The Lights of Home. A Century of Latin American Writers in Paris.* London: Routledge, 2003.

Whitehead, Laurence. "The Alternatives to 'Liberal Democracy': A Latin American Perspective." *Political Studies* 40 (1992): 146–159.

Whitehead, Laurence. "Three International Dimensions of Democratization." In *The International Dimensions of Democratization: Europe and the Americas,* edited by Laurence Whitehead. Oxford: Oxford University Press, 1996.

Wollny, Hans. "Asylum Policy in Mexico: A Survey." *Journal of Refugee Studies* 4, 3 (1991): 219–236.

Wright, Thomas C., and Rody Oñate. "Chilean Political Exile." *Latin American Perspectives* 34, 4 (2007): 38.

Wright, Thomas C., and Rody Oñate. *Flight from Chile: Voices of Exile.* Albuquerque: University of New Mexico Press, 1988.

Yankelevich, Pablo. "Memoria y exilio. Sudamericanos en México." In *La imposibilidad del olvido,* edited by Bruno Groppo and Patricia Flier. La Plata: Ediciones al Margen, 2001.

Yankelevich, Pablo. *México, país refugio.* Mexico: Plaza y Valdés, 2002.

Yankelevich, Pablo. "Asilados sudamericanos en México: Luces y sombras de la política de asilo del estado Mexicano durante la década de 1970." Paper presented at the LASA XXVII International Congress in Montreal, September 2007.

Yankelevich, Pablo, and Silvina Jensen, Eds. *Exilios: Destinos y experiencias bajo la dictadura militar.* Buenos Aires: Libros del Zorzal, 2007.

Yashar, Deborah J. *Demanding Democracy: Reform and Reaction in Costa Rica and Guatemala, 1870s–1950s.* Stanford, CA: Stanford University Press, 1997.

Young, Iris Marion. *Inclusion and Democracy.* New York: Oxford University Press, 2000.

Yundt, Keith W. *Latin American States and Political Refugees.* New York: Praeger, 1988.

Zacharia, Janine. "US Forced to Confront its Bolivian Problem." *The Global Edition of the New York Times,* 2 July 2008, p. 2.

Zarco, Isidoro. "El exilio: Ingrato destino de nuestros ex-gobernantes." In *El pensamiento vivo de Isidoro Zarco,* edited by Cesar Brañas. Guatemala: Editorial Jose de Pineda Ibarra, 1973, pp. 125–126.

Zohar, Marcel. *Free my People to Hell: Betrayal in Blue and White; Israel and Argentina: How the Jews Persecuted by the Military Were Neglected.* Tel Aviv: Zitrin, 1990 (in Hebrew).

Zolberg, Aristide. "The Next Waves: Migration Theory for a Changing World." *International Migration Review* 23, 3 (1989): 403–427.

Zorrilla de San Martín, Juan. *La Epopeya de Artigas.* Montevideo: Biblioteca Artigas, 1963, Vol. IV.

Zúñiga Huete, Angel. *Morazán.* Tecigualpa, Honduras: Editorial Universitaria, 1982.

Index

CPSIA information can be obtained
at www.ICGtesting.com
Printed in the USA
LVOW13s1503210118
563427LV00013B/912/P